Biographical Dictionary of Latin American Historians and Historiography

Biographical Dictionary of Latin American Historians and Historiography

Jack Ray Thomas

GREENWOOD PRESS
Westport, Connecticut
London, England

Library of Congress Cataloging in Publication Data

Thomas, Jack Ray.
    Biographical dictionary of Latin American historians
and historiography.

    Bibliography: p.
    Includes index.
    1. Historians—Latin American—Biography. 2. Latin
America—Historiography. 3. Latin America—History—
Bio-bibliography. I. Title.
F1409.8.A2T48   1984   980′.0072022   83-8558
ISBN 0-313-23004-8

Library of Congress Catalog Card Number: 83-8558
ISBN: 0-313-23004-8

First published in 1984

Greenwood Press
A division of Congressional Information Service, Inc.
88 Post Road West
Westport, Connecticut 06881

Printed in the United States of America

10 9 8 7 6 5 4 3 2 1

For my mother and father with love and gratitude

Contents

Preface

History did not become a viable academic discipline in Latin America until the 19th century. To be sure, there was interest in the subject during the colonial age and some histories were written then, but they were not of the analytical, critical variety that we regard today as scholarly production. There were chronicles, like * Bernal Díaz del Castillo's account of Cortés' conquest of Mexico or *Alonso de Ercilla y Zúñiga's epic poem on the Spanish struggle against the Araucanian Indians, and there were some attempts at comprehensive history such as *Father Juan de Velasco's study of Ecuador's past, but even works of this nature were closer to chronicles than true history.[1]

The dearth of historiographic works in the colonial epoch is understandable when the entire cultural and educational life of that period is explored. Few people attended schools of any kind, much less colleges or universities in which the student might prepare himself to become a historian. Even those who did enjoy the opportunity for higher education did not experience much training in the area of history. Some churchmen did encourage their students to work in the history of their local areas and the Jesuits tried to stimulate student interest in the past, but colonial curricula did not include anything more than a quick brush with history, and when the subject was taught, the focus was usually on universal or Church history; America's past was generally ignored.

In the 19th century, however, educational opportunities expanded, and the subject was offered more frequently, although it was still excluded from many schools. When history did find its way into programs of study the interest centered on America, largely because of the successful Wars for Independence that had been fought during the first quarter of the century.[2] This independence struggle led to a tremendous surge of national pride and a desire on the part of leaders to recount the great exploits of their countrymen in the battle for freedom. It was hoped that these glorious events would never be forgotten and that subsequent generations could always refer back to them for inspiration and guidance.

Despite the increased interest in history, the early post-independence age did not produce much in the way of analytical, well-researched works. Historians groped their way during the first half of the century, often writing what they considered to be history but what in reality were personal impressions or outright

---

*Throughout the book, asterisks are used to designate those individuals who are discussed in a separate entry.

political polemics. For example, history was not prominent in the intellectual activity of Chile until the advent of the Generation of 1842.[3] Following that slow start, however, Chilean scholars picked up momentum, and by the 20th century they could boast of a significant number of scholarly studies.[4]

While most of the history production came after 1850, there were some important histories written before the middle of the century. *Carlos María de Bustamante's *Cuadro histórico de la revolución mexicana* (1823–1832) and *Lucas Alamán's *Historia de Mexico* (1849) were outstanding examples. But these books and others like them, while extensively researched, had something of the polemic about them due to each author's inability to submerge his own political convictions when dealing with the past. Nevertheless, neither one of these works can be dismissed as irrelevant because each included a considerable amount of careful historical research and some thoughtful analysis. Yet it remained for the writers of the second half of the 19th century to produce in quantity the more sophisticated works. One of Peru's outstanding historians, *Juan Pedro Paz-Soldán, writing in 1891, complained that it was impossible to write even a partial history of his country because so little had been done prior to 1850 that even the examination of a minor event had to be treated like a definitive study in order to orient the reader to the material at hand. A similar situation existed in Venezuela, where little history was written in the first half of the 19th century. No local historic tradition existed, and none developed until *Rafael María Baralt activated an interest in the discipline in the middle of the century. Baralt wrote his first historical article in 1829, but his major contribution, *Resúmen de la historia de Venezuela desde el año de 1797 hasta èl de 1830*, did not appear until 1841. Meanwhile, in Ecuador, *Pedro Fermín Cevallos did not embark seriously upon his own historiographic career until 1853, when he began to work on his *Cuadro sinóptico*, which became the basis for his later, more famous, *Resúmen de la historia del Ecuador* (1870). This later work is recognized by scholars as the first significant history of Ecuador.

In Brazil, history was more advanced prior to 1850 than in most of the other Latin American countries. The Instituto Histórico y Geographico was founded in 1838, and historical research had been going on for some time before mid-century. But much of the work was done by foreigners. Robert Southey, an Englishman, published his *History of Brazil* between 1810 and 1819, and a German, Karl Friedrich Philipp von Martius, won a prize in 1843 for his essay on how Brazilian history should be written.[5]

It is accurate, then, to note that 19th century Latin American historiography emerged dramatically in the second half of the century and then advanced significantly in the first half of the 20th century. But if the lack of historical production in the colonial period can be explained by educational shortcomings, the failure of extensive historical work before 1850 can be understood in the light of political and military preoccupations in most Latin American countries. For the first quarter of the century the independence wars raged, and during the next quarter the region sought to stabilize itself politically as inexperienced leaders tried to solve the monumental problems that characterized the immediate postwar years. It was only after the passage of a couple of decades that men had the time, interest, training, and inclination to write history. And only when history was regarded as a significant and important facet of intellectual progress and as a stimulus for nationalism did historians begin to explore their craft carefully. They used the experiences of Europeans and North Americans, and they debated the nature and value of history, how it should be written, and why it was significant. Out of the historiographic arguments of the century emerged a better understanding of the discipline and a general consensus that the major goal of history was to find truth in the past. But the method to arrive at that truth remained open for debate well into the 20th century.

It was not until the third decade of the 20th century that history came to be written more by trained scholars than by amateurs. Departments of history were established in the universities, and research theory and techniques became a part of the curriculum after 1930. More objective, less passionate, and more extensively researched books and articles began to appear, and the preponderance of biographies and political histories gave way to economic, social, and even some intellectual studies. Political leanings continued to influence historians with the result that, in addition to national political prejudice, some writers produced histories strongly influenced by fascist, nazi, communist, and socialist ideology. Following World War II a more balanced type of history flowed from Latin American pens, and by the 1970s younger historians were using statistical and computer techniques in their research, and fewer impassioned polemical works appeared. Latin American historians were now carrying out extensive research and producing scholarly, analytical history that compared favorably with historical studies written anywhere in the world.

In this examination, I have used the broadest possible criteria for selecting the writers of history. It is clear that, if one is to study the historiography of this era, one must look at the writers as well as their work. Some are recognized generally as outstanding, and no one could quarrel with characterizing them as historians. But there are also those who did not write any history books or articles or essays on historical events but who did think and write about the discipline of history. These writers must be included in any historiographic study. Similarly, men whose careers were in politics, religion, business, or the professions and who also wrote history must be included. It is a certainty that modern scholars will question the inclusion of some of the authors in this study. But even those who wrote little or no history but who thought and wrote about the discipline of history deserve to be included because of the contribution they made to the philosophy of history.

In the bio-bibliographical sketches that follow the introductory narrative, colonial chroniclers, as well as 19th and 20th century writers are examined. To keep the number of historians manageable I have cited only those 20th century writers who died before 1983. As with the narrative, some who are a part of this section might be challenged as historians, while it may be argued that others who have been omitted should have a place in the book. The major considerations for inclusion were that the writer either produced a significant amount of historical writing or that a portion of his scholarly production was so important to the discipline of history that he could not be excluded. In any case, those who are in the bio-bibliographical section represent a wide spectrum of historical philosophy and production and reflect the tone of Latin American historiography from the colonial age to the last quarter of the 20th century.

In the organization of this book the introduction provides an overview of Latin American historiography from the earliest times to the late 20th century, but the focus is on the 19th century, when the writing of history began to evolve beyond a crude narrative stage and historians began to forge a discipline that ultimately emerged in the 20th century. Their ideas on what history should be and their writing of history formed a solid foundation on which their 20th century counterparts could build.

Since no comprehensive reference work on Latin American historians now exists, the remainder of the book includes bio-bibliographical sketches of historians, both amateur and professional. The sketches are designed to provide the reader first with the vital statistics of each historian. Dates and places of birth and death, educational data, and career activities are listed at the beginning of each entry. In some cases specific verifiable biographical data is unavailable. Following the vital statistics, the first paragraph traces briefly the career of the individual in narrative form. A second paragraph then focuses on the contribution made to historiography by the individual. Finally, each sketch concludes with a bibliography that cites the works produced by the person and then lists the works written by others about the historian. In both cases, citations are limited to six, although in many instances the authors wrote more, or more works have been written about them.

Following the bio-bibliographical sketches, four appendices are provided to assist the user of the volume. The first lists the historians by country, including the city and date of birth, and the second lists them by year of birth. The third appendix divides the historians by the various jobs they held other than writing history. Finally, the fourth appendix is a cross-topical reference citing historians under the major historical topics they investigated.

As with the writing of any book, a number of people assisted in the preparation of this manuscript. I am particularly indebted to the Reference Staff of the Bowling Green State University Library for their efforts at locating necessary data. Kausalya Padmarajan and Catherine Sandy in the Library's Inter-Library Loan Department found many books for me that were essential for the completion of the study. Angela Poulos made several crucial suggestions that aided in the acquisition of needed materials, while Maria Padilla, Bowling Green University Department of History, furnished valuable data on historians of Argentina and Mexico. Dr. Jack Clarke, University of Wisconsin–Madison Library School, read parts of the manuscript and raised numerous significant questions concerning the various philosophies of history discussed in the book. Dr. Joseph Spinelli, Department of Geography and Assistant Dean, College of Arts and Sciences, Bowling Green State University, graciously gave of his time to assist in resolving a number of geographic questions that arose during the final preparation of the manuscript. Throughout the writing of the manuscript Judy Gilbert typed the drafts and prepared the final copy. Laboring under the burden of sometimes barely legible copy, she retained her good nature and patience throughout the ordeal, for which I am very grateful. Finally, my wife Darlene and my sons Jack, Kurt, and Brad all provided understanding, encouragement, and support during the years of research and writing. Obviously, although many people contributed to the project, errors of omission or commission are entirely my own.

NOTES

1. For a discussion of Velasco's work, see Adam Szaszdi, "The Historiography of the Republic of Ecuador," *Hispanic American Historical Review*, 44, No. 4 (November 1964), pp. 508–510. E. Bradford Burns points out that some significant histories were written in the last years of the colonial era in Brazil and important histories were produced in the Spanish American countries as well in this epoch. But the real surge of historiography came in the 19th century. See E. Bradford Burns, *Perspectives on Brazilian History* (New York: Columbia University Press, 1967), p. 3

2. See Domingo Amunátegui Solar, *Don Andrés Bello enseña a los chilenos a narrar la historia nacional* (Santiago: Prensas de la Universidad de Chile, 1939), p. 5; Francisco Bauzá, *Historia de la dominación española en el Uruguay* 3d ed. (Montevideo: Tall Graf "El Democrata," 1929), I, xxii; and Juan de Arona [Juan Pedro Paz-Soldán], *Páginas diplomáticas del Perú* (Lima: Imprenta de la Escuela de Ingenieros, 1891), p. vi.

3. Jack Ray Thomas, "The Impact of the Generation of 1842 on Chilean Historiography," *The Historian*, 41, No. 4 (August 1979), pp. 705-720.

4. Not everyone regards the great outpouring of Chilean history as necessarily beneficial to Chilean letters. The 20th century historian Francisco Encina claimed that these histories were not indicative of increased literary talent in his nation. Instead, he saw the growing interest in history and the production of historic works as symptomatic of a lack of literary acumen. He argued that to write prose and poetry requires imagination but these writers had only the desire to write, not the talent, and consequently they turned to history, which did not require any imagination. Francisco Encina, *La literatura histórica chilena y el concepto actual de la historia* (Santiago: Editorial Nascimento, 1935), pp. 12–25. Another 20th century historian agreed that some of the history written in the previous century lacked artistic quality, but he insisted that the majority of history produced had "scientific value" and advanced man's knowledge about Chile. Guillermo Feliú Cruz, "La literatura histórica chilena: Notes sobre su desenvolvimento," *Atenea*, 68, No. 203 (May 1942), pp. 254–268. For excellent insight into 19th century Chilean historiography, see Allen Woll, "The Philosophy of History in Nineteenth Century Chile: The Lastarria–Bello Controversy," *History and Theory*, 13 (October 1974), pp. 273–290; Allen Woll, "For God and Country: History Textbooks and the Secularization of Chilean Society," *Journal of Latin American Studies*, 7 (May 1975), pp. 23–43; and Allen Woll; "Positivism and

History in Nineteenth Century Chile: José Victorino Lastarria and Valentín Letelier,'' *Journal of the History of Ideas*, 37 (July–September 1976), pp. 493-506.

5. Karl Friedrich Philipp von Martius, ''How the History of Brazil Should Be Written,'' in Burns, *Perspectives on Brazilian History*, pp. 21–41.

Biographical Dictionary of Latin American Historians and Historiography

Introduction

THE MEN WHO WROTE HISTORY

In general, the earliest Latin American historians came from families that enjoyed economic comfort and political influence. They were, for the most part, socially elevated, and their surnames were traditionally renowned, having been familiar in upper-class society for several generations. In short, they fit John Higham's description of early 19th century U.S. writers of history as "patrician" historians, men who were socially prominent, economically prosperous, and involved primarily in some activity other than professional historiography.[1]

The fact that history was written largely by amateurs from the upper-class elite is understandable because writing history required a measure of educational opportunity coupled with leisure time, and only the wealthy and high-born could meet these requirements. In the last years of the 19th century and the first half of the 20th century, when professional historians appeared in greater numbers, it was still true that most came from the upper levels of the class-conscious Latin American society.[2]

Along with acquiring a good general education and reading extensively in history, the Latin Americans prepared themselves for a historiographic career by traveling widely in their own countries, in other American nations, and throughout Europe. Many went abroad as diplomats in the service of their governments, but some journeyed overseas simply because they were wealthy enough to afford such trips and were curious about foreign lands and peoples. Still others went to different areas as exiles after becoming too deeply involved in partisan politics at home. Finally, a few traveled to distant nations solely for the purpose of using archives, libraries, and manuscript collections in their literary and historiographic endeavors.[3]

Experience in foreign countries benefitted the Latin American historians immensely. Not only did they have an opportunity to view firsthand the work of foreign writers but they were also able to associate with them and learn a great deal simply from that contact. *Benjamín Vicuña Mackenna wrote enthusiastically about his meetings with William Prescott in Massachusetts, while a number of historians prized their meetings with European luminaries such as Victor Hugo. At the same time, relationships within Latin America became profitable for some of the travelers. *Bartolomé Mitre and *Diego Barros Arana created a friendship that lasted a lifetime and enabled them to exchange books and ideas on a wide variety of subjects related to historiography.[4]

An additional advantage from foreign travel was access to foreign archives and libraries. Those who traveled as diplomats, exiles, or just plain tourists were able to enjoy these benefits just as much as those who went abroad for the express purpose of researching historiographic topics. In all cases their works were improved by the experiences, but for those who wrote on the colonial period the trip to Europe and particularly to the Archives of the Indies in Sevilla was essential. Two examples bear out the value of foreign travel. *Francisco Adolfo de Varnhagen served as a diplomat in Portugal, Spain, Paraguay, Holland, and Austria. He used the archives in each country, and much of his research was later put to good advantage in his detailed *Historia geral do Brasil*.[5] Diego Barros Arana also traveled widely in Europe, Brazil, Argentina, and Uruguay, although instead of serving his country as a diplomat he was living in exile due to his political activity. But the result of his access to foreign materials was, like Varnhagen's, a lengthy, detailed, in this case, 16-volume history of his native Chile.[6]

Many of the trips abroad occurred when the historians were still very young men, and although educational opportunities in history were limited, the historians, aided by a sound liberal education and experiences at home and abroad, were able to produce some books and articles at surprisingly young ages.

This historiographic and literary precociousness can be explained in part by the nature of the literary world in Latin America. The region was high in illiteracy, and educational opportunities were reserved for the fortunate, small minority represented by the upper classes. Consequently, few people were involved in writing, and the lack of competition made possible the publication of works at an early stage in a writer's career. It must be pointed out also that most of these early writings were not of particularly high quality and that the later, more mature production of these historians, as one might suspect, was far superior to their initial efforts. Even so, the publication of a writer's work at such an early age has to be regarded as a significant accomplishment and as an important training stage in post-independence historiographic development.

Equally important in explaining the nature of the historians and historiographic contributions was the diversity of their interests and careers. Taken together, these historians made up a collage of intellectuals, clerics, politicians, statesmen, creative writers, diplomats, philosophers, and teachers. Unlike the professional historians of the second half of the 20th century who resided on college and university campuses, these men found other methods to sustain themselves and their families. Many were independently wealthy and were seeking only to operate in a milieu that interested them, but some needed the income from other occupations to enable them to live up to the standards of their class. Because history as a discipline did not enjoy any kind of popularity until the second half of the 19th century and therefore the number of professional historians required to staff university courses was minimal, few teaching positions for the professional historian could be acquired. Even in secondary schools, history did not play a prominent role in the curricula, which meant that there was little opportunity for the professional historian to teach his subject at any educational level. In addition, these scholars were restless men of action who were not content to spend their lives in libraries and archives but who wanted instead to make a positive contribution to the literature of their nations while at the same time contributing to their countries' political, religious, or cultural development.

Still another reason for their myriad interests was the wide-ranging opportunities that were open to educated men with influential social and political connections. There was little competition in the intellectual and literary fields so that the scholar might divide his time among several related disciplines such as philosophy, literature and history and make a name for himself in all three. The opportunities were virtually limitless for the ''Renaissance'' man who did not specialize in any one intellectual field or concentrate on any one position. Additionally, the scholar might hold a government job or run for political office or gain a post within the Church.

Due to this interest in other disciplines and other professions and because of the necessity, or simply the desire, on the part of some to pursue other careers, the historiographic production of many historians of the age was naturally curtailed. However, the rich experience brought to history by these men more than compensated for their reduced yield. A 20th century writer, Antonio Castro Leal, deplored the failure of *José Fernando Ramírez to write more because everything he produced was a major contribution to Mexico's historiography. But Ramírez was so deeply involved in politics, administration, and the judicial life of his country that he did not have the time to increase his output.[7] This is not necessarily as great a loss as Castro indicated. It is entirely possible that Ramírez' work might not have been so rich had he not had the governmental and political experience that contributed so much to his knowledge and understanding of Mexico. Phrased another way, the interaction of scholarship and practical action mutually benefitted the histories that each man wrote. Another 20th century historian, Ricardo Donoso, accentuated this view when he proudly wrote that the great Chileans of the 19th century were ''not only historians'' but that their ''vigorous civic action wrote some of our most brilliant history.''[8]

Among the most popular careers for historians were those in law and politics. Given Latin American educational training and the social inclinations of the population in this period, it is not surprising that many historians were also lawyers. The study of law throughout the modern epoch was the major interest of young men, and it did fit neatly into historiography. The study of legal traditions and theories in Europe and America required an interest in the past that could easily be transferred to an examination of military or political exploits of earlier generations. At the same time, those historians who accepted the notion of historiographic research as the concentrated study of documents found such action very close to the preparation of court briefs or the putting together of a complete case based on precedent. Some historians, like *Andrés Lamas and

*José Manuel Restrepo even practiced law while at the same time writing their histories.[9]

This interest in, and training for, the law led also to careers in politics and government service. Bartolomé Mirte was a statesmen, militarist, bibliophile, and historian who eventually reached the pinnacle of political success when he was elected President of Argentina in 1861. A man who wrote less history but who gained a great deal of fame was Domingo Santa María, who occupied the Chilean presidential palace from 1881 to 1886. In the same era, a number of historians ran unsuccessfully for their nations' highest offices. A host of historians gained seats in their national senates or chambers of deputies, while others served as governors or members of state legislatures. Many more held appointive offices as ministers of state, education, agriculture, and/or foreign affairs.

A number of politically oriented historians of this era served their governments abroad. They were selected for diplomatic missions because of their education and training or, in a few cases, because of their social standing. While their nations benefitted, the men themselves were rewarded for their foreign activities. Some wrote about the countries in which they worked, thereby increasing knowledge of these regions for the people at home. The Argentinian *Vicente Gregorio Quesada wrote an eight-volume work on his diplomatic career that included residence in Brazil, Mexico, Rome, and Spain. Even more importantly the diplomat-historians gained access to archival material that aided them in developing their later histories.

While some historians were politicians and diplomats, others served as military officers, usually in the internecine conflicts that occurred all too frequently in the early years after independence. In 1821, *Rafael María Baralt, at the tender age of 11, served as a clerk and standard bearer in the Venezuelan army. He continued his military career into later life and used the experiences to strengthen his understanding of the role of the military in politics for his classic study, *Resúmen de la historia de Venezuela* (1841).

A military career was just as advantageous for historians as were careers in government or politics, perhaps even more so when one considers the influential role played by the military in most Latin American countries as a result of the unending string of civil wars and insurrections in the 19th century. Such experience led the soldier-historians to gain a greater insight into martial life and into the military's position in the Latin American scheme of things. When they set out to write about the past they therefore were much better equipped to put together histories of their nations than were those not as well versed in warfare and violence.

A scientific field for historians was health care. Lisandro Alvarado studied medicine at the Central University of Caracas and graduated with a doctorate in medicine. Nevertheless, he had a greater interest in philosophical and historical speculation and soon turned to writing history. Even so, he made use of his earlier training as he became interested in what we refer to today as psychohistory. In 1895 he published a work entitled *Neurosis de hombres célebres de Venezuela* in which he examined the psychological problems of some of the nation's outstanding past leaders. But Alvarado was not alone in this interest; *Ramos Mejía, an Argentine physician, produced a similar book, *Neurosis de los hombres célebres en la historia argentina.*[10]

The combination of science, medicine, and history was not one that surprised all 19th century observers. Some believed that history itself was a science and that it was not a great departure to move from the hard sciences to the social sciences. In fact, some were convinced that scientists made better historians than those trained in the humanities, religion, or law. Historians needed the scientific background to research and analyze past events, and they could better interpret the past if they had strong scientific training.

Still another career, pursued by some, was that of clergyman. The outstanding examples of clerics who delved into history were *Federico González Suárez in Ecuador and Francisco de Paula García Peláez in Guatemala. Both eventually became archbishops, González of Quito and García of Guatemala. González Suárez ranks as one of the finest historians of Ecuador and of all Latin America. He wrote a general, multivolume history of his country that was generally well received, although part of it angered some churchmen. In his diverse writing and even in some of his histories he generally defended the Church, but when he presented some scandalous evidence regarding conduct of clergymen in the colonial era he suffered vicious attacks from a number of priests. His reasons for writing history fit neatly into his primary career with the Church. He wanted history to provide a basis for morality and to encourage the establishment of good customs among his people. He wrote history, then, because he believed that "there is no civilization without morality, and social well-being is impossible, without good customs."[11] The training received by clerics, their access to extensive libraries, and the scholarly temperament of those who entered the service of the Church all coalesced to make the writing of history an attractive avocation.

Even more logical as a supplementary career for writers of history was that of literature. Since most Latin Americans regarded history as a part of literature, it was inevitable that a number of novelists, poets, and dramatists should fall quite naturally into the writing of history. *José Victorino Lastarria wrote what many regard as Chile's first novel, *El manuscrito del diablo*. In Mexico, *Vicente Riva Palacio wrote a number of historical novels based upon serious historiographic research. His countryman, *Justo Sierra, produced a series of short literary articles between 1868 and 1873, which he called *Las conversaciones del Domingo*, while *Ricardo Fernández wrote short stories dealing with Costa Rican customs. In addition, he also wrote a three-act comedy. In Colombia, *José Manuel Groot was a prose stylist, a painter, and a poet, while in Argentina, *Vicente Fidel López, cast in the mold of romanticism, wrote a novel, *La novia del hereje* (1868), which he modeled after the work of Sir Walter Scott. Another historian who wrote poetry was Rafael María Baralt, and even Bartolomé Mitre fancied himself a poet and dramatist. He hoped to elevate the cultural level of his people not only because he believed this a healthy aspect of a nation's development, but also because he was convinced that culture could be used to elevate the patriotic sentiments of a people, welding them into a cohesive, progressive nation.

Adán Quiroga's intellectual output, while centering on archaeology and history, also touched on poetry and literature. A friend, Leopoldo Lugones, who wrote an introduction to one of Quiroga's books, confided that he once visited his friend's home to see his archaeological collection but stayed until three o'clock in the morning discussing, not archaeology, but rather poetry. Quiroga himself once commented, "I was born a poet." Another writer, noting Quiroga's varied interests, referred to him as a "multiple man."[12] Such a characterization could easily be applied to almost all Latin American historians of this epoch, and nowhere is their concern for diverse disciplines more evident than in their literary production.

Another career related to literature that historians followed was journalism. The historians were writers, and since they had varied interests and were held in some esteem in their nations, it is to be expected that they would find journalism to their liking. The career had the added advantage of providing supplemental income for those who needed it. A journalist could earn far more than a professional historian because newspapers circulated widely, whereas history books did not enjoy an extensive audience. At a young age Francisco Bauzá began his journalistic career, and he ultimately became editor and director of several Montevideo publications while he continued to write articles on political and philosophical-religious subjects.[13] Diego Barros Arana wrote for a number of newspapers and periodicals, and his fellow historian Benjamín Vicuña Mackenna contributed to many Santiago publications. Rubén Dario described Vicuña Mackenna as "an incomparable journalist" because of his articles in *La Nación* and *El 21 de Mayo* and because of the large number of pieces he placed in *El Mercurio de Valparaiso*. José Manuel Restrepo wrote for a weekly newspaper, *El Semanario del Nuevo Reino de Granada*. In 1809 he published a series of articles on the geography, population, and industry of the Province of Antioquia.

Along with literary and journalistic achievement, oratorical prowess seems to have been a common trait among historians. Francisco Bauzá was an eloquent speaker who was once called "the most outstanding parliamentary orator of the country in the past century,"[14] but he was also a man who possessed a great deal of information, and he knew how to use it to advantage when he found himself in a public speaking situation. Another observer revealed that Bauzá's orations were "magesterial oratorical pieces," standing above most other orations in a region where public speaking was so prized and outstanding speeches were so common.[15]

Because of the political activity, the writing and speaking talent, and the general reputations gained by historians, they turned frequently to journalism either to set forth some new concept in the discipline that interested them at the time or to champion some political cause that preoccupied them. In any case, the interaction of journalism, prose, poetry and history all aided them in developing acceptable and sometimes outstanding literary styles. These were men who had to place their thoughts before the reading public no matter what the subject. Whether or not they were well versed in a given discipline, they never hesitated to make known their views. The end result of this was a good deal of material that was shallow and sometimes misinformed. But in general their histories benefitted from such flights into other, related disciplines.

Some writers of history after the mid-19th century turned to teaching. Historians taught in secondary schools and universities, and some held administrative posts in institutions of higher learning or served the government in a variety of capacities associated with public education. But as noted earlier, through the first years of the 19th century such positions were few in number and consequently difficult to obtain. As the century wore on and particularly into the 20th century, as more courses came to be taught, paralleling the rise of government interest in public education, more openings occurred and some historians found at least partial employment in the field of education. Diego Barros Arana became an outstanding teacher and in 1863 assumed the role of Rector of the Chilean National Institute. Later he moved up to become Rector of the University of Chile, and he held a seat on the Council of Public Instruction.[16] *Miguel Luís Amunátegui followed a similar path to become Secretary General of the University, while in other countries José Manuel Groot, *Alejandro Marure, and Lisandro Alvarado were master teachers.

Many historians worked in educational administration. José Manuel Restrepo served as Director General of Public Instruction in Colombia from 1832 to 1842. José Ramírez was Rector of the Colegio de Abogados on two different occasions in Mexico, while Carlos Martínez Silva became minister of Public Instruction in Peru and Vicente Fidel López served as Minister of Public Instruction in Buenors Aires in 1852. *Lucas Alamán was convinced of the necessity for education, and he brought from France teaching machines for the hard sciences. He also provided a library for the Colegio de Guanajuato. He was responsible for opening the Escuela de Agricultura and the Escuela de Artes in 1844. Alamán once said of education, "Without it there can be neither freedom nor equality." He also noted that formal primary instruction received all the attention, but he believed that "moral and public education" should be an important part of the educational system. Governments should provide books for those who could read or else they would read trash "that is apt to corrupt them, making them lose respect for authorities and even for moral and public decency." In this type of education the lives of illustrious men were important, and their deeds had to be recorded so that their actions and their virtues could serve as examples to subsequent generations.[17]

In summary, it is possible to characterize 19th century Latin American historians as well educated, although oftentimes self-taught, with varied interests and professions separate from the writing of history. They were politically oriented, traveled widely, and fancied themselves as men of literature even if some of their contemporaries derided the literary quality of their work. They focused historiographic attention primarily upon their own countries, although experiencing life abroad, and they were preoccupied mainly with the independence and immediate post-independence periods. Such interests were natural since the acquisition of freedom from Spain came early in the 19th century and seemed to many to be the most important event in all the world, for all time. Nationalism and patriotism were important in creating the powerful interests in their own histories and particularly in the modern era.

Twentieth century historians, with the advantage of a more structured education in the discipline, became professional historians. They gave less attention to other occupations and interests, and they broadened their historical interests to include European, United States, and world history. In dealing with their own past, these historians turned away from a preoccupation with the colonial and independence periods that had characterized 19th century scholarship and instead worked in the post-independence era. Then, too, some by the second quarter of the 20th century began to show interest in the history of ideas. The great Argentine historian *Ricardo Rojas pioneered intellectual history and provided inspiration for subsequent generations.[18] Meanwhile, in almost every country revisionist historians were at work attempting to alter long accepted views of the past. Those nations with significant Indian populations experienced Indianist movements in historiography as they reevaluated the native population's contribution to the region's development.[19] In other countries, great 19th century political leaders underwent closer scrutiny, and new analyses based on more rigorous research revealed new interpretations of leaders like José de San Martin and Juan Manuel de Rosas in Argentina, Gabriel García Moreno in Ecuador, Bernardo O'Higgins in Chile, and the Emperor Dom Pedro II in Brazil, to mention only a few.

While the 20th century historians displayed striking differences from their predecessors, they did share a strong interest in the discipline of history, and their attitudes toward the subject were just as diverse. Almost everyone had a distinctive view on the nature of history and its function in man's world, and all were more than willing to publicize their ideas on history along with their narratives on the past.

THE MEANING OF HISTORY

Latin American historians entertained a wide variety of attitudes relative to the meaning, value, and utility of their discipline. They were influenced by European and North American writers and by historians who preceded them in other Latin American countries or in their own nations. Moreover, political and social realities of the age played a role in molding their historiographic attitudes. Some presented exceedingly simplistic definitions of history, while others saw it in far more complex terms. The writers' personal lives and academic training, or lack of training, also influenced their thinking. But all had some definite view of the nature and objectives of history. Each man also sought to justify his discipline in terms of its value not only to scholars but to society as a whole. A Central American writing in 1895, *Enrique Gómez Carrillo, expressed a view held by many of his fellow historians when he wrote that all mankind has an inherent interest in the past. Obviously, most people were more curious about the immediate past, but there were those who found even the remote, ancient period fascinating. This concern for things that had happened resulted "because it is very natural for man to want to inform himself on the origin and development of the social body to which he pertains." He elaborated on this theme when he added that history "is a study that is interesting to all because there is, in man, a natural wish to know that which occurred in the world," and that "knowledge brings great advantages, teaching that which it is convenient to do or to avoid for the sake of truth and for the good that we must search for in the land."[20]

A Colombian journalist who brightened the Chilean literary scene at mid-century, *Juan García del Río, agreed. He wrote that the human spirit has an irrefutable desire to fix itself on the past in an effort to learn lessons that might be helpful for the present and the future. "Looking at history in this manner . . . , it is a religion with its mysteries, its dogmas, its obligations and its end."[21] A more prominent historian of the age concurred when he commented: "There is in men and in societies a natural propensity to evoke memories of the past that becomes irresistible when uncertainty and vacillation increase and skepticism develops. The retrospective look brings light and breath and serves many times over the principal objective of repairing the injustices committed."[22]

The Chilean José Victorino Lastarria was yet another writer who felt that interest in history was natural. He suggested that there is a correlation between the individual who has amnesia, and is therefore obsessed with events that occurred in his life but that he cannot recall, and societies that become troubled when their backgrounds are lost.[23] Human nature requires that both persons and civilizations know something of their past in order to find tranquility of mind in the present.

Most of the preceding arguments exploring the value of history convey a negative attitude. They express the mental and emotional problems that might arise if history is not studied or if it is studied and not understood. But little is mentioned about the benefits that history bestows when it becomes known to societies or individuals. One writer who did speculate on the more positive impact of the discipline, however, was *Juan Vicente González. He took the same basic argument used by Lastarria and *Pedro Fermín Cevallos but expressed it in a much more affirmative form. He wrote that history provides man with a limitless fount of knowledge from which all may draw as they seek fulfillment in their lives. In this way the experiences of the past served to improve life in the present.

Meanwhile, *Francisco Bilbao had his own ideas relative to the nature and utility of history. Bilbao was a strange combination of a practical, realistic activist who sought social and political reform in his country and an idealistic, meta-physical dreamer. His ideas regarding history tended to gravitate to this latter penchant for seeking meaning in the spiritual realm. He defined history as ''reason judging memory and projecting obligations of the future.'' There is, he noted, no history without memory, and men cannot have a conscience without memory. Consequently, history is essential for binding together man's total conscience, as it existed historically in time and space, with its present conscience. If history did not provide this service of putting together the myriad events of the past, then man would have no examples for living and no conscience attuned to past moral and ethical values, which are so necessary for present orderly living. Without history the world simply slides into social chaos.[24]

Others agreed with Bilbao, but in general, spiritual attitudes were in the distinct minority. Scientific concepts influenced most historians, and they renounced any belief in divine intervention in the historic process. By the 19th century, science was supreme, and the positivistic philosophy of Auguste Comte, with its emphasis upon modernization and scientific advance, gained a wide audience. As the accentuation of science increased in the second half of the century, there was a concomitant decline is support for the old spiritual, scholastic philosophy that had been so influential in medieval Europe and colonial Latin America. The result was that those who wrote and thought about history tended to discount any concept that related to a spiritual philosophy of the discipline.[25]

Another factor that turned historians away from regarding their subject as a spiritual phenomenon was the growth in political liberalism that included an antimetaphysical bias. This same movement was usually strongly anticlerical. Liberals, in their anxiety to discredit the Church, often attacked spiritualism, even when it did not directly involve religion. Consequently, many historians of liberal persuasion denounced the extreme providential theories of history such as those that had been expressed in an earlier age by the French writer Bishop Bossuet and parroted by his later admirers in America.

One idea related to a religious interpretation of history that did have some currency was that the study of history, while not divinely inspired, was certainly good for the soul. Gómez Carillo noted, ''The noble tendencies of Hispanic America incline one to the study of history; and as this contributes to elevate the soul and to fortify it with sane examples, it is hoped that the desire to cultivate such an important realm of human knowledge will never be lost.''[26] Gómez' idea of the soul comes through his philosophy very much resembling Bilbao's ''conscience.'' Both men believed that an awareness of the past improved man morally and ethically. Consequently, Bilbao's creation of a conscience through understanding history and Gómez' ''elevation of the soul'' are one and the same concept with only semantic differences. In both cases the writers thought in terms of moral advance for the individual, and that advance could be achieved either through the soul or the conscience.

But should history speculate to an inordinate degree on spiritual, natural, and metaphysical matters? For most historians the answer was an emphatic no. Ricardo Fernández Guardia denounced such an idea on the grounds that history must revolve around man, not abstractions. He set forth his view succinctly with the simple statement, "History is the true relation of the events of humanity."[27] Not all, but most of the historians approximated this view toward their subject. They regarded history as more than just another academic discipline that was studied because it was interesting, exciting, or titillating. Instead, they believed it was essential for the well-being of mankind. History was a force that had to be studied and understood before man could reach his full potential. Hence, it was logical that history was written not only by what we might loosely term professional historians but also by politicians, statesmen, military officers, clerics, journalists, and philosophers. It was simply too important to be left in the hands of a small elite group of historians; it had to be examined by the best minds, no matter what their profession.

Objectives of History

Just as all recognized the overriding importance of understanding history, nearly all who wrote history believed that the written product must have some specific objective. Naturally, since writers of history were from varied backgrounds and professions their objectives in writing about the past were different. For one like Francisco Bilbao it was enough just to resurrect earlier events. But his countryman Diego Barros Arana believed that history had a moralizing mission. Another historian agreed with Barros Arana when he wrote, "History also ought to be considered as the most beautiful code of morality. It is a loyal picture of customs and passions, a most lively portrait of the human heart." Still another author stated that his interest in writing about the past was not to win glory for himself or to make money but rather to serve his fellow man. He wanted to reproduce faithfully for all mankind its past so that man might find guidance in the experience of his ancestors.[28]

But more practical objectives were also in the minds of some historians. Antonio García Reyes wrote a history of the Chilean navy, in part because he wanted to impress upon the people the importance of their navy and thereby induce young Chileans to pursue a naval career rather than entrust their defenses to foreigners.[29]

Of great concern to many historians was the image of Latin America in Europe, and they used history to improve that image. Writing in 1823, Domingo Juarros justified his writing a history of Guatemala with the argument that Spanish America was bound to become "an extensive field for the employment of British capital and British industry, and ultimately prove an inexhaustible source of advantage to the various branches of our manufactures and commerce." Consequently, information that could be gleaned from Guatemala's past would be of use to the British as they aided the economic development of the region.[30] Manuel de Mendiburu, writing in Peru, expressed much the same opinion. He hoped that his *Diccionario histórico-biográfico de Perú* would serve to "rectify the many errors" held as fact by Europeans regarding his country and that it would project an image of Peruvians who loved culture, learning, and knowledge as much as civilized men from any country in the world. Such an image could eliminate the misconception, frequently held by Europeans, that Peru and the rest of Latin America was a barbaric jungle.[31]

*Domingo Sarmiento set forth the same argument when he wrote a review of *Claudio Gay's history of Chile. Sarmiento pointed out that Gay's book had the advantage of presenting to Europeans a more detailed knowledge of Chile than had any previous work. Sarmiento, too, was certain that given a clear understanding of the country people and business would be more easily attracted to the nation, which prior to Gay's study many Europeans perceived to be a land "overrun by savages." Even in the 20th century this determination to acquaint Europe and the rest of the world with Latin America was a motivation for writing history. Central Americans were anxious to bring their region to the attention of the nations of the world, which led some of them to focus their studies on economic history, which they hoped would advance their relations with other countries. They wrote about the interdependence of the world and used diplomatic history to foster that notion and to enhance their role in the world community.[32]

This attempt to "sell" Latin America to Europe through history violated one of the basic premises regarding historiography held by the men of this age. The historian who set out to write a history for any purpose other than acquisition of the truth was immediately placing himself in danger of shaping his data to fit his objective. Should this happen, the end result then became something much less than true history. On the other hand, if one wrote his history and then concluded that it would make a positive contribution to international understanding, then the history would remain valid. In the case of many Latin Americans, their histories were objective studies that could be used to exalt the fatherland abroad, and they did not suffer excessively from a lack of objectivity.

In line with the attempt to improve the image of Latin America overseas was the parallel objective of impressing the Latin Americans themselves with their past glories. History in this way became a force for the generation of patriotism. During the Wars for Independence in the first quarter of the 19th century, it was not difficult to create a national sentiment. The fighting against Spain took care of that chore. But as the decades wore on after independence, some intellectuals noted that their countrymen were losing their patriotic zeal amid the omnipresent political rebellions and civil wars. To regain the advantages of patriotism, which some viewed as essential for progress, historians wrote national histories. The Uruguayan Francisco Bauzá noted that each generation in Latin America had its own distinctive task. His generation's grandparents had conquered the country for Christian civilization; his parents had won independence and created nations; and to his generation was left the task of cementing nationhood and creating a national literature that favorably reflected the customs and character of the age. To his way of thinking, a national literature was bound to exalt the national spirit and enhance the Latin American drive toward progress.[33]

When the Brazilians founded their Institute of History and Geography in 1839, one of the major reasons set forth was to glorify the fatherland. Brazil's outstanding 19th century historian Francisco Adolfo de Varnhagen wrote that readers would find in his work a "noble patriotism" but it would not be a glorification of the nation by attacking everything foreign. Instead, he would through documents highlight the many good aspects of his country. Varnhagen also noted in his *Historia general* that one of the major thrusts of historians should be to form and improve the "general national spirit."[34] Meanwhile, Carlos María Bustamante published his *Cuadro histórico* in a period of political turmoil in Mexico in the hope that it would inspire his contemporaries "to rise against their tyrannical oppressors and imitate the actions of the heroes who have preceded them and died to save them."[35]

In Argentina, historians after 1810 became obsessed with the ideas of freedom and nationalism, and the resultant historic production dwelled upon La Plata's struggle for independence from autocrats and dictators, be they Spanish or Argentine. Andrés Lamas emphasized the battle for liberty in his writing and thereby contributed to the growth of a proud national spirit. Meanwhile, in Peru, Manuel de Mendiburu frankly used his *Diccionario histórico-biográfico del Perú* to honor the nation's past heroes, and he used their fame and glory as examples for his contemporaries.

The problem of building nationalism and patriotism in Argentina, Chile, and elsewhere was monumental, but nowhere was it more difficult than in Mexico. In that country the racial, social, and economic diversity was so great that any sense of nationhood was difficult to create. Mexican historians recognized these divisions, and in particular they concentrated upon the difference between the Spanish and Indian background. Some writers viewed their history as a struggle between these two basic forces, out of which emerged the synthesis of the *mestizo* that gave Mexico its distinctive character. José Ramírez believed that Mexican historians who were either Spanish or Indian could not do an effective job on Mexico's past and that the true history of controversial events like the conquest could be written ony by a *mestizo*. The *mestizo* was not only a detached, disinterested observer—unlike either Spanish or Indian historians—but he also understood the character of his nation better than the pure bloods. The famous late 19th century historian, Justo Sierra, agreed. He wrote, "Mexicans are the children of two peoples and two races; we were born of the conquest; our races are in the land that the aboriginal people inhabited and in the Spanish soil. This fact dominates our history; to it we owe our soul."[36] When Mexicans embraced this concept of a duality in racial stock, it was then but a short step to accept the spirit of Mexican nationalism. Such a realization was bound to strengthen their nation and curtail the localism and regionalism that had been present from the time of the colonial period to the 19th century.

The determination to build patriotism was also pronounced in those countries where political chaos was rampant and where nations were involved in foreign wars. For example, Venezuelan and Colombian historians wrote about patriotism and national unity as crucial objectives for history amid the conservative–liberal struggles, or while dictators flourished. Likewise, Chilean historians emphasized patriotism during the war against the Peru–Bolivian Confederation and during the War of the Pacific. Once these wars ended successfully, the great outburst of national pride also contributed to the desire to spread patriotism among all the people.

Nationalism, however, was not the only goal of patriotic writers who tried to use history for more than an intellectual exercise. Some of the historians also believed that history should serve as a guide for society in its quest for progress. They believed that every epoch contributes something to the total development of man. Nations and races had been formed in antiquity, but by the 19th century a significant change had occurred when religion came under greater attack and gradually became separated from the temporal order.[37] This meant that Christian religious teaching, which had directed society for 1,800 years, suddenly lacked the power to continue to act as a guide. The decline of the Church as moral leader of the people did not mean that it was destroyed completely as the teacher and leader of mankind, but now secular philosophies and ideas were coming more into play and confusing the once clear role of the Church relative to the people. In such a situation, history might serve to aid religion in leading the people of the world down the straight, narrow, and virtuous path.

One of the historians who believed firmly that history had such a role to pursue was Rafael María Baralt. He suggested that the history of a people should be taken into account by society when plans were made for the future and when decisions were made for the present. He wrote that the customs of a people are determined by climate, geography, laws, and governments and that all these are inextricably bound together. Because of this union it is essential to study customs of the past when attempts are made to resolve issues of the present and future. History can also be used, according to Baralt, to understand these past customs and their operation and in this way serve peoples who might wish to avoid or overturn a dictatorship. The customs and actions of their predecessors might provide for the insurgents the insights needed to effect such a change.[38]

José Lastarria put the same idea a different way. He wrote, "Society must respond to history. History must guide society in its future endeavors in the search for happiness. Only in history can be found the immutable laws of happiness or decadence; the course that brought progress or the path that led to ruin. Public men must know the history of the people they guide."[39] This argument introduced a new ingredient into the concept of using history as a guide for society—laws of history. It is one thing for random aspects of past events to be taken and used to guide the present; it is quite another to indicate that laws are at work in history which make that guidance valid.

History: Science or Art

Many historians simply accepted history as a science and made no effort to justify such an assumption. After all, history made use of auxiliary sciences in opening the mysteries of the past, and therefore history must itself be a science. Geography in particular was a science that historians found essential to their work. Juan Vicente González wrote that history had to be accompanied by geography. Historians must know the places where events transpired or their accounts will be faulty.[40] A supporting view on the nature of history came from Federico González Suárez, but he went back to archaeology to demonstrate the value of auxiliary sciences to history. In his work he personally relied heavily upon both archaeology and geography in reconstructing the past.[41] Gómez Carillo added chronology to the list of valuable auxiliary scientific disciplines. He argued that chronology divided, ordered, and computed time for the historian, thereby making it possible to keep historic events in their proper perspective.[42]

But does the mere use of auxiliary sciences mean that history is itself a science? Not all historians accepted this idea, but some, notably Bartolomé Mitre, did sanction such a view. He stated emphatically that historians who stayed close to their documentation and who put that documentation into logical, readable form were actually working at a scientific method. He wrote, "As the philosophy of history cannot be written without history, history cannot be written without documents...because documents of any manner constitute more than its protoplasm...[they] constitute its essence."[43] Other historians and writers alluded constantly to "the science of history" without developing their reasons for such a characterization, but many of those influenced by the strongly scientific positivism of August Comte believed that their research into old documents and their use of that material in rebuilding the past was clearly scientific.[44] One example of this penchant for science was *Juan Zorrilla de San Martín, who constantly referred to the "historic sciences" and "auxiliary sciences," which combined to make the labors of the historian easier and enhanced his conclusions. Zorrilla referred also to the "scientific labor" of history, not in the sense of its being only partially scientific but rather implying that the discipline is totally and completely a science.[45]

Federico González Suárez regarded history as a science but not a hard science. Instead, he saw it as a "science of social morality." He picked up this attitude from Cesar Cantú. Early in his life he read all he could find on history and developed a deep love for the discipline. Among these early books was one written by Cantú, the Italian author of *Historia universal*. González had been counseled by churchmen not to read the book, but he went ahead and was profoundly impressed by Cantú's social morality concept. Cantú's argument, and González' as well, was that history judged the past and by so doing it established norms of morality for the future. Individuals and societies must then build their values on these moral norms. Such norms were scientifically arrived at and could be scientifically maintained. Consequently, history was a science of social morality. González believed also that only the Catholic historical school was in the possession of true history as a science of social morality. This was the case "because the Catholic church is the only one that teaches the exact truth respecting Divine Providence and human liberty." History, therefore, considered from a philosophical point of view cannot be the mere narration of past events but it is a science of social morality, a science that is beneficent for mankind.[46]

Antonio Batrés was another who believed strongly in the scientific nature of history. He wrote that history was able to "wrest from nature" many of its greatest secrets. He saw the universe as a union of forces that were essentially harmonious in what he called the "great laboratory of nature." Consequently, his attitude toward the universe was that it was a scientifically guided phenomenon that could be tested scientifically and that revealed attitudes and ideas that might serve as guides for contemporary and future societies. In the midst of this scientific universe was man. From ancient times geniuses had sought to discover scientific principles and varied knowledge in a wide range of disciplines. Now, in the 19th century, in what Batrés called the modern epoch. "specialists exist who concentrate their studies on a single realm of knowledge, making it easier to achieve rapid and practical progress, favored by the known freedom to think and the stimulus accorded to merit."[47] Those who specialized in history were dealing with the scientific knowledge of the past, and, as a result, history itself became a science.

By the later years of the 19th century some histories with scientific themes did appear. In particular José María Ramos Mejía and Lisandro Alvarado produced several works of psychohistory. Ramos was particularly interested in mental problems suffered by monarchs and dictators because the people had no control over them no matter how troubled or demented they might become. Pablo Groussac was skeptical of the value of this kind of history and of the psychiatric method employed, but he did believe that Ramos' books were important, not so much in the scientific parts as in their "erudite and literary aspects."[48] Vicente Fidel López was more emphatic in proclaiming Ramos' work scientific. He even referred to one book as "pure science," while he praised Ramos for his innovative study in what he called "medical-social history."[49]

Such studies were generally applauded by those positivist and scientific historians who believed that the investigation, verification of documents, and analysis of historic data was unscientific. However, few works about science existed as the focus continued to be on biography and politics. Still, even for these works, a so-called scientific method satisfied the craving for scientific legitimacy on the part of historians, who lived in an age of technological and scientific advance and who wanted desperately to legitimize their endeavors as scientific.[50]

In contradistinction to the history-as-science attitude was the view that history is, in reality, art. Vicente Fidel López illustrated his support for this argument when he described history in terms of color, imagination, oral tradition, and literature.[51] A host of others agreed, many of whom wrote history as literature, utilizing the historic novel or the epic poem as the vehicle to present their research and ideas to the reading public. Even some of those who wrote general histories conceived of their work as literature and art. The old argument that history dealt with man and man was unpredictable was used to counteract the history-as-science notion. For the historians who accepted this idea, a science had to be based upon the assumption that one's subject, whether alive or inanimate, would always react in the same way in a controlled situation. Man, it was argued, did not always respond to a stimulus in the same way, and therefore the study of man could not be regarded by any stretch of the imagination as a science.

A third group of historians, and the largest number, went down the middle of the road between the science and art extremes. One writer representative of this attitude was Juan Vicente González, who deplored the emphasis upon industrial development and material well-being at the expense of the traditions of the past. While he was unhappy with his generation's preoccupation with the material world, he nevertheless referred to history as a science. At the same time, however, he implied that history was not entirely scientific but rather a combination of art and science. He spoke of "grace and beauty" within history and the correlation between the arts and works of nature.[52]

A more important spokesman for this view was *Pablo Groussac, who was interested in folklore, social customs, and literature as well as history. Groussac was a historian who believed that historic research must have a scientific base to be effective. But while he consciously supported this concept, he also wanted to save a part of history for the philosophical or artistic historian. He once asked, "How much more vast would be the general knowledge of the vocational historian, and more complete the documental apparatus that he utilizes in his scientific reconstruction of the past, if the part of imaginative and subjective evocation would be increased?"[53]

Groussac believed that scientific activities can play a part in history as the historian seeks to uncover the true facts concerning events that transpired earlier. But he wrote that historic facts do not repeat themselves, and therefore history cannot be an exact science. A science must revolve around hard data and events that in given situations react the same way. Historic events, guided by unpredictable human beings, cannot be examined like animal behavior or chemicals in a test tube. History cannot be compared with geology because "historic events are singular and accidental," whereas geological events are guided by natural laws. History cannot be a science because "it cannot order in series its constituted elements" or "apply to successive facts determinist laws of generalization and causality (as is intended in the philosophy of history and sociology) but also by the scarcity and insufficiency of tested documents in ancient times or its discordant abundance in modern times." There are, then, some scientific aspects to historiography, such as the use of auxiliary sciences, but when the scholar puts together his history it becomes a work of art. True history is like architecture; it is neither all science nor all art but a combination of both. When the architect drafts his plans he is performing a work of art, but when the plans are transformed into the actual structure the building is scientifically constructed to ensure strength and durability. Following this line of thinking, then, there are two separate parts to history. The first is the "erudite preparation," or research, and the second is the "creative or constructive faculty." The first can be scientific in nature, but the second is pure art. The historian is the artist who harmonizes the two parts into a workable and worthwhile whole. To each problem in his study the historian must apply his critical ability, along with his sagacity and "his supreme talent of expression."[54]

In a later reference to historiography Pablo Groussac's concept of his discipline remained fairly constant, but he appended a third dimension. Now, he wrote in the preface to his biography of Santiago Liniers in 1907, that history was composed not only of science and art but of philosophy as well. He noted that there was little difference in these parts to history because he saw them as all compatible and logically coexistent.[55] He phrased his argument in this fashion:

Very far from having incompatibility between history considered as science, as art, as philosophy, it must be noted that no essential difference exists; when prolonged sufficiently, any of the convergent routes leads to an encounter with the remaining, making it possible to say, according to the formula of Bacon, that if a superficial knowledge is separate from art and philosophy, a more profound knowledge will return us to them.[56]

The histories written during the 19th century reflect clearly the science versus art debate. For example, Mitre's *Historia de Belgrano* is a meticulous study put together after assiduous research in primary documentation, in short, a product of the history as science school. On the other hand, Vicente Riva Palacio's *Calvario y Tabor: Memorias de las luchas de la intervención*, while based on documents of that age, placed the work in the genre of the historical novel, an obvious work of the historian who viewed his craft as pure art. Finally, representative of the science *and* art view is Pablo Groussac's *Santiago de Liniers: Conde de Buenos Aires, 1753–1810*, a well-researched study that is presented in the interesting and readable style of the artistic "literato."

Lessons in History

While there was no consensus on the science–art issue, Latin American historians did agree that history had valuable lessons to pass on, not only to contemporary society but to future generations as well. A Chilean wrote that history was the "oracle of the gods," which counseled and taught people to build happier and more contented lives for themselves.[57] José Antonio Saco, in Cuba, wanted to use history to inform his people, and for that purpose he sought always to present accurate facts. He was mainly interested in social and political problems of his day, but he assumed that history could aid in moving the population toward lofty objectives. Sebastián Lorente, Diego Barros Arana, *Andrés Bello, Joaquín Acosta, Miguel Amunátegui, Justo Sierra, and many others argued that the first objective of history must be to instruct and provide examples for contemporaries.[58]

A major argument presented at this time for the discipline's educative value was that history repeats itself, and consequently, when events occur again and again individuals will know how to handle problems by simply looking at the action taken by their predecessors. Some believed that history did repeat itself. They drew a parallelism between the history of Spain and the history of La Plata as proof of similarities in different generations. Thus, the policies of Bernardino Rivadavia from 1821 to 1828 could be seen as imitations of the policies of King Charles III, who ruled Spain from 1759 until 1788.[59] Those who supported this idea did not have in mind an exact repetition of the past because in the comparison between La Plata and Spain they recognized that they were talking about two very different geographic and cultural regions and even about two very different political systems, one monarchical and the other republican. Therefore, when they stated that history repeated itself, they had in mind the similarity of political policies at different times in history.

Francisco Bauzá believed that there are lessons to be learned from history because the same things that transpired 2,000 years ago could apply in his own day. For example, Aristotle's argument that nations with a middle class are more stable than those devoid of such a class was as true in 1876 as in fifth century Athens. The factors that impeded progress in classical Athens prevailed in Latin America. "Ignorance or total despotism; slavery or abject misery; we have here that which destroyed republican Greece, and that which perhaps can destroy us." There was in Uruguay no middle class and consequently no political stability.[60] But Bauzá never concluded that history repeated itself exactly; he believed only that similar situations existed from age to age. However, even this similarity could be very important in instructing people of later generations.

Some historians, notably Lucas Alamán, found that history taught lessons in specific areas. To Alamán, history was invaluable for learning something about contemporary politics, and he was confident that history could guide his generation in political matters. He sought to learn about the influence that ideas had on the people and their impact on the morality of the age. This was a period in which the political system changed dramatically and in which political alterations influenced changes in attitudes toward religious beliefs and customs. Therefore, he hoped that his history of this significant era would instruct future generations to be more cautious. This type of lesson, he believed, was "the greatest good that can result from the study of history." But Alamán also hoped that the instructive value of his history would not be limited only to Mexico. He believed that other nations might learn a great deal from Mexico's experience and profit from the knowledge because man acted in similar ways no matter in what country he resided. All people, whatever their nationality, could find some value from seeing "how the errors of men can make the most beautiful presents of nature useless."[61]

Other historians believed that history could provide important lessons even for science. Alejandro Marure noted that history "presents to us the scale of human knowledge; the successive graduations through which men have passed before elevating themselves to perfection; discoveries that have served as a bane to their different systems; the methods that have been employed in order to accelerate their advances; the genius that has given impulse to their progress."[62]

At the same time, history was significant in that it could help people in Latin America improve their mental state and gain a measure of happiness. R. Rafael

Pérez wrote that, in the early years after independence, history had been important mainly to provide Europeans with a clearer and more accurate picture of the region than they then possessed. But by the last years of the 19th century this need no longer existed. Now, he felt, the major function of history was to provide Latin Americans with the knowledge that would enable them to live better, happier, and more prosperous lives.[63] Pérez did not elaborate on how this might be achieved, but he appeared convinced that knowledge from the past could work such a miracle.

A few historians recognized the educational value of history but in a more intellectual way. The Guatemalan Domingo Juarros found history ''delightful for the mind'' as it recounted important events and relived the exploits of heroes. But, in addition, history taught

the manner in which we ought to conduct ourselves on occasions of difficulty, by holding up to view what prudent and sensible men have done in similar circumstances; it will animate us to the performance of noble actions, by setting before us the glorious examples of our predecessors; and it will eternalize the memory of heroes, long since withdrawn from the great theatre of life, who by their achievement have dignified the human race.[64]

Gómez Carillo tended to agree as he argued that the major utility of the study of history was that it delighted man, ''instructing him profitably, at the same time inclining him to sympathize with the good and hate the evil.''[65]

This attitude toward history is reminiscent of the view that St. Augustine took toward ancient Greek philosophers when other churchmen denounced their work out of hand because they were pagan. Augustine argued that the works of Aristotle and others should be read not for their content but to sharpen the wit of the reader. These Latin American historians inferred that history might also be used, not in place of lessons or content, but in addition to them as a means to hone the minds of the readers. The phrase, ''delights the mind,'' is used frequently, and the indication is that history might be significant as a means simply to prepare or improve the mind for the study of other disciplines.

While the role of history in the total educational process was recognized as important, most historians saw its greatest value in the influence it had upon the young. González Suárez taught in the University of Ecuador and revealed that he used history to inculcate in his students his own political ideas. He deplored despotic governments and tried to pass on to those in his classes this hostility toward tyrants. He regarded history as ''the permanent lesson that is given to generations with past facts.''[66]

Juan García del Río, writing in his Chilean publication *El museo de ambas Américas*, also had some thoughts on the teaching worth of history. He insisted that history must be an impartial judge of the past. Readers of history want to learn the lessons of the past, and it is up to the historian to fulfill that longing. He commented that in the 19th century not only kings were the oppressors but commoners as well, with the result that the ''practical utility of history has made itself extensive to all classes of society.''[67]

In general, there was agreement among the historians that history had a great deal to offer in helping people learn about politics, morality, economic development, and the way to lead a prosperous and contented life. The lessons of history had many practical applications, and the subject deserved to be written if only for these hints at self-improvement and national improvement as well. But history was more than a practical blueprint for the good life. It was also a spiritual and intellectual stimulus that could sharpen the wit and not only strengthen knowledge of the past but aid in an understanding of man and of his religious background. For all these reasons it was worth writing and studying, and since it was so important, it was worth doing well. Therefore, these same historians had some very pronounced ideas about how history should be researched and then presented in written form.

HISTORIC TRUTH AND THE WAY TO FIND IT

Latin American historians selected for investigation topics ranging from distant world history events to contemporary national issues. Some examined pre-Columbian America, while others dealt with the colonial era, but most concentrated on events in the independence and post-independence periods. Political history predominated, with little or no attention given to social or economic themes.[68] Biographies of illustrious political leaders and military heroes attracted widespread attention, particularly among those who were interested in advancing patriotism among their countrymen.[69] Of even greater interest were the lengthy, detailed, multivolume national histories that became commonplace in the 19th century. These histories were encouraged by scholars and politicians alike. Political figures were interested in comprehensive national histories for the purpose of stimulating patriotism and thereby binding the nation's population closer together. Some also believed that the people needed a general awareness of their past in order to cope better with the present and the future. Then, too, there were other government officials who doubtless believed they might enhance their own popularity by demonstrating, through history, the wickedness of their predecessors.

Whatever the motivation for national histories they appeared in abundance in both the 19th and 20th centuries. Their popularity was heightened by the fact that some governments subsidized this type study. Those men who were fortunate enough to gain official patronage had distinct advantages over their fellow scholars even beyond the financial remuneration that was naturally an important consideration; governments could be very helpful in providing access to documents, and they could also smooth the path to publication, which was not always an easy one.

Official historians were not political hacks but many were accomplished scholars, and their contributions to historiography were significant. For example, *José Milla, commissioned by the Guatemalan government to write a history of Central America from the discovery of the region by the Spanish to the independence epoch, was a corresponding member of the Royal Spanish Academy and an honorary member of the International Library Society. In addition, he was a Guatemalan delegate to the Congress of Americanists.

Men such as Milla had no difficulty in deciding their areas of research interest because their governments made that decision for them. But most were moved to write national histories for other reasons, and even Milla wrote his *Historia de la América Central* in the belief that it would be of use to later historians and provide a base for what he hoped would be their more sophisticated work. If his study did lay the foundation for future research, he felt that the confidence of his government in selecting him to write a national history would have been warranted. Others believed that they were doing the spadework for future generations, but they held no illusions about the permanence of their efforts. They believed that, as their nations progressed and as scholarship improved, some of their work, or perhaps all of it, would be rendered anachronistic.

Most of the historians were confronted with situations in which little historiographic work had been done. Consequently, almost any topic could be justified on the grounds of virginity. But beyond this there were many other considerations that led to the selection of specific topics. Sebastián Lorente wrote his history of Peru because he had studied his country's past for many years and still had difficulty understanding it. He believed the reason for this was that earlier historians had not started at the beginning, and without a solid background, modern history became incomprehensible. As he phrased it, Peru's history was for him "an undecipherable enigma." Lorente was certain that history was bound together chronologically and that one must master the whole to understand any of its parts. He linked causes and consequences and studied history progressively for a lengthy period of time, after which he concluded that "the situation of the republic cannot be understood without having studied the colonial epoch, colonial period without study of the conquest, the conquest without forgetting the Inca empire, and the empire, if the primitive culture is unknown."[70]

Some historians chose topics for study because they disagreed with existing interpretations. Their work was initiated to correct what they believed to be erroneous examinations of particular periods or events. Federico González Suárez read carefully through the five-volume *Resúmen de la historia de Ecuador* written by Pedro Fermín Cevallos, making marginal notes of discrepancies or corrrecting obvious errors. When he looked at all these notes, he concluded that the colonial period in particular had been handled badly by Cevallos, and he decided to write a history of this age. The end result was much broader as he wrote his *Historia general de Ecuador*, in which he included events beyond the colonial era. In this work he said that he wanted to look at Ecuador as a biographic subject rather than as a national history. Using this method he could "deduce from the facts conclusions that served the present generations as moral conductors."[71]

Once the historian decided on the subject he wished to research, he then had to try to discover what actually occurred in the past. While some polemicists wrote history to advance a political cause or set forth their own personal views, most of the writers sought what historians have always wanted—true, objective studies. Just as these historians found truth in history important for an understanding of life or for the justification of history, when they wrote they were conscious of the need for accuracy and objectivity, which could lead them to the acquisition of truth.

Pablo Groussac reflected the general sentiment when he wrote that history's raison d'être was the search for truth. Consequently, the finished product had to be constructed on a solid base of documentation from which deductions and inferences could be supported. But what method might one use to secure the truth? Most historians agreed that every document on a given subject had to be examined carefully before a historic work could be produced. In theory this was the way history must be written, but in practice this technique was unworkable. Histories, except those extensive multivolume works on narrow topics, would, in the words of Groussac, "always be incomplete." Consequently, historians should not seek to do anything more than arrive at a "very relative approximation of absolute truth." For Groussac this approximation of the truth was enough, given the difficulties of achieving objectivity. Since the individual constructs the work and criticizes and selects sources, part of his ideology is bound to creep in, no matter how carefully he might try to eliminate his personality from the study. Therefore, getting close to the truth was about all that man could hope to accomplish.[72] This was exactly why historians argued that their discipline was not an exact science. Materials out of which histories were constructed were imperfect because it was frequently impossible to prove their veracity. Therefore, conjecture and hypothesis were oftentimes of necessity substituted for exact truth. But this is precisely where art entered into history and science left off. At this point a solution to a problem depended upon the investigator's talent in achieving as close an approximation of the truth as possible.[73]

A major concern was that even the truth would not be accepted by the entire reading public. Past leaders had supporters who would not accept criticism of their heroes as valid. Conversely, those who hated historic figures would not accept a balanced account since they were determined to perpetuate the satanic image of these men. One historian who acknowledged this problem wrote that he was certain of the objectivity of his research despite the appearance of "diatribe" and "excessive eulogy" in his sources. But he was also aware that some people would reject his work because of "passion or partisanship."[74]

This longing for impartiality was uppermost in the minds of a majority of the scholars. Yet few believed they could achieve complete, total truth. A Peruvian wrote that he would not attempt to moralize but instead would note evil when it existed, either "with horror or with pity," and then move on to commiserate with the unfortunate people who had suffered as a result of evil acts. He preferred to dwell more on that which was good in society and to emphasize beauty in an effort to inspire his countrymen to follow the examples of their outstanding ancestors.[75] While this pledge for devotion to the truth was sincere, the historian's comments concerning the method employed to find that truth and the projected thrust of his history indicate that he was not going to reach that ultimate goal of historiography. If evil existed, the historian must not shun it in favor of the more happy events that have transpired. If he does so he fails to live up to the high standards of objectivity that can lead to an approximation of the truth.

Miguel Luís Amunátegui warned against just such action when he pointed out that historians generally avoided unpleasantness in writing their histories and that it would be difficult, although extremely desirable, for men of his generation to avoid that pitfall. He held out little hope for this change in attitude, however, when he recalled that English historians had been largely silent about the lewdness of Charles I and Henry VII and that Spanish historians had little to say about the seamier side of Philip IV. Without such material history was not only inaccurate but was also dry and uninteresting. Amunátegui pleaded with his fellow historians to make the 19th century an age in which reality was revealed no matter how unpleasant it might be.[76]

The other side of this argument was that too many historians emphasized evil because people were more interested in the bizarre and spectacular and would devote more attention to any history that included a generous portion of wars, killings, rebellion, and intrigue. Rafael María Baralt confronted this issue and pointed out that earlier historians had been "more inclined to recount battles and surprising events than to conserve facts relative to industry, commerce, and civilization, which are things that form the most useful part of history if it is true that history is more a lesson than an entertainment."[77] He also wrote, "The works of peace do not matter to history; interest ends when great crimes, bloody battles, or calamitous events cannot be included."[78] It must be noted, however, that while Baralt deplored interest in the spectacular, he fell into the same trap as those he condemned when he wrote his history of Venezuela. In volume I of his *Resúmen de la historia de Venezuela*, he devoted 14 chapters to bloody battles and only 8 to peaceful institutions.[79]

The emphasis upon spectacular events was not the only threat to finding historic truth. The problem of excessive nationalism was also one that had to be confronted. Throughout much of the 19th century and into the 20th the xenophobia generated during the Wars for Independence continued at a high level. It was impossible for a historian writing on his country's past to escape completely the adverse effects of this pious devotion to the fatherland. Manuel Mendiburu, while affirming his unflinching search for the truth, created some suspicion in his readers' minds when he also noted that he sought to honor his country. He never made an attempt to explain how he proposed to handle situations in which the truth might not be in line with Peru's honor. He did admit that "fables, falsehoods, and exaggerations" made the task of writing history very difficult, but he had been able to attain historic truth by using the "least partial authors." Even so, he recognized that some question of veracity might emerge, and in some cases he left the question of authenticity to "the reader's judgment." Despite his monumental hedging in this vein, Mendiburu did try to come close to the truth. He believed that most controversial issues are fathomable when the historian relies on logic and when he employs doubt in preference to "adventurous opinions."[80]

Most historians agreed that truth was the essential ingredient in history. Many pledged their determination to learn the truth by eliminating errors and misconceptions and by a diligent examination of the documents. But more was needed than careful research. The historians tried to divest themselves of their preconceptions and biases before initiating their work. Alamán summed up this attitude when he wrote, "It is necessary to dress ourselves in the character of philosophers, who look for nothing more than the truth, and to employ with rigor and sincerity the criticism that serves to encounter it."[81]

Not all believed that Alamán or others could follow these words judiciously. Critics charged that Alamán did not write with the object of finding the truth as he frequently insisted. One opponent acknowledged that Alamán had an excellent critical sense but he too often acted the role of the partisan politician.[82] Alamán himself believed that he was objective and that rather than presenting a partisan view he was in fact clearing up distortions that other historians had inflicted upon the reading public. He revealed that many people were surprised to find that much of what they had learned about the colonial period was fantasy rather than fact. Others wrote him letters congratulating him on depicting events in history as they really happened not as others imagined they happened.[83]

Among all historians concern for objectivity in the work of others as well as in their own research was uppermost in their minds. Recognizing the difficulty of finding historic truth, they nevertheless believed that the writer who sincerely sought it was doing the best job possible. They understood that the lack of documents and the loss of some of those that had existed earlier were obstacles to the acquisition of historic truth. But they also noted the errors caused by the incomplete researcher and the inability of some to understand an earlier epoch. Studies that were not carefully researched, for whatever reason, put into print errors that were often perpetuated by subsequent historians who blindly accepted such work. Consequently the accomplished historian had to be careful of all histories, lest he be misled by his predecessors.

Equally perplexing was the problem of the impassioned historian who attacked races, religions, classes, political parties, and individuals in his work because of his own prejudices. These writers had no interest in justice and no love of truth. The result was a totally unjust view of history that again might be perpetuated by later historians.[84]

Still, it was not only the dishonest, vulgar writer who did a disservice to the past. Historians of some reputation, men who attained popularity and stature in their professions, contributed to the perpetuation of falsehoods, as they failed to examine documents carefully enough, or on occasion, not at all, thereby continuing and giving added vitality to lies. *García Icazbalceta was one of the many who recognized that the attempt at objectivity was difficult and that preconceived ideas influenced strongly all historians. After all, historians were also human and subjected to all the pressures and prejudices that plagued every individual. But each historian had to make the effort to free himself from the partisan ideas that he held and to make a concerted effort at objectivity.

Recognizing the danger of partisanship was only part of the problem. An additional obstacle lay with the historian who found that injustice had been done to an event or a person in history and who believed it was his duty to rectify the injustice at all costs. He might then go too far in the other direction, finding little or nothing reprehensible about the man or the event. For example, Joaquín García Icazbalceta, as he set out to prove that Bishop Zumárraga was not an ''ignorant friar'' or a destroyer of Mexican civilization, became so committed to this cause that he lost his determination to approach the subject objectively. He found Zumárraga an ''apostolic hero'' and a practical man who may have erred from time to time but only because he was human and because of the era in which he lived.[85] Consequently, García removed from Zumárraga any responsibility for his own actions, and the result was a glowingly favorable biography. Such an assessment is just as detrimental as the relentless criticisms of the man, despite the fact that García was attempting to acquire the truth of his subject's life. But when dealing with events and personages removed from Zumárraga, García was adamant in his devotion to veracity.

Two areas of history that were extremely difficult for the historian to remain dispassionate about were Spain's role in America and, as suggested by García, the Church. In both cases hostilities were heightened by the independence war waged against Spain, in which the Church generally allied itself with Spain. The conquest as well as the colonial period and independence were topics that either incited the writer to denounce Spain and/or the Church or led the writer to apologize for the mother country and religion. José Victorino Lastarria became one of the strongest critics of Spain, contributing to the Black Legend that had been initiated centuries before. But Spain had its supporters in writers like Lucas Alamán, and Juan Vicente González. González argued that religion had a place in historiography even though scientific theory was in vogue in the second half of the 19th century when he wrote his *Manual de historia universal*. He pointed out in the preface to that work that critics had accused him of giving too much importance to religion in this book. His answer to that charge was that every writer had convictions, and since he was Catholic he believed that it was appropriate for him to write about his church. But González did not feel that this attitude in any way hampered his quest for objective history. He insisted that the man of conviction had to be certain only that his conviction was ''free and intelligent'' and that the attempt to justify a belief would not lead him to ''denaturalize the facts'' and accept equivocal testimony.[86]

Other historians were not at all concerned about any sentiment or conviction; they simply argued for truth in history with no mention of any extenuating circumstances. One of the most outspoken of this group was F. A. Berra. Writing in his book *Bosquejo histórico* in 1881, Berra set forth his historiographic philosophy. He wrote that in all his work he narrated the facts as he knew them and he based his judgments on those facts. He went on to write that he had not concerned himself with "flattery or with mortified sentiments" but instead had confined himself "scrupulously to the rules of morality and justice." In another passage later in the same book, Berra elaborated on his view of the historian's quest for accuracy. He wrote that historians must be slaves to the truth and inflexible in judging that truth. They are obliged to praise meritorious events and to condemn errors and crimes. It is the historian who applies moral laws to the past, and his task is to make that application rigorously, without hesitation, and without being influenced by any personal sentiments.[87]

While this hard line of historic truth was accepted by many historians of the age, there were those who did not pursue it to the satisfaction of Berra. He detected two schools of historiography even within the relatively small La Plata area of South America. The first school paid little attention to the facts and generally embellished many events that should have been censured. Members of this group found trivialities that supported their position and blew them out of proportion, making virtually insignificant episodes appear as great historical events. In this fashion the writers of this category used lies and half-truths to appeal to the vanity of the public by creating a fictionalized history that was far removed from the truth. For Berra this type of historiography could be described only as "corrupt."

The second school of historiography was inspired by different objectives. These writers, among whom Berra included himself, investigated carefully all events, tested all documentation, and then used their research without distorting it in any way. Such a technique Berra viewed as being "eminently moral." Writers of this school were, in effect, teachers of society. They learned themselves what was good and what was evil, and their work inspired the people to avoid the evil and gravitate to the good. In addition, these historians' examinations of customs led to their determination as to whether or not such customs were moral or immoral and then they could suggest that people embrace the one and avoid the other.

Not all historians were so convinced of their skill in seeking out the truth. *Ernesto Quesada had doubts about the complete authenticity of his work, but he remained confident that he had come as close to the truth as possible in his study of the difficult Rosas era in Argentina. He recognized that his study was not definitive, not because of any methodological failure on his part but because not all documents were available to him. Letters, memoirs, diaries, and other primary sources that might alter his conclusions were undoubtedly locked away in private archives or simply stored in dusty attics and therefore unattainable. Since he did not know of their existence, he had no way of finding them. But he did not want to postpone the publication of his work until every shred of evidence had been uncovered; this probably would not occur in his lifetime. On the other hand, the publication of the Rosas study might have the effect of bringing out clarifications and corrections from others who knew the whereabouts of additional information. This would be a positive accomplishment even if the study itself was proved wrong by the additional information. Summing up his feelings on the subject, Quesada noted that there probably were errors in his book, but he insisted that these were not errors of passion or prejudice or preconceived ideas. Instead they were the result of deficient information. Moreover, Quesada revealed that those who might justly and earnestly question his work would meet only with respect from him, but he hoped that they would show him the same consideration for his judgments and for his ideas.

Quesada brooded over the fact that his historic effort could not be definitive, but he consoled himself with the rationalization that everything he wrote could become a cog in the wheel of history that eventually would have to be considered before any definitive history could be written. He reasoned that while his work surely would be corrected in the future, in the light of new evidence, it was significant because he was searching for the truth, and if all historians sought only the truth those who came along later would move very close to that definitive history.[88]

But not all historians were as optimistic. Some were dubious about the possibility of finding truth and, beyond that, about the human capacity for overcoming one's preconceptions. Juan García del Río wrote, 'The major part of human judgments are erroneous.'' Often in the quest for complete truth it appears better to believe the opposite of what García called the ''vulgar, authorized, sanctioned, accredited opinion.'' Passions and interests spread a veil over the truth that cannot be penetrated. Like the European historians Sismondi, Guizot, and Thiers, García del Río also found ''crass lies'' in history because judgments of historians had been colored by preconceptions and personal attitudes.[89]

On the whole, however, 19th century historians believed that they and their contemporaries produced many objective works amid the polemics, political harangues, and impassioned pleadings for causes that were mistakenly labeled history. Some of the assessments of 19th century historians by their successors in the 20th century are revealing. One described José Fernando Ramírez as a ''jurist'' who ''distributed the truth.'' The same writer linked Ramírez with Joaquín García Icazbalceta, *Manuel Orozco y Berra, and Alfredo Chavero and called them all outstanding Mexican historians of the 19th century. But Ramírez had his own doubts about arriving at the truth. He wrote that ''materials of history rarely present the bare truth, it being very common for the editor to write them with the design of disfiguring them.'' This should not surprise anyone since the task of history as conceived by historians might be impossible. The true historian is expected to carry out too many functions that are incompatible within one mind. He must be a storyteller but at the same time a stern judge of facts. As the raconteur he is expected to make his offering interesting and perhaps even entertaining, which sometimes requires an embellishment of the truth, but as the austere judge of historic fact he is supposed to decide coldly and unemotionally what is fact and what is fiction. Can these two functions be carried out by one person without each one adversely affecting the other? Ramírez concluded that this could seldom occur, but he did agree that while the odds against success were astronomical, the effort had to be made by anyone calling himself an historian.[90]

Others also questioned the feasibility of finding complete truth but, again, held out the belief that some had come very close to that prized goal. One of the biographers of Pedro Fermín Cevallos wrote that his subject "possesses as few others absolute objectivity in history" and that this was partly explained because he wrote history "with the severity of a notary, with the cool sincerity of philosophy."[91] And still other historians, such as Mitre and Groussac in Argentina, Barros Arana and Vicuña Mackenna in Chile, González Suárez in Ecuador, Varnhagen and *Capistrano de Abreu in Brazil, and José Manuel Groot in Colombia have been praised for their objectivity and for their devotion to truth. At the same time one might also compile a list of those who became politicized, such as Lastarria in Chile, Vicente Fidel López in Argentina, Justo Sierra and Lucas Alamán in Mexico, and *Manuel de Montúfar in Central America. But even those who tended to present a partisan point of view in their histories or who launched into a topic with preconceived notions about the men and events in that subject believed for the most part that they were purveyors of truth. They did not regard themselves as historiographic prostitutes for having a firm conviction and for finding support for that conviction in their research. This in no way justifies their sometimes uncritical stance, but it does explain why and how their production could be both historical from their point of view and polemical from ours, as we enjoy the advantages of hindsight.

Criticism and Use of Sources

Accepting the fact that the search for truth was paramount in the interest of legitimate historiography, the historians of this age then had to approach their research with an eye to accuracy. The historian's work with his sources began sometimes with simply taking notes on books he read or on making marginal notations on articles or books that interested him. Most were curious, and this curiosity led them to seek other sources on the same topic until they ultimately collected enough material on which to construct their own histories. Pedro Fermín Cevallos began his multivolume history of Ecuador in just this manner.[92] Through the first part of that study, the work was based upon secondary sources. Cevallos compiled materials but made no effort to verify or criticize them. For the study of aboriginal Ecuador he simply took the work of Juan de Velasco and transferred it to his own history without any close analysis. For the colonial period he used William Prescott and other secondary sources. In his defense, however, the documentation in Ecuador on these periods was quite scarce when Cevallos wrote, making any kind of definitive study impossible without travel in other areas.[93]

Finding the sources, then, was a problem as well, but of even greater consequence was determining the veracity of those books and documents. Most recognized this pitfall and agreed that they could not be free from errors without a careful scrutiny of their sources and a close testing of materials for accuracy. Earlier chroniclers had not always been impartial, particularly when writing about such controversial events as the conquest of the Indians. Therefore, their work could not be accepted out of hand, but it did serve a purpose for the later historians because the chronicles placed the reader in the period in which they were written, clarified customs of that age that were different from later periods, and created the milieu of that earlier event in the mind of the historian. Thus, the setting for a history could be molded from the chronicles and books of an earlier age, but as historic evidence they had to be handled with extreme care.

Consequently, tiresome, monotonous work was required in archival material to learn exactly what had happened in the past. This necessitated patience and miniscule analysis, beginning with the establishment of the veracity of the material under study.[94] Almost all the historians of the 19th century were preoccupied with the task of verifying the author of a book or document, but Pablo Groussac believed that authorship was only one aspect of the successful scientific method that historians must follow. He agreed with his contemporaries that truth emerges from well-criticized primary sources. But he noted that the digging for and collecting of materials was fairly well completed by the end of the 19th century. At that point the major task became one of employing a scientific method of analysis. Consequently, historians in the 20th century would have to confine their work to documentary criticism rather than to the search for basic documents.[95] Pursuing this theme, Groussac sought to set an example for his own students by refusing to accept any document as valid until he tested it thoroughly. He subjected documentary collections to close study as he was suspicious of even the traditionally accepted materials. While some historians felt that it was enough to determine that documents and writings were in fact produced by the cited author, Groussac saw this as only a starting point in his research. He believed that one had to be certain that the author's work was accurate, and simply verifying authorship did not ensure the validity of the study. For example, the memoirs of the independence hero Manuel Belgrano were filled with inaccuracies and omissions. Belgrano was an old, infirm man when he wrote his memoirs. Consequently, verifying the fact that Belgrano wrote the material was not enough; a closer inspection for accuracy through comparison with documents and oral tradition was essential.

Groussac was also interested in interpreting the materials he used. He wrote that sources that were not interpreted were virtually valueless. Even psychological examination was important for determining why an opinion was given or an action was taken. This was all part of a methodological technique that all historians should use, but Groussac stopped short of setting up a narrow method that all historians must use. Instead he wrote that the technique varied with the historian, and rightly so. The method employed depended upon the "perspicacity" of the individual and his judgment. To find the truth then, Groussac suggested that "it is indispensible to listen to all testimony, to practice a complete and miniscule inventory of all unedited documents." He taught his students to "reject any notion of reflex, to doubt everything that had not been verified personally, to meditate long hours even over a theme without importance.[96]

Earlier, Groussac's fellow historian Bartolomé Mitre had set the tone for scientific study of documentation in Argentine research. He insisted on extensive and careful analysis of primary sources in a scientific manner. After his verbal battle with Vicente Fidel López over documentary research versus philosophical interpretation of secondary materials, young historians chose generally to follow his lead and to dig into the basic research materials.[97]

In addition to teaching his scientific method, Mitre also tried to convince young historians that they did not have to travel far and wide to find the necessary ingredients for writing sound history. In a letter to a friend and fellow historian, Andrés Lamas, he remarked that Buenos Aires was an excellent place to carry out the study of Argentina's past. He believed that there was more material on the old viceroyalty of Potosí in Buenos Aires than in Potosí itself. And the neighboring city of Montevideo could be used fruitfully as well; its libraries were particularly rich in the "periodical papers of the revolution."[98]

Research in other than the pre-Columbian and colonial periods presented distinctive problems for the researcher. For example, in studying Uruguayan independence, materials that existed in Argentina on Uruguayan history were generally antagonistic to that country because the official histories of the revolution were written by Rio Platanese monarchists whose memoirs and documents filled the national archives. Bauzá complained that republicans all over Latin America, after winning their independence, found themselves with the difficult task of governing new nations and consequently spent little time documenting their work. As a result, monarchist sympathizers dominated the publishing scene and provided their own partisan rendition of the independence movement.[99]

Similarly, *Gonzalo Bulnes, in writing his history of the Chilean war against the Peru–Bolivian Confederation, found gigantic problems. Materials were so biased and prejudiced that it was next to impossible to verify specific events in the war. He tried to use newspapers such as the Chilean *El Mercurio* and *El Araucano*, but both of these were so emotional over the war that anything resembling impartiality in their pages was impossible to find. However, consulting the official newspaper of the Confederation, *Eco del Protectorado*, along with other Peru–Bolivian documents, and comparing their context with the Chilean press, he was able, in his own mind at least, to approximate the truth.[100]

Some historians, among them Lisandro Alvarado, put a good deal of faith in periodicals and other contemporary publications. This use of contemporary material was dangerous, however, in that it increased the possibility of the researcher becoming prejudiced in his account because the event was a part of his era and he might even have been a prominent participant in developments that he now wrote about. In such a situation the historian's judgment obviously would be clouded, if not downright biased. Alejandro Marure, along with several others, recognized this problem and noted a concomitant difficulty. He cautioned that the historian writing on recent events must put aside all affections and friendships for persons involved in the topic on which he worked. He believed that this was not impossible if the historian was dedicated to his task and cognizant of the necessity for impartial history.[101]

Lucas Alamán also was confronted with this problem. He wrote about events in which he participated, and he still tried to remain impartial. He has been criticized for always having preconceived notions, even though he is generally praised, even by his most outspoken detractors, for his exhaustive research. Alamán tested and analyzed his sources, but the events were too fresh in his mind and many of the sources he used belonged to friends or members of his family who shared his views. As a consequence, their materials contributed nothing toward the impartiality of his work.[102] Despite the many examples of difficulty in finding unbiased contemporary sources, it is true that some historians were able to present reasonably objective views of contemporary events, but most found it virtually impossible.

Another phenomenon of this age was the historian who dealt with all periods of history, far removed and contemporary, who did not trust himself to interpret the past. Instead, influenced by the Rankian school of scientific historiography, he tried to avoid this danger by presenting data without interpretation. Those who did make some strides in this direction relied heavily on careful analysis of sources and on extensive criticism of those same sources. But many historians believed that their interpretations of data were not in the best interest of sound historiography. Alamán argued that personal observations should be excluded as much as possible by any author, thereby leaving it to the reader, with all the facts before him, to judge the data presented by the historian.[103]

Joaquín Acosta also hesitated to make his own views a part of his history but for a different reason. He feared that he did not possess the talent required to handle facts in this way. But this did not really matter, according to Acosta, because if the facts are presented clearly and in logical order then all readers will probably reach the same conclusion. This meant, however, that the narration had to be concise, with the result that he could not discuss the virtue of one source over another in the text, nor could he explain why he believed one source valid and another inaccurate. Then, too, he must not dwell upon the most interesting and dramatic parts of the history, which, in his words, was a "natural tendency" of historians; this became unnecessary when one realized that the facts themselves were attractive enough to interest and stimulate the imagination of the reader.[104]

Other historians held views roughly the same and simply presented the details without any methodological explanation appended to their studies. But while they were willing to let the reader perform the analysis, there were more historians who were anxious to analyze their sources and present a point of view to the reader. Writers like Mitre and Groussac in Argentina, Barros Arana and Vicuña Mackenna in Chile, González Suárez in Ecuador, and Lisandro Alvarado in Venezuela, to mention only a few, delighted not only in recounting the past but also in building from the data their own interpretations of the history they studied.

Their analyses may not always have been accurate, but they made the effort that some of their fellow historians shunned. And for that effort their histories became considerably more than shallow, one-dimensional narratives. Then, too, while they themselves might fail in their interpretive study, they at least were laying the foundation for a more profound type of history that followed in the later years of their own century and on into the 20th century[105]

It is to the credit of these historians that they recognized that their work, despite long months and sometimes years of research and writing, was not errorless. They did not regard themselves as infallible because they understood that as human beings they could not escape the many pitfalls that adversely affected their judgment. Nevertheless, they hoped that these errors could be kept to a minimum and that later historians would correct their inaccuracies.[106] Lucas Alamán made an open appeal for assistance in which he assured his readers that he would accept every ''rational'' criticism in the spirit of cooperation and that he would answer all the objections that were raised. In this way the reader might actually contribute to the accuracy of the study.[107]

This kind of help through criticism worked very well in the 19th century because many of the histories were published first serially in newspapers or periodicals and only put together in book form after the serial had been completed for some time. Consequently, the advice or objections received by the historian could be considered and, if found reasonable, included in the final book form. One writer, Ernesto Quesada, even chose his topics on the basis of reader participation. He avoided a long definitive work on Argentina's civil wars because he believed many sources were as yet undiscovered. Therefore, he believed that a series of short, monographic studies might elicit from readers new documents or insights that could be used later in a more detailed study. Such data could alter the author's judgment and render the lengthy work valueless, but if the history was done in short stages and corrected along the way, with new information, then the final work would be truly definitive. This technique makes everyone a historian. Anyone who reads has the opportunity to get into the production of a historic work. A side benefit of this method was the growth of a more nationalistic sentiment, which in the case of Argentina was necessary after the long, divisive civil struggle that had plagued the nation. At the same time, viewed in a more cynical light, this tactic made possible the use of a good deal of free research assistance for the author.

Still another beneficial effect of including the public in the writing of history was the increased interest in historic studies that resulted when people participated, or had the opportunity to participate, in their preparation. Enticing people to read was a difficult task, and any gimmick that induced people to spend time reading was well worthwhile. Ernesto Quesada believed that his call for research aid at the outset of his work would encourage a more severe criticism than otherwise might be forthcoming. Critics realized that he was asking for help and therefore would not be overly wary about their criticism.

Another view on the subject of historic criticism came from Alfredo Chavero, who believed that each individual historian had the duty to correct his own errors that appeared after publication of his work. When he found mistakes in his earlier works, he was the first to point them out and often the first to make the alterations. This led his contemporary, García Icazbalceta, to write, "Chavero with his writings is the same as posterity." But beyond his own close attention to possible errors, Chavero also heeded the critics and their attitudes toward his writing, even when their criticisms severely censured his work.[108]

Mitre was one of those historians who saw the correction and alteration of previous histories as natural and valuable. This to him was merely a routine, ongoing historic method. New materials were always going to turn up, and these must always be integrated into older works. All these men were realistic enough to recognize their shortcomings and to profit from their mistakes. Instead of carping at their critics, they evaluated the criticisms and in subsequent editions modified their works accordingly. Anyone who has ever written anything and endured criticism realizes that this is not always an easy attitude to assume. Human nature being what it is, writers sometimes take a hostile view of criticism, even of the constructive variety. These Latin Americans displayed a high degree of devotion to their subject and a remarkably reasonable attitude toward those who found their works to be lacking in one way or another. They regarded themselves as intellectuals and tried to act as they believed such an elevated station in society required them to act.

From the Río de la Plata to the Río Grande, 19th and early 20th century historians plied their craft with both personal documentation, sometimes collected at great expense, and public materials found in the emerging national archives and public libraries of Europe and America. The earliest 19th century historians did not place as much emphasis on Spanish archives for colonial research, but by mid-century the best historians realized the necessity for visiting Spain when dealing with colonial American history. At the same time, early national writers were forced into the use of personal libraries due to the shortcomings of public archives and libraries. And even at a later date, when governments devoted greater financial support to such institutions, personal collections continued to be of inestimable value for many historians.[109]

By mid-century the history of the independence movement had surpassed the colonial era as the chronological period in which most historians were interested. Writers might still use Spanish sources for the Wars for Independence, but they also had a plethora of material in America on which to base their research. Then, in the second half of the 19th century, contemporary history became fashionable. This type of historiography required a vast range of personal papers, documents, and archives usually held by people, still living, who had participated in events now studied.

Following 1940, for example, former participants in the Mexican Revolution of 1910 wrote about that major event in their history. Their recollections, combined with the steady emergence of documents from that age, led to important books and articles that illuminated the revolution.[110] Other 20th century events also commanded the attention of historians as they moved away from colonial and independence themes. In many of these works the authors no longer collected research materials for their personal use but now turned to the use of public archives and libraries that had not been available to their 19th century counterparts. Nonetheless, recent historians have been just as jealous as their predecessors in guarding their precious documentary materials. They have worked long and hard to keep all archival and library material in their own countries so that future scholars and students can benefit from their use.

The personal archive and library, along with the public documentary collections, became the basic tools for Latin American historians, tools without which many of the outstanding histories of the past century, as well as the current, could not have been written.

With the materials collected and with a means employed to analyze documents, historians then turned to the task of preparing their research for the reading public and of presenting it in a readable, interesting, literary prose that would be attractive to the potential reader but would also reflect the historians' view that history was in fact literature and must be handled in the same way as any other literary genre.

LITERARY STYLE AND TYPES OF HISTORY PRODUCED

Once historians completed collecting data, analyzing documents, and interpreting their sources and decided upon the technical format to be followed, they turned their attention to the problem of putting their thoughts to paper. It was one thing to be a competent, studious researcher; it was quite another to develop an effective writing style that smoothly communicated ideas to the reader. For this reason literary style was a primary concern of the historians, and some of them experimented with approaches to presenting their histories other than the traditional history book or biography. In all cases, they kept foremost in their minds their conviction that history was a branch of literature and that the literary quality of their work was of equal importance with the research.

The major historians of the period were influenced either consciously or unconsciously by grammarians who insisted upon grammatical precision and the integrity of the Hispanic language. Chile's experience in the matter of style is representative of most of Latin America. The dominant Chilean linguist was Andrés Bello. Bello was interested in anything that appeared in print, and while not a historian himself, he had written reviews of histories and essays on the nature of history. He influenced all Chilean historians of the 19th century, including Barros Arana, Vicuña Mackenna, and Miguel Amunátegui.[111] He insisted on the purity of the Spanish language and frequently deplored the interjection of "gallicisms" into the tongue. He believed that literary inspiration had to come from past Spanish writers and that less attention should be paid to the exciting French writers of the 18th and 19th centuries. Not all of Bello's students accepted his views, but nevertheless his strict attention to correct grammar rubbed off on most of them. Barros Arana, in his early years, wrote in a manner that left a good deal to be desired. One 20th century scholar regarded his style as "weighty and defective." However, with the passage of time, Bello's example, and a great deal of effort, this facet of his work improved and his narrative talent grew more interesting without any decline in critical ability.[112]

Vicuña Mackenna clearly bore the mark of Bello. At age 18 he published articles, but Bello told him to concentrate more on grammar and to be certain that his writing followed a logical course. After these suggestions Bello went on to encourage him to continue writing because he found real talent in Vicuña's prose.[113] He also impressed upon Vicuña the idea that style was as important in history as it was in any other literary genre. He fervently believed his own dictum: "If it is written well, it will be read well."

Of all the Chilean historians of this epoch, Lastarria was the only one who did not rely heavily upon Bello for stylistic assistance, but even he was influenced by the master because he had earlier studied under him. Later critics found Lastarria's writing style "generally correct" but "arid." Perhaps had he paid closer attention to his teacher he might have escaped such criticism.[114]

Despite Bello's wide reputation as a literary scholar, his own writing was not above criticism. Lastarria found it grammatically correct but believed that in making it so perfect Bello had sacrificed any spirit his style might possess for what Lastarria termed literary convenience.[115] This criticism notwithstanding, Chilean historians regarded Bello as the final word on style, and many profited from their association with him. A later Chilean observer even went so far as to suggest that Bello taught Chileans how to write history, particularly through his work with the annual university historical memorial. Domingo Amunátegui concluded that Bello's "mature and reflective criteria" was found in all memorials, with the possible exception of the one presented by Lastarria. He went on to argue that Chile's impressive activity in history in the 19th century was owed largely to Bello.[116] This is an exaggeration, but Bello's role in the literary quality of his nation's historiography cannot be denied.

Chile was not an isolated area in the literary quest for excellence, as concern for writing quality was in evidence throughout Latin America. The difference from region to region and writer to writer was only in degree. Some writers used generally correct styles following the Bello pattern, but oftentimes they were charged with dullness and with presenting uninteresting works. Others did not concentrate on grammatical accuracy but received praise for the excitement and beauty of their works. One such grammatical illiterate was Baralt, who wrote in a natural style without any concern for grammar. Nevertheless, one scholar characterized his history of Venezuela as "one of the dozen most beautiful books in the Spanish tongue."[117]

Other historians were intrigued by the styles not only of their countrymen but of foreigners as well. One U.S. historian, William Prescott, was revered for his "narrative writing."

Some historians were so conscious of their literary capabilities that they exaggerated their writing styles, with the result that the work appeared to be artificial. Carlos María Bustamante used a florid, exaggerated style in his histories. He was self-assured and convinced that his writing ability was superior to that of other writers of the age. In an introduction to his *Cuadro histórico*, he wrote that he did not want to speculate on the merits of his book and would leave that for the reader. But he did confide that, after completion of such a difficult enterprise, he personally admired the result.

A number of historians had pleasant styles largely because they avoided the artificiality displayed by some 19th century writers and they consciously kept their work simple. Andrés Lamas used common, natural words, which made for a clear presentation. At the same time, this technique made it possible for him to explain even the most difficult themes in a readable and enjoyable fashion. His thoughts were not trapped in vocabulary and grammar, as sometimes happened to other writers of this era. Alejandro Marure wrote also in an elementary fashion, disdaining anything that would make his work appear artificial. He relied on short, rapid sentences to drive home his points in his biographies and histories.[118]

Perhaps the most significant attitude toward style among the Latin American historians was that expressed by Pablo Groussac. Being a native of France, he had to work very hard at mastering the Spanish language. His greatest aid in this endeavor was his work as a journalist. Writing for a newspaper-reading public taught him to keep his work simple and clear. Once he achieved the excellence of language he sought, he then reflected upon the role of style in historiography. He argued persuasively, as noted earlier, that history was both a science and an art, and in supporting the latter category he stated that the historian, after collecting and testing his sources, became the artist who had to present his ideas in an appealing fashion to the reading public. Groussac was certain that the power of expression was fundamental to sound historiography, but he lamented that nature bequests this talent to very few people. Others not so blessed must strive to approximate the level of stylistic achievement of those with natural talent. Groussac once wrote, in discussing the history craft, that "the artist, and he alone, is the one who erects its [history's] beauty."[119] Based on his own experience he believed that anyone could write well but only a few could ever be great writers. Nevertheless, everyone must strive to write in the most interesting manner because ideas presented in a poorly written work would find a small audience. Additionally, those ideas might become so clouded in a work of low literary quality that they would be misunderstood or misinterpreted. In any case, style was extremely important for the historian's work.

There were those who paid some attention to style but who did not agree with Groussac on the importance of the writing. Pedro Fermín Cevallos did not write particularly well. In fact, contemporaries criticized him for writing in a "stiff and taut" manner.[120] Such attacks did not trouble him too much because he did not strive for literary excellence. He wanted only to write a smooth, flowing narrative. Beyond that he was not prepared to go because, as he phrased it, "no one sacrifices thought for style."[121]

Another type of historian simply did not care about correct grammar or stylistic considerations. Representing this group was Juan Vicente González. He was a fiery, impetuous writer who could not be constrained by rules. In assessing his own work he stated that he did not labor or "sweat" over style but instead simply wrote as he felt. The end result was "multiform and extravagant," but it did convey his true sentiments and this was for him the most important consideration. His determination to write what he felt was molded by experience as a journalist and then carried over to his more scholarly endeavors.[122] Whatever the grammatical shortcomings of his writing, his ideas did come through clearly and forcefully, and no one can demand more of a historian.

Still other historians had trouble with their styles. José Manuel Groot was one of those whose historic method was regarded as sound but whose style left much to be desired. His writing has been characterized charitably as 'simple, frank, natural, positive, without pretensions or artificial affectations.'' This is praiseworthy, but he also was given to grammatical slips and he frequently introduced French words into the text, which disturbed many of the Hispanic purists. Nevertheless, despite his uneven style, his *Historia eclesiástica* is regarded as a solid work.[123]

One of the least effective writers was Manuel de Mendiburu. Surprisingly, he recognized and admitted his stylistic shortcomings, and because of his realization that writing was a problem, he concluded that he could not write a historic monograph or a general history. Still, he loved history and wanted to make a contribution to its literature. The solution to his dilemma was to write a dictionary of Peruvian history in which he could trace his nation's past but in which he would not be called upon to construct a work of literature.[124]

If there was anything approximating a consensus regarding the role of style in historiography, it was that one's work must be readable and unencumbered with grammatical problems but style must always be a secondary consideration to content. Research, analysis, and interpretation were of primary importance and must never be inhibited by literary considerations. This attitude was somewhat surprising in light of the 19th century concern for literary quality in Europe and the United States and the influence that these areas had in general on the Latin American intellectual world. However, because historiography was in its infancy, the basic and fundamental aspects of the discipline received the greatest attention. This is not to suggest that Europe and the United States did not have any influence at all on Spanish American historiography. On the contrary, Latin Americans were conscious of trends and developments abroad, and some were strongly influenced by these currents.

Francisco Bulnes agreed that an historian's style was important, but he went beyond mere style to list all the qualities he believed necessary for writing successful history. He then postulated that such a man could never exist. In matters of style, his basic argument was that every writer must be himself. He must not try to imitate other writers from his own country or from foreign lands, living or dead. Instead, he was obligated to retain, develop, and utilize his own natural technique. In this way a native historiography would emerge that would be far superior to anything built on the imitation of others.[125]

Philosophical Versus Narrative History

Just as historians did not always agree on research techniques or share ideas on the value of style, they found little common ground on the kind of history they should write. That is, they were not always sure about the nature of the finished product, as to whether it should be a narrative recounting of the past or a philosophical speculation on a given historical person or event. They even had difficulty in deciding which periods were fair game for study and which should be avoided. These diverse views present an insight into the thinking of the historians on their subject, how they perceived of their discipline, and how they believed history should be presented to the reading public.

Two philosophical historians of the century stand out above all the others— Vicente Fidel López and José Victorino Lastarria. López was influenced in his historiographic career by Johann Gottfried Herder, Jules Michelet, and Edgar Quinet. Herder believed that the most important things in history were the relationships of man with nature and of men among men. López accepted this concept and concluded that history was humanity. He viewed history as a reciprocal struggle between those who wished to detain progress and those who wished to push steadily forward.[126] Herder was constantly concerned with the philosophical foundations of history and concluded that the narrative, factual brand of historiography was invalid because history is really the history of ideas and it is ideas that guide the moral condition of the humanity that is hidden in the human mind. For this reason, the mind and its ideas must be explored, not the data of countless factual events. He also believed that history taught lessons that were invaluable for the patriot, the citizen, or simply the moral man. These lessons could better be expressed through a philosophical history than through a narrative treatment.[127] López was in complete agreement with all of these attitudes.

The other great philosophical historian, José Lastarria, knew López from his exile days in Santiago, and they both expressed their views on history in speeches at roughly the same time. López presented a speech to the Faculty of Philosophy and Humanities at the University of Chile in 1845, about a year after Lastarria delivered his famous philosophical memorial on the colonial history of Chile. Like López, Lastarria was influenced by Herder and mentioned the German philosopher by name in his address. Like López also, his views on the philosophy of history found little sympathy among his Chilean contemporaries, who generally sided with the narrative approach then in vogue. One observer called Lastarria a man alone whose "philosophical-historical speculations" found little currency even in his own country.

Lastarria sought to philosophize about the past, but he did not rely heavily enough on primary data. This was the major criticism not only of Lastarria but of López and other philosophical historians as well. The widespread feeling was that they sought to build systems out of the past but that their facts were not strong enough to substantiate their ideological assumptions. For Lastarria the important part of history was not the event itself but rather the idea behind the event. He devoted his efforts to understanding these ideas. He once wrote, "Philosophy of history presents to us the logic of events." One opponent of this view suggested that it was not the logic of events that attracted Lastarria to this type of historiography but instead his inability to follow one train of thought consistently.[128]

Lastarria agreed that Herder's concept of the philosophy of history was valid except in one area. Herder based his views on the supposition of "a fatal and necessary evolution of humanity, without any participation from the liberty of man." But Lastarria insisted on independence for human nature in history. Herder in his *Las ideas sobre la filosofía de la historia* and Giambattista Vico in his *Ciencia nueva* removed that freedom from mankind and founded their theories on the supernatural conception of human history. For Lastarria, no providential hand guided mankind; instead, history was "founded on the liberty and progress of humanity."[129]

Another Chilean, Francisco Bilbao, also favored the philosophy of history concept, and like Lastarria, he rejected the fatalistic philosophy. He argued that such thinking excused all mistakes, absolved all crimes, and vindicated all despots and kings. Actually it was a "cowardly doctrine" that eliminated all responsibility from "peoples and governments." Lastarria praised Bilbao, although he did note that mysticism and metaphysics tended to disfigure his work slightly. Bilbao believed, "The truth is the vision of justice that determines life. This is the base of the new philosophy of history that we present to the New World."[130]

In other Latin American countries, scholars were also taking a long look at the philosophy of history. Lisandro Alvarado remarked that Professor Rafael Villavicencio, a teacher of universal history at the Central University of Venezuela, had worked with innovations in history and had instituted a course on the philosophy of history. In this course narrative fact was considered far less important for an understanding of history than was familiarity with Auguste Comte's positivism. Using positivism as a frame of reference, a model of the past could be constructed that might then serve to instruct the youth in events of an earlier age.

Although support for philosophical history was in evidence throughout Latin America and its proponents were firmly committed to it, others found it detrimental to historiography. One of the problems with philosophical history that was always cited by its opponents was its supporters' inclination to downgrade the value of basic factual research completely. Barros Arana in Chile complained that as a youth he was aware of a group of men who considered themselves philosophical historians but who "aspired only to know the laws of that philosophy of history derived from events, without knowing the events themselves intimately.''[131] Andrés Bello also complained about the system builders and argued that their method was not valid because it was contrary to the ''general principles'' that had guided historiography for many centuries. Basic research and criticism of sources remained for Bello the fundamental method for successful historiography. And he was not alone in Chile, or for that matter in Latin America. A committee of Chilean historians charged with selecting the best history for a prize remarked of Lastarria's *Bosquejo histórico de la constitución de gobierno de Chile* that, while the work was interesting and valuable, the committee wished that he had placed more emphasis on the facts rather than on his philosophical model. The committee members argued that he could have moved naturally into theory if he had at first set forth the facts.[132]

The history of which the committee members spoke was narrative history. This was the type that dealt in great detail with events of the past. Its adherents were primarily concerned with complete documentation and with long study in archives. Their goal was detailed, documented, objective history with little or no regard for an extensive analysis that might lead to the erection of philosophical systems. Mitre in Argentina, Bello and Barros Arana in Chile, González Suárez in Ecuador, Baralt in Venezuela, Varnhagen in Brazil, and many others chose this brand of history. Some of them argued that the stage of historiographic development in Spanish America prevented a successful philosophy of history in the 19th century. Quesada, for example, acknowledged that it might be interesting to develop a philosophy of history out of the Rosas era, but he contended that to do so was at that time impossible. He insisted that all the facts had to be known before a valid philosophy could be developed, and he pointed out the obvious fact that Argentina and other Latin American countries were still in their infancy in historic works and thus were not ready for that type of history. Along the same lines, Pablo Groussac complained that some methodologists tended to denigrate narrative history, but he charged that it was the narrative type alone that led to exactitude and the approximation, at least, of truth.[133]

The philosophical historians seemed to feel superior to the narrative breed. They were enamored of philosophy anyhow, and much of their education had revolved about philosophical and theological subjects. Consequently, they felt prepared to cope with any phase of philosophy, and they categorized those who did not think along these same lines as intellectual lightweights. The level of tolerance on both sides was quite low, as witness the polemics that raged throughout the century. But just as many writers believed that pure creative literature was far superior to historiographic literature, which they regarded as lacking in imagination, the philosophers of history regarded the narrative practitioners as inferior to them and to their thoughtful histories. It appears that both sides overstated their cases. Philosophies of history were not totally deficient in data or in the use of primary source materials. Conversely, the narrative historians did not simply present only the facts and neglect any analysis of the events they described. Somewhere between these two extreme views the majority of historians worked and produced their histories, not all of which could be described as classics but the majority of which were solid historiographical endeavors.

The types of history written—philosophical or narrative—and the methods employed to present the end product in an interesting manner indicate a degree of professionalism and interest among the Latin American historians that might be missed in light of their sometimes polemical works. An additional testament to this attitude is to be found in the numerous and sometimes lengthy quarrels over interpretation of historic episodes and over historiographic methodology that raged throughout the national period.

HISTORIOGRAPHIC POLEMICS

Latin American historians of the 19th century delighted in the combat of historiographic polemics. They seemed to thrive on the competition of these written clashes. It might have been that for the macho-conscious writer who had given up warfare or who had never participated in military activity the polemic was a substitute for the display of masculinity that accompanies physical violence. Others, such as Bartolomé Mitre and Benjamin Vicuña Mackenna, had nothing to prove in this direction since both had been active warriors. As they grew older, however, and as their nations became more stable and peaceful, the chance for winning acclaim on the battlefield was no longer present, but they still could enjoy combat of a verbal nature as they battled over concepts and ideas. A good example of this was the sentiment revealed by Vicente Fidel López in 1842 over the prospect of a literary polemic with Chilean writers. He expressed great joy that the Chileans had taken up the challenge and were prepared to wage an all-out war of words in the press.

In all the historiographic polemics, whether extended or short, participants were convinced of the righteousness of their views, and they were determined to win converts to their side of the argument. In the process of these debates, the historians had to think through their own views on history and historiography before they could enter the various frays. Consequently, some of the arguments were well received and reasonable and contained the writer's innermost thoughts on the subject. At the same time, polemics were competitive, and the object was to destroy the opponent's arguments as well as to make one's own unassailable. As a result, an endless preoccupation with minutiae sometimes dominated the debates.

Many of the historians participated not only in historiographic arguments but also in conflicts waged over religious matters, political quarrels, literary disagreements, or economic differences of opinion. Juan Vicente González was, as one historian remarked, "always the polemicist."[134] This same characterization could apply to a host of other writers of the age. José Manuel Groot was fond of polemics of all types, but he was especially addicted to religious clashes. At the same time, Pablo Groussac was a critic of a writer's works, and he was always a formidable polemicist no matter what the subject.

While many historians indulged themselves in historiographic, political, or religious debates, there were those who recognized that such a genre was not conducive to the best scholarship method. Passions and emotions were too strong to permit objective appraisal of evidence, and too frequently the historian became more interested in besting his polemical opponent than in discovering the truth. Yet the very issue of objectivity and the search for the truth was the central theme in many of the encounters, and most of the historians did not long lose sight of their major task of attaining the truth. One of the shorter but nevertheless significant polemics erupted in Chile, where the great Andrés Bello stepped into the historiographic wars to confront a youthful poet, Jacinto Chacón, who represented a point of view that Bello believed was inappropriate for the development of historical literature in the nation.

Andrés Bello Versus Jacinto Chacón

As noted earlier Andrés Bello was not primarily a historian but he was the intellectual leader of Chile, a nation that gave the world a host of outstanding historians. Bello naturally then had to think and write about history. His view on the subject did not coincide with the ideas of the young writers of the mid-19th century, and finally he entered into a brief published discussion with Jacinto Chacón in which the protagonists set forth two principal schools of historical thought[135]

Chacón was a young writer who had not gained great eminence at the time of the clash, whereas Bello was the master scholar. Bello had initiated the practice of an annual historical memorial presented by a member of the faculty of the University of Chile to the assembled scholars. José Victorino Lastarria wrote the first, and Bello commented upon it. He also reviewed subsequent memorials and occasionally devoted a column in one of Santiago's newspapers to historical topics. His attitude toward history was generally traditional in that he favored the straight, narrative approach. Lastarria, on the other hand, was bored with a faithful recounting of the past and chose instead to pay less attention to facts and more to an analysis of events. He regarded this as philosophical history, and he firmly believed that his was the only valid historical technique. But this major ideological struggle over narrative versus philosophical history included Lastarria only indirectly. Chacón became his spokesman and as such he took on Andrés Bello.

In 1847 the University of Chile established a tournament for national histories. Lastarria entered his *Bosquejo histórico de gobierno de Chile durante el primer período de la revolución desde 1810 hasta 1814*. According to a 20th century writer, *Domingo Amunátegui, the book was a "philosophical" type of history, and it had literary merit. Amunátegui saw the work as one that came close to the truth even though Lastarria did not use primary documentation or emphasize factual material as did narrative historians. Having said this, however, Amunátegui suggested that the study was not really that profound or even worthy of characterization as an exemplary history. He argued that good writers in Chile were scarce at the time so that even mediocre efforts were well received. Meanwhile, one of Lastarria's biographers, *Alejandro Fuenzalida, came to his subject's defense when he wrote that the *Bosquejo histórico* could not be condemned for not containing facts, as some contemporaries had done, because Lastarria did use primary sources, although he did not develop them logically to describe the nature of political parties. More important to Fuenzalida, however, was Lastarria's ability to find a logical relationship between cause and effect that might modify societal arrangements.[136]

Another commentator on the mid-19th century argued that Lastarria was a philosophical historian rather than a narrative one because "he could never follow one train of thought consistently." Isaac Cox agreed and added that Lastarria's histories were "bold in thought and well written, but they were polemics rather than histories and their conclusions have been largely superceded."[137]

Although criticized by contemporaries and modern writers, Lastarria did have supporters during his lifetime. Bello's view of his first historical presentation to the university was generally laudatory. Another giant of 19th century literature, Domingo Sarmiento, also praised this work. In the Santiago newspaper *El Progresso*, Sarmiento wrote that Lastarria's book was written in a "lucid, easy language" and that the ideas contained in the study were well conceived. In general, he viewed the work as one that was "as complete as possible."[138]

It was not, however, this earlier work but rather Lastarria's *Bosquejo histórico* that launched the argument between Bello and Chacón. The judging committee for the 1847 tournament included Antonio García Reyes and Antonio Varas, both of whom had written some histories but neither of whom could be characterized as a historian. Both were preoccupied with government service. Each man was a close friend of Lastarria, and they agreed that Lastarria should win the prize but only if he made some changes that would bring his book closer to the kind of history advocated by Bello. Lastarria naturally refused to rewrite the study, and the prize went to another entrant.

When the book was published, Chacón, as one of Lastarria's few historiographic followers, wrote the prologue, in which he denounced the emphasis upon narrative history in the university and throughout the nation. Chacón characterized Lastarria's work as constitutional history, which, he argued, was the highest form of historiography. Such history, according to Chacón, can be written only after historiography has passed through a progressively more sophisticated scale from simple chronicle to complex philosophical history. It can be written only after all is known about a society, about its politics, religion, morality, literature, economy, and customs. Since this kind of historic investigation had been done only in the 19th century, it was logical, wrote Chacón, that constitutional history could be written only after 1840. Throughout the prologue he drew a sharp distinction between constitutional and political history. Political history was ineffective if constitutional history was not completely understood. It was constitutional history that put together the facts and ideas that demonstrated trends toward new ideas. Put another way, it was constitutional history that illuminated the move toward social revolution.[139]

Chacón depicted Lastarria not as "a mere chronicler" of facts but as a man who explored the center of social movements. Consequently, Lastarria was the first constitutional historian. As a constitutional historian, Lastarria examined the entire life of a people and concluded that proponents of the old system were steadfastly refusing to change. Political historians, on the other hand, only scratched the surface of civilizations' secrets. Unlike them, Lastarria had moved directly to the heart of a people with his *Bosquejo histórico*.

Chacón also took the opportunity to expound the virtues of the constitutional historian in general as opposed to what he considered the less sophisticated "political historian." Only the constitutional historian, he wrote, could provide a clear development of political events because of his analysis of the facts in all areas of man's progress. He then expanded on this theme. "Only the constitutional historian...can give us the true causes of political events, presenting to us an illustration so brief, logical, and clear, of the march of revolution, and to judge with elevation and impartiality the men and things of the constitutional period through whose labyrinth he leads us."[140]

When Chacón so boldly condemned all other types of history except the constitutional variety, he invited rebuttal from those who did not work in this genre. This was a conscious effort on his part because he wished to take to task those who had rejected Lastarria's *Bosquejo histórico* as a prize-winning effort, and more importantly from his point of view, he wanted to show up their arguments against Lastarria as unworthy of literary tournament judges. In the process of seeking vindication for his friend, Chacón lashed out at narrative history. He wrote that it was one thing to learn facts but quite another to use those facts to see the larger scheme of history. It was this use of data that was "the importance and utility of history." The possessor of facts who did not use them to draw the large historic story together could write history and make it interesting, but it would be sterile and unsophisticated. On the other hand, the constitutional historian with his grasp of the age and his knowledge of society could present "the true explanation and the exact understanding of the life of a people." More important, however, he could then show the lessons that were to be gained from this past experience and aid in the future development of humanity. This was Lastarria's contribution to scholarship.[141]

The man who took up the challenge of Chacón's arguments was Andrés Bello. He did so in a series of articles, first reviewing Lastarria's *Bosquejo histórico* and then exploring the problem of historical writing. Bello first complimented Lastarria on his book and praised him as being "among the most distinguished and industrious members of the University and the National Institute." He noted that the book had been considered for a prize but that the judges had found it lacking and had chosen to present the award to another author. Bello defended their decision, but he would not go as far as they had in opposing Lastarria's work. While the judges had criticized Lastarria for not preparing the groundwork for his study with proper research, Bello argued that the *Bosquejo histórico* was more than an unsupported collage of "principles and generalities." It was a respectable "political history."

Bello was less gracious with Chacón. In particular he was disturbed by Chacón's insistence that history could be rated on a scale beginning with chronicles at the bottom and progressing to constitutional history at the top. Chacón's argument that this height of constitutional history could be reached only in the 19th century, after history had passed through all the lesser stages, particularly nettled his adversary. Bello insisted that all types of history are of equal value and that chronicles, constitutional history, and philosophical history all occupy the same level of importance. He cringed under the charge that narrative, factual studies were inferior to philosophical history. In a second article, Bello hauled out some of the leading European historians to support his thesis. He cited Agustín Thierry and Jean Charles Sismondi and their statements that facts are the basis of history. Bello modestly explained his use of renowned historians by stating that his words carried little weight in this discipline but few could deny the arguments of the great men in European historiography. Mentioning Chacón again by name, Bello stated that the "trite road to history" referred to by Chacón, that is, the reliance on facts, was the only true method to accurate, complete history. Only after careful consideration of the facts could the historian arrive at a philosophy of a civilization or a society.[142]

In discussing the philosophy of history of Lastarria and Chacón, Bello divided it into two categories. One was a general study of humanity, such as man's morality and man's laws. The second was more specific in that the facts of a society or a people were studied. In this latter category the various influences on the people could be discerned and ideas could be traced as the facts unfolded. A general philosophy of history used truths found in one area and applied them to another. Since certain laws of humanity applied anywhere in the world in a general sense, in a philosophy of history all experiences of all peoples could be used. On the other hand, the second type of philosophy of history required a different tack. In specific matters there were no generalizations that applied to all peoples so that the approach that worked for general history was valueless for the second type. In this area everything had to be studied. The historian "must examine the spirit of a people in its geographic location, its laws, its religion, its industry, its artistic productions, its wars, and in its letters and sciences." This task would be impossible if history did not reveal itself through its facts. It would be impossible to understand this kind of history without a "complete exposition of the facts."[143]

After providing the reader with his own thoughts on the philosophy of history, Bello lashed out again at Chacón. He denied that the judges had rejected Lastarria's book only because of "intolerance and exclusiveness" or from a desire to have all history written only with the objective of presenting the facts. Bello wrote that if the commission's views on Lastarria's work represented "intolerance and exclusiveness" then the whole discipline of literary criticism was dead in Chile. Lastarria had the right to produce any book he chose, but he and Chacón must also recognize the rights of others to examine and criticize the book.[144]

In another article published in the semi-official newspaper *El Araucano*, Bello went into the question of the proper kind of history. For the second time he defended the commission's stand on Lastarria's book. The commission's point that the book lacked the factual data necessary to make valid judgments on the period under consideration was, for Bello, a supportable appraisal. He then went back to the basic argument over narrative versus philosophical history. He conceded that for some countries or some areas of the world where extensive histories had already been written, a reevaluation of the past might be in order. Certainly historians were then in a position to philosophize about history, having extensive data readily available for their scrutiny. But Chile had not reached this level. Little had been written about the independence era so it was necessary to dig into sources and present the facts in a narrative way. Bello, in essence, believed that both methods of history were valid but that in Chile's peculiar situation only the narrative brand was legitimate.[145]

Bello's strongest argument came at the conclusion of this article. He pointed out that there was no good reason why the one history should be exalted over the other or, more importantly, why both methods could not be employed in a single study. A combination of narrative with philosophical history was for him sound. But Bello feared that, if Lastarria's outspoken emphasis on philosophical history passed unchallenged, students would follow his lead and produce history that was not based on verified fact. Bello had detected an eager interest in history among Chile's youth, and he wanted to make certain that young scholars were educated properly in their search for truth.[146]

The polemic died with Bello's article. It seems incredible that this resolution of the argument could not have been invoked from the very beginning. To a degree both sides were correct. True history required both the factual and the philosophical approaches. Yet Lastarria had been so outspoken in defending the correctness of his methodology in preparing his university memorial in 1844 that Bello felt constrained to overstate the case for factual, narrative history at the expense of philosophical analysis. Consequently, both Lastarria and his followers, chief among them Chacón, and Bello and his supporters share responsibility for instituting and perpetuating a futile debate over historic method when their energies could have been directed to enriching the intellectual scene in other areas. This having been said, however, it must also be pointed out that the polemic, while not adding much in the way of scholarship, did serve to publicize the discipline of history and to hold students' attention on it, at least while the discussion lasted. Later events indicate that interest did not decline after 1848 but continued on throughout Chile's development down to the very present. In this light, then, the polemic did make a positive contribution to Chilean intellectual and historiographic progress.

Some years later, across the Andes in the Argentine, three historiographic

debates raged that were more protracted and became more famous than the Bello–
Chacón confrontation. All three involved Bartolomé Mitre, and two of the three
centered on his two-volume book, *Historia de Belgrano*, which he wrote in
1859.

Bartolomé Mitre Versus Dalmacio Velez Sarsfield

The first polemic that evolved from the publication of Mitre's biography of
the independence hero Manuel Belgrano included the respected scholar Dalmacio
Velez Sarsfield, who took exception to a number of points made by Mitre in the
book. Velez' objections were included in four newspaper articles published in
El Nacional. Mitre's answers appeared in a series of articles in *La Nación
Argentina*, but all articles by both men were collected almost immediately and
published in book form in 1864.

Velez was particularly disturbed by Mitre's statement in the book that General
Belgrano had to stimulate the people of the Argentine interior to support the
independence movement in 1812. Belgrano had written in a letter to a friend
that in some parts of the interior it was like moving through enemy territory
where, if people were not hostile, they were at least apathetic about independence.
Velez charged that Mitre had accepted this one letter as an authoritative statement
on the sentiment of the provinces when in reality it was only Belgrano's personal
impression and not at all accurate. Instead, Velez insisted that it was really all
the people who made the revolution, and independence leaders like Belgrano
were oftentimes more a hindrance than an asset.[147]

Mitre responded that Velez' judgment was subjective in nature; that he offered
no new proof of the validity of his view over that of Mitre; and that he provided
no evidence that Belgrano was wrong in his assessment of the situation in 1812.
This set the tone for the entire debate as Mitre insisted that biography and history
must be based upon tested documentation and not upon emotion. He claimed
that his judgments were the result of clear evidence in the form of primary
documents and that his conclusions could be destroyed only by "other facts
plainly justified and by other documents of more value than those which served
in making the study." But Velez had used only "vague memories and incomplete
reminiscences." He did not analyze any documents, and his "appreciations are
exaggerated, his judgments are absolute, and all his assertions or nega-
tions. . .have no more foundation than his anonymous and unauthorized word."[148]

As a result of Mitre's position, the polemic moved quickly into a disagreement
over historical method, and particular points raised by Velez were overshadowed
by Mitre's insistence on the proper way to carry out historiographic research
and present it to the reading public. But Velez countered with the argument that
facts did support his contention that the people were already behind the war. He
pointed out that citizens of Tucumán joined Belgrano's army even though they
did not know him and had only heard his name in connection with his unsuccessful
campaign in Paraguay. Would such a reputation enable him to stir the apathetic
population to support the war against the Spaniards? Not in the mind of Velez.

He said that such action on the part of the people clearly indicated that revolutionary zeal was already present and did not have to be dragged from the populace, as Mitre contended. Velez closed his first article by stating that it was the people who held the enthusiasm for independence and it was they who led the leaders in the struggle against Spain.[149]

This parting shot by Velez added a new dimension to the polemic that the great Argentine historian *Ricardo Levene viewed as crucial for his country's historiographic development. The clash had now broadened because a social concept had been introduced. That is, were the real heroes of independence a handful of educated, well-to-do men, or was it the people of the hinterland who deserved credit for the victory?[150] Velez believed that the latter view was accurate, while Mitre continued to exalt individuals as heroes.

Mitre told the reading public that he was not anxious to get involved in the argument with Velez but that he was aware that his silence on the subject would be construed as acceptance of the criticism so that he had to continue the verbal battle. He noted that Velez' criticisms had pointed out the existence of two different historic schools that examined and probed the causes and evolution of the Argentine struggle for independence. One group of writers tried to prove that an enlightened minority of the population planned, directed, and carried off the movement exclusively without the assistance of the popular forces in the nation. A second group went the opposite direction and gave almost exclusive glory to the people for the independence success. In the process this element downgraded traditional heroes to an inconsequential role in the battle with Spain. These were both extreme views, but there was very little backing off from either extreme by even distinguished Argentine writers up to the second half of the 19th century. And Velez Sarsfield even went so far as to deny the traditional heroes any significant leadership role in the success of the revolution. Mitre unhappily noted, however, that at the same time Velez blamed the leaders for any mistakes that were made. This for Mitre was the height of illogical thinking. If the heroes had no important leadership function, then they could not be blamed for the mistakes that were made. Beyond that, Velez also credited Martín Guemes with great importance and saw him as more significant than San Martín and almost as important as Bolívar in the total picture of South American independence. This stance suggested that Velez did not regard all leaders as insignificant but only some few, among whom was Belgrano.

For Mitre both schools of history were inaccurate and their judgments were impossible to surport with documentation. History teaches, said Mitre, that any great revolutionary movement has to have popular support or it will not succeed. At the same time, men of action are necessary to lead the masses. Argentina provided clear proof of this since the famous leaders drafted the political and military plans that helped bring about success. In defense of his book *Belgrano*, Mitre wrote that he tried "to paint the real life of a memorable epoch, using unedited documents, up to that time unknown." In this way he hoped to "humanize" revolutionary war heroes. He included their great achievements but did not ignore their "human weaknesses." He freely placed responsibility on them for the errors he believed they committed. Of more importance, he based his study on documents and facts, and he tested the facts in a most critical way. Mitre stated frankly and immodestly, "A book written along these lines could not propose to create heroes with attributes which they never had.[151]

Velez attacked Mitre on another aspect of the same issue. Mitre claimed to have verified his facts by testing them against official documents. Velez, however, argued that it was common knowledge among intellectuals in Argentina that these documents were notoriously unreliable. Consequently, they were not capable of leading Mitre to the truth he sought. Coming in for greater criticism from Velez was Mitre's lack of concern for the common people. It was not only Mitre's refusal to depict them in a glorious fashion that disturbed Velez but Mitre's refusal to delve deeply into the social and cultural history of the independence age that upset him as well. Mitre had written that he wished to write about the "real life of a memorable epoch," but Velez claimed he did not accomplish this because he was preoccupied with individuals, not with the customs or opinions of the masses.

All great historians, according to Velez, wrote about an entire age, not just the glorious figures in that period. But Argentine historians had been glaringly deficient in this type of historiography as they continued to dwell upon the heroics of a few chosen individuals. Mitre was not alone in this; most of the other Argentine writers did the same thing, but neither did Mitre break out from this inappropriate type of historiography and therefore he deserved criticism for his work.[152]

Mitre denied these allegations, insisting instead that he was dealing with the entire period and not just with a single individual or a few heroes. Beyond that, to the charge that any number of men could have done as well as Belgrano did in 1812, Mitre responded that such suppositions had no place in scholarly research. Velez listed the names of a number of those he believed could have accomplished the same as Belgrano, but Mitre refuted the list with the charge that one was not even a military man and another was not even a front rank officer.[153]

Velez was not overly caustic and bitter in his criticisms of Mitre, and for this reason the debate never really heated up as did many of the other polemics of the 19th century. Velez at times praised Mitre's work as the "best history we have" of 1810. His strongest objection to the biography came when Mitre got to 1812. He also referred to the early "interesting articles" written by Mitre in the serialized version of the book.[154] These statements came in Velez' third article and the first one that he signed. Up to this point Mitre was not certain who his antagonist was but now he knew for certain, and because of his respect for the scholarly ability of Velez and perhaps also because Velez in the third article even became complimentary, Mitre's position softened.

In Mitre's answering work he praised the third article written by Velez as far better than the other two and he took pains to depict his adversary in a favorable light. He said that Velez was an authority on men and events in the revolution and that even when he was not a participant in the events he was a valuable resource because he had a feel for the emotions and sentiments of the age. Mitre even went so far as to write that Velez made some telling points in his criticism of *Belgrano* that could be utilized to great advantage by other historians. Having said this, however, Mitre then returned to the fray with the statement that Velez had "not responded to the fundamental rules of good historic criticism" and that he had not brought anything new to the polemic insofar as additional facts were concerned. Mitre was particularly miffed at the practice of denying the validity of documents without showing evidence as to why they were inaccurate. Moreover, Velez never attempted to offer anything in place of the documents to support his own views.[155]

By the time of Velez' last article, both parties were anxious to bring the polemic to an end in an amicable fashion. Now Mitre was referring to Velez as the "illustrious critic" and the "distinguished writer," with no hint of sarcasm or petulance. For his part Velez claimed a victory in at least one area when he noted that Mitre had, in response to his criticism, acknowledged a more prominent role in the revolution for General Guemes.

But Mitre generally held to his views and stated plainly that he had not seen any new documents that would lead him to alter his general characterization of Belgrano and that leader's role in the independence wars. He did concede that much work remained to be done on that period in Argentina's history, and he did not claim that his biography of Belgrano was a definitive work. But he did insist that his book came close to that definitive history.

In another part of his final article, Mitre recalled that he wrote *Belgrano* "precisely...to wake up the sentiment of Argentine nationalism deadened then by the 1858 division of the people." When he showed errors and internal troubles, he was simply trying to demonstrate the greatness of the nation as it overcame such obstacles on its path to mature development. He studied the origins of his country's sentiments and attitudes and showed how these led to independence. But throughout the book his major consideration was not the stimulation of patriotism or national pride but rather the search for truth. For Mitre the fundamental reason for writing any history or any biography was simply to find truth, a truth that he could support with authentic documentation. Mitre believed that he had achieved that end insofar as extant documentation would permit.[156]

Finally, both Mitre and Velez concluded the polemic with the hope that their debate had added to the maturation of Argentine historiography.[157]

In comparison with other polemics in which Mitre was involved, and those that took place in other countries on historiographic matters, this debate was mild, reasoned, and unemotional. Both men believed that they made telling arguments in support of their own views, and yet each was willing to make concessions to his adversary. In this way, it was a profitable exchange of ideas from which the reading public and Argentine historiography benefited.

A second polemic involving Mitre and his biography of Belgrano was much more lengthy as books, rather than articles, became the vehicles of expression for the participants. It was much more emotional and the language more caustic. The arguments ranged over a wider area and opened up additional areas of disagreement among Argentine historians.

Bartolomé Mitre Versus Vicente Fidel López

Vicente Fidel López was an outstanding writer of the 19th century. He, like Mitre, had fled the Rosas dictatorship to take up residence in Chile, where he and Domingo Sarmiento became journalists of some note. He participated in the literary quarrel with members of Chile's Generation of 1842 and later returned home to Argentina following the defeat of Rosas to continue his writing. He and Mitre were longtime friends and remained so throughout the debate, although from time to time, as the arguments became more intense, that friendship sometimes appeared strained. The same was not true of their respect for one another; that remained strong even amid the most sharply worded attacks on each other's work.[158]

At the time of the polemic in 1881 and 1882, Mitre's stature as a historian was already recognized and López was just beginning to acquire a solid reputation. The exact cause for the initiation of the discussion is disputed by each participant. Mitre wrote the first articles in defense of his *Historia del Belgrano*, which López had criticized in the prologue to his book on Argentine independence, *Historia de la Revolucíon argentina*. Mitre then began to publish articles entitled *Comprobaciones históricos* serially in Argentine newspapers. These were later collected and published in book form. López then charged that Mitre had initiated the polemic by attacking his comments about *Belgrano*. But Mitre argued that the assault on Belgrano was in reality an attempt by López to avenge statements made by Mitre in an article written in 1875 in a Chilean journal in which Mitre criticized the historiographic ability of López. This, however, might have been occasioned by López' criticism of the first edition of *Belgrano*. In any case, the article in the Chilean journal carried a blunt appraisal of López as a historian. Mitre wrote:

Excuse me for saying that this writer [López] ought to be taken with caution because he writes history with philosophical tendencies, more according to a theory based on hypothesis than in accordance with a methodological system of verification. Outside of the documents printed in periodicals the historical baggage of López is very light. Guiding himself by the compass of his theory, illuminating himself along his road by preconceived ideas, affirming dogmatically ideas that are contrary to those who base their work on unedited documents that he has not consulted, he incurs grave errors, notwithstanding the literary beauty of many of his animated pages, which, however, he has not adjusted to historic truth.[159]

Mitre believed that López stewed over this criticism for six years and then took out his wrath on his friend in the prologue to his book. And well he might suspect that this article was the cause of López' attacks on *Belgrano*. In his

three-volume defense, *Debate histórico*, López announced that he had not pre-
cipitated the clash with Mitre but had earlier, in 1872, praised the biography of
Belgrano. Then three years later Mitre published his article in Chile belittling a
number of Argentine historians, among them López. When Mitre discredited
Argentine writers, wrote López, he violated the rules of urbanity and provoked
López, who now stated that he did not wish to be courteous in his style, particularly since Mitre had characterized him as a historian of "doubtful credit."
It would have been bad enough had this been written in a private letter to a
countryman, but it was published openly and, to make it much worse, directed
at a foreign audience.[160] This reference to a private letter seems to support the
contention of Ricardo Rojas that López probably was aware of a personal letter
written to another friend who was coeditor with López of *Revista del Río la
Plata*. In that letter, which López probably saw, Mitre wrote, in reference to
López: "It is a pity that with such beautiful gifts of the historian he writes without
documents and asserts with such frequency the contrary to that which the documents say and verify."[161]

Whatever the immediate cause of the polemic, it was a lengthy and exceedingly
important event in Argentine historiographic development. In fact, the 20th
century Argentine historian Ricardo Rojas contends that it was one of the two
most important literary polemics in 19th century Argentine history.[162]

In the debate, Mitre's articles were carried in *Nueva Revista de Buenos Aires*
and *La Nación*. López published his articles in *El Nacional*. The articles were
then collected in books, which roughly amounted to eight hundred pages for
each man. Consequently, the smallest detail was often scrutinized from every
possible angle, and dozens of pages were written about the use of one word or
the interpretation of one word. Despite this tedious preoccupation with minutiae,
the main themes of the polemic were not obscured. Fundamentally, the difference
of opinion centered around the manner in which each man believed history should
be researched and written. For Mitre the method was simplicity itself. The
historian must examine all documents, published and unpublished alike, and
then test each document against other information such as oral tradition. Then,
only after carefully sifting all available information, could he discern the truth.
That to Mitre was the ultimate objective of all history: the acquisition of the
truth.

Throughout the argument, as with his earlier confrontation with Velez, Mitre
centered his attention on the analysis and testing of documents and observations
in his defense of *Belgrano* and, in a larger sphere, his defense of his brand of
historiography. But he also took the offensive in many cases to criticize López,
usually castigating him for not using documents but at times also finding stylistic,
geographical, historical, and chronological errors.[163] This was not difficult since
López wrote the articles over a brief period of time and did not devote much
time or effort to making them grammatically or stylistically correct. He wrote
the two volumes, later divided into three, of his *Debate histórico*, in a few
months. Another cause of errors was that he did not write the material but rather

dictated it. While this made mistakes more numerous, it did give his ideas more force because the articles sounded like conversation and dramatized what Ricardo Rojas called "oratorical vehemence."[164] Still, his overriding concern was the proper historic method.

For López the kind of research advocated by Mitre was sterile, boring, unimaginative, and primitive. He agreed that sources were important and that they must be consulted, but this in itself was not enough. Philosophical tendencies should be included in all research to lend color, understanding, and the broad picture to the completed work. López went on to argue that great historians in other countries such as Hume, Macaulay, Carlyle, Buckle, Thiers, Michelet, Guizot, and Taine all wrote works which Mitre described as pervaded with "philosophical tendencies." None of these great writers confined themselves to Mitre's system, which, according to López, was nothing more than "documentation."

López gave a further hint of his idea of what history should be when he defended himself from a Mitre attack on his too brief and rapid treatment of specific events in the independence wars. He wrote that he was "too rapid and brief" in his treatment to give the episode "animation and fire." He saw no reason to introduce minutiae and trivia into the story. In his mind too much detail tried the reader's patience. Consequently there was a good, solid literary reason for brevity.

This points up another basic difference in the thinking of the two men. Mitre insisted upon careful research first and literary quality second, although it is true that his works were, in a literary sense, excellent. On the other hand, López was willing to sacrifice some detail in order to make the finished product more readable.

Mitre's answer to all this was that detail was important not only because every minor point is significant in the overall picture but also because mistakes in dealing with detail or omission of detail cause the reader to lose confidence in the historian. For Mitre a small error regarding the use of one cannon or more than one in a given battle made López' entire history suspect. López retorted that Mitre also made errors and did not believe that his work was weakened by them.

While López was not enthralled with detailed historiography, he decided that the best tactic in combatting the charges of Mitre was to go back to the documentation and show clearly that Mitre was wrong in his interpretation of primary documents. At this point he could not resist taking a swipe at Mitre's vaunted personal library, which the owner claimed contained 100,000 documents. López asked, whether this meant that Mitre was a bigger man and better historian than Diego Barras Arana, whose library was reputed to hold only 8,000 documents.

The debate generally, however, centered upon one man's analysis of documents or the other's interpretation of words. Consequently, chapters were written on the translation from English of a word or phrase. Carefully, each man examined the movements of troops through the city of Buenos Aires when the

English invaded, and they quarreled over street names and over the number of troops involved from each side. Mitre was able to get the argument over to a discussion of detail, which López looked upon as being less than essential to good historiography. In this respect he was able to fight out the battle on his own ground in an atmosphere much more familiar to him than to López.

But López had the literary style, and some of his barbs were not only sharp but cleverly phrased. He charged, at one point, that if Mitre "had a clearer understanding of literature and was more competent in saying what he wished to say," López would agree with some of his conclusions. But, he continued, it was well known that Mitre was inclined "to pontificate with the metaphor." His metaphors, insisted López, were inconsistent and had little resemblance to the matter with which they dealt.[165]

Mitre's style was not as smooth as his adversary's, but he believed that style was of less importance than content. Just as he insisted that historical works be based upon assiduous collection and examination of data, he chose to rely on documentation in his polemical struggle with López. He went back to the sources and hauled out the materials that he had used to discover historic truth. He then cited passages from López juxtaposed to his own earlier passages and demonstrated with the sources that his conclusions were accurate and that López' arguments were false.[166]

But he also used the debate to expound further his own philosophy of history and to set down his view of what the historian should be doing. He saw as the primary need the discovery of new documents that would fill in the many gaps in Argentina's history or additional documentation that might clarify events that to his age were still murky and shadowy.

Mitre went on to discuss his idea of documental research. By use of the term *documents* he did not mean isolated papers but rather a cohesive system of materials that augment and correct each other. "It is not enough to know one or a few documents," he wrote. "It is necessary to know them all, because one alone that is lacking can annul or give diverse significance to all the rest. But López based his work on the testimony of two contemporary historians, and he brought out only one new fact in the entire book. This is not the kind of work that was then needed when so much digging in documentation was still to be done on the independence period.[167]

Later in this book Mitre conceded that López had made a contribution to independence history beyond introducing one new fact. But his contribution was not in the realm of research, rather it was a contribution of interpretation. Once again, however, this was not what Argentina needed at that time. The nation's history was not ready for that kind of scholarship but still needed extensive basic research.

After taking López to task for his methodology and for his lack of a significant contribution, Mitre then took the opportunity to boost his own role in Argentine historiography. He stated bluntly that his book on Belgrano "marked an epoch in our mode and method of writing history in our country, and the hero and the public conscience have gained something with the reading of its pages.''[168] Two outstanding later Argentine historians agreed. Ricardo Rojas and Ricardo Levene viewed Mitre's work on Belgrano and the subsequent polemics that it inspired as the initiation of a school of historiography that served to push forward along the correct path the study and writing of history in Argentina.[169] Mitre also took credit for making the debate more than it started out to be. He believed that he had "widened the field of discussion" by getting away from only specific criticisms of parts of López' work and tackling the greater problem of historic method in general.[170]

As one might suspect in this type of writing, both authors frequently overstated their cases. López certainly had something to do with moving into various areas that at first neither man had chosen to examine, but Mitre gave him no credit for this at all. On the other side, Mitre over and over insisted that López brought nothing new to the discussion. Yet on close inspection it is obvious that López was not interested in bringing new facts to the public because he argued in favor of a synthesis of facts already known as opposed to documentary research. Mitre also boasted that his work, *Comprobaciones*, had been published in all the Argentine press and picked up by foreign periodicals as well. He noted that it could "be read as any other book of historic narrations without the reader suspecting it as part of a polemic." López' *Refutaciones*, he charged, was not as widely read, nor was it something that one could profit from except insofar as it was critical of Mitre.[171]

Mitre's boast about his wide audience and his subsequent inference that this popularity of his writing was evidence that he had bested López in the debate are not valid. It must be kept in mind that Mitre was an ex-president of Argentina and that his name alone could get material published and attract the reading public. López, on the other hand, while also possessing a reputation as a literary figure, could not command the prestige or audience of his adversary. Mitre's second point about the nature of his *Comprobaciones* as opposed to *Refutaciones* is well taken however. More often than not Mitre chose to discuss the larger issues in historiography, while López frequently quibbled over minute details.

Mitre made a point of not opposing the concept of philosophical history. He noted that he had no objection to this type of historiography as he understood it. That school of history was one in which the historian sought for the ideal but within the facts. This was not López' system however. López wanted to build a philosophy of history that as yet had not been written. His philosophy of history then was based on conjecture rather than fact, and as such it was not really a philosophy of history. This was Mitre's fundamental objection to López. His disagreement was not with philosophy of history but rather with a philosophy based on conjecture rather than fact. In addition, Mitre believed that something positive must be contributed by each historical work, and he could find little of value in López' history of independence. He wrote: "And in the matter of history, he who does not enrich it with facts, with documents, with ideas, with new views, or with forms that rejuvenate the old offers nothing but words that would better remain quiet in the dictionary.''[172]

López, however, found Mitre's method of researching and writing history to be ''cold'' and detached. By relying solely on documents to the exclusion of reminiscences, oral tradition, and deduction, Mitre produced a work that was lifeless history. He did not take into account ''passions'' of the participants, nor did he examine their divergent natures. His history then was mechanical, sterile, and bereft of any strain of humanism. History, said López, cannot be totally mechanical, scientific, and molded within an established scientific framework. Why? Because history is a work of ''art''; not Mitre's history, which was a simple work of register and annotation of detailed facts, but the true history, the philosophy of history that takes into account society and man and passion, things that cannot be gleaned from civil and official records and letters. Mitre called documents the ''meat on the bone of history'' (still another metaphor). But he ignored an even more important ingredient in the finished product—imagination. He also ignored the very important oral tradition. According to López the great historians of the past, Sallust, Tacitus, Thucydides, and Macauley, were not archivists, nor were they preoccupied with documentation. Instead they used oral tradition, people's emotions, and their imaginations to formulate their great histories that became classics. These historians presented little that was new. Others writing before them had gone over the same ground. But despite this, their works remain ''literary monuments.'' For Mitre the merit of a book was the number of documents used to write it. Imagination, style, grouping of facts had no value for him, according to López.[173]

López had shown himself to be especially thin-skinned when he brooded for six years over Mitre's criticism of him in the article published in Chile. He rankled under subsequent assaults on his work and in defense lashed out at his antagonist, oftentimes in ill-advised and shallow attacks. Mitre, too, was sensitive to criticism of his work, but his earlier polemic with Velez had toughened him to criticism so that he was willing to accept constructive suggestions. He demonstrated this clearly by bringing out a revised edition of *Belgrano* after the Velez polemic in 1876–1877. And following the debate with López, he published still another revised edition in 1887. While he was willing to profit from the polemics, he did insist that the criticism of his work be ''just and objective.'' He remarked also that ''every book gains from being impartially and severely examined.'' And he believed that true criticism strengthened a book and complemented it.[174] López even noted the changes in the various editions of *Belgrano*, although he used these to support his argument that the original was not such a great history, but as Velez and he pointed out the weakness of *Belgrano*, Mitre hastened to take advantage of their comments to strengthen his work.[175]

Mitre concluded his portion of the debate with the comment that in 54 chapters of his work on the polemic he had ''opened new roads to history and historians, broadening their horizons, or changing points of view, and we believe we fixed some doubtful points with a complete and correct documentation.''[176] López, on the other hand, continued to believe that he had defended the position of philosophical history in a satisfactory fashion and that he had proven to Mitre that the earlier judgment of his ''light baggage'' as a historian was not an accurate appraisal of his scholarship.[177]

Both men appeared satisfied with their roles in the discussion. And subsequent Argentine writers agreed that the debate was indeed beneficial for their country's intellectual and literary development. Certainly one of the major outgrowths of the clash was the increased interest in archival work. People familiar with the discussion realized that archives could provide at least some answers to the questions debated by the participants. Students would now be required to display some ability in working with original documents.[178] In addition to pointing the way to the archives, the writings of Mitre and López also provided the youth of the nation with a clear picture of two different historic methods, one based on careful documentation and studied judgment, and the other brilliantly conceived and written themes without extensive, tedious documentation.[179]

This battle aided historiographic growth in Argentina not merely by popularizing history but also by laying out the path that historiographic scholarship should take. Both schools of historiography were clearly delineated, and those who fancied either one had a model to follow and a hero to emulate. No matter which man or which method was chosen, Argentina benefitted because despite their deep differences both were right in their assessment of historic scholarship. Documentation was essential and scientific scholarship was admirable. But at the same time, the synthesis and analysis of facts already proven by scholars also had a place in historiography when handled with a talented, literary flair. In this sense both were right, just as history is both a science and an art. The secret is not to overemphasize one aspect at the expense of the other but to combine them both so that the end product is a rich, scholarly, literary job; informative yet entertaining.

Bartolomé Mitre Versus Pablo Groussac

Late in the 19th century, Mitre felt compelled to embroil himself in a third polemic, which again revolved about the historiographic treatment of Argentine independence. This time his adversary was Pablo Groussac, the well-known, respected intellectual who had written histories, essays and bibliographies.

This debate was a very brief one and went over some of the same ground explored in the two earlier confrontations. Groussac wrote a piece in 1897 about the independence period to which Mitre took exception. In May 1897, Mitre attacked Groussac's work in *La Nación*. Mitre was again piqued because, in his biography of Santiago Liniers, Groussac had mentioned Mitre's *Belgrano* and his *Comprobaciones* and had taken exception to some of the points made by the great historian, who was now nearing the end of his brilliant career and life. In response, Mitre charged that Groussac had been too kind to Liniers, probably because of the "native sentiment" that led him to exalt a man who, while significant, did not merit the kind of treatment accorded him by his French countryman. This blatant charge of partisanship was tempered somewhat by Mitre's acknowledgment that the work did add something to Argentine history and that Liniers was deserving of some glory, although not in the amount parceled out by Groussac.[180]

Mitre did not want to get into specifics in this polemic, as he had done earlier with López, but rather sought to answer some of the charges of arbitrary judgments and lack of understanding of military tactics, and of topographical references in documents of the independence wars. Such things as the size and positioning of the British line in the battle of Buenos Aires in 1807, which Groussac had questioned, were defended by Mitre. He cited his sources just as he had done in the earlier debates, but Groussac was unimpressed. Instead he pointed out that the source used by Mitre, General Whitelock's statements at his trial in England, was confused and self-serving and that, instead of using the General himself, Mitre would have done better to use the proceedings of the Whitelock trial, which were clearer and more objective.[181]

Here was a classic example of Mitre being caught by his own arguments and a partial, at least, vindication of one of López' favorite contentions, namely, that not all documents should be taken as gospel. Mitre's statements in support of archival research throughout the 19th century were significant for the progress of historiography in his country, and no historian can dispute the value of this type of basic research. However it is true that different historians might view primary documents in different ways and interpret them differently so that it is not always justified to state flatly that because a thesis is based upon primary documentation it is valid.

But Groussac's challenge to Mitre was not strong. He was talking about peripheral events, and he did not in any way challenge the validity of the entire Belgrano book. In fact, he showed great deference to the old master. He wrote that he had tremendous respect for Mitre and that his questions on *Belgrano* did not amend in any way the "importance" of that work. He wrote that he knew from the beginning of the discussion that Mitre would be the victor since he was a "high personality" whose "authority exercises in the public spirit the fortunes of dictatorship." In the eyes of public opinion, Mitre could never lose a polemic, no matter how serious the charges against him. But Groussac reiterated that he was calling to task not the entire book but only some passages within it.[182]

This mild polemic ended the controversy that had welled up around Mitre and his book on Argentine independence. All three battles had served to bring forth important questions and in some cases significant answers. Mitre's book went through four revised editions so that the finished product was far superior to the initial version. In addition, the ideas of his adversaries that emerged from their criticisms of his book contributed to Argentine historiographic advance. As new concepts appeared and old ones survived critical examination, Argentine historians moved into a more advanced stage of their craft. Mitre, Vélez Sarsfield, López, and Groussac all contributed to that progress.

The Federico González Suárez Polemics

Meanwhile, in Ecuador, another series of historiographic debates were taking place. Here the central figure was the outstanding historian Federico González Suárez. These polemics differed from others of the age in that no single important opponent of González emerged to challenge him. Instead, a host of clerics and members of religious orders took it upon themselves to attack him, and in defense he wrote articles and finally a book, *Defensa de mi criterio histórico*. In addition, he also touched on the polemics in his book *Memorias íntimas*. Through most of his adult life he was embroiled in one controversy or another.

His major historiographic argument resulted from a monumental history of Ecuador, which he wrote in the last years of the 19th century. He began to publish volumes in this history in 1890, and by 1894 he had brought out volume IV. This was the crucial part of the history and the one that excited so much opposition. It dealt with Ecuador's colonial past and particularly the role of ecclesiastical orders in Ecuadorean society. González noted carefully the many scandals of religious groups, particularly the Dominican order, that were recorded in the documents in which he carried out his research. He wrote later that the histories he had written earlier had not caused much of a stir. People met his work "not only with indifference, not only with disdain, but with disgust." When he wrote a history of the Canary Islands, people called it "useless" and condemned him for taking time away from his priestly duties to write such drivel.[183]

Volume IV of his *Historia*, however, touched the nerve endings of the regular clergy in Ecuador, and they leaped to defend from what they considered vicious attacks by a fellow clergyman who obviously wished to harm them. A number of articles appeared questioning his motives, his research, and his conclusions. Throughout 1894, González remained silent as he prepared his defense. Then, in 1895, he came forth with his *Memorias íntimas*. In this work he listed his critics and noted the accusations they had made against him. He also took time to discuss his concept of history and set down the methods he had employed to arrive at his conclusions.[184]

González was no stranger to polemics or to published attacks on his work or his person. For example, in 1877 he had taken exception to an article in which the author had attacked Ecuadorean prelates for opposing revolutionary principles. In a published answer, González pointed out the numerous errors in the work and then produced a second study in which he showed that much of the work had been plagiarized from European books. Later he took on a Radical party member, José Peralta, over articles that were carried in Peralta's weekly newspaper, *El Constitucional*. This was a particularly bitter encounter that quickly deteriorated into a personal war between the two men. It served to sharpen

González' pen for his later historiographic polemic, and it also enhanced his national reputation. Consequently, when the attacks came in 1894, he was prepared to defend himself and his history.

González needed all the skill and talent that he possessed to head off the passionate denunciations of his work. At one point some of his severest critics asked the Vatican to put volume IV on the Index. The Vatican remained silent on the proposal, thereby giving its temporary tacit approval to the request. Another request of the Vatican asked that González be branded an enemy of religious orders. At this point the Roman Curia asked González for a declaration that included his avowal of support for religious orders and, among other things, that he state plainly that if he had foreseen the scandal of his volume IV he would not have published it. Now it was González' turn to remain silent. He made no statement on the request, but he later wrote that he could not in good conscience agree to its stipulations because such a statement would prove him to be a historian who was unaware of what he had written. He knew full well what the results of the volume would be, but as a historian he could not suppress what he believed to be the truth. He told the Papacy that he could not make the statement it desired, and if this were to cost him his bishopric then so be it. He later remarked: "I had the firm resolution even of renouncing my Ecuadorean nationality and exiling myself away from Ecuador before retracting volume IV."[185]

Pope Leo XIII ruled on the issue and agreed that no public statement need be made. However, he did want to hear González' side of the argument in private, not as a prerequisite for González' holding his bishopric but only for the "knowledge" of the Papacy. González apparently convinced the Pope that his action was legitimate and his work accurate because he was never reprimanded for any of the things he wrote in his histories.

González wrote that he was accused by his adversaries in the historiographic polemic of "heresy, radicalism, lying, calumny, hypocrisy, immorality, perversity, impiety, thievery, and atheism." Some clerics tried to ban the book, others told their parishioners not to read it, and from the pulpit and confessional González was denounced as corrupt. Such intemperate remarks played into the hands of political enemies of González and gave them extensive ammunition for their attacks upon him. Opponents initiated rumors that the Pope had branded the book an "infamous libel," which was not true. But the one aspect of the entire battle that troubled González the most was that his critics for the most part never read volume IV of his history. They did, however, read everything that others wrote in condemnation of it. Consequently, the entire case against him was based upon hearsay.[186]

Many of his Ecuadorean critics were not of the clergy but were his political opponents. For example, Pablo Herrera, who had been his friend, joined in the attacks against him, probably because on the floor of the Senate González had spoken against a measure proposed by Herrera. González found it equally interesting that most of the opposition from churchmen came from foreigners. The loudest attacks were launched by two Italians and a German. Despite the controversy raging around the book both inside Ecuador and abroad, González refused to retract any part of volume IV. He indicated that he had not written the book to make money or to win glory for himself but rather to provide a service for his countrymen. Consequently, he would not have lied in the book because he would have been cheating them, and he regarded lying as one of the worst vices. He continued to insist that he spoke only the truth in the book and in fact had even greater scandals that he could have revealed had he believed them essential to his history.

In reflecting on the historiographic polemic, González concluded that his only "crime" was in staying carefully within the boundaries of truth. He refused to delete essential but embarrassing material, and he devoted his life to the pursuit of the truth. For this he was branded a virtual criminal. But by the turn of the century he began to witness others writing history in the manner he set forth, and now he was no longer alone. He was also happy to witness the growth of the Ecuadorian Society of American Historical Studies, which ensured the continued development of historians who would be well trained in their craft and committed to the acquisition of truth as he had always been.

In defense of his work, González felt constrained to set forth his philosophy of history and his ideas on methodology. He stated that truth was the "soul of history" and that every facet of historical research and writing had to focus on the search for the truth. For González, the two great threats to accurate history were "flattering panegyric" and "passionate hatred." The panegyric apologized for every institution and individual with which the author agreed under the pretext of honoring country, religion, or attitude. In this way history was destroyed amid personal interests. On the other hand, hatred tended to hide the historic truth and removed any possibility that that truth might be included in the finished product. History then must move between these two dangerous extremes, always keeping sight of the ultimate goal—truth. Without truth, history became nothing more that "a fable."

These ideas are commendable and demonstrate the advanced historiographic thought of González. Unfortunately, however, he could not escape his religious training and his deep religious commitment, both of which made him intolerant of other views. His religious attitudes formed an important segment of his philosophy of history. He wrote that history was a science of social morality and that Catholic historians were the only ones capable of writing perfect history because they alone taught the exact truth respecting Divine Providence and human liberty.[187] With such intolerance of other religions, it is not surprising that González would be regarded through much of his life as a staunch supporter of the Church. However, when he came to write about Ecuador's colonial past, he encountered facts about the monasteries and convents in his country that he believed could not be glossed over. He called this age "the most sober, the most sad, the most lamentable of our history." This he found to be the truth and he wrote it. As he put it, he was not writing *A Thousand and One Nights*. As a historian he could not ignore important events that were public knowledge when they occurred and that continued to be public knowledge even in his lifetime. All anyone had to do was to go to the Archives of the Indies and collect the data. He would not be regarded as much of a historian if he suppressed the information and then in subsequent generations historians encountered the evidence he passed by.[188]

He did, however, seek to defend the holy orders of the colonial period. He noted that they were important in civilizing the Indians and in building the Spanish colonies. Most of the orders were admirable in their devotion to the people, but one has to recall that religious orders are peopled with human beings who are capable of error. Therefore, one need not condemn all religious orders for the work of some individuals. In response to the suggestion that he should not have made known the scandals in the orders because liberals and other opponents of the Church could then use the information for their own purposes to denigrate the entire Church, González answered that if he had not mentioned the scandals and liberal historians had encountered the information in their research then they would have been much less objective about it and the condemnation of orders and Church would have been much greater.

Detractors suggested that González had no business including religious issues in the general history of Ecuador. But González answered that it was impossible to separate religion from history. History could not be understood without knowledge of the peoples' religious beliefs. The historian can never omit anything so important as a nation's religion. He supported this view with a quote from Cicero which held that the historian has two virtues: he never says anything false; and he never is afraid to tell the truth. González' guide as a historian had been these virtues. He wanted only to tell the truth, and consequently he could not hide the truth out of fear.[189]

A final significant point made by González dealt with government or Church control of reading. He argued that book banning can work against the Church when books are suppressed arbitrarily and without an impartial and honest judgment. As an example, the placing of Galileo's *Dialogues* on the Index was a distinct mistake and a long-range problem for the Church. This book was banned for no other reason than Pope Urban VIII's resentment. As a result the Catholic church had not been able to come to terms with the sciences from that day on.[190]

As a parting shot, González said that his characterization of the colonial period might be supported by the fact that, although there were thousands and thousands of clerics in Ecuador during the 300-year colonial period, not one saint was ever produced from that country. This, according to González, has to say something negative about the religious people who operated there.

Despite his criticism, González made one concession. He admitted that the general history he produced was not "an artistically literary book." This, he agreed, was a legitimate reason for criticism, and he was not proud of this shortcoming. But all other charges were false because the book was rooted in truth and extensive research not only in Ecuador but in the Archives of the Indies in Sevilla as well.

On into the 20th century González continued to be a controversial figure, but he generally held to his views. He continued to insist that through research, a love of the truth, and a desire to perform a service for a people by recounting their past, all historians were pursuing a perfect historiographic course to the utmost of their abilities.

Like most of the other historiographic polemics in this age, the Ecuadorean experience had clear beneficent effects on the history that was subsequently written. Young Ecuadoreans now turned more attention to archival work, and those who studied the colonial period realized that a trip to Sevilla was essential. Others came to understand that objectivity and a love of the truth were characteristics that a historian could not do without, and consequently they worked toward such goals. González himself had said that by the late 19th century historical studies were still new for Ecuador. His standards and his determination to fight his detractors in the historiographic debate contributed greatly to the development of this nascent discipline.

CONCLUSION

The polemics waged in Chile, Argentina, and Ecuador were symptomatic of the growing interest in letters in general and history in particular in the 19th century. While the psychological lure of verbal combat should not be discounted as a reason for the new discussions, a more significant reason for their existence was the novelty of historical studies and, as with any new endeavor, the many attitudes and ideas that were set forth, challenged, tested, and finally used. All this was to the benefit of the historians, and it most assuredly aided in the growing sophistication of the histories they produced. Consequently the polemics were an important ingredient in pushing forward history as an important, viable, legitimate, and respectable intellectual discipline.

With restricted educational opportunities in the 19th century, there was little interest in history as a formal discipline in the schools. Consequently there was little effort to develop professional historians until the latter years of the century. Instead, the writing of history was more an avocation than a career. Then, too, the reading public was small, due partly to high illiteracy, and the publishing scene was dominated by fiction, poetry, general essays, and political works. Making it even more difficult for writers of history was the poor economic condition that existed in most countries, preventing all but a few people from buying books. Even newspapers and periodicals were scarce because their cost was outside the reach of a large proportion of the population. Finally, political chaos prevented any dramatic increase in educational opportunities and preoccupied the minds of most of the literate public. Only when histories could be used for political purposes or to stimulate nationalism were they encouraged.

Yet, while publication opportunities for the historian were meager because of all these obstacles, the best histories did find their way into print even in the early years of the century; later even works of inferior quality appeared as the popularity of history increased.

The nonprofessional aspect of historiography was not the problem that it might at first appear. The diverse careers of the historians were beneficial to them because their wide political, economic, social, and religious activities enriched their lives and gave them a more realistic view of their own world as well as the earlier world about which they wrote. These were no ivory tower scholars removed from reality. They were Renaissance men who dabbled in a vast number of activities and interests, many of which would be used to increase their understanding of man, thereby helping them to explain better man's sometimes incomprehensible acts.

While few of these historians devoted full time to researching and writing history, it is remarkable that many of them relied heavily upon primary documentation in their quest for the truth about the past. Some were synthesizers, to be sure, but the best works reflected long, arduous study in archives and libraries. Not only did the writers seek the documents of a period about which they were writing, but they were skeptical enough to test the veracity of their sources and to compare them with other materials, hoping that the truth would sift out after extensive testing and examination. In this way some definitive works were written, and many of the histories from this century reflected at least some significant research even if the total work on occasion might have been something less than profound historical scholarship.

Equally important was the 19th century devotion to history as literature. The Latin Americans spoke frequently of the "science" of history and praised "scientific" historical research, but at the same time they were committed to writing histories that held the interest of the reader, not only by the appeal of the material covered but through a pleasant literary style as well. Some even went so far as to use their research to build historical novels, but even those who wrote monographs and definitive multivolume national histories tried, often with great success, to present their work in an attractive literary manner.

While there was some unanimity in the idea of seeking literary excellence, writers of history differed greatly in their attitudes toward what history was, what it should do, and how it should be researched and written. Their divergent attitudes burst forth in a series of written debates that took place throughout Latin America. These polemics enabled the historians to think out their own views on the subject and to stimulate public interest in history. The verbal clashes made the discipline more visible, and the public developed a greater interest in it. At the same time, history was becoming an important part of the Latin American curriculum, so that by the first quarter of the 20th century the subject was far more significant and popular than it had been in the earlier years following independence.

Meanwhile, political participation by historians and the conscious use of history for political purposes was commonplace in this era. For men who engaged in political struggles and wrote history at the same time it was inevitable that their two interests would overlap. They used history to attack figures or ideas that ran counter to their own philosophies. Given this atmosphere, it is surprising that so many objective, professional histories were written in these years.

Nineteenth century Latin American writers were political men. With independence a recent accomplishment, they were always conscious of their heritage and cognizant of their unique positions as spokesmen for their countrymen. Many could not divorce their histories from their political careers, and the result was sometimes subjective, partisan examinations of the past. But even this kind of writing included valuable research, sometimes of an eyewitness nature and, at times, sound judgments, when the narrative strayed from purely political subjects. The work of Alamán and Bustamante in Mexico, Montúfar in Central America and Vicuña Mackenna, Barros Arana, and Miguel Amunátegui in Chile is representative of this kind of writing. But these were vigorous, aggressive men of action who happened to have a deep interest in history and a talent for research and writing that enabled them to publicize their work and their views, be they social, economic, or political. Some of them, as they matured, departed from partisan work to produce outstanding objective histories and to build international reputations.

In most works of the period, the guiding historiographic force was the quest for truth. Whether the motivation for writing history was to create a piece of literature, stimulate patriotism, strengthen a partisan political view, or simply explain some aspect of the past, the search for accuracy and truth was paramount. However, there was no consensus on how to find historical truth. Most agreed on the examination, verification, and analysis of primary documents, but even on this point there was some disagreement as the so-called philosophical historians placed less emphasis on primary research and chose instead to concentrate on building analytical frameworks for periods in the past. This disagreement did not inhibit or distort historic production but helped to stir debate and discussion in the discipline, which was important for its continued progress. Additionally, even among the philosophical historians there was agreement that truth must be the primary objective of historians.

Because of the devotion to truth, scholarship, and intellectual progress, Latin American historians created a historiography that was far richer than one might have expected, given the political turbulence and economic and social problems of the region. The output of the writers of history was substantial, and the quality of the work generally high, despite the fact that obstacles were always monumental. Confronting their problems head on, they laid the foundation for a mid-20th century Latin American historiography that ranks favorably with the historical output from any area of the world, if not in total production, then certainly in the quality of the histories written. As many of the 19th century historians realized, they were breaking new ground and performing the basic historical spadework upon which later generations could build.

Twentieth century historians, trained in research techniques in universities, were able to push forward the basic ideas of their predecessors into such areas as intellectual, economic, social, and cultural history and even into quantitative studies. They utilized the research of social science disciplines to delve deeply into historical themes. The new methods and more sophisticated training of the historians led to significant revisionist studies in every country of Latin America, and the discovery of unused documentation contributed to the production of works in areas that had not been touched by earlier historians. Consequently, by the last half of the 20th century Latin American historiography realized its potential, and the historical works that were produced in every country reflected the long, arduous growth and development of historical writing that began far back in the colonial period and advanced steadily in the 19th and early 20th centuries. By 1980 well-researched, creative, and thoughtful studies were commonplace throughout the region.

NOTES

1. John Higham, *History: Professional Scholarship in America* (New York: Harper & Row, 1965), p. 4.

2. See, for example, Julio César Jobet, "Notas sobre la historiografía chilena," *Atenea*, 95, Nos. 291–292 (September–October 1949), pp. 354–359.

3. Anonymous, "Biografía de don Lucas Alamán," in Lucas Alamán, *Historia de México* (Mexico City: Victoriano Agüeros, 1883), I, p. 6; Alberto Quirozz, *Lucas Alamán* (Mexico City: Cuadernos de Lectura Popular, 1967), pp. 10–14.; and *Apuntes para la biografía del d. Lucas Alamán* (Mexico City: Sagrado Corazón de Jesús, 1897), pp. 7–13; Eugenio Larrabure Unanue, "Juan de Arona," in Juan de Arona [Pedro Paz-Soldán], *Cuadros y episodios peruanos y otras poesías, nacionales y diversa* (Lima: Calle de Melchormalo, 1867), p. xxiv; Francis Gall, *José Milla y Vidaurre* (Mexico City: Instituto Panamericano de Geografía e Historia, 1966), pp. 40–41; Antonio Castro Leal, "Prólogo," in José Fernando Ramírez, *Fray Toribio de Motolinía y otros estudios*, 2d ed. rev. (Mexico City: Porrúa, 1957), p. xvi; and Federico González Suárez, *Memorias íntimas: Apuntes sobre asuntos personales escritos esclarecer algunos hechos, cuyo conocimiento podra convenir, acaso, ãl la posteridad, año de 1844–1895*, included as an appendix to Nicolás Jiménez, *Biografía del ilustrisimo Federico González Suárez* (Quito: Talleres Tipográficos Municipales, 1936), p. lxiv. José Luís Coto Conde, *Don Ricardo Fernández Guardia: Ensayo biográfico* (San José: Imprenta Nacional, 1957), p. 6; Alfonso Toro, "Don Lorenzo de Zavala y su obra," in Lorenzo de Zavala, *Ensayo histórico de las revoluciones de México desde 1808 hasta 1830*, 3d ed. (Mexico City: Oficina Impresora de Hacienda Dept. Editorial, 1918), I, p. v; Miguel Antonio Caro, *D. José Manuel Groot* (Bogotá: Prensas del Ministerio de Educación Nacional, 1950), p. 14; Alfonso Laferrere, "Noticia Preliminar," in Pablo Groussac, *Páginas de Groussac* (Buenos Aires: Talleres Gráficos Argentinos L. J. Rosso, 1928), p. xviii.

4. See Jack Ray Thomas, "The Role of Private Libraries and Public Archives in Nineteenth-Century Spanish American Historiography," *The Journal of Library History*, 9, No. 4 (October 1974), pp. 334–351.

5. Pedro Moacyr Campos, "Outline of Brazilian Historiography," in E. Bradford

Burns, *Perspectives on Brazilian History* (New York: Columbia University Press, 1967), pp. 57–58. See also Francisco Adolfo de Varnhagen, *Historia geral do Brazil*, 2 vols. (Rio de Janeiro: E. & H. Laemmert, 1854–1857).

6. Guillermo Kaempffer Villagran, *Asi sucedió: Sangrientos episodios de la lucha obrera en Chile, 1850–1925* (Santiago: Arancibia Hermanos, 1962), pp. 30–32; and Samuel A. Lillo, *Literatura chilena*, 2d ed. (Santiago: Minerva, 1920), p. 133.

7. Castro Leal, "Prólogo," p. ix.

8. Ricardo Donoso, *Don Benjamín Vicuña Mackenna: Su vida, sus escritos y su tiempo, 1831–1886* (Santiago: Imprenta Universitaria, 1925), p. 7.

9. Ricardo Levene, *Mitre y los estudios históricos en la Argentina* (Buenos Aires: Academia Nacional de la Historia, 1944), pp. 58–59; and José Manuel Restrepo, *Autobiografía: Apuntamientos sobre la emigración de 1816, e índices del "Diario político"* (Bogotá: Biblioteca de la Presidencia de Colombia, 1959), p. 10.

10. J. Fombona–Pachano, "Alvarado visto por J. Fombona-Pachano," in Lisandro Alvarado, *Los delitos políticos en la historia de Venezuela* (Caracas: Biblioteca de Cultura Venezolana, 1954), pp. 138–319.

11. Federico González Suárez, *Defensa de mi criterio histórico* (Quito: Publicaciones del Archivo Municipal, 1937), p. 12.

12. Ernesto Morales, "Noticia biográfica," in Adán Quiroga, *La cruz en América* (Buenos Aires: Editorial Americana, 1901), pp. xi–xii.

13. Francisco Bauzá, *Discursos apologéticos* (Montevideo: Mosca Hermanos, 1952), p. 2.

14. Arturo Sergio Visca, "Prólogo," in Francisco Bauzá, *Estudios literarios* (Montevideo: Ministerio de Instrucción Pública y Previsión Social, 1953), p. 2.

15. Bauzá, *Estudios literarios*, p. xv.

16. Carlos Orrego Barros, *Diego Barros Arana* (Santiago: Universidad de Chile, 1952), pp. 14–15; and Lillo, *Literatura chilena*, p. 134.

17. *Apuntes para la biografía del D. Lucas Alamán*, pp. 19–20, 28–29; "Biografía de don Lucas Alamán," I, pp. 3–4; and Quirozz, *Lucas Alamán*, pp. 28–37.

18. Joseph R. Barager, "The Historiography of the Río de la Plata Area, Since 1830," *Hispanic American Historical Review*, 39, No. 4 (November 1959), pp. 588–642.

19. See Charles Arnade, "The Historiography of Colonial and Modern Bolivia," *Hispanic American Historical Review*, 42, No. 3 (August 1962), pp. 333–384.; Louis A. Perez, Jr., "In the Service of the Revolution: Two Decades of Cuban Historiography, 1959–1979," *Hispanic American Historical Review*, 60, No. 1 (February 1980), pp. 79–87; Robert A. Potash, "Historiography of Mexico Since 1821," *Hispanic American Historical Review*, 40, No. 3 (August 1960), 383–424; and Adam Szaszdi, "The Historiography of the Republic of Ecuador," *Hispanic American Historical Review*, 44, No. 4 (November 1964), pp. 503–550.

20. Agustín Gómez Carrillo, *Elementos de la historia de Centro-América*, 5th ed. (Guatemala City: Encuadernación y Tip. Musical, 1895), pp. 8–9.

21. Juan García del Río, "La historia," *El museo de ambas Américas*, I, No. 8 (August 1842), pp. 318–319.

22. Fernando Cruz and Antonio Machado, *José Batres Montúfar y Alejandro Marure*, 2d ed. (Guatemala City: Editorial del Ministerio de Educación Pública, 1957), p. 105.

23. José Victorino Lastarria, *Investigaciones sobre la influencia social de la conquista y del sistema colonial de los españoles en Chile* (Santiago: Universidad de Chile, 1843), p. 2.

24. Francisco Bilbao, "Lei de historia," *Obras completas* (Santiago: El Correo, 1897–1898), I, pp. 131-133.

25. See Isaac J. Barrera, *Historiografía del Ecuador* (Mexico: Instituto Pan Americano de Geografía e Historia, 1956), p. 66; Lastarria, *Investigaciones*, p. 10; Bilbao, "Lei de historia," pp. 140–145; and Juan García del Río, "Delicias y ventajas del estudio," *El museo de ambas Américas*, II, No. 13 (January 1843), p. 31. See, for example, Charles A. Hale, *Mexican Liberalism in the Age of Mora, 1821–1853* (New Haven: Yale University Press, 1968).

26. A. Gómez Carrillo, *Compendio de historia de la América Central*, 3d ed. (Guatemala City: La República, 1906), p. 8.

27. Ricardo Fernández Guardia, *Cartilla histórica de Costa Rica* (San José: Avelino Alsina, 1909), pp. 4–5.

28. Bilbao, "Lei de historia," p. 131; Guillermo Felíu Cruz, *Barros Arana, historiador*, 5 vols. (Santiago: Ediciones de los Anales de la Universidad de Chile, 1959), V, p. 36; Ernesto Chinchilla Aguilar, *El historiador guatemalteco don Alejandro Marure* (Mexico City: Instituto Panamericano de Geografía e Historia, 1966), p. 11; and González Suárez, *Memorias íntimas*, p. lxi.

29. Antonio García Reyes, *Memoria sobre la Primera Escuadra Nacional, leida en la sesion pública de la Universidad de Chile el 11 de octubre de 1864* (Santiago: Universidad de Chile, 1847), pp. v–xiv.

30. Domingo Juarros, *A Statistical and Commercial History of the Kingdom of Guatemala in Spanish America*, trans. J. Baily (London: John Mearne, 1823), p. v.

31. Manuel de Mendiburu, *Diccionario histórico-biográfico del Perú*, 2d ed. (Lima: Enrique Palacios, 1931), I, p. 9.

32. Domingo Sarmiento, "Los trabajos de Claudio Gay," *El progresso* (Santiago), July 22, 1843, reprinted in Domingo Sarmiento, *Obras completas* (Buenos Aires: Luz del Día, 1948), II, p. 171. For a recent examination of Gay's work, see Carlos Stuardo Ortiz, *Vida de Claudio Gay, 1800–1873: Escritos y documentos*, 2 vols. (Santiago: Nascimento, 1973). This work contains a distinguished 225-page look at Gay and his work by Guillermo Felíu Cruz, which complements admirably Stuardo Ortiz' biographical study. See also William J. Griffith, "The Historiography of Central America Since 1830," *Hispanic American Historical Review*, 40, No. 4 (November 1960), pp. 548–569.

33. Bauzá, *Discursos apologéticos*, pp. 191–192. See also E. Bradford Burns, "Ideology in Nineteenth-Century Latin American Historiography," *Hispanic American Historical Review*, 58, No. 3 (August 1978), p. 420.

34. Campos, "Outline of Brazilian Historiography," p. 59; and Varnhagen, *Historia geral do Brazil*, I, p. 61. See also *Revista no Instituto Histórico e Geográfico do Brazil*, 2d ed. (Rio de Janeiro: Typografía Universal de Laemmert, 1956), pp. 7–11.

35. Carlos María de Bustamante, *Cuadro histórico de la revolución mexicana comenzada en 15 de septiembre de 1810*, 2d ed. (Mexico City: I. Cumplido, 1846), I, p. iii.

36. Justo Sierra, *Prosas*, 3d ed. (Mexico City: Universidad Autónoma de Mexico, 1963), p. 112.

37. Batres, *Estudios históricos y literarios*, p. 8.

38. Augusto Mijares, "Baralt historiador," in Rafael María Baralt, *Obras completas* (Maracaibo, Venezuela: Universidad de Zulia, 1960), I, pp. xxxiv, 62–63.

39. Lastarria, *Investigaciones*, pp. 11–12.

40. Juan Vicente González, *Manual de historia universal* (Caracas: Rojas Hermanos, 1869), p. 1.

41. Barrera, *Historiografía del Ecuador*, p. 67.

42. Gómez Carrillo, *Elementos de la historia de Centro-América*, p. 8.

43. Angel Acuña, *Mitre historiador*, 2 vols. (Buenos Aires: Coni, 1936), I, p. 149.

44. Armando Donoso, *Recuerdos de cincuenta años* (Santiago: Nascimento, 1947), p. 26; and García del Río, "La historia," pp. 322–323.

45. Juan Zorrilla de San Martín, *Conferencias y discursos* (Montevideo: Ministerio de Instrucción Pública y Previsión Social, 1965), I, pp. 152–153.

46. González Suárez, *Memorias intimas*, p. lix; and Barrera, *Historiografía del Ecuador*, pp. 57–66.

47. Batrés Juaregui, *Estudios históricos y literarios*, p. 5.

48. Pablo Groussac, "Introducción," in José María Ramos Mejía, *La locura en historia* (Buenos Aires: Talleres Gráficos Argentinos, 1927), p. iv.

49. Vicente Fidel López, "Introducción," in José María Ramos Mejia, *Las neurosis de los hombres célebres en la historia argentina*, 2nd ed. rev. (Buenos Aires: Talleres Gráficos Argentinos, 1927), pp. 69–77.

50. See Luís Galdames, "Concepto de la historia," *Atenea*, 95, Nos. 291–292 (September–October 1949), pp. 297–308; and Valentín Letelier, *La evolución de la historia*, 3d ed. (Santiago: Cervantes, 1900), II, p. 334, who believed that the testing and analysis of sources turned historic study into the "science of history."

51. Acuña, *Mitre historiador*, I, p. 156.

52. Juan Vicente González, *Historia moderna* (Caracas: Bolívar, 1925), p. ii.

53. Quoted in Laferrere, "Noticia Preliminar," p. xxxiv.

54. Pablo Groussac, *Mendoza y Garay: Las dos fundaciones de Buenos Aires, 1536–1580*, 2d ed. (Buenos Aires: Jesús Mendendez, 1916), pp. xx–xxii.

55. This theme is examined also in Rómulo D. Carbia, *Historia crítica de la historiografía argentina desde sus origines en el siglo xvi* (Buenos Aires: Coni, 1925), I, p. 76.

56. Pablo Groussac, *Santiago de Liniers: Conde de Buenos Aires, 1753–1810* (Buenos Aires: Arnoldo Moen y Mermano, 1907), p. xi.

57. Lastarria, *Investigaciones*, p. 8.

58. Marriano Sánchez Roca, "Nota introductoria," in José Antonio Saco, *El juego y la vagancia en Cuba*, (Havana: Lex, 1960), p. 9; Sebastián Lorente, *Primeras lecciones de historia del Perú: Adoptada como texto por la honorable Municipalidad de Lima para sus escuelas* (Lima: Librerería Universal, 1872), p. 9; Feliú Cruz, *Barros Arana historiador*, V, p. 36; Diego Carbonell, *Escuelas de historia en América* (Buenos Aires: Lopez, 1943), p. 205; Andrés Bello, *Obras completas* (Santiago: Pedro G. Ramírez, 1884), VII, p. xxxiii; and Joaquín Acosta, *Descubrimiento y colonización de la Nueva Granada* (Bogotá: Biblioteca Popular de Cultura Colombiana, 1942), p. xvii.

59. Carbia, *Historia crítica de la historiografía argentina*, p. 50; and Vicente Fidel López, *Historia de la revolución argentina* (Buenos Aires: n.p., 1881), pp. 71–72.

60. Francisco Bauzá, *Tres ensayos sobre la formación social y económica del Uruguay* (Montevideo: Facultad de Humanidades y Ciencias, 1965), p. 1.

61. Lucas Alamán, *Historia de México* (Mexico City: Victoriano Agüeros, I, 47–48.

62. Quoted in Chinchilla Aguilar, *El historiador guatemalteco Don Alejandro Marure*, p. 11.

63. Rafael Perez, *La compañía de Jesús en Colombia y Centro-América después de su restauración* (Valladolid, Spain: Luís N. de Gaviria, 1896), p. vii.

64. Juarros, *A Statistical and Commercial History of the Kingdom of Guatemala in Spanish America*, p. 1.

65. Gómez Carrillo, *Compendio de la historia de la América Central*, p. 7.

66. Juan Vicente González, *Páginas escogidas* (Caracas: Antologia "Victoria," 1921), p. 145.

67. García del Río, "La historia," pp. 320–321.

68. Julio César Jobet, *Temas históricos chilenos* (Santiago: Empresa Editorial Nacional Quimantu, 1973), p. 15; Jobet, "Notas sobre la historiografía chilena," pp. 347–348, 355; and Alberto J. Pla, *Ideología y método en la historiografía argentina* (Buenos Aires: Nueva Visión, 1972), p. 15. Some economic and social histories were written in the 19th century beginning as early as 1813, but they were the exception rather than the rule. See Sergio Villalobos Rivera, "La historiografía económica en Chile, sus comienzos," *Historia*, 10 (1971), pp. 7–13.

69. See, for example, Januario de Cunha Barbosa, "Iconographia brazileira," *Revista do Instituto Histórico e Geográfico Brasileiro*, XIX (1856), p. 353.

70. Samuel Lorente, *Historia del Perú bajo la dinastía austríaca: 1598–1700* (Paris: A.E.Rochette, 1970), I, p. 9; José María Luís Mora, *México y sus revoluciones* (Mexico City: Porrúa, 1950), p. 5; Alamán, *Historia de México*, I, p. 41; Alamán was very cautious about his choice of topics and always moved slowly, with an eye on public opinion. Before bringing out the first volume of his *Historia de México*, he tested the reading public with his *Biografía de D. Carlos María Bustamante*, which was published anonymously. In this book Alamán criticized Bustamante in the same way that he planned to attack him in his *Historia*. If the reaction was favorable on such an appraisal, he would go ahead and publish his *Historia* under his own name. The public accepted the Bustamante biography, and Alamán brought out his *Historia*. See Anonymous, *Biografía de Alamán*, pp. 29–30.

71. Barrera, *Historiografía del Ecuador*, pp. 55–56.

72. Pablo Groussac, *Mendoza y Garay: Las dos fundaciónes de Buenos Aires, 1536–1580*, pp. xxiv–xxix. See also Juan Gómez Millas, "Las tendencias del pensamiento histórico," *Atenea*, 95, Nos. 291–292 (September–October 1949), p. 17.

73. Groussac, *Páginas de Groussac*, pp. 328–329.

74. Quoted in Cota, *Don Ricardo Fernández Guardia: Ensayo biográfico*, p. 13.

75. Lorente, *Historia del Perú*, I, p. 19.

76. Miguel Luís Amunátegui, *Estudios sobre instrucción pública* (Santiago: Imprente Nacional, 1897), pp. 232–235.

77. Quoted in Antonio Mieres, *Tres autores en la historia de Baralt* (Caracas: Instituto de Estudios Hispanoamericanos, Facultad de Humanidades y Educación, Universidad Central de Venezuela, 1966), p. 30.

78. Baralt, *Obras completas*, I, p. xxxiii.

79. Mieres, *Tres autores en la historia de Baralt*, p. 54.

80. Mendiburu, *Diccionario histórico-biográfico del Perú*, pp. 91–113.

81. Lucas Alamán, *Disertaciones sobre la historia de la República Megicana desde la época de la conquista que los españoles hicieron a fines del siglo XV y principios del XVI de las islas y continents americano hasta independencia* (Mexico City: Jus, 1942), pp. 7, 12; and Alamán, *Historia de México*, I, p. 43.

82. Arturo Arnaiz y Freg, "Prólogo," in Lucas Alamán, *Semblanzas e ideario* (Mexico City: Ediciones de la Universidad Nacional Autónoma, 1939), p. xxxi.

83. Quoted in Antonio Ferrer del Rio, "D. Lucas Alamán: su vida y sus escritos," in Alamán, *Disertaciones sobre la historia de la República Megicana*, p. xxiv.

84. José Fernando Ramírez, *Noticias históricas de la vida y hechos de Nuño de Guzmán* (Guadalajara, Mexico: Circulo Occidental, 1962), pp. 17–18, 82; and Joaquín García Icazbalceta, *Don Fray Juan de Zumárraga: Primer obispo y arzobispo de México* (Mexico City: Porrúa, 1947), I, p. 4.

85. García Icazbalceta, *Don Fray Juan de Zumárraga: Primer obispo y arzobispo de Mexico*, I, pp. 7–10.

86. González, *Manual de historia universal*, pp. viii–ix.

87. F. A. Berra, *Bosquejo histórico de la república del Uruguay*, 2d ed. rev. (Montevideo: Librería Argentina de Francisco Ibarra, 1881), pp. 6, 218.

88. Ernesto Quesada, *Época de Rosas* (Buenos Aires: Artes y Letras Editorial, 1927), II, p. 11.

89. Juan García del Río, "Errores de la historia: Patria de Cristóval Colón," *El museo de ambas Américas*, I, No. 2 (February 1842), pp. 50–53.

90. Castro Leal, "Prólogo," pp. ix–xvi.

91. Augusto Arias Robalino, *Biografía de Pedro Fermín Cevallos* (Quito: Colegio Central Técnico, 1948), p. 75.

92. Ibid., p. 68.

93. Isaac J. Barrera, *Pedro Fermín Cevallos: Estudio y selecciones* (Puebla, Mexico: J. M. Cajica Jr., 1960), pp. 18–24. Baralt is also an example of this type of research, which frequently yielded a compilation rather than a history. See Mieres, *Tres autores en la historia de Baralt*, pp. 35–36, 150–157.

94. Juarros, *A Statistical and Commercial History of the Kingdom of Guatemala*, p. 2; José Milla, *Historia de la América Central: Desde el descubrimiento del país por los españoles (1502) hasta su independencia de la España (1821)* (Guatemala City: El Progresso, 1879), p. iii; Feliú Cruz, *Barros Arana, historiador*, I, pp. 10–11; Diego Barras Arana, *Estudios históricos-bibliográficos* (Santiago: n.p., 1910), p. 138. Also quoted in Carbonell, *Escuelas de historia en América*, pp. 82–83, 131–132, 206; and Vicente Riva Palacio, *Resúmen integral de Mexico a través de los siglos* (Mexico City: Compañía General de Ediciones, 1951), p. 7. Like von Ranke, the Latin Americans believed that the historian had only to verify his documents in order for them to serve as a basis for gaining historic truth.

95. Groussac, *Páginas de Groussac*, pp. 322–324.

96. Quoted in Leferrere, "Noticia preliminar," pp. xxxi–xxxii.

97. Ricardo Levene, *Las ideas históricas de Mitre* (Buenos Aires: Coni, 1948), p. 8.

98. Bartolomé Mitre, *Correspondencia literaria histórica y política del General Bartolomé Mitre* (Buenos Aires: Coni Hermanos, 1912), I, p. 44.

99. Francisco Bauzá, *Historia de la dominacion española en el Uruguay*, 3d ed. (Montevideo: Tall Graf "El Democrata," 1929), I, pp. xxiv–xxv.

100. Gonzalo Bulnes, *Historia de la campaña del Perú en 1838* (Santiago: Los Tiempos, 1878), p. vi.

101. Chinchilla Aguilar, *El historiador guatemalteco Don Alejandro Marure*, pp. 14–15.

102. Arnaiz y Freg, "Prólogo," pp. xxxi–xxxvi.

103. Alamán, *Historia de Mexico*, I, p. 43.

104. Acosta, *Descubrimiento y colonización de la Nueva Granada*, p. xviii.

105. See especially Ramírez, *Fray Toribio de Motolinía y otros estudios*; García Icazbalceta, *Don Fray Juan de Zumárraga*; and Alvarado, *Los delitos políticos en la historia de Venezuela*.

106. Yáñez, "Prólogo," in Mora, *Mexico y sus revoluciones*, p. xx; José María Luís Mora, *Ensayos, ideas y retratos* (Mexico City: Ediciones de la Universidad Nacional Autónoma Mexico, 1941), pp. 203–204; and Arias, *Biografía de Pedro Fermín Cevallos*, p. 77.

107. Alamán, *Disertaciones sobre la historia de la República Megicana*, pp. 12–13.

108. García Icazbalceta, *Don Fray Juan de Zumárraga*, p. 4; and Alfredo Chavero, *Obras del lic. don Alfredo Chavero* (Mexico City: Victoriano Agüeros, 1904), p. xxii.

109. Thomas, "The Role of Private Libraries and Public Archives in Nineteenth Century Spanish American Historiography," pp. 334–351.

110. Potash, "Historiography of Mexico Since 1821," p. 410.

111. Feliú Cruz, *Barros Arana, historiador*, I, pp. 10–11.

112. Carbonell, *Escuelas de historia en América*, p. 131; and Feliú Cruz, *Barros Arana, historiador*, V, p. 30.

113. Feliú Cruz, *Barros Arana, historiador*, I, 31. For a generally sympathetic treatment of Vicuña Mackenna's style, see Guillermo Feliú Cruz, "Interpretación de Vicuña Mackenna: Un historiador del siglo XIX," *Atenea*, 95, Nos. 291–292 (September–October 1949), pp. 144–181.

114. Raúl Silva Castro, "Ensayo sobre Lastarria," *Cuadernos americanos*, 16, No. 1 (1957), pp. 235–236.

115. José Victorino Lastarria, *Suscrición de la Academia de Bellas-Letras, Santiago de Chile, a la estatua de Don Andrés Bello* (Santiago: Librería del Mercurio, 1874), p. 85.

116. Domingo Amunátegui Solar, *Don Andrés Bello enseña a los chilenos a narrar la historia nacional* (Santiago: Prensas de la Universidad de Chile, 1938), pp. 10–16.

117. Visca, "Prólogo," p. xv; and Francisco Bauzá, Isidoro de María and Daniel Muñoz, *Crónicas del Montevideo antiguo* (Montevideo: Universidad de la República, Departamento de Publicaciones, 1966), p. 9; and Mijares, "Baralt historiador," p. xliv; and Mieres, *Tres autores en la historia de Baralt*, p. 24.

118. Benjamin Fernández Medina, "Apuntes biográficos del Dr. D. Andrés Lamas," in Andrés Lamas, *La obra económica de Bernardino Rivadavia* (Buenos Aires: Comité Sudamericano para el Impuesto Único, 1917), p. xxii. See also Chinchilla Aguilar, *El historiador guatemalteco Don Alejandro Marure*, pp. 10–15.

119. Groussac, *Páginas de Groussac*, pp. 330–331.

120. Barrera, *Pedro Fermín Cevallos*, p. 38.

121. Arias, *Biografía de Pedro Fermín Cevallos*, p. 39.

122. González, *Historia moderna*, p. v.

123. José Caicedo Rojas, "Don José Manuel Groot," in José Manuel Groot, *Historia eclesiastica y civil de Nueva Granada* (Bogotá: Biblioteca de Autores Colombianos, 1953), pp. 36, 54.

124. Mendiburu, *Diccionario histórico-biográfico del Peru*, p. 7.

125. George Lemus, *Francisco Bulnes: Su vida y sus obras* (Mexico City: Ediciones de Andres, 1965), p. 82.

126. Raul A. Orgaz, *Vicente F. López y la filosofía de la historia* (Córdoba, Argentina: Rossi, 1938), pp. 48–59.

127. Vicente Fidel López, *Memoria*... (Buenos Aires: Nova, 1943), pp. 16–17.

128. Quoted in Isaac Joslin Cox, *Some of Chile's Historians as Viewed by Their Fellow Craftsmen* (New York: H. W. Wilson, 1939), p. 59.

129. Lastarria, *Recuerdos literarios*, pp. 238–243.

130. See Francisco Bilbao, "Evangelio," in *Obras completas*, I, pp. 247–249; and Lastarria, *Recuerdos literarios*, p. 291.

131. Quoted in Feliú Cruz, *Barros Arana, historiador*, IV, pp. 72–74.

132. Lastarria, *Recuerdos literarios*, pp. 245–246; and Alfonso Bulnes, "Bello y la historiografía chilena," *Atenea*, 160, No. 410 (October–December 1965), pp. 33–40.

133. Quesada, *Época de Rosas*, I, p. 29; and Groussac, *Mendoza y Garay*, p. xxiv.

134. Mariano Picón Salas, "Notas sintética sobre el escritor," in Juan Vicente González, *Páginas escogidas* (Caracas: Antologías "Victoria," 1921), p. 10.

135. An excellent article on this polemic is Allen Woll, "The Philosophy of History in Nineteenth Century Chile: The Lastarria–Bello Controversy," *History and Theory*, 13 (October 1974), pp. 273–290.

136. Alejandro Fuenzalida Grandón, *Lastarria i su tiempo (1817–1888): Su vida, obras e influencia en el desarrollo político e intelectual de Chile* (Santiago: Barcelona, 1911), p. 145.

137. Cox, *Some of Chile's Historians as Viewed by Their Fellow Craftsmen*, pp. 59–60.

138. Sarmiento, *Obras completas*, II, p. 215.

139. Jacinto Chacón, "Prólogo," in José Victorino Lastarria, *Obras completas*, IX, pp. 37–38.

140. Ibid., pp. 43–50.

141. Ibid., p. 50.

142. Andrés Bello, *Obras completas de Don Andrés Bello* (Santiago: Pedro G. Ramírez, 1884), VII, p. 112.

143. Ibid., pp. 112–114.

144. Ibid., p. 117.

145. Ibid., p. 119.

146. Ibid., p. 184.

147. Dalmacio Velez Sarsfield, "Rectificaciones históricas: Artículos publicados en 'El Nacional," in Bartolomé Mitre, *Estudios históricos sobre la revolución argentina: Belgrano y Guemas* (Buenos Aires: Comercio del Plata, 1864), pp. 217–219, 231–232.

148. Mitre, *Estudios históricos sobre la revolución argentina: Belgrano y Guemes*, pp. 5–6.

149. Velez, "Rectificaciones históricas," pp. 222–225.

150. Levene, *Mitre y los estudios históricos en la Argentina*, p. 88.

151. Mitre, *Estudios históricos sobre la revolución argentina: Belgrano y Guemes*, pp. 7–15.

152. Velez, "Rectificaciones históricas," pp. 233–234.

153. Mitre, *Estudios históricos sobre la revolución argentina: Belgrano y Guemes*, pp. 32–36.

154. Velez, "Rectificaciones históricas," pp. 234–235.

155. Mitre, *Estudios históricos sobre la revolución argentina: Belgrano y Guemes*, pp. 135–140.

156. Ibid., pp. 144–147.

157. Velez, "Rectificaciones históricas," p. 262.

158. Ricardo Rojas, "Prólogo," in Bartolomé Mitre, *Comprobaciones históricas* (Buenos Aires: Librería La Facultad de Juan Roldán, 1916), I, pp. xix–xx.

159. Bartolomé Mitre, "Algo sobre literatura americana," *Revista chilena* (October 1875), IV, pp. 499–500.

160. Vicente Fidel López, *Debate histórico: Refutación a las comprobaciones históricos sobre la historia de Belgrano* (Buenos Aires: Librería La Facultad de Juan Roldán, 1921), I, pp. 17–21.

161. Rojas, "Prólogo," p. xxii.

162. Ibid., p. ix.

163. Mitre, *Comprobaciones históricas*, I, pp. 28–29.

164. Ricardo Rojas, "Noticia preliminar," in López, *Debate histórico*, I, pp. 11–13.

165. López, *Debate histórico*, I, pp. 27–50, 83–84, 254–259.

166. Mitre, *Comprobaciones históricas*, I, pp. 14 ff.

167. Ibid., pp. 197–200.

168. Ibid., p. 341.

169. See Levene, *Mitre y los estudios históricos en la Argentina*, pp. 88 ff.

170. Mitre, *Comprobaciones históricas*, II, p. 16.

171. Ibid., II, p. 25.

172. Ibid., II, pp. 26–28.

173. López, *Debate histórico*, II, pp. 228–243.

174. Mitre, *Comprobaciones históricas*, I, pp. 359–360.

175. López, *Debate histórico*, I, pp. 86–88.

176. Mitre, *Comprobaciones históricas*, II, p. 388.

177. López, *Debate histórico*, III, pp. 325–327.

178. Carbia, *Historia de la historiografía argentina*, pp. 70–71.

179. Laferrere, "Noticia preliminar," p. xxxi.

180. Groussac, *Santiago de Liniers: Conde de Buenos Aires*, pp. 413–414.

181. Ibid., p. 431.

182. Ibid., p. 458.

183. González Suárez, *Defensa de mi criterio histórico*, p. 5.

184. See Jiménez, *Biografía de Ilustrisimo Federico González Suárez*, pp. 113–114.

185. Ibid., pp. 115–116.

186. González Suárez, *Memorias íntimas*, pp. lxi–lxiii.

187. González Suárez, *Defensa de mi criterio histórico*, pp. 6–26.

188. Ibid., pp. 45–68.

189. Ibid., pp. 81–84.

190. Ibid., pp. 102.

Bio-
Bibliographical
Sketches

A

ABREU Y LIMA, JOSÉ INÁCIO (6 April 1794, Recife, Brazil–8 March 1869, Recife). *Education*: Graduated with the rank of Captain of Artillery, Royal Military Academy of Rio de Janeiro, 1816. *Career*: Officer in the Brazilian Army; fought with Simón Bolívar in Venezuela, 1818–1821.

Having been active in the Latin American struggle for independence both in his native Brazil and with the forces of Simón Bolívar in Venezuela, following the liberation of New Granada, Abreu y Lima traveled to the United States and Europe. In 1832 he returned to Brazil, where he began to write historical and political books. He was concerned on a theoretical basis with the plight of the common man and with the development of socialism in Europe. But practically he was interested in strengthening the role of commoners through the use of the electoral process. He recognized the fraudulent schemes that prevailed in Brazil, and he railed against them in print. His solution to the problem was direct elections by qualified voters over the age of 25, a plan he urged on the nation.

In his historical writing Abreu y Lima was interested in the development of socialism, but his major effort was a short history of Brazil. Because he was a liberal, open to all ideas and philosophies, movements such as socialism held a good deal of fascination for him. This interest led him to touch on class differences in his development of the history of Brazil, preventing it from becoming just another political history. Still, his history was not above criticism from contemporary historians, especially *Francisco Adolpho Varnhagen, the 19th century giant of Brazilian historiography. Varnhagen was disappointed with Abreu y Lima's failure to consult all available documents before embarking upon his history of Brazil. In Varnhagen's mind Abreu y Lima had relied too heavily on histories that themselves were inaccurate and weak. He did not analyze these histories carefully and therefore simply perpetuated the mistakes the earlier authors had made. Additionally, Varnhagen charged that he had not researched extensively enough and that there were thousands of documents in existence of which Abreu y Lima was simply unaware. Consequently, the history was grossly deficient in revealing the truth of Brazil's past, which was the major aim of all historical research.

A. *Bosquejo histórico, político e literário do Brasil* (Niteroi, Brazil, 1835); *Cartilha do Povo* (Pernambuco, Brazil, 1849); *O socialismo* (Recife, Brazil, 1855); and *Reforma eleitoral* (Recife, Brazil, 1862).

B. José Honorio Rodrígues, *Historia e historiadores do Brasil* (São Paulo, Brazil, 1965), pp. 62–72.

ABRIL Y OSTALO, MARIANO (25 May 1862, San Juan—1935, San Juan). *Career*: Journalist in Puerto Rico and Madrid; Delegate Puerto Rican Legislature, 1904; Senator from Guayama, 1917; Senator, 1920; Official Historian of Puerto Rico, 1931; Member, Board of Trustees, University of Puerto Rico, 1931.

In the midst of the struggle for Puerto Rican independence from Spain a number of intellectuals took the lead in denouncing Spanish rule. Abril y Ostalo was among this group, and for his outspoken articles in such newspapers as *El clamor* and *La democracia*, both of which he edited, he was jailed in Spain after a trial that condemned him as a dangerous subversive. Upon his release from prison he returned to Puerto Rico no less determined to aid in the acquisition of his country's independence. When Spain was finally driven from Puerto Rico, Abril y Ostalo became involved in Puerto Rican politics with the same controversial, outspoken attitudes that had characterized his position in the independence movement. A liberal, he seldom missed an opportunity to chastise the conservatives and to point out in print their many errors. Eventually he held important elective offices, which provided him with a forum for his liberal political philosophy. Meanwhile, he continued to write poetry throughout his long political struggle, and he never lost interest in researching and writing history.

Abril's work in the discipline of history gained him a measure of fame and eventually, in 1931, led to his appointment as the Official Historian of Puerto Rico. While he had labored long in the political arena, his historical interests were not limited to political history, as was the case with many Latin Americans at the turn of the century. Instead, he was enthralled with intellectual history, and he explored the philosophies that were having an impact on the 20th century world. In particular he was interested in socialism and its role not only in Puerto Rico but throughout the world as evidenced by his work *El socialismo moderno*. Indeed, his willingness to study and research the history of Europe set him apart from most Latin American historians, who confined their research to their own countries. While his output was far less than that of some other outstanding Latin American historians, this broader interest in historical subjects was a major contribution to Puerto Rican historiography.

A. *Sensaciones de un cronista* (San Juan, 1903); *El socialismo moderno* (San Juan, 1911); *Alemania (ante el conflicto europeo)* (San Juan, 1915); *Un heroe de la independencia de España y América; Antonio Valero de Barnabe* (Puerto Rico, 1929).

B. Kenneth R. Farr, *Historical Dictionary of Puerto Rico and the U.S. Virgin Islands* (Metuchen, N.J., 1973), p. 1; Donald E. Herdeck, ed., *Caribbean Writers: A Bio-Bibliographical-Critical Encyclopedia* (Washington, D.C., 1979), p. 629; and Percy Alvin Martin, *Who's Who in Latin America* (Stanford, 1936), pp. 2–3.

ACEVEDO DÍAZ, EDUARDO (20 April 1851, Unión, Uruguay—1924, Buenos Aires). *Education*: Bachelor's degree, Universidad de Montevideo, 1869 studied law. *Career*: Participated in a rebellion against the government, 1870; exiled; founded the newspaper *La república* and wrote for *La democracia*; imprisoned and exiled again for anti-government writing, 1875; exiled in Buenos Aires for eight years; Member, Council of State, 1898; Senator, 1898–1903; Envoy Extraordinary to the United States, Mexico, and Cuba, 1903; Minister to Paraguay and Argentina, 1906; Minister to Italy and Switzerland, 1908; Minister to Brazil, 1911; served in Austria-Hungary and Switzerland, 1916; pensioned from public life, 1920.

In the midst of internal chaos in his country Acevedo Díaz tried to assist the rise of something resembling democracy, and when he failed he paid for his audacity with exile. But whether in Uruguay or outside he could still write, and he was still in a position to oppose political ideologies with which he disagreed. But for that disagreement he spent long years as an exile in Argentina and Brazil. Back in Uruguay he again became embroiled in the political maneuvering of his country, and when in 1903 he tried to help the opposition candidate to gain the presidency, he was drummed out of the Blanco party.

Acevedo Díaz' contribution to Uruguayan historiography consisted of fictional historical novels based upon well-researched historical sources. He wrote a trilogy that covered the era of Uruguay's war for independence from the Spanish. Later he wrote another historical novel on the gaucho, which is considered to be his finest book. By combining fiction with historical fact he was able to reach a wider audience for his work, his ideas, and his perception of the history he wrote. Acevedo Díaz is generally regarded as the first novelist of Uruguay, and from that lofty position he was able to influence other writers and encourage them to use historical data in writing their fiction. But his contribution to history did not stop with the historical novel. He also wrote chronicles and narrative histories on the early period of Uruguayan history, and he eventually wrote a history textbook. Finally, he put together a solid study of the role of militarism in 19th century Uruguay.

A. *Grito de Gloria* (La Plata, 1893); *Ismael* (Montevideo, 1894); *Mines* (Rome, 1910); *Lanza y sable* (Montevideo, 1911); *El mito del plata* (Buenos Aires, 1917); *América y Argentina* (Buenos Aires, 1940); and *La vida de batalla de Eduardo Acevedo Díaz* (Buenos Aires, 1941).

B. Helen Delpar, *Encyclopedia of Latin America* (New York, 1974), p. 3; Michael Rheta Martin and Gabriel Lovett, *Encyclopedia of Latin American History* (Indianapolis, 1968), p. 2; William Belmont Parker, *Uruguayans of To-Day* (New York, 1967); and Jean L. Willis, *Historical Dictionary of Uruguay* (Metuchen, N.J., 1974), pp. 2–3.

ACOSTA, CECILIO (1 February 1818, San Diego de los Altos, Venezuela— 8 July 1881, Caracas). *Education*: Bachelor of Civil Law, University of Caracas, 1838. *Career*: Taught political economy, University of Caracas, and philosophy and literature at other institutions in Venezuela; poet, essayist, orator, legislator, polemicist, social scientist, and historical theorist.

Born into a poor agricultural family in the rural regions of Venezuela, Acosta and his widowed mother moved to Caracas when he was five. He planned to join the priesthood but instead became enthralled with literature, and although he graduated with a degree in law, as was true of most young men of his era, his heart was always in writing and teaching. He made his mark on his native land with his wisdom and his erudition, but he never realized any material gain.

Acosta did leave a great legacy for Venezuela, however. Not only was he one of the outstanding writers and thinkers of the 19th century, he was also a political analyst who opposed dictators and who wrote lucid, logical tracts condemning tyrannical and dictatorial government and championing democracy. Several of these pieces were collected and published in 1913 as *Opúsculos críticos*, but his antidictatorial attitude was also set forth in correspondence with friends and scholars. These letters were published in 1918 under the title *Cartas venezolanas*. His study of Venezuela led him to espouse sociology along with political economy and literature as well as to look carefully at Venezuela's past to explain its present and probe its future. Still, he did not confine his thoughts to a single country, and his ideas and research had relevance for all of Latin America. When he opposed Venezuelan dictators he did not limit his opposition to his own country but saw the danger in all Latin American dictators. His work was not only Venezuelan, it was American, and he counted among his friends and admirers such outstanding Latin Americans as the Cuban José Martí, who pronounced a funeral oration for him while visiting Caracas.

Acosta, a determined patriot, believed in the value of history for the progress of any people and nation. He was, at the same time, committed to the idea of education. If more people could be educated, he reasoned, many of the problems of his era could be wiped out. And as a part of that education, knowledge of the past was essential. In his written work he exalted the study of history and supported the concept of extended, detailed research for the writing of history. At the same time, he knew that a literary bent would help to win wider audiences for written history, and so he advocated history with a literary flare. In his own work he sought always clarity of thought coupled with a clear, logical style, and he mastered the Spanish language to the extent that he was able to present his thoughts and arguments in a manner that the reading public found attractive.

A. *Cosas sabidas y cosas por saberse* (Caracas, 1856); *Opúsculos críticos* (Paris, 1913); *Estudios de derecho internacional* (Madrid, 1917); *Cartas venezolanas* (Madrid, 1918); *Doctrina* (Caracas, 1950); *Pensamientos y sentencias* (Caracas, 1952).

B. *Diccionario biográfico de Venezuela* (Madrid, 1953), pp. 1–2; Donna Keyse and G. A. Rudolf, *Historical Dictionary of Venezuela* (Metuchen, N.J., 1971), p. 10; César Humberto Soto, *Personajes célebres de Venezuela* (Caracas, 1946), pp. 165–170; and Arturo Uslar-Pietri, *Letras y hombres de Venezuela* (Mexico, 1948), pp. 98–112.

AGUIRRE, JUAN FRANCISCO (18 August 1758, Donamaria, Spain—February 1877, Asturias, Spain). *Education*: Studied at the Spanish Naval Academy. *Career*: Fought in various naval campaigns and promoted to Lieutenant; assigned to commissions studying the boundaries between Spain and Portugal in South America; returned to Spain, was promoted to Captain, and held several military posts.

Aguirre spent 12 years in Paraguay awaiting the commissioners from Portugal in order to draw firm boundary lines between Brazil and Spanish America. During that time he kept a diary in which he revealed what he had learned about the region and about the historical development of the La Plata area. In 1796 he was assigned to Buenos Aires, and two years later he was ordered back to Spain, where he finished his diary while fulfilling several military posts. When the French invaded Spain, however, he was persecuted by the Napoleonic troops, and he went into hiding from the French authorities in the province of Asturias, where he remained until his death.

Aguirre's diary was a monument to ethnography and history. He was a careful observer of a restricted field of interest, Paraguay and the Río de la Plata region. In that area he had a clear view of events, peoples, and natural developments. His work could fit neatly into the modern discipline of sociology, but he was also a historian who sought the truth of the past about which he studied. He wrote about the social, economic, and historic reality of Paraguay. His diary is filled with detailed information that aids the modern researcher in understanding the development of the region. Some critics charged that he did not work in the archives and in documental sources and that the historical part of his work was therefore deficient. More recent scholarship, however, suggests that he did do work in primary documents and that his research was based upon sound scholarship principles known at that time. One writer has pointed out that there is not a paragraph of his diary pertaining to history that does not contain the results of study in some original document. This use of primary sources is even more significant than it might otherwise be because every document he used has subsequently been lost or destroyed. Therefore, Aguirre's diary is all that remains of much of the original documentation.

A. *Historia del diario* (Asunción, 1793); *Etnografía del Chaco* (Buenos Aires, 1899); *Juan Francisco de Aguirre: Discurso histórico que comprende el descubrimiento, conquista y establecimiento de los españoles en las provincias de la Nueva Vizcaya, generalmente conocidas por el nombre de Río de la Plata* (Buenos Aires, 1947).

B. Efraím Cardozo, *Historiografía paraguaya* (Mexico City, 1959), pp. 435–448; Francisco Esteve Barba, *Historiografía indiana* (Madrid, 1964), pp. 599–601.

ALAMÁN, LUCAS (17 October 1792, Guanajuato, Mexico—2 June 1853, Mexico City). *Education*: Studied at the Real Seminario de Minería, Mexico City, and in London and Paris. *Career*: Mexican Deputy to the Spanish parliament, 1821; Minister of Foreign Relations, 1823–1825, 1830–1832, 1853; leader, Conservative political faction; created financial and industrial organizations such as the Banco de Avio, La Junta de Fomento de la Industria, and the textile industry in Orizaba and Celaya; Director of Industry, 1842–1846; organized the Archivo General de la Nación and the Museo de Antiguedades.

Throughout the first half of the 19th century, a tumultuous, chaotic period in Mexican history, Lucas Alamán functioned as a political leader, industrial capitalist, and historian. Because he was leader of the Conservatives, he became associated with dictators like Antonio López de Santa Anna, and when criticism was heaped upon that individual the hostility spilled over onto Alamán. Then, too, later historians of liberal persuasion tended to criticize him because of his politics. Unfortunately, while opposition to his political action can be understood, there should not be the same hostility to his written work.

Alamán was a bright, well-educated, well-traveled man with a variety of interests, like most other young men of his class in Mexico. His talents were directed largely to industry and politics in the early years of his life, but later he turned to the writing of history. His histories are rich in firsthand information because he lived in the period he wrote about and he was a prominent figure who knew the other leaders of the nation. With the tremendous experience he had gained in his early life he wrote about Mexico's past. Opposition figures challenged his historical work as they challenged his political views, and when writing about politics he was not an unbiased observer. Nevertheless, he put together some historical articles, read them publicly, and then collected them for publication as a history of Mexico. He used as sources memorials, official documents to which he had access, articles in periodicals, and his own personal correspondence. He also had memories of many of the events, which he incorporated into the study. His work, although lacking objectivity in political matters, was generally of high quality. His style was sincere, correct, and precise, and his thought was logical and clear. In his major historical work *Disertaciones sobre la historia*. . . he remained faithful to his views and to his documentation. But in some other pieces he gave free reign to his imagination, which then made for more exciting reading. In particular a small piece in his book *Semblanzas y Ideario*, 1833, about the reception by Father Hidalgo of the news that authorities had uncovered the plot against the Spanish was a masterful piece of writing as he described the priest's actions and thoughts in that critical moment of his life.

Alamán was an outstanding writer whose *Historia de México* has been described by one North American historian as "magesterial." In that work he sought to demonstrate that the Spanish background to Mexican independence was not a detrimental period in the nation's development. Instead, he argued that the 300 years of Spanish control prepared Mexico well for its independent course and that the liberals who castigated everything Hispanic should recognize the great value in the Spanish cultural background that so enriched the Mexican people.

A. *Memoria que el secretario de estado y del despacho de relaciones presenta al soberano congreso constituyente* (Mexico City, 1823); *Disertaciones sobre la historia de la República mexicana desde la época de la conquista que los españoles hicieron a fines del siglo XV y principios del XVI de las islas y continente americano hasta la independencia*, 3 vols. (Mexico City, 1844–1849); *Historia de México desde los primeros movimientos que prepararon su independencia en el año de 1808 hasta la época presente* (Mexico City, 1849–1852); *Obras de d. Lucas Alamán*, 5 vols. (Mexico City, 1899).

B. Juan Bautista Alamán, "Apuntes para la biografía del excelentisimo señor don Lucas Alamán," in Lucas Alamán, *Historia de México* (Mexico City, 1942), pp. ix–xlvi; Helen

Delpar, *Encyclopedia of Latin America* (New York, 1974), p. 13; *Diccionario Porrúa de historia* (Mexico City, 1976), I, pp. 47–48; Moises González Navarro, *El pensamiento político de Lucas Alamán* (Mexico City, 1952); and Robert A. Potash, "Historiography of Mexico Since 1821," *Hispanic American Historical Review*, 40, No. 3 (August 1960), pp. 383–424.

ALCÂNTARA MACHADO D'OLIVEIRA, JOSÉ DE (19 October, 1875, Piracicaba, Brazil—1941, Rio de Janeiro). *Education*: Bachelor of Judicial Science, School of Law, University of São Paulo, 1893; Bachelor of Social Sciences, 1894; Doctor of Law, 1895. *Career*: Alternate Professor of Legal Medicine and Public Hygiene, 1895, Full Professor, 1925, Vice-Director, 1927, Director, 1935, School of Law of São Paulo; Municipal Councilman, São Paulo, 1911–1916; State Deputy, 1915–1924; President, Paulista Faculty of Letters and Philosophy, 1921; State Senator, 1924–1930; Vice-President, Penitentiary; Member, Council of the State of São Paulo, 1928; President, Superior Council, School of Politics and Sociology of São Paulo, 1933.

As a lawyer and public figure Alcântara was active in the political activity of his home state of São Paulo, while at the same time he built a solid reputation as a teacher and administrator in higher education. His educational background in legal studies and his practice of law generated in his mind a commitment to a strict discipline for the people of his nation. This same devotion to living by the rule of law and an acceptance of the idea of strict discipline in life as well as in the writing of history enabled Alcântara to produce some effective historical studies.

Alcântara's work in historical research proved to be extremely important for the history of Brazil. He studied state and local records and reviewed the wills of many of the early Paulistas. This research revealed that the Brazilian frontiersmen, the Bandeirantes, lived in virtual poverty, whereas tradition held that they were wealthy and lived in aristocratic splendor after their early forays into the interior. Alcântara's work in medical law eventually led him to write on medical subjects, especially on the use of hypnotism in treating mental patients. Finally, he was conscious of political action in his country, and he wrote on the development of city governance and local political problems. While not in the forefront of Brazilian historians, Alcântara by means of creative historical themes contributed to the broadening of historical study in Brazil from a concentration on political themes.

A. *Do momento da formacão dos contratos por correspondência* (São Paulo, 1892); *A embriaguez e a responsabiliadade criminal* (São Paulo, 1893); *O hipnotismo* (São Paulo, 1895); *Problems municipais: Os honorarios médicos* (São Paulo, 1922); *Vida e morte do bandeirante* (São Paulo, 1929); *Brasilio Machado (1848–1919)* (Rio de Janeiro, 1937).
B. Robert M. Levine, *Historical Dictionary of Brazil* (Metuchen, N.J., 1979), p. 6; and Percy Alvin Martin, *Who's Who in Latin America* (Stanford, 1936), pp. 9–10.

ALEGRE, FRANCISCO JAVIER (12 November 1729, Veracruz, Mexico—16 August 1788, Bologna, Italy). *Education*: Elementary studies at home; secondary studies at the Real Colegio de San Ignacio de la Puebla; studied law in Mexico City and theology at Puebla. *Career*: Entered the Jesuit order, 1747; taught grammar in secondary school in Mexico City; gave grammar classes in Veracruz; taught rhetoric and philosophy for seven years in Havana; taught canon law at Mérida, Yucatán.

Clerics from both Spain and America, especially members of the regular orders, were scholars and teachers in the colonial era, and many of them also wrote history. Francisco Alegre wrote and studied in Mexico, in Cuba, and finally in Italy following the expulsion of the Jesuits from America in 1767. He was renowned for his erudition as he studied and taught Latin, theology, and mathematics. He wrote poetry as well as scholarly treatises, and he knew Latin, Greek, Hebrew, and English fluently. He worked in the classics, and many of his written works revolved about classical themes such as a poem that focused on the conquest of Tiro by Alexander the Great. Alegre also translated the *Iliad* of Homer from Greek to Latin. Because of his scholarly activities he was well known and respected in Europe and America.

Alegre was asked by his religious order to continue writing the *Historia de la provincia* that had been initiated by Father Francisco de Florencia. He worked on this project at the Real Colegio Seminario de San Ildefonso de Mexico. He also wrote a history of the Jesuit order at about the same time that he was working on the earlier history, but he never completed it. Back in Europe after the expulsion of the Jesuits he wrote on a variety of subjects, but his histories were of greatest importance. He was regarded as one of the best writers in Mexico in the 18th century, and his scholarship was well respected. He wrote in a simple, easy style that led Europeans after the expulsion to conclude that Mexican ignorance was only a myth. His history of the Jesuit order in America was a narrowly focused study on the order itself rather than a broadly based work uniting the history of the order in America with the history of America itself, as was true of many of the Jesuit histories. He wrote about the Jesuits' activities, problems, and achievements in Mexico, but the book turned out to be a defense of the Jesuits from the attacks lodged against them by their critics. Still, the book is valuable because of the large amount of data it included on the expeditions in which the Jesuits participated, particularly the material on the erection of Jesuit missions in northern New Spain. As history, however, the book lacks objectivity since it was a defense of the Jesuits and made no effort to treat the other side of the question. As one modern writer phrased it, "The book's partiality was notorious."

A. *Institucionces teológicas*, 7 vols. (Bologna, Italy, 1789); *Historia de la Compañía de Jesús en Nueva España* (Mexico City, 1841–1843); and *Memorias para la historia de la provincia que tuvo la Compañía de Jesús en Nueva España* (Mexico City, 1940–1941).
B. Donald C. Briggs and Marvin Alisky, *Historical Dictionary of Mexico* (Metuchen, N.J., 1981), p. 8; *Diccionario Porrúa* (Mexico City, 1976), pp. 63–64; Aurora M. Ocampo de Gómez and Ernesto Prado Velázquez, *Diccionario de escritores mexicanos* (Mexico City, 1967), pp. 8–9; and A. Curtis Wilgus, *The Historiography of Latin America: A Guide to Historical Writing, 1500–1800* (Metuchen, N.J., 1975), pp. 233–234.

ALESSIO ROBLES, VITO (14 August 1879, Saltillo, Mexico—11 June 1957, Mexico City). *Education*: Secondary education at the Ateneo Fuente; civil engineering degree and commission as lieutenant in the Corps of Engineers, National Army, Military Academy of Chapultepec, Mexico City, 1903; Colegio San Juan de Nepomuceno; Pestalozzi Institute; Ateneo Fuente, Saltillo. *Career*: Officer, Corps of Engineers, 1903–1913; taught military tactics, Military Academy of Chapultepec, 1902; taught mathematics and military evolution, Colegio Civil of Monterrey, 1904; taught campaign communications, Military Academy of Tlalpan, 1909–1913; taught American history and mathematics, National University of Mexico, 1935–1938; Chief of the General Staff of the Secretary of War and Marine, 1912; Inspector General of the Police of the Federal District, 1911–1912, 1914; Secretary, Revolutionary Convention of Aguascalientes, 1914; Military Attaché, Mexican legation to Italy, 1912–1913; Federal Deputy, 1920–1922; Managing Director of the newspapers *El heraldo de México*, 1920, and *El demócrata*, 1920–1923; Federal Senator, 1922–1926; Minister Plenipotentiary to Sweden, 1925–1926; President National Anti-Reelection party, 1927–1929; President, National Revolutionary party, 1927; Governor, Federal District.

As a young army officer Alessio Robles fought against the Yaqui Indians in a major campaign in the state of Sonora early in the 20th century. He returned to Mexico City when the campaign ended and assumed teaching responsibilities in the Military Academy in Tlalpan. When the revolution against Porfirio Díaz began in 1910, Alessio Robles returned to military duty to fight against the revolutionary forces. After Francisco I. Madero assumed the presidency, he named Alessio Robles Chief of Staff, despite the fact that Alessio had fought against him. When the confused violence continued, Alessio Robles joined the army of General Venustiano Carranza and was sent to Washington on a special mission for the general. Finally, as the fighting subsided, Alessio Robles returned to his civilian career as a civil engineer, but he retained enough influence in national politics to win the presidency of the PNR, the major political party of the nation. In 1934 he returned to private life and concentrated his attention on the study of history.

In addition to his interest in historical research, Alessio Robles also taught history at the National Preparatory School and the National School of Music, and in 1945 he was named Chairman of the History of the Internal Provinces of New Spain at the National University. As a researcher he used his appointment to Sweden to stop over in Spain and spend some time in the Archives of the Indies. His major interest was the history of his home state of Coahuila, and his major research effort was in this direction. His primary concern was the many errors and inaccuracies he found in books and articles dealing with Coahuila, and he was determined to correct all of them. In addition to his monographs, he also edited several historical documents that related to the history of northern Mexico. He worked long and hard to elevate history to a proximity of truth and away from the continual repetition of errors that plagued many studies, but most especially, from his point of view, those on the history of Coahuila. Consequently, while his focus was local, his impact on improving and upgrading the histories produced was national. For this reason he is respected as one of Mexico's outstanding 20th century historians.

A. *Bibliografía de Coahuila histórica y geográfica* (Mexico City, 1927); *Como se ha escrito la historia de Coahuila: Una crítica mezquina sobre la obra "Francisco de Urdinola y el Norte de la Nueva España"* (Mexico City, 1931); *Acapulco en la historia y en la leyenda* (Mexico City, 1934); *Monterrey en la historia y en la leyenda* (Mexico City, 1936); *Los tratados de Bucareli* (Mexico City, 1937); *Coahuila y Téxas en la época colonial* (Mexico City, 1938).

B. Robert O. de Vette, "Vito Alessio Robles (1879–1957)," *Hispanic American Historical Review*, 38, No. 1 (February 1958), pp. 51–57; *Diccionario Porrúa*, 4th ed. (Mexico City, 1976), pp. 60–61; Percy Alvin Martin, *Who's Who in Latin America*, 2d ed. rev. (Stanford, 1940), pp. 13–14; and Robert A. Potash, "Historiography of Mexico Since 1821," *Hispanic American Historical Review*, 40, No. 3 (August 1960), p. 398.

ALFARO, RICARDO JOAQUÍN (20 August 1882, Panama City—23 February 1971, Panama City). *Education*: Colegio Balboa; University of Cartagena, Colombia; Doctor of Laws and Political Science, National School of Laws, Universidad de Panama; honorary degree, University of Southern California, United States. *Career*: Undersecretary of Foreign Relations; Judge, Mixed Commission of Arbitration Between Panama and the United States; teacher, Instituto Nacional; teacher, Escuela Nacional de Derecho; Secretary of Government and Justice; Magistrate, International Court of Justice, The Hague, 1962; Minister of Foreign Relations; President of the Republic, 1931–1932; unsuccessful candidate for the presidency, 1940.

An active political figure throughout much of his life, Alfaro never gave up his interest in intellectual or literary pursuits. As a result of his literary, judicial, and political careers he gained recognition not only at home but in all of Latin America, the United States, and Europe. He received decorations from twenty foreign governments, and his published work was well received abroad. His interests were varied, and he was particularly enthusiastic about the study of philology. His book *Diccionario de anglicismos* was widely used throughout the Spanish-speaking world, and it was praised by those who favored the preservation of the purity of the Spanish language. In addition to his philological studies, he also wrote poetry and biographies.

Alfaro's historiographical contribution was largely in the field of diplomatic history and studies on the independence movement. He was conscious of the world about him, and he even wrote some of his books in French and English. He was a global man, and his reputation was international in scope. Foreign academic institutions and foreign governments were well acquainted with this work, and he became the most conspicuous of Panama's intellectuals. In his history as well as other work he was conscious of his use of the language, and generally he wrote in a correct, precise manner. One observer characterized his work as "sincere elegance," to which most would agree.

A. *Vida del general Tomás Herrera* (Barcelona, Spain, 1908); *El panamericanismo*

bolivariano y el actual (Washington, D.C., 1926); *Los últimos días del Libertador* (Washington, D.C., 1930); *Contribuciones de América al derecho internacional* (Washington, D.C., 1937); *Diccionario de anglicismos* (Panama City, 1950); *Panorama internacional de América* (Cambridge, Mass., 1958).
B. Helen Delpar, *Encyclopedia of Latin America* (New York, 1974), p. 18; Anne K. and Basil C. Hedrick, *Historical Dictionary of Panama* (Metuchen, N.J., 1970), p. 9; Percy Alvin Martin, *Who's Who in Latin America* (Stanford, 1936), p. 12; Juan Almela Melia; *Guía de personas que cultivan la historia de América* (Mexico City, 1951), pp. 9–10; and Unión Panamericana, *Diccionario de la literatura latinoamericana: América Central: Honduras, Nicaragua y Panamá* (Washington, D.C., 1963), pp. 238–239.

ALVA IXTLILXOCHITL, FERNANDO DE (1577, Teotihuacán, Mexico—1648, Mexico City). *Education*: Graduated with distinction, Colegio de Santa Cruz de Tlaltelolco. *Career*: Governor of Texcoco, 1612; Governor of Tlalmanalco, 1617; Indian interpreter to the Viceroy; landholder.

Alva Ixtlilxochitl was a mestizo who frequently wrote from the Indian perspective on the conquest and colonization of America. As the grandson of the Emperor of the Chichimecas, he was acquainted with the pre-Columbian aspect of Mexican history, and when he wrote he made use of the knowledge about the past he had acquired as a consequence of his royal birth. He also learned a great deal about the Spanish from the paternal side of his family, and most importantly, he learned the Spanish language. Once King Philip III sanctioned a grant of land to Alva as a part of his royal inheritance, he had leisure time to devote to historical studies. He collected Toltec and Aztec manuscripts and gained a great deal more information from interviews with the natives. He possessed an extensive library for that period from which he worked. From all of this source material he put together several histories of New Spain.

One of Alva's histories began with the creation of the world and ran to 1521, when the Spaniards attacked Tenochtitlán. His *Historia general de la Nueva España* is regarded as his major work because he included in its preparation a vast number of prehistoric archeological artifacts and because it was the most complete history of the Chichimeca Indians compiled up to that time. While some later historians criticized this and other histories as confused and sometimes illogically developed, others regarded his work more highly. Carlos María de Bustamante called him the American Cicero, and others praised his simple, eloquent style as well as his presentation of material that came from sources later lost and not now available to historians. His defenders point out that Alva, along with other chroniclers, while charged with confusion and sometimes with using data not entirely accurate, nevertheless provided a major service. They were, after all, not historians but chroniclers, and their work provided historical sources that frequently are not now available to the researcher. Therefore, their histories and chronicles become important sources for modern historians. Another criticism of his work was that of impartiality. He was one of the first mestizo historians of Mexico who wrote in the 17th century, and this in itself produced a change in Mexican historiography because prior to this time all historians had been Spanish and had presented the Spanish point of view. Alva reversed that trend and wrote from the Indian perspective. Thus, while his work was sympathetic to the Indians, it served as a counterpoise to the earlier works that were partial to the Spanish. While some 19th century historians charged that his sources were not accurate, later scholarship has taken the view that his data were "absolutely true" and of tremendous value to Mexican colonial historiography. Another critic accused him of impatience in working with documents, which may have contributed to some of the inaccuracies and chronological problems that annoyed later historians. But few deny that his books are valuable sources today for early Mexican history and that they are also significant as early examples of Mexican literature.

A. *Horribles crueldades de los conquistadores de México y de los indios que los auxiliaron para subyugarlos a la corona de Castilla* (Mexico City, 1829); *Historia chichimeca* (London, 1831); "Romances de los señores de la Nueva España" (unpublished).

B. *Diccionario Porrúa* (Mexico City, 1976), I, p. 83; A. Curtis Wilgus, *The Historiography of Latin America: A Guide to Historical Writing, 1500–1800* (Metuchen, N.J., 1975), pp. 143–144.

ALVEAR Y PONCE DE LEÓN, DIEGO DE   (13 November 1749, Montilla, Spain—15 January, 1830, Madrid). *Career*: Participated in an expedition to the Philippines as a navy guard, 1770; took part in a campaign against the Portuguese in Montevideo, 1775; participated in the drawing of boundary lines with Portugal, 1783; promoted to Captain of the Navy, 1794; gave up his commission, 1801; regained his rank and eventually bacame Commandant of Cádiz, 1807.

In 1783, Alvear y Ponce de León, who had earlier participated in several other colonial adventures in Asia as well as America, was appointed to a special commission assigned by the Spanish crown to investigate and define the boundary limits between the Spanish and Portuguese colonies as defined by the 1777 Treaty of San Ildefonso. While on the assignment in South America he kept a diary that became a chronicle of the age and eventually reached the proportions of a five-volume work.

Alvear's diary contains geographic, ethnographic, and historical information. He traced the development of the region in which the Guaraní Indians resided from the conquest by the Spanish to the time in which he wrote the diary. At the same time, he traced the growth of the Jesuit missions and of each one of the reduction stations that was established. Finally, he devoted some attention to the governmental structure of the region. The diary was also important because it included a natural history of Paraguay and because it was a compilation of Alvear's duties on the boundaries commission. Since his charge was to fix the boundary lines around the Jesuit missions, it was logical that he devoted most of his attention in the diary to that question. For this task he accepted the work of the classical chroniclers without subjecting them to serious criticism. The historical significance of this study was not so much in the chronicling of the event in which he participated as in the development of the internal regime and the culture of the Guaraní people as it was affected by the expulsion of the Jesuits in 1767. He noted that, while the economy of the mission area declined, which was to be expected, the religious devotion of the Indians continued unabated even without the direction of the Jesuits. That order, after two centuries of proselytizing, had done its job well, and Alvear recognized the continued faithfulness of the Indians who lived in the missions. Alvear's historical method was not rigorous and critical; rather, he sought to justify the work of the Jesuits and the Spanish boundaries in the Río de la Plata region.

A. *Relación geographica histórica de la provincia de misiones, del brigadier d. Diego Alvear, primer comisario y astronómo en gefe de la segunda división de limites por la Corte de España, en América* (Buenos Aires, 1836).

B. Efraím Cardozo, *Historiografía paraguaya* (Mexico City, 1959), pp. 449–454; Francisco Esteve Barba, *Historiografía indiana* (Madrid, 1964), pp. 601–602; and Charles J. Kolinski, *Historical Dictionary of Paraguay* (Metuchen, N.J., 1973), p. 8.

AMUNÁTEGUI, MIGUEL LUÍS (11 January 1828, Santiago—22 January 1888, Santiago). *Education*: Studied humanities at the Instituto Nacional Santiago. *Career*: Taught literature in the Instituto Nacional, 1847; worked in the Oficina Estadistica, 1848; began writing history with his brother, Gregorio, 1849; commissioned by the President of the Republic to write a defense of Chile's claim to Patagonian islands that were also claimed by Argentina, 1853 and 1855; named Chief of Instruction, Ministry of Justice, Education, and Public Instruction, 1853; taught at the University of Chile, 1852; Undersecretary of Interior, 1862; wrote for and edited periodicals and journals; President, Chamber of Deputies, 1867; Minister of Interior and Foreign Relations, 1868; President, Chamber of Deputies, 1871; unsuccessful candidate for the presidency, 1876; Minister of Foreign Relations, 1887.

Amunátegui was one of a group of outstanding 19th century Latin American historians who dictated the nature of historiography in their country. But he worked extensively for political causes of the liberal persuasion as well. He championed the separation of church and state, without much success, and he was a champion of female education throughout the nation, adopting a program whereby women could take examinations to gain professional titles. In addition, he founded a newspaper, *El independiente*, which was a political organ and in which he contributed his political ideas.

Although he rose to high-ranking positions in the government, Amunátegui was more significant as one of the leading historians of his age. He worked extensively in primary documents, building his histories from the unedited works to the more readily available secondary studies. He was a champion of detailed work in archives, and like many of his contemporaries he built a personal library that was impressive. He used also private papers, diaries, and correspondence to write effective biographical studies of important figures in Chilean history. As he wrote his histories and biographies, he liked to bring forth the unedited documentation rather than to analyze the subject. He did occasionally examine a thesis, as in his book *La dictadura de O'Higgins*, but he was far more comfortable with the clear, definitive narration of past events. Much of his early work was coauthored with his brother Gregorio, with whom Miguel carried forward the ideals of historiography of a politically liberal nature. Some modern historians have suggested that he was the most significant Chilean historian of the 19th century behind only Diego Barros Arana.

A. *La dictadura de O'Higgins* (Santiago, 1853); *Descubrimiento y conquista de Chile* (Santiago, 1862); *Narraciones históricas* (Santiago, 1876); *La crónica de 1810*, 3 vols. (Santiago, 1876–1899); *Vida de don Andrés Bello* (Santiago, 1882); *Don Salvador Sanfuentes: Apuntes biográficos* (Santiago, 1892).

B. Domingo Amunátegui Solar, *Archivo epistolar de don Miguel Luís Amunátegui*, 2 vols. (Santiago, 1942); Salvatore Bizzarro, *Historical Dictionary of Chile* (Metuchen, N.J., 1972), pp. 27–28; Helen Delpar, *Encyclopedia of Latin America* (New York, 1974), p. 26; Michael Rheta Martin and Gabriel Lovett, *Encyclopedia of Latin American History* (Indianapolis, 1968), p. 15; Unión Panamericana, *Diccionario de la literatura latinoamericana: Chile* (Washington, D.C., 1958), pp. 4–6; and Gertrude Matyoka Yeager, "Barros Arana, Vicuña Mackenna, Amunátegui: The Historian as National Educator," *Journal of Inter-American Studies and World Affairs*, 19, No. 2 (May 1977), pp. 173–199.

AMUNÁTEGUI SOLAR, DOMINGO (21 October 1860, Santiago—4 March 1946, Santiago). *Education*: Studied humanities, National Institute; law degree, University of Chile, 1881. *Career*: Taught at the National Institute and the School of Humanities, University of Chile; Director, Instituto Pedagogico; Dean, School of Humanities; Minister of Justice and Public Instruction, 1887, 1907, 1909, 1910; Deputy, National Congress, 1890; Rector, University of Chile, 1911–1922; Minister of the Interior, 1918, 1923; participated in writing the Chilean Constitution of 1925; active Liberal party member; journalist.

The son of Miguel Amunátegui, the great 19th century Chilean historian, Domingo Amunátegui followed his father's interests in writing history and in political activity. Domingo did not write in other genres as was true of most Latin American historians of his era. Instead, he devoted his literary career almost entirely to history. For his efforts he won the acclaim of fellow historians and the respect of his countrymen. He became a Corresponding Member of the Royal Academy of History, Madrid in 1909, and a Member of the Hispanic Society of America in New York in 1914. He also received commendation from the Italian Crown in 1914 and became a Corresponding Member of the Royal Spanish Academy of Languages of Madrid in 1915. Finally, in 1923 he was named an Official of the Italian Order of San Lázaro. Meanwhile, his governmental career and his educational administrative duties gained him stature as one of Chile's prominent leaders. As such he was called upon often as a public speaker on both educational and political subjects, and he also contributed many perceptive articles for the press on both politics and history.

In his historical writing Amunátegui preferred to concentrate upon the development of education in Chile, as in *Los primeros años del Instituto Nacional, 1813–1835*, and to focus on biographies, such as *José Toribo Medina*, 1932. Later in life he turned also to topics that dealt with political matters. While his father, as a leading Chilean Liberal, had denounced the Spanish influence on Latin America, Domingo, also a Liberal, took the opposite view, arguing that the Spanish colonizing period had in fact been an advantage for the region because it brought Spanish culture to the Western Hemisphere. He argued as well that the Spaniards had not wiped out the native population found in America but instead preserved the Indians and incorporated them into the mainstream of society, particularly through miscegenation. Consequently, while Domingo's noneducational histories were generally of a political nature, he did move into the realm of social history in the last years of his career. He wrote all his history simply but with great clarity, and while his style lacked the elegance of many of the historians of his age, his books were hallmarks of interesting reading. Much of his historical production came after his retirement from public life, and he filled his last years with some of his finest work, carrying on the family tradition of historical writing and winning for himself the plaudits of scholars in every corner of Latin America and in the United States as well.

A. *Los primeros años del Instituto Nacional, 1813–1835* (Santiago, 1889); *El Instituto Nacional bajo los rectorados de don Manuel Montt, don Francisco Puente y don Antonio Varas, 1835–1845* (Santiago, 1891); *La sociedad chilena del siglo XVIII: mayorazgos y titulos de Castilla*, 3 vols. (Santiago, 1901–1904); *Don Francisco Solano Astaburuaga* (Santiago, 1905); *El progreso intelectual y político de Chile* (Santiago, 1936); *La democracia política en Chile: Teatro político, 1810–1910* (Santiago, 1947).

B. Isaac Joslin Cox, "Death of Domingo Amunátegui Solar," *Hispanic American Historical Review* 26, No. 2 (May 1946), pp. 274–276; Guillermo Feliú Cruz, *Caracterización de la obra histórica de d. Domingo Amunátegui Solar* (Santiago, 1940); Percy Alvin Martin, *Who's Who in Latin America* (Stanford, 1936), p. 10; William Belmont Parker, *Chileans of To-Day* (New York, 1920), pp. 11–15; Raul Silva Castro, *Don Domingo Amunátegui Solar: Su vida y sus obras* (Santiago, 1935); and Unión Panamericana, *Diccionario de la literatura latinoamericana: Chile* (Washington, D.C. 1958), pp. 6–8.

ANCONA, ELIGIO (1 December 1836, Mérida, Yucatán, Mexico—3 April 1892, Mexico City). *Education*: Preparatory studies at the Seminario Clerical de San Ildefonso; law degree, Universidad Literaria del Estado, 1862. *Career*: Regidor of Ayuntamiento; Interim Governor of Yucatán; Deputy, National Congress; Circuit Judge; Magistrate, Supreme Court of Justice; founder of the political periodical, *Sombra de morelas*, of the pro-Juárez newspaper, *La pildora*, and of a political newspaper, *Yucatán*.

Ancona was a liberal and a supporter of Benito Juárez in the mid-19th century. As such he challenged the right of the Archduke Maximilian and his French supporters to rule Mexico, and he fought against the imperial government from the pages of several publications and newspapers. Following the expulsion of the French, Ancona held political appointments in the Juárez government. Along with his journalistic talent he also wrote novels, which he based upon historical incidents. Consequently, he wrote not only histories of Mexico, primarily regional histories of his home state of Yucatán, but historical novels that brought history to the wider audience of fiction readers. He remained active politically, particularly following the expulsion of the Emperor Maximilian, when he participated in a defense of the government from Ignacio Comonfort, who sought to take power.

In both his histories and historical novels Ancona tended to reflect his liberal political philosophy. He castigated the Church for its support of what he considered to be Spanish oppression in the colonial and independence periods. At the same time, he championed the role of the Indians in the development of his country in a historical novel *Los martires del Anáhuac*, written in 1870 on the 16th century conquest by Hernán Cortés. This was the first historical novel written in Mexico about that stage of the nation's development. He was also something of an expert on customs, which was reflected in his historical novels, and while his plots were sometimes intricate and difficult to unravel, his tracing of the customs of the people of Yucatán was valuable for the literature and the history of that region. Ancona's contribution to history was less than that of some other 19th century historians, but he did play a role because he helped to create a national literature with a historical flavor and he popularized the concept of history among the Mexican population. Although he was not a profound researcher, he did manage to provide some significant information on Yucatán's historical development.

A. *La mestiza* (Mérida, Mexico, 1861); *El filibustero* (Mérida, Mexico, 1864); *La cruz y la espada* (Mérida, Mexico, 1864); *Los martires del Anáhuac* (Mexico City, 1870); *Historia de Yucatán desde la época más remota hasta nuestros dias*, 4 vols. (Mérida, Mexico, 1878–1880); *Memorias de un Alférez* (Mérida, Mexico, 1904).

B. Donald C. Briggs and Marvin Alisky, *Historical Dictionary of Mexico* (Metuchen, N.J., 1981), p 12; *Diccionario Porrúa* (Mexico City, 1976), I, p. 104; Aurora M. Ocampo de Gómez and Ernesto Prado Velázquez, *Diccionario de escritores mexicanos* (Mexico City, 1967), p. 18; and J. Lloyd Read, *The Mexican Historical Novel, 1826–1910* (New York, 1939), pp. 140–159.

ANDRADE, ROBERTO (26 October 1852, Parroquia, Bolívar, Ecuador—30 October 1938, Guayaquil, Ecuador). *Education*: Colegio de San Diego de Ibarra; University of Quito; Colegio de Jesuitas de Quito. *Career*: Professor of Grammar and History, Colegio Internacional de Lima, 1888; Rector, Colegio Olmedo, Manabi, 1898; Director, Normal Institute in Quito; Senator and Deputy, Ecuadorean National Legislature, 1897–1908; Minister of the Tribunal of Accounts of Guayaquil, 1900.

Dictatorships were common in Ecuador following independence, and political turmoil was the rule rather than the exception. Roberto Andrade was one of a group of passionate opponents who sought to unseat the conservative dictatorship of Gabriel García Moreno, and he was part of the group that assassinated the dictator on 6 August 1875. From that point on Andrade was persecuted, hounded, and besieged by supporters of the fallen García; however, he seemed to glory in the notoriety he received for his role in the assassination. Meanwhile, he fought back against his enemies by producing pamphlets, books, novels, and histories. He attacked in print the Venezuelan President of Ecuador, Juan José Flores, with the words of a patriot who could not condone a foreigner holding political power in Quito. His opposition was significant and aided in building opposition to Flores. Meanwhile, Andrade continued to write about García Moreno in an even more passionately subjective manner than before the assassination. The political liberal in Andrade could not tolerate the conservative García Moreno any more than it could accept a foreign president in his beloved country. Other political figures who paraded across Ecuadorean history were treated in the same way, either with damning criticism, if Andrade opposed them, or with glowing praise, if they agreed with his political philosophy. As his political activity continued he suffered additional adverse consequences, which included imprisonment. His fame as a revolutionary leader grew dramatically as a result of his imprisonment, however, and he was easily elected to the National Congress in 1896.

For the polemicist, critic, journalist, or columnist, it is a danger to write about events and people that elicit such powerful emotions as was the case in the late 19th century in Ecuador, but for the historian, partisan, impassioned sentiment is disastrous. Knowing that complete objectivity cannot be achieved by mortals, nevertheless, the historian must at least make the effort at impartiality. Andrade never did make that attempt, and he even defended his work from those who charged that he was too passionate. He argued that passion in a writer was not a liability until passion led him to support injustice. Such arguments, however, hardly applied to the historian, who has to seek objectivity if he wants to earn the title historian. Despite his prejudice and direct involvement in events he chronicled, Andrade did produce a major seven-volume history of his country, *Historia del Ecuador*, that was well written and that in parts was outstanding. Ecuadorean historians usually point to the parts that deal with the revolution of 1808 as exemplary. Cevallos in his multivolume history covered the period 1808 to 1812, but Andrade, using Cevallos' material, expanded upon it and amplified it by using documents that he found in Bogota's archives. This reworking of the treatment accorded the independence epoch by Cevallos was a major contribution to Ecuadorean historiography. But Andrade also had a negative impact on Ecuadorean historiography when he rehashed the work of earlier historians and then included his own political and religious prejudices.

A. *Seis de agosto, o sea muerte de García Moreno* (Portoviejo, Ecuador, 1896); *Vida y muerte de Eloy Alfaro* (New York, 1915); *Lecciones de historia del Ecuador para los niños* (Quito, 1917); *Estudios históricos: Montalvo y García Moreno* (Guayaquil, Ecuador, 1925); *Antonio, José de Sucre* (Havana, 1930); and *Historia del Ecuador*, 7 vols. (Guayaquil, Ecuador, 1936).

B. Isaac J. Barrera, *Historiografía del Ecuador* (Mexico City, 1956), pp. 106–108; Helen

Delpar, *Encyclopedia of Latin America* (New York, 1974), p. 29; Percy Alvin Martin, *Who's Who in Latin America* (Stanford, 1936), pp. 19–20; and Adam Szaszdi, "The Historiography of the Republic of Ecuador," *Hispanic American Historical Review*, 44, No. 4 (November 1964), pp. 520, 523–525.

ARGUEDAS, ALCIDES (15 July 1879, La Paz—6 May 1946, Chulumani, Bolivia). *Education*: Colegio Nacional, 1898; law degree, Universidad de La Paz, 1903; Collège Libre des Sciences Sociales, Paris. *Career*: Journalist for *El comercio*; Secretary of the Bolivian legation in Paris and London, 1910–1915; founded *Los debates* in La Paz; Member, Chamber of Deputies, 1916; Diplomatic Agent of Propaganda in France and Spain, 1919; Consul General of Bolivia in Paris, 1922; Minister of Bolivia in Colombia, 1929; Senator from La Paz, 1940; Minister of Bolivia in Venezuela, 1941.

Arguedas spent the better part of 25 years outside his country as a diplomat in Europe and other Latin American countries. Still, he returned periodically to gain elective office, to work as a journalist, and to write novels. In his written work he projected an angry attitude regarding Bolivian society, particularly his sociological study *Pueblo enfermo*, which he published in 1909. In this work he denigrated the Bolivian people, criticizing them as lazy, treacherous, and dishonest. But he explained these defects as resulting from the hundreds of years of oppression in Bolivian history. This oppressive atmosphere had brutalized not only the Indian majority but the white and mestizo minorities as well. This pessimistic, accusatory account of Bolivian life made a strong impact on both the nation and the outside world and opened up a discussion among those who read it of social conditions in Bolivia. Additionally, Arguedas carried his theme into his historical works, thereby keeping the social questions before the reading public.

Called by some the foremost historian of Bolivia, Arguedas produced a formal history, *Historia general de Bolivia: el proceso de la nacionalidad, 1809–1921*, that traced Bolivian development by periods, from independence to 1921. The same accusatory tone that marked *Pueblo enfermo* is found in his histories, a fact that ensured the controversial nature of his books. He was a blunt, outspoken writer who was incapable of satire or irony and who was humorless in the delivery of his message. This style was another reason for the controversy that surrounded his historical and sociological work. But although the style was colorless, it was full of vitality, descriptive but insolent in tone. He was a follower of *Gabriel René-Moreno, but unlike his model he was incapable of the deft touch in making his arguments. Instead he was brutal, arrogant, inflexible, moralizing, but sincere. Yet his message was so important to Bolivia that Arguedas' histories are among the most significant ever produced in that country, and he remains as one of the outstanding Bolivian historians.

A. *Pueblo enfermo* (La Paz, 1919); *Historia de Bolivia: La fundación de la República* (La Paz, 1920); *Historia general de Bolivia: El proceso de la nacionalidad, 1809–1921* (La Paz, 1922); *Historia de Bolivia: Los caudillos letrados, la confederación peru-*

boliviana, Ingavi; o la consolidación de la nacionalidad, 1828–1848 (Barcelona, Spain, 1923); *Historia de Bolivia: La plebe en acción, 1848–1857* (Barcelona, Spain, 1924); *Historia de Bolivia: La dictadura y la anarquía, 1857–1864* (Barcelona, Spain, 1926). B. Charles Arnade, "The Historiography of Colonial and Modern Bolivia," *Hispanic American Historical Review*, 42, No. 3 (August 1962), pp. 333–384; Helen Delpar, *Encyclopedia of Latin America* (New York, 1974), p. 38; Dwight B. Heath, *Historical Dictionary of Bolivia* (Metuchen, N.J., 1972), p. 25; Percy Alvin Martin, *Who's Who in Latin America* (Stanford, 1936), pp. 28–29; William Belmont Parker, *Bolivians of To-Day*, 2d ed. rev. (New York, 1967), pp. 27–29; and Unión Panamericana, *Diccionario de la literatura latinoamericana: Bolivia* (Washington, D.C., 1958), pp. 5–8.

ARGUELLO MORA, MANUEL (5 July 1845, San José—8 March 1902, San José). *Education*: Studied at the Universidad de San Thomás, San José; law degree, Universidad de Guatemala, 1857. *Career*: Judge; Magistrate, Supreme Court of Justice; Interim Rector, Universidad de San Thomás; worked in agriculture and commerce; took part in politics; founded the weekly newspaper, *La reforma*.

Along with most of the other Latin American historians of the 19th century, Arguello Mora was involved in a variety of activities in addition to writing history. An orphan, he was raised by his uncle, Juan Rafael Mora, President of Costa Rica. In 1859, when Mora's government was overthrown, Arguello Mora went into exile for the first time. He returned home to Costa Rica for good in 1871.

In his literary efforts Arguello was fond of both novels and history. Consequently, his novels usually had a historical setting, and factual historical events served to inspire the fiction. In his histories he was careful with detail, and his style was absolutely correct. He was a 19th century historian who had been influenced strongly by his European visits, and the European concern for proper style was uppermost in his mind when he wrote. He was also significant because he was one of the first Costa Rican writers to show much interest in history. He was a prolific writer of both fiction and history, and he also wrote about Costa Rican customs and legends. In all of this work he was interested in morality and ethics, and his own personal values provided him with a gauge for those in the past. His efforts were distinctly 19th century. In contrast to his political life, which was marked by the chaos and turmoil of political instability, his literary life was traditional in all respects. His histories were syntheses of the original work of other historians, but the history he produced was beautifully written in an elegant literary style. His use of history in fiction was also important. Many Latin American historians of the 19th century believed that historical novels were as significant as historical monographs because they showed more imagination, talent, and mental agility. They were also regarded highly because the assumption prevailed that more people would read a historical novel and thereby learn history from it than would read a history monograph. Arguello Mora believed that the two genres of fiction and history were eminently compatible and provided the realm of history with a dimension impossible to achieve in a studied historical narrative.

A. *Cuestión Mora y Aguilar, réplica* (San Salvador, 1861); *Páginas de historia: Recuerdos e impresiones* (San José, 1898); *Costa Rica pintoresca: Sus leyendas y tradiciones; colección de novelas, cuentos, historias y paisajes* (San José, 1899).

B. Abelardo Bonilla, *Historia y antología de la literatura costarricense*, Vol. 1 *Historia* (San José, 1957), pp. 130–132; and Unión Panamericana, *Diccionario de la literatura latinoamericana: América Central; Costa Rica, El Salvador y Guatemala* (Washington, D.C., 1963), II, pp. 3–4.

AZARA, FELIZ DE (18 May 1752, Barbunales, Spain—17 October 1821, Huesca, Spain). *Education*: Studied legislation and philosophy at the University of Huesca, Spain, 1757–1761. *Career*: Served in the army; Member, Comisión demarcadora de los límites con el Portugal, 1781; named Chief of the group in charge of designating borders for Paraguay and took up headquarters in Asunción, 1784; mapped and described historically and geographically the colony of Paraguay; assigned to several commissions by the Viceroy of Buenos Aires, 1796; refused the Viceroyalty of Mexico; studied and wrote about America.

Azara was an engineer and soldier who became interested in the physical and historical nature of South America, particularly the Río de la Plata region. He was involved in the attempt to draw satisfactory boundary lines between Portuguese Brazil and the Spanish colonies in South America. He returned to Spain in 1801 and continued to hold various positions in the Spanish government, but his major interest now reverted to Paraguay and the Río de la Plata. He began to publish books and articles and soon gained fame as an expert on the American region, but his reputation was based largely on geographic and botanical work; his historiographic reputation was virtually nil, and in fact some Paraguayan historians charged that his histories had only negative effects.

Unlike some other colonial historians he was not rigorous in his assessment of the works that already existed on the Río de la Plata and Paraguay. Instead, he generally accepted the views of chroniclers unquestioningly and included their work in his own studies of the conquest of the area. But his histories were important because they provided the flavor of the region in which he lived and worked. Additionally, his philosophy of history was far more rationalistic than that espoused by the Jesuits in the region of Paraguay. He gave much less attention to religion and far more to the strictly naturalistic interpretation of the history. For him evangelization and religious acts were not as important as the tracing of the natural development of man. But his history was more than simply a natural history of the region; it was a forerunner of the later, more sophisticated histories of the Río de la Plata region in which society, government, religion, and culture were integrated into a comprehensive study of the historic progress of the region.

A. *Viajes por la América del Sur, se Don Felix de Azara, comandante de la Comisión de límites española en la sección del Paraguay. Desde 1789 hasta 1801, en los cuales de dá una descripción geográfica, política y civil del Paraguay y del Río de la Plata:*

La historia del descubrimiento y conquista de dichos países, con numerosos detalles sobre la historia natural y sobre los pueblos salvajes, que habitan en la expresada región, a la que se acompaña una explosición de los medios empleados por los jesuítas para sujetar y civilizar los naturales de la citada sección de la América (Montevideo, 1846); *Descripción e historia del Paraguay y del Río de la Plata: Obra póstuma de don Felix de Azara brigadier de la Real Armada, y autor de las obras titulades "Apuntes para la historia de los cuadrúpedos y pájaros del Paraguay" de otras* (Madrid, 1847).

B. Efraím Cardozo, *Historiografía paraguaya* (Mexico City, 1959), pp. 401–435; Francisco Esteve Barba, *Historiografía indiana* (Madrid, 1964), pp. 593–598; Charles J. Kolinski, *Historical Dictionary of Paraguay* (Metuchen, N.J. 1973), p. 18.

B

BÁEZ, CECILIO (1 February 1862, Asunción—18 June 1941, Asunción). *Education*: Bachelor's degree, Colegio Nacional, 1882; studied law at the Law School attached to the Colegio Nacional; Doctor of Laws, University of Asunción, 1892. *Career*: Taught in the School for Notaries, 1893–1913; Professor of Civil Law, 1913; Rector, University of Asunción, 1920; Minister to Mexico, 1901; Minister to the United States, 1904; Minister of Foreign Affairs; Provisional President of the Republic, 1905–1906; Member, High Court of Justice, and Minister of Paraguay in Europe, 1917–1919.

While pursuing a career in public service, Báez was also an outstanding historian and philosopher. He gained enough respect from his fellow citizens to win the presidency on a provisional basis for a short period, but his contribution to Paraguay went far beyond that short stint as leader of the nation. He also served well in diplomatic posts, and he became Paraguay's expert in the Chaco boundary disputes with Bolivia, amassing a large amount of data to support Paraguay's claims. Meanwhile, he taught at several schools and ultimately achieved the highest educational administrative post available when he was named Rector of the National University in 1920.

Báez' historical writings were based on his acceptance of the philosophy of positivism, which placed a premium on technological and scientific education. He regarded history as a science and historical research as scientific rather than humanistic. Báez wrote a general history of Paraguay, *Resumen de la historia del Paraguay*, 1910, along with some monographs that dealt with specific events in Paraguay's development. But he also was interested in the medieval period of European history and did some work in that field as well, which indicated a broader range of interest than that possessed by most of the Latin American historians of his generation. In dealing with the colonial period of his own country's history he relied excessively upon the Spanish chroniclers, especially the Jesuits, when examining the role of the Guaraní indians. But this work was significant because he approached it from the sociological perspective rather than from a governmental, organizational point of view. Consequently, Báez made a major contribution to social as well as to political and diplomatic history. His major efforts, however, were directed toward the War of the Triple Alliance and Francisco Solano López' role in that war and in the history of Paraguay. He was a member of the Liberal party and he hated López, who represented all the worst of the Conservative party. His work on the war, then, was not an unbiased account but rather a partisan denunciation of Solano López. This was not an individual perspective, however, because most of the members of the Paraguayan Generation of 1900 reflected the political partisanship of Báez, just as most were transfixed by the war and Solano López.

A. *La tiranía en el Paraguay* (Asunción, 1903); *Cuadros históricos y descriptivos del Paraguay* (Asunción, 1907); *Resumen de la historia del Paraguay* (Asunción, 1910); *Le Paraguay* (Paris, 1924); *Historia colonial del Paraguay y Río de la Plata* (Asunción, 1926); *Historia diplomática del Paraguay*, 2 vols. (Asunción, 1931–1932).

B. Joseph R. Barager, "The Historiography of the Río de la Plata Area, Since 1830," *Hispanic American Historical Review*, 39, No. 4 (November 1959), p. 599; Efraím Cardozo, *Historiografía paraguaya* (Mexico City, 1959), pp. 20, 43; Helen Delpar, *Encyclopedia of Latin American History* (New York, 1974), p. 57; Charles J. Kolinski, *Historical Dictionary of Paraguay* (Metuchen, N.J., 1973), p. 18; Percy Alvin Martin, *Who's Who in Latin America* (Stanford, 1936), pp. 35–36; and William Belmont Parker, *Paraguayans of To-Day* (New York, 1967), pp. 11–13.

BALBUENA, BERNARDO DE (1562, Valdepeñas, Spain—11 October 1627, San Juan). *Education*: Universidad de Mexico, 1585–1590; Doctor of Theology, Universidad de Siguenza, Spain. *Career*: Chaplain, Audiencia de Guadalajara; parish priest, San Pedro Lagunillas; Abbot of Jamaica, 1610; Bishop of Puerto Rico, 1622.

A Spanish priest from the colonial era, Balbuena lived in Mexico and the Caribbean as well as Spain. He served in low clerical offices for 10 years until he decided that he would have a better opportunity to publish his written work if he were assigned to a larger city. He moved to Mexico City in 1602 and published some of his works. In 1606 he transferred to Spain, acquired his doctorate in theology, and received recognition at court, which led to his appointment as Abbot of Jamaica. After he was named bishop, the port of San Juan was taken by Dutch pirates, the town was sacked, and Balbuena's valuable library was destroyed.

At this time in the history of Latin America many of the historic works were written as epic poems, and Balbuena's extensive work—he wrote 40,000 stanzas—was in this genre. It was influenced by the Italian Renaissance and by his extensive interest in humanism, which was prevalent throughout Europe in this age. One observer ranked Balbuena along with Ercilla as the two foremost Latin American epic poets of the golden age of Spain in the 17th century. His writing was smooth and fresh and he described in verse the climate, people, and institutions of Mexico in the 17th century. Unlike Ercilla's description of battles and struggles, Balbuena's poem was more a social study of the Mexican population as well as a look at the geographic features of the region. Not only was the information valuable for later historians of the age, but it was written in a pleasant style that places the work among the finest colonial poems of Mexico. Such works as these won for Balbuena respect and admiration from his contemporaries.

A. *La grandeza mexicana* (Mexico City, 1604); *Siglo de oro en las selvas de Erifile* (Madrid, 1608); *El Bernardo Victoria de Roncesvalles* (Madrid, 1964).

B. Donald C. Briggs and Marvin Alisky, *Historical Dictionary of Mexico* (Metuchen, N.J., 1981), p. 18; *Diccionario Porrúa de historia* (Mexico City, 1976), I, pp. 205–206; and Aurora M. Ocampo de Gómez and Ernesto Prado Velázquez, *Diccionario de escritores mexicanos* (Mexico City, 1967), p. 32.

BARALT, RAFAEL MARÍA (3 July 1810, Maracaibo, Venezuela—4 January 1860, Madrid). *Education*: Studied philosophy, law, and Latin at the University of Sante Fé, Bogotá. *Career*: Practiced law; lieutenant in the Venezuelan army; functionary in the Ministry of War; diplomatic agent of Santo Domingo in independence negotiations with Spain; journalist and poet.

Born into a martial family, Baralt throughout his early life was subjected to military action, and he served in the Venezuelan army for a time. He grew up during the tumultuous independence struggle and went to school amid the chaotic and confused early years of independence. The political problems of Venezuela depressed him, and he eventually went to live in Europe, where he produced most of his literary work. In addition to writing poetry and history in Europe, he also worked as a diplomat for the Venezuelan government. He also wrote articles for Madrid reviews and journals, causing himself considerable trouble with the authorities and leading in one case to his expulsion from the job of director of the review, *Gaceta de Madrid*. At another time he was fired from his job as Minister Plenipotentiary of Santo Domingo for expressing political views that were not consistent with those of the authorities. Politically he was a liberal living in conservative Spain, and the misfortunes that he encountered could have been predicted from such a relationship. Yet, while his politics might have been deplored and might have caused him extensive difficulty, the Spanish government recognized his talent in the intellectual and literary fields by appointing him to the prestigious academies and awarding him various literary honors.

Although his poetry was adequate, Baralt's literary mark was made in articles and books that dealt mainly with history and linguistics. His major historical work was in the field of contemporary political history and was written at a time when national leaders had little patience with criticism from anyone, including historians. His three-volume history of Venezuela included the colonial period, but he carried it through the independence struggle and the immediate post-independence era, thereby encompassing analyses of the activities of people who were still alive, prominent, and, in some cases, powerful. For this reason he found the climate of Madrid more comfortable than that of Caracas. Yet he did feel deeply about his native country and in some of his articles the pain of living outside one's homeland crept into his work. In all his prose his style was fluid and his thinking lucid and eminently logical. Venezuelan writers of the 20th century conclude that in style and in the development of his ideas and arguments he was at least the equal of the great Andrés Bello. Despite his major contributions to the history of Venezuela and the recognition he received in Europe, he died in virtual poverty and without public notice. The Venezuelan scholar *Rufino

Blanco-Fombona went to Madrid in the 20th century and searched carefully throughout the cemeteries of the Spanish capital without the least bit of success in tracing down the grave of the great Venezuelan writer.

A. *Oda a Cristóbal Colón* (Madrid, 1850); *Catecismo de la historia de Venezuela desde 1489 hasta 1811* (Caracas, 1865); *Resúmen de la historia antigua y moderna de Venezuela*, 3 vols. (Curaçâo, 1887); *Apuntes para la historia del golpe de estado del 14 de Marzo de 1892 en Venezuela* (Maracaibo, Venezuela, 1893).

B. *Diccionario biográfico de Venezuela* (Madrid, 1953), pp. 111–114; Donna Keyse and G. A. Rudolf, *Historical Dictionary of Venezuela* (Metuchen, N.J., 1971), p. 19; and César Humberto Soto, *Personajes célebres de Venezuela* (Caracas, 1946), pp. 157–159.

BARRERA, ISAAC J. (4 February 1884, Otalvo, Ecuador—27 June 1970, Quito). *Education*: Colegio de San Gabriel, Quito. *Career*: Editor, *El comercio*, 1934; literary critic; taught Spanish and Latin American literature at the Universidad Central and the Instituto Nacional Mejia; Deputy and Senator on several occasions; held governmental positions; founded and directed the review, *Renacimiento*.

Like many Latin American writers, Barrera was first a journalist and a literary critic before he turned to a study of history. Additionally, he was interested in bibliographical work and in literary history. While pursuing these many interests he found time to teach and to hold several political offices. In the 20th century he became one of the outstanding men of letters in Ecuador, as renowned for his columns on literary criticism as for his biographical and literary history work.

Deeply committed to literary history and to biography, Barrera spent his life researching and writing in these areas. He was not content merely to describe the plot of a writer's work. Instead he wrote about groups of authors, how they compared with each other, schools of literature, the theory behind the works, and the schools of literature to which various works pertained. As a critic he was just as thorough as he examined carefully every facet of the piece and the author who produced it. His greatest contribution to literature and to the history of literature was his monumental *Historia de la literatura ecuatoriana*. In Ecuador the works of literary figures were scattered and difficult to find when he wrote this work. In painstaking fashion he collected the data and the books of the writers and information about the authors themselves to put together this study. It was also a difficult task because many of the authors had not written books but their work appeared in reviews, journals, and periodicals, which had to be ferreted out with patience and energy. He loved literature and believed the work to which he committed himself was essential for the literary growth of the nation, and consequently he made the effort, knowing full well that the glory and fame was not going to attend such studies as it would novels or other literary endeavors. But he did move into other literary fields with his biographical studies. His biographies were sincere efforts at objectivity, and he refrained from giving his imagination free reign as he stayed with the documented parts of the lives of his subjects. One writer said that it would be impossible to get a balanced

and complete picture of Ecuadorean literature without consulting the works of Isaac Barrera, so great was his contribution to the field of letters in his country.
A. *Rocafuerte: Estudio historico-biográfico* (Quito, 1911) *Quito colonial, siglo XVIII, comienzos del siglo XIX* (Quito, 1922); *Historia de la literatura ecuatoriana*, 2 vols. (Quito, 1944): *La prensa en el Ecuador* (Quito, 1955): *De nuestra América: hombres y cosas de la República del Ecuador* (Quito, 1956); *Historiografía del Ecuador* (Mexico City, 1956).
B. Augusto Arias: *Panorama de la literatura ecuatoriana* (Quito, 1946), pp. 231–234; Isaac J. Barrera,'' *Revista de historia de América*, No. 71 (January–June 1971), pp. 153–156; and Unión Panamericana, *Diccionario de la literatura latinoamericana: Ecuador* (Washington, D.C., 1958), pp. 88–91.

BARROS ARANA, DIEGO (16 August 1830, Santiago—4 November 1907, Santiago). *Education*: Studied law at the National Institute. *Career*: Taught history at the University of Chile; political exile in Europe and Latin America; Rector, National Institute, 1863–1872; taught history at the National Institute until 1907; began a diplomatic mission to negotiate a boundary dispute with Argentina, 1876; served also in Brazil and then returned to Europe; named Dean, Faculty of Philosophy and Humanities, 1892, Rector, 1893–1897, University of Chile.

Diego Barros Arrana stands as the leader of Chilean historiography even today. He was devoted to the study of his nation's past, and even from a young age he envisioned writing Chile's history. Toward that end he very early in life began to collect books, articles, and other data that could be used later in his research. He was also a journalist and editor, creating *El museo* in 1853 as a literary journal and in 1857 *El páis* as a political journal. He also wrote for *Revista de ciencias y letras*, 1857; *Anales de la Universidad de Chile*; *La semana*, 1859; *Revista del Pacífico*, *El ferrocarril*, 1863; *La república*, 1871; *Revista de Valparaiso*, 1873; *Revista de Chile*; *La lectura*, 1884; and *La libertad electoral*, 1886. In 1862 he established another literary review, *El correo del domingo*. In addition to his literary, teaching, and political activist careers, he was also a diplomat who served in Argentina, Uruguay, and Brazil.

Barros Arana represents a form of historiography that was popular in 19th century Latin America. He wrote extensive detailed accounts of his nation's history culminating in his massive, 16-volume *Historia general de Chile*. Such types of history were logical given the nature of the historical genre at that time, when history was just beginning to be written and historical data were just being collected. It was advantageous for the history profession to have writers like Barros Arana, who could run through several hundred years of history in an interesting style. These volumes continue today to be valuable research aids for anyone dealing with Chile's early history. But Barros Arana was more than a narrator of Chile's past; he was also a perceptive, analytical student of his country's history, and in other long works, such as *Un decenio de la historia de Chile, 1841–1851*, he scrutinized Chilean developments carefully. He was a researcher who knew how to organize vast amounts of data logically and whose method of testing each piece of primary evidence was emulated by subsequent Chilean scholars. Like most of his contemporaries he was interested primarily in the history of his own country, and he laid the foundations for 20th century Chilean historians. His vast library of documents and books was donated upon his death to the Biblioteca Nacional, and a Barros Arana Room was created for those materials and for some of his personal artifacts.

Historia general de la independencia de Chile, 4 vols. (Santiago, 1854–1858); *Cuadro histórico de la administración Montt* (Santiago, 1861); *Vida y viajes de Hernando de Magallanes* (Santiago, 1864); Compendio de historia de América, 2 vols. (Santiago, 1865); *Historia general de Chile*, 16 vols. (Santiago, 1884–1902); *Un decenio de la historia de Chile*, 2 Vols. (Santiago, 1905–1906).

B. Helen Delpar, *Encyclopedia of Latin America* (New York, 1974), p. 70; Ricardo Donoso, *Barros Arana educador, historiador y hombre público* (Santiago, 1931); Michael Rheta Martin and Gabriel Lovett, *Encyclopedia of Latin American History* (Indianapolis, 1968), p. 40; Carlos Orrego Barros, *Diego Barros Arana* (Santiago, 1952); and Unión Panamericana, *Diccionario de la literatura latinoamericana: Chile* (Washington, D.C., 1958), pp. 18–21.

BARROS BORGOÑO, LUÍS   (1858, Santiago 1943, Santiago). *Education*: Bachelor of Philosophy and Letters, National Institute, 1876; law degree, University of Chile, 1880. *Career*: Taught history at the National Institute; named Chair, Documentary History, Pedagogical Institute, 1883; Head of the Diplomatic Section, Ministry of Foreign Relations, 1883; appointed to Army of Occupation in Lima, 1883; Reporter to the Supreme Court, 1884; Minister of War and Navy, 1889; Provisional Secretary of War, 1891; Treasurer, of the Caja de Crédito Hipotecario, 1892–1901; candidate for President of the Republic, 1920; Minister of Interior, 1925; Interim President for two months, 1925; Ambassador to Argentina, 1925–1928.

Beginning as a history teacher Barros soon became embroiled in public life and did not devote full time to the profession of history. Instead he researched and wrote while holding governmental positions and amidst sometimes perilous activities such as the 1891 revolution. He represented the Conservative cause in the 1920 presidential election against the popular Liberal candidate Arturo Alessandri, who eventually won the close election.

Barros Borgoño's historiographic activity was not extensive, but when he wrote he concentrated upon national history and upon political subjects. He was also fond of writing biographies and of dealing with the historic development of education in his country. The study of Patricio Lynch, *El vice-admirante d. Patricio Lynch*, was a sympathetic look at the life of a military leader. His writing was clear and interesting, but it lacked the eloquence of some of his contemporaries. In other books he defended Chile's role in the War of the Pacific. Nonetheless, the few works produced are significant enough to warrant his inclusion among the leading historians of the early 20th century in Chile.

A. *La misión del vicario apostólico d. Juan Muzzi (1823–1825)* (Santiago, 1883); *El vice-admirante d. Patricio Lynch* (Santiago 1886); *Compendio de historia antigua de los pueblos de Oriente* (Santiago 1888); *Las reformas de la enseñanza secundaria* (Santiago, 1888); *La negociación chileno-boliviana* (Santiago, 1897); *La cuestión del Pacífico y las nuevas orientaciones de Bolivia* (Santiago, 1922).

B. Salvatore Bizzarro, *Historical Dictionary of Chile* (Metuchen, N.J., 1972); p. 39; Michael Rheta Martin and Gabriel Lovett, *Encyclopedia of Latin American History* (Indianapolis, 1968), p. 40; Percy Alvin Martin, *Who's Who in Latin America*, 2d ed. rev. (Stanford, 1940), p. 54; and William Belmont Parker, *Chileans of To-Day* (Santiago, 1920), pp. 67–70.

BASADRE, JORGE (12 February 1903, Tacna, Peru—29 June, 1980, Lima). *Education*: Graduated from the Colegio Alemán, Lima; Doctor of Literature, 1928, Bachelor of Laws, 1931, and Doctor of Laws, 1936, Universidad de San Marcos, Lima. *Career*: Member, School of Law, Universidad de San Marcos, 1931–1980; Chair of Peruvian History, 1928–1954; Chair of History of Peninsular Law, 1938–1954; Director of the Library, Universidad de San Marcos, 1930–1931, 1935–1942; Visiting Scholar of Library Science, Carnegie Foundation, United States, 1931–1932 Visiting Scholar, University of Berlin, 1932; Professor, Centro de Estudios, University of Sevilla, Spain, 1933; Secretary General, Congress of Americanists in Lima, 1939; Professor, School of Letters, University of Buenos Aires, 1942; Minister of Public Education, 1945; Director, Biblioteca Nacional del Perú.

Born in Chilean-occupied Tacna following the War of the Pacific, Basadre attended clandestine Peruvian schools before entering the Colegio Alemán in Lima and later the Universidad de San Marcos in the same city. He emerged from his training a committed scholar and as a Peruvian determined to aid his country by working in government. He was from a Peruvian generation that was influenced by both the Mexican Revolution of 1910 and the Russian Revolution of 1917. Basadre and his friends were also influenced by World War I, university reform movements, and active nationalists who sought social and political reform. Out of this milieu Basadre emerged as a champion of academic freedom in colleges and universities and political freedom for the Peruvian population. But he was more than a protestor for change; he became Director of the San Marcos library. Later, when a disastrous fire all but destroyed the National Library in Lima in 1943, Basadre became the Director of that institution and set about the monumental task of rebuilding the collection. For five years he carried out a national and international campaign to replace the books and manuscripts that were lost, with remarkable success. Additionally, he donated his own library to the nation, enriching the National Library and hastening its renaissance. He was so successful that today Peru's national library stands as one of the finest in Latin America.

Basadre researched in the modern period of Peruvian history, while many of his contemporaries preferred to write about the pre-Hispanic era or the colonial age coupled with the independence and immediate post-independence eras. In addition he was unwilling to devote his complete attention to political history as he looked at social themes and at regional Peruvian development. Then, too, he wrote about the growth of the legal traditions of Peru, and he tried his hand at a lengthy, multivolume general history,. which eventually ran to 17 volumes and went through six editions. In such a study he was able to provide an immense amount of detail, but this did not prevent him from developing a general assessment of Peruvian history. Another characteristic of his historical work was his generally optimistic outlook concerning Perú's ability to resolve its difficulties in public life and build a strong, viable, progressive nation. He saw in Peruvian and Latin American history a steady progress toward a richer, more satisfying existence. He acknowledged that the objective of a better life had not been realized, but he was optimistic that eventually that goal would be achieved. That objective, he wrote, inspired scholars and artists and motivated small elites as well as the vast masses, all of whom were working toward a better life for all. For all these reasons he has been called by one U.S. historian the "outstanding historian in 20th century Peru and possibly in all of South America."

A. *La multitud, la ciudad y el campo en la historia del Perú* (Lima, 1929); *La iniciación de la República*, 2 vols. (Lima, 1929–1930); *Perú: problema y posibilidad* (Lima, 1931); *Historia de la República, 1822–1899)*, 17 vols. (Lima, 1939); *Los fundamentos de la historia del derecho* (Lima, 1956); and *La historiografía de hoy* (Lima, 1973).

B. Marvin Alisky, *Historical Dictionary of Peru* (Metuchen, N.J., 1979), pp. 16–17; Thomas M. Davies, Jr., "Jorge Basadre (1903–1980)," *Hispanic American Historical Review*, 61, No. 1 (February 1981), pp. 84–86; Helen Delpar, *Encyclopedia of Latin America* (New York, 1974), p. 70; Percy Alvin Martin, *Who's Who in Latin America* (Stanford, 1936), p. 42; César Pacheco Velez, "Jorge Basadre," *Revista de historia de América*, No. 92 (July–December 1982), pp. 195–213.

BATRES MONTÚFAR, JOSÉ (18 March, 1809, San Salvador—9 July 1877, Guatemala City). *Education*: Taught at home by his mother; studied at Escuela de Cadetes, Guatemala, 1824; taught himself Italian and English; engineering degree, Academia de Ciencias, Guatemala, 1835. *Career*: Army officer; poet; chronicler; engineer in San Juan, Nicaragua, and in interoceanic explorations, 1837; Corregidor of Amatitlan; taught at the University of Guatemala; Deputy, Guatemalan legislature.

Batres was born in El Salvador, but moved to Guatemala when he was 13 years old. Upon graduation from the military academy, he fought against El Salvador and was captured and imprisoned for a year. While in prison he worked to improve his knowledge of the English language. When he was freed he studied engineering and changed his career. But he did not work long as an engineer and soon gained teaching and political positions. All the while he was soldiering, working as an engineer, teaching, and holding political positions, he wrote poetry, ultimately becoming one of the outstanding poets produced by Guatemala.

Some of Batres Montúfar's poetry was aimed at examining the society in which he lived. His life was sad and difficult; he lost a beloved brother in 1837, and the family periodically fell into difficulty. Perhaps for this reason some critics describe him as cold and aloof and some of his poetry as sarcastic and bitter. Yet the fluidity and smoothness of the verses in most of his work gained him a widespread reputation as a man of letters. In the poetry that dealt with life in his era he was an astute, observant chronicler. Cloaking his work in tragic-comedie fashion, he carefully drew a poetic picture of the people and events of the early half of the 19th century. Additionally, he wrote poems about the colonial age, once again faithfully depicting that era of Spanish control in narrative verse. He was not a great researcher of Guatemala's past, but his significance to history lies in his description of 19th century Guatemala as a rural nation of villages and small towns inhabited by industrious Indians led by the descendants of the Spanish colonizers. Perhaps because of the bleakness of his own life, he was able to delve deeply into Guatemalan developments in the 19th century and present a picture that, balanced with histories of the age, could enable later historians to achieve a valid accounting of life in that period.

A. *Poesías de José Batres Montúfar* (Guatemala City, 1845); *Poesías de José Batres Montúfar; homenaje de la Sociedad de Geografía e Historia de Guatemala* (Guatemala City, 1944); *Poesías líricas* (Guatemala City, 1952).

B. Philip F. Flemion, *Historical Dictionary of El Salvador* (Metuchen, N.J., 1972), p. 25; Richard Moore, *Historical Dictionary of Guatemala*, rev. ed. (Metuchen, N.J., 1973), p. 34; and Unión Panamericana, *Diccionario de la literatura latinoamericana: América Central; Costa Rica, El Salvador y Guatemala* (Washington, D.C., 1963), II, pp. 91–93.

BELLO, ANDRÉS (30 November 1781, Caracas—15 October 1865, Santiago). *Education*: Studied law and medicine at the Central University of Venezuela. *Career*: Poet; lawyer; teacher; journalist; Senator; statesman; politician; man of letters.

Bello became involved in the Venezuelan independence struggle, and in 1810 he went to England along with Simón Bolívar in an effort to raise funds for the revolution. He also tried to recruit some soldiers to fight in the ranks of the rebels. He remained in London as representative of the revolutionary government until 1829, when he transferred to Chile, where he spent the rest of his life. He taught school, wrote articles and books on a variety of subjects, served the Chilean government in various capacities, and eventually became Rector of the University of Chile (1843–1865). For the government he drafted a new civil code and found time to write a Spanish grammar that is still recognized as one of the finest ever written. He was interested in history and worked on an edited version of *El Cid*, and at the same time he studied Greek and Latin works of the ancient and mediaval periods. Among his students are counted some of the finest Chilean historians of the 19th century.

Bello wrote almost no history himself, but he is, nonetheless, significant for the development of history in Chile. As teacher of some of the brightest and, eventually, most successful scholars in the nation, he had a hand in formulating their ideas on literature and on history at the same time. Caught up in a bitter literary polemic with Domingo Sarmiento in the middle of the 19th century, he espoused firmly the cause of neoclassicism as opposed to Sarmiento's romanticism. Bello argued that the Spanish past had been beneficial for Latin America and that the Spanish culture should be studied and pursued instead of turning to France for cultural leadership, as advocated by Sarmiento. In this argument he became the father of the Chilean Generation of 1842, which produced some excellent literature and brought into politics some of Chile's outstanding leaders, among them José Victorino Lastarria, Francisco Bilbao, and Benjamín Vicuña Mackenna, all strongly influenced by Bello's philosophy. That influence was also strong in the nascent historiography of 19th century Chile. While some of his students, influenced by romanticism, wanted to follow the lead of French historians and build historical models out of past events in what they called the philosophy of history, Bello insisted that the historiographic development of Chile did not warrant such philosophizing about the past but that at this beginning stage of historical production historians had to work in the documents, archives, libraries, and private data collections to develop the truth of the past. Only after this, said Bello in a famous polemic with Jacinto Chacón, could historians begin to speculate about epochs as philosophical models. He agreed that the kind of historiography that he advocated might be less glamorous and far more tedious than that espoused by José Victorino Lastarria and Chacón, but to Bello's mind it was the only viable type of history possible for Chile in the 19th century.

A. *Tratado de derecho internacional* (Santiago, 1834); *Principios de la ortografía y métrica* (Santiago, 1835); *Teoría de entendimiento; filosofía del entendimiento* (Santiago, 1843); *Código civil* (Santiago, 1855); *Historia de las literaturas de Grecia y Roma* (Madrid, 1916); and *Derecho internacional* (Santiago, 1932).

B. Salvatore Bizzarro, *Historical Dictionary of Chile* (Metuchen, N.J., 1972), pp. 41-42; Helen Delpar, *Encyclopedia of Latin America* (New York, 1974), p. 75; Donna Keyse and G. A. Rudolf, *Historical Dictionary of Venezuela* (Metuchen, N.J., 1971), p. 20; Michael Rheta Martin and Gabriel Lovett, *Encyclopedia of Latin American History* (Indianapolis, 1968), p. 43.

BENAVENTE, FRAY TORIBIO (MOTOLINÍA)   (1520, Villa de Benavente, Zamora Province, Spain—9 August 1569, Mexico City). *Education*: Unknown. *Career*: Joined the Franciscan order; sent to Mexico in 1524 with the so-called First Twelve; missionary in Guatemala, Mexico, and Nicaragua; founded the convent of Concepción in Granada, Nicaragua; Provincial Vicar, Mexico, 1546; Provincial of the Franciscan order, 1548–1551.

Among the first Franciscan friars to travel to Mexico was Toribio Benavente, who was sometimes known as Benavente Motolinía. Motolinía meant poor man in the Nahuatl language, and the Indians assigned it to him because of his ragged clothing and his humble bearing. He accepted it as an apt description and used it thereafter. Benavente fought not only to convert the Indians but also to protect them from the Spanish authorities. Although he and Bartolomé de las Casas both worked to defend the Indians and both went to Guatemala to bring Christianity to the Indians there, Benavente and Las Casas quarreled over doctrinal issues. The quarrel resulted partly from the general animosity between the Franciscan and Dominican orders in America and partly from confessional rules issued by Las Casas but opposed by Benavente. Consequently, Benavente asked and was granted permission from the order to return to Mexico. However, he had been instrumental in establishing convents, monasteries, and churches in Guatemala, Nicaragua, and Mexico during his missionary activity. He was also party to the religious quarrels that evolved in that period over the method of converting the Indians and the nature of the sacrament of baptism; the polemic over this issue eventually made its way to the Pope himself. Benavente was zealous, enthusiastic, and committed to his religious duties, which led him into another quarrel when he carried out mass baptisms of Indians. It was reported that he baptized some 400,000 Indians in Nicaragua, Guatemala, and Mexico.

While he was converting Indians, building clerical establishments, and quarreling with other friars, Benavente was also busy collecting information about the Indians. Since he quickly learned the Nahuatl language, he was able to communicate with the Indians from an early period of his activity in America, and he learned a great deal about them. With the information that he gained from interviews, codices, and other documents, he constructed a major history of pre-Hispanic Mexico that was one of the first chronicles written in the country. He managed to collect many facts about the cultural lives of the Indians, and his work is especially important for that information. He wrote about the Aztec religion, the conversion of the Aztecs to Christianity, and the Aztec character. He also described Mexican flora and fauna. While the books he wrote are valuable for the information they provided later historians, it must be kept in mind that Benavente was not an objective, analytical historian. Evidence of that runs throughout his histories, which include details of many miracles and his own participation in some of them. He was also given to digressive anecdotes. Nonetheless, the information he did provide was significant, and as a cleric he was extremely important.

A. *Traducción de las vidas y martirios que padecieron tres niños principales de la ciudad de Tlaxcala, la cual practico el interprete general de esta real audiencia en virtud de lo mandado por el exmo. sr. Conde de Revillagigedo, virrey, governador y capitán general de este reino* (Mexico City, 1856); *Historia de los indios de Nueva España in collección de documentos inéditos para la historia de Mexico publicada por J. García Icazbalceta* (Mexico City, 1858) I, pp. 1–249; *Memoriales* (Mexico City, 1903); *Carta al emperador, refutación a Las Casas sobre la colonización española* (Mexico City, 1949); *Carta de fray Toribio Motolinía y fray Diego de Olarte a don Luís de Valasco, virrey de la Nueva España, sobre los tributos que pagaban los indios antes de su conversión* (Mexico, n.d.). B. Donald C. Briggs and Marvin Alisky, *Historical Dictionary of Mexico* (Metuchen, N.J., 1980), pp. 22–23; Helen Delpar, *Encyclopedia of Latin America* (New York, 1974), p. 76; *Diccionario Porrúa de historia* (Mexico City, 1967), I, p. 1,432; Aurora M. Ocampo de Gómez and Ernesto Prado Velázquez, *Diccionario de escritores mexicanos* (Mexico City, 1967), pp. 39–41; and A. Curtis Wilgus, *Historiography of Latin America: A Guide to Historical Writing, 1500–1800* (Metuchen, N.J., 1975), pp. 54–55.

BILBAO, FRANCISCO (9 January 1823, Santiago—16 February 1865, Buenos Aires). *Education*: Studied at the National Institute, Santiago; studied astronomy, geology, and chemistry in Paris. *Career*: Wrote for the press of Chile; traveled to Europe for the government; worked in the Office of Statistics, 1850; exiled for political activity and publication of an anticlerical article; spent the remainder of his life in Argentina, where he continued writing until his death.

Bilbao was one of the restless young writers of the mid-19th century in Chile who attacked the Conservative government and the Catholic church. Of all the writers of this type, Bilbao was the most outspoken and received the harshest treatment at the hands of the established government and its supporter, the Church. In many respects *José Lastarria and others shared Bilbao's beliefs, but they expressed them in more subdued terms and managed to survive the attacks of their opponents.

As a writer Bilbao rambled, digressed, and indulged in extensive symbolism. He was obsessed with religious themes, and no matter what subject he wrote about, eventually he wove into his work some religious thought. He had studied under Andrés Bello, but he was a staunch advocate of romanticism rather than the neoclassicism of Bello. He did not write much history, but he was interested in the writing of the past and he expressed some definite views on the discipline for others to consider. He believed strongly in the utility of history and perhaps even the necessity for civilization to cultivate history. As he expressed this idea in an article entitled "Lei de historia," he argued that man must search for some spiritual justification in the past. It was history, he argued, that created a morality and a universal conscience for mankind, a conscience that was essential if people were to live together in harmony. History, then, set examples that people could follow in building meaningful lives for themselves, but without history and without the guidance of the past, society would crumble into disarray. These ideas were expressed in the usual convoluted style that Bilbao used in all his work. Beneath all the rhetoric, anticlerical intimations, and generally verbose style was a decided belief that history was an essential ingredient for man's cultural development. It was this idea that presented a major contribution to history from Bilbao.

A. *Boletines del espíritu* (Santiago, 1850); *Santa Rosa de Lima* (Lima, 1852); *La revolución en Chile y los mensajes del proscrito* (Lima, 1853); *Iniciativa de la América* (Paris, 1856); *La América en peligro* (Buenos Aires, 1862); *El evangelio americano* (Buenos Aires, 1864).

B. Salvatore Bizzarro, *Historical Dictionary of Chile* (Metuchen, N.J., 1980), pp. 43–44; Helen Delpar, *Encyclopedia of Latin America* (New York, 1974), p. 78; Armando Donoso, *Bilbao y su tiempo* (Santiago, 1913); Zorobabel Rodriguez, *Francisco Bilbao: Su vida y sus doctrinas* (Santiago, 1872); Unión Panamericana, *Diccionario de la literatura latinoamericana: Chile* (Washington, D.C., 1958), pp. 24–26.

BILBAO, MANUEL (1827, Santiago—14 August 1895, Buenos Aires). *Education*: Law degree, National Institute, Santiago, 1850. *Career*: A founder of the Sociedad de Igualdad; edited the periodical *La barra*; exiled after the rebellion of 20 April 1851; edited *Revista independiente* in Lima; exiled to Ecuador, 1854;

went to Buenos Aires, where he continued to write for the press and edited the newspaper *La república*, founded *La libertad*, and edited *La prensa* of Buenos Aires.

The brother of the more famous *Francisco Bilbao, Manuel was influenced strongly by the activities of Francisco. When Francisco went into exile in Peru and then was subsequently exiled from Peru to Ecuador, Manuel followed. Upon Francisco's return to Lima from Ecuador, it was Manuel who defended him in the Peruvian courts and won freedom for him. Then both men moved on to Buenos Aires. Writing for the press of Argentina, Manuel was inclined to defend his brother from the assaults of his enemies. In a series of letters in the press in 1875, he defended his brother from the attacks of *Domingo Sarmiento, who had lived in Chile when Rojas was the dictator of Argentina. In 1883 Manuel published the memoirs of a man who had been a minister in the Rosas government, presumably as a means to nettle Sarmiento, who was the mortal enemy of Rosas. While living in Argentina Manuel Bilbao came to adopt the Argentine position in a major boundary dispute with Chile, and he published articles enunciating his arguments in defense of Argentina. He returned briefly to Chile in 1878, but his writings on the boundary question so incensed the Chilean public that he was encouraged to leave and return to Argentina, which he did, never again returning to his native country.

Manuel was much more the historian than Francisco, but he had a difficult time winning acceptance either in Chile or in Argentina. In Chile his reputation was tarnished because of his support for his brother, who had been driven into exile, and for his defense of Argentina's claims in the boundary dispute with Chile. At the same time, Argentine scholars were unimpressed because of his clash with Sarmiento, a national hero, and again because of his association with his controversial brother. Additionally, he chose to take an unpopular position relative to the dictatorship of Juan Manuel Rosas. Instead of castigating Rosas, as was the popular line, Bilbao found grounds to defend the dictator. He argued that Rosas' attempts at federalism could be justified by the colonial experience of Argentina, and he sought a detached, balanced evaluation of the dictatorship. Not surprisingly, his work, *Historia de Rosas*, was not well received. Some critics accused him of altering history, and the book itself was viewed as something less than objective history. While some writers tried to defend the book and Bilbao, the fact that he was Chilean, although his mother was an Argentine native, served to inhibit any popular support he might otherwise have acquired.

A. *Historia del general Salaverry* (Lima, 1853); *Compendio de la historia política del Perú* (Lima, 1856); *Historia de Rosas* (Buenos Aires, 1868); *Cuestión chileno-argentina: Artículos publicados en El ferrocarril* (Santiago, 1878); *Vindicación y memorias de don Antonio Reyes* (Buenos Aires, 1883).

B. Rómulo D. Carbia, *Historia crítica de la historiografía argentina desde sus orígenes en el siglo XVI* (Buenos Aires, 1925), pp. 266–268; and Unión Panamericana, *Diccionario de la literatura latinoamericana: Chile* (Washington, D.C., 1958), pp. 26–27.

BLANCO, EDUARDO (1839, Caracas—3 January 1912, Caracas). *Education*: Studied humanities, Colegio El Salvador del Mundo, Caracas. *Career*: Served in the army reaching the rank of Colonel and gaining an assignment on the General Staff; writer; historian; Minister of Public Instruction; Founding Member, National Academy of History; Secretary to President Páez.

Any young student is fortunate to have the opportunity to study with a figure of great renown in his community, but Blanco had the good fortune to study under one of the greatest literary personalities in Venezuelan history, Juan Vicente González. At the same time, he came from a military family and therefore served in the army for a time, participating in a civil war during his term in the service. As he worked on various history and folklore projects, he also wrote novels and books about Venezuelan customs. His novel *Zárate* was one of the first novels in Venezuela to deal with Creole customs, and it was also one of the best written. This work made his reputation as a writer, but he also gained fame through articles in a number of Venezuelan reviews. Finally, he capped his literary career with works of poetry, which led to his receiving an award as a Venezuelan poet in 1911.

Along with his many accomplishments as a writer, Blanco was one of Venezuela's more creative historians. He was a devoted, patriotic son of the nation, and he used history to glorify the past leaders and military heroes. In particular he wrote about the independence wars in the early 19th century, and he put together a lengthy study called *Venezuela heróica*, which depicted the glorious victories of Bolívar and others over the Spanish. These were not analytical accounts of military exploits but narrative descriptions that were beautifully written and that caught the fancy of the reading public, making Blanco one of the most popular writers of the 19th century. His other history books were not as well received, but they fit into the same mold, as he was always conscious of the style of his work and the literary quality of everything he published. One Venezuelan critic later referred to his *Venezuela heróica* as the Venezuelan Iliad; another wrote that Blanco did not write history but rather painted in words a beautiful picture of a historic event.

A. *Una noche en ferrara* (Caracas, 1875); *Zárate* (Caracas, 1882); *Las queseras y boyacá* (Bogotá, 1891); *Tradiciones épicas* (Paris, 1914); *Venezuela heróica* (Caracas, 1927); and *Las noches de Panteón* (Caracas, 1954).

B. *Diccionario biográfico de Venezuela* (Madrid, 1953), p. 156; Donna Keyse and G. A. Rudolf, *Historical Dictionary of Venezuela* (Metuchen, N.J., 1971), p. 22; and César Humberto Soto, *Personajes célebres de Venezuela* (Caracas, 1946).

BLANCO-FOMBONA, RUFINO (17 June 1874, Caracas—1944, Buenos Aires). *Education*: Attended Universidad Central de Venezuela. *Career*: Founded a publishing house, Madrid, 1915; Governor of Navarre, Spain; Venezuelan Minister to Uruguay; Governor of the Amazonas territory, southern Venezuela, 1905; Venezuelan and Peruvian Consul in Philadelphia, 1894; Consul of the Dominican Republic in Boston, 1899; Attaché of the Venezuelan delegation,

The Hague, 1896; and Venezuelan Consul to Amsterdam, 1901–1904; pole-micist, writer, poet, journalist, politician, traveler, diplomat, and political activist.

Born into a family of writers, Blanco-Fombona published his first poem at the age of 20 in 1895. The work was well received, and he then embarked upon a lengthy, prolific literary career. He was a leader in and chronicler of the modernist movement in Latin America. While he was creating both prose and poetry, he was also involved in the politics of Venezuela, and in 1910 he openly opposed the dictatorship of Juan Vicente Gómez, which led to his first imprisonment and then to his exile in Europe. While in jail he wrote poems of incarceration and exile and later published them in Europe. Eventually he took up residence in Madrid, and in 1915 he opened a publishing company. After his exile of 20 years he returned to Caracas in 1935 as a respected and revered literary figure. By that time he had encountered other political forces that were as frightening to him as dictatorship, and he wrote against the growing outside interference in Venezuela's politics and economy. In particular Blanco-Fombona feared the domination of his country by the United States, and he made no effort to conceal his fears, or to hide his hostility to Yankee imperialism.

Although he gained fame primarily because of his novels and poetry, Blanco-Fombona was also an accomplished historian, combining the traits and skills of observation with the technical talent to produce outstanding works of fiction or factual accounts of life in Venezuela's past. He was also a master of satire, which he put to good use in his study of political life in Caracas. He was cut from the Nietzschean mold of focusing his interest and analysis on the great men of history, the supermen of the past who led the people either to progress or to stagnation. Because of this attitude he was loathe to enter into any project of social history or of mass movements; instead, he dealt with individuals prominent in Venezuela's history. In this way Blanco-Fombona reflected the 19th century historical current in the 20th century, but although his work might be construed as anachronistic, while the 20th century historians broadened their fields of interest, Blanco-Fombona's finished product was usually a literary work of art. Again, like so many 19th century historians, he was obsessed with the style of his work, and the substance seemed to be of secondary importance. Nonetheless, Blanco-Fombona's works on the Venezuelan independence hero Simon Bolívar have remained significant for modern historians and are generally regarded as being of very high quality.

A. *El hombre de hierro* (Caracas, 1907); *La evolución política y social de Hispano América* (Madrid, 1911); *Bolívar pintado por si mismo*, 2 vols. (Paris, 1913); *El hombre de oro* (Madrid, 1915); *The Man of Gold*, trans. Isaac Goldberg (New York, 1920); *El conquistador español del siglo XVI* (Madrid, 1935); and *Bolívar y la guerra a muerte* (Caracas, 1942).

B. *Diccionario biográfico de Venezuela* (Madrid, 1935), pp. 160–161; Donna Keyse and G. A. Rudolf, *Historical Dictionary of Venezuela* (Metuchen, N.J., 1971), p. 22; Michael Rheta Martin and Gabriel Lovett, *Encyclopedia of Latin American History* (Indianapolis,

1968), p. 45; Percy Alvin Martin, *Who's Who in Latin America* 2d ed. rev. (Stanford, 1940), pp. 71–72; and Arturo Uslar Pietri, *Letras y hombres de Venezuela* (Mexico City, 1948), pp. 138–139.

BRICEÑO-IRAGORRY, MARIO (15 September 1897, Trujillo, Venezuela—6 June 1958, Caracas). *Education*: Elementary and secondary studies in Trujillo; law degree, University of Mérida, 1920; Doctor of Political Science, University of Caracas, 1925. *Career*: Taught in the universities of Caracas and Mérida and in several different secondary schools; served the government in several different ministries and in courts of Justice; held posts in state legislatures, National Congress, various state governments, and the Archivo General de la Nación; served in the Foreign Service, working his way up from Consul to Ambassador.

Venezuela was under the dictatorial rule of Juan Vicente Gómez for the first third of the 20th century, a period when Briceño-Iragorry was growing to adulthood and gaining an education. He was a participant in the political activity of the nation, and he held a number of ministerial and executive branch positions, while spending some of his time teaching in secondary schools and universities. He continued to be an opponent of dictatorial government throughout his lifetime, and when Marcus Pérez Jiménez took control in the early 1950s, Briceño-Iragorry went into exile, where he continued to write against the dictatorial regime while at the same time carrying out historical research. He returned to his native Venezuela in January 1958, following the overthrow of Pérez Jiménez, but he lived only a few months under the nascent democratic government.

As a scholar Briceño-Iragorry was prolific in publishing his research. He wrote 29 books, 91 brief discourses, short monographs, and short articles, and 20 prologues for books written by others. He was mainly a political historian, producing such works as *Los Riberas: Historias de Venezuela*, and he concentrated on the colonial period for his research, although he did write some local history on his home state, some history of education, and some cultural studies on Venezuela in the colonial period. His interest in political history was natural given his own participation in political clashes, and his longstanding interest in teaching made it natural for him to work in the history of education. Finally, the cultural studies of the colonial period stemmed from his literary and linguistic work that he pursued when time permitted.

A. *Historia de la fundación de la ciudad de Trujillo* (Caracas, 1929); *Tapices de historia patria: Esquema de una morfolgía de una cultura colonial* (Caracas, 1934); *Casa León y su tiempo: Aventura de un anti-héroe* (Caracas, 1946); *El regente Heredia; o, la piedad heróica* (Caracas, 1947); *Introducción y defensa de nuestra historia* (Caracas, 1952); *Los Riberas: Historias de Venezuela* (Caracas, 1957).

B. Hector García Chuecos, "Mario Briceño-Iragorry (1897–1958)," *Hispanic American Historical Review*, 40, No. 1 (February 1960), pp. 75–78.

BULNES, GONZALO (19 November 1851, Santiago—7 August 1936, Santiago). *Education*: Humanities degree, National Institute, 1869; studied in Europe until 1874. *Career*: Worked in agriculture; Undersecretary of War and Navy, 1891; Minister Plenipotentiary in Berlin and Rome; wrote for the newspaper, *La tarde*; elected Deputy, 1884, 1898; Senator, 1912–1924; Ambassador to Argentina, 1927; Governor of Tarapacá, 1883.

The son of a former president of the republic, Gonzalo Bulnes was taken into the confidence of the leadership of the nation. He was a member of the economic and intellectual elite of the country, and as such his future was secure. He widened his horizons with travel in Europe and by serving as a diplomat abroad. Consequently, when he wrote political articles or when he moved into the writing of history he was well prepared for the task. Because of his position he was able to collect relevant information from the participants in the events he studied, and he also interviewed many of them personally. Consequently, his research was extensive and solid and the product he provided the Chilean public was generally of outstanding quality.

Because his father and uncle were famous military men and because he himself sought unsuccessfully to fight in the 1891 Balmaceda revolution, his historical interests turned to military activity. Yet he did not write as an apologist for militarism; instead, his book on the *War of the Pacific* credits the Chilean population for the victory over Peru and Bolivia. The civilian leadership, supported by the total population brought success to Chile, according to Bulnes. Because of this point of view critics have charged that Bulnes was overly nationalistic and patriotic and that he used history as a means to praise his country rather than find truth in past events. His research was questioned, understandably, by Bolivian and Peruvian historians, who believed that he was uncritically praising his countrymen to the detriment of valid history. He was affiliated with a group of historians that has been labeled as conservative by 20th century Chilean writers, historians who supported the Church, conservative political ideals, and the economic predominance of the traditional elite class. Even taking all this criticism into account, however, it is undeniable that Bulnes ranks as one of the finest Chilean historians of his age. His literary style is praiseworthy, and he wrote with enthusiasm, clarity, and considerable knowledge on the great military events in Chile's past. His books won accolades from some of the great historians of the 19th century, such as the Argentine scholars *Bartolomé Mitre and *Vicente Fidel López, the Peruvian *Pedro Paz-Soldán, and Bulnes' countryman, *Benjamín Vicuña Mackenna.

A. *Historia de la campaña del Perú en 1838* (Santiago, 1878); *Historia de la expedición libertadora del Perú (1817–1822)*, 2 vols. (Santiago, 1885); *Últimas campañas de la independencia del Perú (1822–1826)* (Santiago, 1897); *Guerra del Pacífico*, 3 vols. (Santiago, 1911–1919); *Las causas de la guerra entre Chile y el Perú* (Santiago, 1919); and *1810, nacimiento de las repúblicas americanas*, 2 vols. (Buenos Aires, 1927).

B. Julio César Jobet, "Notas sobre la historiografía chilena," *Atenea*, 95, Nos. 291–292 (September–October 1949), p. 317; Raul Marin, *Gonzalo Bulnes, recuerdos personales* (Santiago, 1940); William Belmont Parker, *Chileans of To-Day* (Santiago, 1920), pp. 150–152; Unión Panamericana, *Diccionario de la literatura latinoamericana: Chile* (Washington, D.C., 1958), pp. 38–40.

BUSTAMANTE, CARLOS MARÍA DE (4 November 1774, Oaxaca, Mexico—21 September 1848, Mexico City). *Education*: Graduated from secondary school with a major in the arts; studied jurisprudence in France; acquired title of lawyer in Guadalajara, 1801. *Career*: Practiced law; founded the newspaper *Diario de México*; published *El juguetillo*, a revolutionary propaganda periodical; served as an army officer in the war for independence; accompanied Emperor Agustín de Iturbide as his secretary; president of the Congress of 1822; Deputy for 24 years; Auditor of War, 1827.

Through most of the chaotic first half of the 19th century in Mexico, Bustamante was directly involved in the activities of his government, first as an independence war leader and later as a writer who supported liberal and patriotic causes. He was on the scene when independence was achieved, but he was captured by the Spanish forces late in the war and jailed for a year. When Mexico became independent Bustamante took part in the new Mexican government, but he also wrote for the press and found time to record the history of Mexico during these same years. Later he was distressed by the U.S. invasion of his country, and he wrote articles denouncing the Yankees. His histories presented the liberal point of view as contrasted to *Lucas Alamán's conservative interpretation of Mexican history. The two were major historians of the early 19th century, and both made significant contributions to the Mexican historiography of that era.

Bustamante was a prolific writer. One hundred and seven titles have been found over his signature. He devoted time and attention to the colonial age of Mexican history and to many of the principal figures of that era. But his most famous and valuable work, *Cuadro histórico de la Revolución de la América Mexicana*, dealt with the independence struggle in Mexico. Because he was a participant in that action he brought a great deal of eyewitness material to his work, but at the same time he carried with him prejudices that had been nurtured during the long war for independence. Moreover, as a political liberal his histories reflected a passionate liberalism and led to denunciation of conservative activity at this stage of Mexican history. Later Mexican historians found his history to be uneven and his research technique to be deficient in that he was not always able to distinguish between fact and fiction, between truth and lies. The strong parts of his work were weakened by his susceptibility and gullibility along with his partisan political view. Nevertheless, he was an important early 19th century Mexican historian because he collected a great deal of source material from the periods in which he was active for later historians to use, perhaps more rigorously in their research than he did himself.

A. *Galería de antiguos príncipes mexicanos* (Puebla, Mexico, 1821); *Cuadro histórico de la revolución de la América mexicana*, 6 vols. (Mexico City, 1823–1832); *Los tres siglos de México durante el gobierno español hasta la entrade del ejército trigarante* (Mexico City, 1826–1838); *México por dentro y por fuera bajo el gobierno de los Virreyes* (Mexico City, 1831); *La aparición guadalupana en México* (Mexico City, 1843); *Apuntes para la historia del gobierno del general don Antonio López de Santa Anna* (Mexico City, 1845).

B. *Diccionario Porrúa de historia* (Mexico City, 1976), I, pp. 304–305; Michael Rheta Martin and Gabriel Lovett, *Encyclopedia of Latin American History* (Indianapolis, 1968), p. 63; Aurora M. Ocampo de Gómez and Ernesto Prado Velázquez, *Diccionario de escritores mexicanos* (Mexico City, 1967), pp. 48–49; and Victoriano Salado Alvarez, *La vida azorosa y romántica de don Carlos María de Bustamante* (Madrid, 1933).

C

CAILLET-BOIS, RICARDO R. (7 September 1903, Buenos Aires—16 July 1977, Buenos Aires). *Education*: Graduated from the Division of History, National Institute of Secondary Education. *Career*: Taught at the National Institute of Secondary Education, National University of Buenos Aires, 1928, National University of La Plata, 1929, Escuela Superior de Guerra, 1933, and Colegio Nacional de Buenos Aires, 1935; Vice-Rector and Rector, Colegio Nacional de Buenos Aires, 1935; Director, Instituto de Investigaciones Históricas, Universidad Nacional de Buenos Aires, 1955; President, Consejo Nacional de Educación, 1957; Ambassador to Unesco in Paris; Director, Museo de la Casa de Gobierno, 1959; Editor of *Mayo* and *Boletín del Instituto*; twice Argentine representative to the Pan American Institute of History and Geography; and President, Academia Nacional de la Historia, 1970–1972.

In a period when much of Argentine history was written by men whose primary occupations were in medicine, law, politics, or engineering, Caillet-Bois was a professional historian whose career centered on teaching, educational administration, and historical research. He was caught in the tumultuous Perón period, and when Perón was in control Caillet-Bois left his teaching position; when Perón was overthrown, Caillet-Bois returned to the classroom at the Universidad Nacional de Buenos Aires, where he remained until his death. He did accept some brief public assignments in diplomatic and museum posts, but his major interest was teaching and researching, and to these pursuits he remained loyal throughout his active career.

In his research Caillet-Bois was interested in a wide variety of historical problems relating to his country. He wrote more than two dozen books and countless articles on themes that ranged from the later colonial period to the mid-1960s, but mainly on Argentine diplomatic history and Argentine political developments. His scholarship was generally thorough, and he presented his research in a powerful style that enhanced his ideas and gained for him a solid reputation as one of Argentina's outstanding 20th century historians. Unlike most of his contemporaries he did not confine himself to Argentine themes. He wrote about revolutionary France, 18th and 19th century England, and the 19th century United States. Although he bound most of his research to Argentine developments, his interest in global topics was more extensive than that conducted by most other Latin American historians of his era.

Yet his influence in dealing with domestic issues was extensive. In two books he sought historical justification for the Argentine claim to the Falkland Islands, arguing at great length for the position that most of his countrymen shared. These books, written in 1948 and 1953, presaged the emotional appeal of the issue that led ultimately to the Argentine invasion of the islands in 1982.

A. *Alejandro Duclos Guyot, emisario napoleónico antecedente de las invasiones inglesas de 1806–1807* (Buenos Aires, 1929); *Ensayo sobre el Río de la Plata y la revolución francesa* (Buenos Aires, 1929); *Una tierra argentina: Las Islas Malvinas* (Buenos Aires, 1948); *Las Islas Malvinas* (Buenos Aires, 1953); *Cuestiones internacionales, 1952–1966* (Buenos Aires, 1970).

B. Percy Alvin Martin, *Who's Who in Latin America*, 2d ed. rev. (Stanford, 1940), p. 88; and James R. Scobie, "Obituary: Ricardo R. Caillet-Bois (1903–1977)," *Hispanic American Historical Review*, 59, No. 1 (February 1979), pp. 120–121.

CAPISTRANO DE ABREU, JOÃO (23 October 1853, Maranguape, Ceara, Brazil—13 August 1927, Columinjuba, Brazil). *Education*: School of Arts, Recife, 1859. *Career*: Journalist, 1875; teacher at Aquino College, 1876–1879; Official at the National Library, Rio de Janeiro, 1880; Chair of Brazilian History, College of Pedro II, 1883–1899.

Abreu began to think about writing a new history of Brazil when he was just 20 years old. A decade and a half later the job had not yet been launched, and he again wrote about the desirability of producing a new and better history of his country. At this point in his career he began to work in the National Library among the manuscripts that were so essential to the writing of Brazil's history, and Abreu was able to complete his project, which he entitled *Capitulos de historia colonial, 1500–1800*. In his work he used not only the primary and secondary sources at hand in the library but also solicited documents from other parts of the country and from outside Brazil in order to strengthen his study. As a historian Abreu was not locked into one philosophy of history or one methodology; as he matured and studied, he altered his attitude toward his discipline. Early in his career he was influenced by Auguste Comte's philosophy of positivism, which swept through Brazil in the 19th century and gained devoted adherents by the thousands. This philosophy led him to regard Brazil as an inferior nation. Then he found the German school of historiography, and he shifted his thinking away from positivism to the rigorous, scientific historical method of the Germans, leading him to become a critic of other historians as well as a writer of history in his own right.

Following the Rankian scientific school of German historiography, Abreu concentrated upon rigid criticism and interpretation of documents rather than searching for the positivistic laws that governed history. He was determined to find truth as it was revealed in authentic documentation; historical reality was now more important to him than some philosophical system that might govern historical development. But he was not content simply to narrate events of the past. Instead, he used his extensive documentation to interpret Brazilian history, which led him in turn to expand his thinking beyond the political realm to include social, cultural, and economic history. In this fashion Abreu uplifted Brazilian historiography and initiated a style and methodology that influenced 20th century Brazilian historians. While he was devoted to the scientific methodology of historical research, Abreu was also aware of the reading public and did not want his work to become narrowly pedantic so that it would be read by only a few historians. He chose rather to produce a history that the general public could understand. To that end, he synthesized a mountain of documents to bring out a book that the public could read, understand, and enjoy and from which they could learn about their own past. One historian calls Abreu's history of Brazil "the most condensed and the most lively colonial history of Brazil." Additionally, he expanded Brazilian historiography, being the first Brazilian historian to find some historical significance in Brazil's hinterland, thereby opening up a new, fertile field for historical investigation. For all of his work and his thoughts on history Abreu became the leader of modern Brazilian historiography, paving the way for the later 20th century historians who adopted his views on the writing of history and who have reconstructed Brazil's history in an authentic and splendid fashion.

Another major contribution to his nation's historiography was Abreu's defense of *Adolfo de Varnhagen as a major historian. While others criticized Varnhagen's efforts, Abreu argued that Varnhagen worked tirelessly to upgrade the quality of history produced in Brazil. More importantly, he pointed out, Varnhagen did not limit his research to political events but instead touched on industrial development, the progress of the mining industry, cultural advance, and exploration into the interior. Because of his work in these fields of history, where others had not yet ventured, Varnhagen deserved to be called the father of Brazilian historiography, according to Abreu. At the same time Abreu strengthened his own role in Brazil's historiography by his serious treatment of Varnhagen's work as well as by his innovative and thoughtful histories of Brazil.

A. *O Brasil no seculo XVI* (Rio de Janeiro, 1880); *O descobrimento do Brasil e o seu desenvolvimento no seculo XVI* (Rio de Janeiro, 1883); *Os capitulos de historia colonial* (Rio de Janeiro, 1907); *O descobrimento do Brasil* (Rio de Janeiro, 1929); *Antigos e o povoamento do Brasil* (Rio de Janeiro, 1930); and *Cartas de Capistrano de Abreu a lino de assuncao* (Lisbon, 1946).

B. E. Bradford Burns, "Ideology in 19th Century Latin American Historiography," *Hispanic American Historical Review*, 58, No. 3 (August 1978), p. 427; E. Bradford Burns, *Perspectives on Brazilian History* (New York, 1967), pp. 157–180; Robert Conrad, "João Capistrano de Abreu, Brazilian Historian," *Revista de historia de América*, No. 59 (January–June 1965), pp. 149–162; Helen Delpar, *Encyclopedia of Latin America* (New York, 1974), p. 2; José Honorio Rodrígues, "Preface," in Capistrano de Abreu, *Capitulos do historia colonial (1500–1800)* (São Paulo, 1954), pp. 5–8; Thomas E. Skidmore, "The Historiography of Brazil, 1889–1964, Part I," *Hispanic American Historical Review*, 55, No. 4 (November 1975), pp. 716–748.

CARBIA, RÓMULO D. (15 September 1885, Buenos Aires—1944, Buenos Aires). *Education*: Doctor of History, Pontifical University of Sevilla, Spain.

Career: Staff member of the Buenos Aires daily newspaper, *La prensa*, 1906–1911; Professor, Colegio Nacional, 1915; Librarian, School of Philosophy and Letters, University of Buenos Aires, 1916–1918; Professor, University of La Plata, 1919; Professor, University of Buenos Aires, 1922.

Like many Latin Americans who grew up in the late 19th and early 20th centuries, Carbia was vitally interested in religion, and his early education was designed to prepare him for an ecclesiastical career. However, he chose to become a teacher rather than a priest and devoted his life first to journalism and later to the study and teaching of history. His journalistic career, while successful, was of secondary importance to his overriding passion, which was to research and write history. As he traveled widely in South America and Europe for the press he not only filed stories for *La prensa* but took the opportunity to investigate materials in foreign libraries and archives that applied to Argentina.

Carbia's histories, not surprisingly in view of his early education, focused on Church history, although later in life he turned to an examination of the discovery, conquest, and colonization of America. Of perhaps greater importance was his work on Argentine historiography. In this area he sought to provide present and subsequent generations with knowledge of past histories and historians to clarify the discipline and to serve as a guide for younger historians. In a 1925 book, Carbia emphasized the old maxims on historical research emphasized by *Bartolomé Mitre and *Pablo Groussac that placed them in the erudite school of Argentine historiography. Carbia accepted their belief in careful, critical, and exhaustive research into primary source materials as being essential for the acquisition of historical truth. Consequently, he became the leading figure in the so-called New School of Argentine historiography, which, as Carbia saw it, was a logical continuation of the work of Mitre and Groussac. Both schools owed their philosophy of history to the Germanic 19th century scientific historiography taught by Leopold von Ranke.

A. *Historia eclesiástica del Río de la Plata* (Buenos Aires, 1914–1915); *La Revolución de Mayo y la iglesia* (Buenos Aires, 1915); *Lecciones de historia argentina* (Buenos Aires, 1917); *Historia de la historiográfica argentina* (Buenos Aires, 1925); *Nueva historia del descubrimiento de América* (Buenos Aires, 1936); *Historia crítica de la historiografía argentina desde sus origenes en el siglo XVI* (Buenos Aires, 1940).

B. Joseph R. Barager, "The Historiography of the Río de la Plata Area, Since 1830," *Hispanic American Historical Review*, 39, No. 4 (November 1959), pp. 588–642; Percy Alvin Martin, *Who's Who in Latin America* (Stanford, 1936), p. 72; William Belmont Parker, *Argentines of To-Day* (Buenos Aires, 1920), I, pp. 488–490; and Ione S. Wright and Lisa M. Nekhom, *Historical Dictionary of Argentina* (Metuchen, N.J., 1978), p. 146.

CARDOZA, RAMÓN INDALECIO (16 May 1876, Villarrica, Paraguay—1942, Asunción). *Education*: Graduated from the Colegio Nacional, Asunción, 1895; teaching degree, Escuela Normal, 1898. *Career*: Director, Superior School of Villarrica, 1898–1914; teacher at the Escuela Normal; Paraguayan delegate to the Second Congress for the Welfare of Children, Montevideo, 1919; Director and Professor of Pedagogy, Escuela Normal, Villarrica, 1914–1921; Professor, Colegio Nacional, Villarrica; elected to the Senate, 1909; Director General of Schools and President, National Board of Education, 1921–1932; Professor of Philosophy, Escuela Militar de Asunción, 1921–1930; Professor of Child Psychology, Escuela Normal de Asunción, 1921–1927; teacher of history, Colegio Internacional de Asunción, 1928.

One of the few Latin American historians to devote the vast majority of his time to teaching and research, Cardoza was more like the 20th century professional historian than were his fellow Paraguayans. He deviated from the norm of political and diplomatic service that characterized Latin American historians in the 19th and through much of the 20th century. Free from the pressures and time-sapping duties of government, Cardoza was able to concentrate upon teaching and research. He did, however, work in pedagogical administration, organizing the elementary Normal School in his hometown of Villarrica. The results of this effort were so dramatic that Paraguay's leaders asked him to organize other schools throughout the nation. In 1924 he introduced major reforms in Paraguay's primary instruction system by abandoning the so-called encyclopedic method and by encouraging more technical training along the lines of modern-day vocational education.

In his historical work Cardoza was a regionalist as he concentrated upon the history and development of his home city of Villarrica. Additionally, he was one of the organizers of the Instituto Paraguayo de Investigaciones Históricas, the nation's major historical association. He advocated profound research in primary documents for all historians, and he followed that pattern in his own work. As a regionalist he was representative of several other Latin American historians who worked in the late 19th and 20th centuries. While researching and writing on local topics, however, he did not fail to place his studies into a national context, thereby making a contribution not only to regional but to national history as well.

A. *Pestalozzi y la educación contemporánea* (Asunción, 1905); *Proyecto de legislación escolar* (Asunción, 1919); *Memoria sobre el estado de la educación*, 5 vols. (Asunción, 1926–1930); *El Guayra, historia de la antigua provincia, 1554–1676* (Buenos Aires, 1938); *La antigua provincia del Guaira y la Villa Rica del Espíritu Santo* (Buenos Aires, 1938); *Melgarejo, fundador de la ciudad de Villa Rica del Espíritu Santo* (Asunción, 1939).

B. Efraím Cardozo, *Historiografía paraguaya* (Mexico City, 1959), pp. 117, 475; Percy Alvin Martin, *Who's Who in Latin America* (Stanford, 1936), p. 76; and William Belmont Parker, *Paraguayans of To-Day* (New York, 1967), pp. 177–178.

CARDOZO, EFRAÍM (16 October 1906, Villarrica, Paraguay—1973, Paraguay). *Education*: Studied at the Colegio Nacional; Doctor of Law and Social Sciences, University of Asunción, 1932. *Career*: Secretary to the President of the Republic, 1928–1932; Secretary of the Paraguayan delegation to the League of Nations Commission on the Chaco question, 1933–1934; Professor, Colegio

Nacional de Asunción; United Press correspondent in Paraguay; Secretary of the National Boundary Commission; Director of the daily newspaper, *El liberal de Asunción*, 1934; founder of the newspaper, *El guaireño*, 1917.

Following the practice of most Paraguayan historians of his generation, Cardozo was a multitalented literary and political figure who acquired fame and respect within his country and whose historical works gained recognition in foreign nations as well. Serving in the executive branch of his government for a time, he later was elected to the Chamber of Deputies and the Senate, and he carried out diplomatic tasks for the government. In 1971 he was elected President of Paraguay's Liberal Radical party. Meanwhile, he held professorships at both of Paraguay's major universities, as he combined his political activities with teaching.

As a historian Cardozo made good use of his political experience when he devoted his scholarly attention to Paraguay's boundary disputes. He was able to combine his historical interest with contemporary problems as he sought to unravel the complexities of Paraguay's boundaries with its neighbors. Yet he was less partisan in these studies than others, and he employed scrupulous research techniques to seek the truth on the drawing of boundaries. Cardozo reflected a more impartial attitude in all his historical work than many of his predecessors, who tended to reflect a greater nationalistic sentiment that weakened their objectivity. In addition to boundary questions, Cardozo also devoted considerable attention to Paraguayan historiography and to social and political themes of the colonial period. While he was not preoccupied with the War of the Triple Alliance, as were many of his predecessors, he did write on this theme and on the life of the dictator Francisco Solano López, who guided the nation during that war. Cardozo is indicative of Paraguayan historians of both the 19th and the 20th centuries who simply could not put that 19th century disastrous war to rest. However, the struggle was so important to the nation's history that it would be illogical to expect Paraguayans to turn their backs on a catastrophe that came close to destroying their nation.

A. *El Chaco en la régimen de las intendencias* (Asunción, 1930); *Paraguay independiente* (Barcelona, Spain, 1949); *Vísperas de la Guerra del Paraguay* (Asunción, 1956); *El Paraguay colonial: Las raíces de la nacionalidad* (Asunción, 1959); *Historiografía paraguaya* (Asunción, 1959); *Breve historia del Paraguay* (Asunción, 1965).

B. Charles J. Kolinski, *Historical Dictionary of Paraguay* (Metuchen, N.J., 1973), p. 44; Percy Alvin Martin, *Who's Who in Latin America*, 2d. ed. rev. (Stanford, 1940), p. 76; and Dennis Joseph Vodarsik, "Efraím Cardozo (1906–1973)," *Hispanic American Historical Review*, 54, No. 1 (February 1974), p. 116.

CARRERA STAMPA, MANUEL (21 October 1917, Portsmouth, England— 14 June 1978, Mexico City). *Education*: Degrees in law and history, National University of Mexico; studied anthropology at the Escuela Nacional de Antropología; attended the Centro de Estudios Históricos de El Colegio de Mexico; Doctorate of Historical Sciences, El Colegio de Mexico, 1953; postgraduate work at Northwestern University and Georgetown University, United States. *Career*: Established the International Committee on Archives of the Panamerican Institute of Geography and History; Professor, University of Mexico; Secretary, Academia Mexicana de Historia.

Carrera Stampa worked in four areas of historiography. He was vitally interested in the history of art in the early years following graduation from the University of Mexico, and he continued throughout his lifetime to research and write in this field. Meanwhile, he developed a fondness for archival work and published a number of significant studies relating to archivology. By the 1950s Carrera had turned away from his earlier interests, although still publishing infrequently in those fields, and had taken up economic history. Among his works in this genre were some that dealt mainly with economic developments in the colonial era, particularly as they applied to the creation and development of craft guilds. Finally, he turned his attention in the late 1950s and in the 1960s to Mexican Indian history, which occupied him for most of the remainder of his life. In addition to these major fields of study, he worked as well in the history of the Mexican Post Office, the creation and development of Mexico City, and the historical progress of the Academia Mexicana de la Historia.

In researching and writing his histories on these various topics, Carrera proved to be a thorough scholar who paid very close attention to detail. He was less an analyst of Mexican history than a compiler of historical data, some of which he assessed but much of which he simply provided for the reader to assimilate and evaluate on his own. Some of his work was centered on the compilation and annotation of data, which he collected over long periods of time. Up to 1949 he was known primarily for his articles, but in that year he published four major works, three books and one article in the *Hispanic American Historical Review*. These four included archival studies, material on the development of Mexico City, guides to archives, and an article on weights and measures in colonial Mexico. Most of his work, spanning the first three quarters of the 20th century, fit this same pattern as he collected and organized data that was useful for other historians and archivists.

A. *Guía del Archivo del antiguo ayuntamiento de la ciudad de México* (Mexico City, 1949); *Misiones mexicanas en archivos europeos* (Mexico City, 1949); *Planos de la ciudad de México desde 1521 hasta nuestros días* (Mexico City, 1949); "The Evolution of Weights and Measures in New Spain," *Hispanic American Historical Review*, 29, No. 1 (February 1949), pp. 2–24; *Archivalia mexicana* (Mexico City, 1952); *Los gremios mexicanos* (Mexico City, 1954).

B. Charles Gibson, "Manuel Carrera Stampa (1917–1978)," *Hispanic American Historical Review*, 59, No. 3 (August 1979), pp. 476–477; Instituto Panamericano de Geografía e Historia, *Guía de personas que cultivan la historia de América* (Mexico City, 1951), p. 88.

CAVO, ANDRÉS (13 February 1739, Guadalajara, Mexico—1803, Rome). *Education*: Studied within the order of the Jesuits; achieved a degree in philosophy, 1758. *Career*: Ordained a priest, 1764; taught at the Seminario de San

Ignacio de Puebla at San Jeronimo, Puebla, and at the mission of Santisima Trinidad until 1767; historian.

Along with all other Jesuit writers in the late 18th century, Cavo was expelled from America with his order. Upon landing in Spain he was informed that if he left the order and secularized himself he would be permitted to return to Mexico. He followed this advice but soon learned that it was not accurate, and he spent the remainder of his life in Italy. Cavo was a quiet, pious individual who wanted only to carry out his clerical duties and to write history. Perhaps because he was not aggressive, his personal life, following his exile to Italy, declined steadily, and he lived the last years in extreme poverty. He made one last attempt to return to Mexico, but his request was denied and he died in Rome.

Cavo's historical efforts were thwarted because when he wrote most of his history of Mexico he was in Rome without the necessary documentation to do a complete job. His study was not uncovered until 1836, when *Carlos María de Bustamante found the manuscript and published it in 1836–1838. The study covered Mexican history from 1521 to 1766, but 19th century historians criticized it as being seriously deficient. This is understandable since most of it was written outside Mexico, but Cavo was also criticized for his verbose style that included lengthy digressions and the inclusion of considerable extraneous material. Then, too, his history was little more than an enumeration of facts, which dwelled upon the election of local officials in a year by year account. Still, the work did have value because it included information that could not be found in other places. Mexican historians have been harsh in their criticism, and while Hubert Howe Bancroft, the respected U.S. historian of Latin America, criticized it for many of the same reasons, he did point out its value as a source of events, if not as a well-researched and analytical history.

A. *De vita Josephi Juliani Parrenni, Havanensis* (Rome, 1792); *Historia civil y política de México*, published by Carlos María de Bustamante under the title, *Los tres siglos de México, durante el gobierno español hasta la entrada del ejército trigarante*, 4 vols. (Mexico City, 1836–1838).

B. *Diccionario Porrúa de historia* (Mexico City, 1974), pp. 414–415; Aurora M. Ocampo de Gómez and Ernesto Prado Velázquez, *Diccionario de escritores mexicanos* (Mexico City, 1967), pp. 76–77; and A. Curtis Wilgus, *The Historiography of Latin America: A Guide to Historical Writing, 1500–1800* (Metuchen, N.J. 1975), pp. 235–236.

CERVANTES DE SALAZAR, FRANCISCO (1514, Toledo, Spain—14 November 1575, Puebla, Mexico). *Education*: Studied canon law at the Universidad de Salamanca, Spain; Bachelor of Canon Law; Master of Arts and Doctorate in Theology, University of Mexico. *Career*: A secretary in the Royal Council of the Indies; Professor of Rhetoric, University of Osuna, 1550; taught Latin in a secondary school in Mexico; Professor of Rhetoric, Universidad de Mexico, 1553–1557; took holy orders, 1554; Deputy of Finance, University of Mexico, 1567; Rector, University of Mexico, 1572; representative of the Cathedral of Puebla to the Inquisition, 1572.

In the 16th century Spanish clerics dominated learning in the American colonies and coupled their teaching with missionary activity among the indians. Cervantes de Salazar was not particularly interested in converting the Indians, but he was devoted to teaching and writing. Because history was not a major subject for that era in either the secondary schools or the universities, he taught Latin, rhetoric, and theology, but he wrote history. He has been called the father of Mexican humanism because of his translations of famous humanists into Spanish. He also wrote poetry that was not particularly distinguished. Finally, he was named the official chronicler of New Spain and contributed a major work entitled *Crónica de la Nueva España*. Considered more valuable by contemporaries was his work in the Latin language, which was designed to facilitate the use of Latin by Spaniards and Americans because the language was at that time the only one recognized for the use of scholars. He was also an eyewitness to much of the material that appeared in his chronicle. He knew Hernán Cortés, the conqueror of Mexico, personally and dedicated a book to him.

Cervantes de Salazar's chronicle was commissioned by the Spanish crown, which hoped to learn as much as possible about its American possessions from works such as these chronicles. But in addition to this study he wrote *Dialogos* which was a significant social and cultural history. Moreover, he covered the initial organization of the University of Mexico, which came into existence in this period. He described at some length the primitive organization of the school at this time, and he devoted many pages to a recounting of the customs and habits of the people who lived in colonial Mexico. Consequently, his chronicle was a major historical record of 16th century Mexico.

A. *México en 1554* (Mexico City, 1554); *Tumulo imperial* (translation of the work of Oliva y Vives) (Mexico City, 1554); *Crónica de Nueva España*, 3 vols. (Mexico City, 1936).

B. Joaquín García Icazbalceta, "Dr. Francisco Cervantes de Salazar," in Manuel Orozco y Berra, *Diccionario* (Mexico City, 1874–1875), II, pp. 305–306; and Aurora M. Ocampo de Gómez and Ernesto Prado Velázquez, *Diccionario de escritores mexicanos* (Mexico City, 1967), pp. 79–80.

CEVALLOS, PEDRO FERMÍN (7 July 1812, Ambato, Ecuador—21 May 1893, Quito). *Education*: Colegio de San Luís, Quito; jurisprudence degree, University of Quito, 1838. *Career*: Deputy, National Congress, 1844; General Minister in the Executive Branch, 1851; Minister of the Supreme Court of Quito; Professor of Law, Universidad Central, 1865; elected Senator, 1867.

While Cevallos was deeply involved in political matters, he never lost interest in teaching and in writing history. Some of his tasks as a political leader were of great significance for the nation. For example, he authorized the decree for the expulsion of the Jesuits, and he served as judge and legislator on several occasions. Yet his major interest appeared to be the writing of the history of his country.

Cevallos published an article on Ecuador's history, a chronology of historical events, that he hoped would excite interest among Ecuadoreans for their history. Putting that piece together he concluded that there was much research left to be done despite the existence of the first comprehensive history of Ecuador, written by the Jesuit historian* Juan de Velasco earlier. In his research Cevallos detected errors as well as gaps that existed in this generally important work of Velasco. Velasco had been an amazingly inventive author, revealing the existence of giants and Amazon women warriors in his history. This 18th century study was not published until 1842 in Quito, and it served as a background for Cevallos' research into Ecuadorean history. Because of its obvious shortcomings as scholarly history, Cevallos then decided to write another history of Ecuador, carrying it beyond the 18th century, up to 1845. For important events, such as the independence war, Cevallos was particularly valuable as a historian because he participated in those monumental struggles and he could bring an eyewitness view to the documentation that he used in writing that portion of his multivolume history. But critics of his history assailed Cevallos because he did not interpret the history he presented. Instead, he merely provided a chronology of events and permitted the reader to do the interpreting. But even the collection and systematic organization of the data was an important contribution to Ecuadorean history, providing the basis for the most important Ecuadorean history, written later by *Federico González Suárez. Almost equally important, the Cevallos study was beautifully written in proper and precise Spanish. Cevallos was so conscious of his style and grammar that he even wrote a book cataloging the most common mistakes made in the Spanish language. Another Ecuadorean historian, *Isaac J. Barrera, wrote that a good historian who is writing for the people respects the language he uses and takes pains to make certain that it is correct in all ways. Barrera noted that Cevallos was a linguistic perfectionist in the extreme, using the proper words and grammar in all his written work. In fact, other historians have found his style dull because of its correctness. But because he noted the errors in other histories and in documentation in his work, he also made a major contribution to the development of correct usage of the Spanish language in Ecuador. Barrera also points out that Cevallos was the second major Ecuadorean historian and that his chronological position in the historiography of his nation alone warrants a careful study of his work and merits praise from those historians who came later. It must be pointed out, however, that González Suárez wrote the third major national history of Ecuador to correct some of the errors perpetuated and sometimes initiated by Cevallos.

A. *Breve catálogo de los errores que se cometen en el lenguaje familiar* (Quito, 1862); *Instituciones del derecho práctico ecuatoriano* (Quito, 1867); *Resumen de la historia del Ecuador desde su orijen hasta 1845*, 5 vols. (Lima, 1870); *Breve catálogo de errores en ordena la lengua i al lenguaje castellanos* (Ambato, Ecuador, 1880); *Ecuatorianos ilustres* (Quito, 1912).

B. Augusto Arias, *Vida de Pedro Fermín Cevallos* (Quito, 1946); Isaac J. Barrera, *Historiografía del Ecuador* (Mexico City, 1956), pp. 43–54; Albert William Bork and

Georg Maier, *Historical Dictionary of Ecuador* (Metuchen, N.J., 1973), p. 40; and Unión Panamericana, *Diccionario de la literatura latinoamericana: Ecuador* (Washington, D.C. 1958), pp. 9–10.

CHAMORRO, PEDRO JOAQUÍN (1891, Managua—1952, Managua). *Education*: Studied at secondary schools in Nicaragua and El Salvador; Doctor of Law, University of Oriente y Mediodia, Granada, Nicaragua, 1918. *Career*: Secretary of the Nicaraguan legation in Italy and at the Holy See, 1921; Secretary of Government, 1928; owner and director of *La prensa* in Managua, 1928; Secretary at the conferences on the boundaries between Nicaragua and Honduras, San José, 1938; President of the Nicaraguan delegation to the Congress of the Language Academy, Mexico City, 1951.

As a teacher, journalist, politician, and diplomat, Chamorro was in the forefront of Nicaragua's intellectual development in the first half of the 20th century. He cherished the idea of freedom of thought, and he fought to gain and hold the concept of a free press in a free society. Such principles and ideas led authorities to attack him viciously and to silence his newspaper, *La prensa*, on several occasions. Eventually he was even exiled from the nation. But he persistently took up the challenge when the government changed and the opportunity presented itself for him to move into the sphere of free journalistic activity once again.

Intellectually, Chamorro was a Hispanist, and he was unhappy with the sometimes brutal attacks upon Latin America's Spanish past. He defended Spain from the Black Legend assaults of those who found everything wrong in Latin America to be the fault of the Spanish. Yet he was not willing to let Spain's role in America pass without a critical evaluation, and he found some failures along with what he perceived to be achievements in Spain's action in the Western Hemisphere. He also defended the Catholic faith in its activities in America, but once again, he was not an uncritical supporter of the Church. Instead, he sought a balance between the prerogatives of the Church and those of the government, remaining an admirer of Catholicism, a practicing Catholic, and a staunch Nicaraguan patriot.

Chamorro's histories were in the traditional, narrative vein as he recounted the bitter civil struggles of the 19th century. He denounced the old liberals, whom he blamed for the dislocations and crises of the age of the Central American Federation. But he was also critical of outside interference in the region, particularly the invasion by the North American, William Walker, in 1856. His most lasting contribution to Nicaraguan historiography was his collection of documents on the Central American Federation that he collected not only in the region but in Europe and the United States as well. In 1951 he published these documents in a work entitled *Historia de la federación de la América Central, 1823–1840*, which has become indispensable for the study of the federal period. A. *Recuerdos de nuestra misión a Roma* (Granada, Nicaragua, 1925); *Entre dos filos* (Managua, 1927); *Obras históricas del licenciado Jerónimo Pérez* (Managua, 1928); *El*

último filibustero (Managua, 1933); *Límites de Nicaragua* (Managua, 1938); and *Historia de la federación de la América Central (1823–1840)* (Madrid, 1951).
B. Ernesto Mejía Sanchez, ''Pedro Joaquín Chamorro,'' *Revista de historia de América*, No. 34 (December 1952), pp. 545–548.

CHÁVEZ OROZCO, LUÍS (15 April 1901, Irapuato, Mexico—16 September 1966, Mexico City). *Education*: Studied at the Sollano Institute and the Preparatory School of Leon; social sciences degree, National Autonomous University of Mexico. *Career*: Director of Libraries, Ministry of Education, 1935–1936; Undersecretary of Public Instruction, 1936–1938; Administrator of Domestic Affairs, 1938–1940; President, Intercongress of Patzcuaro, Michoacán, 1940; Member, Counsel of the President of the Republic; Chief, Department of Publicity; first Secretary General, National Teacher's Union.

Throughout his career Chávez Orozco held administrative positions in the government and the teacher's union. He gained the respect and admiration of bureaucrats, politicians, and teachers for his integrity and for his clear grasp of issues and problems that confronted the agencies and offices he represented. Additionally, he was a bibliophile who believed that the records, documents, and books of the nation had to be preserved and made available to scholars, teachers, and students. All the while that he served Mexico in various political positions and in the teaching profession, he was above all an accomplished historian who published countless articles and several significant books.

Chavez Orozco was concerned with more than a political reconstruction of the past. He believed that social, economic, and intellectual history were essential for an understanding of history, and he was also convinced that it was not enough to know the history of one country but that the interrelationships of nations in the world required a comparison of development in different nations. Consequently, he did not confine himself to a study of Mexico's past alone but wrote about U.S. relations with Mexico and about Mexico's relations with Cuba, Colombia, and Peru. He was not content to confine his studies to Latin America alone, however. He also studied U.S. colonial history and wrote articles on Thomas Jefferson and on U.S.–English relations. Additionally, he compiled collections of documents on Mexican history and eventually published economic history documents in 12 volumes.

As a historian Chávez conceived of his discipline as one that not merely recounted the past but rather interpreted the past for use in the present. History, then, had the value of teaching lessons that were not only useful but essential for the present. For him, history was necessary to pursue current politics effectively and to find answers for the social problems that confronted governments throughout Latin America. At the same time he regarded history as necessary for an understanding of economic problems, and he wrote economic and social history as well as political studies. His histories, then, were not only highly regarded by other historians and scholars but were valued by Mexico's leaders, who recognized their practical value in dealing with current problems. This recognition pleased him because he once wrote, "History is the beginning of our civic values. History is the base of our social conception. History is the road for the development of our politics." That his histories contributed to an understanding of present problems was extremely gratifiying for him.

A. *El sitio de Puebla en 1863* (Mexico City, 1927); *Prehistoria de socialismo en México* (Mexico City, 1936); *Revolución industrial revolución política* (Mexico City, 1937); *Ensayo de crítica historia* (Mexico City, 1939); *Historia de México época precortesiana* (Mexico City, 1939); and *La crisis agrícola de México en 1908* (Mexico City, 1954).

B. Donald C. Briggs and Marvin Alisky, *Historical Dictionary of Mexico* (Metuchen, N.J., 1981), p. 44; *Diccionario Porrúa de historia* (Mexico City, 1976), I, pp. 592–593; and Luis Rubluo, 'Luís Chávez Orozco,'' *Revista de historia de América*, Nos. 61–62 (January–December 1966), pp. 241–244.

CIEZA DE LEÓN, PEDRO DE (1519, Sevilla, Spain—1554, Sevilla). *Career*: Chronicler and solider.

In 1534, at the beginning of the conquest and colonization period in Latin America, Cieza de León left Spain and traveled to New Granada, where he spent the next 17 years of his life. He kept a diary of what he saw about him, and because he was an observant individual he included a good deal of the detail of the turmoil of early colonization. His diary was also revealing because he recorded the quarrels between rival Spanish factions, while at the same time writing of the Incas and their society. Like others among the conquering forces he shifted allegiances, which led eventually to his being named the official chronicler. Because he was embroiled in some of the battles among Spanish forces, he became a firsthand witness to much of the bickering and battling that predominated in this era. When he returned to Spain with his diary and notes, he wrote and published the first part of his *La crónica del Perú*. This book was soon picked up by other publishers and it appeared in Rome and Antwerp; much later an English version emerged. Cieza de León planned to publish four volumes, but volume three has never been found. The other three volumes covered the conquest, the Spanish internecine struggles, and the life of the Inca Indians at the time of the conquest.

Cieza de León has been compared with other early Spanish chroniclers of Latin America, particularly Bernal Díaz del Castillo who, like Cieza de León, fought in battle and then spent his leisure time taking notes and observing carefully the land and the people. Both were careful of their sources, and both relied heavily upon what they themselves witnessed, which made their books valuable for a study of this period in Latin American history. Not a historian in the modern sense of that term, Cieza de León is nonetheless significant for the chronicling not only of early Peru but also of early Ecuador, which was a part of colonial Peru and about which he wrote in his book. His firsthand account of the Peruvian conquest and the civil war that accompanied it was a remarkably impartial effort. He included geographical description, discussed the Inca civilization, and did not try to gloss over the civil war waged among the Spanish conquerers. Consequently, his chronicle is regarded as a basic source for the colonial history of Peru.

A. *La crónica del Perú*, 3 vols. (Sevilla, Spain, 1553); *The Travels of Pedro de Cieza de León*, trans. Clements R. Markham (London, 1864); *Civil Wars in Peru: The War of Las Salinas*, trans. Clements R. Markham (London, 1923).

B. Albert William Bork and Georg Maier, *Historical Dictionary of Ecuador* (Metuchen, N.J., 1973), p. 43; Helen Delpar, *Encyclopedia of Latin America* (New York, 1974), p. 140; and A. Curtis Wilgus, *The Historiography of Latin America: A Guide to Historical Writing, 1500-1800* (Metuchen, N.J., 1975), pp. 68–69.

CLAVIJERO, FRANCISCO JAVIER (6 September 1731, Veracruz, Mexico—2 April 1787, Bologna, Italy). *Education*: Studied French and music under his parents; learned aboriginal languages; studied Latin and philosophy, Colegio de San Jeronimo and Semenario de San Ignacio, both in Puebla. *Career*: Joined the Jesuit order, 1748; Prefect of Studies, Seminary of San Ildefonso de Mexico; founded a school in Bologna, Italy; taught for five years at the Colegio de San Gregoria and later at the Colegio de San Javier, Valladolid, 1764.

Many Jesuit friars in America collected data and wrote about the New World, either for the benefit of the crown or for religious information to aid in the conversion of the Indians. Most of these chronicles were primitive, containing many inaccuracies and written in an excessively florid style. A major exception to this characterization was the work of Francisco Clavijero, whose education was extensive and independent. He always insisted upon his Mexican nationality, and his instruction was far more liberal than that of the vast majority of clerics. He had little interest in theology and instead read many of the great writers of his age and from antiquity, including many whose works had been banned by the Church. From such writers as Cervantes, Descartes, Newton, and even the Mexican poetess, Sor Juana Inés de la Cruz, he learned a variety of philosophies. Having immersed himself in this kind of literature from an early age, he developed a writing style that one Mexican has described as "brilliant and clean." He was also a linguist who knew most of the Western world's languages, from Greek and Hebrew to German and English. More importantly for his historiographic work, he knew the Indian language of Náhuatl, and some reports suggested that he knew 20 indigenous languages reasonably well. Consequently, he was admirably prepared to write the history of pre-Hispanic and colonial Mexico. His training and his study led him to think about more liberal education, and when he found in his position as Rector of San Ildefonso de Mexico that he could not institute the type of program he wanted, he asked to be removed from the job and his request was granted. Relieved of the responsibility of this duty, he could then devote more of his time to collecting sources and preparing his material for eventual publication. When the Jesuits were expelled from Mexico, Clavijero traveled to Italy and opened a school in Bologna, but it never really got off the ground. He spent the remaining years of his life writing history under difficult circumstances. He was far removed from the site of his work, and he was so poor he could not afford to buy the books he needed for his research.

Despite these obstacles he was able to produce two excellent studies, *Historia antigua de Mégico*, 1826, and *Historia de antigua Baja California*, 1852.

When Clavijero returned to Europe in exile he realized that almost every European was amazingly ignorant about America. This was true not only of the average citizen but also of historians, intellectuals, and scholars. Therefore he was determined to write the true and accurate history of Mexico. He attacked earlier historians and chroniclers for their inaccuracies, especially those who wrote about the pre-Hispanic age in Mexico. At the same time, he took the opportunity to defend the Society of Jesus that was now in exile and coming under fire for its action not only in America but throughout the world. His histories have been described as the first true history of New Spain because, in addition to narrating events and listing bibliographic material, Clavijero noted his critical judgments on each theme. This critical ability was true of all his works, both in history and in other disciplines, and sets him apart from most of the colonial chroniclers. He also dug deeply into the sources, and his linguistic talents enabled him to consult material that was unavailable to others who could not handle the variety of languages, both Indian and European. His major contribution, in addition to this basic historiographic accomplishment, was his even-handed treatment of the subject. He was determined to present a valid picture of the Indians and their culture without in any way denigrating unjustly the Spanish. Such an objective approach was almost unique in his age and would not be found again in more than a few instances until well into the 19th century.

A. *Historia antigua de Mégico: Sacada de los mejores historiadores españoles y de las pinturas antiguas de los indios: Dividida en diez libros, adornada con mapas y estampas, e ilustrada con disertaciones sobre la tierra, los animales y los habitantes de Mégico* (London, 1826); *Historia de la antigua Baja California* (Mexico City, 1852).

B. Donald C. Briggs and Marvin Alisky, *Historical Dictionary of Mexico* (Metuchen, N.J., 1981), p. 48; Helen Delpar, *Encyclopedia of Latin America* (New York, 1974), p. 143; Luís González Obregón, *Cronistas e historiadores* (Mexico City, 1936), pp. 83–126; Aurora M. Ocampo de Gómez and Ernesto Prado Velazquez, *Diccionario de escritores mexicanos* (Mexico City, 1967), pp. 80–82 and A. Curtis Wilgus, *Historiography of Latin America: A Guide to Historical Writing, 1500–1800* (Metuchen, N.J., 1975), pp. 236–237.

COELLO, AUGUSTO C. (1 September 1884, Tegucigalpa, Honduras—7 September 1941, San Salvador). *Education*: Secondary school training at the Colegio Eclesiastico; law degree, School of Law, Central University of Tegucigalpa, Honduras. *Career*: Elected Deputy, 1904; Secretary to the President of Honduras; Undersecretary and Minister of Foreign Relations; journalist while in exile in Costa Rica; in exile in San Salvador, 1906–1907; attached to the Honduras Legation in Washington, D.C.; delegate to the Seventh International Conference, Montevideo, 1933; negotiated a boundary dispute with Guatemala; Governor, Department of Itimbucá.

In many countries of Latin America, families perpetuated literary traditions from generation to generation. Coello's father and brother were prominent writers, and from the age of 12 Coello himself wrote poetry. He traveled widely and observed carefully all that passed before his eyes, retaining a good portion of the experience to be used in later work. He was particularly interested in international law and in sociological matters, and he put these interests to good use when he negotiated several boundary disputes for his country. Meanwhile, he became embroiled in political clashes that led to a period of exile in Costa Rica, where he could not resist the attraction of political involvement which got him into trouble with the authorities of that nation. When not caught up in political warfare, however, he continued to write, and he gained considerable fame from his poetry, which was widely read and appreciated and led to his creation of the national anthem in 1915. He was a sensitive writer who used words to evoke emotions from his audience, and he was generally successful in stirring the reading public to heights of patriotism.

In addition to his sonnets and his political pieces Coello also wrote on international law, history, and biography. Using the successful style of his poetry and prose, he wrote with feeling and with a great deal of knowledge as well. He tried to clarify complex events that were beyond the comprehension of the reading public and sought to explain both contemporary and historical events in his books. His travels in foreign countries as an exile and as a diplomat contributed to his knowledge of Central America and the entire Western Hemisphere and sharpened his appraisal of events in his own country, while at the same time making him more perceptive in analyzing important men of his own age as well as the important figures of history. While his career was built on poetry, he was equally adept at writing prose and history. In all genres he perpetuated the family tradition of literary excellence.

A. *El Tratado de 1843 con los indios moscos* (refutación a don Diego Manuel Chamorro) (Tegucigalpa, 1923); *Las Islas del Cisne: Estudio hecho en virtud del decreto legislativo número 57, de 23 de febrero de 1922* (Tegucigalpa, 1926); *La imprenta y el periodico oficial en Honduras: Ligeros apuntes por Augusto C. Coello* (Tegucigalpa, 1929); *La epopeya del campeño* (San Pedro Sula, Honduras, 1938); *Biografía de Léon Alvarado* (Tegucigalpa, n.d.); *Biografía del doctor Ramón Rosa* (Tegucigalpa, n.d.);

B. William J. Griffith, "The Historiography of Central America Since 1830," *Hispanic American Historical Review*, 40, No. 4 (November 1960), p. 561; Harvey K. Meyer, *Historical Dictionary of Honduras* (Metuchen, N.J., 1976), p. 81 and Unión Panamericana, *Diccionario de la literatura latinoamericana: América Central; Honduras, Nicaragua Panamá* (Washington, D.C., 1963), pp. 141–143.

COMAS CAMPS, JUAN (1900, Alajor, Menorca, Baleares, Spain—18 January 1979, Mexico City). *Education*: Graduated from the Escuela Normal, Madrid; studied pedagogy, Escuela de Estudios Superiores del Magisterio, Madrid; studied in the School of Biological Sciences, Universidad Central de Madrid; studied pedagogy and anthropology at the Universidad de Ginebra. *Career*: Served the Spanish Republican government in a variety of capacities, such as inspector in school zones, Director General of Primary Education, and one of the founding professors of the National School of Anthropology and History in Mexico; Secretary General, National School of Anthropology and History; Director, *Boletín Bibliográfico de antropología americana*, 1943–1952; Investigator, Instituto de Investigaciones Históricas, National University of Mexico, 1955–1979; instrumental in founding the Sección de Investigaciones Antropologicas, National University of Mexico, 1974.

Born in Spain, Comas was a member of a family that supported the Republican government and he grew up in the liberal atmosphere that prevailed in his social circles. He was educated in the nation when the Republican government was in power, and he gave allegiance to that government wholeheartedly. Consequently, when the Civil War began he served the Loyalists in a variety of capacities, and in 1936 he took charge of a project to organize colonies for refugee children in France, the Soviet Union, and Mexico. In 1939 he was forced to leave Spain and he moved to Mexico, which was one of the nations in the world that welcomed Spanish Loyalists and that benefitted from the talents of these Spaniards.

Having studied in Spain and France, Comas brought a rich intellectual and academic background with him to Mexico. He had been trained as both a teacher and a researcher in Europe, and he continued those pursuits in Mexico. At the same time, he combined his interests in anthropology and history and taught both disciplines while researching and publishing in both areas. In addition to his administrative and editorial tasks in Mexico City he continued to publish the fruits of his research while not slowing down his teaching activities. His interest centered on the prehistoric period of Mexican development, and he focused his attention on paleontology and physical anthropology, as in *Paleoantropología y evolución*. His activities as a researcher were applauded by fellow scholars, and his reputation rested as much upon his own research as upon his influential activity in international scholarly organizations. In any case, his work was regarded highly enough to warrant its translation into English, French, Italian, Russian, and Hindi.

A. *Paleoantropología y evolución* (Mexico City, 1959); *La antropología física en México, 1943–1959* (Mexico City, 1960); *Una decada de Congresos Internacionales de Americanistas, 1952–1962* (Mexico City, 1960); *Manual de antropología física* (Mexico City, 1966); *Introducción a la prehistoria general* (Mexico City, 1971); *Cien años de Congresos Internacionales de Americanistas* (Mexico City, 1974).

B. Miguel León-Portilla, "Juan Comas Camps (1900–1979)," *Hispanic American Historical Review*, 60, No. 1 (February 1980), pp. 95–96.

CORTÉS, MANUEL JOSÉ (10 April 1815, Coragaita del Distrito de Potosí, Bolivia—16 February 1865, Sucre, Bolivia). *Education*: Law degree, Universidad de San Francisco Javier, Sucre, Bolivia. *Career*: Judge, of the Supreme Court; Attorney General of the Republic; twice elected to the National Congress and served as President of the Congress, 1861 and 1864; diplomat in Peru; Minister of Public Instruction.

In the turbulent history of 19th century Bolivia, intellectuals were interested in political developments and the reasons for the political instability that plagued the young nation. While they speculated on contemporary problems, Cortés sought answers to political questions in the history of the nation. He was himself a participant in some of the events of the age, particularly as an officer in the Battle of Ingavi. Later he was exiled three times for his political views, and on another occasion he voluntarily took up residence in Argentina. He was, like many of his contemporaries, vitally interested in a variety of subjects, and during his career he wrote poetry, dramas, and legends along with his histories. After 1833 he also wrote articles for a number of periodicals. Politically, Cortés was impatient with dictatorship and tyranny, and he was a champion of democracy and liberty. As one writer expressed it, his main objective was to serve liberty either with the sword or with the pen.

As one of the first Bolivian historians, Cortés had a deep curiosity concerning the history of the world in general and Bolivia in particular. In his histories he departed from the traditional narrative history of political events to examine the philosophical underpinnings of events as they had transpired in the nation's early national period. He also examined the past in a sociological way. His style was clear and literary, and his work reflected a sincerity and an objectivity. Still, his histories did not put Bolivia into a world or hemispheric perspective. They were narrowly of the Bolivian contemporary variety and did not include the relationship of Bolivia to the rest of the world. However, he was a product of the romantic movement in his poetry, literature, and history. He analyzed the fundamental institutions of Bolivia in the context of a new, free, and independent society. But his major contribution to Bolivian historiography was that he was the first to write a well-documented, studied, objective, readable history of Bolivia, which he called *Ensayo sobre la historia de Bolivia*.

A. *Bosquejo de los progressos de Hispano-América* (Valparaiso, Chile, 1858); *Ensayo sobre la historia de Bolivia* (Sucre, Bolivia, 1861); *Introducción al derecho* (Sucre, Bolivia, 1862); *Galería de hombres célebres de Bolivia* (Santiago, 1869).

B. Dwight B. Heath, *Historical Dictionary of Bolivia* (Metuchen, N.J., 1972), p. 84; and Unión Panamericana, *Diccionario de la literatura latinoamericana: Bolivia* (Washington, D.C., 1958), pp. 23–25.

COSÍO, JOSÉ GABRIEL (18 March 1886, Accha, Peru—1973, Lima). *Education*: Secondary Education in the Seminario de San Antonio, Cuzco, 1894–1902; bachelor's degree, University of Cuzco, 1907; doctorate, University of Cuzco, 1908. *Career*: Journalist and editor of the newspaper, *La unión*; taught ancient, modern, American, and Peruvian history in several different secondary schools in Cuzco; Professor of Spanish language and literature, National School of Sciences, 1917; Member of the City Council, Cuzco; Lieutenant Mayor of Cuzco; Inspector of Instruction, Cuzco; Professor, University of Cuzco, 1910–1936; Secretary, University of Cuzco; Director, Colegio Nacional de San Carlos of Puno, 1927–1931; Director, Colegio Nacional de Trujillo, 1931.

José Cosío divided his time between teaching and journalism and occasionally held political office, although usually on the local level. He was active in university affairs beginning while still a student. He was one of the leaders of the student body, and because of the efficient manner in which he carried out his duties, the university administration consulted with him after graduation. In particular, his views were sought on reorganization of the school because of his intimate knowledge of the operation of the institution. Additionally, Cosío was a member of the famous Hiram Bingham archeological expedition of 1912 that sought the ruins of the ancient Inca civilization. He was named to that group as the Peruvian government's official representative.

Cosío was interested in archeology and anthropology as well as history. These interests led him to break with the vast majority of Latin American historians, who generally wrote histories of their own countries. While Cosío was devoted to the study of Peru's past, he was also vitally interested in European, Asian, and ancient Near Eastern history. He was able to put his knowledge of other parts of the world to good use when he researched Peru's past because he had the advantage of comparison with other parts of the world that was lacking in the work of many other historians of his generation.

A. *La civilización de los antiguos peruanos comparada con la de los pueblos primitivos del antiguo continente* (Cuzco, 1907); *El americanismo literario* (Huaraz, Peru, 1909); *Trabajos de la comisión científica de la Universidad de Yale* (Cuzco, 1912); *El Cuzco prehispanico y colonial* (Cuzco, 1918); *Cuzco: The Historical and Monumental City of Peru* (Lima, 1924); *Cervantes i quijotismo* (Trujillo, 1932); *Fonetismo de la lengua quijotismo* (Trujillo, 1932).

B. Percy Alvin Martin, *Who's Who in Latin America* (Stanford, 1936), p. 109; and William Belmont Parker, *Peruvians of To-Day* (Lima, 1919), pp. 597–599.

COSÍO VILLEGAS, DANIEL (23 July 1898, Mexico City—10 March 1976, Mexico City). *Education*: Bachelor of Arts and Bachelor of Letters, National Preparatory School; studied engineering, philosophy, literature, and law; law degree, National School of Jurisprudence, 1925; studied economics at Harvard University; studied agricultural economics at University of Wisconsin; Master of Arts, Cornell University; studied economics at the London School of Economics; studied political science at the École Libre des Sciences Politiques, Paris. *Career*: Taught sociology, political economy, and economic doctrines, National School of jurisprudence and the School for Advanced Studies; worked in the Ministry of Education; taught in the National Preparatory School, the Schools of Law and Philosophy and Letters at the National University, the National School of Economics, National University, the Central University of Madrid, and the Institute of Latin American Studies, University of Texas in Austin; founder of *El trimestre económico*, *Historia mexicana*, and *Foro internacional*; Secretary General, National University of Mexico; directed the National School of Economics, 1933; founded the publishing house, Fondo de Cultura Económica, 1935, and served as Director, 1935–1949; cofounder, School of Economics, University of Nuevo León, and the Casa de España which later became the Colegio de Mexico; economic and financial adviser to the Secretary of Treasury and Public Credit, Bank of Mexico, National Bank for Mortgages and Public Works, and Mexican Embassy in Washington, D.C.; attended numerous international organizations for Mexico; headed the Mexican legation in Portugal, 1936–1937; Mexico's special ambassador to the Economic and Social Council of the United Nations, 1957–1968; President, United Nation's Special Fund, President, Coordination Committee, United Nation's Economic and Social Council.

Pursuing a multifaceted career like so many other Latin American intellectuals of the 19th and 20th centuries, Cosío was a historian, political scientist, economist, essayist, publisher, teacher, and diplomat. He was successful in all endeavors and was rewarded with the acclaim and adulation of his nation's intellectual community. He began teaching ethics at the National University when he was just 17 years old, and he later worked as a banker and economist. Meanwhile he worked as a journalist, thereby enhancing his reputation as an astute observer of the political, social, and educational areas of Mexican life. Yet he did not confine his energies to any narrowly Mexican theme; he was interested in the international scene, and in the 1930s he made possible the transference of Spaniards caught in the Civil War to Mexico, assisting them to continue their academic and scholarly work during their exile. His Colegio de Mexico became the center for graduate study in Mexico in the social sciences, and he served as President of the Colegio from 1958 to 1963. Out of his teaching experience at the Colegio he was able to produce the nine-volume *Historia moderna de México* (1955–1972).

Cosío was fascinated with history. In the previous generation the Díaz regime had encouraged historical studies and this led to the publication of an enormous number of histories, but most of these books were more propaganda than history and their value was negligible. Cosío, however, was determined to write sound history, especially about the political development of Mexico. In writing his histories he concentrated on the presidency and on the personality of the presidents; he also wrote some contemporary works about the Mexican government in which he was quite willing to criticize the President in office. His books were filled with anecdotes that were informative and entertaining, and they were written in a readable style. He was critical of his sources and attempted to recount the truth of the past. However, his partisan political views could not always be suppressed so that some of his history is not objective.

A. *Los Estados Unidos contra Porfirio Díaz* (Mexico City, 1956); *La constitución de 1857 y sus críticos* (Mexico City, 1957); *Historia Moderna de México*, 5 vols. (Mexico City, 1963); *Labor periodística, real e imaginaria* (Mexico City, 1972); *La sucesión: Desenlace y perspectivas* (Mexico City, 1975); *La sucesión presidencial* (Mexico City, 1975).

B. Donald C. Briggs and Marvin Alisky, *Historical Dictionary of Mexico* (Metuchen, N.J., 1981), p. 57; Percy Alvin Martin, *Who's Who in Latin America*, 2d ed. rev.

(Stanford, 1940), p. 142; and Martin Needler, "Review Essay: Daniel Cosío Villegas and the Interpretation of Mexico's Political System," *Journal of Inter-American Studies and World Affairs*, 18, No. 2 (May 1976), pp. 245–251.

CUE CÁNOVAS, AGUSTÍN (28 August 1913, Villahermosa, Tabasco, Mexico—23 April 1971, Mexico City). *Education*: Attended the Escuela Normal Superior, 1928; attended El Colegio de Mexico; law degree, Universidad Nacional Autónomo de Mexico, 1932; *Career*: Taught at the Escuela Normal Superior, the Escuela Nacional de Maestros, the Instituto Politecnico Nacional, and the Universidad Nacional Autónoma de Mexico; embarked upon a brief political career; remained active in the Socialist party of Mexico.

Although trained as a lawyer, Cue Cánovas devoted his life to teaching, to journalism, and to historical research. He wrote articles on political themes for such publications as *El nacional*, *El día*, *El popular* and *Política* and he was anxious to expand on his political and social views for the press or at public gatherings. But he was primarily a teacher and a historian, and it was in these areas that he made his most significant mark on Mexico. His primary teaching was in normal schools so that his ideas had an impact on vast numbers of Mexican students who themselves went on to teach.

In his teaching and in historical research Cue Cánovas was interested primarily in Mexico's independence struggle, in the Reform era and the life of Benito Juárez, and in the Revolution of 1910. He also worked in biography with his study of the life of Father Hidalgo, *Hidalgo*, a major effort. With his concern for social problems he was naturally lured to work in the Reform period of the mid-19th century in Mexican history, and once again he wrote about the leading figure in that movement, Benito Juárez. In his books and articles on this period Cue Cánovas displayed sympathy and admiration for Juárez and for his efforts at altering Mexico during the Reform period. In his studies of this important age in Mexican history, Cue Cánovas listed the reasons for the ascendency of Juárez and the reaction of the nation to his leadership. He then concluded that *La Reforma* was a positive time in Mexico's political development and an important step in the intellectual progress of the nation.

In studying the 1910 Mexican Revolution Cue Cánovas was again sympathetic to the movement and in agreement with the philosophical and practical objectives of the leadership. In discussing the views and accomplishments of such 1910 revolutionary leaders as Francisco I. Madero, Lázaro Cardenas, and Emiliano Zapata he was lavish in praise, and, perhaps because his own political philosphy, which centered on significant social reform, could find a reflection in that movement, he championed the revolution. He argued that the nation needed a revolution at that time in the early 20th century and concluded that the revolution was continuing into the second half of the century. He found this revolutionary atmosphere productive and essential for the nation, and he hailed the continuing struggle. Beyond the borders of Mexico he argued that the 1910 revolution was an important event and would have a profound impact on the entire world, not just Mexico and Latin America.

A. *Historia social y económica de México, 1521–1810* (Mexico City, 1945); *El tratado Mac Lane-Ocampo: Juárez, los Estados Unidos y Europa* (Mexico City, 1956); *Historia política de México* (Mexico City, 1957); *Historia mexicana*, 2 vols. (Mexico City, 1959 and 1962); *Constitución y liberalismo* (Mexico City, 1963); and *Los EE. UU. y el México olvidado* (Mexico City, 1970).

B. Ernesto de la Torre Villar, "Agustín Cue Cánovas," *Revista de historia de América*, No. 72 (July-December 1971), pp. 535–541; and *Diccionario Porrúa* (Mexico City, 1976), I, p. 2458.

CUERVO, LUÍS AUGUSTO (14 February 1893, San José de Cúcuta, Colombia—13 May 1954, Bogotá). *Education*: Doctorate, National University of Bogotá, 1915. *Career*: Mayor of Bogotá, 1919; editor of *Boletín de historia y antiguedades*; Representative, National Congress; President, Chamber of Deputies; Governor of Santander; Dean of the Consular Body and Minister of Colombia in Bolivia; Member, Colombian Academy of Language; Member, Bolivarian Society of Colombia; Member, Assembly of Cundinamarca; President, Municipal Council of Bogotá.

Like many of his contemporaries Cuervo successfully linked a political career with the teaching and writing of history. Additionally, he worked for a time as a diplomat, which was characteristic of most historians of the age. Finally, he sought to create and develop organizations that would assist historians in their work and provide them with the opportunity to exchange ideas and research materials. He was the motivating force behind the Academia Colombiana de Historia, and as a further contribution to the historiography of his country he edited with distinction the *Boletín de historia y antiguedades*.

Cuervo's own scholarly activities centered on legislative and political history with attention given to linguistic studies and cultural affairs. His research was basic primary work in archival and documentary collections. He was aware that his efforts could be used by later historians as a foundation for their own research. While two or three of his books were fundamental to Colombian historiography, Cuervo added a dozen others, in addition to a hundred or more articles, speeches and historiographic reports. Cuervo specialized in the history of the republican era in Colombia, focusing on the immediate post-independence epoch and its early leaders. He was interested in particular in the various conventions, congresses, and meetings that were held in the early republican period, when Ecuador, Venezuela, and Colombia were joined together into the nation of Gran Colombia. He was also vitally interested in the later breakup of that union and the early independent stage in Colombia's development. His scholarship was sound, his style readable, and his primary research significant for later historians.

A. *La monarquía en Colombia* (Bogotá, 1916); *Apuntes historiales* (Bogotá, 1925); *Notas históricas* (Bogotá, 1929); *La juventud de Santander* (Bogotá, 1936); *Introducción al estudio de la filosofía de la historia* (Bogotá, 1938); *Ensayos históricos* (Bogotá, 1947).

B. Instituto Panamericano de Geografía e Historia, *Guía de personas que cultivan la historia de América* (Mexico City, 1951), p. 115.

CUNHA, EUCLIDES DA (20 January 1866, Province of Rio de Janeiro, Brazil—15 August 1909, Santa Cruz, Brazil). *Education*: Studied liberal arts at the Aquino, Rio de Janeiro; attended the Polytechnic School, Rio de Janeiro, 1884; attended the Brazilian Military School, Rio de Janeiro, 1886. *Career*: Army engineer, 1893–1896; civil engineer, 1896; journalist; government surveyor; teacher at the Pedro II Institute, 1909.

At the beginning of the republican era in Brazil, young intellectuals found themselves actively engaged not only in planning political strategies but in trying to understand the society, history, and government of the country. Among those young men was Euclides da Cunha, who adopted the positivistic philosophy that was so prominent in the Brazil of the late 19th century. He was committed to technological and scientific advance for his country, and his career reflected that commitment as he became an engineer and served in the military, where positivism was particularly strong since officers believed that they had the advantage of a greater technical and scientific education than civilians. Da Cunha accepted these ideas until he finally decided that a military career was not for him and became fearful that the new military-dominated republican government was weakening the nation. He turned then to journalism as a career but later returned to service as a military engineer. Following a second tour he went back to civilian life as a surveyor and civil engineer, a career he followed, along with literature, until his death.

Euclides da Cunha's great work on a military attack against the backland people of the northeast of Brazil, *Os sertões*, is a classic in Brazilian literature, and it is also an outstanding work of social history. It was not just an account of a military operation against a rural part of the nation but a social history of the era and of the people who resided in that poor, drought-ridden, region of Brazil. Da Cunha analyzed the assault on Canudos as a major scandal in Brazil's history and as a clash between two cultures, the politically dominant coastal part of Brazil and the backward, politically impotent interior of the nation. The work not only chronicled the assault, which da Cunha witnessed, but was also a geographic study of the region and of Brazil, a military chronicle of the attack on Canudos, and a social commentary on Brazil in the 19th century. For all of these reasons and for the literary quality of the book, da Cunha's study has gone through 16 editions and has been translated into several languages. It has been called the "Bible of Brazilian nationality," and the "greatest and most distinctive" book ever produced in Brazil. But da Cunha also chronicled other events in Brazilian history to which he was party, and these too have received wide acclaim from Brazilian and foreign critics. His short life was marred by tragedy, but his literary production and his insight into the social history of Brazil provided his people with a monumental look at their 19th century past.

A. *Os sertões* (Rio de Janeiro, 1902); *Contrastes y confrontos* (Porto, Brazil, 1906); *Relatorio da Comissão Mista Brasileiro-Peruano de Reconhecimento do Alto-Perú* (Rio de Janeiro, 1906); *Perú vs. Bolivia* (Rio de Janeiro, 1907); *A marjem de historia* (Porto, Brazil, 1909); *Canudos: Diario de uma espedicão* (Rio de Janeiro, 1939); *Rebellion in the Backlands*, trans. Samuel Putnam (Chicago, 1944).

B. Helen Delpar, *Encyclopedia of Latin America* (New York, 1974), pp. 196-197; Robert M. Levine, *Historical Dictionary of Brazil* (Metuchen, N.J., 1979), pp. 71–72; and Samuel Putnam, "Brazil's Greatest Book: A Translator's Introduction," in Euclides da Cunha, *Rebellion in the Backlands* (Chicago, 1944), pp. iii–xviii.

D

DECOUD, HECTOR FRANCISCO (9 July 1855), Asunción—1930, Asunción). *Education*: Attended schools in Asunción. *Career*: Fought in the War of the Triple Alliance, 1865–1870; District Attorney, 1882; Deputy, National Congress, 1883–1887; Editor of *El heraldo*, 1884, and *La república*, 1890; wrote for the newspaper, *La regeneración*.

As a young boy during the War of the Triple Alliance, Decoud was imprisoned, along with his mother. This interrupted his education and left him with a lifelong loathing for both war and the Paraguayan dictator, Francisco Solano López. When the war ended Decoud turned his attention to journalism, writing for several newspapers and eventually becoming an editor. Meanwhile, he embarked upon a political career that proved quite successful as he gained office in the national government. Along with his journalistic and political activity Decoud found time to research and write history books and articles. He reflected a contemporary historiographical theory that found nothing wrong with working one's political prejudices into historical studies. Within the ranks of the Generation of 1900, of which he was a part, this political partisanship was accepted practice.

Decoud's interest in historical subject matter again reflected his era. Like most members of the Generation of 1900, he focused his attention on the War of the Triple Alliance, in which he had been involved. Although his accounts of the war are biased for the most part, they are significant as contemporary evaluations of the war. Again like most others in the Generation of 1900, Decoud had an unabiding hatred of the dictator Francisco Solano López and his accounts of López' acts can hardly be viewed as objective history. He denounced the dictator roundly for his domestic policies and for his role in the War of the Triple Alliance.

A. *Compendio de geografía e historia del Paraguay* (Asunción, 1896 and 1901); *Una decada de vida nacional* (Asunción, 1925); *Sobre los escombros de la guerra: Una decada de vida nacional, 1869–1880* (Asunción, 1925); *Guerra del Paraguay: La masacre de Concepción ordenada por el mariscal López* (Buenos Aires, 1926); *La revolución del comandante Molas* (Buenos Aires, 1930); *Elisa Lynch de Quatrefages* (Buenos Aires, 1939).

B. Joseph R. Barager, "The Historiography of the Río de la Plata Area, Since 1830," *Hispanic American Historical Review*, 39, No. 4 (November 1959), p. 599; Charles J. Kolinski, *Historical Dictionary of Paraguay* (Metuchen, N.J., 1973), p. 79; and William Belmont Parker, *Paraguayans of To-Day* (New York, 1967), pp. 305–306.

DÍAZ DEL CASTILLO, BERNAL (1492, Medina del Campo, Spain—1580, Guatemala City). *Education*: Minimal formal education. *Career*: Served in the Spanish army in the West Indies, 1514; participated in various conquests of America; honored as the oldest conquistador in New Spain.

A number of soldiers who participated in the conquering expeditions into various parts of Latin America chronicled their adventures, either in verse, as did *Alonso de Ercilla, or in prose, as did Bernal Díaz. The latter's work on the conquest of Mexico carried out by Hernan Cortés became the best known of this genre in America and is to this day widely read in both Spanish and English editions. As a captain in Cortés' army, Bernal Díaz was aware of the strategy employed in the conquest, and he was able to write about the expedition with considerable knowledge and authority. Because of his service to Cortés and the crown, Bernal Díaz was rewarded with lands in New Spain, but he went into Honduras with Cortés, after which he received additional lands and a position on the Municipal Council of Guatemala. In 1550 he returned to Spain and was surprised at the fame and honor he had acquired as a famous conquistador in his own right.

Díaz had not intended to write a history of the expeditions to New Spain, but when he encountered the histories written by others, particularly that produced by *Francisco López de Gómara in 1552, he decided that there were so many inaccuracies that he had to set the record straight with a history of his own. Without any formal training and without literary experience, and after the passage of half a century, he wrote his history of the conquest of Mexico. It was done from memory and without extensive research, which placed it in the category of a chronicle, but it was a major history of the event despite the fact that he was 70 years old when he finally wrote down his thoughts and recollections. Although the language was simple and straightforward, the book became a classic and gained him a reputation he did not envision when he wrote the manuscript. Bernal Díaz proved to be a good storyteller, but he also provided vivid descriptions of places and events despite the passage of 40 years. He wanted to make clear that the troops were as important as Cortés, but the great leader emerged from the pages of this book as a successful conquistador. Bernal Díaz' chronicle first appeared in 1632, when the Mercedarian friars in Madrid published his manuscript, which they changed to suit themselves. The original manuscript was not uncovered until nearly 300 years after it was written, in 1904–1905. While it was not a history book because he did not research the topic but recorded his recollections, it is an important document because of the firsthand accounts of the action in the conquest. Moreover, Bernal Díaz pointed out the errors of others and the nature of the actual events as he witnessed and remembered them. It is also a clear reflection of Spanish attitudes toward the Indians and the mentality of the 16th century Europeans relative to America. As such, this modest memoir became a major contribution to the history of Mexico.

A. *Historia verdadera de la conquista de la Nueva España* (London, 1908–1916); *Cortez and the Conquest of Mexico*, trans. B. G. Herzog (New York, 1942); *The Discovery and Conquest of Mexico, 1517–1521*, trans. A. P. Maudslay (Mexico City, 1953).

B. Helen Delpar, *Encyclopedia of Latin America* (New York, 1974), pp. 193–194; Luís González Obregón, *Cronistas e historiadores* (Mexico City, 1936), pp. 11–82; Aurora M. Ocampo de Gómez and Ernesto Prado Velázquez, *Diccionario de escritores mexicanos* (Mexico City, 1967), p 98; Unión Panamericana, *Diccionario de la literatura latinoamericana: América Central: Costa Rica, El Salvador y Guatemala* (Washington, D.C., 1963), II, p. 118; and A. Curtis Wilgus, *Historiography of Latin America: A Guide to Historical Writing, 1500–1800* (Metuchen, N.J., 1975), pp. 47–49.

DÍAZ DÍAZ, OSWALDO (1910, Gachetá, Colombia—15 December 1967, Bogotá). *Education*: Doctor of Law, National University, Bogotá. *Career*: Playwright; teacher of literature and history at the secondary school and university levels; Secretary, Academia Colombiana de Historia, 1961.

As a playwright Díaz Díaz wrote long and effectively, gaining fame for his dramas that eventually filled four volumes, which were published between 1963 and 1967. At the same time, he wrote many historical articles on Colombian history that won the respect of the historical community in his country. Ultimately, he zeroed in on a study of the historical period from 1816 to 1819, when Colombia was in the midst of its independence campaign against the Spanish. He concentrated upon nationalism and patriotism in this era and produced one book, entitled *Los Almeydas: episodios de la resistencia patriota contra el Ejército Pacificador de Tierre Firme*, that traced the independence activity of an *hacendado* family that led a guerrilla movement in the northeastern highlands of Colombia. While this study was nationalistic and patriotic in nature, it was based on solid research carried out in private archives and libraries.

In a subsequent study published in 1964–1967, Díaz Díaz continued his examination of the independence period of Colombian history but broadened his coverage and delved into a wider array of manuscript sources. His conclusion in this work was that there was an extensive resistance to a movement to restore Spanish rule in Colombia once independence was assured. In the work he linked the patriot cause to concurrent social change. Additionally, he set forth the view that the success of Simón Bolívar's climactic Colombian campaign at Boyacá in 1819 was in reality based on the success of patriot guerrilla activity carried on against the Spanish in the period 1817–1819. This same patriot action, Díaz Díaz believed, was responsible not only for independence but for significant social change as well. Thus, the independence movement can be construed, in his view at least, as a social revolution.

A. *El país de Lilac* (Bogotá, 1938); *La gaitana: Drama de la ocupación española en América basado en los relatos algunos cronistas* (Bogotá, 1941); *Blondiette* (Bogotá, 1942); *Comedia famosa de doña Antonia Quijana* (Bogotá, 1947); *Los Almeydas* (Bogotá, 1962); *La reconquista española* (Bogotá, 1964–1967).

B. J. Leon Helguera, "Oswaldo Díaz Díaz (1910–1967)," *Hispanic American Historical Review*, 48, No. 3 (August 1968), pp. 440–441.

DÍEZ DE MEDINA, EDUARDO (8 February 1881, La Paz—27 June 1955, La Paz). *Education*: Law degree, University of La Paz. *Career*: Second Officer,

Ministry of Foreign Relations, 1899; Chief, Diplomatic Section, 1901; diplomatic service in Argentina, Cuba, Chile, Spain, the United States, Great Britain, Japan, Mexico, Paraguay, Peru, and Uruguay; Professor of International Law, University of La Paz; President, Municipal Council of La Paz; Minister of Foreign Relations; negotiated and signed the peace treaty that ended the Chaco War with Paraguay, 1938; Prefect of Oruro.

Many Latin Americans were educated in the law, and since legal training seemed important for an understanding of diplomatic problems, a logical career for a young man with such training was in the foreign service. Díez de Medina is a good example of a career diplomat who also taught, wrote poetry, essays, and history. Additionally, he translated poetry from Brazil, France, and England. In keeping with his literary interests he founded the literary reviews *Literatura y arte* and *Atlántida*, and he also created the *Revista de derecho internacional americano*. But he was, at the same time, in the forefront of diplomatic activity and he worked on a number of boundary disputes in which Bolivia became involved with its neighbors.

At the turn of the 20th century Latin American historians were writing national histories, either of the lengthy, multivolume variety or the brief single-volume historical description. Díez de Medina chose the latter vehicle to convey his views on Bolivian history. His work was typical of the production of others in his era because it included geographic material and natural history along with extensive coverage of political developments. Conversely, Díez de Medina's histories were also different from other histories of that age because some of them had immediate, practical value for the Bolivian government. He wrote on boundary disputes between Bolivia and its neighbors, and that material kept Bolivian negotiators and the leaders of the nation informed of past practices and events that could be used to justify Bolivian claims to disputed territory.

A. *Breve resumen histórico, físico y político de Bolivia* (La Paz, 1901); *Variando prismas* (La Paz, 1908); *La Sentence arbitrale argentine dans le litigo entre la Perou et la Bolivie* (Brussels, 1909); *El problema continental* (La Paz, 1921); *La cuestión del Pacífico y la política internacional de Bolivia* (La Paz, 1923).

B. Percy Alvin Martin, *Who's Who in Latin America* (Stanford, 1936), pp. 124–125; and Unión Panamericana, *Diccionario de la literatura latinoamericana: Bolivia* (Washington, D.C., 1958), pp. 31–32.

DOBLES SEGREDA, LUÍS (17 January 1890, Heredia, Costa Rica—7 September 1956, Heredia). *Education*: Studied in the Colegio San Luís; graduated from the Escuela Normal de Costa Rica, 1918. *Career*: Taught Spanish and geography at the Liceo de Heredia; Director, Instituto de Alajuela and Liceo de Costa Rica; Secretary of Public Education; Visiting Professor of Geography, Marquette University; Visiting Professor of Spanish, Louisiana State Normal College; diplomat in France, Belgium, Holland, Spain, Italy, Argentina, and Chile; President, Municipal Council of Heredia; Deputy to the National Congress.

Uniting teaching, writing, political activity, and diplomacy, Dobles Segreda built a multifaceted career of service to his country and as contributor to scholarly knowledge. He used the experience of each of his interests and positions to strengthen the others and in this manner became successful at each one of his chosen professions. His literary production and his administrative success gained him an international reputation that resulted in teaching positions in the United States and recognition for his academic accomplishments and his diplomatic achievements in Europe. He represented his nation at international congresses on education, agriculture, philosophy, and international cooperation that met in North America, Latin America, and Europe.

Dobles Segreda wrote histories of a local nature, centering his work on Heredia, the city where he was born and raised. At the same time, his major interest was cultural history, and his work dealt mainly with the customs of the people of Heredia and its surrounding area. He had a deep love for the people and their simple, traditional customs, and this affection colored every word he wrote on the subject. Dobles Segreda himself acknowledged that the subjects rather than his own talents made his work appealing and popular with the reading public. He wrote that if his writing was beautiful it was because the subjects he wrote about were beautiful. When he produced his last book, *Fadrique Gutiérrez, hidalgo extravagante de muchas andanzas*, it was a reconstruction of colonial life in his home city of Heredia based upon anecdotes, legends, and his own memory of the city in the 19th century. His history was not born of difficult, painstaking archival research but rather of collecting stories and information either written or orally transmitted and then building an entertaining story around them. In this way he was accorded the distinction of being one of the "outstanding figures of the cultural history of Costa Rica." In addition to this type of history he was also a bibliographer, collecting important documents and studying those materials that existed in archives, libraries, and private collections. He put together a nine-volume bibliography of Costa Rica that is today a fundamental work for the historian of that nation.

A. *El clamor de la tierra: De un optimista a un pesimista* (San José, 1917); *Rosa mística* (Heredia, Costa Rica, 1920); *Vida heroica: Elogio de Marcelino García Flamenco* (San José, 1924); *Indice bibliográfico de Costa Rica*, 9 vols. (San José, 1927–1936); *Julio Sánchez Lépiz: Non omnis moriar* (San José, 1934); *Fadrique Gutiérrez, hidalgo extravagante de muchas andanzas* (San José, 1954).

B. Abelardo Bonilla, *Historia y antología de la literatura costarricense* (San José, 1957), I, pp. 171–174; Theodore S. Creedman, *Historical Dictionary of Costa Rica* (Metuchen, N.J., 1977), p. 57; Unión Panamericana, *Diccionario de la literatura latinoamericana: América Central: Costa Rica, El Salvador y Guatemala* (Washington, D.C., 1963), II, pp. 12–14.

DOMÍNGUEZ, MANUEL (1869, Asunción—1935, Asunción). *Education*: Bachelor's degree, Colegio Nacional, 1890, Doctor of Laws, National University of Paraguay, 1899. *Career*: Taught arithmetic, geography, zoology, Roman history, Paraguayan history, anatomy, physiology, and hygiene at the Colegio Nacional, 1899–1904; Professor of Constitutional Law, 1904–1906; Rector of the National University; Chief, National Archives; Deputy, National Legislature, 1896; Minister of Foreign Affairs, 1902; Vice-President of the Republic, 1902–1904; Minister of Justice and Education; Minister of Finance; Envoy Extraordinary to Bolivia, 1908–1912; Director, Colegio Nacional and Universidad Nacional.

Manuel Domínguez devoted his life to public service and to scholarly research. His career carried him into various disciplines, which he taught and in some of which he carried out research. He was caught in the political clashes of his country, and when his faction gained control of the government he served in many executive and legislative posts. However, when the opposition took control of the government Domínguez returned to teaching and research until the political climate improved for him. While he gained a measure of fame for his political activity, it was his academic and scholarly career that gained the highest regard from his contemporaries, who considered him one of the greatest intellectuals ever to live in Paraguay.

At the same time his career in journalism also won him the plaudits of his countrymen. He founded and then edited the periodical *El tiempo* in 1891. Through his articles he carried the message of Auguste Comte's positivist philosophy to the Paraguayans. He argued that technical growth and an emphasis upon science and technology were required for the development of Paraguay and for the progress of all Latin America.

Domínguez worked in widely diverse fields of historical study, but he concentrated upon the boundary problems that existed between his nation and Bolivia in the Chaco region. His most famous research job was to study and investigate historically the claims of Paraguay to this area. Because of the expertise gained through his research he was chosen as a delegate to the conference that dealt with the Chaco dispute before the war broke out in 1932. His work on the Chaco, along with the research of *Cecilio Baez, is considered the strongest Paraguayan justification for claims to the Chaco. In other historical research he focused on the period of Francisco Solano López and the War of the Triple Alliance. However, as a Colorado party member he championed the career of Solano López, which was a major departure from the work of other members of the Generation of 1900, just as it was a sharp break from the writings of earlier 19th century Paraguayan historians. Domínguez emerged with histories that resembled those of Juan Emiliano O'Leary, which praised lavishly and uncritically Solano López and his regime.

A. *Discusión sobre filología etnográfica y geografía histórica* (Asunción, 1899); *La nación* (Asunción, 1908); *La constitución del Paraguay*, 3 vols. (Asunción, 1909–1912); *Paraguay–Bolivia* (Asunción, 1917); *El alma de la raza* (Asunción, 1918); *Lo que fuimos y lo que seremos* (Asunción, 1920).

B. Joseph C. Barager, "The Historiography of the Río de la Plata Area, Since 1830," *Hispanic American Historical Review*, 39, No. 4 (November 1959), p. 599; Helen Delpar, *Encyclopedia of Latin American History* (New York, 1974), p. 195; Charles J. Kolinski, *Historical Dictionary of Paraguay* (Metuchen, N.J., 1973), p. 86; William Belmont Parker, *Paraguayans of To-Day* (New York, 1967), pp. 299–302.

DURÓN, RÓMULO E. (6 July 1865, Comayuga, Honduras—13 August 1942, Tegucigalpa). *Education*: Studied at the Colegio Nacional; philosophy degree, Academia Científica-Literaria; degree in jurisprudence and social science, Universidad Central, 1885. *Career*: Wrote poetry; founded and edited the periodical, *El trabajo*; taught grammar and geography in secondary schools; secretary of the School of Jurisprudence and Social Sciences, Universidad Central; Rector of the Universidad Central; Member of the Supreme Court; Deputy from the Department of Tegucigalpa, 1910; Minister of Public Instruction, 1915; Deputy from the Department of La Paz, 1917; Minister of Foreign Relations, 1929–1932.

All the time that he dispatched his duties in government, teaching, diplomacy, and journalism, Durón was publishing poetry and writing on a number of diverse subjects. His work in history and geography won him the attention of scholars from other nations, and he received honorary degrees from the University of El Salvador and from the University of Lisbon. Meanwhile he spent time mediating international disputes among Central American countries, and he traveled to the United States on a number of occasions to represent his country at various international gatherings. He was one of a number of Latin Americans who worked with the Carnegie Institute in Washington in an effort to secure international peace. He also found time to translate the works of Byron, Moore, Poe, and Longfellow and to write many articles on literary subjects in reviews, newspapers, and periodicals.

Durón was the premier Honduran historian of the early 20th century. He concentrated upon political history, as did most Latin Americans, but he also devoted some attention to literary and intellectual history. Additionally, he tried his hand at writing biographies in which he analyzed not only the subject but also the times in which his subject lived. Durón was mainly interested in political figures and the political climate in which they functioned. Beyond biography he worked in drama but without a great deal of success. His histories were generally patriotic in tone, and he was not the dedicated researcher in primary materials that characterized some other Central American historians. Yet his work was thoughtful, analytical, and influenced by his own political, judicial, and teaching careers, the experience from which he brought to his historiographical and biographical work. His books carried him to the forefront of Central American historiography in the late 19th and early 20th centuries.

A. *Diccionario biográfico hondureño* (Tegucigalpa, 1904); *La provincia de Tegucigalpa bajo el gobierno del Mallol: Estudio histórico, 1817–1821* (Tegucigalpa, 1904); *Rectificaciones históricas* (Tegucigalpa, 1906); *Efemérides de Honduras* (Tegucigalpa, 1914); *Bosquejo histórico de Honduras, 1502 a 1921* (San Pedro Sula, Honduras, 1927); *Biografía del doctor Marco Aurelio Soto; tomada de la galeria de gobernantes de Honduras por el mismo autor* (Tegucigalpa, 1944); *Historia de Honduras, desde la independencia hasta nuestros días* (Tegucigalpa, 1956).

B. William J. Griffith, ''The Historiography of Central America Since 1830,'' *Hispanic*

American Historical Review, 40, No. 4 (November 1960), p. 555; Harvey K. Meyer, *Historical Dictionary of Honduras* (Metuchen, N.J., 1976); and Unión Panamericana, *Diccionario de la literatura latinoamericana: América Central: Honduras, Nicaragua y Panamá* (Washington, D.C., 1963), II, pp. 144–147.

E

EDWARDS, ALBERTO (1873, Valparaiso, Chile—3 April 1932, Santiago). *Education*: Law degree, University of Chile, 1896. *Career*: Minor official in the Ministry of Treasury, 1891; wrote for the liberal daily newspaper, *El heraldo* (Valparaiso); studied in Europe; Deputy, National Congress, 1909; entomologist and climatologist at the Museum of Valparaiso; Minister of the Treasury, 1914–1915, 1926–1927; Minster of Education, 1930 and 1931; Director General of Statistics, 1916–1927; Chief, Department of Administrative Geography, Ministry of Interior, 1927.

Alberto was a member of a prominent family in Chile, and from an early age he began to write for the press and to work for the government. He was a journalist and politician as well as a historian. But he was interested in a wide variety of intellectual disciplines from the humanities to higher mathematics. His public service was extensive, as was expected of the Chilean elite in the early years of the 20th century. He also wrote detective novels in which the major character resembled Sherlock Holmes.

Edwards wrote short historical pieces for the press throughout his career, but his major efforts were studies on Chilean politics and society. His most famous work, *La fronda aristocrática en Chile*, was this type of study. It was an analytical examination of the role of the Chilean aristocracy in the development of the nation. Edwards took a cerebral look at the past, and his work influenced subsequent historians who researched the period he covered. His basic premise was that the aristocracy was in conflict with the Chilean government, which was supposed to rule without advantage to any class. *Julio César Jobet has pointed out, however, that the basic argument is indefensible since the aristocracy and the state were one and the same in the 19th century. Nevertheless, Jobet acknowledges the value of Edwards' study from the perspective of opening this type of historical speculation as opposed to the traditional narrative historical accounts that predominated in an earlier age. Jobet agrees that Chilean historiography owed much to this pioneering work by Edwards. In addition, Edwards wrote about the great men of Chile's past, and in particular, he held up for example the career of Diego Portales, the 19th century dictatorial leader of Chile's early independent government.

A. *Reflexiones sobre los principios y resultados de la Revolución de 1891* (Valparaiso, Chile, 1899); *Bosquejo histórico de los partidos políticos chilenos* (Santiago, 1903); *La fronda aristocrática en Chile* (Santiago, 1928); *El gobierno de don Manuel Montt (1851–*

1861) (Santiago, 1932); *La organización política de Chile* (Santiago, 1943); *Páginas históricas* (Santiago, 1945).
B. Julio César Jobet, "Notas sobre la historiografía chilena," *Atenea*, 95, Nos. 291–292 (September–October 1949), p. 350; William Belmont Parker, *Chileans of To-Day* (Santiago, 1920), pp. 193–194; and Unión Panamericana, *Diccionario de la literatura latinoamericana: Chile* (Washington, D.C., 1958), pp. 64–66.

EGUIARA EGUREN, JUAN JOSÉ DE   (February 1696, Mexico City—29 January 1763, Mexico City). *Education*: Studied the arts, philosophy, and theology, bachelor's degree, 1712, Doctorate of Theology, 1715, Real Pontificia Universidad, Mexico City. *Career*: Held a number of teaching and administrative positions in higher education; held local political jobs; taught philosophy and theology; Treasurer of the Cabildo, Mexico City.

In his era Eguiara Eguren was famous as an orator and as a talented defender of the Church. He spoke often at religious events and occasionally at academic affairs and always enthralled his audience with the wisdom of his arguments and the clarity with which he presented them. He was astonished to learn that some priests wrote what he considered injurious statements about Mexico, and he passionately defended his country from what he considered unwarranted attacks based on a lack of knowledge. He sought to organize and systematize the literary and scientific work of Mexico in order to prove the progressive nature of the New World in general and Mexico in particular. His work covered the period from the pre-Hispanic era up to his own time, but not all of it was published and even today only a part of his bibliographical study has appeared in print.

Eguiara Eguren was not so much a historian as a bibliographer. He compiled historical information on the work of writers and their literary production. In his discussions on the material he became impassioned and polemical, but despite this problem and other defects in the work, it remains one of the major aids to historical study in the colonial era.
A. *Vida del venerable padre don Pedro de Arellano, y Sosa, Sacerdote, y primer preposito de la Congregación del Oratorio de México* (Mexico City, 1735); *Bibliotheca mexicana sive eruditorum historia vivorum* (Mexico City, 1746); *Praelectio theologica in sorte oblatam distinctionem vigesimam libri secundi magistri sententiarum* (Mexico City, 1746); *Selectae dissertationes mexicanae ad scholasticam spectantes theologiae tribus tomis distinctae* (Mexico City, 1746); *Sor Juana Inés de la Cruz* (Mexico City, 1936).
B. *Diccionario Porrúa de historia* (Mexico City, 1967), I, p. 691; and Aurora M. Ocampo de Gómez and Ernesto Prado Velázquez, *Diccionario de escritores mexicanos* (Mexico City, 1967), p. 106.

ELGUERO, FRANCISCO   (24 March 1856, Morelia, Mexico—17 December 1932, Morelia). *Education*: studied in the Ateneo Mexicano headed by Celso Acevedo and a student of Rafael Angel de la Peña: professional studies at the Seminario Conciliar of Morelia; recognized as a lawyer, 1880. *Career*: Practiced law in Morelia; worked as a journalist; founded the periodical, *El derecho* *christiano*; Judge of Zamora, 1881-1883; practiced law in Mexico City; Deputy, Union Congress, 1912-1913; taught at the Escuela Nacional de Jurisprudencia.

In addition to his law and historical career Elguero was also a journalist and essayist. He founded the periodical, *El derecho christiano*, in Morelia and later in life opened *Reliquias de América española, Museo intelectual*, and, with others, *América española*. Along with his journalist activities he also found time to write and publish poetry and to translate the works of many Europeans. He studied philosophy, theology, law, sociology, history, and Latin, English, French, Spanish, and Italian literature. He combined the applied work of the practicing attorney with the idealistic attitude of the writer. In addition, he spent some of his time traveling. He lived for two years in the United States and for nearly three years in Havana during the violent period of the Mexican Revolution of 1910. He was active politically and was always a patriot. While in the United States he wrote a history of Mexico's reform laws and covered the fall of Porfiro Díaz; in Havana he published some 330 articles, many of which were on historical topics. Back in Mexico he was elected to the National Congress and proved to be an outstanding orator whose patriotic speeches gained wide attention and won considerable fame for him.

As a historian Elguero not only focused upon political history and the development of the 1910 revolution but was also involved in writing intellectual history. He looked at religious views and theological treatises and in one book sought to reconcile the spiritual and scientific worlds. Additionally, he wrote about educational development in Mexico and even produced a three-act play. With his many interests and his prolific production, mainly in articles for the press, Elguero advanced the historiographic cause in his country at the same time that he wrote contemporary history. When writing about the 1910 revolution or Porfiro Díaz, he was in part at least an eyewitness to the events he described, and as such his work takes on the value of a memoir as well as a chronicle.

A. *La inmaculada* (Mexico City, 1905); *Efemérides históricas y apologéticas* (Madrid, 1920); *La anarquía demogógica y la administración de justicia en Michoacán* (Mexico City, 1922); *Reliquias de América española* (Mexico City, 1922); *La erección de la Colegiata de San Juan de los Lagos, apuntaciónes históricas* (Mexico City, 1925); and *Vanguardia* (Mexico City, 1928).

B. *Diccionario Porrúa de historia* (Mexico City, 1967), I, pp. 695-696; Gabriel Mendez Plancarte, *Horacio en México* (Mexico City, 1937), pp. 181-186; and Aurora M. Ocampo de Gómez and Ernesto Prado Velázquez, *Diccionario de escritores mexicanos* (Mexico City, 1967), pp. 106-107.

ENCINA Y ARMANET, FRANCISCO ANTONIO (10 September 1874, Talca, Chile—August 1965, Santiago). *Education*: Studied Law at the University of Chile, 1892; earned the title of lawyer, 1896. *Career*: Worked in agriculture and commerce; held a seat in the Chamber of Deputies; historian; Member, Commission on Uniform Legislation; Member, General Customs Board; represented Chile at various Pan American conferences.

Nineteenth century historiography in Latin America was characterized by vast multivolume national histories, which were less in evidence following the turn of the century. But Encina, despite the existence of *Diego Barros Arana's 16-volume history of Chile, put together his own national history that went into 20 volumes. The history was not only long and detailed, it was also a revisionist look at Chile's past. It might be regarded as a new synthesis of Chilean history from a conservative perspective rather than the liberal bent of Barros Arana's earlier history. In addition to this monumental task Encina wrote numerous monographs and articles on Chile's history. He was an indefatigable researcher who worked 10-hour days in the National Library up to the time he was 80 years of age, while at the same time continuing to carry out his agricultural activities. He began an intense study of history from the age of 11, and he continued reading and studying until his death. He was familiar with the great classical writers, as well as medieval and early modern European writers. He read Michelet, Momsen, Shakespeare, von Ranke, and the Italian historian Cesar Cantu. Consequently, he was well versed in world history and culture, but like most of his contemporaries, when he wrote his themes were confined to Chilean history.

Encina's first major effort was a study of the Chilean economy and its problems, *Nuestra inferioridad economica, sus causas, sus consecuencias*, 1912. He concluded that lack of education was responsible for the economic backwardness of his country. He was also critical of earlier historians, attacking them for a lack of intellectual depth. He even took to task the great Diego Barros Arana for the simplicity of his efforts and for his liberal political bias. But he did concede that the stage of historiographic development of Chile probably necessitated the type of history written by Barros Arana. The reading public was not prepared for more profound works, and the documentation that would permit such studies was not yet amassed. Not only did Encina criticize other Chilean historians but he was extremely critical of many of the heroes of Chile's past. He charged that Diego Portales, to many a hero of the early independence era, was a Chilean Borgia, and he ridiculed others for their lack of intelligence, for their excessive pride, and for their many other human frailties. Meanwhile, he came under criticism for his verbosity in developing his histories. One critic pointed out that a large nation such as France had histories of 250 pages while a small country like Chile had a national history of 20 volumes. Despite these criticisms Encina ranks as one of the foremost 20th century Latin American historians.

A. *Nuestra inferioridad económica, sus causas, sus consecuencias* (Santiago, 1912); *Portales: introducción a la historia de la época de Diego Portales (1830-1891)*, 2 vols. (Santiago, 1934); *La literatura histórica chilena y el concepto actual de la historia* (Santiago, 1935); *Historia de Chile desde la prehistoria hasta 1891*, 20 vols. (Santiago, 1940-1952); *La presidencia de Balmaceda*, 2 vols. (Santiago, 1952); *Resumen de la historia de Chile: Redacción, iconografía y apendices de Leopoldo Castedo*, 3 vols. (Santiago, 1954).

B. Charles C. Griffin, ''Francisco Encina and Revisionism in Chilean History,'' *Hispanic*

American Historical Review, 37, No. 1 (February 1957), pp. 1-28; Julio César Jobet, "Notas sobre la historiografía chilena," *Atenea*, 95, Nos. 291-292 (September-October 1949), pp. 352-355; Percy Alvin Martin, *Who's Who in Latin America*, 2d ed. rev. (Stanford, 1940), p. 169.

ERCILLA Y ZÚÑIGA, ALONSO DE (7 August 1533, Madrid—29 November 1594, Madrid). *Education*: Studied humanities in Madrid. *Career*: Page for Prince Philip, who later became King Philip II; traveled with the Prince in Europe; was in England when Philip married Mary the daughter of English King Edward VI; went to Chile to fight against the Araucanian Indians; returned to Spain and served as a diplomat.

Ercilla was a young man of adventurous spirit, and the Spanish expedition to Chile and Peru in 1557 appeared to be a great opportunity for him. He participated in the struggle against the Indians, and it was in the midst of this great clash that he began to write his only major work, the epic poem *La Araucana*, which he completed after his return to Europe.

La Araucana is the only major piece of poetry produced by Ercilla, but it is extremely significant, not only as poetry but because it chronicles the war against the Araucanians. Critics have pointed out such weaknesses as a lack of unity in the narrative, digressions, unequal treatment, attributing eloquent phrases to the Araucanians, and some artificial techniques borrowed from Homer and Virgil. Despite all of this, however, this was one of the best epic poems of the 16th century, and it gained wide acceptance in Europe. Cervantes in his *Don Quixote* mentions it as one of the three books worth saving from Quixote's library, and Voltaire commented that part of it compared favorably with Homer. Its historical value is unquestioned, as Ercilla gave a balanced account of the fighting and even praised the enemy for his bravery. The Araucanian chieftain Caupolican emerged from the poem as larger than life and has become a great hero among the Chileans. The epic was not only an account of war but also a study of the customs of the Araucanian people and a description of the Chilean experience in the 16th century. The major thrust of the poem, however, is the military conflict, and here again Ercilla captured the participants eloquently in their strife. He noted that he wrote parts of the poem on the battlefield itself, writing on scraps of letters and pieces of leather so that it has the full flavor of an eyewitness account. As a chronicle of the conquest of Latin America it is outstanding, and one scholar has written that it was a shame that Cortés in Mexico had no chronicler of the stature of Ercilla with him to recount the conquest of the Aztecs. *La Araucana* remains a significant record of the Spanish conquest of the Araucanians.

A. *La Araucana*, 3 pts. (Madrid, 1569, 1578, and 1589) (first complete edition, Madrid, 1589-1590); *The Araucaniad*, trans. Charles Lancaster and Paul Manchester (Nashville, Tenn., 1945).

B. Salvatore Bizzarro, *Historical Dictionary of Chile* (Metuchen, N.J., 1980), pp. 127-128; Helen Delpar, *Encyclopedia of Latin America* (New York, 1974), p. 220; Michael Rheta Martin and Gabriel Lovett, *Encyclopedia of Latin American History* (Indianapolis,

1968), p. 130; Walter Owen, *La Araucana: The Epic of Chile by Don Alonso de Ercilla y Zúñiga* (Buenos Aires, 1945), pp. xiii-xxxiv; and Unión Panamericana, *Diccionario de la literatura latinoamericana: Chile* (Washington, D.C., 1958), pp. 76-78.

ERRÁZURIZ VALDIVIESO, CRESCENTE (28 November 1839, Santiago—5 June 1931, Santiago). *Education*: Educated at the Seminario Conciliar Santiago; received holy orders, 1863. *Career*: Secretary to Archbishop Rafael Valentín Valdivieso, his uncle, with whom he traveled in Europe; Editor, *Revista católica* and *El estandarte católico*; joined the Dominican order, 1884; took charge of the order's library; Prior, Convent of the Congregación de Santo Domingo, 1898-1907; Archbishop of Santiago, 1918-1931.

One of the careers sometimes pursued by historians in Latin America was that of the clergy. Errázuriz stands out as one of the successful historians who served the Church well as a priest, a member of the Dominican order, and finally as Archbishop. In the latter capacity he was the leader the Chilean church when the constitution of 1925 officially separated church and state in the nation. He kept calm within the ranks of the clergy and made possible the acceptance of the Church's new role in Chilean society without major incident. He was also an accomplished journalist and polemicist. His articles were lively, sophisticated, and erudite, especially those that dealt with canon law; he served as a professor of canon law at the University of Chile. In all his endeavors he was eminently successful, and that success was recognized both by those within the Church and by secular intellectual organizations.

Errázuriz concentrated on the early years of Chile's development when writing his histories. When he made a trip to Europe early in his career he collected documents that he could then use upon his return to write a history of the Church in Chile and to write about the illustrious early leaders of the country. Later, when he entered the monastery, he used his time as a recluse to research carefully historical topics that he wrote about when he left the monastic sanctuary later on. Some of his biographies of conquistadors and colonial leaders of Chile are regarded as classics, largely because of his rigorous adherence to authenticated documentation and his objective approach to history. In addition to books he wrote many articles of a historical nature, and these too were well received by secular Chilean historians. However, it is true that he is regarded as a conservative historian by modern Chilean historians. This does not detract from his historiographical competence, but the belief persists that he devoted too much attention to religious themes and to support for the elite of Chilean society. Along these lines, he concentrated upon political and religious subjects and did not deal with economic matters or with the social problems of the Chilean people. Nonetheless, he is one of the best known and most widely respected historians of his generation.

A. *Los orígenes de la iglesia chilena* (Santiago, 1873); *Seis años de la historia de Chile*, 2 vols. (Santiago, 1881); *Historia de Chile durante los gobiernos de García Ramón, Merlo de la Fuente y Jaraquemada*, 2 vols. (Santiago, 1908); *Historia de Chile: Pedro*

de Valdivia, 2 vols. (Santiago, 1911-1912); *Historia de Chile sin gobernador (1554-1557)* (Santiago, 1912); *Don García de Mendoza* (Santiago, 1914).
B. Carlos Fernandez Freite, *Biografía de d. Crescente Errázuriz* (Santiago, 1935); Michael Rheta Martin and Gabriel Lovett, *Encyclopedia of Latin American History* (Indianapolis, 1968), p. 130; William Belmont Parker, *Chileans of To-Day* (Santiago, 1920), pp. 4-6; and Unión Panamericana, *Diccionario de la literatura latinoamericana: Chile* (Washington, D.C., 1958), pp. 78-80.

EYZAGUIRRE GUTIÉRREZ, JAIME (1908, Santiago—17 September 1968, Santiago). *Education*: Attended the Colegio del Verbo Divino; law degree, Universidad Católica, 1928. *Career*: Professor, Universidad Católica and Universidad de Chile.

Although trained as a lawyer, Eyzaguirre was primarily a teacher and a historian. He was educated in a theological setting, and his views on history were highly traditionalist and doctrinaire. Theologically, he developed a philosophy in which his fervent Catholicism centered on the importance of mankind. Perhaps because of his religious conviction he followed a traditional kind of historiography, resisting the revisionist historians that emerged in Chile in the 1930s. In writing upon the early years of Spanish colonization in Chile, he supported the concept of Spanish glory and the value for nationalist Chile of the Hispanic colonial age. He advocated the idea of *hispanidad* in his histories and in his biographies. A later biography of Chile's independence hero, Bernardo O'Higgins, was, however, an objective treatment of Chile's great hero and the Hispanist that had emerged in his earlier writing was now subdued. This work won praise throughout Latin America, the United States, and Europe and underwent several editions.

When Eyzaguirre turned from biographical works to studies of Chile, he produced books that were welcomed because he did not treat his homeland as an isolated nation. Instead he placed Chile within the framework of the Western Hemisphere and Latin America. These studies were also marked by his use of his legal background to explain the many complex issues in the nation's development.

A. *La vida de un funcionario de la administración colonial española* (Santiago, 1930); *Privilegios diplomáticos* (Santiago, 1932); *Viejos imagenes* (Santiago, 1947); *El Conde de la conquista* (Santiago, 1951); *O'Higgins* (Santiago, 1965); and *Ventura de don Pedro de Valdavia* (Santiago, 1968).
B. *Eugenio Pereira Salas, "Jaime Eyzaguirre Gutiérrez," Revista de historia de América*, Nos. 67-68 (January-December 1969), pp. 346-347.

F

FAVARO, EDMUNDO J. (25 June 1907, Montevideo—1 September 1957, Montevideo). *Education*: Bachelor's degree, University of Montevideo. *Career*: Worked in commerce and public administration; served in the Ministry of Public Health and the Office of Foreign Relations; Associate Editor, *Hispanic American Historical Review*.

Favaro was a dedicated scholar as well as a public functionary. He concentrated his literary attention upon the study and writing of history. From his almost compulsive affinity for the past he gained an equally great fondness for the libraries and archives where he carried out his historical research. He personally collected many historical books and documents, but he also spent a considerable amount of time in the public archives and libraries of both Uruguay and Argentina.

Because of his short life he did not produce vast amounts of historical studies, and unfortunately he had many unfinished manuscripts underway when he died. The work he did complete, however, ranks with the finest historical studies produced in Uruguay. One of his major works, a biography of Dammaso Antonio Larrañaga, won a prize, while his article on the Congreso de Tres Cruces is generally recognized as his best analytical work. In addition to his monographs and well-researched articles on historical studies, he also published bibliographies for the assistance of other scholars.

A. "Ensayo histórico sobre los antecedentes del himno nacional," *Boletín latino-americano de música*, 4 (1937), pp. 571-634; *Dammaso Antonio Larrañaga, su vida y su época* (Montevideo, 1950); "El Congreso de Tres Cruces y la Assemblea del año XIII,"*Revista del Instituto Histórico y Geográfico, Montevideo*, 19 (1952), and 20 (1957); *Catálogo de la Exposición Bibliografíca, Iconográfica e Histórica de Francisco Acuña de Figueroa* (Montevideo, 1957).

B. Julían Garcés, "Edmundo J. Favaro," *Revista de historia de América*, No. 47 (June 1959), pp. 167-168; Edmundo M. Narancio, "Edmundo J. Favaro (1907-1957)," *Hispanic American Historical Review*, 38, No. 1 (February 1958), pp. 58-59.

FERNÁNDEZ DE PIEDRAHITA, LUCAS (6 March 1624, Bogotá—1688, Panama City). *Education*: Studied in the Colegio de San Bartolomé; Doctor of Divinity, Universidad Tomística de Bogotá. *Career*: Governor of the Archbishopric of Bogotá; Bishop of Santa Marta, Colombia, 1699; missionary among thhe Indians and mestizos of the Caribbean; Member, Bishopric of Panama, 1676; Curate of two Indian towns; Canon of the Cathedral of Bogotá.

As a member of the clergy Father Fernández de Piedrahita devoted his considerable energies to administrative and missionary activities within the Church. However, in 1661 he was charged by a royal investigator with irregularities while in office, and he was sent to Spain for a hearing before the Royal Council of the Indies. He was subsequently exonerated of the charge and was given the position of Bishop of Santa Marta, an appointment that was confirmed by the Pope. Later in his career he became an active and outspoken defender of the Indians, and he strongly supported missionary and conversion activity in Central America.

Fernández de Piedrahita's major historical contribution was the work entitled *Historia general de las conquistas del Nuevo Reino de Granada*. It was designed to be a two-volume study, but he died before completing the manuscript. The history began with the creation of the world and continued up to 1563, but its main theme was the conquest of New Granada. This was the first attempt to clarify and explain the conquest of northern South America, and it was remarkable for the outstanding literary style utilized by the author. One scholar suggests that the Spanish was so clear that it came close to modern Spanish. Fernández was preoccupied with the Chibcha Indians, and his account of life among these Indians was graphic and informative. While he appeared sympathetic to the Indian cause, he was generally impartial and sought the truth in his work. He documented his material well and enhanced it with an elegant literary style. The work was based, to some degree, upon the manuscripts of the conqueror of New Granada, *Gonzalo Jiménez de Quesada, which Fernandez found and used at the Archives of the Indies in Sevilla, Spain, when he was in that country to defend himself from the charges of impropriety leveled against him by royal investigators. In addition to the Jiménez de Quesada notes, he also used other chronicles of America, which broadened the scope of his book. He freely admitted that his history was not a work conceived in primary documentation, but he argued that its merit was in the updating of earlier chronicles and the modernizing of the Spanish from the earlier language. He was, then, a general historian of the conquest and early colonial periods of Colombia. He also commented upon the philosophical character of the Chibchas and discussed the morality of these people. The work was full and readable and served as a foundation for later studies of this period of Colombian history.

A. *Historia general de las conquistas del Nuevo Reino de Granada* (Bogotá, 1881).

B. Robert H. Davis, *Historical Dictionary of Colombia* (Metuchen, N.J., 1977), p. 112; Antonio Gómez Restrepo, *Historia de la literatura colombiana* (Bogotá, 1940), II, pp. 165-170; Unión Panamericana, *Diccionario de la literatura latinoamericana: Colombia* (Washington, D.C., 1959), pp. 39-41; and A. Curtis Wilgus, *The Historiography of Latin America: A Guide to Historical Writing, 1500-1800* (Metuchen, N.J., 1975), pp. 161-162

FERNÁNDEZ GUARDIA, RICARDO (4 January 1867, Alajuela, Costa Rica—5 February 1950, San José). *Education*: Studied in Paris and at the Instituto

Nacional de San José, 1873-1878. *Career*: Undersecretary of Foreign Relations, 1896 and 1909; Minister of Foreign Relations; President, Costa Rican Academy of Language; Minister in Rome, 1900, Honduras, Washington, D.C., 1917, Panama, 1920, Mexico, 1921; Ambassador in Guatemala; Minister of Public Instruction; Minister of Justice.

The son of a diplomat and historian, Fernández Guardia spent the first years of his life abroad. He went to school in Paris and learned French better than Spanish. Upon his return to Costa Rica he studied in his country's schools, but when he returned to Europe his higher education was continued abroad. He was very young when he began his diplomatic career, serving with his father in European posts, and from his father he also acquired his interest in history. At the same time, he was committed also to other forms of literature so that eventually he wrote dramas, fiction, and literary and artistic criticism. He wrote about legends that existed in his country, and he wrote some *cuadros de costumbres* (articles about customs) when that genre became so popular in Costa Rica and Latin America. He also gave some attention to comedies in his writing, but he was always devoted to the writing of history.

Fernández Guardia has been called the finest historian produced in Costa Rica in the early 20th century. Because of his European education he adopted the scientific historiographic methods that were in vogue and transferred them to Costa Rica. For this reason he has been labeled the founder of the scientific school of history in Costa Rica. He advocated the extensive use of archival material in preparing histories and also the careful analysis of that documentation. For his own work he prepared the large collection of documents that had been gathered by his father, León Fernández, in an orderly fashion and then analyzed many of those materials. Out of this primary material he wrote a number of fundamental Costa Rican histories in both book and article form. In addition to rigorous testing and interpreting of documents, Fernández Guardia was also an exceptional prose stylist who presented his historic findings in a pleasant, attractive manner. As a novelist he developed a readable style that he then applied to his efforts in the genre of history with great success. That style was evolved from a thorough study and understanding of Spanish classical writing, which was required because he had learned French before Spanish. That traditional background served Fernández well in preparing him for his literary and historiographic careers. The areas that he worked upon were colonial development and the independence age. Not only did he produce monographs on these periods, but he also devoted a great deal of time to editing historical documents relating to the colonial era.

A. *Cuentos ticos* (San José, 1901); *Historia de Costa Rica: El descubrimiento y la conquista* (San José, 1905); *Cartilla histórica de Costa Rica* (San José, 1909); *Reseña histórica de Talamanca* (San José, 1918); *Cuentos Ticos: Short Stories of Costa Rica*, trans. Gary Casement (Cleveland, 1925); *La Guerra de la Liga y la invasión de Quijano* (San José, 1934); *Historia de Costa Rica: La independencia* (San José, 1941).

B. Theodore S. Creedman, *Historical Dictionary of Costa Rica* (Metuchen, N.J., 1977), pp. 71-72; William J. Griffith, "The Historiography of Central America Since 1830," *Hispanic American Historical Review*, 40, No. 4 (November 1960), p. 556; Instituto Panamericano de Geografía e Historia, *Guía de personas que cultivan la historia de América* (Mexico City, 1951), pp. 153-154; Mary B. MacDonald and Dwight H. McLaughlin, "Ricardo Fernández Guardia," in *Vida y obras de autores de Costa Rica* (Havana, 1941), I, pp. 23-29; Percy Alvin Martin, *Who's Who in Latin America*, 2d ed. rev. (Stanford, 1940), p. 183; "Ricardo Fernández Guardia" *Hispanic American Historical Review*, 30, No. 2 (May 1950), pp. 265-266.

FERREIRA, MARIANO   (24 January 1834, Montevideo—1922, Montevideo). *Education*: Educated at the Uruguayan Colegio and at the University of Montevideo; Bachelor of Science and Letters, 1854; Doctor of Laws, 1857; degree of Advocate, 1866. *Career*: Attaché to the Uruguayan legation in Paraguay; served in the Ministry of Finance; Secretary to the Academy of Jurisprudence, 1865; nominated as Judge of the Criminal and Commercial Courts but refused the position; Member, National Administrative Commission, 1868; Special Attorney to the Government; attorney for the poor in civil cases, 1872; President of the Governing Board, Conservatory of Music, 1886; President, National Commission for Charity and Public Beneficence, 1893; Minister of Foreign Affairs, 1897.

Working in a number of public service jobs throughout much of his life, Ferreira gained the respect of the leaders of Uruguay that resulted in his being elected and appointed to commissions, committees, and posts that dealt with cultural affairs for the public. He worked with libraries and organizations that benefitted the poor and unfortunate in society. Meanwhile, he practiced law and at the same time held posts on bodies that governed education, asylums, and musical and artistic organizations. In all of the positons that came to him Ferreira worked well with others and made a significant contribution to the social and cultural agencies for which he labored.

Ferreira's historical research focused upon the independence age in Uruguay and upon the independence hero José Artigas. Since he lived through the immediate post-independence era, he was familiar with stories and legends that came out of the independence struggle, and there were still many people alive and anxious to talk about their own recollections of this dramatic and exciting age in Uruguayan history. Additionally, members of Ferreira's family had participated in the struggle against Spain and actually fought alongside Artigas. With this knowledge, in addition to the documents to which he had access, Ferreira was able to put together some historical studies of the glorious independence era in Uruguay. He was not an accomplished researcher, but he was able to put the events of independence into a readable form that could be enjoyed by the public.

A. *Apuntes biográficos de la familia Artigas y Ferreira* (Montevideo, 1919); *Memorias del doctor Mariano Ferreira*, 2 vols. (Montevideo, 1920-1921); *Reseña histórica de la Biblioteca y Museo Nacional* (Montevideo, 1920).

B. William Belmont Parker, *Uruguayans of To-Day* (New York, 1967), pp. 225-228.

FIGAROLA-CANEDA, DOMINGO (17 January 1852, Havana—14 March 1926, Havana). *Education*: Studied at the University of Havana. *Career*: Director, Biblioteca Nacional, 1901-1926.

Like many other scholars in the late 19th century, Figarola-Caneda devoted his life to the cause of Cuban independence from Spain. He joined the Independence party and worked tirelessly to free his nation from Spanish control. He was also committed to the growth of the discipline of history, and toward that end he worked extensively. In 1910 he created the Academy of History, and as an aid to historical studies he also founded the National Library of Cuba. Not content with merely collecting books and documents and maintaining the collection for scholars, he was also determined to facilitate the publication of historical research. Consequently, he established a section of the Academy of History that was to oversee the publication of historical scholarship. Eventually, he assumed the title Director of the Publications of the Academy, and he saw to it that the research carried out by Cuban historians reached the reading public.

While his efforts as Director of the Cuban Academy of History were vital to the development of the history discipline in Cuba and while his publication work was significant, Figarola-Caneda was also a historian in his own right. His own publications, however, were not monographs but instead collections of data that were important for the work of other historians and scholars. He collected and published bibliographies on both narrow subjects and broad fields of study, all of which became valuable for the Cuban researcher.

A. *Bibliografía de Rafael María Merechán* (Havana, 1905); *Cartografía cubana de British Museum* (Havana, 1910); *Escudos primitivos de Cuba* (Havana, 1913); *Bibliografía de Luz y Caballero* (Havana, 1915); *Diccionario cubano de seudónimos* (Havana, 1922); and *Centón epistolario de Domingo del Monte*, 7 vols. (Havana, 1923-1957).

B. "Notes and Comment," *Hispanic American Historical Review*, 7, No. 1 (February 1927), pp. 131-132; 7, No. 2 (May 1927), p. 227; and 8, No. 4 (November 1928), p. 586.

FINOT, ENRIQUE (16 September 1891, Santa Cruz de la Sierra, Bolivia—23 December 1952, Santa Cruz de la Sierra). *Education*: Studied at the Seminario de Santa Cruz and the Colegio Nacional de Santa Cruz; graduated from the Escuela Normal de Profesoras y Preceptores de Sucre, 1908. *Career*: Taught cartography and drawing at the Escuela Normal, 1911; Inspector of Primary Instruction, Department of Chuquisaca; Director, Escuela Modelo, La Paz; Secretary, Directorate of Public Instruction, 1914; First Secretary of the Bolivian legation in Peru; Deputy from Santa Cruz; Minister in Chile; Confidential Agent in the United States; Bolivian delegate to the League of Nations; Ambassador to Cuba; Minister of Foreign Relations; Minister in Argentina; and Ambassador to Mexico.

For Bolivian historians a diplomatic career seemed almost essential. Finot, like several others, devoted a good portion of his life to diplomatic pursuits, along with teaching, journalism, and writing history. He was a close friend of the outstanding Bolivian historian *Gabriel René-Moreno, and with him he shared many ideas on historiography. Finot was curious, competent, and scrupulous with the use of documents in his research. He was primarily interested in the history of Bolivia without evidencing much concern for the rest of Latin America or for world history. In one area, however, he did tend to link Bolivian experience with that of the remainder of Latin America: the conquest and early colonization. He wrote about what came to be called the third stage of colonization, or conquest beyond the capital cities. As the Spaniards pushed out from the capital centers, they launched a civilizing wave and created a series of new communities around the capital. From that initial expansion there emerged communication and transportation lines that enabled the Spaniards to establish their colonies on a firm, safe footing.

In the process of writing his histories Finot paid close attention to the documentation that existed, and in the process of his research he uncovered errors that had been made by earlier historians and by chroniclers. But he also covered new ground, largely untouched by previous or contemporary historians, and in this way he made a major contribution to Bolivian historiography. His work also contrasted to other Bolivian historians' in that he was less concerned with literature and more devoted to scientific methodology. In part of his last book, *Nueva historia de Bolivia*, he concentrated on the facts of Bolivian development and on sociological aspects of the nation's history. But the literary Finot could not be completely suppressed so that the end result of his work was not only informative and well researched but readable as well.

A. *Noticia sobre la instrucción pública de Bolivia, su historia, organización y desarrollo* (La Paz, 1916); *Historia de la pedagogía boliviana* (La Paz, 1926); *La historia de Bolivia en imagenes* (La Paz, 1928); *Nueves aspectos de la cuestión del Chaco* (La Paz, 1931); *Historia de la conquista del Oriente boliviano* (Buenos Aires, 1939); *Historia de la literatura boliviana* (Mexico City, 1943); and *Nueva historia de Bolivia* (La Paz, 1954).

B. Fernando Díez de Medina, *Literatura boliviana* (La Paz, 1953), pp. 280-283; Dwight B. Heath, *Historical Dictionary of Bolivia* (Metuchen, N.J., 1972), p. 101; Percy Alvin Martin, *Who's Who in Latin America* (Stanford, 1936), p. 149; William Belmont Parker, *Bolivians of To-Day* (New York, 1967), pp. 121-122; and Unión Panamericana, *Diccionario de la literatura latinoamericana: Bolivia* (Washington, D.C., 1958), pp. 34-36.

FUENTES Y GUZMÁN, FRANCISCO ANTONIO DE   (1643, Santiago de los Caballeros de Guatemala—1700, Sonsonate, Guatemala). *Education*: Self-taught through extensive reading in the Spanish classics. *Career*: Mayor of Santiago twice; Prefect, Municipal Council of Guatemala; Mayor of Totonicapán, 1661; Mayor of Sonsonate, 1669; Captain in the Spanish army.

In the colonial age in Central America it was not uncommon for sons of prominent families to hold important political positions and, at the same time, to publish poetry and literature. Fuentes y Guzmán was a military officer who held several political posts during his lifetime but who also made a contribution to Guatemalan literature. As an administrator he was instrumental in constructing roads from Sonsonate to the capital city for the benefit of people in both regions. But his major contribution to his country was his written work.

Fuentes y Guzmán collected source materials on the colonial age and then used them to write history. At the same time, he wrote poetry, one of the most significant poems of which was a description in verse of the Cathedral of Guatemala, while another was a descripiton of fiestas. Even his poetry took the form of chronicles as he discussed life in colonial Guatemala, but his major prose efforts were in the area of history. He confided that one of the histories he wrote was motivated by his love for Guatemala and because he did not want the documents in his possession to pass into obscurity without being used to document the history of Guatemala. He applied to Spain to be named Royal Chronicler of Guatemala but his petition was refused. Parts of his manuscript on the history of Guatemala were lost, but others remained in the archives in the Guatemalan municipality and in the National Museum. Fuentes believed that he was using the best of sources for his history, but he chose the ones he wanted and overlooked others. He also used a rambling, verbose style. Additionally, he frequently made errors in fact that were later accepted by historians, who continued the errors he made. Fuentes did write a manuscript on the nature of history, suggesting that it should be written after careful evaluation of sources even though he himself did not always follow carefully this advice. He was an intense patriot and he was committed to the production of sound history and eloquent poetry.

A. *Descripción de las fiestas hechas en Guatemala al cumplir Carlos II la edad de trece años* (Guatemala City, 1675); *Historia de Guatemala o Recordación florida*, 2 vols. (Madrid, 1882-1883); *Recordación florida*, 3 vols. (Guatemala City, 1932-1933); *Preceptores historiales* (Guatemala City, 1957).

B. Richard Moore, *Historical Dictionary of Guatemala*, rev. ed. (Metuchen, N.J., 1973), p. 89; Unión Panamericana, *Diccionario de la literatura latinoamericana: América Central; Costa Rica, El Salvador y Guatemala* (Washington, D.C., 1963), II, pp. 101-104; and A. Curtis Wilgus, *The Historiography of Latin America: A Guide to Historical Writing, 1500-1800* (Metuchen, N.J., 1975), pp. 148-149.

FUENZALIDA GRANDÓN, ALEJANDRO (21 December 1865, Copiapó, Chile—1942, Santiago). *Education*: Studied at the Liceo de Atacama; law degree, University of Chile, 1889. *Career*: Journalist for *El atacameno* and *El positivista*; taught history and geography, National Institute and University of Chile, 1894-1918; worked in the Ministry of Public Instruction, 1892-1899; Professor of Administrative Law, University of Chile, 1900-1901; on the Board of Examiners.

Fuenzalida devoted his career to teaching and to writing. Because of the prominence he acquired through his publications, he represented the Chilean government on international scientific meetings. The government also commissioned him to study the Prussian public instruction system in 1911, and he was charged with the task of looking into the organization of public museums in Europe. He fulfilled all these jobs admirably and used the experience to broaden his historical perspective. As a young man he had become acquainted with the positivistic philosophy of Auguste Comte that nurtured the discipline of sociology. Writing articles for the positivist organ, *El positivista*, Fuenzalida Grandón became one of the leading advocates of the exciting new philosophy in Chile.

With his positivist convictions and his consequent tendency to move toward sociology, Fuenzalida applied sociological ideas to history. The result was a social and intellectual study of Chile's past. He focused on the history of teaching in one of his books, which was used extensively by the great Chilean bibliographer and historian *José Toribio Medina as a basis for a later book on the subject. Some of Fuenzalida's other works were of less value, but probably his major contribution to Chilean historiography was his study on the life of *José Victorino Lastarria, *Lastarria y su tiempo*. This was a well-researched effort that brought out in fine detail the character and personality of the great 19th century Chilean politician, writer, teacher, and historian. Additionally, Fuenzalida was aware of the value of the historical novel in promulgating historical knowledge, and in 1889 he published a book on that subject as well. Because of his belief in the value of historical novels and due to his skill as a journalist, he wrote in a pleasant, uncluttered style, which made his histories attractive to the general reading public.

A. *El valor histórico de la novela contemporánea* (Santiago, 1889); *Historia desarrollo intelectual de Chile* (Santiago, 1903); *La evolución social de Chile* (Santiago, 1906); *Lastarria y su tiempo*, 2 vols. (Santiago, 1911); *La enseñanza en Alemania* (Santiago, 1913); and *Don Valentín Letelier y su labor intelectual* (Santiago, 1943).

B. Francisco Encina, "Breve bosquejo de la literatura histórica chilena," *Atenea*, 75, Nos. 291-292 (September-October 1949), p. 62; Percy Alvin Martin, *Who's Who in Latin America*, 2d ed. rev. (Stanford, 1940), pp. 197-198; and William Belmont Parker, *Chileans To-Day* (Santiago, 1920), pp. 64-66.

FUNES, GREGORIO (26 May 1749, Córdoba, Argentina—10 January 1829, Córdoba). *Education*: Studied at the Jesuit Colegio de Monserrat; Doctor of Theology, University of Buenos Aires; law degree, University of Alcalá, Spain. *Career*: Vicar General, Bishopric of Córdoba, 1793; Archdeacon and Dean, Cathedral of Córdoba, 1793; and Rector, University of Córdoba, 1808.

Funes was deeply interested in a religious career but he was also committed to education. Additionally, he became intrigued with the revolutionary activities of the independence era, and he developed a penchant for political activity. As an educator he introduced new methodological concepts, but more importantly he made curricular changes, which included the teaching of French, geography, music, and arithmetic, trigonometry, and algebra. When the independence struggle began in 1810, Funes turned his attention to the war and was elected a representative from Córdoba to the Buenos Aires junta that directed the independence effort. In Buenos Aires he cooperated in the publication of *La gaceta*, a revolutionary newspaper to which he contributed articles. The next few years were stormy ones for both Argentina and Funes. At the center of the problem was not only revolution but the kind of political system that Argentina would adopt once independence was achieved. Funes supported the provinces against the dominance of Buenos Aires in this bitter clash, and he was eventually imprisoned and told to stay out of all public affairs. When he was released to return home to Córdoba, he wrote and contemplated, but then in 1815 he was back in politics once again, this time as Deputy from Córdoba to the Congress of Tucumán, which ultimately declared independence from Spain. In 1818, Funes was elected Deputy from Córdoba to the Congress in Buenos Aires, and for the remaining years of his life he served a variety of political positions while continuing to write.

Funes was an enlightened man of his age, possessing vast knowledge about education, religion, and political science. He was in the midst of the turmoil of the independence era, and he expressed numerous ideas concerning the way the nation should evolve. These were set forth not only from his congressional seats but also in the press. In fact, one of his major positions was his insistence on freedom of the press for the new nation, which led him to draft Argentina's first freedom of the press law in 1811. In his historical research he was determined to use the past for the purpose of exalting the nation and assisting in the construction of a new country. He once wrote that he wanted his histories to reveal the tyranny of Spain and to champion the cause of Argentine independence. Because of these views his history was often inexact by modern standards, but he, like many others of his age, was less interested in historic truth than in the value of history as a tool to propagate the independence movement and the newly independent Argentine government.

A. *Ensayo de la historia civil del Paraguay, Buenos-Ayres y Tucumán*, 3 vols. (Buenos Aires, 1816-1817); *Ensayo de la historia civil de Buenos Aires, Tucumán y Paraguay*, 2 vols. (Buenos Aires, 1856).

B. Roberto F. Giusti, *Diccionario de la literatura latinoamericana: Argentina* (Washington, D.C., 1961), pp. 53-55; and Ione S. Wright and Lisa M. Nekhom, *Historical Dictionary of Argentina* (Metuchen, N.J., 1978), p. 334.

FÚRLONG CÁRDIFF, GUILLERMO (21 June 1889), Villa Constitución Santa Fé, Argentina—1974, Buenos Aires). *Education*: St. Bartholomew's College of Rosario, 1898-1900; Colegio de la Inmaculada de Santa Fé, 1900-1903; Colegio de Córdoba, 1903-1910; Ph.D., Georgetown University, Washington, D.C., 1914. *Career*: Entered the Jesuit order; taught English at the Colegio del Salvador, Buenos Aires; taught at the Colegio del Sagrado Corazón, Montevideo; Director, Academia de Letras del Plata and Editor of its review, *Estudios*.

As a traveler who lived in a variety of foreign countries, Fúrlong was interested in a wide range of subjects and disciplines. He was involved in geographic explorations and conducted ethnological and linguistic studies of Argentine Indian tribes who had been found initially by the missionaries of the colonial age. His publications included work on music, libraries, architecture, mathematics, medicine, and natural history. He even did some work on the role of women in society at a time when women's history was just beginning to elicit some interest from the male-dominated history profession.

Throughout Latin America the Jesuits had kept detailed archives from the colonial age. In the 19th and 20th centuries Jesuit historians researched these collections and produced monographs on the major events in the colonial era. Fúrlong's primary historical interest was the activity of the Jesuits as colonizers in Argentina and as chroniclers and historians of the pre-independence period. In the course of his research he uncovered manuscripts written by several Argentine Jesuit missionaries, which he published along with biographical information on each man. In 1969, as a capstone to his long and distinguished 40-year career, Fúrlong published a three-volume history of colonial Argentina. In all of his published work he relied heavily on the archival material available in Argentina, and this enabled him to resurrect some important individuals from the colonial age who had been forgotten. He stoutly defended religion and Argentina in his publications because he was fiercely loyal to both the Jesuit order and his country. He wrote that he sought the truth concerning the people and events of a historical era. Fúrlong wanted to revive faithfully the colonial age in the Río de la Plata region, and his long career enabled him to produce many important studies on colonial Argentina.

A. *Glorias santafesinas* (Buenos Aires, 1929); *El p. Pedro Lozano, S.J.: Su personalidad y su obra: Biobibliografía* (Montevideo, 1930); *Los jesuitas y la cultura rioplatenese* (Montevideo, 1933); *Nacimiento y desarrollo de la filosofía en el Río de la Plata, 1536-1810* (Buenos Aires, 1952); and *Historia social y cultural del Río de la Plata: 1536-1810*, 3 vols. (Buenos Aires, 1969).

B. Rómulo D. Carbia, *Historia crítica de la historiografía argentina desde sus orígenes en el siglo XVI* (La Plata, 1939), pp. 20-25; Percy Alvin Martin, *Who's Who in Latin America*, 2d ed. rev. (Stanford, 1940), p. 198; Magnus Morner, "Obituary: Guillermo Furlong Cardiff (1889-1974)," *Hispanic American Historical Review*, 55, No. 1 (February 1975), pp. 92-94; Juan Pinto, *Diccionario de la República Argentina* (Buenos Aires, 1949), p. 274; and Ione S. Wright and Lisa M. Nekhom, *Historical Dictionary of Argentina* (Metuchen, N.J., 1978), pp. 334-335.

G

GALDAMES, LUÍS (1881, Santiago—1941, Santiago). *Education*: School of Law, University of Chile, 1903; graduate degree, Pedagogical Institute, University of Chile, 1906. *Career*: Lawyer; Chair of Chilean History and Civic Education, University of Chile; a leader in national education; Rector, Liceo M. L. Amunátegui; Director General of Primary Instruction; Dean of the Faculty of Philosophy and Education, University of Chile; traveled throughout America on various educational missions and on research projects.

A longstanding tradition of Chilean historiography was the writing of national histories. The multivolume, detailed accounts of *Diego Barros Arana and *Francisco Encina were accompanied by a large number of one- or two-volume national histories that appeared throughout the 19th and into the 20th centuries. Among those who wrote these books, Luís Galdames was one of the most successful, producing a study that so impressed the U.S. historian Isaac Joslin Cox that he translated it into English and published it in the University of North Carolina series of Latin American national histories. But Galdames was more than a chronicler of Chile's past, and he produced a number of other works in biography and in constitutional history that were equally well received.

In 1929 Galdames wrote an article in which he expressed clearly his view of Chilean historiography. He noted that for a time Chile was recognized as a nation in the forefront of historical writing in Latin America,, and the methods employed by Chilean historians—rigorous research of the data and accuracy of description—contributed to the high standing of the Chileans. But Galdames concluded that these same qualities, admired in the 19th century, were not necessarily admirable in the 20th. Extensive detail was no longer regarded as virtuous, and books on almost every person in the nation's past were looked upon as excessive biographical scrutiny. Finally, the almost exclusive emphasis upon political history had ceased to be accepted as the proper method. By 1929 Galdames argued that the time had come to amplify the history that had already been produced by moving into social, economic, intellectual, moral, and juridical history to complement the already well-studied political past of the nation. Since he believed that history was the product of the collective action of many people, Galdames disdained the tendency toward biography and argued for a greater study of ideas that motivated groups of peoples as well as individuals. This, for Galdames, was the essence of the new historical method he advocated. Finally, he insisted that the narrative style of writing history that had predominated in the 19th and early 20th centuries must now give way to a synthesis of past events, including an explanation of why these events occurred. It was no longer valid, according to Galdames, merely to refer to events in the past; it was essential now to explain why and how these events came to pass. Simply stated, this argument was a refutation of the *Andrés Bello method of historiography and a movement toward the *José Lastarria concept of the 19th century, acknowledging that Galdames did not advocate Lastarria's views but something far beyond because Lastarria favored political and constitutional history and did not opt for emphasis on the other fields. Nonetheless, the Galdames argument was an indication that Chilean historiography was outgrowing, or had already outgrown, the earlier Bello method.

A. *El Decenio de Montt* (Santiago, 1904); *Estudio de la historia de Chile* (Santiago, 1906); *Geografía económica de Chile* (Santiago, 1911); *La evolución constitucional de Chile* (Santiago, 1911); *Valentín Letelier y su obra, 1852-1919* (Santiago, 1937); *A History of Chile*, trans. Isaac Joslin Cox (Chapel Hill, N.C., 1941); "Concepto de la historia," *Atenea*, 95, Nos. 291-292 (September-October 1949), pp. 297-308.

B. Percy Alvin Martin, *Who's Who in Latin America*, 2d ed. rev. (Stanford, 1940), p. 199.

GÁMEZ, JOSÉ DOLORES (12 July 1851, Granada, Nicaragua—8 July 1918, Rivas, Nicaragua). *Education*: Attended secondary school at the Instituto Nacional de Oriente; entered the School of Jurisprudence and Social Sciences, Universidad Nacional de El Salvador; self-educated. *Career*: Worked in commerce; wrote for the press; learned typography and telegraphy; founded the newspaper, *El termómetro*, in Rivas, 1878; delegate from Nicaragua to negotiations over a border dispute with Honduras; elected Deputy to the Legislative Assembly, 1896; President, Legislative Assembly; Secretary of Foreign Relations.

A political as well as a literary figure, Gámez figured prominently in Central American political and diplomatic activity while at the same time building a reputation as a journalist and historian. Because of his political activity he was exiled first to Costa Rica and later to Guatemala. He also participated actively in several battles between Nicaragua and El Salvador in 1885. Throughout his career he wrote constantly and published many of his literary works, which included novels, essays, and histories.

Many Central American writers of history preceded Gámez, but few were as thorough in tracing the development of the region. His books frequently stirred opposition and launched polemics, but he generally defended himself well because he had researched carefully in the archives and he had the documentation to support his arguments and his views. He worked mainly in the conquest and colonial periods, clarifying points that had been made by other writers and analyzing carefully the events of his nation's history, looking at the lives and contributions of men and at the temper of the times in the nation. He stirred so much opposition and hatred with his history that he did not continue publishing it in subsequent volumes as he had planned because he wanted to avoid the hostility and clamor that had come his way with the earlier work. Thus, much of his historical effort remained unpublished at the time of his death. But his published efforts set the stage for later literary activity in the nation, and he not only provided commentary on the past but chronicled his own age in periodicals and newspaper articles. He looked carefully at the ideas of the post-independence period and how they affected his native country and Central America as a whole. Gámez was a passionate, partisan political figure who could never escape from the political wars that surrounded him, and he found himself more than once involved in the struggle that so intrigued him. But because of his personal political exierence he was able to bring to his political histories an understanding and sensitivity that historians who were not directly involved could not approximate. He was a major Central American historian who like a number of others from this region also wrote *artículos de costumbres* (articles about customs), which reflected his interest in society as well as history and which enhanced his historical efforts.

A. *Catecismo de historia patria* (Managua, 1889); *Historia de Nicaragua desde los tiempos prehistóricos hasta 1860, en sus relaciones con España, México y Centro-América* (Managua, 1889); *Archivo histórico de la República de Nicaragua* (Managua, 1896); *Compendio de historia de Centro-América* (Managua, 1900); *Rafael Carrera y Justo Rufino Barrios ante la historia; discusión entre José Dolores Gámez y Enrique Guzmán en el año de 1889* (Managua, 1907); *Historia de la Costa de Mosquitos (hasta 1894) en relación con la conquista española, los piratas y corsarios en las costas centro-americanas, los avances y protectorado del gobierno inglés en la misma costa y la famosa cuestión inglesa con Nicaragua, Honduras y El Salvador* (Managua, 1915-1939).

B. Unión Panamericana, *Diccionario de la literatura latinoamericana: América Central; Honduras, Nicaragua y Panamá* (Washington, D.C., 1963), pp. 210-211.

GARCÍA, GENARO (17 August 1867, Fresnillo, Mexico—26 November 1921, Mexico City). *Education*: Primary studies in San Luis Potosí; secondary and professional training in the law, Mexico City. *Career*: Director, National Preparatory School; Director, National Museum; Professor, the National Conservatory of Music and the School of Jurisprudence; admitted to the practice of law, 1891.

The son of Trinidad García, who was a member of President Porfirio Díaz'cabinet, Genaro García was far more interested in a scholarly and academic career than fighting on the political battlefields of 20th century Mexico. While he did pursue an administrative career in the academic world, he was more the scholar whose intense historical curiosity carried him to publish almost 100 works in his 30-year career. Many of these books were collections of documents on Mexican history, but others were scholarly monographs that illuminated various facets of Mexico's past. Unfortunately, the last year of his life was a painful experience as he suffered from pernicious anemia that immobilized him and ended his scholarly career.

As a knowledgeable intellectual and writer, García became involved in several polemics that were waged through the periodical press of Mexico. The most extensive quarrel erupted over the ethics and righteousness of the Spanish conquest of America, while another polemic was fought over the use and morality of the duel, which was quite common in that period. But García's primary writing focused upon historical monographs that covered events in the colonial and independence periods of Mexican history, works such as *Carácter de la conquista española en América y en México*. With these books García built a solid reputation not only among Mexican scholars but with foreigners as well. To produce these books he required primary and secondary documentation, and he collected materials carefully over his lifetime. Some Mexican scholars believed that he had, at the time of his death, the richest personal historical library in all of Mexico.

A. *Apuntes sobre la condición de la mujer* (Mexico City, 1891); *Carácter de la conquista española en América y en México* (Mexico City, 1901); *Bernal Díaz del Castillo* (Mexico City, 1904); *Don Juan de Palafox y Mendoza* (Mexico City, 1906); *Documentos históricos mexicanos*, 7 vols. (Mexico City, 1910-1911); *Bibliografía de la independencia de México* (Mexico City, 1937).

B. *Diccionario Porrúa de historia* (Mexico City, 1967), I, p. 818; "Notes," *Hispanic American Historical Review*, 4, No. 1 (February 1921), p. 213; and Herbert I. Priestly, "Death of Genaro García,"*Hispanic American Historical Review*, 4, No. 4 (November 1921), pp. 772-773.

GARCÍA, JUAN AGUSTÍN (12 April 1862, Buenos Aires—23 June 1923, Buenos Aires). *Education*: Doctor of Law, University of Buenos Aires. *Career*: Professor of Law and Sociology, University of Buenos Aires and University of La Plata; Professor of World and American History, School of Philosophy and Letters, University of Buenos Aires.

At the turn of the 20th century Argentine literature was still influenced by the great writers of the mid- to late 19th century. García, who had earned a Doctor of Law degree before he was 20, was deeply affected by the atmosphere of the traditional type of letters as opposed to the modern. Like his 19th century predecessors, he did not limit his teaching to history but also taught classes in law and sociology and wrote in these disciplines as well. He believed that if Argentine intellectuals were to be able to build a national culture, which many sought at the time, they would have to use history to achieve that aim. He argued that scholars must find points of agreement in the past concerning Argentine politics, sociology, economics, and sciences. García felt that sociology was a national social science, and he adhered closely to the philosophy of sociology's founder Auguste Comte but went beyond Comte to link sociology to an awareness of history.

As a historian García was devoted to extensive archival research combined with rigorous critical analysis. His major contribution to the study of the past was his relentless examination of the papers of the Municipal Council (Cabildo) of Buenos Aires during the independence war and his subjection of these documents to the scrutiny of sociological methodology. The result was significant basic research in an important period of Argentine history. Stylistically, García's histories were a little cold and aloof, even when dealing with a period of history in which passions were almost constantly heated. Some critics objected to this type of history, but his work, nonetheless, was well received and he was regarded by his peers as one of the most accomplished Argentine historians of the 20th century.

A. *El régimen colonial* (Buenos Aires, 1898); *Introducción al estudio de las ciencias sociales argentinas* (Buenos Aires, 1899); *La ciudad indiana: Buenos Aires desde 1600 hasta mediados del siglo XVIII* (Buenos Aires, 1900); *Memorias de un sacristán* (Buenos Aires, 1906); *Historia de la universidad de Buenos Aires y de su influencia en la cultura argentina*, 5 vols. (Buenos Aires, 1921).

B. Rómulo D. Carbia, *Historia crítica de la historiografía argentina desde sus origines en el siglo XVI* (La Plata, 1939), pp. 283-290; and Roberto F. Giusti, *Diccionario de la literatura latinoamericana: Argentina* (Washington, D.C., 1961), pp. 55-56.

GARCÍA, RODOLFO (25 May 1873, Ceará-Mirim, Río Grande do Norte, Brazil—14 November 1949, Rio de Janeiro). *Education*: Ginásio Pernambucano; LL.B., University of Recife, 1908; Escola Militar in Ceará and Rio de Janeiro. *Career*: Journalist; Professor in Pernambuco, 1895-1912; Director, Museu Histórico Nacional, 1930-1932; Director, Biblioteca Nacional, Rio de Janeiro, 1932-1946.

Trained as both a scholar and a military officer, García devoted his life to intellectual pursuits while shunning his martial background. He was also interested in journalism early in his career, and from this association he developed a crisp, concise, informative writing style, which he carried into his historical writing. He did not produce much of a scholarly nature in comparison with many of his contemporaries, but his books and articles were sound, scholarly, and important for use by other scholars. Not only did he work in the discipline of history but he also wrote in the field of languages, and he was always interested in archival, library and bibliographical materials. In addition, he was an editor of the work of others and brought into print several significant pieces of scholarship that might never have become available to the public without his efforts.

García compiled bio-bibliographical essays on noted Brazilians such as *Francisco Adolfo de Varnhagen, and he annotated documentary materials that dealt with Brazilian history. Ultimately, he served as a general editor of the Documentos Históricos series. Meanwhile, he shifted the emphasis of his historical work to focus upon political history. When he died he left in manuscript form a political history of Brazil that was published posthumously. Although his historical production was comparatively sparse, he was highly regarded by his contemporaries and enjoyed a respected scholarly reputation not only in Brazil but in Uruguay and Europe as well. His contributions to Brazilian historiography were appreciated mainly by scholars since he was little known among the general Brazilian reading public.

A. *Dicionário de brasileirismos* (Rio de Janeiro, 1915); *Ensaio biobibliográfico sobre Francisco Adolfo de Varnhagen, Visconde de Porto Seguro* (Rio de Janeiro, 1928); *Cartas do Brasil do Pe. Manoel da Nobrega* (Rio de Janeiro, 1929); *Diálogos das grandezas do Brasil* (Rio de Janeiro, 1930); *Nomes do parentesco em lingua tupi* (Rio de Janeiro, 1944).

B. Ronald Hilton, *Who's Who in Latin America: Brazil*, pt. 6 (Stanford, 1948), p. 102; "Personal News," *Hispanic American Historical Review*, 30, No. 4 (November 1950), pp. 565-566.

GARCÍA DEL RÍO, JUAN (1794, Cartagena, Colombia—13 May 1856, Mexico City). *Education*: Studied in Cádiz, Spain, but generally self-taught through extensive reading of French and English authors. *Career*: Journalist; Minister of State in Peru under José de San Martín; founded the Biblioteca Nacional in Peru; sent by San Martín to London to attempt to set up non-Spanish monarchies in Latin America; Senator of the Republic of New Granada; Minister of Finance in Ecuador; Minister of Finance in Peru; founder and editor of *El argos de Chile, El museo de ambas Américas*, and *El mercurio* in Chile; traveled through Mexico.

García del Río was one of a group of 19th century Latin Americans who lived and worked in countries other than those of their birth. These wandering writers moved from nation to nation with the same ease that most people moved from city to city within a country. The result was that García del Río was not well known at home in Colombia because he spent so much time abroad. As a young man, while living with relatives in Spain, he attended parliamentary meetings and listened to the speeches of the Spanish politicians expressing their disdain for the colonies. This experience turned him into a liberal revolutionary and excited in him the patriotism of being an American. Once Cartagena was declared independent, he returned to Colombia and edited a liberal journal. In 1815 he fought to defend Cartagena from a Spanish counter attack. When the province fell he was exiled to Chile, where he founded two literary publications. Meanwhile, he continued his political activity in addition to writing for the press, and he became a friend of the great Venezuelan writer and scholar who spent most of his life in Chile, *Andrés Bello. In Santiago, García del Río helped launch the Generation of 1842, a surge of intellectual activity that sought to bring Chile into the forefront of literary production in Latin America.

Politically, García del Río was a monarchist who favored a non-Spanish royal system for Latin America. When he realized that this was impossible, he then accepted republicanism and worked to make the democratic system work. He admired both San Martín and Bolívar and wrote sympathetically about both men. His histories also included not just biographical material or political narrative but also political ideas and philosophies. He was a writer with a clear style and a logical perspective on political, historical, and literary subjects. His view of history was that it was essential for the human race in order to understand the present and prepare for the future. In one article he likened history to a religion with mysteries, dogmas, and doctrines to which adherents ascribed fully. History was a teacher that could advance man's knowledge of himself and his culture and could also favorably affect his political system. History determined the advantageous methods of political rule as well as the detrimental ones, and in each case could illustrate to the people how their lives should be led and their governments function. In his own histories he sought to instruct future generations about the independence era and about independence leaders.

A. *Meditaciones colombianas* (Bogotá, 1829); *Consideraciones sobre la política y el caracter del Dictador de la República Argentina* (Valparaiso, Chile, 1842); *Sitio de Cartagena de 1815* (Bogotá, 1843); *Biografía del General San Martín (Paris, 1844); Pizarro: Traducción de la tragedia de Mr. Sheridan* (Valparaiso, Chile, 1844); *Página de oro en la historia de Colombia* (Bogotá, 1897).

B. Antonio Gómez Restrepo, *Historia de la literatura colombiana* (Bogota, 1943), III, pp. 175-197; and Unión Panamericana, *Diccionario de la literatura latinoamericana: Colombia* (Washington, D.C., 1959), pp. 45-47.

GARCÍA GRANADOS, RAFAEL (20 February 1893, Mexico City—7 January 1955, Mexico City). *Education*: Instituto Científico de Mexico; St. Louis College, Texas; bachelor's degree in agricultural engineering, Institute Agricole de l'Etat, Gembloux, Belgium; master's degree in historical sciences, University of Mexico. *Career*: Professor of Ancient Mexican History and the History of the Conquest; Chairman, Department of History, National University of Mexico; Director, Historical Institute, National University of Mexico, 1949; Professor of Ancient Mexican Historical Sources, National School of Anthropology; Chairman, Department of History, National School of Anthropology; President, Sociedad de Estudios Cortesianos; Visiting Professor, University of Seville, Spain, 1935; lectured at various U.S. universities, 1942.

The great-grandson of the renowned Mexican historian *José Fernando Ramírez, Rafael García Granados gravitated naturally to the study of his nation's past. He was not as diverse in his activities as his illustrious ancestor, confining himself rather to a career in teaching and researching history, anthropology, and archeology. He enjoyed visiting pre-Colombian sites, where he perused carefully artifacts and decaying buildings from Mexico's prehistoric and early colonial days. He liked to study ancient cathedrals, bridges, and convents, and he learned a great deal about Mexico's early years from these remains. As a teacher he was an inspiration to an entire generation of students that he guided through the historical maze to mold into accomplished historians and anthropologists. In his classes he seldom lectured but instead outlined a historical problem and set the students to work in documents and archeological digs to solve it. Not only was he an outstanding teacher but he was also an important asset to his historical colleagues. As Director of the Historical Institute he published many historical monographs written by colleagues, and he gave each one his own personal attention. Every book he published was carefully prepared for the press so that each publication became something of which he and the authors could be proud.

Teaching and some educational administrative work were important parts of García's life, but his major interest was historical research. He spent long hours each day poring over documents and primary source material to be used in his own monographs and articles. Beyond his personal use, however, he wanted other historians to be aware of the sources he uncovered. To that end he ordered and classified data, making it available for all to use. He did not think only in terms of Mexican scholars in his bibliographical work but instead tried to improve the research climate for historians from all lands. Anthropologists and historians from many countries visited with him and learned about the materials available for their projects from him. Of his own work, the best-known piece is his three-volume bibliographical dictionary of ancient Mexican history, *Diccionario biográfico de historia antigua de México*, but he also wrote many articles and several books on the colonial era in Mexican history.

A. *Historia de Porfirio Díaz*, 4 vols. (Mexico City, 1928); *Huexotsingo: La ciudad y el convento franciscano* (Mexico City, 1934); *Xochimilco* (Mexico City, 1934); *Sillería del coro de la antigua iglesia de San Agustín*, 2 vols. (Mexico City, 1941); *Diccionario biográfico de historia antigua de México*, 3 vols. (Mexico City, 1952-1953); *El hospital de Jesús* (Mexico City, 1956).

B. Charles Dibble, "Obituary Note: Rafael García Granados (1893-1955)," *Hispanic American Historical Review*, 36, No. 3 (August 1956), pp. 381-384; *Diccionario Porrúa de historia* (Mexico City, 1967), p. 827; and Robert A. Potash, "Historiography of Mexico Since 1821,"*Hispanic American Historical Review*, 40, No. 3 (August 1960), p. 396.

GARCÍA ICAZBALCETA, JOAQUÍN   (21August 1825, Mexico City—26 November 1894, Mexico City). *Education*: Studied under tutors; aided by his father in preparing written work for publication. *Career*: Wrote historical articles and books, some of which he published on his own press; wrote books on biography, linguistics, and language development.

For many Mexicans the independence war period was a traumatic and difficult age. Especially for those of some wealth, the struggle for freedom from Spain and the subsequent turmoil as the new nation sought to establish itself on firm ground was extremely difficult. When García Icazbalceta's parents were confronted with this situation they opted to leave Mexico and return to Spain. In 1829, when García was but 4 years old, the family settled in Cádiz, and his early formative years were spent under the Spanish monarchy. The family did not return to Mexico until he was 11 years old, in 1836. He was a precocious young boy who began writing and editing at a youthful age. As a young man he translated Prescott's *History of the Conquest of Peru* into Spanish. At the same time, he studied philology and subsequently wrote books on the Spanish language. He worked extensively in the classics, and his love of the language and of classical literature was sharpened during this period of his life. But his major interest was history, and throughout his life he worked in historical subjects and wrote on historical themes. Moreover, he copied and published many manuscripts written by others that were in danger of being lost.

During his lifelong work in history, García collected documents, chronicles, and important manuscripts that he used in writing his various historical studies, until he built a large, important personal library. When he could not acquire the materials he needed, he took notes on them in libraries and archives and used the notes for his sources. He was primarily interested in the history of 16th century Mexico, which he regarded as the most significant era in Mexican history because it bound together all other historical periods. In addition to his talent for research and his analytical abilities, García Icazbalceta was also a master prose stylist. His graceful literary style was honed on the classics during his youthful years. It has been said of his work that he could make even the most arid material into a pleasant reading experience. He worked mainly in Mexican history but built a reputation among historians in other countries as well as his own. He was also a major biographer of Mexicans, and perhaps his most famous work was his biography of Juan de Zumárraga, the first Bishop and Archbishop of Mexico, *Don Fr. Juan de Zumárraga primer Obispo y Arzobispo de México*. In this work Garcia revealed a considerable talent for analyzing material and for a critical attitude that would not permit him to accept details at face value without careful scrutiny and analysis to determine veracity and authenticity.

A. *Carta de Hernán Cortés al Emperador Carlos V* (Mexico City, 1865); *Don Fr. Juan de Zumárraga primer Obispo y Arzobispo de México* (Mexico City, 1881); *Bibliografía mexicana del siglo XVI* (Mexico City, 1886); *Carta acerca del origen de la imagen de Nuestra Señora de Guadalupe de Mexico, escrita al Ilmo. señor Arzobispo don Pelagio Antonio de Labastida y Dávalos* (Mexico City, 1896); and *Descripción del Arzobispopado de México hecha en 1570 y otros documentos* (Mexico City, 1897).

B. Donald C. Briggs and Marvin Alisky, *Historical Dictionary of Mexico* (Metuchen, N.J., 1981), pp. 91-92; *Diccionario Porrúa de historia* (Mexico City, 1967), I, p. 828; and Aurora M. Ocampo de Gómez and Ernesto Prado Velázquez, *Diccionario de escritores mexicanos* (Mexico City, 1967), pp. 127-129.

GARCÍA ORTIZ, LAUREANO (19 July 1867, Río Negro, Colombia—4 November 1945, Bogotá). *Education*: Colegio de la Paz and Colegio de Martínez y Herrán, Medellín, Colombia; School of Natural Sciences and Agronomy, National University, Bogotá. *Career*: Diplomat, teacher, editor, banker, bibliophile, and historian; Owner and Director of the newspaper, *El liberal*, 1917; Representative from Antioquía, Chamber of Deputies, 1917; Senator from Santander, 1930; Minister of Foreign Affairs, 1918-1921; Ambassador on special assignment to Rio de Janeiro, Santiago, and Buenos Aires, 1925; Minister Plenipotentiary to Chile, 1933-1934; Professor of Political and Diplomatic History, National School of Law, 1939; and Member, National Economic Council, 1939.

Through much of the later 19th and into the first half of the 20th centuries Colombia was wracked by profound political struggles that on more than one occasion burst forth in violent insurrections and civil wars. The career of Dr. García Ortiz paralleled this bitter political warfare, which influenced his thinking and scholarship. Politically he was one of the nation's foremost liberals so that his fortunes rose and fell with the success or failure of that political force. He was partially insulated from the immediate clashes, however, by virtue of his diplomatic activity, which carried him outside the country for long periods of time. However, he also spent considerable time in Bogota, holding appointive and elective domestic offices when the liberals were in control.

García's contributions to Colombian historiography were mainly twofold. He was an inveterate bibliophile who collected books, manuscripts, and documents throughout his lifetime and preserved them in his personal library. Shortly before his death a part of the library was acquired by the Banco de la República, where it remains available for scholars to use. Besides his bibliographical proclivities, García was an accomplished scholar who, unfortunately, because of his other interests and his political and diplomatic careers, had too little time to devote to publishing the fruits of his research. However, he did make a singular contribution to Colombian letters with his studies of the early independence leader Francisco de Paula Santander, which he published in one volume in 1918 under the title, *El caracter del General Santander*. These profiles of Santander were well researched and carefully analytical as García presented a generally objective account of the independence hero's contributions to Colombian independence and early nationhood.

A. *El caracter del General Santander* (Bogotá, 1918); *Conversando* (Bogotá, 1925); *Estudios históricos y fisionomias colombianas* (Bogotá, 1938); *La sociología del nacionalismo moderno, y un ensayo sobre la democracía* (Quito, 1938); *Las Ciudades confederades del Valle Cauca en 1811* (Bogotá, 1943).

B. "Death of Laureano García Ortiz,"*Hispanic American Historical Review*, 26, No. 2 (May 1946), pp. 276-277; Percy Alvin Martin, *Who's Who in Latin America*, 2d ed. rev. (Stanford, 1940), p. 210.

GARCILASO DE LA VEGA (12 November 1539, Cuzco, Peru—22 April 1616, Córdoba, Spain). *Education*: Early education under the direction of clerical tutors; learned Quechua and Latin. *Career*: Enlisted in Philip II's Spanish army; served as a captain, 1564-1574; took minor religious orders; Chief Steward, Hospital of the Immaculate Conception, Córdoba; writer.

As a young boy living in Cuzco, Garcilaso grew up listening to tales of the pre-Hispanic Inca civilization of which his mother was a member. His father was a Spaniard. Garcilaso was enthralled with the stories his mother and others told of this early period, and throughout his lifetime he maintained an active interest in this period of Peruvian history. When his mother and father died he left Peru and took up residence in Spain, where he met and talked with conquistadors and others who had visited the New World. His economic situation was not very secure following a stint in the Spanish army, and he wrote to maintain himself, albeit at a low level. He published translations and wrote a story of the activity of Hernando de Soto in Florida. This was reportedly based on an eyewitness account that he managed to acquire. However, his major effort was a study of the pre-Hispanic period in Peruvian history.

The work on the pre-Colombian era, *Comentarios reales*, became widely read and greatly respected. The study was based upon an account written in Latin by a Jesuit priest, Blas Valera, which came into Garcilaso's possession when he lived in Córdoba, Spain. Once his interest was excited he wrote back to friends in Peru for Inca records, and he of course remembered all the exciting tales that his mother and others had told him as a child. Consequently, a part of the book resembles a memoir, but the rest of it was based on Spanish chroniclers who worked in Peru. Garcilaso complained, however, that their work was too partisan, without understanding that his own *Comentarios* were also partisan. But Garcilaso's study was of immeasurable importance because of the feeling that he had for the era and the people and because, instead of a Spanish chronicler, he was a mestizo writer who provided the Inca side of the story of Peruvian pre-Colombian history. He became symbolic of the mestizo race in America, and although much of his history was idealistic and romantic, when discussing his own experiences it was authoritative. Garcilaso has been criticized by later scholars for his lack of rigorous analysis of sources, but he was not a historian in the modern sense of that term; instead, he was a preserver of facts and legends of the pre-Hispanic era and as such, vitally important for an understanding of the Inca Indians.

A. *La Florida del Inca* (Lisbon, 1605); *Comentarios reales de las Incas* (Lisbon, 1609); *First Part of the Royal Commentaries of the Yncas*, trans. Clements R. Markham (London, 1869-1871); *Works: A Critical Text*, trans. Hady Ward Keniston (New York, 1925); *The Incas*, trans. Alain Gheerbrant (New York, 1961).

B. Marvin Alisky, *Historical Dictionary of Peru* (Metuchen, N.J., 1979), p. 44; Helen Delpar, *Encyclopedia of Latin America* (New York, 1974), pp. 248-249; Francisco Esteve Barba, *Historiografía indiana* (Madrid, 1964), pp. 470-475; and A. Curtis Wilgus, *The Historiography of Latin America: A Guide to Historical Writing, 1500-1800* (Metuchen, N.J., 1975), pp. 70-73.

GARIBAY K., ÁNGEL MARÍA (18 June 1892, Toluca, Mexico—19 October 1967, Mexico City). *Education*: Studied at the Seminario de Mexico; ordained to the priesthood, 1917; studied French, Italian, German, English, Greek, Latin, Hebrew, and Nahuatl. *Career*: Parish priest among the aboriginal peoples, Central Mexico; wrote articles for periodicals and reviews; named Extraordinary Professor of the School of Philosophy and Letters, Universidad Nacional Autónoma de México, 1952; Director, Seminario de Cultura Nahuatl, Institute of History, Universidad Nacional Autónoma de México, 1956.

Among 20th century Mexican scholars there has been a continuing interest in the pre-Columbian period of their nation's history. One of the scholars at the forefront of this interest was Ángel Garibay, a priest who lived among the Indians of the central plateau for 20 years, learning the languages, studying the cultures, and amassing a vast amount of knowledge about these descendants of pre-Hispanic societies. At the same time, he studied the classics and learned the classical languages so that he translated from the Greek the works of Sophocles and Euripides and from Hebrew, the Bible. He wrote articles about the Indians and about languages that appeared in a large number of journals, and he displayed an active interest in the development of folklore as a discipline. After leaving the Indian communities he became a teacher and an educational administrator, but he continued to write about the pre-Columbian cultures and to perpetuate his interest in classical languages.

Garibay's major historical work was in Nahuatl literature. He immersed himself in all the available examples of this material, and because of his close contact with Indian communities he was able to emerge ultimately as the major authority on the subject. He worked extensively with Aztec poetry and epic poems that led to greater knowledge of the Indian culture and that opened new areas for study of the Indian past. Meanwhile, his work in literature pointed up the knowledge that pre-Hispanic Mexican literature played a significant role in the development of the rich culture of the region. He was also different from many of the other writers of history in the 20th century in that he did not write only about his native country but instead made translations of works from other nations and from earlier periods of time. His interest in the Indians extended his curiosity into the ancient Greco-Roman world, and his work in the period gave a richness to his Indian studies and a better understanding of the Indians than otherwise would have been possible.

A. *Épica náhuatl* (Mexico City, 1945); *La conquista espiritual de México* (Mexico City, 1947); *Historia de la literatura náhuatl*, 2 vols. (Mexico City, 1953-1954); *Supervivencias de cultura intelectual precolombina entre los otomies de Huitzquilucan* (Mexico City, 1957); *Vida económica de Tenochtitlán* (Mexico City, 1961).

B. *Diccionario Porrúa de historia* (Mexico City, 1967), p. 834; and Aurora M. Ocampo de Gómez and Ernesto Prado Velázquez, *Diccionario de escritores mexicanos* (Mexico City, 1967), pp. 133-135; Ernesto de la Torre Villar, "Ángel María Garibay Kintana," *Revista de historia de América*, Nos. 63-64 (January-December 1967), pp. 181-182.

GARZÓN MACEDA, CEFERINO (25 August 1895, Córdoba, Argentina—29 March 1969, Córdoba). *Education*: Law degree, University of Córdoba, 1918. *Career*: Taught history at the National University of Monserrat, juridical and social sciences at the National Univeristy of the Litoral, 1920-1921, economic history at the National University of Córdoba, 1940-1946, contemporary political theory at the University of Puerto Rico (Río Piedras), 1949, economic sciences at the University of Córdoba, 1955; social and economic history at the University of Córdoba, 1956; named Director, Institute of Americanist Studies, University of Córdoba, 1956; Director, School of Philosophy and Humanities, University of Córdoba, 1960-1962.

Garzón Maceda was one of the most innovative historians of Argentina in the 20th century. He worked extensively in social and economic history when these areas were just beginning to attract the attention of sholars. Then, too, he recognized the value of archives and of archival research, and he studied and worked in archival administration until he gained recognition as one of the major archival administrators in Latin America. At the First Inter-American Meeting on Archives held at Washington, D.C., in 1961, he presented a paper that reflected his thinking on the value of archives, "Professional Relations Between Archivists and Historians in Argentina.'' Garzón Maceda then returned to Argentina to help establish the School of Archivists in the National University of Córdoba.

Meanwhile, he continued his social and economic history research, and in 1941 he wrote a short paper that was widely acclaimed, ''An Economic Depression in Córdoba in the 18th Century.'' But he relied on techniques that were seldom used in Argentina or in other Latin American countries. For example, he added demographics to his economic studies. Even more innovative was his use of quantitative methods, systematizing data on computers, to develop his economic and social histories. The end result of his quantitative research was two articles on the economic history of Tucumán from the 16th to the 18th centuries. Although important to Argentine historiography, Garzón wrote much less than other Argentine historians of his age. Instead, he helped his students to put together their work, which did end in publication. Therefore, he was indirectly responsible for much Argentine statistical, quantitative, and demographic history, though he himself did not publish the research.

A. *Relaciones professionales entre los archiveros y los historiadores en Argentina* (Córdoba, Argentina, 1961); *Economía del Tucumán, siglos XVI-XVII: Economía natural y economía monetaria, rentas ecclesiásticas* (Córdoba, Argentina, 1965); and *Economía del Tucumán: Economía natural y economía monetaria; sigloso XVI, XVII, XVIII* (Córdoba, Argentina, 1968).

B. Emiliano Endrek, ''Ceferino Garzón Maceda,'' *Revista de historia de América*, No. 69 (December 1970), pp. 128-131.

GAVIDIA, FRANCISCO (27 December 1863, San Miguel, El Salvador—23 September 1955, San Salvador). *Education*: Completed primary school in San Miguel, 1880; attended the Liceo Nacional de Oriente; entered the National University of San Salvador to study law, but then turned to the study of literature and art; self-taught in many languages. *Career*: Corresponding Member, Royal Spanish Academy, 1885; taught languages at the University of El Salvador and at various secondary schools; Secretary of Public Instruction, 1895-1896; founded the Universidad Libre; Honorary President, Ateneo de El Salvador and Academia Salvadorena de la Lengua.

A true scholar of literature and language, Gavidia wanted to read all the great works, not in translation but in the original language. Beginning serious scholarship at the age of 15 he taught himself Greek, Latin, German, French, Italian, English, Sanskrit, Arabic, and Maya-Quiche. Not only could he read these languages but he was accomplished enough to translate poetry from them to Spanish and to maintain the approximate meter. As Secretary of Public Instruction he introduced new teaching methods and imported foreign educational material, but he also brought party politics to the university, which the President of the Republic ordered closed because of political differences with Gavidia. Later he gained a hemisphere-wide reputation by advocating the creation of an American philosophy, and when Ruben Dario visited San Salvador in 1882 he met Gavidia and the two became friends. As a result of that friendship Gavidia became a strong advocate of modernism in Latin American literature.

A student of poetry in a variety of languages as well as a poet in his own right, Gavidia contributed effectively to the literary development of El Salvador. In literature he was a follower of romanticism throughout his lifetime, although in other matters he was a modernist and a humanist. His life was varied and exciting. He was a journalist who wrote for periodicals in El Salvador, Guatemala, and Costa Rica. He also wrote dramas in which he used historical settings for his plots. He translated classics from the Greek, Latin, Italian, and English in addition to his original work. His interest in history was focused on his own country, and the major historical piece he produced was a general history of El Salvador, *Historia Moderna de El Salvador*, in which he emphasized the Spanish contribution to the political unity of Central America. Unlike many other historians of his era he also studied world history and world literature, utilizing the linguistic skills he had acquired during a lifetime of study. His style was sometimes confusing and obscure, but at other times it was clear and appealing. In all instances his work, whether in history or literature, was profound and, without question, erudite.

A. *Pensamientos* (San Miguel, El Salvador, 1880); *Salvadorenos ilustres* (San Salvador, 1901); *Lectura, ideológica o metódica* (San Salvador, 1905); *Historia moderna de El Salvador* (San Salvador, 1917-1918); *La formación de una filosofía propia o sea latino-americana: Discurso de apertura de clases de la Universidad de El Salvador* (San Salvador, 1931).

B. Philip F. Flemion, *Historical Dictionary of El Salvador* (Metuchen, N.J., 1972), p. 57; William J. Griffith, ''The Historiography of Central America Since 1830,'' *Hispanic American Historical Review*, 40, No. 4 (November 1960), p. 554; and Unión Panamericana, *Diccionario de la literatura latinoamericana: América Central: Costa Rica, El Salvador y Guatemala* (Washington, D.C., 1963), II, pp. 58-62.

GAY, CLAUDIO (18 March 1800, Draguignan, France—3 November 1873, Paris). *Education*: Studied natural science at the collège de Draguignan; studied also at the Museum d'Histoire Naturelle, Paris, and at the Sorbonne. *Career*: Taught physics and chemistry at the Colegio de Santiago, 1829; contracted with the Chilean government for a study of Chile's natural history; commissioned by the Chilean government to write a political history of the nation, 1836; research in Peru and the Archives of the Indies in Spain.

It appeared to the Chilean government in the generation after the independence wars that Chile was lagging behind other Latin American nations in the area of letters and intellectual development. Consequently, Mariano Egaña contacted the French naturalist Claudio Gay, who was carrying out a scientific study of Chile for Diego Portales, to ask that he write a general history of Chile. Gay began to collect materials for the study in 1838, and the work was published between 1844 and 1871 in eight volumes of text and two volumes of documents. Although he was not primarily a historian, Gay collected a vast amount of documentation that served later Chilean historians in their more specialized histories of the nation. Gay was sensitive to the developments in Chile, and he put into perspective the activities of the independence leaders of the nation. *Francisco Encina has noted that histories written in the 19th century on the independence era owed their fundamental base to Gay and his work. Encina went on to write that even as late as 1949 a history of the independence era could not be written without consulting Gay.

It is also of considerable interest that Gay's historical methodology fit neatly into the prevailing Chilean scheme developed by *Andrés Bello, which was to investigate sources exhaustively, submit the sources to a rigorous criticism, and present the findings in a clear, logical narrative account. There was in Chile another methodology advocated by *José Victorino Lastarria, which maintained that true history could be written only by fitting the past into philosophical models. The philosophical system builders believed that narrative history was anachronistic and too simplistic and only philosophical history had any validity. When critics attacked Gay's work on the grounds that it was narrative and not philosophical, he responded in a letter to Manuel Montt dated 7 September 1845, in which he argued that Chilean historiography had not at that time developed its basic research to the point where philosophical speculation was possible. The philosophical method might be valid for England or France but not for Chile, where the basic, fundamental histories had not yet been written. When that stage of historical development was reached, then, Gay assured Montt, he would suppport the philosophical historians. Interestingly, this is the same argument that Andrés Bello used in his historiographical polemic with Jacinto Chacón in defending narrative history.

A. *Historia civil de Chile*, 8 vols. (Santiago, 1844-1871); *Historia física y política de Chile según documentos adquiridos en esta república durante doce años de residencia en ella y publicada bajo los auspicios del supremo gobierno*, 2 vols. (Paris, 1844-1871); *Historia de la independencia chilena* (Paris, 1856).

B. Francisco Encina, "Breve bosquejo de la literatura histórica chilena," *Atenea*, 95, Nos. 291-292 (September-October 1949), pp. 38-40; and Guillermo Feliú Cruz, "Claudio Gay, historiador de Chile: Ensayo crítico," in Carlos Stuardo Ortiz, *Vida de Claudio Gay, 1800-1873*, 2 vols. (Santiago, 1973).

GAY, JOÃO PEDRO (20 November 1815, Altos Pirineus, France—10 May 1891, Montevideo). *Education*: Studied at the Seminary of Embrun de Gap, France. *Career*: Secretary to the Bishop of Gap; ordained in the priesthood, 1840; foreign missionary in Latin America; established a church for French immigrants in Uruguay; assigned to Brazil, first in Santa Catarina and then in Rio de Janeiro; taught French and mathematics at the Colégio do Padre Saraiva.

A priest who lived in various parts of South America, Gay was interested in writing history and in studying linguistics. He worked on mastering the Guarani language and the history of Jesuit missions in the La Plata region until he finally settled in Brazil, where he devoted his attention to his missionary activity and to study. Following the invasion of Brazil by the Paraguayans in the War of the

Triple Alliance, Gay fled to Uruguay, where he continued to write on aspects of Brazilian history until his death. Because of his activity in Brazil, his visits to historical sites, and his long scholarly career, Gay knew more about the history, geography, and indigenous languages of southern Brazil than most other people. Scholars from both Brazil and abroad consulted him about this Brazilian region, indicating that he had acquired by the time of his death a worldwide reputation. He was a political liberal who did not refrain from giving partisan sermons from the pulpit, but although he became involved in political questions, his main interest remained scholarship. He amassed an extensive bibliography of published books and unpublished manuscripts that covered a wide range of Brazilian history and that eventually became valuable not only for the information contained in them but as collectors' items. Gay's extensive knowledge of southern Brazil was important to the Brazilian nation in its boundary disputes with Argentina, and he was called upon by the Brazilian government to support its claims along the border with Argentina.

Father Gay's view of history was a relatively simplistic one. He believed that history in a general sense was the narration of facts. These facts could be gleaned from written eyewitness accounts or from oral testimony of participants in the event. Once the facts had been acquired it was then the task of the historian to use this material to develop the spirit of an era, to investigate the causes of events and the effects. The essence of Gay's historiography was the collection of extensive sources, the evaluation of tradition, and the interpretation of the material collected with the objective of arriving at the truth. He also believed that theology was an asset in mastering history because it enabled the historian to understand human beings, their society, and the actions they took. His major contribution was his *Historia de República jesuítica no Paraguai*, which was a clear example of his solid, analytical historical talent. This work displayed clearly his philosophy of history and his concept of the proper historical method.

A. *Historia de República jesuítica no Paraguai* (Rio de Janeiro, 1863); *A invasao Paraguay a na fronteiro brazileira do Uruguai* (Rio de Janeiro, 1867).

B. José Honorio Rodrigues, *Historia e historiadores do Brasil* (São Paulo, 1963), pp. 73-90.

GIL FORTOUL, JOSÉ (17 November 1861, Barquisimeto, Venezuela—15 June 1943, Caracas). *Education*: Doctor of Laws, Central University of Venezuela, 1895; attended classes given by José Martí in the Colegio Santa María and the Colegio Villegas. *Career*: Consul of Venezuela in Burdeos; delegate to several conferences and meetings in Europe; delegate to the Second Pan American Conference in Mexico City, 1902; served in the Venezuelan legation in Mexico City, 1933; Minister of Public Instruction, 1911-1912; President of the Senate, 1913 and 1915; President of the Council of Government; President of the Republic when the dictator Juan Vicente Gómez turned the government over to him while Gómez led troops against nonexistent invaders in 1913 in an effort to consolidate his hold on the nation.

Although completing his education in the field of law, Gil Fortoul early launched a career as a novelist while pursuing diplomatic activities. But after three mediocre novels he chose to follow the path of historical writing. Meanwhile, he continued his political career, which paralleled that of the long-term Venezuelan dictator Juan Vicente Gómez. In many of his public jobs Gil Fortoul sincerely attempted to function effectively and efficiently and to bring needed reforms, especially to the Ministry of Public Instruction, but the dictatorship was not conducive to change or reform, and before the end of his life Gil Fortoul frankly admitted that his public life had been based on mistakes and errors and his support of the dictator had itself been unfortunate. Nevertheless, he maintained the respect of his countrymen and with his fiction and nonfiction and his parliamentary oratory he gained fame and support from a large portion of the nation's population. This lofty position was solidified because of his success in diplomatic posts, which he fulfilled with distinction.

Gil Fortoul's literary reputation was based largely upon the histories he wrote. His inclination was to develop history through a series of chronological periods rather than to deal with specific events in monographic form. With this broad treatment he was able to bring more understanding to Venezuelan history than were those historians who confined their research to narrow subjects. Additionally, he did not restrict his work to political history, as was the practice in the 19th century and on into the early years of the 20th. Instead he wrote about the economic development of the country, about the society that was developing, and about the constitutional history of the nation. He also speculated upon psychological factors in politics and about ethics in government. Because he had been a long-term participant in the political leadership of the nation, the insights he brought to these questions concerning political development evolved not only from research but from his own practical experience. By combining research and experience he was able to produce several outstanding history books. Meanwhile, he championed the historical techniques of well-known European historians such as Oswald Spengler and Hipolito Taine, and he accepted the linkage of geography, sociology, psychology, and political science in writing history. Such a broadened outlook on historiography placed him in the forefront of the development of history in the 20th century in Venezuela, and his ideas and works carried a significant impact even beyond the boundaries of his native land to the other countries of Latin America.

A. *Filosofía constitucional* (Paris, 1890); *Filosofía penal* (Brussels, 1891); *El hombre en la historia* (Paris, 1896); *Historia constitucional de Venezuela* (Berlin, 1907); *De hoy para mañana* (Caracas, 1916); and *Páginas de ayer* (Caracas, 1944).

B. *Diccionario biográfico de Venezuela* (Madrid, 1953), pp. 437-438; Donna Keyse and G. A. Rudolf, *Historical Dictionary of Venezuela* (Metuchen, N.J., 1971), p. 62; Percy Alvin Martin, *Who's Who in Latin America* (Stanford, 1936), p. 218, and Arturo Uslar Pietri, *Letras y hombres de Venezuela* (Mexico City, 1948), p. 132.

GODOI, JUAN-SILVANO (12 November 1850, -1926, Assunción). *Education:* Studied at the Academy of the Immaculate Conception of Santa Fé,

Argentina. *Career*: Clerk, Superior Court; Deputy to the Constitutional Convention; leader of the 1877 and 1879 rebellions; Director General of the Library, Museum, and Archives of Paraguay, 1902; Minister Plenipotentiary to Rio de Janeiro; member, High Court of Justice; Delegate to the 17th Congress of Americanists; founder of the daily newspapers, *La discusión* and *Las provincias*, in Argentina.

Paraguay was ravaged by the War of the Triple Alliance in the 19th century, a war in which the nation's male population was decimated. Consequently, when the war finally ended the leaders who remained had to reestablish a government for the defeated country. To this end a constitutional convention was called, and Godoi, only 19 years old at the time, was selected one of the delegates. The constitution that emerged from the convention was a liberal document that coincided with the political philosophy of Godoi. In addition to his public service and his journalistic activity, Godoi was also an art collector. His collection, the Museo Histórico y de Bellas Artes de Juansilvano Godoi, was established in 1885 in Buenos Aires, a city where Godoi spent a good deal of his life, living in exile because of his political activities. Later the collection was moved to Asunción, where it is even today one of Paraguay's finest collections of art work, numismatics, and historical relics. Godoi also collected books and historical documents that were important for the development of later histories of Paraguay.

Godoi's historical works focused on biography, but he made use of the extensive collections of resource materials that he and others collected in the second half of the 19th century. He believed in complete study of all available materials before producing a history, but his major contribution was in the collection of materials that could be used by scholars for the production of historical studies. He did not limit himself to the printed word, and his museum collection is also a significant contribution to historiographical studies in Paraguay. One of the reasons he worked in the field of history was his conviction that history could be used to restore the morale of the Paraguayan people following the disastrous defeat suffered in the War of the Triple Alliance. Consequently, his histories are excessively patriotic, and most are now outdated by later, more objective studies.

A. *Monografías históricas* (Buenos Aires, 1893); *Mi misión a Río de Janeiro* (Buenos Aires, 1897); *Últimas operaciones de guerra* (Buenos Aires, 1897) *La muerte del mariscal López* (Asunción, 1905); *El baron de Rio Branco* (Asunción, 1912); *Documentos históricos* (Asunción, 1916).

B. Joseph R. Barager, "The Historiography of the Río de la Plata Area, Since 1830," *Hispanic American Historical Review*, 39, No. 4 (November 1959), p. 599; Efraím Cardozo, *Historiografía paraguaya* (Mexico City, 1959), p. 25; Charles J. Kolinski, *Historical Dictionary of Paraguay* (Metuchen, N.J., 1973), p. 108; and William Belmont Parker, *Paraguayans of To-Day* (New York, 1967), pp. 15-17.

GÓMARA, FRANCISCO LÓPEZ DE (2 February 1511, Gomara, Spain—1560, Spain). *Career*: Became a priest before the age of 20; participated in the siege of Algiers; chaplain to Hernán Cortés after his return to Spain.

Gómara met Cortés following the return of the famous conquistador to Spain, where he planned to live out the remaining years of his life. As Cortés' chaplain Gómara spent a good deal of time with Cortés and from him heard about the fantastic conquest of Mexico. Gómara then decided to set down for posterity this fabulous tale of courage, adventure, and glory, in spite of the fact that he never set foot in New Spain and that his primary source for the book, Cortés, could hardly be considered an impartial and objective witness. When in 1552 he tried to publish his work, he was amazed to learn that the Spanish authorities suppressed it because, in their judgment, it was not entirely accurate or factual. Yet other countries gained possession of the manuscript, and it was published in Italy, France, and England.

The study by the Spanish priest was challenged by many of his contemporaries who were less than sympathetic with Cortés, who was glorified by Gómara. His lack of documentation and the one-sided account were cited as shortcomings. The book so upset *Bernal Díaz del Castillo that he began his own book in order to set the record straight about the Mexico conquest. While the research of Gómara is open to question, he was able to produce a volume that described the American continent for Europeans who had not had the opportunity to cross the Atlantic. It is also true that while Bernal Díaz del Castillo set out to disprove Gómara's account of the conquest of Mexico, Cortés emerged from Bernal Díaz' book with nearly as much glory as he had received from Gómara. Since Cortés was the primary source for the work, the book does reflect the conquistador's attitude toward the conquest, which was an important source for later histories of this monumental event.

A. *La historia de las indias y conquista de México* (Zaragosa, Spain, 1552); *Annals of the Emperor Charles V*, trans. Roger B. Merriman (Oxford, 1912).

B. John A. Crow, *The Epic of Latin America* (New York, 1946), p. 71; A. Curtis Wilgus, *The Historiography of Latin America: A Guide to Historical Writing, 1500-1800* (Metuchen, N.J., 1975), pp. 15-16.

GÓMEZ CARRILLO, ENRIQUE (27 February 1873, Guatemala City—29 November 1927, Paris). *Education*: Studied in the primary schools of Santa Tecla, El Salvador; received lessons from his mother; entered the Colegio La Enseñanza, Guatemala City, Instituto Nacional de Varones, Colegio Villatoro. *Career*: Worked in a commercial house; proofreader for *El guatemalteco*; reporter for *El imparcial*; wrote about Guatemala in Europe under a government stipend; wrote novels, criticism, and short stories; Consul General, Paris, 1898; Vice-Consul of Argentina in Paris, 1924.

Gómez Carrillo was an undisciplined youth whose parents transferred him to many different schools in the hope that he would take an interest in education and develop serious scholarly habits. They were never successful at this effort, and finally Gómez left secondary school to work for the press. When Ruben Dario visited Guatemala in 1890, he met Gómez Carrillo and suggested to the government that it send Gómez to Europe to write favorable accounts of Guatemala for the European press. Gómez was sent first to Paris and then to Madrid. Meanwhile he wrote several novels and short stories and gained a measure of fame. In 1895 he returned to Guatemala, surviving a shipwreck on his return passage. He visited Venezuela and stayed for a time in El Salvador. He continued to write and then returned to Paris and Spain in 1898. Also in 1898 he was named Consul General in Paris. At that time Ruben Dario arrived in Paris and roomed with Gómez. In 1905 Gómez visited Russia to cover the Russo-Japanese War. Later he traveled in India, China, and Japan as a reporter. In 1906 he toured Greece, Egypt, and the Holy Land, and in 1914 he served as a war correspondent in Europe for various newspapers, especially *La nación* of Buenos Aires, and in 1916 he assumed direction of *El liberal*.

Gómez' contribution to history was mainly in chronicling the events of his generation and in the development of the historical novel. Because of his adventurous, often turbulent, personal life and because he roamed so widely throughout the world in the midst of major global events, his views on Latin America and on life in general were regarded as important. His total lack of self-restraint contributed to a literary style that was exciting and emotional and thereby attractive to a wide audience. His historical novels were highly regarded both for their quality and for the style, which was a departure for this genre at the turn of the 20th century. Gómez was the first in Central America to adhere to the modernist literary school, which represented a significant change from the romantic historical novelists of the 19th century.

A. *Maravillas* (Madrid, 1899); *Flores de penitencia* (Paris, 1912); *Del amor, del dolor y del vicio* (Paris, 1913); *Treinta años de mi vida*, 3 vols. (Buenos Aires, 1919-1920); *Tres novelas immorales* (Madrid, 1920); *El evangelio de amor* (Madrid, 1922).

B. Richard Moore, *Historical Dictionary of Guatemala*, rev. ed. (Metuchen, N.J., 1973), p. 94; and Unión Panamericana, *Diccionario de la literatura latinoamericana: América Central; Costa Rica, El Salvador y Guatemala* (Washington, D.C., 1963), II, pp. 105-107.

GÓMEZ HARO, ENRIQUE (14 July 1877, Puebla, Mexico—9 February 1956, Puebla). *Education*: Studied law at the Universidad Católica. *Career*: Taught international, constitutional, and administrative law at the Universidad Católica; taught logic and Mexican history at the Normal Católica and the Católica Preparatoria, Puebla; held judicial posts in Puebla and Cholula; Secretary, City Council of Puebla; Editor, *Boletín municipal*; Honorary Consul of Venezuela in Puebla; lawyer; Commissioner of Historical Investigations and Inspector of Archives and Libraries, Puebla.

Gómez Haro was a scholar who taught philosophy, literature, and history and who published several collections of poems, all of which were well received by the literary community of his home state. Additionally, he practiced law and represented various prominent clients. Supporting himself in this manner he then had time to research historical themes and to publish his findings for his countrymen. Therefore, although he wrote poetry, his literary career rested more on his historical publications and on his skill, talent, and reputation as a historian.

Gómez' historical curiosity centered upon his home state of Puebla. As a regional historian he collected a vast amount of documentation that he used in developing the history of this area of Mexico. He was regarded by contemporaries as an able researcher in regional history who also had some success writing historical biography. Here again, however, he concentrated upon those figures who resided in Puebla. He was also a social and cultural historian who wrote about the historic development of music and poetry, and he did devote some time to researching and studying religious history. Although Gómez cannot be considered one of the primary historians of Mexico, he ranks among the best of the regional historians of his country.

A. *El episcopado y la civilización en Puebla* (Puebla, Mexico, 1907); *Puebla, cuna de la diplomacía mexicana* (Puebla, Mexico, 1933); *El venerable Palafox y Mendoza, bien-hechor de Puebla y de los indios, 1640-1940* (Puebla, Mexico, 1940; *Existencia legal de los seminarios lo que han sido para México* (Mexico City, 1944); *El lirio de Puebla* (Puebla, Mexico, 1947), *Hablan las calles* (Puebla, Mexico, 1951).

B. *Diccionario Porrúa de historia* (Mexico City, 1967), I, p. 886; Instituto Panamericano de Geografía e Historia, *Gúia de personas que cultivan la historia de América* (Mexico City, 1951), pp. 177-178; Aurora M. Ocampo de Gómez and Ernesto Prado Velázquez, *Diccionario de escritores mexicanos* (Mexico City, 1967), pp. 139-140.

GONZAGA JAEGER, LUÍS (10 July 1889, Bom Jardim, Río Grande do Sul, Brazil—21 January 1963, Pôrto Alegre, Brazil). *Education*: Studied at a semi-naray in Río Grande do Sul; transferred to the Jesuit College of Campolide, Portugal, 1909; completed his formal education at São Leopoldo, Río Grande do Sul; ordained in the Jesuit order, 1922. *Career*: Taught at the Colegio An-chieta, 1924-1963; Editor of the monograph series, *Jesuítas no Sul do Brasil*, which he began in 1952; Cofounder, Instituto Anchietano de Pesquisas, 1956.

Among the historians of Latin America a few have been members of religious orders, and several of those belonged to the Jesuit order. Father Jaeger was one of those who combined his commitment to the Church with his love for teaching and scholarship to become one of the outstanding Brazilian historians of the 20th century. He answered the call to a religious career early in life, and after studying in Brazil he was fortunate to have an opportunity to move to Portugal to continue his education. However, he was in Portugal at the time of a political upheaval that led to his imprisonment, along with many of his fellow students. While incarcerated he contracted tuberculosis, and upon his release he returned to Brazil to begin recuperation. Consequently, he was not ordained until 1922, 13 years after he began Jesuit training. Despite his misfortune he finally realized his dual goal of becoming a Jesuit and a teacher.

Although his education had not centered upon the discipline of history, once he became committed to the teaching and study of the past he soon emerged as one of the outstanding researchers in Brazil. His major historical interest was the Jesuit order in southern Brazil, and his research, although not limited to that theme, was heavily tilted in that direction. Yet he qualifies also as a regional historian as he examined economic and social developments in the state of Río Grande do Sul. However, he was most effective in writing about the Jesuits in Brazil, and to this end his research efforts were directed. He combined his historical study with his role as Vice-Advocate for the canonization of three Brazilian Jesuits, which resulted in a well-researched and heavily documented book, *Os três mártires río-grandenses*. His efforts in Jesuit and regional Brazilian history were significant for the total development of Brazilian history, and his work in the Instituto Histórico e Geográfico do Río Grande do Sul was beneficial to other scholars and to Brazilian students of history.

A. *As invasões bandeirantes no Río-Grande-do-Sul (1635-1651)* (Pôrto Alegre, Brazil, 1940); *Historia da introducão do gado no Río Grande do Sul (1634)* Pôrto Alegre, Brazil, 1943); *O heroi do Ibia* (Pôrto Alegre, Brazil, 1943); *São Leopoldo no seu primeiro centenario* (Pôrto Alegre, Brazil, 1947); *Indios río-grandenses civilizados pelos antigos jesuítas* (Pôrto Alegre, Brazil, 1954).

B. Rollie E. Poppino, "Luís Gonzaga Jaeger, S.J. (1889-1963)," *Hispanic American Historical Review* 45, No. 1 (February 1965), pp. 99-100.

GONZÁLEZ, JUAN VICENTE (28 May 1811, Caracas—1 October 1866, Caracas). *Education*: Bachelor's degree, Central University of Venezuela. *Career*: Taught grammar and history in various secondary schools, Caracas; opened his own school, El Salvador del Mundo, in which he also taught, 1849; National Deputy from Caracas, 1848; journalist; founder and Director of *La revista* (Caracas).

Juan Vicente González was one of the Venezuelan writers and scholars most adversely affected by the political chaos of the 19th century. He was a political conservative and served a term in the National Congress, but it was precisely at that time that one of the contending political-military factions chose to assault the Congress building, bringing casualties to those inside. González never forgot the bloody scene, and he longed for stable, peaceful government. But his prominence as a journalist and as a scholar would not permit him to avoid the struggles. Finally, his outspoken opposition led to an order for his exile, which was rescinded at the last moment, but he was briefly imprisoned in Caracas. As the nation settled down from its violent rampage, González was able to use the columns of Caracas newspapers and periodicals to attack what he believed to be injustice and errors in government. He became one of the most feared polemicists in the country as he slashed at his adversaries with sarcasm, knowledge, and a caustic writing style. This in addition to his irascible personality gained him a wide reputation as a major critic of Venezuela's political system..

González attempted to write poetry, but his major success was in journalism and in writing history. During his three-month imprisonment he wrote what became his most famous book, *Manual de historia universal*, which eventually emerged as a standard textbook for secondary school history classes. González wrote the book without books or source materials of any kind, putting it together completely from memory. Consequently there are obvious errors, but González acknowledged in the preface that such would be the case. He also wrote frankly of his conservative philosophy and of his staunch support for the Catholic faith, making it clear to his readers that these biases were bound to influence his work. His philosophy of history was basically attuned to the romantic school and was influenced by many of the European romantic historians. Additionally, he pioneered in Venezuela a new kind of study. He wrote a biography of José Félix Ribas, which turned out to be more a history of the period in which Ribas lived rather than a narrow biography of the subject. González was also fascinated by Venezuela's independence age and by the exploits of the great liberator Simón Bolívar. He championed the activities of the independence heroes and wrote sympathetically of their exploits, thereby feeding the patriotism of his countrymen through an appreciation of their history.

A. *Manual de historia universal* (Caracas, 1863); *Biografía de José Félix Ribas* (Paris, 1913); *Historia moderna* (Caracas, 1925); *Las mesenianas* (Caracas, 1932); *Historia y pasión de Venezuela* (Washington, D.C., 1950); and *Historia del poder civil* (Caracas, 1951).

B. *Diccionario biográfico de Venezuela* (Madrid, 1953), pp. 451-454; Donna Keyse and G. A. Rudolf, *Historical Dictionary of Venezuela* (Metuchen, N.J., 1971), p. 63; César Humberto Soto, *Personajes célebres de Venezuela* (Caracas, 1946); and Arturo Uslar Pietri, *Letras y hombres de Venezuela* (Mexico City, 1948), pp. 75-97.

GONZÁLEZ, OBREGÓN, LUÍS (25 August 1865, Guanajuato, Mexico— 19 June 1938, Mexico City). *Education*: Studied in the Escuela Nacional Preparatoria. *Career*: Founded the Liceo Mexicano Científico y Literario, 1885; wrote historical articles for *El nacional*, 1890; worked in the Museo Nacional de Antropología e Historia; Director of the commission to reorganize the National Archives, 1911; Director, National Archives; Chief of the National Archives' Historians, 1919.

González Obregón researched and wrote mainly about Mexico City. He published anecdotes and historical data about the city in newspapers, reviews, and periodicals. Many of these articles were later collected and put into book form. Few other Mexican historians have been as popular as González Obregón because he made history attractive and comprehensible to the man in the street. Writing in newspapers he acquainted Mexicans with their capital city and with life in and around that city from colonial times to his own era. While his work was sometimes light and frequently amusing stories were included, it was also scholarly because he had access to the archives of the nation and worked in them to build his articles and his books. He was so popular that the street on which he lived was renamed after him; up to that time in Mexico no street had ever been named for a living person.

Some contemporaries argued that González Obregón's work was not really history but instead a collection of amusing and sometimes informative tales. But his defenders responded that even if what he wrote was not history it was more valuable than history. It had all the research and thought behind it, and it was far more readable than much of the history that was circulating at the time. Likewise, it stirred the interest of the public because his work was so colorful and his depiction of the customs of the people so interesting to the public. Others suggested that his work was misleading. It appeared to lack sincerity and erudition, although it was supported by extensive labor in primary documents, which he knew how to interpret and analyze. Beyond the documents, however, González Obregón also read widely in the books and articles that had been written about Mexico and about the fables that had been transmitted over the generations so that he was able to capture faithfully life in Mexico City from the colonial age to the 20th century. Another observer wrote that González did not parade names and facts across the pages of his work but instead, like an artist, created a word picture that all could enjoy and from which everyone could profit. Still another writer suggested that he was the complete historian. He worked in documents, he related the material well, he possessed vast knowledge of his subject, and he had an easy literary style that enabled him to present his material in a pleasant fashion. He also possessed the imagination that permitted him to bring alive events from the distant past without losing the authenticity of his work. He brought Mexico's early social life to the people of his generation, and they were delighted to find the information presented so smoothly and in a readable form.

A. *Acta de la inauguración de las obras del desague del Valle de México* (Mexico City, 1900); *Breve reseña de las obras del desague del Valle de México* (Mexico City, 1901); *La limpia y desague de la ciudad de México al traves de los tiempos* (Mexico City, 1903); *Las sublevasciones de indios en el siglo XVII* (Mexico City, 1907); *La Biblioteca Nacional de México* (Mexico City, 1910); *La vida en México en 1810* (Mexico City, 1911).

B. A. Ma. Carreno, *El cronista Luís González Obregón* (Mexico City, 1938); *Diccionario Porrúa de historia* (Mexico City, 1967), I, p. 903; Percy Alvin Martin, *Who's Who in Latin America* (Stanford, 1936), p. 178; Aurora M. Ocampo de Gómez and Ernesto Prado Velázquez, *Diccionario de escritores mexicanos* (Mexico City, 1967), pp. 151-153; and Frederick Starr, *Readings from Modern Mexican Authors* (Chicago, 1904), pp. 118-131.

GONZÁLEZ SUÁREZ, FEDERICO   (12 April 1844, Quito—1 December 1917, Quito). *Education*: Studied in the School of Laws and Humanities at the University in Quito and at the Seminario de San Luís. *Career*: Member of the Jesuit order, 1862-1872; Secular priest in Cuenca, 1872-1883; Senator, National Congress, 1894; Bishop of Ibarra, 1895; Archbishop of Quito, 1906.

In the historiographic chronology of writers of Ecuadorean national history, González was the third after *Father Juan de Velasco and *Pedro Fermín Cevallos. Yet in terms of the quality of his work he stood head and shoulders above the other two. Despite early family misfortunes, his grandparents assured him an education, and members of the Church assisted in his early academic instruction and probably directed him to a career in the priesthood. While lack of funds was a problem for the young boy, an additional handicap was his poor health, which frequently forced him to stay away from school for long periods of time.

When these afflictions struck, Federico's mother usually continued to teach him at home, and he supplemented these lessons with extensive reading in diverse subjects.

González' work has been outstanding in history but not limited to that discipline. He also made his mark in science, literature, and politics and became a recognized authority in the field of letters. Nonetheless, his efforts in history were extremely important, and his fame is based largely upon historical writing. He read the works of both Father Velasco and Cevallos, and at first he intended only to continue the Cevallos study to bring it closer to his contemporary age. But as he read through the earlier multivolume general histories he made notations in the margins of factual errors and lacunae. When he had finished he found that he had so many comments that he decided to write his own version of Ecuadorian history. Once the decision had been made he began the task but quickly realized that the archives of Quito were not sufficient to carry out the necessary research. He then went to Spain, where he studied in the Archives of the Indies. After two years of exhausting work he wrote volume one of his history of Ecuador. That first volume was important not only as the initial step in his history but also because he linked archaeology with history in tracing the development of the aboriginal people in America. As other volumes appeared it became evident that he was a rigorous taskmaster and that he not only researched extensively but carefully criticized every document to ascertain its authenticity. So determined was he to find the truth that when dealing with the role of holy orders in the colonial period in volume four he criticized the Church and the priests for a number of scandals. In particular, the Dominican order came under heavy fire from González so that when the volume appeared there was a noisy, emotional outburst against it. González was forced to defend his work, and he even made an accounting of it before the Pope. Since the Vatican took no action against him, despite anguished cries from European and Latin American clerics, it appears that he had the evidence to support his contentions. He later wrote that he sought the truth in history and would not lie for any reason, even if his refusal to lie cost him his clerical position. His commitment to extensively researched history was firm and his determination to uphold the tenets of scientific historiography remained intact, despite vicious verbal attacks not only upon his history but upon his person as well. He was the greatest of the 19th century Ecuadorean historians and remains a giant in Ecuadorean historiography to this day.

A. *Estudio histórico sobre los cañaris, antiguos habitantes de la Provinca del Azuay, en la República del Ecuador* (Quito, 1878); *La conversión de San Agustín; discurso pronunciado el 7 de mayo de 1887* (Quito, 1887); *Historia general de la República del Ecuador escrita por Federico González Suárez, presbitero,* 7 vols. (Quito, 1890-1903); *Prehistoria ecuatoriana; ligeras reflexiones sobre las razas indigenas que poblaban antiguamente el territorio actual de la República del Ecuador* (Quito, 1904); *Memorias íntimas* (Quito, 1930); *Defensa de mi criterio histório* (Quito, 1937).

B. Albert William Bork and Georg Maier, *Historical Dictionary of Ecuador* (Metuchen,

N.J., 1973), p. 70; George A. Brubaker, "Frederico González Suárez, Historian of Ecuador," *Journal of Inter-American Studies*, 5, No. 2 (April 1963), pp. 235-248; Helen Delpar, *Encyclopedia of Latin America* (New York, 1974), p. 257; Nicolás Jiménez, *Biografía del ilustrisimo Federico González Suárez* (Quito, 1936); Adam Szaszdi, "The Historiography of the Republic of Ecuador," *Hispanic American Historical Review*, 44, No. 4 (November 1964), pp. 508-509, 511-514; and Unión Panamericana, *Diccionario de la literatura latinoamericana: Ecuador* (Washington, D.C., 1958), pp. 30-34.

GONZÁLEZ VÍQUEZ, CLETO (1858, San José—23 September 1937, San José) *Education*: Graduate of Santo Tomás University, 1889. *Career*: Practiced law; President of the Republic, 1906-1910 and 1928-1932; participated in the boundary dispute settlement with Panama, 1931; Foreign Minister, 1933; granted the award Benemérito de la Patria posthumously, 1944.

As a two-term president of the Republic, González Víquez had an opportunity to translate his ideas on politics and culture into reality. In his second term he relegated military spending to a level lower than that afforded education, with the result that Costa Rica was labeled a nation in which there were fewer soldiers than teachers. González' interest in politics and educational and cultural progress found expression in his historical production. His second term was marked by the disastrous worldwide depression of 1929, but he handled the crisis with such success that, unlike most national leaders of that age, he did not lose much popularity. He was a political liberal who did not want to impose dramatic change upon his people but who instead wanted to keep the nation stable, viable, and on an even keel. As president he emphasized educational expansion through-out the country and the extension of public health care to cover more citizens. Beyond these modest aspirations he advocated very little and never did espouse profound social or economic changes.

In his written work González Víquez dealt with contemporary problems of his nation, but he was also vitally interested in Costa Rica's past. He wrote about the economic and political institutions of the nation, making a significant contribution to the knowledge on these subjects. Additionally, he studied regional historical subjects as he wrote histories of major cities of Costa Rica. But his interests were far broader than those of the regional historian. He devoted con-siderable time to the erection and dissolution of the Central American Federation that emerged following independence. But even when dealing with all of Central America he continued to focus primarily upon his nation of Costa Rica, and he never lost sight of his nationalistic commitment to his homeland. Consequently, while his work on Costa Rica is important, he sacrificed an opportunity to create a comprehensive history of Central America because of patriotic considerations.

A. *Apuntes estadísticos sobre la ciudad de San José* (San José, 1905); *Dos proceres* (San José, 1918); *Carrillo y Costa Rica ante la Federación* (San José, 1919); *Manual para la policía judicial* (San José, 1929); *El sufragio de Costa Rica ante la historia y la legislación* (San José, n.d.).

B. Theodore Creedman, *Historical Dictionary of Costa Rica* (Metuchen, N.J., 1977), pp. 82-85; Helen Delpar, *Encyclopedia of Latin America* (New York, 1974), p. 257;

"González Víquez of Costa Rica Dies," New York *Times*, 24 September 1937, p. 21; and William J. Griffith, "Ths Historiography of Central America Since 1830,"*Hispanic American Historical Review*, 40, No. 4 (November 1960), p. 554.

GROOT, JOSÉ MANUEL (25 December 1800, Bogotá—3 May 1878, Bogotá). *Education*: Studied letters, mathematics, and painting in Bogotá. *Career*: Taught school; served two consecutive terms as Deputy in the National Congress; wrote books, monographs, verses, articles about customs, and hundreds of articles against Protestants, liberals, and "other heretics"; founded and directed for a short time two secondaray schools; and wrote for all the Catholic periodicals of Bogotá.

Groot was a sincere, devout individual who published his ideas on a wide variety of subjects but who was primarily a chronicler of customs and a historian. In all of his writing, both poetry and prose, he incorporated material about the customs of the people of Latin America. At the same time, his religious preoccupation meant that religion would also find a prominent place in his historical works, and he was consistently the defender of the faith in all religious issues. He believed that religion was bound up so close with civil and political history that these disciplines could not be separated. Therefore, he decided to defend the clergy with the true history of Colombia. He also defended the Spanish for their colonial activity, and he believed that he could set the record straight concerning their activity by writing the truth, as he understood it, of their colonial administration. Yet, at the same time, Groot did not quarrel with Colombia's right to independence. He wrote that the child who reaches adulthood has the right to gain his freedom, but he does not then have the right to calumny his father. Colombians did not have the right, in his view, to castigate their Spanish ancestors.

The era in which Groot worked in Colombia was a period in which there were no well-organized archives or libraries. Therefore he became a collector of historical materials, and he copied many of those he needed to explain historical events from official collections. He was sympathetic to the Spanish colonial experience and paid homage in his histories to many Spaniards who worked in colonial America. He was a staunch defender of the Catholic church as well as the Viceroyalty in his histories, but curiously he praised the founders of the independence republican government as well. His style was picturesque but not artistic, and he was not careful of his writing so that factual mistakes frequently crept into his books. He introduced many digressions when writing history and incorporated into his studies moral and philosophical judgments. Additionally, he used anecdotes and lengthy descriptions, which served to break up the narrative. His histories were weakened also because he was so quick to involve himself in polemics and to express his political and religious point of view. Yet his histories were generally complete and are useful as a major source of information. However, when he attacked Protestantism he displayed a general lack of understanding of the Protestant faith and a particular ignorance of the ethical and social aspects of the religion. One of his books challenged the religious views of the Protestant H. B. Pratt, but he was incapable of forging a logical attack on those views because, as one later scholar pointed out, he lacked the philological education to deal on an equal footing with erudite scholars. But Groot's works were not lacking in importance; they contained significant documents for the mid-century intellectual clashes in which he was involved. They were even of some importance outside of Colombia because they circulated throughout Latin America, and while his arguments might frequently have been faulty, the issues he raised were crucial to the mid-19th century.

A. *Los misioneros de la herejía o defensa de los dogmas católicos* (Bogotá, 1853); *Noticia biográfica de Gregorio Vasquez Arce y Cevallos* (Bogotá, 1859); *Refutación analítica del libro de Mr. Ernest Renan, titulado Vida de Jesús* (Bogotá, 1865); *Historia ecclesiástica y civil de Nueva Granada, escrita sobre documentos auténticos*, 3 vols. (Bogotá, 1869-1870); *Réplica al ministro presbiteriano H. B. Pratt* (Bogotá, 1876); *Dios y patria; artículos escogidos* (Bogotá, 1894).

B. José Manuel Groot, *Historia ecclesiástica y civil de Nueva Granada, escrita sobre documentos auténticos* (Bogotá, 1869-1870), I, p. 1; and Unión Panamericana, *Diccionario de la literatura latinoamericana: Colombia* (Washington, D.C., 1959), pp. 52-53.

GROUSSAC, PABLO (15 February 1848, Toulouse, France—27 June 1929, Buenos Aires). *Education*: Self-educated. *Career*: Taught mathematics, Colegio Nacional, 1870; wrote for *Revista argentina*; National Inspector of Education, 1874-1878; Editor of *Sud América*, 1884-1885; Director, Biblioteca Nacional, 1885-1929.

As a young man of 18, Groussac left his native France and sailed for Argentina. There he learned Spanish, wrote for the press, taught school, and held several governmental posts. His literary interests were widespread, including poetry, criticism, fiction, journalism, anthropology, folklore, and history. In his job as director of the Biblioteca Nacional he worked not only to build the library but also to expand the scholarly image of his office and of the library in general. He published scholarly reviews that included articles of a high order, written from materials held in the library. Additionally, he came to be recognized as a major scholar with an international reputation. In the late 19th century he was invited to the United States to read a paper on folklore. While in the United States he observed closely the nation and the people and returned home to write a perceptive account of North American life.

Groussac overcame a major handicap in his literary career by writing in a language other than his native tongue. Yet he became so adept at the Castilian language that his style was one of his strong points. But of greater importance were his ideas on history and how it should be written. He believed that history was both a science and an art, and he argued that primary documents should be examined, evaluated, and analyzed rigorously and scientifically. In this manner the historic truth would eventually emerge. However, as a literary man, Groussac realized that all too often this type of basic research yielded dull history. Consequently, history was also an art in his mind because history was also literature and the literary quality was an important aspect of the finished product. Therefore he believed that history should be interesting, colorful literature and well researched. For Groussac, history as art, as science, and as philosophy was all one; together these forms gave history its distinctive character and significance.

A. *Popular Customs and Beliefs of the Argentine Provinces* (Chicago, 1893); *Del Plata al Niagara* (Buenos Aires, 1897); *Santiago de Liniers, conde de Buenos Aires, 1753-1810* (Buenos Aires, 1907); *Estudios de historia argentina: El padre José Guevara—don Diego de Alvear—El doctor don Diego Alcorta—Las Bases de Alberdi y el desarrollo constitucional* (Buenos Aires, 1918); *Páginar de Groussac* (Buenos Aires, 1928), *Mendoza y Garay* (Buenos Aires, 1949).

B. Joseph R. Barager, "The Historiography of the Río de la Area, Since 1830," *Hispanic American Historical Review*, 39, No. 4 (November 1959), pp. 592-593; Roberto F. Giusti, *Diccionario de la literatura latinoamericana: Argentina* (Washington, D.C., 1961), pp. 70-74; and Ione S. Wright and Lisa M. Nekhom, *Historical Dictionary of Argentina* (Metuchen, N.J., 1978), p. 373.

GUERRA Y SÁNCHEZ, RAMIRO (1880, Havana—31 October 1970, Havana). *Education*: Degree in pedagogy, University of Havana, 1899. *Career*: Professor of Spanish Colonial and Cuban History, University of Havana, 1927-1930; Cuban representative, United Nations Economic and Social Council, 1946; Editor of *Diario de la marina* (Havana), 1946; Cuban delegate, United Nations Monetary and Financial Conference at Breton Woods, 1944; Cuban delegate, San Francisco Conference to complete the Charter of the United Nations Organization, 1943.

Guerra y Sánchez earned accolades for his rigorous historical method based upon extensive research in primary documentation and a careful analysis of his sources. Such work influenced other Cuban historians in the 20th century and led to a general acceptance of this rigorous type of historiography. Beyond his thorough research and studied analysis, Guerra y Sánchez also wrote history from a universal, or global perspective. Even when he was writing about a specific event in Cuban history he saw it as a world event and treated it in that fashion. His handling of Cuba's Ten Years War is indicative of this attitude. He wrote in the preface to that work that he believed it his duty to include every bit of information available on that event and to analyze it carefully. Contemporaries conclude that this book was the most complete on the subject ever written and, at the same time, a work that took into account other Cuban and Latin American developments.

Guerra also believed that his discipline was not static. He wrote that history changes as new materials and new interpretations take place. Each generation, he noted, "must write the history of its community with the materials available at the moment." Consequently, there should be many historical studies of each event in a nation's past, as each new generation makes its contribution to the total history of the nation. Morever, while each event must be recorded and analyzed, there must also be syntheses of the entire past experienced by a people.

For this reason he wrote his *Manual de historia de Cuba*, which he published in 1918. For all of his ideas on historiography and for his research and methodological expertise he has been called the "complete historian" and "the man who has contributed most to the modernization of history in Cuba."

A. *Historia de Cuba*, 2 vols. (Havana, 1921 and 1925); *Un cuatro de siglo de evolución Cubana* (Havana, 1924); *Contribución de las escuelas primarias a la independencia económica de la República* (Havana, 1926); *Azúcar y población en las Antillas* (Havana, 1927); *Manual de historia de Cuba* (Havana, 1938); *Guerra de los Diez Años*, 2 vols. (Havana, 1950-1952).

B. Francisco Dominguez-Company, "Dr. Ramiro Guerra y Sánchez," *Revista de historia de América*, No. 70 (July-December 1970), pp. 498-500; "Ramiro Guerra, 90, Author-Sociologist," New York *Times*, 1 November 1970, p. 84.

GUTIÉRREZ, ALBERTO (18 September 1963, Sucre, Bolivia—30 October 1927, La Paz). Education: Graduated from the secondary school, Colegio Junín de Sucre, at 16; studied law at the University of Charcas. *Career*: Adjutant of the Bolivian legation in Paris, 1882; Undersecretary of Foreign Relations, 1900; Foreign Service officer in the United States; Minister in Chile, Brazil, Ecuador, Colombia, Venezuela, and England; Chancellor of the Republic under Gutiérrez Guerra and Saavedra y Siles; Deputy, 1912-1920; Journalist with *El día* (Sucre) and *El heraldo* (Valparaiso).

In all of his writings Gutiérrez was proper and academically sound. He did not become impassioned in polemical writing or in his scholarly work. He was ever the reasonable advocate of whatever position he was defending, which was a style vastly different from many of the other writers of his era. Nevertheless, his opposition to what he considered dictatorial governments led to his exile in 1892 in Chile, where he remained for six years. It was during these years that he wrote articles for *El heraldo* in Valparaiso in which he defended Bolivia in the press of its mortal enemy, Chile. His lifetime spent in a diplomatic career probably contributed to his gentlemanly image as a writer. He was, like so many Bolivian historians, a follower of *René-Moreno, but he was far more reserved in his literary output than the famous leader of Bolivian historiography.

In his books Gutiérrez used a technique that resembled 20th century psychohistory. He examined documentation concerning the life and character of the primary persons in an age he was studying, concentrating upon their spiritual and emotional characterizations. René-Moreno had earlier worked in this type of history, but he collected his information from archives and libraries. Gutiérrez made use of personal interviews to develop his themes. At the same time, all of his histories were constructed around the idea of patriotism and nationalism tempered with intellectual honesty that led him to examine the findings of other historians and to refute them when he found that they were in error. He was also curious as to why nations accept military dictatorships, and in some of his work he examined this phenomenon. He looked at the Bolivian people and examined the characteristics that might make them susceptible to political tyranny and dictatorial domination. Out of such studies he emerged a political liberal who believed strongly in the dignity and freedom of the individual, and his work contributed to Bolivian discussions on political ethics and the anathema of dictatorships of all types. Finally, like most Latin American historians he wrote in different genres such as sociology and biography as well as history. In all areas he was ever the scholar who presented his work in a correct, elegant style that contributed to his popularity with the reading public.

A. *Notas e impresiones de los Estados Unidos* (Santiago, 1904); *El tratado de paz con Chile* (La Paz, 1905); *Paradojas* (La Paz, 1908); *La guerra de 1879* (Paris, 1912); *El melgarejismo antes y después de Melgarejo* (La Paz, 1916); *Hombres representativos* (La Paz, 1926).

B. Gustavo Adolfo, *Figuras de la cultura boliviana* (Quito, 1952), pp. 269-299; Charles Arnade, "The Historiography of Colonial and Modern Bolivia," *Hispanic American Historical Review*, 42, No. 3 (August 1962), pp. 352-353; Enrique Finot, *Historia de la literatura boliviana* (Mexico City, 1943), pp. 394-398; Dwight Heath, *Historical Dictionary of Bolivia* (Metuchen, N.J., 1972), p. 113; William Belmont Parker, *Bolivians of To-Day* (New York, 1967), pp. 133-135; and Unión Panamericana, *Diccionario de la literatura latinoamericana: Bolivia* (Washington, D.C., 1958), pp. 42-44.

GUTIÉRREZ, JUAN MARÍA (6 May 1809, Buenos Aires—26 February 1878, Buenos Aires). *Education*: Studied Latin, philosophy, and mathematics at the University of Buenos Aires; Doctor of Jurisprudence, University of Buenos Aires, 1834. *Career*: As a student, worked in the Department of Topography and Statistics; turned to writing and became a member of the Literary Salon; combined with Esteban Echeverría and others to create the Association of May; while in exile, wrote, taught, and served as Director of the Naval School, Valparaiso, Chile; assisted in writing the Constitution of the Argentine Confederation; served as Minister of Justice, Religion, and Education; Rector, University of Buenos Aires, 1861-1873.

Gutiérrez was a close follower of the two great intellectuals of 19th century Argentina, Juan Bautista Alberdi and Esteban Echeverría. He shared their fondness for the romantic movement in literature and their hostility to the dictator Juan Manuel de Rosas. Because of his antigovernment position he was imprisoned and then exiled to Montevideo, where he edited some periodicals and won a prize for poetry. He then traveled to Europe with Alberdi. In 1845 he moved to Chile, where a sizable colony of anti-Rosas exiles had taken up residence. Like his compatriots, Gutiérrez spent his exile in Chile teaching and writing, and when Rosas fell he returned to Buenos Aires and held some governmental posts. In 1861 he became Rector of the University of Buenos Aires, where he remained until the later years of his life, leading a literary, academic career, which he favored far more than the political nightmare that had cost him his freedom and led to exile.

In his literary efforts Gutiérrez worked in poetry, fiction, and history. He wrote a number of poems himself but in addition he compiled the poetry that had been written in Spanish America, edited works of individual poets of Chile and Ecuador as well as those of his native Argentina, and compiled biographical data on South American poets. This penchant for compilation carried over into the area of history as well, leading him to put together a bibliography on the history of the press in Argentina. All his literary activities complemented each other and in particular added vitality to his historical works and to his biographies. He sought to bring the truth to the subjects he researched, but like so many others of his era he was plagued by the emotion of the independence age, which led him to denounce Spain for its colonization of America and to exalt everything Argentine with little critical analysis because of his fervent patriotism.

A. *Apuntes biográficos de escritores, oradores y hombres de estado de la República Argentina* (Buenos Aires, 1860); *Noticias históricas sobre el origen de la enseñanza superior en Buenos Aires (1767-1821)* (Buenos Aires, 1865); *Bosquejo biográfico del General José de San Martín* (Buenos Aires, 1868); *Origen y desarrollo de la enseñanza pública superior en Buenos Aires* (Buenos Aires, 1868); *Letras argentinas: Echeverría, De Luca, Fray Cayetano Rodríguez y ostros estudios críticos* (Buenos Aires, 1929); *Escritos históricos y literarios* (Buenos Aires, 1934).

B. Joseph R. Barager, "The Historiography of the Río de la Plata Area, Since 1830," *Hispanic American Historical Review*, 39, No. 4 (November 1959), pp. 588-642; Luís Barros Borgoño, *A través de una correspondencia: Don Juan María Gutiérrez* (Santiago, 1934); Roberto F. Giusti, *Diccionario de la literatura latinoamericana: Argentina* (Washington, D.C., 1961), pp. 80-84; Carlos María Urien, *Apuntes sobre la vida y obras del doctor Juan María Gutiérrez* (Buenos Aires, 1909); Benjamín Vicuña Mackenna, *Juan María Gutiérrez* (Santiago, 1878); and Antonio Zinny, *Juan María Gutiérrez: Su vida y sus escritos* (Buenos Aires, 1878).

H

HENRÍQUEZ UREÑA, MAX (16 November 1885, Santo Domingo—12 January 1968, Forest Hills, New York). *Education*: Bachelor of Science and Letters, Instituto Professional, Santo Domingo, 1906; Doctor of Laws, University of Havana, 1913. *Career*: Journalist in Havana, 1904; practiced law in Havana, 1913-1930; taught in the Escuela Libre de Derecho de Santiago de Cuba; Secretary to the President of the Dominican Republic, 1916; General Superintendent of Instruction, Santo Domingo, 1931; Chancellor, Santo Domingo, 1931-1933; Secretary of State, Dominican Republic, 1931-1933; Professor of Literature, University of Santo Domingo, 1932-1933; Minister Plenipotentiary to Argentina, 1934-1935, to England, 1935; delegate to the League of Nations, 1935; Chief of the Dominican mission, Pan American Peace Conference of Buenos Aires, 1936; drama critic, novelist, playwright, poet, and journalist.

Like his brother Pedro, Max Henríquez was raised in a literary atmosphere as both their mother and father gained reputations as writers. In addition to his extensive journalistic efforts and his literary activity he was also influential in political circles, in education, and in the Foreign Service as well. He was devoted to the maintenance of independence for the Dominican Republic, and for that goal he worked long and hard, lobbying in other Latin American nations for the preservation of his native land. His extensive travel and widespread association with education broadened his perspective and made him a figure recognized throughout Latin America for his literary accomplishments as well as his diplomatic talents.

Max Henríquez' interest in history permeated his other literary endeavors. When he worked in fiction he invariably concentrated upon the historical novel, which was generally set amidst local historical events and included the political maneuvering that he had observed firsthand in his own career. He used his imagination to transform memories of political struggles into exciting stories for the general reading public through the use of an enthusiastic, exciting writing style. He hoped that the general public could become familiar with the history of its nation through his works and the books of others. To that end he determined to make as many books of fiction and nonfiction available to the public as possible. Henríquez created the concept of publishing the best literature in a series that he named the *Minima Dominicana*. The advantage of this series was not only that it brought together the outstanding works of literature but that they were published at a low price for the general reader.

Henríquez Ureña viewed history as an intellectual journey through the past that would enable the population to understand the present. But he was not content simply to narrate events of history. Instead he sought to analyze and evaluate history so that people could understand themselves and, at the same time, become acquainted with what they might be able to achieve in the future. Thus, for Henríquez Ureña, history was not simply an intellectual experience but a utilitarian exercise that could only benefit mankind. His historical criticism and his historical exploration into Hispanic American literature were designed to strengthen man's knowledge and understanding of his life on earth.

A. *Reseña histórica sobre Santiago de Cuba* (Santiago, Cuba, 1931); *Panorama de la República Dominicana* (Buenos Aires, 1935); *La Liga de Naciones Americanas y la Conferencia de Buenos Aires* (New York, 1937); *La independencia efímera* (Paris, 1938); *La conspiración de los Alcarrizos* (Lisbon, 1941); *El continente de la esperanza* (Brussels, 1959).

B. Donald E. Herdeck, ed., *Caribbean Writers: A Bio-Bibliographical-Critical Encyclopedia* (Washington, D.C., 1979), pp. 746-747; Instituto Panamericano de Geografía e Historia, *Guía de personas que cultivan la historia de América* (Mexico City, 1951), pp. 196-197; Percy Alvin Martin, *Who's Who in Latin America*, 2d ed. rev. (Stanford, 1940), pp. 240-241; Manuel Valldepers, "Max Henríquez Ureña," *Revista de historia de América*, Nos. 65-66 (January-December 1968), pp. 164-168.

HENRÍQUEZ UREÑA, PEDRO (29 June 1884, Santo Domingo—1946, Buenos Aires). *Education*: Bachelor of Sciences and letters, Professional Institute of Santo Domingo, 1901; law degree, University of Mexico, 1914; M.A., 1917, Ph.D., 1918, University of Minnesota; validation of the doctorate, University of Mexico, 1922. *Career*: Chief Official, Secretariat of the University of Mexico, 1910-1914; Professor of the Spanish Language, Superior School of Commerce and Administration, Mexico City, 1912; Professor of Spanish and Spanish American Literature, National Preparatory School, Mexico City, 1912-1913; Professor of English and Spanish Literature and of the History of the Spanish Language, School of Higher Studies, University of Mexico, 1913-1914; correspondent for the *Heraldo de Cuba* in Washington, D.C., 1914-1915; Editor of *Las novedades*, New York, 1915-1916; Professor of Spanish, University of Minnesota, 1915-1919, 1920-1921; Professor, Summer School, University of California, 1918, and the University of Chicago, 1919; Director and founder, Summer School, University of Mexico, and its Department of University Interchange, 1921-1923; Director General of Public Education, State of Puebla, 1923-1924; Professor of the Spanish Language and Literature, National University of La Plata, Argentina, 1924-1931; Superintendent General of Education, Dominican Republic; and Professor, University of Santo Domingo, 1931-1945.

Born into a family of eminent scholars and literary figures, Pedro Henríquez emulated his father, mother, and brother, all of whom were literary critics and historians. His long career carried him outside his native country to Mexico and the United States, where he studied, taught, and carried out research. His production was prolific, and he became one of the best-known Latin American writers in the 20th cetury. Both at home and abroad he worked as a journalist, and his columns were carried in a number of Latin American newspapers and periodicals. Like his brother he took part in the campaign to protect the independence of Santo Domingo following World War I. He taught in schools throughout the Western Hemisphere, and his influence on the literature of the Latin American and Anglo-American worlds has been overwhelming. He not only taught in many countries but also studied in universities in several different nations, thereby building a hemisphere-wide philosophy of life in America. He also served as an editor as well as writer and journalist.

A man involved in many scholarly disciplines, Henríquez was respected in almost all, including history. He believed that the historian must search for the truth in his research and that extensive labor in documents or secondary materials had to be complemented with honesty and objectivity. His style of writing was smooth and pure, lending great readability to his scholarly findings. Because he was a poet, philologist, artist, architect, musician, philosopher, and sociologist, as well as historian, he was able to give his history books the broadest possible framework, a trait that made for outstanding works, not only in history but on almost any subject he chose. He was the Renaissance man, the complete scholar, whose works were profound, humane, and thought-provoking.

In particular, his view of the Western Hemisphere was expressed in terms of a single, united region. He wrote about Anglo-Saxon America as well as Hispanic America, and he devoted a good deal of his time to learning as much about his Anglo-Saxon neighbors as about his Hispanic background. Consequently, his literary histories were enriched by his extensive background in all of the Western Hemisphere's literary endeavors.

A. *Horas de estudio* (Paris, 1910); *La enseñanza de la literatura* (Mexico City, 1913); *Estudios sobre el renacimiento en España: El maestro Hernán Pérez de Oliva* (Havana, 1914); *La utopía de América* (La Plata, Argentina, 1925); *La cultura y las letras coloniales en Santo Domingo* (Buenos Aires, 1936); *Las corrientes literarias en la América hispaña* (Mexico City, 1949); *Literary Currents in Hispanic America* (Cambridge, Mass., 1945).
B. Gilbert Chase, "Translator's Preface," in Pedro Henríquez Ureña, *A Concise History of Latin American Culture* (New York, 1966), pp. v-ix; Donald E.Herdeck, ed., *Caribbean Writers: A Bio-Bibliographical-Critical Encyclopedia* (Washington, D.C., 1979), p. 747; and Percy Alvin Martin, *Who's Who in Latin America*, 2d ed. rev. (Stanford, 1940), pp. 241-242.

HENRÍQUEZ Y CARVAJAL, FEDERICO (16 September 1848, Santo Domingo—4 February 1952, Santo Domingo). *Education*: Unknown. *Career*: Held a seat in the Dominican Congress; Director of *La opinión*, 1874; founded and directed *El mensajero*, 1881-1890; founded a literary review, *Letras y Ciencias* and edited it, 1892-1899; taught at the Dominican School, Professional Institute, and the University of Santo Domingo; Director of *El normalismo*, 1901; Director of the Normal School; presided over the Supreme Court of Justice, 1916; Minister of Interior and Police; founded the Dominican Academy of History, 1931, and Director, 1931-1944; created the review, *Clio*, and directed it, 1931-1944.

As a jurist, journalist, playwright, historian, and politician, Henríquez y Carvajal played a prominent role in his nation's development. Early in his career he became a devout disciple of political independence, and his passion became independence for Cuba from Spain. He worked with José Martí and other leaders of Cuban independence, and he raised money for the cause while at the same time writing articles demanding a free Cuba. Following Cuban independence he became embroiled in his own nation's political problems, which included occupation by U.S. troops and internal dissension. He managed to survive the internecine struggle, partly by going into voluntary exile in Cuba, and emerged as an outstanding literary figure, teacher, and journalist in Santo Domingo.

Henríquez y Carvajal transferred his political ideology to his historical activity and concentrated his work on Cuban independence and on the concept of American solidarity. He wrote a history of the Cuban Ten Year's War of 1868 in which he championed the idea of Cuban independence. Being a friend and cohort of José Martí, he wrote a biography of the Cuban independence leader, *Marti*, and worked also on the historical development of nationalism, which fit into his contemporary political philosophy. He believed firmly in an America that was bound together by racial, linguistic, and historical ties, and he became preoccupied with the achievement of hemispheric accommodation and unity. This theme was reflected not only in his political tracts but in his historical studies as well.

A. *Cuba i Quisqueya* (Havana, 1920); *Todo por Cuba* (Santo Domingo, 1925); *Romances históricos* (Santo Domingo, 1927); *Baní; parcela histórica de su vida en la villa i en el valle* (Ciudad Trujillo, 1939); *Duarte* (Ciudad Trujillo, 1944); *Martí* (Ciudad Trujillo, 1945).

B. Carlos Bosch García, "Federico Henríquez y Carvajal," *Revista de historia de América*, No. 34 (December 1952), pp. 549-552; "Dr. F. Henríquez, Dominican Leader," *New York Times*, 22 February 1952, p. 21; Donald E. Herdeck, ed., *Caribbean Writers: A Bio-Bibliographical-Critical Encyclopedia*, (Washington, D.C., 1979), pp. 748-749.

HUAMÁN POMA DE AYALA, FELIPE (ca. 1530, place unknown—1615, place unknown). *Career*: Worked among the Indians as a teacher, interpreter, and lay minister; writer.

Supposedly descended from Inca royalty, Huamán Poma embellished his family's position and his own life when he wrote about himself in his *Nueva crónica*. For much of his life he lived near poverty, eking out a living as an interpreter and teacher. Perhaps because of his dreams of past greatness and the penury that was the reality of his life he came to dislike the Spaniards, and to blame them for his own failures. He was treated poorly by the Spanish, and his conversion to Christianity caused him some difficulty within the Indian community so that his life was not pleasant. But for 30 years he took solace in his work, which was his historical statement of Inca history.

Probably because of his own experience and partly because of Indian memories, Huamán Poma attacked the Spanish in his history. He opposed all Spaniards, whether Creole or Peninsular, and he also opposed the organized Church. He blamed all the Incas' problems on the Spanish, and in his study he was not always scrupulous with the truth when discussing the Hispanic role in America. Generally, however, he was well informed because of his Indian contacts, but he was not committed to ferreting out the truth, especially if sources might contradict his portrayal of the Spanish. In general terms he presented a reasonably accurate account of Inca society, customs, and religion, but the book was strengthened by the inclusion of translated Inca poems and songs that had not been put into Spanish by any other scholar. Even more important were the illustrations that he included. These were done in a primitive manner by Huamán Poma himself, but they represented graphically the manner of living among the Incas. This was the major illustrated chronicle of Peru, a fact that explains why some scholars rank it just behind *Garcilaso de la Vega's *Comentarios reales* in order of importance for ancient Peruvian history. It is significant because it was done by an Indian, from the Indian point of view, as contrasted with the many chronicles written by Spaniards and the few done by mestizos.

A. *Nueva crónica y buen gobierno* (Paris, 1936).

B. Marvin Alisky, *Historical Dictionary of Peru* (Metuchen, N.J., 1979), p. 45; Francisco Esteve Barba, *Historiografía indiana* (Madrid, 1964), pp. 475-481; and A. Curtis Wilgus, *The Historiography of Latin America: A Guide to Historical Writing, 1500-1800* (Metuchen, N.J., 1975), pp. 74-75.

I

IBARGUREN, CARLOS (18 April 1877, Salta, Argentina—23 April 1956, Buenos Aires). *Education*: Doctor of Jurisprudence and Social Sciences with distinction, University of Buenos Aires, 1898; *Career*: Taught history, Colegio Nacional de Buenos Aires, 1900-1910; Professor of Roman Law, University of Buenos Aires, 1905; Professor of History, University of Buenos Aires, 1901-1925; Assistant Secretary of Agriculture, 1901-1906; Secretary, Federal Supreme Court, 1906-1911; Member, National Council of Education, 1912-1913; Minister of Justice and Public Instruction, 1913-1914; Councilor, University of Buenos Aires, 1915-1920; Assistant Dean, School of Law and Social Science, University of Buenos Aires, 1917-1918; vice-presidential candidate, 1916 and 1943; President, Institute of the University of Paris, Buenos Aires, 1921-1929; Democratic party candidate for President of Argentina, 1922; legal adviser to the Buenos Aires Exchange, 1924-1931.

Ibarguren divided his time among teaching, politics, and writing, but he combined all three activities smoothly in his career. He wrote political history and personally was involved in the political activity of his nation. He held appointive government posts and ran for office as well, on two occasions aspiring to the second highest political position in the land. Throughout all this activity he produced several excellent histories that were well received by his countrymen.

The political thinker in Ibarguren came out clearly in his histories. He was a nationalist and his books reflected that attitude, but he was also a traditionalist, which also emerged from his pages. His historical efforts revolved mainly around Juan Manuel de Rosas and his dictatorial reign, and his principal work was *Juan Manuel de Rosas: Su vida—su tiempo—su drama*. He wrote about the Rosas dictatorship and concluded that tyranny was not just something that resulted from power-mad leaders but instead grew from a nation's atmosphere and from circumstances that at a particular time dominated a country. His historical work was generally of the type espoused by Vicente Fidel López, who supported the idea of looking at an age in the past as a philosophical unit without examining every piece of documentation that existed in and out of archives. Instead Ibarguren recreated the Rosas epoch in a colorful, imaginative way. His literary style was smooth, interesting, and exciting, and his treatment of Rosas was innovative and thought-provoking. He was a major contributor to early 20th century Argentine history.

A. *Una proscripción bajo la dictadura de Syla* (Buenos Aires, 1908); *Historias del tiempo clásico* (Buenos Aires, 1924); *Manuelita Rosas* (Buenos Aires, 1925); *Juan Manuel de Rosas: Su vida—su tiempo—su drama* (Buenos Aires, 1930); *Las sociedades literarias y la revolución argentina (1800-1825)* (Buenos Aires, 1937); *La intervención imperialista en el Río de la Plata* (Buenos Aires, 1951).

B. Roberto F. Giusti, *Diccionario de la literatura latinoamericana: Argentina* (Washington, D.C., 1961), pp. 206-209; Percy Alvin Martin, *Who's Who in Latin America* (Stanford, 1936), pp. 193-194; William Belmont Parker, *Argentines of To-Day* (Buenos Aires, 1920), I, pp. 46-47; Juan Pinto, *Panorama de la literatura argentina contemporánea* (Buenos Aires, 1941), pp. 205-206; and Ione S. Wright and Lisa M. Nekhom, *Historical Dictionary of Argentina* (Metuchen, N.J., 1978), pp. 405-406.

ICAZA, FRANCISCO A. DE (2 February 1863, Mexico City—28 May 1925, Madrid). *Education*: Studied at the Liceo Mexicana under Vicente Riva Palacio. *Career*: Second Secretary, Mexican ministry in Spain and Portugal, First Secretary, 1895; Minister Plenipotentiary in Germany, 1904-1912; Minister Plenipotentiary in Spain, 1912.

Some Mexican intellectuals managed to ride out the violent decade of the Mexican Revolution of 1910 by serving in diplomatic posts outside the country. In this manner they did not have to become directly embroiled in the savage fighting that ravaged the country. Icaza was one of those diplomats who returned only infrequently to his native country during that decade of turmoil and chaos. Serving in Europe in second-level diplomatic positions, he was insulated from the politcal machinations that entrapped many Mexicans of this age, and he could concentrate upon literary and historical activities. He was a poet of some prominence and an accomplished novelist as well. His work was well received in Europe, especially Spain, and he won awards and prizes from the Spanish for some of his poetry and novels. He received an honorary degree from the University of Mexico in 1920.

In addition to writing poetry Icaza translated into Spanish the poetry of foreigners. He became an authority on the criticism of Spanish literature and on Latin American history. His historical efforts were extensively researched and presented in interesting, lively prose. His analysis was penetrating, and he used his documentation wisely and carefully to develop his themes. In writing his history he concentrated upon the conquest and colonial periods of Mexico as well as upon literary history. He wrote about some of the outstanding authors of Spain in the 16th and 17th centuries, scrutinizing their works carefully and placing them in historical context.

A. *Efímeras, confidencias, paráfrasis, poemas íntimos, Rivadeneyra* (Madrid, 1892); *Lejanias* (Madrid, 1899); *La canción del camino* (Madrid, 1905); *Antología crítica de poetas extranjeros*, 2 vols. (Madrid, 1919); *Sucesos reales que parecen imaginados, de Gutierre de Cetina, Juan de la Cueva y Mateo Aleman* (Madrid, 1919); *Diccionario autobiográfico de conquistadores y pobladores de la Nueva España*, 2 vols. (Madrid, 1923).

B. *Diccionario Porrúa de historia* (Mexico City, 1976), I, p. 1050; Aurora M. Ocampo de Gómez and Ernesto Prado Velázquez, *Diccionario de escritores mexicanos* (Mexico City, 1967), pp. 178-179.

IGLESIA Y PARGA, RAMÓN (3 July 1905, Santiago de Compostela, Spain— 4 May 1948, Madison, Wisconsin). *Education*: Studied at the University of Madrid, 1920-1925, the University of Illinois, and the University of Wisconsin. *Career*: Fought in the Loyalist army in the Spanish Civil War, 1936; fled to Mexico, 1939; worked at menial tasks; taught at the Colegio de México, Mexico City, 1941-1945, and at the National University of Mexico.

Caught up in the struggle of the Republicans in Spain to maintain their control over the government, Iglesia y Parga fought for three long years in a losing cause. Only when the outcome was certain defeat did he leave his homeland to take up residence in Mexico. In a strange country with little money, he was forced to work long and hard just to keep himself and his family alive. Ultimately he was able to secure a teaching job, and soon he became one of the major historians of Mexico. He had studied and written history before the war, but the experience of battle and misery altered his perspective and made him a better historian. He now had firsthand experience of catastrophic world events, and he could use his own reactions and sentiments in times of crisis to understand better the actions and thoughts of historical figures about whom he wrote. At the same time, he grew intellectually during these tragic years and became far more critical of his sources, even altering one major view he had expressed before the Civil War, namely his evaluation of Hernán Cortés.

In 1936, before the Civil War in Spain, Iglesia y Parga had written an article generally accepting *Bernal Díaz del Castillo's intepretation of Cortés and the conquest of Mexico. Following his military experience and his adoption of Mexico as his country, Iglesia y Parga went back to a study of the Spanish conquest of Mexico and concluded that his earlier work was in error and now, rather than rely on Bernal Díaz' account of the conquest, he concluded that *Francisco López de Gómara was more accurate in his study of that event. This evaluation reestablished Gómara as the major authority on the conquest of Mexico. Iglesia now subjected his sources to more rigorous evaluation, and he destroyed the notion that some of the old authorities, like Bernal Díaz, should be accepted without careful scrutiny. Beyond his tough-minded historical method, which he taught in his classes and practiced in his own work, he was also significant because of his writing style, which he considered a crucial part of any historian's effort. He loved smoothness of language, and he applauded both Bernal Díaz and Gómara for their pleasant styles. He appreciated, too, clarity of thought and economy of words. He wanted history to be not only a careful analysis of data but also a literary work of art, and he believed firmly that even the most effective job of scientific historical research was deficient if the results were not presented in an artistic literary fashion. This combination of scientific method and artistic expression in the historian's craft altered the views of his students and introduced a new historiographical philosophy into Mexican historical scholarship.

A. *Baraja de crónicas castellanas del S. XIV* (Mexico City, 1940); "Two Essays on the Same Topic: Bernal Díaz del Castillo and Popularism in Spanish Historiography, and

Bernal Díaz del Castillo's Criticism of the History of the Conquest of Mexico, by Francisco López de Gómara,"*Hispanic American Historical Review*, 22, No. 4 (November 1940), pp. 517-550; *Cronistas e historiadores de la conquista de México: El ciclo de Hernán Cortés* (Mexico City, 1942); *El hombre Colón y otros ensayos* (Mexico City, 1944).
B. *Diccionario Porrúa de historia* (Mexico City, 1976), I, p. 1015; José Miranda, "Ramón Iglesia Parga,"*Revista de historia de América*, No. 25 (July 1948), pp. 139-143; and "Ramón Iglesia y Parga, 1905-1948,"*Hispanic American Historical Review*, 28, No. 2 (May 1948), pp. 163-164.

IGUÍNIZ, JUAN BAUTISTA (29 August 1881, Guadalajara, Mexico—30 April 1968, Mexico City). *Education*: Secondary studies in the Seminario Conciliar de Guadalajara: higher education in the Museo Nacional de Arqueología, Historia y Etnología de México, Mexico City. *Career*: Worked in the Museo Nacional, Escuela Nacional de Bibliotecario, Archives, and various libraries, Mexico City; served in the Ministry of Foreign Relations; Chief Historian, Ministry of Foreign Relations, 1928-1933; Director, Biblioteca Nacional, 1951-1956; researched at the Instituto de Historia, Universidad Nacional Autónomo Mexicana, 1956; taught at the University of Mexico and various other schools in Mexico City.

Historians need bibliographical assistance in order to carry out their research, and some historians try to assist their compatriots by providing this information while at the same time writing history themselves. One such scholar was Juan Iguíniz. He was fascinated with books, libraries, archives, and research, and he devoted a lifetime to all these areas. He wrote in reviews, periodicals, memorials, and bulletins. His work was published both in Mexico and abroad. While his major concern was bibliographical studies, he also wrote literary criticism, history, travel accounts, geneology, and heraldry.

Iguíniz' major contribution was in the field of bibliography, where he produced an impressive number of publications examining almost every facet of Mexican bibliographical studies. His lengthy production has benefitted scholars who wished to work in historical themes, from a bibliography of Jesuit writers to a bibliography of Mexican novelists. His lifetime spent in libraries and archives has been a major contribution to historical scholarship in his own country, and his work has been recognized by scholarly organizations in Europe and the United States as well. In addition to his scholarly production he was also a major teacher of bibliographical studies in the schools of Mexico, and he taught graphics and library science to many Mexican students, improving in the process the library and bibliographical fields for the Mexican nation.
A. *Apuntes biográficos del doctor D. Francisco Severo Maldonado* (Mexico City, 1911); *La imprenta en la Nueva Galacia* (Mexico City, 1911); *Las publicaciones del Museo Nacional de Arqueología, Historia y Etnología* (Mexico City, 1912); *Instrucciones para la redacción y formación de los catalogos bibliográficos según el sistema de Melvil Dewey adaptadas a las bibliotecas hispano-americanos* (Mexico City, 1919); *Documentos para la historia de Sonora y Sinaloa* (Madrid, 1949); *Breve historia de la Tercera Orden*

Franciscana en la Provincia del Santo Evangelio de México desde sus origenes hasta nuestros días (Mexico City, 1951).
B. Aurora M. Ocampo de Gómez and Ernesto Prado Velázquez, *Diccionario de escritores mexicanos* (Mexico City, 1967), pp. 179-182.

INGENIEROS, JOSÉ (24 April 1877, Palermo, Italy—31 October 1925, Buenos Aires). *Education*: Doctor of Medicine, University of Buenos Aires, 1900. *Career*: Founded the revolutionary periodical, *La montaña*, 1897, and *Archivos de psiquiatría y criminología* and *Revista de Filosofía*, 1915; and contributed to *Revista de derecho, historia y letras*; taught and wrote on neuropathology; Chair of Experimental Psychology, School of Philosophy and Letters, University of Buenos Aires, 1908.

Ingenieros was trained as a physician with a specialty in neurology and psychology. Along with *José María Ramos Mejía, he was an early participant in what is today called psychohistory. But he was also devoted to a study of society and worked with social problems that ultimately led him into the socialist movement. While pursuing his teaching and writing on psychology, criminology, and history, he also devoted some attention to philosophy. He wrote and lectured on morality and on the philosophical development of Argentina. In 1915 he began to publish a popular library that came to include 150 volumes on the primary works of thought in Argentina. This monumental task resulted in a work that is regarded as a standard of excellence throughout Latin America today. Ingenieros also traveled in Europe and the United States to participate in intellectual congresses and symposia, thereby building an international reputation.

In his historical work Ingenieros concentrated upon the history of ideas, but in the process of his research he did not neglect political, social, or economic developments. He traced the course of Argentina through the 19th and 20th centuries, examining carefully the Rosas era and its impact on Argentine history. Much of his work included the theme of morality and its place in history as he wove into his books his philosophical interests. His own philosophy of history was constructed upon the concept that the past has witnessed a never-ending clash between youthful forces that demand change and reform and older elements that seek to preserve the status quo. This titanic struggle permeated his own nation's history, and by implication it could be ascribed to universal history. Ingenieros believed that the youthful forces for change would gain the ascendancy, and this coupled with his unswerving belief in the perfectibility of mankind made him an optimist in spite of his living through such destructive events as World War I.

A. *La evolución sociológica argentina* (Buenos Aires, 1907); *La evolución de las ideas argentinas*, Vol 1, *La revolución* (Buenos Aires, 1918), Vol. 2, *La restauración* (Buenos Aires, 1920); *Las doctrinas de Ameghino, la tierra, la vida y el hombre* (Buenos Aires, 1919); *La locura en la Argentina* (Buenos Aires, 1920); and *Las fuerzas morales* (Buenos Aires, 1922).
B. Hector Pablo Agosti, *José Ingenieros, ciudadano de la juventud* (Buenos Aires, 1945);

Gregorio Berman, *José Ingenieros, el civilizador, el filósofo, el moralista; lo que le debe nuestra generación* (Buenos Aires, 1926); and Roberto F. Giusti, *Diccionario de la literatura latinoamericana: Argentina* (Washington, D.C., 1961), pp. 95-99.

IRARRÁZAVAL LARRAIN, JOSÉ MIGUEL (28 January 1881, Santiago—19 December 1959, Santiago). *Education*: Law degree, Seminario Conciliar, Santiago, 1902. *Career*: Attorney, historian, and lexicographer.

Irarrázaval's first forays into historical writing centered around the very practical problem of boundary disputes between Chile and Argentina. In 1930 he published a book in which he pointed out the historical, geographical, and diplomatic errors that had led to the 20th century quarrel over the boundaries that separated the two nations. This study began with the boundary treaty of 1881 and traced the changes that had taken place in Chilean thinking from that treaty to 1930, when border disputes erupted once again to plague the area.

Irarrázaval also took a close historical look at José Manuel Balmaceda's insurrection against the Chilean parliament in 1891. In that year President Balmaceda closed the congress and ruled as a dictator. Congressional forces fought back and eventually Balmaceda was overthrown, and for the next generation it was the Chilean congress that ruled the nation, not a succession of weak presidents. Irarrázaval concluded that this event was a major part of Chile's history, and he found that it was not a sudden outburst of the executive against congress. Instead he traced the growing power of parliament even before Balmaceda became president, indicating that the whole affair was not a spontaneous rebellion but merely the culmination of a long period of tension between the executive branch and the congress.

Irarrázaval's major historical effort, however, was his research on the independence hero José de San Martín, entitled *San Martín y sus enigmas*. While countless works had been published on San Martín throughout Latin America before Irarrázaval wrote his brief study, none up to that time had been as scrupulous in the examination of the small, often overlooked acts of the revolutionary leader. It was Irarrázaval who took the seemingly unimportant anecdotes from his life and put them together to find a more human, less heroic figure. He sought to understand the human San Martín, and through his assiduous research he succeeded in developing such a biographical study. These small events appeared to him to be the enigmas of San Martín's life, and they served to create a more complete picture of one of Latin America's great heroes.

A. *La Patagonia, errores geográficos y diplomáticos* (Santiago, 1930 ; *El Presidente Balmaceda* (Santiago, 1940); *San Martín y sus enigmas* (Santiago, 1949); *El gobierno y los bancos durante el administración Balmaceda* (Santiago, 1953). *La administración Balmaceda y el salitre de Tarapacá* (Santiago, 1953).

B. Raul Silva Castro, ''José Miguel Irarrázaval Larrain,'' *Revista de historia de América*, No. 49 (June 1960), pp. 204-205.

J

JAIMES FREYRE, RICARDO (12 May 1868, Tacna, Peru—24 April 1933, Buenos Aires). *Education*: Studied at the University of Lima; self-taught. *Career*: Teacher at Colegio Junín de Sucre; Private secretary to President Mariano Baptista; diplomat in Brazil; founded the *Revista de América* in Buenos Aires with Ruben Dario, 1894; taught literature and philosophy, Colegio Nacional, Tucumán, Argentina, 1900-1920; founded *Revista de letras y ciencias sociales*, 1905; Professor at the Escuela Normal of Tucumán and at the University of Tucumán; Councilor from Tucumán, 1917.

Jaimes Freyre was born in Tacna, Peru, where his father served the Bolivian government as consul. After living in Peru he returned to his native country for a brief period of time before moving on to Argentina, where he spent most of his life. Like his father before him, he served for a time as a diplomat and as a journalist, writing for and creating several periodicals. He traveled in South America and also in Europe, where he worked in the Archives of the Indies in Sevilla. In 1916 he became a naturalized Argentine citizen. His parents had both been literary figures, and he continued in the career they had pursued. Like his mother he wrote poetry, and his prose efforts resembled those of his father. Then in 1920 with a change of government in Bolivia he returned home, and in 1921 he was named Minister of Public Instruction. Later he served as Bolivia's delegate to the League of Nations. In 1922 he became Minister of Foreign Relations, and a year later he was transferred to Washington as Bolivian Minister. He ran unsuccessfully for the presidency in 1925, and in 1927 he returned to Buenos Aires to live out his life. Although he had been an important literary figure and a significant diplomat and political leader, Jaimes was virtually penniless in the last years of his life.

Jaimes Freyre was an intellectual giant in South America. He has been characterized as a medieval gentleman who was romantic, correct, and upright. Throughout his work ran a thread of nostalgia, and he was enraptured with the past. One scholar remarked that he did not live in the present; rather his life was committed to history. He was a passionate writer who was intense in his work and who was concerned about the form as well as the content of his writing. Although better known as a poet whose work reflected the modernist strain, he was also an accomplished historian. His histories were for the most part regional studies, and he is known as the greatest historian of Tucumán. But he was also a historian of the Middle Ages, and he drew comparisons between his era and

Europe's medieval past. This kind of interest outside one's country was a rarity for Latin American historians, but his work in European history enhanced all his literature and history.

A. *Historia de la edad media y de los tiempos modernos* (Buenos Aires, 1895); *Tucumán en 1810* (Tucumán, Argentina, 1909); *Historia de la República de Tucumán* (Buenos Aires, 1911); *El Tucumán colonial (documentos y mapas del archivo de Indias)* (Buenos Aires, 1915); *Los conquistadores* (Buenos Aires, 1928).

B. Enrique Finot, *Historia de la literatura boliviana* (Mexico City, 1943), pp. 160-166; Dwight B. Heath, *Historical Dictionary of Bolivia* (Metuchen, N.J., 1972), p. 130; William Belmont Parker, *Bolivians of To-Day* (New York, 1967), pp. 153-154; and Unión Panamericana, *Diccionario de la literatura latinoamericana: Bolivia* (Washington, D.C., 1958), pp. 49-52.

JARAMILLO ALVARADO, PÍO (1889, Loja, Educador—1968, Quito). *Education*: Doctor of Law, University of Loja, Ecuador. *Career*: Governor of Loja Province; practiced law in Quito; wrote a political column under the pseudonym "Petronio" in *El día*; served in the executive branch of government, 1925; exiled to Panama; taught political law and sociology in secondary schools and in the universities of Quito and Guayaquil; served as a diplomat in Peru; founded the Instituto Indigenista to work with the Indians; President, Casa de la Cultura Ecuatoriana, 1947-1948.

In the later 19th and early 20th centuries many Latin American intellectuals believed that the discipline of sociology was the queen of the social sciences, and they worked in that area as well as in other fields. Jaramillo Alvarado was one Ecuadorean who followed this academic and intellectual course. He was especially interested in the Indians of his country, and he not only wrote about them and their lives but also tried to assist them to improve their lot in Ecuadorean society. At the same time, he worked to integrate the eastern part of the nation into the rest of the country, motivated, in part at least, by the same desire to aid the Indians of the Ecuadorean Amazon region. His political activity was also geared to assist the indigenist population. A political liberal, Jaramillo came close to winning the presidency on a couple of occasions. However, he did work in government for educational and social programs. He is also recognized as one of the pioneers of Ecuadorean socialism as he sought to improve the economic and social climate of the country.

In his writing, whether in history, sociology, or some other discipline, he thought of himself less as a literary artist than a social and political activist. Consequently, his written work was generally aimed at some social action. His style was excellent and his Spanish clear and properly constructed. In some of his political articles, however, he could become impassioned and accusatory as he denounced the social and political injustices that he perceived in the nation. Despite his passionate commitment to contemporary causes, he was a dedicated historian. He collected an extensive personal library of books and documents that he then used as a foundation for his histories, which were generally regional in nature. He wrote about his home state and the cities in which he lived. In every case he used his sources well, researched diligently, and then presented his findings in a logical clear, almost pedantic fashion. Yet the work never slips into a tedious recounting of details that distracts the reader; instead his accomplished style enables him to hold the reader's interest. Jaramillo's logical development of premises and formidable development of his ideas makes his work not only informative but readable. He never thought of himself as a literary figure, but his work qualifies him as a *literato*, and one writer calls him one of the outstanding Ecuadorean figures of the 20th century. While he was basically a regional historian, when dealing with Ecuadorean literature he placed the Ecuadorean writers in the perspective of Latin American literature. He became one of the most respected intellectuals of Ecuador as well as one of the country's premier political activists.

A. *El indio ecuatoriano; contribución al estudio de la sociología nacional* (Quito, 1922); *Los tratados con Colombia* (Quito, 1925); *Política tropical: Con un estudio preliminar acerca de la dictadura de Bolívar* (Quito, 1927); *El secreto de Guayaquil en la entrevista de Bolívar y San Martín* (Quito, 1954); and *Historia de Loja y su provincia* (Quito, 1955).

B. Augusto Arias, *Panorama de la literatura ecuatoriana* (Quito, 1946); Albert William Bork and Georg Maier, *Historical Dictionary of Ecuador* (Metuchen, N.J., 1973), p. 86; Adam Szaszdi, "The Historiography of the Republic of Ecuador," *Hispanic American Historical Review*, 44, No. 4 (November 1964), pp. 506-507; Unión Panamericana, *Diccionario de la literatura latinoamericana: Ecuador* (Washington, D.C., 1958), pp. 132-135.

JIJÓN Y CAAMAÑO, JACINTO (11 December 1890, Quito—23 August 1950, Quito). *Education*: Attended the Central University of Quito and studied history under Archbishop Gonzaléz Suárez. *Career*: Industrialist; Conservative politician; Senator from Pichincha Province; unsuccessful presidential candidate, 1940; Mayor of Quito; leader of the Conservative party, 1924-1939; Professor in the Central University of Quito; proprietor of woolen and cotton factories in Ecuador and Colombia.

If *Velasco, *Cevallos, and *González Suárez were the three most significant historians of Ecuador through the colonial period to the end of the 19th century, Jijón y Caamaño was the most accomplished Ecuadorian historian of the 20th century. He was a member of a prominent old family with wealth and prestige to support him in his career activities. He also became a prominent politician and a leader of the Conservative party, which championed the elite to which he belonged. It is not surprising then that he would find himself in close association with the Church, since the Ecuadorian Conservatives and the Church were linked inextricably. As a young man he encountered the great historian González Suárez and became his most accomplished student.

Jijón was interested in many disciplines, especially archeology, and he used them all in writing his histories. He was committed to the auxiliary sciences as the foundation of historiography and for the advancement of the history profession. He was also a dedicated researcher who looked for sources in Europe as well as America and who worked diligently in archives and libraries to amass the data necessary to bring his studies to conclusion. One of his major interests in Europe was to find evidence to support his mentor's arguments that were included in volume four of his history of Ecuador. Soon he had amassed so much documentation that, when a new edition of González Suárez' work appeared, it included a large section of documents that supported the Archbishop's contentions in his earlier work. Jijón also collected documents, and later published them, that were important for the histories of other American countries. He wrote about the role of the city of Quito in the revolution. Not only was he skilled in finding evidence from the past but he was also a tough-minded critic of sources and of other historians. He questioned Velasco's history, which included stories of animals transformed into plants and hair into snakes, but he also wondered how Velasco could know so much about events that had taken place 700 years earlier without written documents and without archeological skills. This attitude led Jijón to concentrate more on archeology and enabled him to strengthen his own history of Ecuador.

A. *Política conservador* (Riobamba, Ecuador, 1929); *Sebastián de Benalcazar* (Quito, 1936); "La fundación de Pasto,"*Segundo congreso internacional de historia de América*, 2 (Buenos Aires, 1938), pp. 286-300; *El Ecuador interandino y occidental antes de la conquista castellano* (Quito, 1940); and *Antropología prehispánica del Ecuador* (Quito, 1952).

B. Isaac J. Barrera, *Historiografía del Ecuador* (Mexico City, 1956), pp. 81-98; Albert William Bork and Georg Maier, *Historical Dictionary of Ecuador* (Metuchen, N.J., 1973), p. 83; Percy Alvin Martin, *Who's Who in Latin America*, 2d ed rev. (Stanford, 1940), pp. 255-256; and Adam Szaszdi, "The Historiography of the Republic of Ecuador," *Hispanic American Historical Review*, 44, No. 4 (November 1964), pp. 509, 514-515.

JIMÉNEZ, MANUEL DE JESÚS (20 June 1854, Cartago, Costa Rica—25 February 1916, Alajuela, Costa Rica). *Education*: Studied at Colegio de San Luís Gonzaga, Costa Rica. *Career*: Worked as an accountant on the family hacienda and in commercial houses; taught history, geography, and literature; Deputy from Cartago to the National Congress; Secretary of Foreign Relations, 1888; unsuccessful candidate for the presidency; Consul of Costa Rica in El Salvador; Prime Minister, 1910.

Costan Rican historians of the 19th century were generally involved in writing *cuadros de costumbres* (articles about customs), novels, short stories, and other forms of literature in addition to their histories. All of this literary activity was interspersed with political and diplomatic duties, which sometimes carried these writers to high public office. Jiménez was typical of this type historian. He was naturally involved in politics because his father was president of the nation and later his brother became president. Therefore, a public career was natural for him. So too was his interest in literature, and although he originally wanted to be a physician like his father, he gave up when the family fortunes dwindled and he turned to teaching and governmental service. Once the decision was made to follow a literary career he fell into the traditional pattern of fiction, short stories, and history. Unfortunately, the last years of his life were marked by illness, and his output was not as extensive as it might have been had his health not deteriorated.

Jiménez was a devout Catholic and an equally committed political conservative. These views carried into his historical work, and like most 19th century historians of Latin America, he focused his attention upon the periods of the conquest and colonization. His histories were generally in article form, and some were almost chronicles of the lives of the great colonial families of Costa Rica. This type of history fit neatly into his other literary activity, *cuadros de costumbres*, in which he sought to describe the customs and lives of people living in Costa Rica. His historical efforts were confined generally to expanding upon works that had been produced by others rather than by digging into archival material to develop his own raw historical data. He also wrote about life in his home city in the 19th century, which was a traditional form of history among Costa Rican writers. His style was clean, sharp, and smooth. Some drama occasionally crept into his work, but for the most part he was content to describe the events that had taken place without much suspense or interpretation, and his language, true to his conservative commitment, was always of the traditionally correct type, with few vulgarisms. He also wrote historical novels using actual events for background to his fiction, or he wove events into a fictional setting. He was not one of the major Costa Rican historians, but his work did achieve some measure of popularity, and his linking of novels and *cuadros de costumbres* with history was in keeping with the trend established by others of his and previous generations in Costa Rica.

A. *Cuadros de costumbres* (San José, 1902); *Noticias de Antaño*, 2 vols. (San José, 1946-1949).

B. Theodore S. Creedman, *Historical Dictionary of Costa Rica* (Metuchen, N.J., 1977), p. 105; Unión Panamericana, *Diccionario de la literatura latinoamericana: América Central: Costa Rica, El Salvador y Guatemala* (Washington, D.C., 1963), II, pp. 26-27.

JIMÉNEZ DE QUESADA, GONZALO (1506, Córdoba, Spain—1579, Mariquita, Colombia). *Education*: Law degree, University of Salamanca, Spain. *Career*: Worked in the Royal Chancelory of Granada until 1535; Justicia Mayor of the 1535 Expedition to Colombia; named general of a force assigned to explore the coast of Tierra Firme; founded the city of Santa Fé de Bogotá, 6 August 1538.

A conquistador, Jiménez de Quesada endured extreme hardships as he marched across northern South America. Despite his success against the Chibcha Indians and his establishment of the city of Bogotá that eventually became the seat of the viceroyalty, he never gained the respect, admiration, and adoration of other conquerors. Instead, his acquisitions of territory were systematically taken from him by other Spanish leaders, and when he complained to the crown his arguments were denied and he was banished from Granada. With his military and political career at a low ebb, Jiménez de Quesada turned to writing and became a successful man of letters. He was also devoted to the law, so that when he lost his case in Spain he accepted the decision. Ultimately, he was restored to some of his former power, and near the end of 1550, after squandering his fortune, he returned to Colombia. In 1565 he was commissioned to lead another expedition into the eastern interior of the viceroyalty. By this time Jiménez was obsessed with the legend of great wealth in the region and the story of the fabulously wealthy Indian king, El Dorado. After three years of fruitless searching, Jiménez de Quesada returned to Bogota, a sick, disillusioned man. He made one final expedition and conquered another tribe of Indians, but then he contracted leprosy and soon after his triumphal return the disease, coupled with old age, led to his death.

Jiménez de Quesada was a man of great faith and a tenacious leader who never gave up hope that he would find El Dorado. He was honest, trustworthy, and brave; it has been noted by historians that he was the only one of the major Spanish conquistadors against whom troops did not rebel at some time during the course of the conquest. Despite the hardships and the difficulty of leading expeditions into unknown territory, Jiménez de Quesada never gave up his interest in, and love for, literature. He kept notes of his experiences and on his observations of the Indians, and later he wrote chronicles on the age. His writing provided the first insight into life in New Granada, and while his literary talents were not great, the information he put on paper was valuable for later historians of the period. His data was sometimes confused and jumbled, but it was indispenable for building the history of northern South America. He covered his own expeditions in his history, but he also had a good deal to say about other conquistadors that was far from complimentary. In addition, he wrote out his political and social views when time permitted, and these assessments of the political situation in Latin America have also proved valuable. Finally, like most Latin American writers, he wrote poetry. Jiménez de Quesada may not be considered a historian, but he was a chronicler who was an eyewitness to many important events in the conquest. For this reason his work became fundamental for later colonial and early modern writers of New Granadan history.

A. *Gran cuaderno* (n.p., 1539); *Epítome de la conquista del Nuevo Reino de Granada* (n.p., 1540); *Anales del Emperador V. La diferencia de la guerra de los dos mundos. Relación sobre los conquistadores y encomenderos. Los ratos de Suesca* (n.p., 1568); *Compendio historial de la conquista del Nuevo Reino de Granada* (n.p., 1572-1573); *Colección de sermones con destino a ser predicados en las festividades de Nuestra Señora* (n.p., n.d.).

B. Antonio Gómez Restrepo, *Historia de literatura colombiana* (Bogotá, 1940), I, pp. 13-28; and Unión Panamericana, *Diccionario de la literatura latinoamericana: Colombia* (Washington, D.C., 1959), pp. 58-60.

JOBET BÚRQUEZ, JULIO CÉSAR (1912, Santiago—1980, Santiago). *Education*: Studied at the University of Chile under the historian Guillermo Feliú Cruz, 1930, degree in history, 1933. *Career*: Taught at several secondary schools, at the Technical State University, and at the University of Chile, 1937-1972; joined the Socialist party, 1933; served in various offices until the party was outlawed in 1973.

Jobet was a young student during the dictatorship of Carlos Ibáñez del Campo in Chile, and he soon became disillusioned with the government and eventually with the capitalist system that led to the worldwide Great Depression. Turning to socialism, Jobet not only became active in the Socialist party but soon became the intellectual spokesman for the party. He published articles in condemnation of the Chilean political system and in support of dramatic and significant change within the nation. Meanwhile, he continued to study and write history, and soon he was one of the leading figures in the Chilean revisionist school of historiography. Jobet was impatient with the historical studies of the political and social elite in his country, and he argued that the continued emphasis on their lives was of no value for an understanding of Chilean history. Instead, he counseled study of economic history and of social developments. Only through studying the workers and their plight could a true picture of Chilean history emerge, according to Jobet.

Publishing extensively in journals and newspapers, Jobet carried his message to the lower classes and became synonymous with socialist philosophy. He devoted some of his research attention to left-wing figures from Chile's past, including the labor leader and progressive economic and political thinker of the early 20th century Manuel Recabarren. He also chronicled the progress of his Socialist party, partially as an eyewitness because he was a member of the party from its inception in the 1930s. But more than simply creating a memoir he looked carefully at the party's development and its participation in the popular front movement of 1938. He recognized the disparate nature of the party, with the social reformers like Marmaduke Grove forming one faction and the Marxist youth forming the other. But for Jobet this was not an unhealthy situation, and he believed that socialism could accommodate a wide variety of philosophies and use them all to mold an effective political force that could lead the nation out of stagnation to prosperity for all Chileans. Probably his most significant study was his *Ensayo crítico del desarrollo económico-social de Chile*, which set forth his view on the bankruptcy of the elite and the importance of the lower classes in Chilean history. The book was highly praised outside Chile and by some of his fellow scholars at home, and it was heralded as a major contribution to the revisionist theme in Chilean historiography that Jobet helped initiate with this and other books and articles.

A. *Santiago Arcos Arlegui y la sociedad de la igualdad (un socialista utopista chileno)* (Santiago, 1942); *Tres ensayos históricos: Los problemas de la historia; Panorama de*

la Revolución francesa; Francisco A. Encina, sociologo e historiador (Santiago, 1950); Ensayo crítico del desarrollo económico-social de Chile (Santiago, 1951); Recabbaren (Santiago, 1955); Los precursores del pensamiento social de Chile, 2 vols. (Santiago, 1955-1956); El Partido Socialista de Chile, 2 vols. (Santiago, 1971).
B. Paul W. Drake, "Julio César Jobet (1912-1980)," Hispanic American Historical Review, 62, No. 1 (February 1982), pp. 121-122.

JUSTIZ Y DEL VALLE, TOMÁS JUAN DE (12 July 1871), Santiago, Cuba—1959, Havana). *Education*: Doctor of Philosophy and Letters, University of Havana, 1899; Licentiate in Law, University of Havana. *Career*: Professor of History, University of Havana, 1901; teacher at the Escuela Normal, 1902; teacher of geography and history, Instituto de Segunda Enseñanza de La Habana, 1905; teacher of Cuban and American history, Instituto de Segundo Enseñanza de La Habana; Editor of *La noche* (Havana); taught geography and history, Colegios La Gran Antilla and San Franco de Paulz, 1909; Secretary, Ateneo de Havana, 1909.

In the Cuba of the early 20th century, literary figures tried their talents at a variety of activities, sometimes including history. Justiz y del Valle was a playwright, novelist, journalist, and teacher. Along with other intellectuals of his age he was also interested in bringing writers of all genres together to discuss mutual objectives and problems. As a playwright and novelist he was criticized for not developing his characters fully and for the weak construction of his plots.

As a historian Justiz del Valle was one of the few in all of Latin America who did much with world history. Most Latin American historians concentrated upon the history of their own countries, and many of them worked on local or provincial history. Justiz y del Valle wrote some of this type of history but also broadened his interests and wrote a world history book. At the same time he taught world history at the University of Havana. His history was not definitive, and he did not work extensively in unpublished, archival sources when carrying out research for the book. Nonetheless, he was one of the few Latin American historians with a broad interest in history outside his own country, and for this he is significant to Latin American historiography of the 20th century.

A. *Histórical universal* (Havana, 1916); *Resumen de las lecciones de historia universal* (Havana, 1916); *Loynaz ideal cubano* (Havana, 1930); *Ecos de un guerra a muerta* (Havana, 1941); *Historia documentada de la Isla de Cuba* (Havana, 1945); *Lecciones de historia contemporánea* (Havana, n.d.).
B. Donald E. Herdeck, ed., *Caribbean Writers: A Bio-Bibliographical-Critical Encyclopedia* (Washington, D.C., 1979), p. 766; Instituto Panamericano de Geografía e Historia, *Guía de personas que cultivan la historia de América* (Mexico City, 1951); Percy Alvin Martin, *Who's Who in Latin America*, 2d ed. rev. (Stanford, 1940), p. 259; and William Belmont Parker, *Cubans of To-Day* (New York, 1919), pp. 153-154.

L

LAFUENTE MACHAIN, RICARDO DE (4 January 1882, Buenos Aires—
10 March 1960, Buenos Aires). *Education*: Doctor of Jurisprudence, University
of Buenos Aires, 1891. *Career*: Practiced law, 1891-1955.

Lafuente Machain worked primarily in geneological studies through much of
his early career. He became interested in his own family, which had migrated
from Paraguay to Buenos Aires, and he began his scholarly activity by inves-
tigating carefully his ancestors through the use of family archives, public records,
and documents he found in Spain and in other Latin American nations. This
study led him to work on the histories of conquerers and early settlers in Latin
America. Additionally, he investigated the histories of the establishment of both
Asunción and Buenos Aires, using the extensive geneological data he had acquired, as well as public documents from the early colonial period. Once again
the use of Spanish archives was essential for these topics, and he paved the way
for later urban history studies for those two cities.

The geneological research of Lafuente Machain also led him to develop biographies of famous colonial leaders in the La Plata region. Later he became
interested in one of Paraguay's early leaders, José Gaspar Rodríguez de Francia,
and he wrote a book on the dictatorship of Francia and his successors. For this
study he introduced the use of oral traditions that had been passed through
families, and he used also little known or used documents that he had encountered
in his other studies. His most enduring historical work, however, came with his
publication of *Los portugueses en Buenos Aires* in 1931. In this book Lafuente
Machain looked at the Portuguese contribution to the development of the Argentine capital city and included a list of all those who were documented as
moving to Buenos Aires. In the list he included their place of birth, profession,
civil status, and other details. Six years later Lafuente Machain published *Conquistadores del Río de la Plata*, a bio-bibliographical dictionary tracing the 16th
century Spaniards through the Argentine conquest. These two works provided
later historians with significant data for their more extensive research on Buenos
Aires and on the conquest of the La Plata region.

A. *La imagen patrona de la Asunción* (Buenos Aires, 1917); *Los Machain* (Buenos Aires,
1926); *Los portugueses en Buenos Aires* (Buenos Aires, 1931); *Don Pedro de Mendoza
y el puerto de Buenos Aires* (Buenos Aires, 1936); *Conquistadores del Río de la Plata*
(Buenos Aires, 1931); and *Buenos Aires en el siglo XVII* (Buenos Aires, 1944).

B. Julian Garces, "Ricardo de Lafuente Machain," *Revista de historia de América*, No.
49 (June 1960), pp. 191-192.

LAMAS, ANDRÉS (10 November 1817, Montevideo—22 September 1891, Buenos Aires). *Education*: Attended the Universidad de la República, Montevideo, Uruguay. *Career*: Edited *El sastre* (Montevideo), 1836; contributed to several other journals; participated in Uruguay's civil war, 1838; founded *El iniciador*; wrote for *El nacional, El comercio del Plata*, and *El conservador*; Uruguayan Minister of Government, Minister of Finance, and Minister of Foreign Relations; chief political administrator during Uruguay's Great War, 1843-1851; worked as a diplomat in Brazil seeking support against the Rosas dictatorship.

Born in Uruguay, Lamas spent some time in Brazil and Argentina before finally settling down in Buenos Aires in 1875. As a political figure he enjoyed considerable success, but when the turmoil of Uruguay subsided and he felt that he was no longer required to contribute to the leadership of the nation, he retired to Buenos Aires to write and study. While he had been in Uruguay and Brazil he had collected documents that he could now put to use in the bibliographical and historical works that he later produced. Lamas' major contribution to Argentine historiography was bibliographical. While he wrote monographs, they did not have the impact on Argentine historical writing that came from his bibliographical studies.

In his bibliographical collections, Lamas familiarized himself with the citations of historical events and ordered them into workable units. He was also an erudite monographer of historical events. In one essay in 1891 Lamas sought to explain the uniformity of the independence movements throughout Latin America by pointing to the similarity of the conquests and the colonial experiences. This hemisphere-wide perspective was not found in many of the historians of his era, most of whom were nationalistic in their philosophies and concentrated their efforts only on the history of their own countries.

A. *Colección de obras, documentos y noticias inéditas o poco conocidas para servir a la historia física, política y literaria del Río de la Plata* (Buenos Aires, 1869); *Juan Díaz de Solis: Descubrimiento del Río de la Plata* (Buenos Aires, 1871); *Escritos políticos y literarios* (Buenos Aires, 1877); *Introducción a la obra del P. Lozano, historia de la conquista del Paraguay, Río de la Plata y Tucumán*, 5 vols. (Buenos Aires, 1873-1875); *Rivadavia: Su obra política y cultural* (Buenos Aires, 1915); *Biografía de don Joaquín Suárez: Su descendencia en el Uruguay, Brazil y Argentina* (Buenos Aires, 1941).

B. Rómulo D. Carbia, *Historia crítica de la historiografía argentina desde sus orígenes en el siglo XVI* (La Plata, 1939), pp. 26-29, 100-106, 131-133; Ione S. Wright and Lisa M. Nekhom, *Historical Dictionary of Argentina* (Metuchen, N.J., 1978), pp. 470-471.

LARRAZÁBAL, FELIPE (1818, Caracas—1873, at sea off New York). *Education*: Doctor of Civil Law, Central University of Venezuela, 1841. *Career*: Musician; journalist; jurist; historian; biographer; founded and directed the periodicals, *El patriota*, 1828, and *El federalista*, 1830; established a short-lived conservatory of music in Caracas; Governor; Deputy, National Congress; Minister, High Federal Court.

Throughout much of the 19th century Venezuelan men of letters gave considerable attention to the life of the great liberator, Simón Bolívar. Larrazábal was especially enamored of Bolívar's exploits, and he devoted his literary career to reconstructing the independence hero's life. In 1865 Larrazábal published two volumes of Bolívar's biography, but he continued to collect data for further study, believing that his initial effort merely laid the foundation for a more detailed account that he would produce later. Meanwhile, Larrazábal served in various political posts and published numerous articles on political themes that contributed to the ongoing 19th century debate over conservative versus liberal politics. He was a passionate polemicist who during the course of his many verbal battles emerged as one of Venezuela's outstanding thinkers and writers. Eventually he amassed a sizable collection of Bolívar's letters, which he planned to publish in Europe. The letters numbered 3,000 and Larrazábal packed them for shipment to Europe. He accompanied the letters on shipboard, but off the coast of New York the ship sank, killing Larrazábal and burying his prized collection of Bolívar's letters at sea.

While Larrazábal's interest in Bolívar's life occupied much of his time, he also wrote historical articles on other themes and a book on religious seminaries. Nonetheless, he was renowned for his work on Bolívar's life. His research on Bolívar was extensive and his documentation generally sound. The work was marred, however, by Larrazábal's frank fondness for his subject, upon whom he heaped praise with little objective material or analysis included. Additionally, he wrote music that was lyrical but excessively sentimental, much like his historical treatment of Bolívar. Later Venezuelans have criticized him for his verbose, digressive writing style. He was influenced by ancient writers such as Thucydides, Livy, and Tacitus, and he incorporated some of their style into his biography of Bolívar. As one writer put it, Larrazábal seemed incapable of understanding that he was a historian and not an epic poet. Then, too, his undisguised love for Bolívar led him to accept almost every act carried out by the Venezuelan hero as right and proper. His biography was deficient in its lack of objectivity, but its one redeeming virtue was that it was the first biography of Bolívar, and in it Larrazábal described the personality of his subject carefully and accurately. Although the work no longer has much value in Venezuelan historiography, its author is regarded as one of the first true biographers in Venezuela and not an amateur who toyed with historical subjects.

A. *Memorias contemporáneas* (Caracas, 1846); *Historia de los seminarios clericales* (Caracas, 1856); *Correspondencia general del libertador Simón Bolívar* (New York, 1871); *Asesinato del general Salazar* (Barranquilla, Colombia, 1873); *Vida de Bolívar*, 2 vols. (Madrid, 1918).

B. *Diccionario biográfico de Venezuela* (Madrid, 1953), pp. 587-588; Donna Keyse and G. A. Rudolf, *Historical Dictionary of Venezuela* (Metuchen, N.J., 1971), p. 73; and César Humberto Soto, *Personajes célebres de Venezuela* (Caracas, 1946), pp. 163-164.

LAS CASAS, BARTOLOMÉ DE (11 November 1484, Sevilla, Spain—18 July 1566, Madrid). *Education*: Gained a solid Latin education in the cathedral academy of Sevilla; self-taught through reading. *Career*: Taught Christian doctrine on Hispaniola, 1502; landholder and encomendero on Hispaniola; first priest ordained in the New World, 1512; entered the Dominican order, 1524; organized a Dominican mission in Guatemala, 1537-1539; lobbied at the Spanish court for the abolition of the encomienda system, 1540; attempted to build a model community in Venezuela, 1520-1521; Bishop of Chiapas, Mexico, 1545-1550.

Although Las Casas was a holder of Indians on his encomienda in the New World he ultimately concluded that they should not be enslaved, and he devoted the remainder of his life to the task of freeing them from Spanish domination. Because he was glib, erudite, and persuasive he was able to convince the Spanish crown that the treatment of the Indians in the New World was barbarous and must be changed. At one point the king stopped future conquest while the crown tried to determine whether the Indians should be treated as human beings. Las Casas' lobbying efforts eventually paid off, and the New Laws of 1542 provided for the gradual abolition of the encomienda system which had mistreated the Indians so severely, according to Las Casas. In 1550 he debated the entire question of conquest and colonization in America with Juan Gines de Sepúlveda. Sepúlveda contended that some people were born to be slaves and that the Indians could be conquered, enslaved, and finally converted to Christianity. Las Casas countered that argument by stating that all men in the world were the same and that they were capable of improving their lot and of being educated. Consequently, he urged that all wars against the Indians be stopped and that they not be forced to work for their Spanish conquerors. His argument was somewhat vitiated by virtue of his earlier call to import Africans to replace the Indians on the encomiendas, but it nonetheless gained a wide audience and provided Spain's antagonists, like England, with ammunition to attack the Spanish for their cruelty and barbarity toward the American Indians. Las Casas was, therefore, a contributor to what came to be called the Black Legend, which was the characterization of the Spanish as excessively cruel, brutal, and barbarous.

Las Casas has been criticized for his histories, which are called biased, overdrawn, exaggerated, and polemical. His books were used to buttress his arguments with the crown on the treatment of the Indians as he carried on his never-ending fight for Indian rights and humane treatment. But his works are also partially eyewitness accounts of the conquest of America and of Indian society in America. In one book he compared the Indians with the Europeans to illustrate his conviction that the Indians were capable of Christianization and of adopting civilized life. In his description of events that he witnessed his books are significant because he was usually faithful to the event and did not overstate his case, as he did when he was arguing for the amelioration of the treatment of the Indians. Although he made little effort at objectivity, his accounts are crucial for an understanding of early colonization, if the reader keeps in mind his polemical bent and his well-known biases, central among which was the conviction that the only defensible justification for the Spanish presence in America was to Christianize and care for the Indians.

A. *Brevíssima relación de la destruyción de las Indias* (Sevilla, 1552); *A Briefe Narration of the Destruction of the Indies by the Spaniards* (London, 1625); *Derecho público* (Madrid, 1843); *Historia de las Indias*, 5 vols. (Madrid, 1865-1876); *Apologética historia* (Madrid, 1909); *Crueldades que los españoles cometieron en los indios mexicanos* (Mexico City, 1926); *Las Antiguas gentes del Perú* (Lima, 1939).

B. Juan Friede and Benjamin Keen, *Bartolomé de las Casas in History* (DeKalb, Ill., 1971); Lewis Hanke, *Bartolomé de las Casas, Bookman, Scholar, Propagandist* (Philadelphia, 1952); Lewis Hanke, *Bartolomé de las Casas, Historian* (Gainesville, Fla., 1952); John L. Phelan, "The Apologetic History of Fray Bartolomé de las Casas," *Hispanic American Historical Review*, 49, No. 1 (February 1969), pp. 94-99; Helen Rand Parish with Harold E. Weldman, S.J., "The Correct Birthdate of Bartolomé de las Casas," *Hispanic American Historical Review*, 56, No. 3 (August 1976), pp. 385-403; and Henry Raup Wagner and Helen Rand Parish, *The Life and Writings of Bartolomé de las Casas* (Albuquerque, N.M., 1967).

LASTARRIA SANTANDER, JOSÉ VICTORINO (22 March 1817, Santiago—14 June 1888, Santiago). *Education*: Law degree, National Institute, Santiago, 1839. *Career*: Leader of the Liberal party; founded the Literary Society of Santiago; founded a newspaper, *El seminario de Santiago*; served in the Ministry of the Interior, 1843; Deputy to Congress, 1843; founded a literary review, *La revista de Santiago*; Plenipotentiary Minister to Peru, Argentina, and Brazil, 1862; Deputy, 1867-1873; founded the Fine Arts Center of Santiago, 1873; Minister, Court of Appeals; Senator, 1876; Minister of the Interior, 1876; Senator, 1879-1885; Supreme Court judge.

In mid-19th century Chile, young intellectuals became restive with the dominance of the Conservative party in government. Lastarria emerged as a leader in the movement to unseat the Conservatives and establish a new liberal regime. The liberals were enamored with the romanticism of the Argentine exile *Domingo Sarmiento and opposed to the neoclassicism of *Andrés Bello. But Bello was the most respected intellectual leader of Chile, and his views prevailed despite the popularity of Lastarria, who was one of the most outspoken supporters of liberalism in politics and romanticism in literature. As part of his views Lastarria demanded a break with Spanish tradition in favor of modern French ideas, which Bello opposed. Along these lines Lastarria wrote a scathing denunciation of Spanish colonial policies, which contributed to the already established Black Legend of Spanish barbarism in the New World.

Lastarria became an important participant in the development of Chilean historiography in the 19th century. He wrote history himself, but his more important contribution was to set forth a view of how history should be written that departed from the form espoused by Andrés Bello. Bello taught that history could be written properly only after extensive research in primary documents that had been rigorously tested for authenticity. Once the research was completed Bello believed that a narrative literary form was the best method to present the findings of research. Lastarria, conversely, disdained this type of history, which he believed to be overly simplistic and ineffective, and he advocated a more complex, sophisticated form, which he called philosophical history. In this method Lastarria was less concerned about detailed research than about sweeping general-izations that one might make from historical events. His first major effort was the initial historic memorial presented to the University of Chile in the series created by Andrés Bello. That study was a comprehensive examination of the colonial age, with a minimum of primary research but a maximum of interpre-tation of already accepted historical data. This same determination to assess ages in history led him to another book, which he thought should have won a prize but which lost out to another study. When that happened Jacinto Chacón, an avid disciple of Lastarria, charged that Lastarria's method was the reason for his loss of the prize and challenged the narrative historians to develop what he regarded as Lastarria's higher form of historiography. Bello took up the chal-lenge, and a brief polemic ensued between Chacón and Bello, with Lastarria's historiographical ideas at the center of the debate. Neither side altered its views, and Lastarria continued to the end of his life convinced that his form of histo-riography was superior to the narrative method of Bello.

A. *Bosquejo histórico de la constitución del gobierno de Chile durante el primer periodo de la revolución desde 1810 hasta 1814* (Santiago, 1847); *Don Guillermo: Historia contemporánea* (Santiago, 1860); *Don Diego Portales* (Santiago, 1861); *Recuerdos literarios*, 2 vols. (Santiago, 1878-1879); *Estudios históricos*, 3 vols. (Santiago, 1909); and *La América* (Buenos Aires, 1965).

B. Helen Delpar, *Encyclopedia of Latin America* (New York, 1974), pp. 324-325; Joaquín Rodrígues Brava, *Don José Victorino Lastarria* (Santiago, 1892).

LEGUIZAMÓN, MARTINIANO (28 April 1858, Rosario de Tala, Entre Rios, Argentina—26 May 1935, La Finca "La Morita," Argentina). *Education*: Studied at Colegio Nacional de Concepcion del Uruguay; Doctor of Jurispru-dence, University of Buenos Aires, 1885. *Career*: Taught history and literature in secondary schools, 1886; held a post in the Ministry of Finance of the prov-incial government of Buenos Aires, 1888; counsel for a Buenos Aires bank; journalist and novelist.

Leguizamón worked in many areas of literature, beginning with poetry, which he produced at a young age, and carrying through journalistic essays, novels, folklore, articles on customs, theatrical dramas, and history. In most of his work he was preoccupied with the gauchos and others who lived in the countryside. His themes were local in nature, and he was, like many of his contemporaries, extremely patriotic, not only for Argentina but for the province in which he lived; as he championed provincial themes he also condemned cosmopolitanism.

In his histories Leguizamón reflected his two preoccupations, patriotism and regional historiography. One scholar has suggested that his "nativist passion" comprised his historical impartiality. For example, as he delved deeply into gaucho history in his search for the true origin of this romantic and important Argentine class, he became enamored with the gauchos. Since he was motivated by a regionalist sentiment, he then concluded that the gaucho originated in Argentina and not Uruguay, as some scholars had suggested. Moreover, he failed to understand the impact of the rest of the nation on the gauchos, just as he did not concern himself with Argentina's influence on his home province. Additionally, he was unable to bind the Spanish culture that had been influential in the creation of Argentina to the modern age in his country. But one positive result from his gaucho research was the creation of an interest in Juan Manuel de Rosas, who used the gauchos in his rise to power in Buenos Aires province and eventually in all of Argentina. Leguizamón published for the first time many of the dictator's papers, annotating and assessing each of them. While he was a champion of the gauchos, this work presented the gaucho leader, Rosas, in a generally unfavorable light. Despite the shortcomings of his work, Leguizamón has been labeled "the patriarch of Creole literature" in Argentina. In all of his literary efforts, including his histories, he wrote in a clear, precise style that drew praise from his contemporaries.

A. *Recuerdos de la tierra* (Buenos Aires, 1896); *Alma nativa* (Buenos Aires, 1906); *La cuna de gaucho* (Buenos Aires, 1916); *Páginas argentinas: Crítica literaria e histórica* (Buenos Aires, 1916); *Rasgos de la vida de Urquiza* (Buenos Aires, 1920); and *Papeles de Rosas* (Buenos Aires, 1936).

B. "Bibliographical Section," *Hispanic American Historical Review*, 16, No. 4 (November 1936), pp. 548-549; Roberto F. Giusti, *Diccionario de la literatura latinoamericana: Argentina* (Washington, D.C., 1961), pp. 104-106; Martin Alberto Noel, *El regionalismo Leguizamón* (Buenos Aires, 1945); Delio Panizza, *Martiniano Leguizamón* (Buenos Aires, 1940); José Torre Revello, *Martiniano Leguizamón: El hombre y su obra* (Parana, Argentina, 1939); and Ione S. Wright and Lisa M. Nekhom, *Historical Dictionary of Argentina* (Metuchen, N.J., 1978), pp. 492-493.

LETELIER, VALENTÍN (1852, Santiago—1919, Santiago). *Education*: Law degree, University of Chile, 1871. *Career*: Politician; writer; historian; Rector, University of Chile, 1906.

Caught up in political activity through much of his career, Valentín Letelier was as much activist as passive scholar. He was a leading member of the Radical party at the turn of the century, and he was among those who forced the overthrow of President José Manuel Balmaceda in 1891. Letelier was instrumental in getting the Radical party to take greater interest in social problems and to forsake the almost total preoccupation with political matters that had characterized the party through much of its history. Additionally, he was committed to the philosophy of positivism, and he was the individual most responsible for the development of that philosophy in Chile. Finally, he worked in the field of pedagogical reform, particularly in the teaching of law.

He carried out historical research not only in Chile but in Germany as well. While in Europe he researched and wrote about Berlin's schools in the belief that an understanding of education abroad would assist the Chileans in solving their own educational problems. Not only did he discuss practical educational developments in Germany, but he also explored the various philosophies of education that he encountered and compared them with Chilean educational theories. Beyond his speculation on education, Letelier worked hard to reform teaching laws in the nation, using the research he had conducted to support his arguments. In this manner, he used historical study to justify political and educational changes in his contemporary world.

A. *El hombre antes de la historia* (Copiapó, Chile, 1877); *De la ciencia política en Chile* (Santiago, 1886); *La acusación* (Santiago, 1890); *El cobro de intereses en el derecho chileno* (Santiago, 1897); *La acción penal dedans entre comuneros escrits hecho para que se tenga presente* (Santiago, 1898); *La evolución de la historia* (Santiago, 1900); *Apuntaciónes de derecho administrativo* (Santiago, 1904).

B. Helen Delpar, *Encyclopedia of Latin America* (New York, 1974), p. 329.

LETURIA, PEDRO DE (26 November 1891, Zumárraga, Spain—20 April 1955, Rome). *Education*: Primary and secondary studies in Orduña, Vizcaya, and Bogotá, Colombia; doctorate, University of Munich, 1914. *Career*: Joined the Jesuit order at the age of 15; taught in Bogotá, 1915-1918; helped organize the Jesuit Historical Institute in Rome; founded the international historical review in Rome, *Archivum historicum, S.J.;* inaugurated the Department of History in the Gregorian University, 1929, and served as Professor and Head of the Department, 1929-1950.

Entering the Jesuit order at a young age, Leturia turned his attention to scholarly pursuits and coupled his clerical duties with diligent study that led him to schools in Spain and Germany. He took his doctoral degree in Germany, where he was trained in the rigorous Germanic school of historiography. Throughout the remainder of his life he studied diligently in archives and worked carefully in private documental collections held by Colombian citizens. In particular, he devoted much time to the materials relating to Latin America in the Archives of the Indies in Sevilla, Spain, and in the archives of the Vatican, Rome, and Simancas. He became one of the major resources of knowledge about materials that existed in these collections, and he was frequently consulted by colleagues from around the world as to what they might find in these major archives.

Father Leturia's major historical interest was in the termination of the role of the Patronato Real in Spanish America, and from the time of his doctoral dissertation this theme occupied much of his scholarly attention. But he also devoted some time to the independence era and to the heroes of that independence and their intellectual as well as military contributions to the achievement of independence. His skill in using archives enabled him to perform the kind of primary research that was essential for other historians to carry out their work. He laid a solid foundation upon which his contemporaries could build.

A. *El ocaso del Patronato Real en la América española, la acción diplomática de Bolívar ante Pio VII* (Madrid, 1923); *Der Heilige Stuhl und das spanische Patronat in Amerika* (Munich, 1926); *Las grandes bulas misionales de Alejandro VI* (Barcelona, 1930); *Bolívar y Léon XII* (Caracas, 1931); *Gregorio XVI y la emancipación de la América española* (Mexico City, 1948); *Ideales políticos religiosos del "precursor" Miranda* (Madrid, 1951).

B. Instituto Panamericano de Geografía e Historia, *Guía de personas que cultivan la historia de América* (Mexico City, 1951), pp. 236-237; "Obituaries," *Hispanic American Historical Review*, 35, No. 3 (August 1955), pp. 441-442.

LEVENE, RICARDO (7 February 1885, Buenos Aires—13 March 1959, Buenos Aires). *Education*: Studied at the Colegio Nacional, Buenos Aires; Doctor of Laws, University of Buenos Aires, 1906. *Career*: Taught history, Colegio Nacional, 1906; Professor of Sociology, University of Buenos Aires, 1911; Professor of Judicial and Social Sciences, University of Buenos Aires, 1914; Secretary, Department of Economics, 1915; Professor of History, University of La Plata, 1919; Professor, University of Buenos Aires, 1920; Dean, School of Humanities, University of La Plata; President, University of La Plata; and President, Argentine National Academy of History.

Ricardo Levene was a leading historian not only in Argentina but in all of Latin America. He combined a respected scholarly career with educational administration to become a prominent figure in Argentine higher education. With the weight of his scholarship giving him added stature as an administrator, he served as President of the National Commission of Historical Museums and Monuments, a position from which he oversaw the restoration and conservation of the nation's archeological and historical remains. He also founded and directed the Institute of the History of Law, and he established the Archivo Histórico de la Provincia de Buenos Aires in 1926. While he did not travel widely outside his country, he maintained a constant contact with scholars in other Latin American countries, the United States, and Europe, and he was quick to assist any historian who needed Argentine source material. As President of the Unversity of La Plata, Levene expanded the curriculum of the institution to include medicine and journalism, and he enlarged the schools of astronomy, agronomy, and veterinary science.

In the early years of his career Levene concentrated upon the independence period in Argentine history as he worked carefully through the archives and libraries to research these topics. Later he studied the history of Argentine law, producing a number of outstanding monographs on this subject. Unlike most 19th century historians, he was also interested in other than political history, and he was the first Argentine to deal with the independence movement from the economic and judicial perspective. He was also intrigued with the idea of comparing Argentine history with the histories of other American nations, something that had not been done to any great extent by earlier Latin American historians. It was this penchant for comparative history that led to Levene's recognition by historians in other countries, and in 1937 he served as Chairman of the International Congress of History of the Americas that met in Buenos Aires. Later he became the editor of the Historia de America project that led to the publication of 14 monographs on the history of individual Latin American countries. Finally, Levene was interested in the lengthy national histories that 19th century historians had frequently found so appealing, and between 1936 and 1942 he published his monumental 10-volume *Historia de la nación Argentina*.

A. *Lecciones de historia argentina*, 2 vols. (Buenos Aires, 1913); *Ensayo histórico sobre la revolución de mayo y Mariano Moreno*, 2 vols. (Buenos Aires, 1920-1921); *Investigaciones acerca de la historia económica de virreinato del Plata*, 2 vols. (Buenos Aires,

1927-1929); *Historia de la nación argentina*, 10 vols. (Buenos Aires, 1936-1942); *Historia de las ideas sociales argentinas* (Buenos Aires, 1947); *Las ideas históricas de Mitre* (Buenos Aires, 1948); *Las Indias no eran colonias* (Buenos Aires, 1951); *El mundo de las ideas y la revolución hispanoamericana de 1810* (Santiago, 1956).
B. Joseph R. Barager, "The Historiography of the Río de la Plata Area, Since 1830," *Hispanic American Historical Review*, 39, No. 4 (November 1959), pp. 603-605; Instituto Panamericano de Geografía e Historia, *Guía de personas que cultivan la historia de América* (Mexico City, 1951), pp. 237-238; José M. Mariluz Urquijo, "Ricardo Levene, 1885-1959,"*Hispanic American Historical Review*, 39, No. 4 (November 1959), pp. 643-646; Percy Alvin Martin, *Who's Who in Latin America* (Stanford, 1936), pp. 212-213; William Belmont Parker, *Argentines of To-Day* (Buenos Aires, 1920), I, pp. 187-188; and Ione S. Wright and Lisa M. Nekhom, *Historical Dictionary of Argentina* (Metuchen, N.J., 1978), pp. 496-498.

LEVILLIER, ROBERTO (1886, Paris—19 March 1969), Buenos Aires). *Education*: Studied in Europe, 1906-1907. *Career*: Wrote for *Caras y caretas* and *La nación*; editor of *El país*, 1900; private secretary to the Intendent of Buenos Aires, Manuel Guiraldes; carried out historical research at the Archives of the Indies in Sevilla, Spain, 1912; Minister Plenipotentiary and Extraordinary Envoy to Peru, 1922; assigned to the Argentine Embassy in Lisbon, 1927; served in Argentine embassies in Czechoslovakia, Poland, and Finland, 1928-1934; Ambassador to Mexico, 1935-1937; Ambassador to Uruguay, 1938-1941.

As a diplomat serving in a variety of foreign countries, Levillier was able to utilize the archival material from those nations to write his histories. At the same time his early training as a journalist provided a clear, interesting writing style that made his books and articles attractive to the reading public. He was committed to the idea that historical research materials should be available to scholars who might not have the good fortune to travel in foreign lands where archives were open to them. Consequently, in 1934 he proposed that the League of Nations Assembly edit a comprehensive history of the primitive cultures of America that would be published in both Spanish and French and would be a cooperative international project of scholars. The League ultimately agreed to the project and authorized the publication of 15 volumes of ethnography and 25 of history. By the time the project was approved and ready for publication, however, it was 1938, and the international problems of that year led Argentina to withdraw its financial support for the project, which was eventually scrapped.

Levillier was able to write many history books on his own, particularly after he retired from diplomatic service following 1942. Prior to that time, however, he used his tour of diplomatic duty in Peru to collect the material for what one Argentine historian called his most important work, *Nueva crónica de la conquista de Tucumán*. Research in the Archives of the Indies in Spain was also used to develop this history, which required four volumes. This work was marked by an introductory essay on prehistorical developments in the La Plata region, which provided a valuable backdrop for the entire study. In his later work Levillier turned to biographies of Spanish conquerors in America and devoted a two-volume work to the life and activity of Amerigo Vespucci in which he defended the contributions made to the Western Hemisphere by Vespucci and concluded that the naming of the continent for him rather than Columbus, as some historians had suggested, was justified. While Levillier concentrated on the colonial period in various regions of South America, he was also an Argentine patriot who devoted many articles and books to the treatment of his nation's history. Yet he has been called "the historian of America" by Latin American scholars, indicating the breadth of his hemisphere-wide interest.

A. *Antecedentes de política económica en el Río de la Plata*, 2 vols. (Madrid, 1915); *Nueva crónica de la conquista del Tucumán*, 3 vols. (Buenos Aires, 1926, 1930, 1932); *Biografía de los conquistadores de la Argentina* (Madrid, 1933); *Don Francisco de Toledo, Supremo organizador del Perú*, 3 vols. (Buenos Aires, 1935, 1939, 1942); *América, la bien llamada*, 2 vols. (Buenos Aires, 1947-1948); *El nuevo mundo, Americo Vespucio* (Buenos Aires, 1951).

B. Ricardo R. Caillet-Bois, "Roberto Levillier (1886-1969)," *Revista de historia de América*, No. 71 (January-July 1971), pp. 156-160; Ione S. Wright and Lisa M. Nekhom, *Historical Dictionary of Argentina* (Metuchen, N.J., 1978), p. 498.

LLAVERÍAS MARTÍNEZ, JOAQUÍN (27 July 1875, Havana—23 November 1956, Havana). *Education*: Bachelor of Arts, University of Havana, 1893; began study toward a degree in medicine, University of Havana. *Career*: Fought for the revolutionaries in Cuba's war for independence from Spain, reaching the rank of Captain, 1898; appointed to a minor position in the Archives of the Island of Cuba, the forerunner of the National Archives of Cuba, 1901; worked in the Archives for the remainder of his life; Editor, Director, and contributor to the *Boletín del Archivo Nacional de Cuba* throughout its existence; represented Cuba at the International Congress of Archivists and Librarians, Brussels, 1910; Director, National Archives of Cuba, 1922-1956.

At the conclusion of the Cuban struggle for independence Joaquín Llaverías, a dedicated patriot who had fought during the war, agreed to take charge of the nation's archival collection. That decision led him to give up a cherished ambition to become a medical doctor, and instead of returning to the university to continue his education in medicine, he devoted the remainder of his life to Cuba's archives. Not only did he give his time and energy to the collection and classification of documents, but he also recognized the need for a forum to acquaint scholars and political leaders, as well as the general public, with the work of the archives. To that end he was instrumental in founding the *Boletín del Archivo Nacional de Cuba*, which he used extensively to further the interests of the archives throughout his lifetime. He also used the *Boletín* to publish some of his own historical articles, which were generally well written and carefully researched. Additionally, he struggled at great length to acquire a suitable building to house the archives, and the building was completed in 1944 after he enlisted the support of those in government as well as many from private life to help convince the authorities that a building was essential. Following the move into new quarters,

Llaverías then added printing equipment, and the archives press was formed to disseminate news about the archives and to give scholars a vehicle to publish their research. In this way he supported not only the archival and bibliographic work of the scholarly community in Cuba but the activity of historians as well.

   Although his major contribution to historical scholarship was in the direction and maintenance of the archives, Llaverías was a historian in his own right. He used the material he assiduously collected and catalogued to write articles and a few books on historical subjects. Moreover, he assisted many scholars by writing introductions to their books, thereby lending his own prestige and the prestige of the archives to many historical accounts. Most of his scholarship revolved around archival matters and he wrote two histories on the development of Cuba's archives, but he did produce a few articles on the history of journalism in Cuba and on specific historical events in the nation. Although his research was careful and profound, his major contribution to historiography remained in the assistance he provided other historians through his archives and his publishing help. Without his aid, the writing of history in Cuba would have been much more difficult in the early and middle years of the 20th century.

A. *Historia de los archivos de Cuba* (Havana, 1912); *Los periódicos de Martí* (Havana, 1929); *Papeles existentes en el Archivo General de Indias relativos a Cuba y muy particularmente a la Havana 1512-1586* (Havana, 1931); *Catálogo de los fondos del Liceo Artístico y Literario de la Habana* (Havana, 1944); *Martí en el Archivo Nacional* (Havana, 1945); *Biografía del Archivo Nacional de Cuba* (Havana, 1954).

B. Roscoe R. Hill, "Joaquín Llaverías Martínez, 1875-1956," *Hispanic American Historical Review*, 37, No. 3 (August 1957), pp. 346-355; Percy A. Martin, *Who's Who in Latin America*, 2d ed. rev. (Stanford, 1940), p. 283.

LÔBO, HÉLIO (17 October 1883, Juiz de Fora, Brazil—1960, Juiz de Fora). *Education*: Bachelor's degree, Law School of Rio de Janeiro, 1902. *Career*: Journalist and polemicist writing for *Revista forense* of Belo Horizonte and *Gazeta jurídica* of São Paulo; named to the commission to negotiate Bolivian-Brazilian boundaries, 1910; First Secretary of the Diplomatic Corps, 1914; served in the Brazilian Embassy in the United States; assigned to the Brazilian mission to The Hague; Secretary to the President of the Republic, 1914-1918; Consul General in London, 1920; taught history at the University of Buenos Aires, Yale University, the University of Pennsylvania, and the University of Montevideo, 1920-1922; served in the Brazilian Embassy in Santiago, 1923; Minister Plenipotentiary to Uruguay, 1928; Extraordinary Envoy to The Hague, 1930.

   Hélio Lôbo's historical activities were aided by his diplomatic career, which enabled him to visit many different countries and to learn about those countries and their relationship with Brazil. His diplomatic assignments also opened up archives and libraries in Europe and the United States that would have been unavailable to him had he not chosen a diplomatic career. When stationed in the United States he examined the idea of democracy from a historical perspective and also wrote about contemporary issues such as prohibition, arms limitation, and imperialism. Eventually he turned his attention to relations between the United States and Brazil and wrote of the need for better understanding between the two nations. His diplomatic histories also dealt with the concept of equality among nations, and he argued that Brazilian diplomatic history had been marked by the desire on Brazil's part to effect equality among nations, a policy inspired by Brazilian ideas of fraternity and justice.

Hélio Lôbo also became interested in economic history and wrote in favor of government involvement in the economy to facilitate production and trade in Brazil. At the same time he studied and wrote about the financial activities of the nation and the organization of the financial structure that was the underpinning of the nation's economy. Some of his research took him into Brazilian political history, and by virtue of his access to diplomatic archives he was able to publish a book in 1916 on the events leading up to the War of the Triple Alliance, 1864-1870.

A. *De Monroe a Río Branco* (Rio de Janeiro, 1912); *Antes da guerra* (Rio de Janeiro, 1914); *Cousas diplomáticas* (Rio de Janeiro, 1918); *Cousas americanas e brasileiras* (Rio de Janeiro, 1923); *Docas de santos* (Rio de Janeiro, 1936); *Panamericanismo e o Brasil* (São Paulo, 1939).

B. Sergio Buarque de Holanda, "Historical Thought in Brazil," in E. Bradford Burns, *Perspectives on Brazilian History* (New York, 1967), p. 187; Virgilio Correa Filho, "Hélio Lôbo," *Revista de historia de América*, No. 49 (June 1960), pp. 192-201.

LÓPEZ, VICENTE FIDEL (24 April 1815, Buenos Aires—30 August 1903, Buenos Aires). *Education*: Doctor of Law, University of Buenos Aires, 1839. *Career*: As an opponent of the Juan Manuel de Rosas dictatorship, went into exile in Chile shortly after graduating; joined fellow exile Domingo Sarmiento to establish a school and create a journal, *El progreso*; fought against the Rosas government; embarked upon a political career as Minister of Public Instruction, Buenos Aires, 1852; Professor of Political Economy, University of Buenos Aires, and Rector, 1868; served in the Argentine National Congress, 1871–1880; President of the Bank of the Province, 1879-1883; Minister of Finance, 1890; created the Bank of the Nation.

López was embroiled in the political activities of his age, spending time in exile in Chile, Uruguay, and Brazil. He was most effective in his anti-Rosas activity with his journalistic endeavors, written while in exile in foreign nations. Following the overthrow of Rosas he devoted attention to both government service and private business, and he was active in the formation of the Radical party. Throughout his public and private business career he continued writing, and along with his friend from exile, *Juan María Gutiérrez and the Uruguayan, *Andrés Lamas, he founded the *Revista del Río de la Plata* in 1871. At the same time he continued to think about and write the history of his nation.

As a youth López knew the leading political figures of the early independence age, and from them he also heard a great deal about the independence struggle itself. When he began to write the history of this age he had the memories of these leaders to guide him and to enliven his narrative. But he was strongly influenced by foreign historians and writers such as Jules Michelet, Thomas Macaulay, and Sir Walter Scott. From them he learned about style and concluded that history must be exciting, interesting, and stimulating, as well as factual. He wanted his readers to feel the emotions of the age that he described, to become a part of these past great events. He also argued that the historian could not remove himself from his theme completely and look upon it in a cold, aloof, strictly objective manner. Linked with this view was his belief that research in primary documents in a somber archive was less desirable than seeking out oral tradition and interviewing the primary figures who made the history. This interpretation of the historian's craft brought him into direct conflict with another great 19th century Argentine historian, *Bartolomé Mitre. The two giants of historiography engaged in a monumental polemic over the proper historic method, with Mitre championing exhaustive study in archives while López advanced his oral tradition concept. After several articles and books the polemic ended with no advantage to either man, but it was extremely significant because it brought into sharp focus the vastly different techniques employed by each man. By participating in this discussion López helped make Argentine historiography of the 19th century far richer than it had been in earlier years.

A. *La revolución argentina: Su origen, sus guerras y su desarrollo político hasta 1830*, 5 vols. (Buenos Aires, 1881); *Debate histórico; refutación a las "Comprobaciones históricas" de Mitre*, 2 vols. (Buenos Aires, 1882); *El conflicto y la entrevista de Guayaquil, expuesta al tenor de los documentos que la esplican* (Buenos Aires, 1884); *Historia de la República Argentina: Su origen, su revolución y su desarrollo político hasta 1852*, 10 vols. (Buenos Aires, 1883-1893); and *Manual de la historia de Chile* (Valparaiso, Chile, 1845); *Memoria sobre los resultados generales...y un estudio preliminar de José Luís Romero* (Buenos Aires, 1943).

B. Joseph R. Barager, "The Historiography of the Río de la Plata Area, Since 1830," *Hispanic American Historical Review*, 39, No. 4 (November 1959), pp. 595-598; Rómulo D. Carbia, *Historia crítica de la historiografía argentina desde sus orígenes en el siglo XVI* (La Plata, 1939), pp. 150-158; Roberto F. Giusti, *Diccionario de la literatura latinoamericana: Argentina* (Washington, D.C., 1961), pp. 103-107; José Victorino Lastarria, *Recuerdos literarios: Datos para la historia literaria de la América española i del progreso intelectual en Chile*, 2d ed. (Santiago, 1885), pp. 89-90, 130-137, 139; Ione S. Wright and Lisa M. Nekhom, *Historical Dictionary of Argentina* (Metuchen, N.J., 1978), pp. 509-510.

LÓPEZ PORTILLO Y ROJAS, JOSÉ (26 May 1850, Guadalajara, Mexico—22 May 1923, Mexico City). *Education*: Law degree, Universidad de Guadalajara, 1871. *Career*: Traveled extensively in the United States, Europe, and the Orient; taught political economy and commercial and penal law, Escuela de Jurisprudencia, 1872; Deputy from Jalisco, National Congress, 1875-1877; journalist; Deputy, National Congress, 1880-1882; Senator, 1882; founded *La república literaria*, 1886-1890; Governor of Jalisco, 1911-1913; Minister of Public

Education; Minister of Foreign Relations under Huerta; taught at secondary schools during the tumultuous decade of the Mexican Revolution.

López Portillo was a good example of the Latin American historian who also worked in many other disciplines and at various jobs. He was a lawyer, philosopher, and politician, and he wrote poetry, novels, religious stories, and legends. He also traveled widely and wrote travel books upon his return. Scholars have placed him somewhere between the romantic and the realist literary movements, and he participated in both so that both schools influenced his work. In the great Mexican polemic over the primacy of the Mexican nationalist or Hispanist literature, he adopted a conservative and traditionalist view. He argued that the rich Hispanic tradition was essential for the progressive development of Mexican literature, and he opposed the use of French words to alter the Castillian language. He believed that Mexicans should assert their nationalism without adulterating the Spanish language by reverting to French literary currents. In his novels he touched on social problems, such as the relationship between large landowners and laborers, and in one novel he wrote about life in an orphan asylum. He defended the social work of the Church and attacked the new reformist secularized philosophy of social activity.

In his historical efforts López Portillo reflected the conservative traditionalist views that could be found as well in his other literary activity. He was pro-Church and pro-Spanish background, while the liberal historians were anticlerical and hostile to the Spanish colonial experience, instead exalting the Indian historians of Mexico and denigrating everything Spanish. He also advocated the dissemination of traditional morality among the people, both in his fiction and in his historical efforts. In this manner he wrote about the colonial period, the Indians, and even about Porfirio Díaz, which was a foray into contemporary history. But he was unlike most Latin American historians of the era in that he did not confine himself exclusively to writing the history of his own country. Instead, he wrote about the Middle East, Europe, and occasionally the United States. This breadth of interest set him apart from many of his contemporaries and earned him a place of prominence among Mexican historians. However, his major niche was in fiction and poetry, not history.

A. *La raza indigena* (Mexico City, 1904); *La doctrina Monroe* (Mexico City, 1912); *Historias, historietas y cuentecillos* (Paris, 1918); *Aztecas y espartanos* (Mexico City, 1921); *Elevación y caida de Porfirio Díaz* (Mexico City, 1921); *Enrique VIII de Inglaterra* (Mexico City, 1921).

B. *Diccionario Porrúa de historia* (Mexico City, 1973), I, p. 1211; Aurora M. Ocampo de Gómez and Ernesto Prado Velázquez, *Diccionario de escritores mexicanos* (Mexico City, 1967), pp. 198-200; Margarita Perez Poire, *Don José López Portillo y Rojas, su vida, su obra* (Mexico City, 1949).

M

MARTÍNEZ, JOSÉ LUCIANO (12 June 1870, Montevideo—18 August 1956, Montevideo). *Education*: Doctor of Laws, University of Montevideo, 1902. *Career*: Commanded a company of the University Battalion while in school; Private of Artillery, 1893; promoted to Ensign, 1895; helped found the Artillery Corps, 1898; promoted to Second Lieutenant, 1898; promoted to First Lieutenant, 1902; fought in the 1904 war; served in the War Department; Secretary to the Governor of Montevideo, 1907; Secretary to the Military Court of Appeals; Military Judge of Instruction, 1912; and finally promoted to Lieutenant Colonel.

Few career military men became so involved in researching and writing history as Colonel Martínez. As a result of his extensive research he gained a reputation as an expert on military history and was in great demand to give addresses and to publish articles in newspapers and periodicals both in Uruguay and abroad. He wrote biographies of famous Uruguayan military leaders, but in addition he also studied historical military strategy in important battles. Additionally, he became involved in a polemic in the Montevideo press in 1917, which provided an opportunity to use his historical knowledge and his literary skill.

A member of the Historical and Geographical Institute, Martínez used his firsthand knowledge of military life to research topics in military history. In this manner he was able to bring to his historical works an expertise that the nonsoldier did not possess. His histories were narrative in nature and not particularly analytical, nor did he delve into the problem of military involvement in politics that afflicted not only Uruguay but all Latin America. Nevertheless, his work brought to his leaders a measure of understanding of the military and the action in which Uruguayans participated.

A. *Cuestas y su administración* (Montevideo, 1904); *Biografía del teniente coronel don Eulogio de los Reyes* (Montevideo, 1907); *Hombres y batallas* (Madrid, 1912); *Batalla del Palmar* (Montevideo, 1935); *Corazones y lanzas* (Montevideo, 1943); *Horas de gloria* (Montevideo, 1951).
B. William Belmont Parker, *Uruguayans of To-Day* (New York, 1967), pp. 317-319.

MARURE, ALEJANDRO (28 February 1806, Guatemala City—23 June 1851, Guatemala City). *Education*: Philosophy degree, Seminario Conciliar, 1822; studied law, University of San Carlos. *Career*: Appointed to a post in the Ministry of Foreign Relations and ultimately became Chief of the department; Deputy to the Legislative Assembly of the Nation, 1831; taught history and geography,

Academia de Estudios, Guatemala City, 1832; prepared, along with others, an atlas of the nation; taught international law, University of San Marcos, 1839; Member, Consultative Council of State, 1839-1849; participated in the breakup of the Central American Federation and the creation of the independent status of Guatemala.

During the second quarter of the 19th century Central America was going through a tumultuous period of attempted unity in the face of widespread sympathy for the creation of separate, independent nations. Marure lived through that age and took part in some of the political events that developed in his home in Guatemala. He carried out missions in Honduras and El Salvador for the Guatemalan government, and he had an opportunity to witness firsthand the wrenching experience for the region. From an early age he had been an outstanding student, and throughout his life he retained the scholarly qualities that early had been nurtured in him. While his political, diplomatic, and teaching duties occupied much of his time, he managed to write for the press and more importantly to produce several outstanding histories of his country. One of his most impressive books was a heavily documented monograph on the social, economic, and political value of an interoceanic canal for Nicaragua entitled *Memoria histórica sobre el canal de Nicaragua.*

Marure wrote contemporary history, which enabled him to live the material about which he wrote. He was a man who seemed to have no personal ambitions either for literary fame or for monetary accumulation. He was the true scholar whose intellectual pursuits were aimed at providing knowledge for others. He found time for political, diplomatic, and journalistic activity, but he did not permit these other interests to color the scholarship of his history. He sought objectivity in his work while recognizing that this elusive goal is even more difficult when writing about contemporary events than when developing accounts from periods long past when the principal actors and their close relatives are no longer present. Marure, recognizing the vicissitudes of his work, managed to produce several fine histories dealing with Central American turbulence in the first half of the 19th century. In one of his books he wrote that he was not interested in gaining plaudits from his contemporaries for his efforts but that he was writing history for subsequent generations, which he suggested should be the goal of all historians. As a researcher he rigorously examined his documentation, believing that the historian's task was not simply to collect documents but also to make certain that they were valid. To ensure validity he believed sources had to be analyzed in the light of events of the age in which they were written. He argued that passions and prejudices had to be eliminated from the mind of the successful historian and once that was achieved an objective account must be the result.

A. *Bosquejo histórico de las revoluciones de Centro-América desde 1811 hasta 1834* (Guatemala City, 1837); *Memoria sobre la insurrección de Santa Rosa y Mataquescuintla en Centroamérica, comparada con la que estalló en Francia el año de 1790, en los departmentos de La Vendée* (Guatemala City, 1837); *Observaciones sobre la intervención que ha tenido el expresidente de Centro-América, general Francisco Morazán, en los negocios públicos de Guatemala durante las convulsiones que ha sufrido este Estado, de mediados de 1837 a principios de 1839* (Guatemala City, 1839); *Catálogo de las leyes del Estado de Guatemala* (Guatemala City, 1841); *Efemérides de los hechos notables acaecidos en la república de Centro-América, desde el año 1821 hasta el de 1842* (Guatemala City, 1844); *Memoria histórica sobre el canal de Nicaragua* (Guatemala City, 1845).

B. William J. Griffith, "The Historiography of Central America Since 1830," *Hispanic American Historical Review*, 40, No. 4 (November 1960), pp. 549-550; Richard Moore, *Historical Dictionary of Guatemala*, rev. ed. (Metuchen, N.J., 1973), p. 129; and Unión Panamericana, *Diccionario de la literatura latinoamericana: América Central; Costa Rica, El Salvador y Guatemala* (Washington, D.C., 1963), II, pp. 121-124.

MEADE SÁINZ-TRÁPAGA, JOAQUÍN FELIPE (5 February 1896, San Luís Potosí, Mexico—3 July 1971, San Luís Potosí). *Education*: Studied English, French, art, and the violin with tutors in his home; attended St. Mary's High School, Kansas, 1908-1910; studied in Beaumont, England; and attended Oxford University in England, 1915. *Career*: Served in the English army, 1918; Honorary Consul of Switzerland in Tampico, 1929; independently wealthy.

Meade had the advantages of family wealth so that he had plenty of time to research and study and the funds to travel in Mexico and throughout Europe and the United States visiting archives and libraries. From 1900 throughout his life he visited Europe and traveled to various sites in Mexico. In 1920 he began seriously to study in the Mexican General Archive and later visited the libraries and archives of the states of San Luís Potosí, Tamaulipas, and Veracruz. At this time he also became interested in archaeology, and through the 1920s he made several explorations in Huastecas, which he photographed. This effort was undertaken at his own expense. After 1934 he focused his research on the history and archaeology of his home state of San Luís Potosí.

Meade's historical work was not primarily analytical or profound. Instead, he concentrated his efforts on collecting information on data, which he then published for other historians and archaeologists to use. He published unedited documents and general histories and guides of cities and archeological sites in Mexico. Additionally, many of his photographs were published in his books, giving them added interest for general readers.

A. *Documentos inéditos para la historia de Tampico. Siglos XVI y XVII* (Mexico City, 1939); *La Huasteca, época antigua* (Mexico City, 1942); *Arqueología de San Luís Potosí* (Mexico City, 1948); *San Luís Potosí* (San Luís Potosí, Mexico, 1953); and *La Huasteca veracruzana*, 2 vols. (Mexico City, 1962-1963).

B. "Joaquín Meade," *Revista de historia de América*, Nos. 73-74 (January-December 1972), pp. 219-221.

MEDINA, JOSÉ TORIBIO (21 October 1852, Santiago—11 December 1930, Santiago). *Education*: Studied humanities and law, National Institute; became a lawyer, 1873. *Career*: Secretary of the Chilean legation, Lima, 1874; visited the Philadelphia World's Fair in 1876; worked at the British Museum in London; fought in the War of the Pacific; named Auditor of War of the Army of the Reserve; returned to Chile to practice law; First Secretary of the Chilean legation, Madrid; studied at the Archives of the Indies, Sevilla, Spain; established his own printing press in his house to publish his books, 1886; and traveled widely in Latin America and Europe in quest of bibliographical materials.

Chile's and perhaps Latin America's greatest bibliographer, Medina traveled extensively to consult and copy documents, mainly from the colonial age, for the history of Chile. He also performed bibliographical research for the Río de la Plata area, during which time he met *Bartolomé Mitre, *Vicente Quesada, and other Argentine historians. For four years he lived in Spain studying at the Archives of the Indies and publishing several works, while at the same time copying manuscripts on Chilean history. From 1896 to 1902 Medina published 78 volumes on bibliography and history. In 1902 he traveled to Lima, Guatemala, and Mexico to continue his studies on early Latin America. From America he went to Paris and Rome to look for additional sources, and he returned to Chile particularly impressed with the Vatican library. In 1923 he donated his own considerable library to the government, and it was housed in a separate room in the National Library. In 1927 Medina made his last trip abroad, visiting the United States and Europe, where he received academic accolades for his lifetime of bibliographical and historical study.

Working in the periods of exploration and the conquest of America in the early years of his bibliographical study, Medina collected documents on Spanish activity not only in Chile but in all areas of Latin America. Additionally, he collected documents for a history of the Araucanian Indians. Later he gathered data for the study of the history of the colonial press in Chile, and he amassed a large collection of coins and medals from all over Latin America. Another area in which he was strongly interested was that of the Inquisition in America. Not only did he copy numerous documents from the Archives of the Indies in Sevilla, Spain, but he also acquired information from the Vatican as well. He was a tireless worker and an astute collector of historical documents. He edited, wrote, corrected, and even printed some of his bibliographies. His efforts were extremely significant to colonial Latin American history as his books became the initial stage in writing the histories of colonial Chile and Latin America.

A. *Historia de la literatura colonial de Chile*, 3 vols. (Santiago, 1878); *Los aborigenes de Chile* (Santiago, 1882); *Colección de documentos inéditos para la historia de Chile desde el viaje de Magallanes hasta la batalla de Maipo (1518-1818)*, 30 vols. (Santiago, 1888-1902); *La primitiva Inquisición americana (1491-1569)* (Santiago, 1914); *La literatura femenina en Chile* (Santiago, 1923); *Ensayo bio-bibliográfico sobre Hernán Cortés* (Santiago, 1952).

B. Victor M. Chiappa, *Noticias acerca de la vida y obras de D. José Toribio Medina* (Santiago, 1907); Salvador Dina-Marca, *Los estudios de Medina sobre Ercilla* (Santiago, 1953); Armando Donoso, *José Toribio Medina (1852-1930)* (Santiago, 1952); Sarah Elizabeth Roberts, *José Toribio Medina: His Life and Works* (New York, 1941); Raúl Silva Castro, *Medina y la historia literaria de Chile* (Santiago, 1953).

MELO MORAIS, ALEXANDRE JOSÉ DE (23 July 1816, Alagoas, Brazil—1882, Rio de Janeiro). *Education*: Taught by his uncles, who were members of the Carmelite order; degree in medicine, School of Bahia, 1840. *Career*: Practiced medicine; became a convert to the medical technique of homeopathy, which he introduced into Brazil; earned a small fortune from books written on homeopathy; directed a homeopathic clinic, 1840-1854.

Melo Morais was trained as a physician and following graduation he practiced medicine in his hometown. But then he became interested in homeopathic medicine, and from that point on he confined his medical attention to this technique, which sought cures by using small doses of drugs that produced the symptoms of the disease being treated. Melo Morais became the leading exponent of homeopathy in Brazil, and through the money he received from several books published on the subject he purchased historical documents for use in his research. He also used part of his own fortune to publish some of the historical documents. Later in life, after he had amassed a large collection of research materials, he offered them for sale to the government. Because he was a Deputy in the Legislature at the time and since he cast the deciding vote in favor of the sale, which returned a handsome financial profit to him, Melo Morais was criticized widely for a conflict of interest.

Melo Morais' historical methodology revolved around the extensive use of primary, archival documentation, and he devoted his life to collecting the important sources needed to build the true history of Brazil. He hired people in other countries to search the archives and libraries for documents relative to Brazil, and he also hired copyists to transcribe data and send them to him. If he found something of interest he acquired it, and in the process he was able to construct the magnificent archival collection that he eventually sold to the government. He also published parts of his collection of documents, but he made little effort to criticize the sources or to organize them logically so that they would be more useful for historians. In truth he seemed to lack the critical ability needed for historical research, and his own methodology was deficient. He also had problems with interpreting the sources and lacked talent in composition. Consequently, his published bibliographies were not well received by the scholarly community. However, he did collect important documents, and he was tenacious in finding important materials so that his bibliographical efforts were important for later historians.

A. *Ensaio corográfico de Império do Brasil* (Rio de Janeiro, 1854); *Brasil histórico* (Rio de Janeiro, 1868); *História do Brasil-reino e Brasil império* (Rio de Janeiro, 1871-1873); *A independência e o império do Brasil* (Rio de Janeiro, 1877); and *Os meus trabalhos sôbre a história do Brasil* (Rio de Janeiro, 1882).

B. José Honorio Rodrigues, *Historia e historiadores do Brasil* (Sao Paulo, 1963), pp. 99-109.

MÉNDEZ PEREIRA, OCTAVIO (30 August 1887, Aguadulce, Panama—14 August 1954, Panama City). *Education*: Teaching degree, Escuela Normal,

Panama, 1906; law degree, Universidad de Chile, Santiago, 1913; studied also in England and France, specializing in law. *Career*: Professor of Spanish, Instituto Nacional, Panama City; Rector, Instituto Nacional; Minister Plenipotentiary of Chile, 1921; Undersecretary of Public Instruction; Secretary of State, 1923; Extraordinary Envoy to England and France, 1927; helped found the Universidad Nacional de Panama, 1935; Rector, Universidad Nacional, 1935-1940; Director of the daily newspaper, *El Panamá-América*; wrote a column on culture for the newspaper, *La estrella de Panamá*; Rector, Universidad Interamericana, 1943; Panamanian representative to the first United Nations meeting in San Francisco, 1945; Regional Director of UNESCO, Havana, 1950; Founded the Museum of Panama.

Méndez Pereira was a teacher, an educational administrator, a literary figure, and a diplomat. In all these areas he excelled, and he managed to build a hemisphere-wide reputation, which also reflected positively upon his country. He traveled and studied in different countries and could speak fluent English and French in addition to his native Spanish. This study abroad also created in his mind a global impression, which he put to good use when he worked with the United Nations. In that capacity he was most concerned with humanitarian causes, for which he received a bust of himself that was displayed at American University in Washington, D.C. Additionally, universities throughout Latin America and the United States bestowed honorary degrees upon him for his outstanding work in cultural development and humanitarian activities.

Méndez Pereira's literary career revolved around poetry, journalistic essays, criticism, and history. He exhorted Panamanian youth to get involved in intellectual matters and to advance the prestige of their nation through their own literary efforts. A great patriot, he was proud of his nation and of its heritage, through which passed all manner of individuals, from priests to pirates, from chroniclers to explorers. In his writing of history he dramatized the varied background of his nation and made it plain that he was a champion of Panama and its people. He was the eternal optimist when writing about contemporary Panama, and his histories also had the tinge of optimism about them. In addition to histories he also wrote historical novels that were enthusiastic, fluid, and beautifully written. In all his work he expressed his ideas in a clear, concise fashion, leaving little room for misinterpretation of his views. His work was dynamic, thoughtful, and patriotic. He supported his nation in all his works, but his histories were not scrupulously objective; instead they were patriotic and strongly supportive of the country.

A. *Justo Arosemena* (Panama City, 1919); *Historia de la literatura española; apuntes tomados de uno de los cursos dictados en la cátedra del Instituto Nacional por el profesor...y publicados por Fabian Velarde* (Panama City, 1922); Congreso Panamericano Commemorativo del Bolívar, 1826-1926 (Panama City, 1927); *Breve historia de Ibero-América* (Panama City, 1936); *Alas en la muletas o la vida ejemplar de Roosevelt* (Panama City, 1945); *Bolívar y las relaciones interamericanas* (Panama City, 1960).

B. Percy Alvin Martin, *Who's Who in Latin America* (Stanford, 1936), p. 248; Juan

Almela Meliá, *Guía de personas que cultivan la historia de América* (Mexico City, 1951), pp. 270-271; and Unión Panamericana, *Diccionario de la literatura latinoamericana: América Central; Honduras, Nicaragua y Panamá* (Washington, D.C., 1963), pp. 265-268.

MENDOZA, CRISTÓBAL L. (9 October 1866, Caracas—26 February 1978, Caracas). *Education*: Philosophy degree, Central University of Venezuela, 1903; Doctor of Political and Social Sciences, Central University of Venezuela, 1907; conferred the title of lawyer, Superior Court of the Federal District, 1907. *Career*: Taught at the Central University of Venzuela, Caracas, and at the Technical Industrial School; wrote for *El tiempo*, and *El cojo ilustrado*; Editor-in-chief of *El tiempo*, 1910-1911; Secretary, National Academy of History, 1933-1937; President, Bolivarian Society, 1949-1964.

Before beginning his teaching career, Mendoza traveled to Europe to study their most modern educational techniques and then returned to Venezuela to implement those ideas in his native country. This devotion to studying carefully all possible information before making a decision or embarking upon a new job marked his entire career. He was devoted also to reforming the political atmosphere of his nation, and while he worked actively to make changes he also wrote about political problems in history to support his views with historical evidence. He was concerned about the unification of America and consequently wrote articles on Simón Bolívar's attempt to bring the newly independent Latin American states together at the Panama Congress in 1826. Mendoza was also concerned about social problems and wanted to illustrate the dire consequences of poverty throughout Latin America through his historical analysis of the region. In a speech he once said that he wanted to help end the poverty of Latin America by "being useful." Conseqently, when he wrote about problems in history he was trying to be useful for the present by illustrating the traditional roots of problems and then hoping to encourage others to work toward their solution.

Beyond his scholarship and teaching Mendoza was also instrumental in the organization of historians into scholarly groups. His work in founding and leading the Venezuelan Academy of History is indicative of his determination to assist the profession in a period of growth and development.

A. *La gloria de Isabel la Católica* (Caracas, 1883); *Estudio sobre la legítima* (Caracas, 1907); *Elogio de Andrés Bello* (Caracas, 1951); *Guerra a muerte* (Caracas, 1951); *Los escritos del Libertador* (Caracas, 1953); *Temas de historia americana* (Caracas, 1963).
B. "Homenaje: Cristóbal L. Mendoza: Trayectoria y voluntad," *Revista de historia de América*, No. 85 (December 1978), pp. 3-7.

MENDOZA, JAIME (25 July 1874, Sucre, Bolivia—26 January 1939, Sucre). *Education*: Attended the Seminario de San Cristobal; degree in medicine and surgery, Universidad Mayor de San Francisco Javier, Sucre, 1901. *Career*: Practiced medicine among the miners who worked for the Uncia and Llallagua mining companies; founded schools, hospitals, and sports centers in the remote mining areas of Bolivia; fought in the Battle of Arce, 1903; furthered his studies in Chile, 1906; traveled in Europe, 1911 and 1914; taught law and medicine, University of Sucre; Director of Manicomios, 1925; Rector, Universidad Mayor de Francisco Javier; Senator, 1931; military surgeon, 1932-1935; Director, National Mental Hospitals; Professor, School of Medicine, Sucre.

As a selfless young man devoted to helping the poor and afflicted, Mendoza worked as a physician in the most difficult regions of Bolivia, among some of the most destitute people. His contributions to their well-being were extensive, and for these efforts he has been characterized as a philanthropist. Not only did he put his talents as a physician at the disposal of the poor, but he also contributed the royalties from one of his books, *Apuntes de un médico*, to a women's mental institution. In addition to his work as a physician he was also a poet and essayist, and his literary career was aided by his widespread travels in both Europe and the Western Hemisphere. On these journeys he encountered such prominent Latin American writers as *Gabriel René-Moreno from his native country, who was living in Chile when Mendoza studied there. He also met Ruben Dario, *Rufino Blanco-Fombona, and Emilio Bobadilla, becoming friendly with all of them and receiving some influence from them in his literary endeavors. From these associations and from his perception of the world around him, Mendoza injected into his novels a strong social flavor, which also found its way into his histories. In the historical genre he was most influenced by his countryman Gabriel René-Moreno.

The influence of René-Moreno was evident in Mendoza's historical work, but Mendoza concentrated upon social history much like *Alcides Arguedas. However, while René-Moreno and Arguedas were pessimistic about Bolivian society and even the future of Bolivia, Mendoza, although never minimizing the problems facing the nation, remained throughout his life optimistic about Bolivia's future. He was an objective historian who wrote in a direct, clear style but with the objective of enlisting the Bolivian people in a monumental task of national development. In this job he set forth his so-called Andinista thesis, which simply pointed out the great influence of the Andes Mountains on the geographic, historical, and social development of Bolivia. He possessed a strong belief, too, in the value of the Indians for Bolivia's future, which led him to become one of the major forces behind modern Bolivian Indianismo. In his historical production he gained widespread respect and admiration, which has been evident among the finest Bolivian historians. For example, *Enrique Finot, himself one of Bolivia's outstanding historians, has written that Mendoza's historical studies were among the most solidly written in Bolivia in the 20th century.

A. *En las tierras de Potosí* (Barcelona, Spain, 1911); *La Universidad de Charcas y la idea revolucionaria* (Sucre, Bolivia, 1924); *Los héroes anónimos* (Cochamamba y La Paz, Bolivia, 1928); *La tesis andinista: Bolivia y el Paraguay* (Sucre, Bolivia, 1933); *La tragedia del Chaco* (Sucre, Bolivia, 1933); *El Chaco en los albores de la conquista* (Sucre, Bolivia, 1937).

B. Charles Arnade, ''The Historiography of Colonial and Modern Bolivia,'' *Hispanic*

American Historical Review, 42, No. 3 (August 1962), pp. 352-353; Fernando Díez de Medina, *Literatura boliviana* (La Paz, 1953), pp. 265-268; Enrique Finot, *Historia de la literatura boliviana* (Mexico City, 1943), pp. 343-346; Dwight B. Heath, *Historical Dictionary of Bolivia* (Metuchen, N.J., 1972), p. 153; William Belmont Parker, *Bolivians of To-Day*, 2d ed. rev. (New York, 1967), pp. 175-177; and Unión Panamericana, *Diccionario de la literatura latinoamericana: Bolivia* (Washington, D.C., 1958), pp. 59-62.

MERA, JUAN LEÓN (28 June 1832, Ambato, Ecuador—13 December 1894, Ambato). *Education*: Self-taught. *Career*: Painted; taught school; edited an official periodical; Governor of Tungurahua Province; Deputy, National Congress, President of the Senate; and Minister, Tribunal de Cuentas de la República.

Juan Mera was one of the few examples of historians emerging from the ranks of the poor in Latin America in the 19th century. Instilled with a great love for books as a child, he could not afford to buy reading materials, but he frequented the libraries and read the classic works in Spanish. As a young man he wrote poetry, but unlike the more prosperous intellectuals of Ecuador he could not indulge himself in pursuits that did not bring in money. Consequently, he turned from poetry to painting, and eventually after selling some of his work he went to Quito to paint with some of the finest artists in the nation. However, he favored writing over painting, and when he became interested in politics he used his writing ability to propose his political ideas. He wrote fables and satires on political points and strongly supported public education. Eventually he held political office, which eased his always difficult financial status. He also wrote the words for the national anthem adopted by the Ecuadorean Congress in 1865.

Mera was a poet, novelist, and folklorist as well as a historian. He was a careful researcher who took great pains to correct errors he found in literary works and to build extensive bibliographies of primary and secondary sources. In his books he utilized the indigenist theme and dwelled upon nativist points, praising the Indian population as heroes. He was a product of the romantic movement in literature, and the emotionalism of that type of work could be found in his histories, legends, novels, and poems. He was also interested in social themes, and again his histories were replete with discussions of the role of groups and individuals in society. He was also committed to interesting the youth of the nation in history and so he exalted the past in the hope of bringing more young men into the area of history writing, not just to explain and appreciate the past but to prepare them for the future. He wrote the first Indianist novel of America. He was also concerned about the territorial claims of Ecuador, and therefore one of his novels dealt with the contested eastern territories of the nation, which he believed belonged completely to Ecuador. These same themes found their way into his histories as he concentrated on political history. He once wrote that he wanted to continue the history of *Pedro Fermín Cevallos from the point at which it ended to his own day, but when he found that he did not have time to carry out this task he wrote shorter monographs on particular themes rather than a definitive national history.

A. *La virgen del sol, leyenda indiana* (Quito, 1861); *Ojeada histórico-crítica sobre la poesía ecuatoriana desde su época más remota hasta nuestros días* (Quito, 1868); *Cumandá o Un drama entre salvajes* (Quito, 1879); *Últimos momentos de Bolívar* (Quito, 1883); *García Moreno; libro inédito* (Quito, 1904); La dictadura y la restauración en la República del Ecuador; ensayo de crítica (Quito, 1932).

B. Luís Felipe Borja, *Juan León Mera; breves apunte críticos* (Quito, 1932); Darío C. Guevara, *Juan León Mera o el hombre de cimas* (Quito, 1944); Unión Panamericana, *Diccionario de la literatura latinoamericana: Ecuador* (Washington, D.C., 1958), pp. 40-43.

MIER NORIEGA Y GUERRA, FRAY JOSÉ SERVANDO TERESA DE
(18 October 1765, Monterrey, Mexico—3 December 1827, Mexico City). *Education*: Doctor of Theology, Colegio de Porta Coeli de Mexico, 1787. *Career*: Member of the Dominican order; Secretary to the Spanish Consul in Lisbon; journalist; member, Mexican Constituent Congress; Deputy, Mexican National Congress; signed the Mexican Constitution of 1824.

In December 1794 Mier Noriega gave a speech on the Virgin of Guadalupe questioning the authenticity of the miracle, and the authorities exiled him to Spain, where he lived as a recluse for 10 years after losing his title of Doctor. In 1808 he fought in Spain against the French invasion, but when the French forces were successful he went to England and then back to Mexico in time to take part in the Hidalgo Revolution for Independence. Mier Noriega wrote tracts and pamphlets in support of independence and once again fell into the hands of Spanish authorities, who convicted him in the Spanish Inquisition. His punishment was exile to Spain but he escaped and fled to Havana, and from there he moved to the United States. Near the end of the independence struggle in Mexico he returned to his homeland to be captured still another time by the Spanish, who now held only the island of San Juan de Ulua in the harbor of Veracruz. Eventually he was freed and became a part of the new government, but he opposed the first emperor of a free Mexico, Agustín de Iturbide, and he was exiled to Santo Domingo. When Iturbide's government fell, Mier Noriega returned to Mexico to serve again in the government.

With all of his activity against the Church in Mexico and Europe and with his fervent participation in the independence struggle in Mexico, Mier Noriega lived an exciting life at the center of the major political maneuvering of the early 19th century. Consequently, much of the history he wrote was of an autobiographical nature or centered on events in which he was a participant. In both cases he wrote from a firsthand vantage point, providing valuable information for later historians. His major work was a study of the independence struggle, and although sometimes he exaggerated the truth and strayed from the documentation that supported his work, it was still an important historical study chronicling events in this era. In all his writing he was an ardent champion of Mexican independence, and that fact, along with his colorful career, has made him a favorite chronicler of the early 19th century period for modern Mexicans.

A. *Historia de la Revolución de Nueva España antiguamente Anáhuac, o verdadero origen y causa de ella con la relación de sus progresos hasta el presente año de 1813* (London, 1813); *Carta de despedida a los mexicanos* (Puebla, Mexico, 1821); *Cartas del Dr. Fray Servando Teresa de Mier al cronista de Indias Doctor D. Juan Bautista Muñoz, sobre la tradición de Ntra. Sra. de Guadalupe de Mexico, escritas desde Burgos año de 1797* (Mexico City, 1875); *Escritos inéditos de Fray Servando Teresa de Mier* (Mexico City, 1944).

B. Donald C. Briggs and Marvin Alisky, *Historical Dictionary of Mexico* (Metuchen, N.J., 1981), pp. 146-147; *Diccionario Porrúa de historia* (Mexico City, 1976), I, pp. 1345-1346; Alfonso Junco, *El increible Fray Servando: Psicología y epistolario* (Mexico City, 1959); Aurora M. Ocampo de Gómez and Ernesto Prado Velázquez, *Diccionario de escritores mexicanos* (Mexico City, 1967), pp. 231-232; and Vito Alessio Robles, *El pensamiento del Padre Mier* (Mexico City, 1944).

MILLA Y VIDAURRE, JOSÉ (Salomé Jil) (4 August 1822, Guatemala City— 30 September 1882, Guatemala City). *Education*: Studied at the Colegio Tridentino until 1846. *Career*: Editor of *Revista de la sociedad económica de amigos del país*; Secretary, Hermandad del Hospital de Guatemala, 1849; held a post in the Ministry of Foreign Relations, 1850; Editor, *Gaceta oficial*; sent on a special mission to Washington, D.C., from Guatemala, 1858; published the periodical *Hojas de avisos*, 1861-1863; edited *La semana*, 1864-1871; wrote for *El correo de Ultramar*; commissioned by the government to write a history of Central America, 1874; Deputy, National Congress, on several occasions.

From an early age Milla displayed scholarly gifts and won a scholarship for his study in literature. He wrote poetry, articles for the press, and articles about customs, as well as history, even though he was well aware that the reading public in Guatemala was sparse and that making a living in literature might be next to impossible. In June 1871, when the conservative government for which he had worked gave way to the liberals, Milla went into exile, traveling through the United States and Italy from 1871 to 1874. He wrote a perceptive study of the countries he visited, particularly the United States. For his literary and journalistic efforts he became recognized as one of the major writers of Guatemala. As a journalist he was calm and reasoned in describing the events taking place in the chaotic Central America of his era. In his articles about customs he described in great detail the life of Guatemala's colonial society.

Milla was always interested in history both for his journalistic endeavors and for his novels. One scholar claims that he was the premier historical novelist in Latin America, publishing the first such book in 1866. But he also worked in traditional history, and he was careful of sources and rigorous in his criticism of documents, books, and other historians. He made significant changes in the work *Recordación florida* by *Antonio de Fuentes y Guzmán. But for his own books he devoted long hours to painstaking research in archives and libraries throughout the nation. He worked mainly in early colonial history beginning with the arrival of the first Spaniard and carrying his study through to independence. He was a penetrating and perceptive scholar who relied on the traditional method of extensive digging into archives and testing of documents for authenticity. But beyond his research capabilities he was also an accomplished prose stylist whose correct language was enlivened by his imaginative re-creation of events. One example of his clever literary activity was found in his study of the United States and Europe. He invented a traveling companion for himself, whom he called Juan Chapin. Into the mouth of Chapin he placed the words that he believed were typical of the average Guatemalan and in this fashion brought home to his fellow citizens some of their prejudices and foibles, while at the same time providing them with a clear interpretation of life in the United States. In 1873 the liberal president of Guatemala was so impressed with Milla's literary work that he personally met him on his return home and commissioned him to write an official history of Central America.

A. *Don Bonifacio: Leyenda antigua* (Guatemala City, 1862); *Los nazarenos: novela histórica* (Guatemala City, 1867); *Un viaje al otro mundo, pasando por otras partes, 1871-1874*, 3 vols. (Guatemala City, 1875); *Historia de la América Central, desde el descubrimiento del país por los españoles (1502) hasta su independecia de la España (1821); precedida de una "Noticia histórica" relativa a las naciones que habitaban la América Central a la llegada de los españoles*, 5 vols. (Guatemala City, 1879-1905); *Historia de un pepe* (Guatemala City, 1887).

B. John L. Martin, "A Note on José Milla, Official Historian of Guatemala," *Hispanic American Historical Review*, 21, No. 4 (November 1941), pp. 673-676; Richard Moore, *Historical Dictionary of Guatemala*, rev. ed. (Metuchen, N.J., 1973), p. 135; Walter A. Payne, *A Central American Historian, José Milla (1822-1882)* (Gainesville, Fla., 1957); Unión Panamericana, *Diccionario de la literatura latinoamericana: América Central; Costa Rica, El Salvador y Guatemala* (Washington, D.C., 1963), pp. 125-127.

MITRE, BARTOLOMÉ (26 July 1821, Buenos Aires—19 January 1906, Buenos Aires). *Education*: Attended secondary schools in Carmen de Patagones and Buenos Aires, along with the Military Academy in Montevideo; largely self-educated. *Career*: Artillery officer, 1839-1849; taught in the Military Academy of Bolivia; journalist in Chile; Minister of Government and Foreign Affairs, 1850s; Governor of Buenos Aires Province, 1860; first President of the Argentine Republic, 1862; Senator; founded the newspaper, *La nación*, 1869.

Mitre spent a good portion of his life in military action as Argentina was embroiled in provincial struggles and international wars. At the same time he became involved in politics, and when the opportunity arrived he served both the provincial government of Buenos Aires and the unified Argentine nation. Amid all the other activities that occupied his life he was always the scholar and writer. He published poems from a young age and was the consummate biblio-phile until his death. His collection of books and documents was a source of great pride, and when he died he left the collection and his home to the Argentine nation. In addition to journalism, poetry, and history, he is also credited with writing the first historical novel of Argentina, entitled *Soledad*. While his military career was not particularly distinguished, he was effective as a political leader and hailed as a successful president of his country. Mitre brought peace to the traditionally antagonistic provinces under his jurisdiction. Additionally, he encouraged economic development and used the government to assist in construct-ing transportation lines and ports to ensure economic growth. Following his presidency Mitre remained active in foreign affairs while serving as Senator from Buenos Aires. In 1874 he ran again for the presidency, but when he lost he declared the election fraudulent and launched a rebellion against the government. His uprising was crushed and Mitre was imprisoned but soon pardoned. While he remained in politics thereafter, he spent most of his remaining years re-searching and writing history.

As a historian Mitre dealt mainly with the independence period in Argentine history, an era only recently ended when his career began and many of whose participants were still alive. When he produced his histories, particularly his *Historia del Belgrano*, which he wrote in 1859, he had to contend with the biases and prejudices of those who actually participated in the independence struggle. He was instrumental in developing the early Argentine historiographic standards for his nation, and some have credited him with establishing a school of history that appeared to fit neatly into the temper of 19th century scholarship. He insisted that the historian must examine all available evidence, especially primary documents, and write his history while paying close attention to these sources. Unlike some contemporaries who found this kind of history dull and uninspired, Mitre insisted that for Argentina, at its particular stage of scholarly development, this kind of detailed, verifiable history was essential. Only after the events of the past had been clarified through careful scrutiny and analysis could historians then turn to the type of history that permitted philosophical speculation and the erection of speculative models of the past. Mitre remains to this day a respected founder and leader of Argentine historiography.

A. *Historia de Belgrano y de la independencia argentina*, 2 vols. (Buenos Aires, 1859); *Estudios históricos sobre la Revolución argentina: Belgrano y Guemes* (Buenos Aires, 1864); *Comprobaciones históricas a proposito e la "Historia de Belgrano,"* 2d ed. (Buenos Aires, 1881); *Nuevas comprobaciones históricas a propósito de historia argen-tina* (Buenos Aires, 1882); *Historia de San Martín y de la emancipación sudamericana*, 3 vols. (Buenos Aires,, 1887-1890); *Obras completas: Edición ordenada por el H. Congreso de Nación Argentina, ley no. 12.328*, 10 vols. (Buenos Aires, 1938-1942).
B. Angel Acuña, *Mitre historiador*, 2 vols. (Buenos Aires, 1936); Rómulo D. Carbia, *Historia crítica de la historiografía argentina desde sus origenes en el siglo XVI* (La Plata, 1939), pp. 161-169; Roberto F. Giusti, *Diccionario de la literatura latinoameri-cana: Argentina* (Washington, D.C., 1961), pp. 136-144; William H. Jeffrey, *Mitre and Argentina* (New York, 1952); Ricardo Levene, *Las ideas históricas de Mitre* (Buenos Aires, 1940).

MONCAYO, PEDRO (1807, Ibarra, Ecuador—1888, Valparaiso, Chile). *Ed-ucation*: Unknown. *Career*: Political figure; writer; journalist; historian.

Born shortly before the war for independence began in Ecuador, Moncayo grew up amid the intrigue, confusion, and tumult of the independence struggle. He became a participant in the post-independence scrambling for power and witnessed the Colombian role in Ecuadorean politics. Foreign domination of the

Ecuadorean government led him to battle for political control, and he participated in the patriotic society called El Quiteño Libre, which published a periodical that assailed the Colombian-dominated regime of Juan José Flores. Because of his political activity he was twice exiled. Following the first exile he returned home to participate in congressional activity. The second exile followed a civil war, and this time he went to Chile. There he wrote on the political and historical events of the nation. In those years he wrote a history of Ecuador. Never published, the manuscript was later destroyed by fire. He wanted to rewrite this study, and his friends and fellow scholars put documentation at his disposal that ultimately enabled him to write *El Ecuador de 1825 a 1875, sus hombres, sus instituciones y sus leyes*. He lived through the age he wrote about so that some of his material was firsthand, and in all of it he had strong feelings, which were reflected in the book.

His history of Ecuador, Moncayo wrote in the preface to the book, could not be a true history because he lacked the energy, health, and materials to write a sound study of that era. This was an accurate assessment, and *Pedro Fermín Cevallos wrote a small pamphlet extensively criticizing Moncayo's work as biased and inaccurate in places. Cevallos also criticized Moncayo's historic method, which was colored by his own political and personal views of the period under study. While this criticism was just for the entire book, it is true that in dealing with individuals whom he knew and with particular events in which he was a participant, Moncayo left a valuable account for later historians of that age. He had an appreciation of the events and of the maneuvering that took place in that chaotic post-independence period, and his recollections of those events and people made a significant contribution to Ecuadorean historiography.

A. *La cuestión de límites entre el Ecuador y el Perú según el uti possidetis de 1810 y los tratados de 1829* (Quito, 1860); and *El Ecuador de 1825 a 1875, sus hombres, sus instituciones y sus leyes* (Santiago, 1885).

B. Isaac J. Barrera, *Historiografía del Ecuador* (Mexico City, 1956), pp. 104-105; and Adam Szaszdi, "The Historiography of the Republic of Ecuador," *Hispanic American Historical Review*, 44, No. 4 (November 1964), p. 519.

MONTÚFAR, LORENZO (11 March 1823, Guatemala City—21 May 1898, Guatemala City). *Education*: Bachelor of Philosophy, Colegio Seminario, 1841; law degree, 1845. *Career*: Taught Roman law and Spanish civil law, University of San Carlos; Deputy, National Legislature; Magistrate, Supreme Court of Costa Rica; Minister of Foreign Relations, Costa Rica, 1856; special envoy to El Salvador, 1857; Rector, Universidad de Santo Tomas, Costa Rica, 1865; Nicaraguan Minister Plenipotentiary to Peru, 1869; Minister of War and Navy, Costa Rica; Minister Plenipotentiary of Guatemala in Washington, D.C., to deal with the problem of boundaries between Mexico and Guatemala.

Caught up in the struggles of Central American countries in the 19th century, Montúfar moved from country to country and at times held diplomatic posts outside Central America in North America and Europe. A political liberal, he frequently found himself at odds with governments of conservative persuasion, and on a number of occasions he was forced to move on to safer regions. He was an impassioned battler for causes that he believed in deeply, and in defense of those causes he was inflexible. He never deviated from the liberal philosophy and consistently opposed such conservative policies as the death penalty and the political power of the clergy. Additionally, he always defended the rule of law, the dignity of man, freedom, and human equality. He fought long and hard for his views through speeches, polemical articles in the press, and political struggles. He remained true to his beliefs, and his honorable battle to realize his objectives won the admiration even of his enemies.

There can be no doubt that Montúfar's passion for political causes had an impact upon his histories. The extent of that impact, however, is open to question. Some have argued that his political action did not color his work or reflect unduly his liberal commitment, while others insist that his history of Central America was rendered useless because of his biased political attitude. One writer claimed that he was so passionate in his beliefs that he even falsified facts to fit his preconceptions. Yet when he wrote about the law, few doubted his sincerity and his objectivity. One book on the rights of people was declared the official text on the subject. Despite critics the general consensus of Central American historians is that Montúfar made a significant contribution to the history of the region with his work, which was spearheaded by a seven-volume history of Middle America, *Reseña histórica de Centro-América.*. This type of multivolume, definitive national history was in vogue in the 19th century and it was this study that came in for much of the criticism that was leveled at him by critics, who viewed it as less an objective history than a political polemic delivered by a committed liberal.

A. *Reseña histórica de Centro-América*, 7 vols. (Guatemala City, 1878); *El evangelio y el syllabus* (San José, 1884); *Un dualismo imposible* (San Salvador, 1886); *Apuntamientos sobre economía política* (Guatemala City, 1887); *Walker en Centro-América* (Guatemala City, 1887); *El general Francisco Morazán; artículos publicados en 1892 y 1893 con motivo de la commemoración del primer aniversario de aquel héroe* (Guatemala City, 1896); *Discursos del doctor Lorenzo Montúfar* (Guatemala City, 1923).

B. William J. Griffith,"The Historiography of Central America Since 1830," *Hispanic American Historical Review*, 40, No. 4 (November 1960), p. 550; Rafael Montúfar, *Comprobaciones históricas; el doctor Lorenzo Montúfar y el partido jesuítico* (Guatemala City, 1899); Richard Moore, *Historical Dictionary of Guatemala*, rev. ed. (Metuchen, N.J., 1973); and Unión Panamericana, *Diccionario de la literatura latinoamericana: América Central; Costa Rica, El Salvador y Guatemala* (Washington, D.C., 1963), II, pp. 129-132.

MONTÚFAR Y CORONADO, MANUEL (1791, Guatemala City—1844, Jalapa, Mexico). *Education*: Unknown. *Career*: Journalist; President, Guatemalan Assembly, 1840.

Montúfar was an independence leader in the struggle against Spain who then went on to participate in the conservative-liberal struggles that wracked Central

America in the early independence era. He wrote articles of a political nature for the newspaper, *El editor constitucional*, and he became an active member of the Guatemalan Assembly. When the Guatemalan leadership prepared to establish a political structure for the nation, Montúfar was a party to the drafting of the first constitution. Later, when liberals and conservatives resorted to open warfare to determine the course of action for the nation, Montúfar fought on the side of the conservatives, and when liberals gained control of the government, Montúfar fled into exile in Mexico, where he spent the remainder of his life. It was from Mexico that he published his account of the revolutionary activity that he had witnessed in Central America.

In the heat of the Central American revolutions of the early independence age most of the chroniclers and historians supported the liberal cause, and when the liberals won the war the published accounts were written by liberals from the liberal point of view. The conservatives did not have an opportunity to make known their side of the argument in Central America, but Montúfar recalled the event from his exile in Mexico and from there he published a conservative interpretation of the political warfare. His work was deficient because he did not have access to the documents and materials of the revolutionary period, but it is significant because it was the only conservative history of Central America written in the first half of the 19th century.

A. *Memorias para la historia de la revolución de Centro-América (Memorias de Jalapa)* (Jalapa, Mexico, 1832); *Memoria del General José Arce* (San Salvador, 1947); and *Memorias del General Miguel García Granados*, 2d ed., 4 vols. (Guatemala City, 1952).
B. William J. Griffith, ''The Historiography of Central America Since 1839,'' *Hispanic American Historical Review*, 40, No. 4 (November 1960), p. 553; Richard Moore, *Historical Dictionary of Guatemala* (Metuchen, N.J., 1973), p. 138.

MORA, JOSÉ MARÍA LUÍS (1794, San Francisco de Chamacuero, Mexico—14 July 1850, Paris). *Education*: Doctor of Theology, Colegio de San Ildefonso, Mexico City, 1819. *Career*: Introduced the first course in political economy at the Colegio de San Ildefonso; taught philosophy, history, and constitutional, commercial, and agricultural law; political theorist who laid the foundations for Mexican liberalism; journalist; member of the Mexican legation in Paris, 1846; Minister Plenipotentiary in London, 1847.

In the midst of the post-independence struggle for political ascendancy in Mexico, Mora emerged as one of the leading political thinkers. Although a priest, he favored secular control over education, nationalization of Church wealth, and other anticlerical concepts. His ideas were used by liberal political leaders to create an effective political force that eventually gained control of the government with the Benito Juárez regime. Some of Mora's ideas also could be found in the Mexican Revolution of 1910 and were major facets of modern Mexican liberalism. The Mexican writer Arturo Arnaiz y Freg wrote that Mora's writing, perhaps unconsciously, laid the primary ideological foundation for the Liberal party, whose policies eventually became converted into constitutional concepts. Mora wrote the constitution for the state of Mexico, which was the major expression of Mexican liberalism.

As the great Mexican political thinker of the 19th century, Mora placed his stamp on the development of his country. But he was also a literary figure and a historian. He was more the intellectual than the active political warrior, but his influence was just as great or greater than those persons who operated actively on the political scene. Mora possessed a tremendous knowledge of Mexico and its political and social system, and he was determined to renovate the nation. He defended his views strongly, and once they were enunciated, he maintained his liberal principles throughout his life. His influence on contemporaries and subsequent generations was profound. He is considered one of the greatest Hispanic American essayists of the 19th century. He wrote in a sober, direct, concise, and energetic style that some have characterized as dry. But style was not of great interest or concern to him; instead he was preoccupied with his ideas. His powers of observation were enormous, and he was able to draw a clear word picture of an event, idea, or person. As a historian he reflected the liberal political view of Mexican history and provided a counterpoise to the conservative history of *Lucas Alamán. While some Mexican historians of the era were concerned about the lack of objectivity in writing about events in which they participated, Mora did not share their concern. He knew that such works could not be objective, but he did not find this fact disturbing. Instead he said that the studies contained valuable information that might otherwise be lost and that the biased work had the value of preserving this information for historians of a later, more disinterested era to use in writing a truly objective history of the event. Mora himself wrote three volumes on Mexican history from the liberal political perspective.

A. *Discurso sobre la naturaleza y aplicación de las rentas y bienes eclesiásticos* (Mexico City, 1833); *Mexico y sus revoluciones*, 3 vols. (Paris, 1836); *Obras sueltas*, 2 vols. (Paris, 1837); *Ensayos, ideas y retratos* (Mexico City, 1941); *El clero, la educación y la libertad* (Mexico City, 1949).

B. Arturo Arnaiz y Freg, *Estudio biográfico del doctor en teología y licenciado en derecho civil, don José María Luís Mora* (Mexico City, 1934); Helen Delpar, *Encyclopedia of Latin America* (New York, 1974), p. 389; Charles A. Hale, *Mexican Liberalism in the Age of Mora, 1821-1853* (New Haven, 1968); Aurora M. Ocampo de Gómez and Ernesto Prado Velázquez, *Diccionario de escritores mexicanos* (Mexico City, 1967), pp. 242-243; Joaquín Ramírez Cabañas, *El doctor Mora* (Mexico City, 1934); and Fulgencio Vargar, *El doctor José María Luís Mora y la educación en Mexico* (Mexico City, 1934).

MORENO, FULGENCIO R. (9 November 1872, Asunción—1933, Asunción). *Education*: Studied at the University of Asunción. *Career*: Journalist; on the staffs of *La unión, El progreso, La tribuna*, and *La prensa*, 1893-1901; an editor of the literary periodical, *La semana*; Editor-in-Chief, *Revista del Instituto Paraguayo*; Clerk in the General Post and Telegraph Office, 1894; Clerk of the Chamber of Deputies; elected Deputy Minister of Finance, 1901; elected Senator, 1903; Minister of Foreign Affairs, 1912; Director, Colegio Nacional de Asunción; Professor of History, Escuela Normal; Minister to Chile and Peru, 1913;

Minister Plenipotentiary Extraordinary to deal with the Bolivian boundary dispute, 1915; Minister to Bolivia, 1918; Minister to Chile, 1919.

The diplomatic career was an attractive one for many literary figures and scholars in 19th and early 20th century Latin America. Moreno was attracted to foreign service, along with his continuing interests in journalism and his devotion to historical and literary production. His terms in the National Congress also placed him in the mainstream of politics in his generation, and he exerted a measure of influence on the governmental activity of Paraguay. Also like many Latin American intellectuals, he managed to combine his career interests by researching and writing on diplomatic topics. In his case, however, Moreno's historical research into boundary claims benefitted Paraguay in the continuing quarrel with Bolivia over the Chaco region, a disagreement that led eventually to war.

Moreno's studies on the Chaco region were based on penetrating research and careful analysis of existing documentation, and they advanced Paraguay's claims to the Chaco region. But this was not his only historical effort. In addition, he wrote on the history of the city of Asunción and provided historical studies on Paraguay's independence period. Paraguay, Argentina, and Uruguay produced more regional and local historians than other areas of Latin America, and Moreno was one of the better writers at this type of history. Additionally, he worked in biography, which was typical of 19th century Latin American historians, but he ignored the political-military heroes who usually received the greatest attention from historians and wrote instead about literary figures, providing a cultural flavor to his historical efforts.

A. *La cuestión monetaria* (Asunción, 1902); *Diplomacia paraguayo-boliviana* (Asunción, 1904); *Estudio sobre la independencia del Paraguay* (Asunción, 1912); *Juan Zorrilla de San Martín* (Asunción, 1915); *Paraguay-Bolivia* (Asunción, 1917).

B. Charles J. Kolinski, *Historical Dictionary of Paraguay* (Metuchen, N.J., 1973), p. 164; and William Belmont Parker, *Paraguayans of To-Day* (New York, 1967), pp. 163-165.

N

NIN FRÍAS, ALBERTO AUGUSTO ANTONIO (9 November 1882, Montevideo—28 March 1937, Montevideo). *Education*: Studied at the College of St. Mark, Windsor, England, La Chatelaine, Geneva; the Municipal Gymnasium, Berne, Switzerland, and the Institute of St. Louis, Brussels; graduated from the University of Montevideo in 1908; M.A., George Washington University, Washington, D.C., and a Ph.D. from the same institution, 1910. *Career*: Librarian, Uruguay's House of Representatives, 1904; Lecturer in French, Preparatory School of the University of Montevideo; substitute lecturer in philosophy and ethics, 1906; Secretary of the Uruguayan legation at Washington, D.C., 1908; Chargé D'Affaires in Washington, D.C., 1909; Secretary of the Uruguayan legation in Brazil, 1910; Chargé D'Affaires in Chile, 1913; Secretary of the Uruguayan legation in Venezuela and Colombia, 1914; Chargé D'Affaires in Venezuela and Colombia, 1915; Professor of Spanish and American History, University of Syracuse, 1915; University Secretary, Y.M.C.A., Buenos Aires; and Vice-Rector, Universidad Popular de Buenos Aires.

Unlike most Latin American historians Nin Frías was educated largely outside his native country, in Europe and the United States. He was fluent in several languages, which made not only his overseas education but also his interest in a diplomatic career logical and reasonable. While he served in many countries and many positions, he never reached the highest levels of the diplomatic profession, but he was important enough in the Uruguayan foreign service to hold many second-level posts. When he gave up his diplomatic career he then turned to teaching and eventually to educational administration.

Nin Frías worked in several academic disciplines, including English, philosophy, Spanish literature, and history. His historical efforts centered on social, religious, and literary history; he was primarily interested in the history of Uruguay, but he also worked in some aspects of world history. His research was seldom in primary sources; he was more a synthesizer of the works of others, and his histories were mainly essays constructed from these secondary sources. Nevertheless, in this form of historiography he excelled, his work was well received, and he enjoyed the respect of intellectuals from his own country and from abroad as well.

A. *Ensayos de crítica e historio* (Montevideo, 1902); *Nuevos ensayos de crítica e historia* (Montevideo, 1904); *Estudios religiosos* (Valencia, Spain, 1909); *Ensayo sobre el In-*

stituto Americano de Acción Social (New York, 1909); *La literatura como factor social* (Buenos Aires, 1914).

B. Percy Alvin Martin, *Who's Who in Latin America*, 2d ed. rev. (Stanford, 1940), p. 352; and William Belmont Parker, *Uruguayans of To-Day* (NewYork, 1967), pp. 377-379.

O

O'LEARY, JUAN EMILIANO (13 June 1880, Asunción—1968, Asunción). *Education*: Graduated from Colegio Nacional, Asunción, 1899; attended the National University of Paraguay. *Career*: Taught American and Paraguayan history, history of Spanish literature, geography, rhetoric, and world history, Colegio Nacional and Escuela Normal de Asunción; Director, Colegio Nacional de Asunción, 1910; Deputy, National Congress, 1917; Minister Plenipotentiary to Spain; Director, National Archives, 1934.

O'Leary devoted his career mainly to teaching and to administrative tasks in the field of education. Additionally, he worked in archives and in the preservation of historical documents. In this regard he was vastly different from most Latin American historians, who spent much of their time involved in political struggles or diplomatic service. He did hold a couple of offices, but he did not have the inclination to spend his time in the political wars of his country. His archival work in particular was significant because he helped to rebuild the Paraguayan archives following their virtual destruction in the disastrous War of the Triple Alliance.

O'Leary's histories have focused on the period of the War of the Triple Alliance, when Paraguay fought Argentina, Uruguay, and Brazil. Commensurate with this interest he developed a passion to study the career of the Paraguayan dictator Francisco Solano López, both from the national political perspective and from the vantage point of Paraguay's leader in the war. O'Leary was a member of the Paraguayan Generation of 1900, but unlike most of his contemporaries he defended Solano López rather than castigating him. O'Leary was a member of the Colorado party, the conservative party to which Solano López belonged. O'Leary's research convinced him that much that had been written earlier that was critical of Solano López was unfounded, and he therefore initiated a revisionist school of historiography relative to the war and to Solano López. In O'Leary's history Solano López emerges as a hero rather than a villain. O'Leary's research on the war was extensive, and he tried to work as much as possible in primary documents from the age he studied. But his interpretation of those sources and his views of the entire mid-19th century Paraguayan experience as expressed in *El mariscal Solano López*, were significant since they created a new approach to the war and to Solano López. Less important than his work on the war was O'Leary's study of Guaraní literature. He collected some Guaraní prose and poetry, and he was well enough immersed in Guaraní poetry to be asked to write a prologue to a 1921 collection of Indian poetry. Still, his major contribution to Paraguayan history was his interpretation of the Solano López epoch.

A. *Frente al pasado* (Asunción, 1916); Nuestra epopeya (Asunción, 1919); *El libro de los heroes* (Asunción, 1922); *El Paraguay en la unificación argentina* (Asunción, 1924); *El mariscal Solano López* (Asunción, 1926); *El centauro de Ybycui; vida heróica de general Bernadino Caballero en la guerra del Paraguay* (Paris, 1929).

B. Joseph R. Barager,"The Historiography of the Río de la Plata Area, Since 1830,"*Hispanic American Historical Review*, 39, No. 4 (November 1959), p. 622; Charles J. Kolinski, *Historical Dictionary of Paraguay* (Metuchen, N.J., 1973), p. 171; Percy Alvin Martin, *Who's Who in Latin America*, 2d ed. rev. (Stanford, 1940), p. 285; and William Belmont Parker, *Paraguayans of To-Day* (New York, 1967), pp. 113-114.

OLIVEIRA LIMA, MANUEL DE (1867, São Paulo Brazil—1928, São Paulo). *Education*: Unknown. *Career*: Diplomat in Lisbon, Tokyo, Venezuela, Brussels, and Washington, D.C.

Oliveira Lima was a diplomat who spent most of his life outside Brazil in the service of his nation. He collected books and documents from libraries and archives in Europe, the United States, and other Latin American countries. Eventually he could boast of a private library of more than 40,000 pieces of historical material, which he used to write his histories. Prior to his death he willed his substantial library to the Catholic University of São Paulo.

Many 19th and early 20th century Brazilian historians focused their attention upon the independence and early imperial periods of Brazilian history. Oliveira Lima was one of those who was enthralled with this era. His histories came on the heels of the substantial efforts of *Francisco Adolfo de Varnhagen, a pioneer in writing Brazilian history, but Oliveira Lima never reached the stature of Varnhagen, although his works were widely read. He did very little work in original source material but instead went over the work of other historians and used their efforts to build a new interpretation of the independence era, particularly the role of the Portuguese King João VI. Unlike other Brazilian historians of his era, he tried to elevate the position of João in the independence and early post-independence ages. At the same time, he studied carefully the activities of the royal court and the imperial bureaucracy, which he sought to integrate into the history of that period. He was not particularly cognizant of the role of the Brazilian people in their own history because he believed that since they had no political power they were not necessary in any recounting of Brazil's past. Oliveira Lima was born and had been raised under the empire, and he was a pro-imperial historian who disliked the republic and never felt quite comfortable living under it. This accounts, in part, for the role of expatriot he played in the last years of his life. In addition to his studies of João and the imperial age in Brazil, he also touched lightly on what we might call today psychohistory, a form of historiography that had little support until the second half of the 20th century.

A. *Aspectos de literatura colonial brazileira* (Leipzig, 1896); *Dom João VI no Brazil*, 2

vols. (Rio de Janeiro, 1908); *América Latina e America Ingleza; a evolucão brazileira comparada dom a hispano-americana* (Rio de Janeiro, 1910); *A conquista do Brazil* (São Paulo, 1913); *Dom Pedro e Dom Miguel* (São Paulo, 1925).
B. Robert M. Levine, *Historical Dictionary of Brazil* (Metuchen, N.J., 1979), p. 152; and Stanley Stein, "Historiography of Brazil, 1808-1889," *Hispanic American Historical Review* 40, No. 2 (May 1962), pp. 234-278.

OLIVEIRA VIANNA, FRANCISCO JOSÉ DE (20 June 1883, Rio de Janeiro—1951, Rio de Janeiro). *Education*: Colegio Carlos Alberto Niteroi; LL.D., University of Rio de Janeiro, 1906. *Career*: Professor of Law, School of Law, Rio de Janeiro; Director, Industrial Institute of the State of Rio de Janeiro, 1926; Member, Consultative Council of the State of Rio de Janeiro, 1931; legal adviser, Ministry of Labor, 1932; member of the special commission to revise the federal constitution, 1933.

As a young man Oliveira Vianna espoused the political causes of his upper-class background and developed an antiliberal political philosophy that he carried throughout his life. Not only did his histories reflect these political views, but when he became an influential political figure in the 1930s he was party to the drafting of laws that regulated labor unions and social welfare programs.

The most articulate of the young right-wing, antiliberal writers of the 1920s, Oliveira charged in his histories that the 19th century Brazilian empire fell not because of the strength of the republican movement but because of inherent weaknesses in the imperial regime. There were, he argued, few adherents to the antiempire forces, but the military was crucial in bringing down the Emperor, Pedro II. In addition to political history, Oliveira Vianna also tried his hand at social history. He did more than any other historian to popularize the notion that the Bandeirantes (Brazilian frontiersmen) were perpetuators of the aristocratic culture in Brazil and that the residents of the state of São Paulo were generally wealthy. This view was challenged by liberal historians, who refuted Oliveira's arguments with documentary evidence. Oliveira also popularized the interpretative essay, based on historical materials, and he worked on the cultural and social developments in Brazil. His works were more anthropological and sociological than historical, but his theses rested on historical research. He eventually concluded that the rural aristocracy was the major force in Brazilian development, and he wrote critiques of liberals in the Brazilian government, indicating their weaknesses. In all of his writing he possessed a smooth, flowing style that attracted many readers and gained some support for his political views. This was particularly true among the elite, which in any case sympathized with his attacks on liberal democratic institutions.

A. *As populações meridionais do Brasil* (São Paulo, 1920); *Pequenos estudos de psycología social* (São Paulo, 1921); *O idealismo na evolução política de imperio* (São Paulo, 1922); *Evolução do povo brasileiro* (São Paulo, 1923); *O ocaso do império* (São Paulo, 1925); *Problemas de política objectiva* (São Paulo, 1930).
B. Sergio Buarque de Holanda, "Historical Thought in Brazil," in E. Bradford Burns, *Perspectives on Brazilian History* (New York, 1967), pp. 190-191; Robert M. Levine,

Historical Dictionary of Brazil (Metuchen, N.J., 1979), p. 153; Percy Alvin Martin, *Who's Who in Latin America* (Stanford, 1936), p. 286; Thomas E. Skidmore, "The Historiography of Brazil, 1889-1964, Part I," *Hispanic American Historical Review*, 55, No. 4 (November 1975), pp. 716-748; Stanley Stein, "Historiography of Brazil, 1808-1889," *Hispanic American Historical Review*, 40, No. 2 (May 1960), pp. 269-270.

OMISTE, MODESTO (6 June 1840, Potosí, Bolivia—16 April 1898, Potosí). *Education*: Studied in Buenos Aires and Chuquisaca; law degree, 1858. *Career*: Founded and edited the daily newspaper, *El tiempo*, in Potosí; Deputy, National Congress, 1874, 1880, 1889, and 1892; Minister in Argentina; diplomat in Venezuela; President, Municipal Council of Potosí.

Omiste was a politically active humanist who functioned primarily on the local level, achieving noteworthy success in advancing social and educational innovations in Potosí. One observer remarked that if Omiste had been as successful on the national scene as he was in his home state, Bolivian education would have advanced by 50 years. He not only fought for educational expansion from his political offices but also championed education in the press. In national politics he was but one congressman among many and did not enjoy enough influence to make any kind of impact on the nation as a whole.

Just as Omiste's major success politically was in his home state of Potosí, his literary and historical activity focused on regional events. He was the historian of Potosí, and when he wrote biography his subjects were native to that region. He was largely a narrative historian who described events faithfully but with little analysis. Likewise his biographies were not probing examinations but rather factual accounts of the lives of illustrious Bolivians from the Potosí area. His histories were more like chronicles than analytical studies of the Bolivian past. His style was clear and simple, and his work was largely informative of the events of Potosí. His major work, *Crónicas potosinas*, was a full account of local traditions.

A. *Historia de Bolivia: Texto para instrucción primaria* (Potosí, Bolivia, 1875); *Indice general de leyes, decretos, resoluciones ordenes y demás disposiciones administrativas de la República de Bolivia desde 1825 hasta 1882* (Rosario de Santa Fe, Argentina, 1884); *La influencia de la mujer en la política de las naciones* (Potosí, Bolivia, 1887); *Monografía del Departamento de Potosí* (Potosí, Bolivia, 1892); *Historia de Bolivia desde la época incásica, hasta la administración del gobierno del dr. Mariano Baptista* (Potosí, Bolivia, 1897); and *Crónicas potosinas*, 2 vols. (La Paz, 1919).

B. Unión Panamericana, *Diccionario de la literatura latinoamericana: Bolivia* (Washington, D.C., 1958), pp. 66-67.

OÑA, PEDRO DE (1570, Valdivia, Chile—1643, Valdivia). *Education*: Attended the Colegio Real de San Martín and the Colegio Mayor de San Felipe in Lima; graduated from the University of San Marcos, 1593. *Career*: Fought on the side of the government to put down a revolt in Quito; served as Corregidor in Lima; wrote sonnets, songs, and poems.

The epic poem has been an important source of knowledge about colonial

Latin America, and Pedro de Oña produced the first book of poetry published in America in 1596, an epic entitled *Arauco domado*. This poem was a result of his interest in the Araucanian Indians in Chile, an interest that led Oña to learn the Indian language and to study the Araucanian civilization. The poem recounts naval battles, struggles against pirates, and most importantly the Spanish battle to defeat the Araucanians. The poem has been compared with Ercilla's *La Araucania*, and some critics have charged that Oña simply used Ercilla's work as a foundation for his own. Whether or not that charge is accurate, both epic poems are significant for an understanding of Chile's Indians and of the Chilean war to defeat the Araucanians.

Oña also has been accused of writing his epic for the express purpose of praising the activities of the Viceroy, Garcia Hurtado de Mendoza. This may or may not have been his motivation, but the evidence suggests that he was more than a little interested in heaping praise upon that individual. The Ecuadorian historian *Isaac C. Barrera notes that in one part of the poem Oña digresses into material that has no relation whatsoever to the topic at hand but does display Hurtado de Mendoza in a favorable light. It would appear then that the poem was written to exalt the career of this Viceroy. However, the epic poem is still important because Oña knew intimately the Araucanians and their civilization, and his recounting of that material is extremely important for a study of early Chilean colonial history.

A. *Arauco domado* (Lima, 1596); *El temblor de Lima* (Lima, 1609); *Sermón* (Rome, 1612); *Ignatius Loyola* (Sevilla, Spain, 1636); *El Ignacio de Cantabria* (Sevilla, Spain, 1639); *Río Lima al Río Tibre* (Madrid, 1643).

B. Isaac J. Barrera, *Historiografía del Ecuador* (Mexico City, 1956), pp. 21-22; Salvatore Bizzarro, *Historical Dictionary of Chile* (Metuchen, N.J., 1972), p. 219; Michael Rheta Martin and Gabriel Lovett, *Encyclopedia of Latin American History* (Indianapolis, 1968), p. 242; and A. Curtis Wilgus, *The Historiography of Latin America: A Guide to Historiographical Writing, 1500–1800* (Metuchen, N.J., 1975) pp. 171–172.

OROZCO Y BERRA, MANUEL (8 June 1816, Mexico City—21 January 1881, Mexico City). *Education*: Colegio Lancasteriano de Octaviano Chausal; Bachelor of Topographical Engineering, 1834, law degree, 1847, Colegio de Minería. *Career*: Practiced law; taught mathematics; Secretary to the Puebla city government; Director, Archivo General de la Nación; official in the Ministry of Development, 1857; Minister of Development, 1862; built the fortifications for Mexico City when the French invaded; Minister, Supreme Court of Justice, 1863; Member, Scientific Commission of Mexico in the Maximilian government; Undersecretary of Development, 1864; Counselor of State, 1865; Director, National Museum, 1866; when Maximilian fell, imprisoned and fined for collaborating with the French; Chair of History and Geography, Colegio de la Paz.

When Maximilian entered Mexico to establish a French-supported imperial government, many Mexican intellectuals were torn between their patriotism and their political views. Conservatives welcomed Maximilian as preferable to the liberal government of Benito Juárez, but foreign domination caused some to act cautiously. Orozco y Berra had supported Juárez and planned to follow him out of the capital city when the French arrived, but family ties prevented him from leaving, and in a short time he accepted Maximilian's leadership and served in his government. Nevertheless, he was not a dedicated conservative or imperialist, and when the French withdrew their support from the Emperor, Orozco told him to leave with the army to avoid unnecessary bloodshed. Consequently, Orozco was not treated as harshly as some others who worked for the imperial government, and he soon was able to regain the stature and respect that he had enjoyed before the arrival of the French. Throughout this exciting and trying time Orozco continued his literary activity, and when he wrote about the period it was from a firsthand perspective.

In his early years Orozco was a journalist, a poet, and a literary essayist, but then he shifted his attention to geography, ethnography, and history. He wrote the first ethnographic book in Mexico in 1856. He followed that up with the *Diccionario universal de historia*, for which he was the major researcher and collector. This work was long a major research tool in Mexico, although now it is antiquated and of limited value. In his historical books Orozco was the first to make extensive use of auxiliary sciences such as anthropology, paleontology, ethnography, and geography. He was also the first to use the entire archival collection of Mexico in writing his histories. This gave his history greater stature in that he was able to reinterpret earlier historians who had not consulted these materials, particularly in the pre-Hispanic age. Orozco was the first to attempt to understand history in its total form by using scientific methods and auxiliary disciplines. He was also the first to use historical and cultural material in his geographies. Orozco was impartial and always submitted his research to a rigorous analysis.

A. *Noticia histórica de la conjuración del Marqués del Valle* (Mexico City, 1853); *Diccionario universal de historia y de geografia*, 7 vols. (Mexico City, 1853-1855); *Apendice al diccionario universal de historia y de geografía*, 3 vols. (Mexico City, 1855-1856); *Memoria para el plano de la ciudad de Mexico* (Mexico City, 1867); *Historia antigua y de la conquista de Mexico,* 4 vols. (Mexico, 1880); Historia de la geografía *en Mexico* (Mexico City, 1880); *Apuntes para la historia de la geografía en Mexico* (Mexico City, 1881); *Historia de la dominación española en Mexico*, 4 vols. (Mexico City, 1938).

B. Aurora M. Ocampo de Gómez and Ernesto Prado Velázquez, *Diccionario de escritores mexicanos* (Mexico City, 1967), pp. 263-265.

OSPINA VÁSQUEZ, LUÍS (1906, Medellín, Colombia—April 1977, Medellín). *Education*: Law degree, National University. *Career*: Served in the Departmental Assembly of Antioquia and the National Senate; University Professor; Member, National Planning Council.

Ospina Vásquez was a wealthy man whose family had also tasted the power of the national presidency. His father had been President of Colombia and his grandfather had also served as President. Perhaps because of the economic wealth and the political tradition in the family Ospina seemed to have no desire to become involved deeply in elective politics. Instead he preferred the placid life of the scholar, working from his coffee finca in southwestern Antioquia, surrounded by his considerable library of historical materials. Unfortunately, during the last decade and a half of his life Ospina suffered from gradual blindness, which curbed his scholarly activity. Therefore, instead of continuing his profound research into his country's history he devoted this time to creating an institute that would concentrate upon the study of Antioquia. This institute opened in 1976 as the Fundación Antiquena para los Estudios Sociales. For this organization Ospina provided the library and financial support. Consequently, through his efforts a continuing research effort will continue even though its sponsor has passed from the scene.

Few Latin American historians of the 19th and 20th centuries concentrated upon economic history, but Luis Ospina's reputation was based largely upon this type of history. He produced one major book on the development of Colombian industry and on the relationship between industrial growth and governmental activity, *Industria y protección en Colombia, 1810-1930*. Chronologically, the book went back to the colonial period and carefully noted Colombia's industrial development through the national period. As Ospina traced this development carefully, basing his conclusions on extensive research and careful analysis, he produced a study that has stood the test of time. Younger scholars have worked in the same area but have not superseded his findings. Consequently, he is regarded as an outstanding economic historian of Colombia.

A. *Industria y protección en Colombia, 1810-1930* (Medellín, Colombia, 1955); *Estructura de la Universidad* (Medellín, Colombia, n.d.).

B. Frank Safford, "Obituary: Luís Ospina Vásquez (1905-1977)," *Hispanic American Historical Review*, 58, No. 3 (August 1978), pp. 466-467.

OTERO, VÉRTIZ, GUSTAVO ADOLFO (8 September 1896, La Paz— 1958, La Paz). *Education*: Colegio Nacional de Ayacucho, La Paz, 1913; Bachelor of Science, University of San Andrés, La Paz, 1914. *Career*: Journalist; wrote for El comercio de Bolivia and *El diario*, both of Bogotá; founded *El fígaro*; contributed to *El diario*, El tiempo, and the illustrated magazine, *Atlántida*; Editor, *La semana*, 1915, and *Lectura*, 1916; Secretary to the President of the Republic, Gutiérrez Guerra, 1917; Secretary, Bureau of Statistics and Geographical Studies, 1918-1920; Consul General in Spain and Italy, 1927; Director, Institute of Fine Arts, and Director, University of La Paz, 1937-1938; delegate to the Book Exposition in Bogotá; Senator from La Paz; Minister of Education; Minister Plenipotentiary in Colombia and Ecuador; Ambassadoro to Ecuador; taught at the Universidad de San Andrés; founded the *Revista de Bolivia*, 1937; Director, University of San Andrés Library, 1938.

Otero was a man with a wide range of interests. He wrote and worked in biography, novels, criticism, essays, geography, sociology, psychology, journalism, drama, and travelogues. He possessed a pleasant, simple literary style that was at the same time clear and elegant, and he employed it to highlight the cultural and social problems of Bolivia. He is also recognized as an accomplished essayist, and his fiction gained attention throughout Bolivia. In 1956 he was awarded the National Grand Prize for Literature, and he was selected to be a member of the Academia Boliviana de la Lengua Correspondiente de la Real Academia Española.

In his historical work Otero was interested in social developments during the colonial period of his nation's past. His work was not extensively researched, but he presented his findings in a readable and clear prose. He seemed more interested in recounting detailed accounts of past events than in analyzing the past, as some earlier Bolivian writers of history had done, such as *Alcides Arguedas and *Jaime Mendoza. This did not trouble Otero, who was content with telling a lucid story that would be interesting instead of digging into the causes and results of historical acts. As noted, his histories were not well researched, and frequently parts of his books were in error. But he popularized history in Bolivia, and for this accomplishment he deserves considerable credit. A group of Bolivian scholars noted in 1947 that Otero was the nation's most important writer. Patriotic and nationalistic, he was a part of Bolivia's "indigeneous movement" seeking political, economic, and social change for the Bolivian people.

A. *El hombre del tiempo heróico: Esquema de un ensayo psicológico y moral de Antonio José de Sucre, Gran Mariscal de Ayachucho* (La Paz, 1925); *La doctrina de Bolívar y la ideología pacifista de Bolivia* (Barcelona, Spain, 1931); *Las atrocidades paraguayas* (Barcelona, Spain, 1933); *La vida social del coloniaje* (La Paz, 1942); *Figuras de la cultura boliviana* (Quito, 1952); *La cultura y el periodismo en América*, 2d ed. (Quito, 1953).

B. Fernando Díez de Medina, *Literatura boliviana* (Madrid, 1954), pp. 321-323; Enrique Finot, *Historia de la literatura boliviana* (Mexico City, 1943), pp. 354-356; "Gustavo Adolfo Otero," *Hispanic American Historical Review*, 40, No. 1 (February 1960), pp. 85-89; Dwight B. Heath, *Historical Dictionary of Bolivia* (Metuchen, N.J., 1972), p. 170; Percy Alvin Martin, *Who's Who in Latin America* (Stanford, 1936), p. 292; and Unión Panamericana, *Diccionario de la literatura latinoamericana: Bolivia* (Washington, D.C., 1958), pp. 69-71.

OVALLE, ALONSO DE (1601, Santiago—11 May 1651, Lima). *Education*: Educated in a Jesuit school and at the Colegio de Córdoba, Argentina. *Career*: Jesuit priest and missionary to the Negroes of Chile; missionary to the Indians in southern Chile; Rector, Colegio de San Francisco Javier, a Jesuit school; traveled in Spain, Peru, and Rome.

As a missionary Ovalle was vitally interested in education, and he devoted most of his life to the conversion of Indians to Christianity and to their education. On a visit to Europe he was so appalled at the ignorance of the people there concerning the colonies in America that he determined to write histories of the region to enlighten the Europeans. From that time on he spent part of the time collecting material for the book and writing it.

Although he traveled widely in Europe, he had intended to return to Chile earlier, but the disastrous earthquake of 1647 destroyed Santiago and created a situation in which he was more helpful in Europe gaining support for rebuilding the city than he would have been at home. Since Ovalle was already in Europe, the city government of Santiago empowered him to deal with the Spanish crown to begin rebuilding Chile as quickly as possible. He raised money in Europe and was on his way home with 16 other Jesuits to assist the country in 1650, when he fell ill and died.

Ovalle's major work was *Histórica relación del Reino de Chile y de las misiones y ministerios que ejércita en el la Companía de Jesús*, which he wrote to inform Europeans of life in the colonies. But it was far more than a simple historical chronicle of the colonies. Ovalle wrote knowledgeably about the Spanish colonials, the natives, and their lives in America. He described society and culture carefully, leading one writer to indicate that it was partly in the genre of *cuadros de costumbres* (studies of customs) that he excelled. He also described the geography of America and wrote about crops and farm life, games, and religious activity. In addition, he concentrated upon the role of missionaries and in particular the missionary activities of the Jesuits. Ovalle had a lively style and was comprehensive in his treatment of life in America. The book was published first in Italy, which was logical since Ovalle wanted to instruct Europe about America. It then was translated into English and published in England. The English version was the most widely circulated for some years. Only in the 19th century did the work find its way to a publisher in Chile. José Toribio Medina published it in his *Colección de historiadores de Chile*, in 1888. Wherever the book has appeared it has provided a clear, readable study of life in America in the colonial era, and literary scholars maintain that the work was the first to differentiate Chilean from Spanish literature. In this light it was not only a historical milestone but a literary one as well.

A. *Histórica relación del Reino de Chile y de las misiones y ministerios que ejércita en él la Companía de Jesús* (Rome, 1646).

B. Salvatore Bizzarro, *Historical Dictionary of Chile* (Metuchen, N.J.), 1972; Francisco Antonio Encina, ''Breve bosquejo de la literatura histórica chilena,'' *Atenea*, 95, Nos. 291-292 (September-October 1949), pp. 28-29; José Toribio Medina, *Historia de la literatura colonial de Chile* (Santiago, 1878), II, pp. 116-130.

OVIEDO Y VALDÉS, GONZALO FERNÁNDEZ   (1478, Madrid—1557 Valladolid, Spain). *Education*: Unknown. *Career*: Page to Don Juan, son of Ferdinand and Isabella, and held several other posts at court; Secretary to Captain Gonzalo Fernández de Córdoba; served under Pedro Arias d'Avila in the expedition to Panama, 1514; Regidor and Teniente in Tierra Firme; Governor, Province of Cartagena; Alcade of Santo Domingo; Regidor of Santo Domingo; Chief Chronicler of the Indies.

Oviedo spent his early years at the Spanish court, reading voraciously and meeting the important figures who visited Madrid. He was particularly fascinated by the conquistadors who returned from America with tales of fascinating things they had witnessed, and he had earlier been present when Columbus returned from his first voyage in 1493. All of this contact with conquistadors and travelers to America led him to make the trip in 1514 with Pedro Arias d'Avila. In return for his services he was granted political offices in Central America and the Caribbean, and he spent 24 years in America. Eventually he was named Chief Chronicler of the Indies and produced two significant histories of Spanish activity in the New World. In addition, he wrote what some scholars regard as the first novel produced in America, *Claribalte*. His activity in America was also marked by a clash with *Bartolomé de las Casas over the attempt to convert the Indians to Christianity.

Oviedo's histories were marked by eyewitness accounts of events in the New World as he chronicled the colonization of the region. Such observations were strengthened because he had been in a prominent political position in Europe and therefore had an opportunity to compare the Old World civilization with America. He was a careful observer and was interested in the way people lived and the way their governments and communities functioned. Like other chroniclers of his era he was interested in a variety of disciplines, including history, so that his historical works include a good deal of geography, archaeology, and ethnology. While overall his research lacked critical analysis, so that historians frequently question its usefulness, the chronicling of events was important to later historians as a basis on which to construct their more analytical works.

A. *Historia general y natural de las Indias* (Sevilla, Spain, 1535); *Histoire du Nicaragua* (Paris, 1840); *Libro de la cámara real del Principe Don Juan y officios de su casa y servicio ordinario* (Madrid, 1870); *La llegada de Gonzalo de Ovideo y de Pedrarias Dávila a la bahía de Santa Marta año de 1514* (Santa Marta, Colombia, 1950).

B. Theodore S. Creedman, *Historical Dictionary of Costa Rica* (Metuchen, N.J.,. 1977), pp. 70-71; Robert H. Davis, *Historical Dictionary of Colombia* (Metuchen, N.J., 1977), p. 112; Helen Delpar, *Encyclopedia of Latin America* (New York, 1974), p. 436; Michael Rheta Martin and Gabriel Lovett, *Encyclopedia of Latin American History* (Indianapolis, 1968), p. 246; and A. Curtis Wilgus, *The Historiography of Latin America: A Guide to Historical Writing, 1500-1800* (Metuchen, N.J., 1975), pp. 26-27.

P

PALMA, RICARDO (7 February 1833, Lima—6 October 1919, Lima). *Education*: Attended primary schools in Orengo and Clemente Noel, Peru; largely self-educated. *Career*: Served in the Peruvian navy; Consul in Para, Brazil, 1864; Secretary to President José Balta, 1868; Senator from Loreto for three terms; fought against Chile in the War of the Pacific; Assistant Librarian of Lima; Director of the newspaper, *La prensa*, Buenos Aires, but remained in Peru to rebuild the National Library, 1853.

With little formal education, Palma joined the navy at an early age and traveled widely. While in the service he was shipwrecked on the southern coast of Peru and later left the navy to become embroiled in politics. In 1860 he took part in an assault on the home of the President, Ramón Castilla, and paid for the failure of the mission with exile in Chile for two years. When the War of the Pacific broke out, Palma enlisted in the reserves and fought in the losing battle of Miraflores. With the Chilean occupation of Peru, his personal library of several thousand books and manuscripts was destroyed, and when he protested the looting of the Peruvian archives by the Chilean occupation forces he was imprisoned on a Chilean warship for 15 days. Through hard work and diligence he managed to rebuild the Peruvian National Library after it too was depleted by the Chileans, and he served for 28 years as Director of the National Library. In rebuilding the library he catalogued more than 20,000 books in less than 4 years.

As a literary figure Palma began by writing verses and then turned to translations of famous European writers such as Victor Hugo. His most famous work, however, revolved around the writing of short stories in which he mixed fact and fiction. These *Tradiciones* were published in newspapers and soon became very popular with the reading public. These stories covered Peruvian history from the time of the Incas to the national period. They were generally well researched, and the nonfiction parts were for the most part accurate. They were also sometimes satirical, and this contributed to their success with the reading public. But critics have charged that his intermingling of historic fact with his imagination was also his great failure. This mixture of fact with fiction was so well done that readers could not distinguish truth from imaginary events, and thus any historical value of the works was destroyed. Palma himself confessed that he did not set out to write history, but he also was quick to point out his debt to history and tradition. Consequently, Palma ranks with those who used history in their literature successfully to bring to the public an awareness of their past that many might otherwise never have found. This mixture of history and fiction was an important part of the historiographic development of Peru and of all of Latin America in the 19th century.

A. *Anales de la Inquisición de Lima* (Lima, 1863); *Armonías* (Paris, 1865); *Pasionarias* (Le Havre, 1870); *Tradiciones, 1st series* (Lima, 1872), *2d series* (Lima, 1872), *3d series* (Lima, 1875), *4th series* (Lima, 1877); *El Demonio de los Andes* (New York, 1883); *Recuerdos de España* (Lima, 1897); *Papeletas lexicográficas* (Lima, 1903); *Mis últimas tradiciones* (Barcelona, 1906); *The Knights of the Cape*, trans. Harriet de Onís (New York, 1945).

B. Marvin Alisky, *Historical Dictionary of Peru* (Metuchen, N.J., 1979), pp. 70-71; Helen Delpar, *Encyclopedia of Latin America* (New York, 1974), p. 440; Sturgis Leavitt, "Ricardo Palma," *Hispanic American Historical Review* 3, No. 1 (February 1920), pp. 63-67; Michael Rheta Martin and Gabriel Lovett, *Encyclopedia of Latin American History* (Indianapolis, 1968), p. 248; William Belmont Parker, *Peruvians of To-Day* (Lima, 1919), pp. 449-455; and Reuben Vargas Ugarte, "Don Ricardo Palma y la historia," *Journal of Inter-American Studies*, 9, No. 2 (April 1967), pp. 213-224.

PARDO GALLARDO, JOSÉ JOAQUÍN (29 December 1905, Guatemala City—31 July 1964, Guatemala City). *Education*: Earned the title of teacher of primary instruction, Escuela Normal Central para Varones, Guatemala City; self-taught in archival organization. *Career*: Director, Archivo General del Gobierno, 1935; placed in charge of consolidating all provincial and municipal archives into a new National Archives; one of the founders of the School of Humanities, 1945; Director, Department of History, and Professor of Central American History and Paleography; taught in the School of Juridical and Social Sciences; Chair of Critical History of Central America, University of San Carlos de Guatemala.

From 1935 to 1954 Guatemala was caught up in struggles among dictators and between communists and noncommunists. This created an often chaotic and turbulent political and social atmosphere that took its toll on scholarly and intellectual activity. Yet Pardo Gallardo was at the peak of his career during these years and managed to avoid the pitfall of political intervention that adversely affected the lives and careers of many other Guatemalans. When in 1934 Pardo and another scholar uncovered the Act of Independence of 1821 and published a report in a Guatemala City newspaper, President Jorge Ubico was furious because he had not been notified beforehand. This act of bypassing the political leadership of the nation even in scholarship matters could have destroyed Pardo's career before it began, but Ubico went ahead and named Pardo Director of the Government Archive, despite his anger. As custodian of the nation's records and documents, Pardo was confronted with a poorly organized archive housed in improper conditions for the preservation of documents, manuscripts, and records. He brought some semblance of order to the archives and launched a lengthy campaign to get a suitable building where the precious materials could be safely housed. All of this activity was carried out amid the most difficult political background, but Pardo managed to stay above politics and in 1956 the new archive became a reality.

Although his major contribution to historiography was as an archivist, Pardo did some original historical research on his own. He studied the colonial period of Guatemalan history and assessed the cultural changes that took place in that era. He was also a fine teacher at the secondary and higher educational levels, and many of his students learned their trade from him. At the same time, his conscientious determination to pursue the correct historical method was passed on to these people, who carried on the work he initiated. Not only did he influence Guatemalan youth but students from Europe, the United States, and other Latin American countries also benefitted from his instruction and guidance. The current generation of Guatemalan historians owes much to Pardo and to his well-ordered archival collections.

A. *Boletín del Archivo General del Gobierno*, 10 vols. (Guatemala City, 1935-1945), *Prontuario de reales cédulas, 1529-1599* (Guatemala City, 1941); *Efemérides para escribir la historia de la muy noble y muy leal ciudad de Santiago de los Caballeros del Reino de Guatemala* (Guatemala City, 1944); *Bibliografía del doctor Pedro Molina* (Guatemala City, 1954); *Indice de los documentos existentes en el Archivo General del Gobierno* (Guatemala City, n.d.); *Proceres y martires de la independencia de Centro América* (Guatemala City, n.d.).

B. Richard Moore, *Historical Dictionary of Guatemala*, rev. ed. (Metuchen, N.J., 1973), pp. 152-153; and Walter Payne, "Obituary: José Joaquín Pardo Gallardo (1905-1964)," *Hispanic American Historical Review*, 45, No. 3 (August 1965), pp. 463-467.

PASO Y TRONCOSO, FRANCISCO DEL (8 October 1842, Veracruz, Mexico—30 April 1916, Florence, Italy). *Education*: Attended the Colegio de San Ildefonso, Mexico City; professional training in the Escuela Nacional de Medicina but failed to graduate after losing interest in two different thesis projects; studied history; learned Nahuatl. *Career*: Visitor to the National Museum, 1888, became Director, 1889; worked in libraries and archives of Madrid and Florence; teacher and scholar.

Paso spent a lifetime copying and analyzing documents that he collected from many libraries in Mexico and many more throughout Europe. He traveled more widely in Europe than other Mexican scholars, visiting libraries, archives, and museums in almost every Western European nation. Once he had collected his vast amount of material he then devoted considerable time to organizing, verifying, and correcting the copies that oftentimes had deviated from the originals after many renditions.

As a historian Paso recognized the tremendous value of using foreign languages in research. This recognition was strengthened when he traveled and worked in so many different European libraries. Therefore, he was committed to learning languages himself, and he advocated extensive language training for all historians. He was a patient, careful researcher who painstakingly verified every document he found. It was his contention that what he learned had to be published instead of collecting dust in some manuscript collection. He said that those who possessed knowledge had to publish it in order to make it availabe for everyone in the world. In addition to using foreign languages to great advantage when writing about Mexico's history he also believed firmly in the value of archaeology for the historian. He carefully studied Indian structures from the pre-Columbian age to better understand the Indians. He also worked in oral history, interviewing contemporary Indians in an effort to learn about their ancestors from hundreds of years earlier. This technique led him to learn considerably more about the Indians of Mexico than might otherwise have been possible.

A. *Descripción historia y exposición del Códice pictórico de los antiguos Náuas* (Florence, Italy, 1898); *Papeles de la Nueva España* (Madrid, 1905); *Los libros de Anáhuac* (Rome, 1906); *Destrucción de Jerusalén* (Florence, Italy, 1907); *Los libros de Chilam Balam* (Mexico City, 1940); and *Espistolario de Nueva España, 1505-1518*, 16 vols. (Mexico City, 1939-1942).

B. Luís González Obregón, *Cronistas e historiadores* (Mexico City, 1936), pp. 175-195; Silvio Arturo Zavala, *Francisco del Paso y Troncoso, su misión en Europa, 1892-1916* (Mexico City, 1938).

PAZOS KANKI, VICENTE (30 December 1779, Ilabaya, Bolivia—28 March 1845, London). *Education*: Studied at El Semanario de La Paz; degree in theology and law, University of Cuzco. *Career*: Joined the priesthood and fought for Latin American independence; wrote in the Argentine revolutionary periodical, *La gaceta*; *El censor*, 1812; fled to England; returned to Argentina to edit a republican periodical, *Crónica argentina*; attended the Congress of Tucumán; Consul General of Bolivia in London, 1829-1838 and 1842-1845.

Pazos Kanki's overriding passion was Latin American independence from Spain. He devoted much of his early life to the goal of freedom for his countrymen, not just in Bolivia but throughout Latin America. He became embroiled in the movement in Argentina and there aided Mariano Moreno in encouraging the Creole population to overthrow the Spanish viceregal government. His journalistic endeavors in this cause were significant, and when the Argentine revolutionaries saw that success was near, Pazos Kanki then turned his literary and oratorical talents to support of republican government once independence was achieved. Once again his activity was significant for the cause he espoused, but in the turmoil and chaos of the last years of the war against Spain and early independence he suffered the fate of many of his countrymen who opposed those who came to power and went into exile. Living in both the Unitied States and Europe, he continued to write and to support the cause of freedom until his death.

A dynamic fighter for politicial causes, Pazos Kanki was also a devoted champion of liberty in the literary world. He was a follower of the early 19th century romantic movement, and the development of his poltical philosophy reflected these literary commitments. He wrote in a simple style and developed his arguments logically and presented them with clarity. Throughout his writing there appears a call for justice and freedom whether he was writing dispassionately about a historic event or passionately in the midst of a heated polemic. In his *Memorias histórico-políticas* he dwelt upon the conquest of Latin America and the colonial age without devoting much attention to the independence period in which he participated. Some Latin Americans have lamented this lack of a memoir of the revolutionary age, but such lacunae do not detract from the value of the book as a solid colonial history. His strength as a historian was in his talent for synthesis and for a clear exposition of the historiographic work already in existence. His main weakness was his failure to exploit primary documentation and his penchant for plagiarizing. Despite this shortcoming he was a great American patriot and an outspoken champion of liberty, which made him an important Bolivian literary figure, even though he spent little time in his native country. Additionally, he was a precursor of the modern Indianist movement in Bolivia, and he went so far at one point as to advocate the reestablishment of the Indian monarchy to lead the political fortunes of Bolivia.

A. *Letters on The United Provinces of South America*, trans. Platt Crosby (New York, 1819); *Compendio de la historia de los Estados Unidos de América* (Paris, 1825); *El evangelio de Jesucristo* (London, 1829); *Memorias histórico-políticas* (London, 1834); *El pacto y ley fundamental de la Confederación Perú-Boliviana* (London, 1837); *Cartas al Señor Antonio Acosta y el Excmo Señor Conde de Aberdeen* (London, 1845).

B. Charles Arnade, "The Historiography of Colonial and Modern Bolivia," *Hispanic American Historical Review*, 42, No. 3 (August 1962), pp. 333-384; Fernando Díez de Medina, *Literatura boliviana* (La Paz, 1953), pp. 177-179; Enrique Finot, *Historia de la literatura boliviana* (Mexico City, 1943), pp. 89-98; Dwight B. Heath, *Historical Dictionary of Bolivia* (Metuchen, N.J., 1972), p. 185; and Unión Panamericana, *Diccionario de la literatura latinoamericana: Bolivia* (Washington, D.C., 1958), pp. 73-75.

PAZ-SOLDÁN, JUAN PEDRO (20 June 1869, Lima—30 May 1944, Lima). *Education*: Studied in the Jesuit School in Lima, at the Colegio de San José, Argentina, and at the Univeristy of San Marcos, Lima. *Career*: Journalist for some of the leading newspapers in Peru; Consul in Santiago, 1894; fought in the civil war of 1895; founded the newspaper, *El halcón*; exiled to Iquique; editor for a number of newspapers for 15 years in Argentina; Consul General of Peru in Buenos Aires, 1902; Consul General in Montevideo, 1902; Editor of the official Peruvian newspaper, *El peruano*.

As the political wars grew heated in Peru in the first years of the 20th century, journalists lined up on one side or the other and put their pens to the service of political factions. Paz-Soldán used his talents to champion his political favorites and denounce his opponents. In the course of this political journalism he wrote for or edited better than a dozen newspapers, and when his opponents gained control of the government he found himself in exile. Consequently, he spent many years of his life outside Peru, but he was able to support himself by holding down diplomatic positions in the countries where he lived or by working on newspapers. He lived for 15 years in Argentina, where he was editor of five different newspapers. Back in Peru, Paz-Soldán founded the newspaper, *La nación* but when the party it supported was overthrown, Paz-Soldán closed it down. Later he opened two more newspapers and briefly revived *La nación*.

Paz-Soldán's historical efforts were centered on the colonial age in Peru, which was in keeping with the general Latin American historical interests of the early 20th century. His journalistic prose led to clean, concise histories, but he was not renowned for exhaustive research in primary documentation. He was a synthesizer of the work of others, but his studies were significant because they brought the past to the general reading public in an attractive and interesting way. Additionally, Paz-Soldán's interest in biography led to short pieces on historical figures and to the publication eventually of a biographical dictionary in 1917.

A. *Cuadros y episodios peruanos y otras poesías nacionales y diversas* (Lima, 1867); *Páginas diplomáticas del Perú* (Lima, 1891); *La inmigración en el Perú* (Lima, 1891); *La ciudad de Lima bajo la dominación española (1535-1554)* (Lima, 1908); *Una revolución famosa (18 de septiembre de 1543)* (Lima, 1909); *Diccionario biográfico de peruanos contemporáneos* (Lima, 1917).

B. Fred Bonner, "José de la Riva-Aguero (1885-1944)," *Hispanic American Historical Review*, 36, No. 4 (November 1956), pp. 490-502; William Belmont Parker, *Peruvians of To-Day*, (Lima, 1919), pp. 267-270.

PERAZA SARAUSA, FERMÍN (7 July 1907, Guara, Cuba—31 January 1969, Miami, Fla.). *Education*: Instituto de Segunda Enseñanza de la Habana, 1921–1925; degree in letters and sciences, Universidad de la Habana, 1927; Doctor of Civil Law, 1930; Doctor of Political, Economic, and Social Sciences, 1937; degree in library science, Havana University, 1950. *Career*: Director, Municipal Library of Havana, 1930–1960; Professor Library School, University of Havana 1946–1960; Director of Library Science, Summer School of the University of Panama, 1949–1950; Professor, Inter-American School of Library Science, University of Antioquia, Medellín, Colombia, 1960–1962; Latin American bibliographer, University of Gainesville, Florida, 1962–1967; Associate Researcher, Center for Advanced International Studies, University of Miami, Florida, 1967–1969.

Many Latin American historians became so enthralled with research that they moved into careers as archive and library directors instead of teaching history and writing on history. Peraza Sarausa became so devoted to bibliographical and library work that he returned to school to study Library Science and eventually earned advanced degrees in that discipline. Because of his outstanding record in library and bibliographical work he gained a reputation throughout the Western Hemisphere, and his expertise was sought from those outside his country. Finally, the political climate of Castro's Cuba became so stifling for him that he went into exile in Colombia and later in the United States. Even outside his homeland he continued his bibliographical research and the writing of bibliographies. In 1937 he began publishing an annual Cuban bibliography, and he continued with this project even after leaving his native country. In 1960 it was published in Medellín, Colombia, and from 1961 to 1965 in Gainesville, Florida.

Another major long-term project was Peraza Sarausa's *Diccionario biográfico cubano*, the first volume of which appeared in 1951 and the final volume in 1968. Along these same lines he published a biographical dictionary, entitled *Personalidades cubanas*, that ran to 10 volumes. These research aids were welcomed by the Cuban scholarly community but were also hailed by scholars in the United States and throughout Latin America. Clear evidence of their importance was the fact that they continued to be published outside Cuba when Peraza Sarausa went into exile, and his annual studies continued to the year of his death. All of these works provide the researcher and the student of Cuban history with invaluable bibliographical tools and research aids.

A. *Anuario bibliográfico cubano* (Havana, 1937–1965), (Medellín, Colombia, 1960), (Gainesville, Fla., 1961–1965), (Miami, Fla., 1967–1968); *Bibliografía de Francisco González del Valle* (Havana, 1943); *Bibliografía de Antonio Maceo y Grajales* (Havana, 1945); *Diccionario biográfico cubano,*, Vols. 1 to 11 (Havana, 1951–1960), Vol. 12 (Gainesville, Fla., 1966), Vols. 13–14 (Coral Gables, Fla. 1968).

B. "Dr. Fermín Peraza, Bibliographer, 61," *New York Times* 2 February, 1969, p. 72; Elena Verez de Peraza, "Fermín Peraza Sarausa," *Revista de historia de América*, Nos. 67–68 (January–December 1969), pp. 350–352.

PEREDA SETEMBRINO, EZEQUIEL (10 April 1859, Paysandú, Uruguay—13 October 1927, Montevideo.) *Education*: Studied at the Liceo del Plata and the Franco-English Institute; tutored. *Career*: Edited the newspaper, *El imparcial*, Paysandú, 1877–1879; Director, Public Library of Paysandú, 1877–1879; Editor, *La democracia de Paysandú*, 1877, 1880; Coeditor, *El Pueblo*; co-owner and Joint Editor, *El Paysandú*; Manager and Editor, *El liberal*, Montevideo; attorney for minors and the indigent at Paysandú; Secretary of the commission that organized the telephone system of the country; Member, National Committee, Colorado party; Member, Board of Directors, Uruguayan Steamship Company, President, Anticlerical League of Montevideo; delegate to the first agricultural cattle-breeding society and various rural cattle associations; Member, Chamber of Deputies, 1899–1905; Senator, 1924.

A member of the landed elite, Pereda was able to fulfill his many intellectual pursuits without concern about his livelihood. He was also a man of varied interests who served in numerous public offices while writing extensively. A member of the liberal political faction, he was anticlerical and a powerful supporter of public education. He was a Freemason who actively pursued the goals and objectives of the organization. Because of his political and Masonic activity, he was forced at one point in his career to go into exile in Buenos Aires, where he wrote articles antagonistic to the Uruguayan government. He was an accomplished journalist who wrote on many political and cultural topics as well as taking ownership of two publications.

Like many literate Uruguayans, Pereda wrote poetry, novels, and nonfiction. His novels were generally historical, and he wrote a couple of biographies of historical figures. He was not a historian who worked in the archives of his

country. Instead he wrote about characters and events that had a popular appeal
for the reading public, and he worked into his histories his liberal political views
and his anticlerical religious attitudes.He was not an objective historian but saw
history as a creative form of literature that did not require a lengthy and arduous
search for the truth in manuscripts and documents. His field of interest was the
independence period and the late 19th century, and he was particularly intrigued
with the role of Garibaldi in Latin America, writing a multivolume study of
Garibaldi's Uruguayan activities.

A. *Una historia como muchas* (Montevideo, 1883); *Garibaldi, An Historical Sketch*
(Montevideo, 1895); *Los extranjeros en la Guerra Grande* (Montevideo, 1904); *Garibaldi
en el Uruguay* 3 vols. (Montevideo, 1914–1916); *El Belen uruguayan histórico, 1801–
1840* (Montevideo, 1923); *Artigas,* 5 vols. (Montevideo, 1930–1931).

B. Percy Alvin Martin, *Who's Who in Latin America* (Stanford, 1936), pp. 305–306;
and William Belmont Parker, *Uruguayans of To-Day* (New York, 1967).

PEREYRA, CARLOS (3 November 1871, Saltillo, Mexico—30 June 1942,
Madrid). *Education*: Escuela Oficial Numero 1, Saltillo, Mexico 1883; Colegio
de San Juan, Saltillo, Mexico, 1885; Ateneo Fuente, Saltillo, Mexico, 1886;
Escuela Preparatoria, Mexico City; and Licenciado en Leyes, Escuela Jurispru-
dencia, Mexico City, 1889. *Career*: Defender of the Office of the Federal District;
Agent of the Public Ministry; Member, Qualification Commission of the State
of the Public Ministry; Member, Qualification Commission of the State of Coa-
huila; founded the newspaper, *El pueblo Coahuila*, 1892; founded *El espectador,*
Monterrey, 1897; taught history and social science, National Preparatory School,
Mexico City; named to Mexican legation in Washington, D.C., 1909; Deputy,
National Congress, 1910; First Secretary, Mexican legation, Washington, D.C.,
1911; diplomatic posts in Washington and Belgium, 1911 to 1917; moved to
Spain, where he spent the remainder of his life writing histories of Mexico.

Caught in the midst of the Mexican Revolution of 1910, Pereyra moved about
constantly both within and outside Mexico. Despite his journalistic and diplomatic endeavors he remained throughout his life devoted to researching and
writing Mexican history. His travels in the United States and Europe enabled
him to gain access to archives and libraries that contained material that could
be used to develop his historical efforts. Additionally, he was able to move into
the area of foreign histories as he wrote on James Monroe, George Washington,
Simón Bolívar, and the Paraguayan dictator Francisco Solano López. Yet his
major interest remained Mexican history, and it was in that area that he published
most of his historical writing.

A fellow Mexican historian has written that Pereyra's contribution to Mexican
historiography was not research in archives or original documents but critical
studies of published works. He was especially interested in revising traditional
Mexican views concerning the role of Spain in America. In particular he sought
to divert attention from Spain's activity in colonial America to English and U.S.
action relative to Spanish America. He was bold and passionate in his criticisms,

and his work was marked by vigorous denunciations of forces that he personally opposed. He has been described as a master of the art of the dialectic, as he defended the Spanish role in America and denounced the English and North Americans. In addition to his later diatribes he did contribute substantially to Mexican historiography early in his career when he helped to collect and publish primary historical documents.

A. *Documentos inéditos o muy raros para la historia de México*, 5 vols. (Mexico City, 1905–1906); *Bolívar y Washington: Un paralelo impossible* (Madrid, 1917); *La disolución de Rusia* (Madrid, 1917); *Rosas y Thiers; La diplomacia europea en el Río de la Plata (1838–1850)* (Madrid, 1919); *Monardes y el exotismo médico en el siglo XVI* (Madrid, 1936); and *El fetiche constitucional americano* (Madrid, 1942).

B. *Diccionario Porrúa de historia* (Mexico City, 1976), II, A 1607; and J. Ignacio Rubio Mane, "Nota necrologica: Carlos Pereyra, 1871–1942," *Revista de historia de América*, No. 15 (December 1942), pp. 325–330.

PICÓN SALAS, MARIANO (26 January 1901, Mérida, Colombia—1965, Caracas). *Education*: Doctor of Philosophy and Letters, University of Chile, 1928, *Career*: Professor of Art History, University of Chile, 1929-1936; Superintendent of Public Education for Venezuela, 1936; led a diplomatic mission to Czechoslovakia, 1937–1938; Professor of General Literature, University of Chile, 1930; Librarian, National Library of Venezuela, 1927; Director of Culture, Ministry of National Education; Professor, Pedagogical Institute, Central university of Venezuela; Dean, School of Philosophy and Letters, Central University of Venezuela, 1946–1947; Visiting Professor, Columbia University, New York, 1950–1951; served on the Venezuelan delegation to UNESCO.

A teacher trained outside his native country, Picón Salas earned a reputation as a writer, scholar, professor, and diplomat in Venezuela through hard work and a prolific literary production. As a writer he was regarded by Latin Americans as one of the finest in that part of the world in the 20th century and his tact, skill, and erudition served him well in the diplomatic field. As a scholar he spoke English, French, and German, possessed some knowledge of Portuguese and Italian, could read Greek and Latin, and knew a little Sanskrit. With such a varied langugage talent he was able to read and digest the major authors in a wide variety of countries and to learn a great deal from them about literature, research, and history. He was not only the author of many literary works but also wrote columns on art and literature for newspapers in Caracas and for periodicals in Colombia and Mexico.

Picón Salas contributed mightily to the development of cultural history in Venezuela and throughout Latin America. His own training in literary and artistic fields prepared him well for the task. He worked in some areas of political and military history, but his major interest was in the cultural development of Venezuela. He believed that a nation's past could not be fully understood or appreciated if its cultural experience was forgotten or ignored.Culture for him was an essential ingredient for the life of a people or a nation, and he was determined to make certain that the cultural heritage of Venezuela was not lost. At the same time, he was interested in the contemporary cultural scene, and he wrote on books, art, and drama in newspapers and reviews. He was the first Venezuelan to place so much emphasis upon the cultural aspect of history, and as such he initiated a shift away from the historical focus that had for so long fallen on the political and military events of the past. In this respect Picón Salas was a precursor for later Latin American cultural historians and helped shape the thinking of those general historians who no longer ignored the literature, art, and music of history. He also collaborated with other scholars of Latin America because of his educational experience in Chile and his teaching positions in the United States. In this fashion he was able to influence scholars not only through his written work but by virtue of his friendship with scholars throughout the Western Hemisphere.

A. *Problemas y método de la historia del arte* (Caracas, 1933); *Formación y proceso de la literatura venezolana* (Caracas, 1940); *De la conquista a la independencia* (Mexico City, 1944); *On Being Good Neighbors*, trans. Muna Lee (Washington, D.C., 1944); *Francisco de Miranda* (Caracas, 1946); *Dependencia o independencia en la historia hispano-americana* (Caracas, 1952); *Los días de Cipriano Castro* (Caracas, 1953).

B. *Diccionario biográfico de Venezuela* (Madrid, 1953), pp. 917–918; Percy Alvin Martin, *Who's Who in Latin America* 2d ed. rev. (Stanford, 1940), p. 394; Donna Keyse and G.A. Rudolf, *Historical Dictionary of Venezuela* (Metuchen, N.J., 1971).

PIMENTEL, FRANCISCO (2 December 1832, Aguascalientes, Mexico—14 December 1893, Mexico City). *Education:* Studied with tutors and individual professors. *Career:* Alderman and Secretary of the Town Council, Mexico City, 1865; Political Prefect of Mexico City during the Maximilian imperial government; one of the founders of the Academia Mexicana Correspondiente de la Real Española, 1875; President, Liceo Hidalgo.

There are some Latin American intellectuals who may not properly be called historians but who made significant historiographical contributions through their research and published materials. Pimentel fits into this category. Well educated by private instructors, Pimentel was from the wealthy class of Mexican society. Not only did the family possess material wealth, but Pimentel inherited the titles of Count of Heras and Vicount of Queréndaro, giving him prestige and social position. He was primarily interested in philology, and he wrote literary criticism. His work centered on a study of the Spanish American language as he sought to explain the impact of the indigenous languages on Spanish. For this work he was roundly praised, and he won scholarly medals in Mexico, at the Philadelphia Exposition, and from French scholarly organizations. Much of his literary history was accepted for its time but was later refuted by subsequent scholars.

For history Pimentel was important for his research activities. For example, he compiled information on poets, grouped them in categories, and then furnished biographical and bibliographical information about them. His work was extremely useful for literary scholars. However, outside of this bibliographical preparation his histories were not particularly valuable. One Mexican scholar notes that Pimentel contributed little historical information that was new, and beyond that he even contributed to the confusion of contemporary and subsequent historians by virtue of the inaccuracies of his material and the inapplicability of his analysis. While he was regarded as a true Mexican intellectual, he did not possess the critical powers nor the skeptical attitude needed for solid historical scholarship. At the same time, he lacked the talent to synthesize the work of others. He seemed to have little interest in his historical work beyond simply putting the material on paper. He was not a passionate researcher, and therefore he never became completely absorbed in his histories. The result was uninspired books. He could not place himself in the era about which he wrote, so that his literary criticism, as well as his history, appears cold and uninspired. Yet his compilations and research have laid the foundation for later studies and provided the spadework for subsequent scholars.

A. *El reino de Michoacán* (Mexico City, 1856); *La monarquía de Texcoco* (Mexico City, 1856); *Cuadro descriptivo y comparativo de las lenguas indígenas de Mexico, o tratado de filología mexicana* 2 vols. (Mexico City, 1862–1865): *Memoria sobre las causas que han originado la situación actual de la raza indígena de Mexico y medios de remediar* (Mexico City, 1864); *La economía política aplicada a la propriedad territorial en Mexico* (Mexico City, 1866); and *Historia crítica de la poesía en Mexico* (Mexico City, 1885).

B. Aurora M.Ocampo de Gómez and Ernesto Prado Velazquez, *Diccionario de escritores mexicanos* (Mexico City, 1967), pp. 291–292; and Francisco Sosa, "Vida y escritos de don Francisco Pimentel," in Francisco Pimentel, *Obras completas* (Mexico City, 1903–1904), I, pp. v–cx.

PINTO, MANUEL MARÍA (1872, Yungas de La Paz, Bolivia—1942, Buenos Aires). *Education*: Studied law in La Paz. *Career*: Practiced law in Buenos Aires; founded the review, *Resurgimiento*, 1899; wrote history and poetry.

Pinto, like so many other Bolivians of his era, spent much of his life in foreign countries, and like many others he chose Argentina for his home. While in Argentina he met Ruben Dario, Leopoldo Lugones, and his countryman *Jaimes Freyre. The impact of their influence led him to accept modernism, and he became one of the most powerful advocates of that movement in Latin America. At the same time that he was pursuing his legal and literary careers he also became involved in political activity, writing various articles on Bolivia and on its problems that grew out of the War of the Pacific against Chile. Throughout his career he never turned his back on his native country, and he continually wrote about the international political scene involving Chile, Peru, and Bolivia. Ever the patriot, Pinto generally supported Bolivia's position in these essays and articles.

Pinto's poetry was musical, sentimental, and filled with images.He was a true disciple of the modernist movement. At the same time he wrote nativist poetry that incorporated folklore in its themes. While he had something of a reputation as a poet, he is far better known in his country as a historian. He documented his histories extensively, but there was a negative, pessimistic tinge to them.

Nonetheless, some Bolivians contend that his study on the Revolution of La Paz, *La revolución de la Intendencía de La Paz*, is one of the most outstanding works ever produced on an aspect of Bolivian history. His style was one of simplicity influenced by modernism, as was his poetry. He focused on an analysis of the facts and on reformist orientations in colonial Bolivia. In his other major work on the international role of Bolivia after the War of the Pacific, *Bolivia y la triple política internacional*, he was also applauded for his erudition, literary style, extensive documentation, and clear development of his ideas. The result was a penetrating study of Bolivia's contentions in its postwar relations with Chile and Peru that stands as one of the most solid studies on this subject to come out of Bolivia.

A. *Bolivia y la triple política internacional* (Buenos Aires, 1902); *La revolución de la Intendencía de La Paz en el Virreinato del Río de la Plata con la ocurrencía de Chuquisaca (1800–1810)* (Buenos Aires, 1909); and *El conflicto del Pacífico* (Buenos Aires, 1918).
B. Fernando Díez de Medina, *Literatura boliviana* (La Paz, 1953), pp. 270–271; Enrique Finot, *Historia de la literatura boliviana* (Mexico City, 1943), pp. 166–168; and Unión Panamericana, *Diccionario de la literatura lationoamericana: Bolivia* (Washington, D.C., 1958), pp. 78–79.

PIZARRO, PEDRO (ca. 1515, Toledo, Spain—9 February 1587, Quito). *Education*: Unknown. *Career*: Served as a page to his first cousin, Francisco Pizarro, in the conquest of Peru; granted large estates and prospered financially following the Spanish conquest.

Pedro Pizarro began his service to the conquest at an early age, and almost from the time the expedition landed in South America he kept firsthand observations while at the same time participating in the actual fighting. Because of the estates he acquired subsequently he was able to find the leisure time to put these notes together in his chronicle of the conquest. It is believed that the manuscript was not printed during his lifetime but found its way into the national library at Madrid, where it was later found and published in 1844. Still later it was translated into English in a two-volume version.

Pizarro's chronicle has been compared to the work of *Bernal Díaz del Castillo on the conquest of Mexico. Their experiences were similar as both wrote amid the fighting and both served as soldiers as well as chroniclers. Pizarro wrote in a direct manner revealing the events as he saw them. He was not objective in his assessment because he had little sympathy for the Indians; instead, he exalted the activity of the Spanish. Additionally, he was sometimes vindictive in discussing the Indians, and his details were not always checked out completely. But even though the work suffered from these deficiencies, it nevertheless remains an important piece of historical work, particularly in the large number of illustrations that he incorporated in the study and in the details it did include that were not available from any other source.

A. *Nuevo crónica y buen gobierno* (Paris, 1936).

B. Marvin Alisky, *Historical Dictionary of Peru* (Metuchen, N.J., 1979), p. 78; and A. Curtis Wilgus, *The Historiography of Latin America: A Guide to Historical Writing, 1500–1800* (Metuchen, N.J., 1975), pp. 73–74.

PORRAS BARRENECHEA, RAÚL (23 March 1897, Pisco, Peru—September 1960, Lima), *Education*: Colegio de la Recoleta, 1906–1911; School of Letters, Universidad de San Marcos de Lima, 1912–1915; School of Law, 1915–1920; law degree, 1922; Doctor of Philosophy, History, and Letters, 1928. *Career*: Jurist; legal commentator; Librarian, Ministry of Foreign Affairs, 1922–1926; teacher, Colegio Anglo Peruano de Lima, Colegio Alemán, Colegio Antonio Raimondi, and Colegio de la Recoleta; Chief of the Archive of Boundaries, Ministry of Foreign Affairs, 1926–1931; Adviser to the Tacna-Arica Boundary Commission, 1926; First Secretary, Peruvian embassy to the Congress of Panama, 1926; Professor, University of San Marcos, 1928–1959; Director, Colegio Universitario, University of San Marcos, 1931; Counselor, Peruvian delegation to the Leticia conferences of Rio de Janeiro, 1933.

A legalist, Porras researched boundary disputes for his country and in 1926 published a definitive study on the topic entitled *Historia de los limites del Perú*. This became a significant reference book, which presented the history of Peru's boundary problems from colonial times to the modern period. He also did a great deal of research on Peruvian civil law and on individuals who were important to that law. In one instance he compiled a guide to the works of the 19th century legal writer Toribio Pacheco. Much of his work centered on the collection and publication of bibliographies, but he was also interested in biographies.

Like a number of other Latin American intellectuals of the 19th and early 20th centuries, Porras combined the teaching of history and other subjects on the secondary level with teaching in the universities. But his kind of history was the utilitarian, nationalistic, political type prevalent in this era. Along with several prominent Paraguayan historians who worked on boundary questions between their country and Brazil, Porras concentrated on the history of the boundaries of his country. Consequently, he was a major resource for the boundary negotiations that raged between Chile and Peru following the War of the Pacific. Because of this and other significant historical research projects Porras was not simply an academic historian who wrote up his research for the intellectuals of the nation and the students in the schools; his was the kind of practical historical research that was of immediate value to his country in the critical period of boundary negotiations with Chile. He was then, in the terminology of 1981 U.S. historiography, a "public historian" of great accomplishment and of inestimable value to the foreign ministry of his country. It is not surprising, then, that in writing about historical methods he emphasized the collection and use of primary documents for the writing of solid history. He once said, "We must not lose sight of the historical maxim that without documents there is no history, and without proceeding from the facts, neither interpretations nor syntheses can be built."

A. *Alegato del Perú en la cuestión de limites de Tacna y Arica* (Lima, 1921); *Historia de los limites del Perú* (Lima, 1926); *José Antonio Barrenechea* (Lima, 1928); *El Congreso de Panamá* (Lima, 1930); and *Historia de la conquista y colonia* (Lima, 1950).
B. Marvin Alisky, *Historical Dictionary of Peru* (Metuchen, N.J., 1979), Romero de Valle, "Raúl Porras Barrenechea," *Revista de historia de América*, No. 50 (December 1960), pp. 512–515; and Percy Alvin Martin, *Who's Who in Latin America* (Stanford, 1936), p. 314.

POSADA GUTIÉRREZ, JOAQUÍN (1797, Cartagena, Colombia—1881, Bogotá). *Education*: Studied in Jamaica, England, and France. *Career*: Fought with Bolívar in the Revolutionary War; served in the Parliament of New Granada; served in Congress; General.

In New Granada's revolutionary age Spanish peninsulars fought to preserve their positions in the colonial government, but some from that class gave their support to the revolutionaries. Posada Gutiérrez came from a prominent peninsular family, but when trouble came to Spanish America his parents sent him out of Colombia to Jamaica and then to Europe, where he spent 10 years gaining an education. However, when he returned he joined the revolutionary army and fought well for the rebels, despite his class association. He was a devoted follower of Bolívar and believed in a strong executive for the political system that was in the process of being established. He defended his political ideas from the national congress seat he held, and he also participated in the many civil wars that plagued Colombia from 1831 to 1876.

The historiographic efforts of Posada Gutiérrez have been heralded by some scholars as "a treasury of news, doctrines, and teachings." His work was impassioned, and he sometimes interjected his own philosophies and prejudices into his work. Moreover, he was not always impartial, and those who read his material had to be careful in accepting the authenticity of his views. He did not write history in the narrative style but instead he commented upon events and explained them to the readers, but always in the light of his own attitudes and philosophies. Despite criticism from contemporaries, his literary talent was heralded by almost all critics. He wrote with clarity and linked historic events together with logic. In a smooth prose he was able to narrate events and at the same time express his opinions on the subject. His descriptions were clear and graphic, and one historian remarked that his work contained a high degree of literary talent. If his historic method came into question and if his objectivity was suspect, no one questioned his ability to write beautiful, impassioned, emotional, and lively prose. Undoubtedly his literary talent was his strongest asset as a historian.

A. *Apuntamientos sobre la Campaña del Sur* (Cartagena, Colombia, 1843); *Memorias histórico-políticas* 2 vols. (Bogotá, 1865–1881); *La batalla del Santuario* (Bogotá, 1936).
B. Antonio Gómez Restrepo, *La literatura colombiana* (Bogotá, 1926), p. 108; José J. Ortega, *Historia de la literatura colombiana* (Bogotá, 1934), pp. 196–198; and Unión Panamericana, *Diccionario de la literatura lationoamericana: Colombia* (Washington, D.C., 1959), pp. 84–86.

PRADO Y UGARTECHE, JAVIER (3 December 1871, Lima—1936, Lima). *Education*: Early education at the Jesuit's school, Lima; Bachelor of Arts and Doctor of Jurisprudence, University of San Marcos. *Career*: Professor of the History of Philosophy, University of San Marcos; Lawyer; Minister to Argentina; Minister of Foreign Affairs; negotiated a successful commercial treaty with Bolivia; Associate Justice of the Supreme Court; Dean, School of Letters, University of San Marcos; Senator from Lima, 1908–1913; Minister of Government and War, 1910; President, Civil party; Senator from Lima, 1919; Rector, University of San Marcos, 1915.

One characteristic of Latin American historians in the 19th and early 20th centuries was the youthful ages at which they began writing. Prado y Ugarteche wrote his first monograph at the age of 20, a work on the historical development of philosophical ideas that gave clear evidence of his scholarship and his originality. But again, like many other Latin American historians, he was involved in diverse activities, from practicing the law to laying plans for the expansion and modernization of Peru's industry. More importantly he carried out the negotiations with Peru's neighbors to resolve longstanding boundary conflicts and diplomatic problems. Within two years he ended border disputes with Bolivia, Brazil, and Chile. His diplomatic and academic activity won him prominence throughout the nation and led to a movement to nominate him for president of the Republic, but because of political factions that he believed could not be overcome for a successful run at the presidency, he withdrew his name and returned for a second term in the Senate.

In his academic and intellectual activities Prado y Ugarteche marked his term as Rector of the University of San Marcos by delivering several inspiring addresses in which he urged the leaders of the population to work to increase interest in the literature and history of Peru. Not only did he encourage others to study history but he built a private library of 20,000 volumes of historical importance and an archeological collection in which the different periods of Peruvian history were traced that gained worldwide fame. His own historical writing centered on the history of ideas and the development of philosophy in Peru. Since not many historians of the era worked in the realm of ideas, his work served as a foundation for later studies in this genre.

A. *El método positivo* (Lima, 1890); *La evolución filosófica* (Lima, 1891); *El estado social del Perú durante la dominación española* (Lima, 1894); *La Teoría de lo bello en el arte* (Lima, 1896); *La educación nacional* (Lima, 1899); *La nueva época y los destinos históricos de los Estados Unidos* (Lima, 1919).

B. William Belmont Parker, *Peruvians of To-Day* (Lima, 1919), pp. 11–17.

PRESSOIR, JACQUES CATTS (2 April 1892, Port-au-Prince—8 September 1954, Port-au-Prince). *Education*: M.D., Ecole de Médicine, Port-au-Prince. *Career*: Taught philosophy, Lycée Pétion, Lycée Toussaint Louverture, Ecole Normale D'Institutrices, and Institut d'Ethnologie.

Trained as a physician, Pressoir quickly found that his interests were in a more scholarly area. He became interested in philosophy and history and taught both subjects in several different Haitian schools. He also belonged to a number of scholarly societies in his native country and in other nations as well, serving as President of the Société Haitienne d'Histoire et de Géographie. He became convinced of the value of cultural interchange among nations, and he traveled widely in the United States visiting international organizations and universities in an effort to promote greater exchange of individuals and ideas between his country and the United States.

In addition to his teaching and traveling Pressoir found time to research and publish his findings on a wide range of historical topics. He produced a multi-volume study of the role of the Protestant church in Haiti and also wrote a single-volume history of Haiti. Additionally, he became interested in archaeology and eventually produced a study of historical and archaeological monuments in Haiti. Finally, he turned his attention to historiography and wrote, in collaboration with Ernst Trouillot and Henoch Trouillot, a study of Haitian historians and their work.

A. *Le Protestantisme en Haiti*, 3 vols. (Port-au-Prince, 1945–1946); *L'enseignement de l'histoire en Haiti* (Port-au-Prince, 1950); *Monuments historiques et archéologiques* (Port-au-Prince, 1952); *Historiographie d'Haiti* (Port-au-Prince, 1953).

B. "Obituaries," *Hispanic American Historical Reivew* 35, No. 3 (August 1955), p. 441.

PRIETO, GUILLERMO (10 February 1818, Mexico City—2 March 1897, Tacubaya, Mexico). *Education*: Self-taught. *Career*: Deputy, Constituent Congress, under Benito Juárez; Minister of the Treasury, 1852, 1855, 1858, and 1861; journalist; *costumbrista* (writer about customs); Secretary to President Anastacio Bustamante; Deputy and Senator; Director, National Postal System, 1856–1857.

In a career that spanned almost the entire 19th century, Prieto was buffeted by the events of that era as much or more than other intellectuals. He was a political liberal who found himself jailed or exiled when the conservatives managed to gain control of the government. Much of his journalistic activity revolved around politics, but he wrote also on a wide variety of subjects. He began with a disordered education, and his thought as a youth frequently lacked coherence, but through diligent work and self-study he overcame these deficiencies and developed into one of the most popular poets of Mexico and certainly the founder of the genre of *cuadros de costumbres* (articles about customs) in Mexico. He was a member of the romantic movement in literature. He supported Benito Juárez in the War of the Reform, 1858–1860, and throughout his lifetime he was a champion of Mexican liberalism and nationalism. His *Romancero nacional*, written in 1885 as a patriotic tribute, was a collection of patriotic poems. His own patriotism was enhanced by his travels abroad, including a trip to the United States, which he recorded in a perceptive book about the Yankees who lived north of Mexico. He wrote about the heroes in Mexican history from the independence period to the reform era, glorifying their contributions to the development of the nation. He also devoted some attention to folklore and to social history as he described the life and times of the common people in Mexico City. The language he used in his books was the language of the commoners, and he wrote realistically about hospitals, jails, lepers, farmers, recreation, and festivals.

In addition to his poetry and his political activity, Prieto chronicled events of the 19th century in his country. He was meticulous in recounting incidents that took place and in describing the individuals involved. His style was lively and the subjects he covered of interest to the common people, which enhanced his own popularity with the Mexican population. He covered the political, religious, and social events of the age with the careful eyes of a dedicated student of his own country. His work was enriched by virtue of his opportunity to compare his native land with other countries, particularly the United States. With this opportunity for comparison he was able to write knowledgeably about Mexico and bring out the salient facts in the 19th century history of his country. Prieto's greatest failing was that he, like many other 19th century Mexican scholars, colored his work with his intense liberal political sentiment. Despite this one difficulty, however, he was a major contributor to the development of history in Mexico in the 19th century.

A. *Viaje a los Estados Unidos*, 3 vols. (Mexico City, 1877–1878); *Musa callejera*, 2 vols. (Mexico City, 1883); *Breve introducción al estudio de la historia universal* (Mexico City, 1884); *El romancero nacional* (Mexico City, 1885); *Lecciones de historia patria escritas para los alumnos del Colegio Militar* (Mexico City, 1886); *Compendio de historia universal* (Mexico City, 1888); *San Francisco in the Seventies: The City as Viewed by a Mexican Political Exile* (San Francisco, 1938).

B. Helen Delpar, *Encyclopedia of Latin America* (New York, 1974), p. 500; Michael Rheta Martin and Gabriel Lovett, *Encyclopedia of Latin American History* (Indianapolis, 1968), p. 271; Aurora M.Ocampo de Gómez and Ernesto Prado Velázquez, *Diccionario de escritores mexicanos* (Mexico City, 1967), pp. 297–299; Salvador Ortiz Vidales, *Don Guillermo Prieto y su época: Estudio costumbrista e historia del siglo XIX* (Mexico City, 1939); and Robert A. Potash, "Historiography of Mexico Since 1821," *Hispanic American Historical Review*, 40, No. 3 (August 1960), pp. 390–391.

PUEYRREDÓN, CARLOS ALBERTO (18 July 1887, Buenos Aires—16 June 1962, Buenos Aires). *Education*: Doctor of Jurisprudence, University of Buenos Aires, 1907. *Career*: Held a seat in the National Congress, 1914; Intendent in the city of Buenos Aires, 1916; founded the Saavedra Historical Museum, 1930; President, Argentine National Academy of History, 1960–1962.

Pueyrredón was deeply involved in the preservation and dissemination of all forms of culture in his nation. He was a poet, novelist, historian, and bibliophile. He amassed an extensive personal library devoted to all the works on Don Quixote, the only one of its kind in Argentina. His personal collection of books and unpublished writings also included histories about Spain and Argentina. He championed the cause of private libraries throughout the nation, and a book he wrote in 1958, *Bibliófilos y libreros anticuarios*, is credited with a decree law that forbade the taxing of private libraries by the government. He was determined to see these libraries perpetuated and extended, and he wanted to be certain that financial considerations would not lead to their destruction.

Many of Pueyrredón's books and articles were written partially from his own library, or else the inspiration for the research came from his own books and documents. In his histories he took great pride in his work in documents and rare books, and he believed that some of these histories were important primarily for the extensive documentation. In the prologue of his book on the role of Francisco de Miranda in the independence movement, he noted that he had visited the Miranda Archive in Caracas and had used the English, Spanish, and Argentine archives to put together his study. He stated flatly that the value of the book, as far as he was concerned, was its extensive documentation. In other books he included facsimiles of rare documents that he used for his research, along with his own study of the theme. The same technique was used in another book on the independence struggle in Argentina.

Pueyrredón's philosophy of history was expressed in both his historical studies and his books on literature and poetry. His book, *El falso Quixote*, published in 1961, included a comment on keeping alive in Argentina the interesting Cervantes and his Don Quixote. He pointed out that the glory that Cervantes won around the world was as much glory for Argentina as it was for Spain because Argentina had emerged culturally from Spain in 1810 with the revolution. He argued that the separation from Spain had not destroyed the cultural bonds between the two countries, nor did it break the tradition or history that the two nations shared. This historical and cultural link, he argued, should be preserved just as the old books in private libraries had to be protected.

A. *Escritos históricos del coronel Manuel A. Pueyrredón, guerrero de la independencia* (Buenos Aires, 1929); *En tiempos de los virreyes, Miranda y la gestación de nuestra independencia* (Buenos Aires, 1932); *La campaña de los Andes, cartas secretas e instrucciones reservadas de Pueyrredón a San Martín* (Buenos Aires, 1942); *1810: La Revolución de Mayo según amplia documentación de la época* (Buenos Aires, 1953); *Bibliófilos y libreros anticuarios* (Buenos Aires, 1958); and *El falso Quixote* (Madrid, 1961).

B. Julian Garces, "Carlos Alberto Pueyrredón," *Revista de historia de América*, Nos. 53–54 (June–December 1962), pp. 220–221.

Q

QUESADA, ERNESTO (1 June 1858, Buenos Aires—6 February 1934, Spiez, Switzerland). *Education*: Attended secondary schools in Buenos Aires; studied Law in Leipzig, Berlin. and Paris; Doctor of Law, University of Buenos Aires, 1882. *Career*: Assistant Librarian, National Library, Buenos Aires, 1877–1878; taught foreign literature, Colegio Nacional, Buenos Aires; held diplomatic posts in Rio de Janeiro and Washington, D.C.; wrote for a variety of publications; Judge, Criminal Court; Justice, Appellate Court; Professor of Political Economy, University of La Plata; taught at the University of Buenos Aires and at the University of Berlin; Member, School of Judicial and Social Sciences, University of La Plata; Visiting Professor of American History and Economics, Harvard University, Cambridge.

As with most intellectuals of the 19th century, Quesada held a variety of jobs ranging from diplomat to judge. But he was always vitally interested in education, whether at home or abroad, and he was determined to improve Argentine instruction. In 1909 he went to Europe to study German methods of teaching history and English methods of testing students. In all, he visited 22 universities and carefully evaluated their curricula and teaching techniques. He paid particular attention to the methods of teaching history, and he was impressed by the German seminar approach, which he advocated for Argentine schools. But all of his thoughts were incorporated in a 1,300 page report that he wrote on European education when he returned to Buenos Aires. His trip to Europe convinced him also that Argentine scholars should devote more energy to collecting documents and then publish the collections for scholars to use in their work. He personally built an impressive library, which he donated to the University of Berlin. While his investigations in Europe focused on education, he did not limit himself to that field. He studied as well real estate laws, science, and international relations. He was active politically in Argentina, and he was a strong nationalist. He defended Argentina's boundary claims against Chile in 1895 with a series of reasoned, logical articles. When World War I arrived, Quesada defended the Central Powers in a book in which he argued that Germany had no designs on South America. Following the war he was influenced by the philosophy of Oswald Spengler, whose views he brought to the Argentine reading public.

Quesada made two major contributions to Argentine historiography. He advocated strongly the introduction of the German school of historical methodology and instruction in Argentina, and he employed the German techniques in his own historical labors in an effort to teach by example. Secondly, he launched a revisionist school of historiography relative to the 19th century dictator, Juan Manuel de Rosas. Argentine historians almost from the time of Rosas' exile to England had been hypercritical of this man who so dominated Argentina in its early independence years. Quesada argued that the time had come to reexamine Rosas now that several decades had passed since his flight from Argentina. His biography of Rosas, published in 1898, naturally excited the ire of many of Rosas' enemies, who challenged Quesada's revisionist argument. But Quesada argued persuasively that while one might disagree with his conclusions, it was imperative to look at Rosas in a more objective way than before. He attempted to place Rosas in the historical milieu of his age and did not evaluate him separately from the nation as his detractors had done previously in biographies and history books that portrayed him as a demonic dictator who had shaped Argentina by his brutality and terror. Quesada insisted that Rosas must be studied scientifically and as a consequence of the times in which he lived. Quesada's book was a dispassionate, unbiased judgment that fit into the mold of the kind of history the Germans advocated and that Quesada suggested for Argentina.

A. *La época de Rosas: Su verdadero caracter histórico* (Buenos Aires, 1898;) *Historica diplomática nacional* (Buenos Aires, 1902); *La guerra civil de 1841 y la tragedia de Acha* (Buenos Aires, 1916); *La ciudad de Buenos Aires en el siglo XVIII* (Córdoba, Argentina, 1918); *La doctrina Drago* (Buenos Aires, 1919); *Acha y la batalla de Angaco* (Buenos Aires, 1927).

B. Joseph R. Barager, ''The Historiography of the Río de la Plata Area, Since 1830,'' *Hispanic American Historical Review* 39, No. 4 (November 1959), pp. 588–642; Rómulo D. Carbia, *Historia crítica de la historiografía argentina desde sus origenes en el siglo XVI* (La Plata, 1939), pp. 267–271; Percy Alvin Martin, ''Notes and Comment: Dr. Ernesto Quesada,'' *Hispanic American Historical Review*, 14, No. 3 (August 1934), pp. 351–352; William Belmont Parker, *Argentines of To-Day* (Buenos Aires, 1920), I, pp. 89–95; and Ione S. Wright and Lisa M. Nekhom, *Historical Dictionary of Argentina* (Metuchen, N.J., 1978), p. 741.

QUESADA, VICENTE GREGORIO (7 April 1830, Buenos Aires—19 September 1913, Buenos Aires). *Education*: Studied law, Buenos Aires; studied library science, Europe. *Career*: Secretary to the Governor of Buenos Aires, 1852; Representative, Confederation Congress; Minister of the Interior; founded the periodical, *La revista de Paraná;* began publication of *La revista de Buenos Aires*, 1863; Director, Buenos Aires Public Library; Deputy, National Congress, 1878–1880; Diplomat in Rio de Janeiro, Washington, D.C., Mexico City, Rome, Paris, and Berlin, 1883–1904; Representative to the First Pan American Conference, 1889–1890.

Quesada was primarily a bibliographer, and his major contribution to Argentine historiography was in this discipline. But he did not confine his activities to bibliographical labors. *President Domingo Sarmiento sent him to Europe at one point to ferret out documents that might be useful in ending Argentina's boundary crises with Bolivia, Chile, and Paraguay. The result of that trip was a report entitled *Las bibliotecas europeas y algunas de América Latina*. He followed this with another report on the same subject, *La Patagonia y las tierras australes del continente americano*. A later study that added to his reports was *El virreinato del Río de la Plata, 1776–1810*. All three works staunchly supported Argentina's boundary claims. A fervent Argentine nationalist, Quesada followed the lead of many of his intellectual compatriots by denouncing the United States' role in the Western Hemisphere as expansive and detrimental to Latin American nations.

In Argentine historiography Quesada fits primarily into the categories of bibliographer and memorialist. He was an inveterate collector and organizer of documents from all the countries he visited, and his professional tasks led him to museums and libraries where he organized these materials. These were not his only historiographical endeavors, but they were his most important. As a memorialist Quesada put together his recollections of his diplomatic career spent in a number of American and European capitals. His primary inclination was to collect data, and while he wrote monographs, essays, and articles on historical themes, his greatest success came in the bibliographical area. In *La Patagonia* (1875) he wrote that the book was not a history but a collection of documents, many of which were rare and unedited. His works are an important contribution to Argentine historiography as he made available for later historians a multitude of rare, previously unknown documents.

A. *La Patagonia y las tierras australes del continente americano* (Buenos Aires, 1875); *El virreinato del Río de la Plata, 1776–1810* (Buenos Aires, 1881); *Los Estados Unidos y la America del Sur: Los yanquis pintados por si mismos* (Buenos Aires, 1893); *Recuerdos de mi vida diplomatica misión en Estados Unidos* (Buenos Aires, 1904); *La sociedad hispano-americana bajo la dominación española* (Buenos Aires, 1893); *Los indios en las provincias del Río de la Plata* (Buenos Aires, 1902); *La vida intelectual en la America española durante los siglos XVI, XVII, y XVIII* (Buenos Aires, 1910).

B. Rómulo D. Carbia, *Historia crítica de la historiografía argentina desde sus origenes en el siglo XVI* (La Plata, 1939), pp. 97–103; and Ione S. Wright and Lisa M. Nekhom, *Historical Dictionary of Argentina* (Metuchen, N.J., 1978), pp. 171–172.

QUINTANO ROO, ANDRÉS (30 November 1787, San Bernabé de Mérida, Yucatán, Mexico—15 April 1851, Mexico City). *Education*: Degree in the Arts and Canon Law; Seminaro Conciliar de Mérida, Real y Pontificia Universidad; apprenticed to a lawyer. *Career*: Journalist who supported independence from Spain; Deputy, Congress of Chilpancingo; presided over the National Constituent Assembly that proclaimed independence in 1813; Undersecretary of Relations, 1822; Judge, Supreme Court of Justice; Vice-President, Institute of Sciences, Literature, and Arts, 1826; Minister of Justice and Ecclesiastical Affairs.

In the midst of the tumultuous independence era in Mexico, Quintano Roo was a participant who used his journalistic talents to advance the cause of Mexcian independence. He held a number of important governmental positions in the administrations of Agustín Iturbide, Guadalupe Victoria, Vicente Guerrero, and Santa Anna. As such he was instrumental in the political maneuvering in the important immediate post-independence age. Throughout this era, in addition to his work with the government, he continued to write poetry, essays, and political articles. In poetry he belonged to the romantic school, but his poetry was basically patriotic in nature and designed to win and hold support for the cause of independence. He immersed himself in the classical works of Horace and Vergil, and this early affection for the classics molded his style in essays and prose. The only major departure from patriotic work was his translation of some of the psalms of David. He also wrote short pieces that were laudatory of independence war heroes.

Quintana Roo's place in historiography is secured by his chronicling of events in prose and epic poems in the independence and immediate post-independence periods. He was not a historical researcher but instead a chronicler of events whose works could be used in later generations to write an accurate history of the early 19th century in Mexico.

A. *La libertad y la tiranía* (Toluca, Mexico, 1820); *Acusación presentada en la Cámara de Diputados el 2 de diciembre de 1830 contra el Ministro de la Guerra* (Mexico City, 1830).

B. Michael Rheta Martin and Gabriel Lovett, *Encyclopedia of Latin American History* (Indianapolis, 1968), p. 276; and Aurora M.Ocampo de Gómez and Ernesto Prado Velázquez, *Diccionario de escritores mexicanos* (Mexico City, 1967), pp. 304–305.

R

RAMÍREZ, JOSÉ FERNANDO (5 May 1804, Villa del Parral, Mexico—4 March 1871, Bonn, Germany). *Education*: Title of Lawyer, Colegio de Durango; studied at the Colegio de San Ildefonso; attended the Colegio de Abogados, Mexico City, 1833. *Career*: Deputy and Senator, National Congress; Escuela Festiva, Chihuahua, 1827; District Attorney, State of Chihuahua; judge; lawyer; writer; bibliophile; member, Council of Government, 1833; represented Durango at the Fifth Constitutional Congress; Secretary of Government, Durango, 1835; Rector Colegio de Abogados, Durango, 1837 journalist; director, National Museum; Minister of Relations; President of Council, 1864–1866; when the empire fell went into exile in Europe.

Ramírez was active in regional politics through most of his life, and at times he became a major figure on the national scene as well. During the U.S. occupation of Mexico City he hid Mexican officers in his home to prevent their capture, but he was equally concerned about the nation's documents, fearing that they would be taken out of the country or destroyed by the invaders. Consequently he devoted most of his time during the occupation to copying the most important manuscripts in the General Archives and in Mexico City's museums. Not only did he copy this data to preserve it, but in the process he collated the material and compared documents to eliminate errors from those that had been copied, sometimes several times removed from the original. Following the war with the United States he was again involved in politics, and in 1855 he was exiled to Europe by Santa Anna. While there he studied in Europe's archives and once again copied documents that he then took back to Mexico with him. When the French invaded Mexico, Ramírez at first refused to participate in the government but later he became a member of the imperial regime, which meant that when Juárez was successful and the French were driven out, Ramírez had to flee to Europe, where he spent the remaining years of his life in exile, studying, writing, and building an impressive personal library. He wanted the library to remain in Mexico, and it was sold to Alfredo Chavero with the understanding that it would never be sold outside the nation, but an English buyer purchased the collection and took it to England.

Ramírez was a great patriot, despite his collaboration with the French imperial government. He loved Mexico and devoted his life to improving literature and intellectual activity there. His histories were thorough, thoughtful accounts of the nation's past activities based upon careful research in primary documentation.

He also published many of the documents he uncovered in his painstaking, lifelong research, making it easier for scholars who succeeded him to acquire the necessary primary sources. He also wrote about events in which he participated, paticularly the war with the United States.In a sense he was both a chronicler of events and an accomplished historian when he wrote about more distant events in Mexico's past.

A. *Diario de las operaciónes militares de la división que al mando del General José Urrea hizo la campaña de Tejas* (Victoria de Durango, Mexico, 1838); *Proceso de residencia contra Pedro de Alvarado* (Mexico City, 1847); *Cuadro histórico-geográfico de la peregrinación de las tribas aztecas que poblaron el Valle de Mexico* (Mexico City, 1853); *Diccionario universal de historia y geografía* 10 vols. (Mexico City, 1853–1856); *Noticias de la vida y escritos de Fray Toribio de Benavente o Motolinía, uno de los primeros misioneros católicos y fundadores de la Provincia Mexicana del Santo Evangelio de Mexico* (Mexico City, 1859); and *Mexico durante su guerra con los Estados Unidos* (Mexico City, 1905).

B. Luís González Obregón, *Cronistas e historiadores* (Mexico City, 1936), pp. 128–171.

RAMÍREZ DE AGUILAR, FERNANDO (4 August 1887, Oaxaca, Mexico—1953, Mexico City) (Jacobo Dalevuelta). *Education*: Attended the Institute of Sciences and Arts, Oaxaca, and the Normal School of Oaxaca. *Career*: Taught history, University of Mexico, and the secondary schools of Mexico City; Chief of Information for the newspaper, *El universal*; Secretary General, Editors Union; Member, Municipal Council of Mexico City, 1930–1931; Professor of Folklore, Summer School, University of Mexico.

In addition to his teaching duties, Ramírez wrote extensively for the Mexican press.He contributed articles to several newspapers on a number of subjects, but he was most fond of describing life in Mexico in the contemporary period and writing articles on the history of Mexico. He has been praised for his perceptive powers of observation, which enabled him to translate to paper the developments he witnessed. Ramírez also liked to examine different regions of Mexico and then write articles about his findings. He wrote a great deal about Oaxaca, his native state, and he used his wide experience to write articles about customs (*articulos de costumbres*). At one time he even tried his hand at writing drama. His major interest, however, was history.

The subjects of his historical study were similar to those of most Mexican historians. He worked on the independence era, and the reform period of Benito Juárez, and he produced some articles on the conquerors and the conquest. Additionally, Ramírez wrote on folklore and legends. While he was not one of the first rank of Mexican historians, Ramírez was a chronicler and historian of national events of some note. He helped organize the First National Congress of Mexican History in 1933, and he was a respected member of the historical profession.

A. *Las fiestas guadalupanas y otras crónicas* (Mexico City, 1922); *Oaxaca, de sus historias y sus leyendas* (Mexico City, 1922); *Desde el tren amarillo* (Mexico City, 1924);

Supersticiones antaño y hogaño en algunas regiones de Oaxaca (Mexico City, 1925); *Nicolas Romero: Un año de su vida (1864–1865)* (Mexico City, 1929); *Don Vicente Guerrero, síntesis de su vida* (Mexico City, 1931).
B. Percy Alvin Martin, *Who's Who in Latin America* 2d ed. rev. (Stanford, 1936), pp. 326–327; Aurora M. Ocampo de Gómez and Ernesto Prado Velázquez, *Diccionario de escritores mexicanos* (Mexico City, 1967), p. 312.

RAMOS, JOSÉ ANTONIO (4 April 1885, Havana—27 August 1946, Havana). *Education*: Self-educated; doctorate, School of Philosophy, University of Havana. *Career*: consular officer, Europe and the United States; librarian, Havana; playwright; teacher; Instructor in Spanish, University of Pennsylvania, 1932; lectured on American literature, University of Mexico, 1933; Consul General of Cuba in Mexico; commissioned to reorganize the Library of the Cuban Foreign Ministry, 1936; Executive Librarian, Cuban National Library, 1938.

As was true of many intellectuals of the early 20th century in Latin America, Ramos traveled widely in Latin America, the United States, and Europe. From 1907 to 1910 he lived in Paris and Madrid, and when he returned home he joined the consular service, which returned him to Madrid and then reassigned him successively to Lisbon, New York, and Philadelphia. While in the last post in 1932 he was dismissed from government by President Gerardo Machado, against whom he worked. With his elimination from the service, Ramos went into exile in Mexico. Before leaving the United States he had taught Spanish literature at the University of Pennsylvania and had continued writing dramas and literary criticism. In addition to his many other endeavors he was a journalist who contributed articles to newspapers, journals, and reviews in Cuba.

While Ramos' major interest was contemporary literature, he was also concerned with the past. He wrote about Cuba's history and worked in the biographical genre as well. He was a social historian, unlike most of those who wrote history in his country in the first half of the 20th century and who concentrated upon political developments. Nothing indicates his progressive historical outlook or his commitment to social history so much as his early study of the role of women in history, written when most other historians inside and out of Latin America were ignoring the contribution of women to historical development. He also included history in his novels providing a cultural aspect for his historical output and advancing the historical novel in his country.
A. *Caliban rex* (Havana, 1914); *El traidor* (Havana, 1915); *El homre fuerte* (Madrid, 1915); *Manual del perfecto fulanista, apuntes para el estudio de la dinámica político-social cubana* (Havana, 1916); *Ensayo de una nueva justificación de la República de Cuba* (Havana, 1921); *Caniqui* (Havana, 1936).
B. Donald E. Herdeck, ed., *Caribbean Writers: A Bio-Bibliographical-Critical Encyclopedia* (Washington, D.C., 1979), pp. 853–855; Percy Alvin Martin, *Who's Who in Latin America* 2d ed. rev. (Stanford, 1940), pp. 327–328.

RAMOS MEJÍA, JOSÉ MARÍA (24 December 1849, Buenos Aires—June 1914, Buenos Aires). *Education*: Attended the University of Buenos Aires.

Career: Practicing psychiatrist; Director, Department of Public Hygiene; Director, Department of Public Assistance; President, National Council of Education.

Ramos Mejía introduced into Argentine historiography the scientific essay. In this particular case the science that he applied to history was psychiatry and the result was a close resemblance, in a primitive stage, to the current field of psychohistory. Ramos Mejía was both a practicing psychiatrist and a historian so that the linking of these two interests appeared logical to him. But he was also interested in education and concerned about the problem of immigrants in Argentina retaining their own cultural backgrounds and failing to integrate themselves into the mainstream of Argentine life. To hasten a greater homogeneity in his country he urged the government to establish a national curriculum that would be less like the European educational system and more American, thereby welding the population into a truly Argentine nation.

In his historiography Ramos Mejía applied his psychological training to prominent individuals in Argentina's past and concluded that many were neurotic and that their actions could be explained by their mental conditions. Such assertions naturally brought out critics who challenged his ability to psychoanalyze people who had died generations earlier and whom he never had an opportunity to examine or interview. Nevertheless, Ramos Mejía's breakthrough into a new field of history was a major contribution to his nation's historiography. His accomplishment was even more remarkable when it is recognized that psychiatry itself, as a discipline, was largely neglected in Argentina at that time. In fact, he has been recognized as the creator of psychiatry in his country. When Ramos Mejía wrote his first book, only seven theses had been written in psychiatry in the entire nation. Therefore he took a relatively new discipline, wedded it to history, and created a new historical field of study. The 20th century Argentine historian *Rómulo Carbia referred to Ramos Mejía as one of the most important scientists of Argentine historiography. The subjects of Ramos Mejía's histories were alive and vibrant, and his books took on the aspect of theater. With the defects of time lapse and the application of psychiatry to individuals and groups alike, the books produced by Ramos have become suspect in the 20th century. But he is regarded as an important innovator in the field of history. He might have written the first great national history, but the field in which he chose to work was so new and so suspect that he did not become one of the major historians of Argentina. However, with his picturesque style, his elegant prose, and the novelty of his approach he was able to make a permanent impression on Argentine historiography.

A. *Las neurosis de los hombres célebres en la historia argentina* (Buenos Aires, 1878); *La locura en la historia: Contribución al estudio psicopatológico del fanatismo religioso y sus persecuciones* (Buenos Aires, 1895); *Las multitudes argentinas: Estudio de psicología colectiva* (Buenos Aires, 1899); *Rosas y su tiempo* 2 vols. (Buenos Aires, 1907); *Rasgos de la vida pública de S.S. el señor brigadier general don Juan Manuel de Rosas* (Buenos Aires, 1942).

B. E. Bradford Burns, ''Ideology in Nineteenth-Century Latin American Historiography,''

Hispanic American Historical Review, 58, No. 3 (August 1978), pp. 427–428; Rómulo D. Carbia, *Historia crítica de la historiografía argentina desde sus origenes en el siglo XVI* (Buenos Aires, 1925), pp. 251–256; and Ione S. Wright and Lisa M. Nekhom, *Historical Dictionary of Argentina* (Metuchen, N.J., 1978), p. 756.

RANGEL, ALBERTO (29 May 1871, Recife, Brazil—14 December 1945, São Paulo). *Education*: Colegios Moretsohn and Americano, São Paulo; Colegio de Itu; Colegio de São Bento; Military Schools of Porto Alegre and Rio de Janeiro; Bachelor of Science and Bachelor of Military Engineering. *Career*: Served in the army as a military engineer; Ataché, Consulates General of Brazil, London, and Paris; Editor, *Commerico do Amazonas*; contributor to the *Revista do Brasil, Revista nova* (São Paulo), *O paiz, Jornal do gremio Euclydes de Cunha*; Director of Lands and Colonization, State of Amazonas; Secretary of the Amazonas state government; collected copies of documents relating to Brazil in the Quai d'Orsay of Paris and the Record Office of London; organized and catalogued the Archives of the Chateau D'Eu, Seine Inferieure, France; resigned from the Brazilian army, 1900.

Although trained to be a military engineer, Rangel devoted his life to literature and history. As a student of Brazil's literary giant, Euclydes de Cunha, Rangel had the benefit of an outstanding educational background for history and literature. Additionally, he was chosen by the Brazilian government to copy documents from foreign archives, which put him in the midst of primary documentation and impressed upon him the necessity for solid research in archival materials when writing history. As a diplomat he also learned a great deal about other cultures and other historical techniques, which he could then use for his own historical research.

In his historical activity Rangel's major interest was in the development of the empire and the imperial government's diplomatic relations with England and France. His work was rigorously researched, and he gained a reputation for expertise in the use of Brazilian and foreign archives. Because he worked so extensively in archival and documental material, scholars both inside and outside Brazil frequently contacted him for assistance, which he willingly provided. In his later years, he became interested in education during the first empire, and he completed a study on the influences, theories, and activities of those who instructed the young man and who became Emperor Dom Pedro II. While his scholarship was impeccable, Rangel was also significant as the popularizer of the short historical study. Dealing with narrow topics he covered themes and subjects thoroughly in a few pages, leaving the larger, broader works to other historians.

A. *Fora da forma* (Belem, Brazil, 1900); *Inferno verde* (Genova, Italy, 1908); *Sombras nagua* (Leipzig, Germany, 1913); *Rumos e perspectivas* (Porto, Brazil, 1914); *Quinzenas de campo e guerra* (Tours, France, 1915); *Dom Pedro I e a Marquesa de Santos* (Tours, France, 1916); *Quando o Brasil amanhecia* (Lisbon, 1919); *Transanteontem* (São Paulo, 1943).

B. Alexander Marchant, "Death of Alberto Rangel," *Hispanic American Historical Review*, 26, No. 2 (May 1946), p. 276; Percy Alvin Martin, *Who's Who in Latin America* 2d ed. rev. (Stanford, 1940), pp. 418–419.

RAVIGNANI, EMILIO (15 January 1886, Buenos Aires—8 March 1954, Buenos Aires). *Education*: Attended the Colegio Nacional, Buenos Aires, and Doctor of Laws, Universidad de Buenos Aires, 1910. *Career*: Professor of Roman Law, Universidad de La Plata, 1913; Professor of Sociology, 1914–1916; Head, Seminary of Economics and Finance, Universidad de Buenos Aires, 1915; taught Argentine history, Colegio Nacional, 1915; planned the history curriculum for the Escuela Normal, 1916; Alternate Professor of American History, Universidad de Buenos Aires, 1919; Deputy, National Chamber of Deputies, 1936–1943, 1946–1950; Dean, School of Philosophy and Letters, Universidad de La Plata, 1923; served in Buenos Aires municipal government; a Radical party leader in the Argentine Congress.

A group of Argentine historians turned to the combination of sociology with history to delve into the nation's past. Ravignani was one of these individuals who combined two disciplines in an effort to explain better the history of the nation. Along with some other historians of a similar bent of mind he wrote *Manual de historia de la civilización argentina* (1917), which decentralized Argentine history by giving less significance to Buenos Aires and including material on all parts of the nation. He also incorporated geography into his histories, and a book on the teaching of cartography made an important new contribution to Argentine teaching methods. The exercises in the book were divided into two groups that were then divided into series, two for Argentine history and three for American history. The units carried keys with them, which served as guides for the instructor.

Ravignani also became involved in politics and held several minor governmental positions in addition to his stint in the Congress. He was a leader of the Union Civica Radical. While a fervent Radical in politics, his histories remained reasonably objective, including those that covered political topics. He was primarily a constitutional historian, although he did some work in other areas as well. He spent some time at the University of Montevideo, helping to organize that school's Institute of Historical Research. He was also Director of the Historical Research Institute of the University of Buenos Aires, a group that contributed strongly to the elevation of Argentine historical production in the 20th century. The Institute published a *Bulletin* that set a lofty goal for other such publications to emulate. Ravignani was a collector and organizer of documents for his own work, and he aided other historians in their research and in finding publishing outlets for their books and articles. Ravignani's myriad interests, in addition to his determination to link sociology, history, and geography, added to the methodological arguments that took place in the nation and provided historians with many possibilities upon which to reflect. His own scholarship was extensive and as varied as his many academic and nonacademic activities.

When he went into exile during Juan Peron's dictatorship he used his ideas on the teaching and writing of history to stimulate Uruguayan historians, and he published documents and other materials in Montevideo while training graduate students in history.

A. *Una comprobación histórica; el comercio de ingleses y la "Representación de hacendados" de Moreno* (Buenos Aires, 1914); *Historia del derecho argentino* (Buenos Aires, 1919); *Cartografía histórica americana: Un censo de la provincia de Buenos Aires en la época de Rosas, año 1836* (Buenos Aires, 1922); *Asambleas constituyentes argentinas, 6 vols.* (Buenos Aires, 1937–1940); *El pacto de la Confederación Argentina* (Buenos Aires, 1938); *El virreinato del Río de la Plata, su formación histórica e institucional* (Buenos Aires, 1938).

B. Joseph R. Barager, "The Historiography of the Río de la Plata Area, Since 1839," *Hispanic American Historical Review*, 39, No. 4 (November 1959), pp. 602–603; Rómulo D. Carbia, *Historia crítica de la historiografía argentina* (La Plata, 1939), pp. 310–315; Percy Alvin Martin, *Who's Who in Latin America* (Stanford, 1936), pp. 330–331; "Obituaries: Emilio Ravignani," *Hispanic American Historial Review*, 34, No. 3 (August 1954), p. 417; William Belmont Parker, *Argentines of To-Day* (Buenos Aires, 1920). I, pp. 121–123; and Ione S. Wright and Lisa M.Nekhom, *Historical Dictionary of Argentina* (Metuchen, N.J., 1978), pp. 758–759.

REAL DE AZÚA, CARLOS (1916, Montevideo—1977, Montevideo). *Education*: Attended Universidad de la República, Montevideo. *Career*: Literary critic, intellectual historian, and political scientist.

In the arena of experimentatíon that was 20th century Uruguay, Real de Azúa was one of the intellectuals most involved in the political maneuvering. While he wrote about the political machinations of the major parties—Colorado and Blanco—he himself underwent some alteration in his own thinking. His family tradition was associated with the Colorado party and was devoutly Catholic in religious affiliation. As time went on Real de Azúa left the Colorado party and eventually the Church as well. As a youth he was enamored of Primo de Rivera's Spanish Falangist movement, but as he moved along in his career he gave up such notions and began to think in more democratic terms. At the same time, he learned the difference between magnificent political theory and realistic political systems. This alteration in his thought and action led him to assess critically political causes and to evaluate political systems carefully and rigorously. He became convinced of the tragic history of Latin American and of the failings of the Uruguayan welfare state that he had earlier supported. He was a militant anti-imperialist and Uruguayan nationalist. Throughout his life Real de Azúa was cognizant of the positions of others, and he could understand their arguments even though he did not agree with them. Because of this understanding he was able to change his own positions and to explore new ideas without the trauma of altering the firm position of earlier days.

In his historical endeavors Real de Azúa utilized the lessons learned from his public life and political activity. He was rigorously critical of his sources in research and could alter his perceptions when he learned through documentation that earlier positions had been inaccurate. He was able to use his experiences in his historical writing and to transfer many of the lessons learned in his public life to his scholarship. Consequently, he was able to produce histories that not only traced the events of Uruguay in the 20th century but also analyzed the nation's experiences and assessed the value of historical events in light of the period in which the histories were written. His works had a serene harmony about them and a balance that reflected a trained, critical, analytical mind at work. His histories explained and evaluated the turbulent 20th century of Uruguayan history when social and political experimentation were the rule rather than the exception. It was Real de Azúa who explained President Batlle's administration with sincerity, understanding, and compassion but with a critical eye that noted its weaknesses as well as its achievements. Real de Azúa wrote of Uruguay's past in the decade of the 1960s, when the nation was faltering and moving toward collapse. His historical work served to trace the path of the nation's experimentation and its eventual problems that led to the destruction of the welfare state that had held out so much hope but was unable to succeed over a protracted period of time.

A. *España de cerca y de lejos* (Montevideo, 1943); *El patriciado uruguayo* (Montevideo, 1961); *El impulso y su freno* (Montevideo, 1964).

B. "Obituary: Carlos Real de Azúa (1916–1977)," *Hispanic American Historical Review*, 58, No. 4 (November 1978), pp. 697–699.

RENÉ-MORENO, GABRIEL (7 November 1836, Santa Cruz de la Sierra, Bolivia—28 April 1908, Valparaiso,Chile). *Education*: Began his studies in his native city; continued his education under the direction of a clerical leader of La Serena, Chile, 1854; studied humanities, Colegio de San Luis; law degree, University of Chile, 1858; self-taught in literature. *Career*: Journalist in Chile; Director, Library of the National Institute, Santiago; taught at the National Institute.

René-Moreno spent most of his life in Chile studying and writing history. He was a student of the great Chilean historian Miguel Luís Amunátegui. Unlike many other Bolivians who wrote history, René-Moreno never wrote poetry, never operated in the political arena, and never pursued a diplomatic career. Instead he concentrated on teaching and writing and emerged as one of the most renowned Bolivian authors of the 19th century. He was a dedicated bibliophile who collected a large number of books and documents. In this penchant for collecting books he was like many other 19th century Latin American historians who also put together impressive libraries. Near the end of his life he gave his library to the government of Bolivia, which passed it on to the National Library of Sucre. Today, the University of Santa Cruz bears his name.

René-Moreno was a major bibliographical and historical figure of his age who loved literature and used the written word in a lively style to bring his views to the reading public. Like many of the great 19th century Latin American historians, he was committed to the exhaustive use of documentation in building his histories. To find the documents he needed René-Moreno traveled throughout Latin American and Europe, leading one writer to call him "a research pilgrim." He was also a severe critic of the written word and rigorous in analyzing essays, poetry, and other histories. His bibliographies were not only lists of works but carefully annotated with long pages of critical examination. Also like other historians of his age, René-Moreno was an accomplished polemicist who used satire and impassioned prose to attack his adversaries. But he was at his best in writing histories of his native country. After extensive research in all available documentation, René-Moreno then developed a literary history that included all the tension, suspense, anxiety, and apprehension of a good novel. He did not write to make money but to satisfy his own curiosity, his passion for history, and his patriotism.One Bolivian has depicted René-Moreno as the pure writer and the great scholar, placing him in the company of the intellectual giants of Latin America—*Andrés Bello, *Domingo Sarmiento, *Ricardo Palma, and several others. He emphasized in Bolivia the historiographical school of extensive research and his views gained wide acceptance among Bolivian historians, who followed his lead and went to work in the primary documents from the nation's past. Finally, although he spent the greater part of his life in Chile he was a Bolivian patriot, and his historical work was dedicated to bringing to light the true history of his beloved nation.

A. *Daza y las bases chilenas de 1879* (Sucre, Bolivia, 1880); *Biografía del general don José Ballivián y Segurola* (Santiago, 1895); *Ultimos días coloniales en el Alto-Perú: Documentos inéditos, 1808* (Santiago, 1897); *Bolivia y Argentina: Notas biograficas y bibliográficas* (Santiago, 1901); *Bolivia y Perú: Notas históricas y bibliográficas* (Santiago, 1901); *Ayachucho en Buenos Aires y prevaricación de Rivadavia* (Madrid, 1917).

B. Valentín Abecja Baldivieso, "El historiador Gabriel René-Moreno," *Revista de historia de América*, No. 88 (July–December 1979), pp. 123–153; Charles Arnade, "The Historiography of Colonial and Modern Bolivia," *Hispanic American Historical Review*, 42, No. 3 (August 1962), 333–384; Fernando Díez de Medina, *Literatura boliviana* (La Paz, 1953), pp. 233–240; Enrique Finot, *Elogio de Gabriel René-Moreno* (Washington, D.C., 1934); Humberto Vázquez-Machicado, "Prólogo," in Gabriel René-Moreno, *Estudios de la literatura boliviana* (La Paz, 1955), I, pp. xiii–lxxvii; and Unión Panamericana, *Diccionario de la literatura latinoamericana: Bolivia* (Washington, D.C., 1958), pp. 83–87.

RESTREPO, JOSÉ MANUEL (31 December 1781, Emvigada, Antioquia Colombia—1 April 1863, Bogotá). *Education*: Studied humanities, Colegio de San Bartolomé de Bogotá; law degree, Royal Audiencia, 1808. *Career*: Wrote for the press; served as judge; sat in the First Congress of the United Provinces, 1811; elected to the triumvirate to exercise public power, 1814; fought for independence against the Spanish; Governor of Antioquia, 1819; Deputy, Congress of Cucuta, 1821; Minister of the Interior under Simón Bolívar; President, Academy of Arts, Sciences and Letters; and Director of Public Credit.

In the midst of the independence struggle in northern South America, many intellectuals not only wrote and spoke in support of independence but also fought on the battlefields to defeat the Spanish. Restrepo was one of the most prominent writers in that early 19th century struggle. When at one point in the war the Spanish were temporarily successful, Restrepo fled for his life to Jamaica and then moved on to the United States, where he lived in exile. He improved his command of the English language and tried to learn as much as possible about politics as practiced in North America. When independence was secured, he went back to Colombia and was immediately called upon to hold political office. He served with distinction during the often stormy years of Simón Bolívar's leadership of Gran Colombia, and he was involved in the administrative details that accompanied the breakup of that union into the three nations of Colombia, Venezuela, and Ecuador. He ended his career holding administrative posts in government and in education, and he eventually put together his diary from his exile in the United States. The diary gave some significant insight into the society of the United States more than a decade before Alexis de Tocqueville made his visit and wrote his classic study of life in the United States. Restrepo's diary was far more personal than Tocqueville's book and much less perceptive, but it remains, nonetheless, of great importance for the Latin American view of the United States at this early stage in North America's development.

As Restrepo lived through the independence period he made a conscious effort to collect documents, newspapers, periodicals, and other materials that would enable him to explain the events at a later date.When his governmental tasks became less demanding he used these sources, collected over a long period of time and in many places through which he traveled, to write the history of the independence war. He tried to chronicle the events of the war, but he was also determined to explain many of the events and analyze their significance. Consequently, his book became a history rather than a chronicle. He hoped to achieve a high degree of objectivity, and for this reason his histories lack the passion and heat of others who wrote about this age in Colombian history. Yet his work is straightforward, clear, and, despite his efforts at objectivity, patriotic. His studies are most important for the primary documentation and his eyewitness accounts.

A. *Historia de la revolución de la república de Colombia*, 10 vols. (Paris, 1827); *Historia de la Nueva Granada* (Bogotá, 1936); *Memoria sobre amonedación de oro i plata en la Nueva Granada desde 12 de julio de 1753 hasta 31 de agosto de 1859* (Bogotá, 1952); *Diario político y militar: Memorias sobre los sucesos importantes de la época para servir a la historia de la Revolución de Colombia y de la Nueva Granada, desde 1819 para adelante* (Bogotá, 1954); *Autobiografía: Apuntamientos sobre la emigración de 1816 e indices del "Diario político"* (Bogotá, 1957). *Diario de un emigrado* (Bogotá, n.d.).

B. Robert H.Davis, *Historical Dictionary of Colombia* (Metuchen, N.J., 1977), p. 192; Antonio Gómez Restrepo, *Historia de la literatura colombiana* (Bogotá, 1943), III, pp. 169–174; Rafael M.Mesa Ortiz, *Don José Manuel Restrepo* (Bogotá, 1948); Joaquín Ospina, *Diccionario biográfico y bibliográfico de Colombia* (Bogotá, 1939), III, pp. 404–406; and Unión Panamericana, *Diccionario de la literatura latinoamericana: Colombia* (Washington, D.C., 1959), pp. 91–93.

RESTREPO POSADA, JOSÉ (1908, Bogotá—28 November 1972, Bogotá). *Education*: Attended Colegio de San Bartolomé de Bogotá. *Career*: Church administrator who rose to the rank of Monsignor; Chancellor, Bogotá Archdiocese; Secretary to Archbishop Ismael Perdomo, Cardinal Crisanto Luque, Cardinal Concha, and Dean of the Cathedral of Bogotá.

As a descendant of two famous Colombian historians, his great-great-grandfather *José Manuel Restrepo and his father, José María Restrepo Sáenz, Monsignor Restrepo followed comfortably in their historiographical footsteps. He was conscious of his heritage, and he collected and preserved the documents and libraries of his famous ancestors. He also published several important works, previously not in print, by José Manuel Restrepo, and he completed a number of major reference works initiated by his father, particularly those of a genealogical nature.

In his own historical research Monsignor Restrepo concentrated on biography, compiling biographical sketches of clerical leaders who had served in the Archdiocese of Bogotá, which he published in a three-volume work. Later he wrote short biographies of 315 canons who had served in the Bogotá Cathedral Chapter from 1550 to 1970. By confining his activity to clerical topics he limited his output, and at the same time he made little effort at impartiality. Yet the documents he uncovered and preserved were important for clerical history and for some political themes as well.

A. *Arquidiócesis de Bogotá: Datos biográficos de sus prelados*, 3 vols. (Bogotá, 1961–1966); *Arquidiócesis de Bogotá: Cabildo eclesiástico* (Bogotá, 1971).

B. J. León Helguera, "Obituaries: José Restrepo Posada (1908–1972)," *Hispanic American Historical Review*, 54, No. 1 (February 1974), pp. 114–115.

REYES, OSCAR EFRÉN (18 June 1896, Baños de Tungurahua, Ecuador—1 December 1966, Quito). *Education*: Attended primary and secondary schools in Quito; graduated from the University of Quito, 1914. *Career*: Undersecretary of Public Education; Chief, Technical Department, Ministry of Public Education; Rector, Colegio Nacional Juan Pío Montúfar; delegate from Ecuador to the Inter-American Conference on Education held in Chile, 1938; and Professor, University of Quito.

Oscar Reyes was a liberal who believed that only the liberal political philosophy could effectively guide Ecuador to progress and security. Consequently, his political convictions crept into his written work and rendered his histories less objective than they otherwise might have been. He was also determined to disseminate education throughout the nation in order to strengthen the total population, and to that end he taught and worked in educational administration.

As a historian Reyes worked in Indian history and contemporary political history along with biography. Perhaps his most famous work was a biography of the darling of 20th century Ecuadorean liberal, Juan Montalvo. Montalvo was a 19th century liberal who gained fame and prestige from his undying opposition to the dictator Gabriel Garcia Moreno. In the Reyes biography of Montalvo the subject emerged as a powerful figure who was held up for the praise of posterity. Yet Reyes wrote the biography not so much to glorify Montalvo as to defend the political philosophy of liberalism. Consequently, the book became an unqualified champion of liberalism and Montalvo a hero of that political philosophy. Yet Ecuadoreans regard this biography as the best work on Montalvo produced up to the middle of the 20th century. Reyes' histories of Ecuador and of Local regions of the nation are also highly regarded, although once again his passion for liberalism colored his work at least partially.

A. *Historia de la República* (Quito, 1931); *Los Incas, políticas* (Quito, 1936); *Mayas y Incas* (Quito, 1940); *Vida de Jaun Montalvo*, 2d ed. (Quito, 1943); *Descubrimiento y conquista del Ecuador* (Quito, 1948); and *Breve historia del Ecador* (Quito, 1950).

B. Albert William Bork and Georg Maier, *Historical Dictionary of Ecuador* (Metuchen, N.J., 1973), p. 126,; Instituto Panamericano de Geografía e Historia, *Guía de personas que cultivan la historia de América* (Mexico City, 1951), p. 354; and Adam Szaszdi, "The Historiography of the Republic of Ecuador," *Hispanic American Historical Review* 44, No. 4 (November 1964), pp. 520, 529.

RIQUELME, DANIEL (1857, Santiago—9 August 1912, Lausanne, Switzerland). *Education*: Studied humanities at the National Institute, Santiago; studied law at the University of Chile. *Career*: Edited the literary periodical, *El Alba*; founded *El Sud América*, a literary periodical, 1873; founded with the Colombian poet Adolfo Valdes a literary and dramatic journal *El entreacto*, 1873 wrote for *El heraldo*, Santiago, and for *El correo quillota* and *La reforma*, La Serena; officer in the Ministry of Finance; fought in the War of the Pacific; named Section Chief, Ministry of Industries and Public Works, 1888; Secretary of the Chilean legation in Bolivia, 1897.

Working in many journalistic and literary capacities, Riquelme developed a devotion to history and biography. But his major efforts throughout his lifetime were in journalism. In creating and editing numerous newspapers and journals he generally maintained a high level of quality, writing articles that were created by a clear, logical mind. Additionally he wrote, along with Isidoro Errázuriz, an account of the political and military events of the War of the Pacific, in which he had also participated. Like many other Chilean historians, his travels in other countries broadened his perspective and contributed to the success of his histories.

Although Riquelme is recognized as one of the outstanding journalists of Chile, his histories were also important. He relied on two main themes for his studies: the war against Peru and Bolivia; and events in Santiago. He was so well versed in the life of his native city that he incorporated into his journalistic articles and in his histories background material on the city and its inhabitants. In the category of Santiago events he wrote a fine study on the 1851 rebellion, which wracked the city and the nation. It was a careful, perspicacious narrative of the events leading up to the outburst and then the actual tragedy that led so many young liberal intellectuals to exile in foreign lands. His history was of the detailed, narrative kind that incorporated less extensive research than personal knowledge of events. Nevertheless, several of his works are of significance in that type of history.

A. *Chascarrillos militares* (Santiago, 1885); *El incendio de la iglesia de la Compañía el 8 de diciembre de 1863* (Santiago, 1893) *La revolución del 20 de abril de 1851* (Santiago, 1863); *Compendio de la historia de Chile* (Valparaiso, Chile, 1899); *Páginas de sangre de la historia de Chile* (Santiago, 1932); *Bajo la tienda: recuerdos de la campaña al Perú y Bolivia, 1879-1884* (Santiago, n.d.).

B. Mariano Latorre, *La chilenidad de Caniel Riquelme* (Santiago, 1931); Domingo Melfi, *Estudios de literatura chilena* (Santiago, 1938), pp. 49-63; Unión Panamericana, *Diccionario de la literatura latinoamericana: Chile* (Washington, D.C., 1958), pp. 164-166.

RIVA AGUERO Y OSMA, JOSÉ DE LA   (26 February 1885, Lima—26 October 1944, Lima). *Education*: Colegio de la Recoleta de Lima, 1893-1901; bachelor's degree in literature, 1905, doctorate in history, doctorate in jurisprudence, Universidad de Lima. *Career*: Traveled in France, Belgium, Italy, and Spain; a founder of the National Democratic party, 1915; traveled in Bolivia; Peruvian delegate, Historical Congress of Sevilla, Spain; Official Orator, University of San Marcos, 1916; Professor of Incan History, University of San Marcos, 1918; and Mayor of Lima.

The great-grandson of the first president of the Peruvian republic, Riva Aguero worked in both literature and history. He was one of the first Peruvians to give much attention to historical criticism. Meanwhile, he was active in political circles. In 1907 he encouraged students of military age at the university to enter the service because of the danger of a war with Bolivia and Ecuador. He set an example for his fellow students by being among the first to volunteer for military service. While his patriotism was unquestioned, he got into difficulty with the government when he wrote an article demanding amnesty for all political prisioners, a recommendation for which he was briefly imprisoned. When he was freed, following an uprising of students on his behalf, the government granted the full amnesty that he had suggested. Riva Aguero became more conservative as he grew older, however, and he grew increasingly suspicious of democracy. His political philosophy held that an enlightened elite should wield political power rather than trusting the masses with a voice in their own government. This political philosophy led him to espouse fascism in the 1930s, and he supported the fascist line until his death in 1944. He was also a staunch supporter of the Catholic church after 1930, when he returned to Peru following 11 years of exile in Europe for political action.

His histories were centered in the area of the general history of Peru and the development of the Incan empire prior to the arrival of the Spanish. He advocated extensive research and the testing of sources when putting together a history. He also wrote a history of Peruvian historiography in which he evaluated Peruvian historians and their work. He in turn was criticized by his peers for relying too heavily upon *Garcilaso de la Vega in his history of the Incas. But he was applauded by some Peruvians for his philosophy, which insisted that the historian must build a national soul through his work. History, he believed, led people to accept national duty and to perform in a heroic fashion in times of crisis. Unfortunately, his patriotic preachings were mitigated by his acceptance of fascism, which was destroyed in World War II, and his credibility suffered proportionately to the demise of the fascist philosophy.

A. *Carácter de la literatura del Perú independiente* (Lima, 1905); *Examen de la primera parte de la Comentarios Reales de Garcilaso de la Vega* (Lima, 1908); *La historia en el Perú* (Lima, 1910) *Concepto del derecho, ensayo filosofía juridíca* (Lima, 1912); *Garcilaso de la Vega* (Lima, 1916); and *El Perù, histórico y artístico* (Santander, Colombia, 1921).

B. Fred Bonner, "José de la Riva-Aguero (1885-1944)," *Hispanic American Historical Review*, 36, No. 4 (November 1956), pp. 490-502; Helen Delpar, *Encyclopedia of Latin America* (New York, 1974), pp. 532-533; Percy Alvin Martin, *Who's Who in Latin America* (Stanford, 1936), pp. 339-340; William Belmont Parker, *Peruvians of To-Day* (Lima, 1919).

RIVA PALACIO, VICENTE (16 October 1832, Mexico City—22 November 1896, Madrid). *Education*: Law degree, Colegio de San Gregorio, 1854. *Career*: Alderman, 1855; Deputy and Secretary to the Mexico City Municipal Council, 1856; Deputy, 1861; Governor of the State of Mexico, 1862; Governor of the State of Michoacán, 1865; General-in-Chief of the Central Army; fought for Juárez against the Maximilian government; elected Judge of the Supreme Court; ran unsuccessfully for President of the Supreme Court of Justice; Minister of Fomento, 1876; Minister of Mexico to the Court of Spain, 1886.

Along with many of his fellow writers and scholars of the 19th century, Riva Palacio was a multitalented individual. He was a novelist, poet, dramatist, storyteller, critic, satirist, orator, journalist, soldier, politician, jurist, and historian. He was most famous, however, for his historical novels. Because he held in his possession a large part of the archives of the Mexican Inquisition, he used these sources as a basis for many of his novels. He was also a firsthand observer of the French intervention and he personally battled against the imperial takeover. Consequently, his books on the imperial period have a great deal of authenticity, not only as well-researched history but as studied observations by one of the participants in the events. While Riva Palacio's novels were based on historical research and on eyewitness accounts, he did include fiction in his stories, but usually only to add adventure that made the plot more exciting.

Riva Palacio was influenced by European writers in the mold of Alexandre Dumas, and he wrote poetry and satire along with his novels. Some of his novels were clarion cries against the French and Maximilian and calls to the liberals to defend the homeland from the European interlopers. His prose was caustic and biting on the one hand, and satirical on the other. In all cases he drove home his points with vigor and audacity. While not primarily a historian, his historical novels were among the best of that genre written anywhere in Latin America in the 19th century. They represented an effort to bring to the reading public history in literary form, a practice that was favored by many of the writers of the region in the 19th century, keeping to their belief that history was not just a form of literature but that it was, in itself an art, to be transmitted to the public by artistic methods.

A. *Calvario y Tabor* (Mexico City, 1868); *Martín Garatuza, Memorias de la Inquisición* (Mexico City, 1868); *Monja y casada, virgen y martir: Historia de los tiempos de la Inquisición* (Mexico City, 1868); *La vuelta de los muertos* (Mexico City, 1870); *Memorias de un impostor, don Guillen de Lampart, rey de Mexico* (Mexico City, 1872); *Mexico a través de los siglos* (Mexico City, 1884–1889).

B. Aurora M. Ocampo de Gómez and Ernesto Prado Velázquez, *Diccionario de escritores mexicanos* (Mexico City, 1967), pp. 325–327.

ROJAS, ARÍSTIDES (November 1826, Caracas—3 March 1894, Caracas). *Education*: Doctor of Medicine and Surgery, Central University of Venezuela, 1853; postgraduate work in the United States and Europe. *Career*: Practiced medicine; opened a bookstore in Caracas with his brothers.

Although trained as a physician Arístides Rojas soon turned to a literary career. He practiced medicine for 12 years but spent part of his time writing and collecting material for his books. He also devoted some energy to philology and to bibliographical work. He amassed a large collection of books and research sources that went into his extensive personal library. Not only was his bookstore in Caracas a place where books could be purchased, but he and his brothers turned it into a cultural center where writers and intellectuals could meet and discuss the literary, political, and cultural issues of the day. Rojas wrote elemental textbooks and articles for use in teaching such subjects as geology, seismology, statistics, and history. He also prepared instructional aids that could be used in teaching Venezuela's Indian population. He was an editor, translator, and compiler of books dealing with bibliographic subjects. To prepare himself for his natural science studies he traced the route of Alexander von Humboldt, exploring Venezuela in its mountains, rivers, plains, and coastline. It was during these journeys that he became a champion of the Indian population and saw the need to educate the native Americans. The results was a series of textbooks written especially for the Indian population.

Rojas was not a traditional historian but instead was fond of linking history with poetry and writing epic poems on themes that he had researched. He was convinced that history was literature and that it had to be presented to the readers in a manner that emphasized the literary quality of the work. At the same time, his scientific training had taught him to carry out careful, extensive research, whether his topic was geography, geology, or history, so that his historical efforts benefitted from his medical and scientific background and interests. He was one of the first Venezuelan historians to study the life of the great Venezuelan precursor of independence, Francisco de Miranda, and he wrote other studies on the independence era and its major participants. He also was cognizant of the value of primary documents for historical writing, and to assist other historians he compiled, edited, and published collections of documents. He wrote in a simple, clear, yet attractive style that won readers for his books and gained for him a reputation as a major literary figure as well as a historian. Rojas was one of several Latin American scholars who combined a scientific background and career with history. But he differed from the others in that he also wove poetry into his work and sought to combine both poetry and history into an interesting, exciting literary piece, which he managed with some success.

A. *Recuerdos de Humboldt* (Puerto Cabello, Venezuela, 1874); *Estudio histórico* (Caracas, 1884); *Historia patria: Leyendas históricas de Venezuela*, 2 vols. (Caracas, 1890–1891); *Capítulos de la historia colonial de Venezuela* (Madrid, 1919); *Crónica de Caracas* (Buenos Aires, 1946); *Ideas educativas de Simón Bolívar* (Madrid, 1952).

B. *Diccionario biográfico de Venezuela* (Madrid, 1953), p. 1018; César Humberto Soto, *Personajes célebres de Venezuela* (Caracas, 1946), pp. 174–176; and Donna Keyse and G. A. Rudolf, *Historical Dictionary of Venezuela* (Metuchen, N.J., 1971), p. 102.

ROJAS, RICARDO (16 September 1882, Tucumán, Argentina—29 July 1957, Buenos Aires). *Education*: Attended secondary schools in Santiago de Estero and Buenos Aires as well as the University of Buenos Aires; Honorary Doctor of Letters, School of Philosophy of Letters, University of Buenos Aires, 1921. *Career*: Journalist on the newspaper, *El país* and contributed articles to *La nación*; taught school at the secondary and university level; Professor of Literature, University of La Plata, 1909–1920, and University of Buenos Aires, 1913–1946; Dean, Institute of Argentine Literature, 1926–1930; and Rector, University of Buenos Aires, 1926–1930; initiated the Chair of Hispanic American Studies, University of Madrid, 1928.

Ricardo Rojas was a true man of letters in Latin America. His activities were varied, and he contributed publications to many of the disciplines that caught his fancy, including poetry, philosophy, aesthetics, education, politics, folklore, history, criticism, drama, oratory, and chronicles. His writings required 40 volumes with many other unfinished pieces not included. He published his first poems and articles at the age of 15 and hardly paused in his efforts until his death 60 years later. In addition to becoming a prominent literary figure in his own country, he received praise from Europe and North America for his extensive works. He traveled in Europe at the turn of the 20th century, and while he was there, some of his books were published in Paris and Spain. Along with his teaching, journalistic career, and writing, he also became involved in politics, which resulted in his contributing to the development of the Radical party in the 1930s and serving as a party leader in the same decade. Because of his opposition to government policies he was sent to prison on Martin García Islan in the Río de la Plata and exiled to Tierra del Fuego in 1934. In 1946 he ran for the Senate and continued his political activity thereafter, but his reputation was built mainly around his literary contributions.

In his histories, as in many of his other works, Rojas exalted Western culture.

He was particularly concerned about blending Argentine developments with those of America and the Western world, and his work tended to emphasize this desire. At the same time, he opposed cultural regionalism in his own country and tried to foster a national spirit through his writing and teaching. One of his early books, *La restauración nacionalista* (1909), was designed to inform the Argentine intelligentsia on the teaching of history in Europe, but in the process he emphasized the deficiences of education in Argentina. Rojas was genuinely troubled over the Argentine immigrants' continued devotion to Europe, and he wanted to teach them more about their adopted country in order to strengthen their national pride. He also wanted to spread the concept of perfecting humanity and toward this end he set forth examples of the heights that human beings can achieve with biographies of José de San Martín and *Domingo Sarmiento. In his historical work he held up for example the advantages of political democracy and liberalism, but unlike some of the other Argentine liberal historians of the 19th century he made no effort to divorce the role of Spain from the growth of the Argentine culture. Instead, he combined the Spanish background with the Argentine present to produce stylistically excellent prose. He is deserving of all the honors, accolades, and praise that have been heaped upon him and his work, not only in his native Argentina, but throughout the Western world.

A. *Cartas de Europa* (Barcelona, Spain, 1908); *La restauración nacionalista* (Buenos Aires, 1909); *Eurindia: ensayo de estética fundado en la experiencia histórica de las culturas americanas* (Buenos Aires, 1924); *El santo de la Espada: Vida de San Martín* (Buenos Aires, 1933); *El profeta de la Pampa: Vida de Sarmiento* (Buenos Aires, 1945); and *Ensayo de crítica histórica sobre episodios de la vida internacional argentina* (Buenos Aires, 1951).

B. Joseph R. Barager, "The Historiography of the Río de la Plata Area, Since 1830," *Hispanic American Historical Review*, 39, No. 4 (November 1959), pp. 588–594; Helen Delpar, *Encyclopedia of Latin America* (New York, 1974), pp. 538–539; Roberto F. Giusti, *Diccionario de la literatura latinoamericana: Argentina* (Washington, D.C., 1961), pp. 167–171; Earl T. Glauert, "Ricardo Rojas and the Emergence of Argentine Cultural Nationalism," *Hispanic American Historical Review*, 43, No. 1 (February 1963), pp. 1–13; Percy Alvin Martin, *Who's Who in Latin America* (Stanford, 1936), pp. 354–355; and William Belmont Parker, *Argentines of To-Day* (Buenos Aires, 1920), pp. 555–559.

S

SAHAGÚN, BERNARDINO DE (1500, Sahagún, Spain—1590, Mexico City). *Education*: Studied at the University of Salamanca, Spain. *Career*: Took Franciscan vows, 1524; served as a missionary in Mexico, 1529; taught at the Imperial Colegio de Santa Cruz de Tlaltelolco, where the children of Indian royalty were educated.

In the early colonial period of Latin America, missionaries from the various orders went to America to work with the Indians, and several of them learned to communicate with the Indians in their own language, which enabled them to learn a great deal about Indian culture and history. Sahagún was one of the most important of those missionaries who wrote history in America. Because of his close contact with the Indian leaders he was able to amass a large amount of documentation, both written and oral, on the Indian history of Mexico. He wrote out his manuscript in Nahuatl and then gave it to Indian leaders to verify. The extensive study contained a tremendous variety of material. Since some of it was embarrassing to the Church, Sahagún's superiors wanted to suppress portions of his book. To accomplish this, parts of the 12-book manuscript were sent among the religious houses for their verification or refutation. Sahagún, however, had a copy in Nahuatl, which he sent to the President of the Royal Council of the Indies, who ordered that the manuscript be sent back to the author and translated into Spanish. The completed manuscript required two volumes and was sent to Spain but then lost for the remainder of the colonial period and was not published until 1829–1830 by the Mexican historian *Carlos Maria de Bustamante.

Sahagún's work was filled with material about the Indians of New Spain, and it became a major source for pre-Hispanic history in the region. Most of it was accurate, and Sahagún was careful that his facts were tested for authenticity.Still, it was not a completely unbiased work, and Sahagún accepted a good deal of Indian testimony as truth without supporting data. Sahagún generally supported the Indian cause and displayed sympathy for Indians in their relationship with the Spanish.The manuscript was generally acceptable in style, but it was not particularly well written. Much of the book has been criticized as dull and uneventful, yet in the modern era it has been regarded highly by Mexican historians, who have praised the work because it served as one of the major sources for knowledge about the way of life of the Mexican Indians.

A. *Historia de las cosas de la Nueva España* (Mexico City, 1829); *La conquista* (Mexico

City, 1929); *A History of Ancient Mexico* (Nashville, Tenn., 1932); *Los cantares a los dioses* (Mexico City, 1938); *Breve compendio de los ritos idolátricos de Nueva España* (Roma, 1942); and *Ceremonias que se hacian a hora del demonio* (Mexico City, 1954). B. Alfredo Chavero, *Sahagún* (Mexico City, 1877); Helen Delpar, *Encyclopedia of Latin America* (New York, 1974), pp. 545–546; Aurora M. Ocampo de Gómez and Ernesto Prado Velázquez, *Diccionario de escritores mexicanos* (Mexico City, 1967), pp. 348–349; and A. Curtis Wilgus, *The Historiography of Latin America: A Guide to Historical Writing, 1500–1800* (Metuchen, N.J., 1975), pp. 58–59.

SALADO ÁLVAREZ, VICTORIANO (30 September 1867, Teocaltiche, Mexico—13 October 1931, Mexico City). *Education*: Taught by his family from its large library; law degree, Escuela de Leyes, Guadalajara, Mexico, 1890. *Career*: Wrote for periodicals; perpetual secretary of La Academia Mexicana, 1925; taught Spanish at the Escuela Nacional Preparatoria; Deputy and Senator, National Congress, 1902–1906; Secretary of Government, State of Chihuahua, 1906; Secretary to the Ambassador of Mexico in Washington, D.C., 1907; Undersecretary of Foreign Relations, 1911; Minister Plenipotentiary in Guatemala, El Salvador, and Brazil, 1911–1915; from exile wrote for a large number of Mexican newspapers and also contributed articles to two U.S. papers.

Salado Álvarez has been referred to in Mexico as the "academic cream." He was cultured, moderately conservative, and competent in the use of the Spanish language. He possessed a critical mind and his scholarship was rigorously pursued. He opposed the drift to modernism in literature and involved himself in an important polemic over the issue with Francisco Monterde. The most significant outcome of this clash was the popularization of the novelist Mariano Azuela and his novel *Los de abajo*. Politically, Salado Álvarez opposed the Venustiano Carranza regime and was forced out of diplomatic service and into exile for a time. From exile he wrote extensively for the press while at the same time preparing his own historical novels. With the fall of Carranza he returned to Mexico and continued his scholarly career in his homeland.

As was true of many Latin American historians who traveled or lived abroad, Salado Álvarez took the opportunity to use archives and libraries in foreign lands. During his diplomatic years he became acquainted with the research materials available, and he soon was using them for his histories and for historical novels. Additionally, he wrote biographies and compiled bibliographies of materials available for research abroad. He wrote mainly about national political events from Santa Anna to Benito Juárez in his historical monographs as well as in his historical novels. He reserved the contemporary period for his articles in newspapers and periodicals. His style was correct and his stories were readable and interesting for the public. Salado Álvarez' place of prominence in Mexican literature was secured by the enormity of his output and the variety of the work he produced. More importantly, he was not an innovator in literature but represented the traditional literary current, and his battle to preserve some of the traditional beliefs in modern literature gained him a wide and well-deserved reputation. While this tendency to preserve the past in literature was present in his mind, it was also true that he was a traditional historian, working in the political history of the 19th century and using biography as well as historical monographs to cover the periods that he researched. Beyond that he was also among those in Mexico and throughout Latin America who believed that history was art and that the historical novel, well researched and carefully written, while fiction, could make a major contribution to the historical literature of the region. Consequently, while Salado Alvarez' reputation is based largely upon his literary production in fiction, he was also a major contributor to the historical profession of his nation.

A. *De autos* (Guadalajara, Mexico, 1901); *Episodios nacionales mexicanos*, 4 vols. (Mexico City, 1902–1906); *Refutación de algunos errores del sr. d. Francisco Bulnes: El papel de Juárez en la defensa de Puebla y en la campaña del 63* (Mexico City, 1904); *Breve noticia de algunos manuscritos de interés histórico para Mexico, que se encuentran en los archivos y bibliotecas de Washington* (Mexico City, 1908); *La conjura de Aarón Burr y las primeras tentativas de conquista de Mejico por americanos del Oeste* (Mexico City, 1908); *La novela vivida del Primer Ministro de Mexico en los Estados Unidos* (Mexico City, 1933).

B. Max Henríquez Ureña, *Breve historia del modernismo* (Mexico City, 1954), p. 485; Aurora M. Ocampo de Gómez and Ernesto Prado Velázquez, *Diccionario de escritores mexicanos* (Mexico City, 1967), pp. 350–351; J. Lloyd Read, *The Mexican Historical Novel 1826–1910* (New York, 1939), pp. 293–303; and Frederick Starr, *Readings from Modern Mexican Authors* (Chicago, 1904), pp. 288–300.

SALGADO, JOSÉ (29 March 1875, Montevideo—1948, Montevideo). *Education*: Law degree, University of Montevideo, 1895. *Career*: Taught civil law at the University of Montevideo; Professor of History, University of Montevideo; Deputy, National Congress, 1919; Member, Constitutional Convention, 1916.

Salgado was a politician and historian dividing his time between each career. His political activity was confined largely to the Chamber of Deputies, where he served as representative from two different districts. He contributed also to the Constitutional Convention of 1916, and in the Chamber of Deputies he served on some of the most significant committees, such as Foreign Affairs, Powers of the Chamber, Committee on Codes, and the Standing Committee. In addition he taught history and law at the university.

Salgado wrote a good deal on Uruguayan history, and his studies have been valued highly both in Uruguay and in other parts of the world as well. He was elected to membership in the Historical Institutes of Brazil, Argentina, and Uruguay and to the Geographical Societies of Rio de Janeiro and Lisbon. Salgado was also selected as a delegate to the Congress of Americanists that met at Buenos Aires in 1910. He wrote poetry and has published studies on legal subjects, but he did his history research on the colonial era with a study on *los cabildos colonials* and wrote a five-volume general history of his country, *Historia de la República Oriental del Uruguay*. The latter work was in the mold of other Latin American multivolume, definitive histories published in the late

19th and early 20th centuries. He did not devote much time to profound research in monographic subjects but rather wanted to look at the full scope of Uruguayan history, a task that he fulfilled well with his book.

A. *Canto a la paz* (Montevideo, 1904); *Historia de la República Oriental del Uruguay*, (Montevideo, 1905); *Tratado sobre la possesión* (Montevideo, 1905); *Los cabildos colonials* (Montevideo, 1910); *Historia diplomática de la independencia oriental* (Montevideo, 1925); and *El federalismo de Artigas, génesis de la orientalidad* (Montevideo, 1945).

B. Percy Alvin Martin, *Who's Who in Latin America*, 2d ed. rev. (Stanford, 1940), p. 466; and William Belmont Parker, *Uruguayans of To-Day* (New York, 1967), pp. 467–468.

SAMPER ORTEGA, DANIEL (1895, Bogotá—2 November 1943, Bogotá). *Education*: Seminario Conciliar and Military School of Colombia. *Career*: Director, National Library of Colombia, 1930–1938; Director, Gimnasio Moderno, Bogotá; President, Academia Colombiana de Historia; Editor, *Seleccion Samper Ortega de literatura colombiana*; taught in the school of army officers; Member, Ministry of National Education; National Director of Fine Arts; Minister of the Colombian Embasy at Washington, D.C.

A renowned Colombian scholar, Samper Ortega was both a historian and a bibliophile. As Director of the National Library he carried out an extensive program of reorganization in the library and brought it into a new, modern building for the 1930s. At the same time, he kept abreast of the state of historical research in his country and contributed some work of his own. Yet his most famous endeavor was as editor of a collection of scholarly and creative works that became classics of Colombian literature, named appropriately for him. Before his death he published 100 of these great Colombian works. His bibliographical knowledge was enhanced by his travel abroad, especially as a diplomat. This contact with other cultures afforded him the opportunity to broaden his perspective and his knowledge of books and bibliographical material that existed not only in his own country but in other lands as well. With his expertise he was able to strengthen the Colombian National Library and to write about other areas of the world outside the narrow confines of Colombia.

Samper Ortega's bibliographical efforts led him to recognize other significant writing styles and research methods, and he was committed to the laborious task of long, patient work in archives and in primary documents. Yet he was also aware of the reading public, and he believed that historical works should be well written in a literary fashion so as to appeal to the widest possible audience. Consequently, a good deal of his work had a definite literary quality about it, which tended to hide his firm belief in exhaustive, detailed primary research.

A. *Entre la niebla* (Bogotá, 1923); *Conferencía sobre fray Luís de León* (Bogota, 1928); *Colombia* (Madrid, 1929); *Colombia: Breve reseña de su movimiento artístico e intelectual* (Madrid, 1929); *Bogotá (1538-1938)* (Bogotá, 1938); and *Don José Solis, virrey del Nuevo Reino de Granada* (Bogotá, 1953).

B. "Daniel Samper Ortega," *Hispanic American Historical Review*, 24, No. 2 (May 1944), p. 360; Percy Alvin Martin, *Who's Who in Latin America*, 2d ed. rev. (Stanford, 1940), pp. 468-469,

SANTOVENIA Y ECHAIDE, EMETERIO (23 May 1889, Mantua, Pinar del Río, Cuba—18 November 1968, Miami, Fla.). *Education*: Provincial Institute of Pinar del Río; Bachelor of Letters and Sciences, 1917, Doctor of Civil Law, 1920, University of Havana. *Career*: Editor of several newpapers in Havana; primary school teacher; Professor of Public Instruction; Notary Public, Havana; Lawyer; Senator; Secretary to the President of the Republic; President, National Bank of Agricultural and Industrial Development; Director, Cuban Archives.

As a man of letters in Havana, Santovenia devoted a great deal of his time and talent to journalistic pursuits. Not only was he a successful editor of various newspapers but he also contributed articles to his own and other papers and periodicals. When not writing for the press he labored in the discipline of history and wrote for periodicals and reviews as well as publishing numerous books.

As a historian Santovenia entered several literary contests in Havana and gained fame in these for his research and for his literary style. He concentrated his efforts in the area of biography and political history, but occasionally he turned out a work in the area of technical or business history, which was not typical for the age in which he wrote. His works were marked by imagination, extensive research, and high literary quality, which gained for him the respect of the community of historians in Latin America.

Meanwhile, he became a prominent statesman and opposed those governments that he believed were depriving the cuban people of their rights. Because of his outspoken political activity he was elected to the Senate, and eventually he was appointed to positions in the National Archives, the National Library, and the National Museum. He used his political influence to expand all of these institutions, and he also aided in the construction of new buildings to house their collections. At the same time, he carried out a program to copy documents from other archives and libraries that pertained to Cuban history and to bring them to Havana. Finally, he was active in the Cuban Academy of History, which he joined in 1918 and of which he was elected President in 1941.

A. *Gonzalo de Quesada* (Pinar del Río, Cuba, 1915); *Los arroyos de Mantua puerto habilitado para el tráfico marítimo* (Havana, 1915); *Del pasado glorioso* (Havana, 1927); *El espiritú frances y la nación cubana* (Havana, 1937); and *Historia de Cuba* (Havana, 1939).

B. "Emeterio S. Santovenia," *Revista de historia de América*, Nos. 65-66 (January-December 1968), pp. 168-172; Percy Alvin Martin, *Who's Who in Latin America* (Stanford, 1936), p. 375; and William Belmont Parker, *Cubans of To-Day* (New York, 1967), pp. 103-104.

SARMIENTO, DOMINGO FAUSTINO (15 February 1811, San Juan, Argentina—11 September 1888, Asunción). *Education*: Attended primary and secondary schools in San Juan; largely self-educated. *Career*: Taught in a provincial school; worked for the provincial government; fought against the dictatorship of Juan Facundo Quiroga and fled into exile in Chile; taught school and wrote for several Chilean newspapers; commissioned by the Chilean government to reorganize teacher training in Chile; sent by the Chilean government to Europe and the United States to study their educational systems: Governor of San Juan, 1862, Ambassador to the United States; and President of Argentina, 1868–1874.

Sarmiento early came to deplore dictatorship, and for a good portion of his life he fought against dictatorial regimes either on the battlefield or in print. As an exile in Chile he expanded both his educational and journalistic horizons as he taught school and wrote for the Chilean newspapers *El mercurio* and *El progreso*. Coming from Argentina, which was at mid-century intellectually advanced over Chile, Sarmiento became embroiled in polemics with *Andrés Bello over the direction Chilean literature should take. Youthful members of the Chilean Generation of 1842 had to confront Sarmiento's cultural views and compare them with those of Bello. Sarmiento believed that romanticism should be pursued and that the neoclassicism of Bello was outdated. Bello insisted upon maintaining the purity of the Spanish language, while Sarmiento looked to the French for inspiration. His newspaper articles, sometimes signed with pseudonyms such as Pinganilla, forced the Chileans to explore their own literary and cultural ideas before accepting the views of Bello. As President of Argentina, Sarmiento strengthened education and introduced extensive material reforms. But because of his fondness for the United States and Europe he was sometimes resented by his countrymen, who believed that he was willing to make Argentina into a British colony and that he viewed the United States in an uncritical manner. While he had political detractors, few challenged his literary and intellectual predominance.

In his attitude toward history Sarmiento saw the possibility of using history to advance the nations of Latin America materially. For example, in reviewing an early 19th century history of Chile, Sarmiento pointed out that the work could serve to better acquaint Europeans with Latin America and the result of that familiarity could be a greater willingness to invest in this developing region. In his own writing, history played a role as he analyzed dictatorship in his most famous work, and he traced the historic background of Argentina in several of his other books. But Sarmiento also saw that history could be used for specific purposes. His *Facundo* was an attack upon dictatorship not just in one province but throughout Argentina and the world. Consequently, the study was an effort to use history to build opposition to the Buenos Aires dictator, Juan Manuel de Rosas. History for Sarmiento was literature and literature could be used for political purposes. Throughout his life he wrote in all genres aggressively, polemically, and with an eye to instituting change in his country.

A. *Civilización i barbarie; vida de Juan Facundo Quiroga, aspecto físico, costumbres, i abitos de la República Argentina* (Santiago, 1845); *Argirópolis; o la capital de los Estados Confederados de Río de la Plata* (Santiago, 1850); *Recuerdos de provincia* (Santiago, 1850); *Life in the Argentine Republic in the Days of the Tyrants* (New York, 1869); *A Sarmiento Anthology*, trans. by Stuart Edgar Grummon (Princeton, N.J.: 1948).

B. Allison Williams Bunkley, *The Life of Sarmiento* (Princeton, N.J., 1952); Frances W. Crowley, *Domingo Faustino Sarmiento* (New York, 1972); Helen Delpar, *Encyclopedia of Latin America* (New York, 1974); Roberto F. Giusti, *Diccionario de la literatura latinoamericana: Argentina* (Washington, D.C., 1961), pp. 173–179; Michael Rheta Martin and Gabriel Lovett, *Encyclopedia of Latin American History* (Indianapolis, 1968), p. 300; and Ione S. Wright and Lisa M. Nekhom, *Historical Dictionary of Argentina* (Metuchen, N.J., 1978), pp. 881–883.

SARMIENTO DE GAMBÓA, PEDRO (1530, Alcala de Henares, Spain— 1591, Peru). *Education:* Unknown. *Career:* Navigator; cosmographer; historian. Adviser to Viceroy Francisco de Toledo in Peru; took part in various exploratory expeditions in America.

Sarmiento's life appears more fictional than real as he passed from one adventure to another, each more amazing than the preceding. He was a part of the expedition that discovered the Solomon Islands in 1567, and a decade later he headed an expedition to explore the Straits of Magellan. As an adviser to the Vicerory Toledo in Peru he traveled throughout the colony becoming familiar with the entire region. The Viceroy eventually wanted a history of the Viceroyalty of Peru, and he commissioned Sarmiento to prepare the study for him. The objective of the history was to prove that Spain had the right to take control of Peru.

Sarmiento's history of the Viceroyalty of Peru is almost directly opposite to that of Garcilaso de la Vega's later study, which praised the Inca rulers. Sarmiento's study found the Incas to be barbaric tyrants who had illegally gained control of Peru and who were therefore in no position to challenge Spain's claim to the territory. The study was not impartial or objective, but did satisfy the aims of the political leadership. However, it was an important book because of the firsthand, eyewitness accounts it included. In this regard it became a primary source for later historians, even though overall it was a biased endeavor.

A. *Narratives of the voyages of Pedro Sarmiento de Gamboa to the Straits of Magellan* (London, 1895); *Historia de los incas* (Buenos Aires, 1942); *Historia indica* (Buenos Aires, 1942).
B. John A. Crow, *The Epic of Latin America* (Garden City, N.Y., 1946), p. 173; and Helen Delpar, *Encyclopedia of Latin America* (New York, 1974), p. 599.

SIERRA, JUSTO (26 January 1848, Campeche, Mexico—13 September 1912, Madrid). *Education:* Studied at the Liceo Franco-Mexicano, Mexico City; law degree, Colegio de San Ildefonso, 1871. *Career:* Journalist; wrote a column, "Conversaciones del domingo," in *El monitor republicano*, 1846–1890; wrote novels, drama, and poetry; taught history, sociology, and education at the Escuela Preparatoria, Mexico City; Undersecretary of Public Instruction; Deputy, National Congress; Judge, Supreme Court; Minister of Public Instruction and Fine Arts, 1905–1911; Minister Plenipotentiary in Madrid, 1912.

Justo Sierra was a major literary figure, historian and educational reformer. He reorganized the National University, encouraged curricular reform, and tried to expand the opportunities for Mexican youth to attend schools of higher education. Meanwhile, he served in political and diplomatic posts and wrote newspaper articles, poetry, and history. These combined efforts are among the richest literary production in Mexico from the late 19th and early 20th centuries. Sierra's work served as an inspiration for the youth of Mexico, and even members of the famous Ateneo de la Juventud, an influential intellectual organization, looked favorably on the life and work of Sierra. His fiction, drama, and poetry were written early in his life, while in later years he concentrated upon history and articles dealing with education. But it was history that was perhaps his most enduring legacy for Mexico.

Sierra's historical production was headed by a general history of Mexico, entitled *Evolución política del pueblo*. In this work he began a new trend in Mexican historiography by elevating the role played in the development of the nation by the mestizos, whereas earlier historians had chosen to emphasize either the Indian or Spanish contribution. Some lavish praise of his contribution has even linked his name with such other great Latin American literary figures as José Martí, *Domingo Sarmiento, and *Andrés Bello, all of whom reflected the conscience of America. Sierra's other major historical work was *Juárez; su obra y su tiempo*, a sympathetic study of the great 19th century reformer. A Mexican scholar has pointed out that Sierra was a combination of accomplished historian and intuitive philosopher. The union of these two talents set him above the other historians of his generation.

A. *Mexico: Su evolución social* (Mexico City, 1900–1902); *Mexico: Its Social Evolution*; trans. G. Sentiñon, 2 vols. (Mexico City, 1900–1904); *Juárez: Su obra y su tiempo* (Mexico City, 1905); *Evolución política del pueblo mexicano* (Mexico City, 1910; *Ensayos y textos elementales de historia*, Vol. 9, *Obras completas* (Mexico City, 1948); *Historia de la antiguedad*, Vol. 10, *Obras completas* (Mexico City, 1948); and *Historia general*, Vol. 11, *Obras completas* (Mexico City, 1948).

B. William Rex Crawford, *A Century of Latin American Thought* (Cambridge, Mass., 1944); Helen Delpar, *Encyclopedia of Latin America* (New York, 1974), pp. 562–563; Michael Rheta Martin and Gabriel Lovett, *Encyclopedia of Latin American History* (Indianapolis, 1968), p. 301; and Aurora M. Ocampo de Gómez and Ernesto Prado Velázquez, *Diccionario de escritores mexicanos* (Mexico City, 1967), pp. 361–364.

SIERRA O'REILLY, JUSTO (24 September 1814, Tixcacaltuyú, Yucatán, Mexico—15 January 1861, Mexico City). *Education*: At the Seminario Conciliar de Mérida; Studied philosophy and theology; studied jurisprudence, canon law, and Civil Law; law degree from the Colegio de San Ildefonso, Mexico City, 1838; Doctor of Canon Law and Doctor of Civil Law, Universidad Literaria de Yucatán. *Career*: Fought for states' rights against the central Mexican government; Judge, 1839; founded and wrote for four periodicals; sent to the United States by the Yucatán government to enlist support against Indian raids on estates; agent of the Ministry of Development of Yucatán; edited Civil Code for Mexico.

A Yucatán intellectual, Sierra O'Reilly was caught in the midst of a states' rights battle between the leaders of his home state and the central government in Mexico City. Because of almost constant turmoil in the capital, the government of Mexico could not furnish services to the states; in particular, it could not provide protection from Indian incursions in Yucatán. Sierra and others believed that the United States could be induced to come to the aid of the province, which would secede from Mexico if the United States would agree to send aid and then annex the state. When Washington refused, Sierra O'Reilly returned home, and the dream of a link with the United States was shattered. While he held a number of political and judicial posts, Sierra O'Reilly collected documents for his historical studies. Unfortunately, a mob assaulted his home because of his participation in political action and destroyed his historical documents, some from the official archives that had been lent to him for his historical writing.

Sierra O'Reilly worked in a number of literary genres including history, biography, and the historical novel. He was also a journalist who participated in the political quarrels fought out in the Mexican press. He was prone to write on economic questions and to work in international politics. His major contribution to history was his production of historical novels that were carefully researched for historical authenticity but that included fictional characters. Despite the fictional aspects, the novels were historically valuable for the well-researched material that was included. Additionally, Sierra wrote travel books on his many sojourns throughout Mexico and to other areas of the world. He was one of the first successful Mexican journalists to publish literary materials in the press, and he introduced the short novel that was published in newspapers serially or in small pamphlet form.

A. *Un año en el Hospital de San Lazaro* (Yucatán, Mexico, 1845–1846); *Impresiones de un viaje a los Estados Unidos de América y al Canada*, 4 vols. (Campeche, Mexico, 1851); *Los indios de Yucatán; Consideraciones históricas sobre la influencia del elemento indígena en la organización social del país* (Campeche, Mexico, 1857); *Proyecto de Código Civil Mexicano* (Mexico City, 1861); *Algunas leyendas* (Mérida, Mexico, 1892); *Diario de nuestor viaje a los Estados Unidos* (Mexico City, 1938).

B. Aurora M. Ocampo de Gómez and Ernesto Prado Velázquez, *Diccionario de escritores mexicanos* (Mexico City, 1967), pp. 364–365; and J. Lloyd Read, *The Mexican Historical Novel, 1826–1910* (New York, 1939), pp. 98–108.

SIGÜENZA Y GÓNGORA, CARLOS DE

SIGÜENZA Y GÓNGORA, CARLOS DE (1645, Mexico City—22 August 1700, Mexico City). *Education*: Studied at the Jesuit Colegio in Puebla. *Career*: Secular priest; taught cosmography and mathematics at the Universidad de Mexico, 1672; Chaplain, Hospital del Amor de Dios, 1682–1700; Geographer to the King; took part in an expedition to map the coast of Pensacola Bay, Florida; appointed Royal Cosmographer, 1689.

Scientifically inclined members of the priesthood were not in large numbers in the 17th century, but Sigüenza y Góngora was a tough-minded, determined scientist who insisted upon finding scientific explanations for events that others explained by mystical or miraculous causes. In his most famous participation in one of these controversies over religious versus scientific explanations of natural phenomena, he explained scientifically a comet that had been visible in 1681 and 1682, contradicting the miraculous explanation offered by the respected cleric Father Eusebio Francisco Kino. Sigüenza y Góngora was a man of many interests who worked in the fields of poetry, journalism, mathematics, astronomy, geography, cosmography, and history. Throughout his lifetime he collected documentation for his research, and he left to the Jesuit order his rich library filled with historical documents, despite the fact that the Jesuits had expelled him early in his career.

Sigüenza's work was largely ignored or challenged in his own lifetime, and many of the things he wrote have been lost down through the years. Mexicans charge that some of his manuscripts were lost when the United States invaded Mexico in 1847. Yet it is now clear that he was one of the most erudite men of his age, and he is generally regarded as a scholar of first rank in the colonial period. He was in the forefront of research and far ahead of the majority of his contemporaries. He brought honor to himself and to his country by his scientific and historic work. He was symbolic of the intellectual growth of Mexico in the colonial age, despite the fact that he was isolated in an area far removed from the European centers of scientific and literary activity. He was also on the cutting edge of Mexican and Latin American historiography. Sigüenza's work is now regarded as imprecise and faulty, but it helped pave the way for later, more sophisticated histories to be written in Mexico. Sigüenza worked also in archaeology, and he wrote biographies of Saint Francis Xavier and Hernán Cortés. But another great contribution he made to scholarship was his saving of records for the Municipal Council of Mexico City, which were threatened by a fire set amid the popular riots of 1692 in Mexico City. These research materials were preserved and used by later Mexican historians.

A. *Piedad heróica de don Hernando Cortés, Marqués del Valle* (Mexico City, 1689); *Libra astonómica y filosófica* (Mexico City, 1690); *Relación de lo sucedido a la Aramada de Barlovento* (Mexico City, 1691); *The Mercurio Volante of Don Carlos de Sigüenza y Góngora*, trans. Irving A. Leonard (Los Angeles, 1932).

B. Helen Delpar, *Encyclopedia of Latin America* (New York, 1974), p. 563; Irving A. Leonard, "Sigüenza y Góngora and the Chaplaincy of the Hospital del Amor de Dios," *Hispanic American Historical Review*, 39, No. 4 (November 1959), pp. 580–587; Michael Rheta Martin and Gabriel Lovett, *Encyclopedia of Latin American History* (Indianapolis, 1968), p. 301; and Aurora M. Ocampo de Gómez and Ernesto Prado Velázquez, *Diccionario de escritores mexicanos* (Mexico City, 1967), pp. 366–367.

SIMONSEN, ROBERTO COCHRANE (18 February 1889, Santos, Brazil— 25 May 1948, São Paulo). *Education:* Civil engineering degree, Polytechnic School of São Paulo, 1909. *Career*: Industrialist; financier; Federal Congressman, 1924–1927; Senator, National Congress, 1947; Professor of Economic History, Escola Livre de Sociologia e Politica and the University of São Paulo; founder and President, Cia. Construtora de Santos; President, Cia. Frigorífica de Santos, 1916–1919.

Through the 19th and into the 20th century Brazilian historiography focused on political and biographical studies. Roberto Simonsen, a businessman of some importance in his home state, also had an interest in history, and he combined his business and financial expertise with his penchant for historical research to produce the first major economic history of Brazil, a two-volume study that appeared in 1937. *História econômica do Brasil*. These two volumes covered only the colonial period of Brazil's economic history, but they were crucial to stimulating other historians to work in fields apart from the political and bio-graphical. Simonsen followed up his initial study with several other books on economic themes, and he continued to teach economic history to ever larger classes as this new historical endeavor gained additional adherents among students.

Simonsen was an innovator in Brazilian historiography with his economic studies, and soon his initial effort stirred others to follow along the same lines. His research was careful and studied, but he was more the synthesizer than the original researcher. For the age in which he wrote, however, Simonsen's work of synthesis was exactly what Brazilian history needed, and he filled the void that had for so long existed in the area of economic history. He planned to follow up his initial economic history with subsequent volumes in order to bring the study to the chronologically modern period of Brazilian history. He did not add volumes to his study but instead brought out two different books, one on the economic history of coffee and the other on Brazil's industrial history. These works, like the first study, were well received, and he gained a measure of influence in the academic and historiographical world of São Paulo and all of Brazil.

A. *A orientacão industrial brasileira* (São Paulo, 1928); *As crises no Brasil* (São Paulo, 1930); *A industria em face da economica nacional* (São Paulo, 1937); *História econômica do Brasil* 2 vols. (São Paulo, 1937); *Aspectos de história econômica do café* (São Paulo, 1938); *Evolução industrial do Brasil* (São Paulo, 1939).

B. Sergio Buarque de Holanda, "Historical Thought in Brazil," in E. Bradford Burns, *Perspectives on Brazilian History* (New York, 1967), pp. 194–195; Ronald Hilton, *Who's Who in Latin America*, Part 4, *Brazil* (Stanford, 1948), p. 238; and Alexander Marchant, "Death of Roberto Simonsen," *Hispanic American Historical Review*, 28 No. 4 (November 1948), pp. 630–631.

SOSA, FRANCISCO (2 April 1848, San Francisco de Campeche, Mexico— 9 February 1925, Coyoacán, Mexico). *Education*: Studied philosophy, Latin, and law at Mérida. *Career*: Journalist; Prefect of Coyoacán; Deputy and Senator; wrote for liberal periodicals; Director, Biblioteca Nacional.

Interested in many disciplines and in a variety of careers, Sosa worked at one time or another in almost all the literary genres, but his most successful work was in the area of history. He wrote biographies of great Mexican leaders that were generally impartial, interesting, and informative. He also wrote on and studied oral legends and stories. A political liberal, Sosa wrote numerous articles for liberal organs such as *El siglo XIX, El interino, El radical, El eco de ambos mundos,* and *El federalista*. Despite his political leanings, when he wrote history he displayed a measure of impartiality and objectivity that was not always present in the work of Latin American historians.

Sosa worked on regional Mexican history and on the Indian and early Spanish contributions to Mexican development. His research on legends was also significant as he fit the legends into a historical framework that contributed a cultural aspect to the political history of the earlier ages. He was a cultural historian as he wrote about fine arts, architecture, statues, and literature. Most of his work focused upon Mexico, but occasionally he dealt with other parts of the world and with scholars from other countries, as was the case with his article on *Juan Zorrilla de San Martín published in 1890.

A. *Manual de biográfía yucateca* (Mérida, Mexico, 1866); *El monumento de Colón* (Mexico City, 1877); *Efemérides históricas; biográficas* 2 vols. (Mexico City, 1883); *Apuntamientos para la historia del monumento de Cuauhtemoc* (Mexico City, 1887); *Conquistadores antiguos y modernos* (Mexico City, 1901); *Caracter de la conquista española en América y en México* (Mexico City, 1901).

B. Aurora M. Ocampo de Gómez and Ernesto Prado Velázquez, *Diccionario de escritores mexicanos* (Mexico City, 1967), pp. 370–372.

SOTOMAYOR VALDÉS, RAMÓN (30 April 1830, Santiago—15 June 1903, Santiago). *Education*: Studied humanities at the National Institute. *Career*: Journalist; edited *El mensajero,* 1853, *El diario de Valparaiso, El ferrocarril,* 1855, and *El conservador*; went to serve as Minister Plenipotentiary in Mexico, 1863; returned home to teach at the University of Chile, 1865; elected Deputy, 1866; served as a diplomat in Bolivia, 1866; served in the Ministry of Finance until 1886.

As both a journalist and diplomat, Sotomayor Valdés managed to put his talents to use in writing history. His style was elegant and his form was impeccable. While on diplomatic missions he collected data on the countries he visited, but he wrote mainly about Bolivia. His studies on that country are regarded as accurate and perceptive as he was present when some of the political turmoil about which he wrote transpired. While in Mexico he had encountered the chaos of the establishment of the Maximilian imperial government, and the notes he sent back to Santiago are regarded as an indispensable source for determining the thoughts and attitudes of the diplomatic corps when Maximilian controlled Mexico.

Sotomayor Valdés was a contemporary of *Diego Barros Arana, annd he worked in the same generation as *Benjamín Vicuña Mackenna, *Miguel Amunátegui and *Crescente Errázuriz, but he managed to attain solid credentials as a historian himself. His research was thorough, and he was less passionately involved in the period he wrote about than were some of the others. He also narrowed the scope of his study of Chilean history to a short chronological period, which provided the oportunity to become totally familiar with the available source material and to put that material to exceptionally good use. *Francisco Encina pointed out that, of all the great 19th century Chilean historians, Sotomayor Valdés had the greatest literary talent. He was a probing historian, and he was always curious about the reasons for political decisions made by leaders. He tried to understand the thought process of the historic figures and to explain the reasons for their actions. He was less renowned than his famous contemporaries and it was once believed that his work was not carefully researched, but later 20th century scholars disproved that assertion and Sotomayor Valdés must be recognized as an outstanding researcher and writer of history.

A. *Formación del diccionario hispanoamericano* (Santiago, 1866); *La Legación de Chile en Bolivia desde septiembre de 1867 hasta fines de 1870* (Santiago, 1872); *Estudio histórico de Bolivia bajo la administración del general José María de Achá* (Santiago, 1874); *Historia de Chile durante los 40 años transcurridos desde 1831 hasta 1871*, 2 vols. (Santiago, 1875–1876); *Campaña del ejército chileno contra la confederación Perú-Boliviana en 1837* (Santiago, 1896).

B. Fidel Araneda Bravo, *Don Ramón Sotomayor Valdés, 1830–1903* (Santiago, 1938); Francisco Encina, "Breve bosquejo de la literatura histórica chilena," *Atenea*, 95, Nos. 291–292 (September–October 1949), pp. 47–49; Luís Galdames, *Ramón Sotomayor Valdés* (Santiago, 1931); and Unión Panamericana, *Diccionario de la literatura latinoamericana: Chile* (Washington, D.C., 1958), pp. 180–190.

T

TABORGA, MIGUEL DE LOS SANTOS (5 July 1833, Sucre, Bolivia—5 December 1905, Sucre). *Education*: Studied for the clergy and took holy orders in 1857. *Career*: Rose through the ranks of the clergy to become Archbishop of Charcas, 1888; journalist and editor of newspapers and journals.

In addition to his ecclesiastical work, Taborga was also interested in political activities, and he held parliamentary positions from time to time. In 1872 he presided over the National Congress, and he was a member of the Convention of 1880. On two different occasions he traveled in Europe. He was also an accomplished polemicist writing passionately on religious, nationalistic, and historiographical subjects. Taborga's journalistic activity revolved around political and religious topics, while his book-length work was in the historical genre. He was a political conservative who defended the Church and attacked political liberalism and the widely popular positivism of Auguste Comte. He was the intellectual defender of the faith, but like so many other Latin American intellectuals, he was enraptured with polemics, which gave him the opportunity to compete with other minds over a variety of questions. Being a man of action but at the same time a man of God, he could satisfy the competitive urge through polemics without direct physical action in the political or military arena.

Although he objected strongly to positivism, Taborga had in common with the positivists a great respect for science. But he was also devoted to philosophy, theology, and history, In his historiographical efforts he had an opportunity to apply scientific research techniques, which he did scrupulously. He was committed to detail, and he ferreted out all the documentation available when researching a topic. He worked in rare documents that others seldom used. He was a careful researcher who was conscious of the historian's search for truth, and he believed that truth could be found only through exhaustive examination of historical data. Taborga was a patriot who championed the cause of his nation in the struggle against Chile, and he was bitterly disappointed when Chile ultimately won the war. His writing was frequently dramatic and impassioned, particularly when he participated in polemics or in discussing Bolivia's international problems. He worked in the pre-Columbian period of Bolivian history, and he was also a bibliographer of Bolivian historical events.

A. *Biografía del R.P.Mariano Jacobo M. Ramallo* (Sucre, Bolivia, 1868); *Constitucionalidad de la candidatura del señor Aniceto Arce* (Sucre, Bolviia, 1884); *Crónica de la revolucion del 8 de septiembre* (Sucre, Bolivia, 1888); *Un capítulo de la historia de la época colonial* (Sucre, Bolviia, 1905); *Estudios históricos de monseñor Miguel de los Santos Toborga* (Sucre, Bolivia, 1908); *Documentos para la historia de Bolivia. Aclaraciones sobre el 25 de mayo. Investigaciones históricas sobre la triple misión de Goyeneche. Crónicas de la catedral de Sucre. Idea de una introducción a la historia de Bolivia* (n.p., n.d.).

B. Enrique Finot, *Historia de la literatura boliviana* (Mexico City, 1943), pp. 223, 227–228, 236, 394; and Unión Panamericana, *Diccionario de la literatura lationoamericana: Bolivia* (Washington D.C., 1958), pp. 96–97.

TARQUÍNIO DE SOUSA, OCTÁVIO (7 September 1889, Rio de Janeiro—22 December 1959, Rio de Janneiro). *Education*: Attended the secondary and superior schools of Rio de Janeiro. *Career*: Functionary in the Postal Service and in the Ministry of Justice; literary critic; began work as a historian in 1931.

With the worldwide depression of 1929–1930, several Latin American governments fell, among them Brazil's. The 1930 Revolution not only brought Getulio Vargas to the presidency for a lengthy period of dictatorial rule but also launched Brazil into a period in which the people became obsessed with their past and history blossomed as never before. Brazilians wanted to learn all they could about their ancestors and about the historic development of the nation, and historians like Octávio Tarquínio were present to write biographies of prominent Brazilians to satisfy the craving of the people for knowledge of those who came before them. This was a period of national introspection that Tarquínio and other historians served well with their biographies and their histories. At the same time that his books were gaining stature throughout the nation, Tarquínio was also writing literary criticism, but when Getulio Vargas launched his takeover of the government in 1937 to continue his dictatorial rule, Tarquínio gave up criticism and concentrated upon history from that point onward. In addition to his biographical studies he wrote on the late colonial period and the early independence age, seeking to illuminate the era of the rupture from Portugal.

Tarquínio was an objective historian who was committed to presenting his research findings in a clear, lucid, readable style. He worked in primary sources and was determined to consult all available data before organizing and presenting his findings. In particular, he sought to present a fair, acurate, objective depiction of the men who played major roles in the nation's historical development during the imperial age. For him, Brazil's history was a personal matter, and he wrote the political history of his country from a very personal perspective. He saw his biographical subjects as the true movers of historical creation. He tied tightly together the relationship between the lives of heroes and the historical process of Brazil. Additionally, he united smoothly the search for the truth of historical personalities and events with a lively imagination that enabled him to bring to the reading public interesting, informative, objective accounts of Brazil's past. Tarquínio himself wrote in an introduction to his 10-volume biographical study that he was attempting to link men to events so that the men would appear alive, not as abstract individuals with whom few readers could identify. He wanted to find the tie between his historical characters and the environment in which they lived.

A. *Bernardo Pereira de Vasconcellos e seu tempo* (Rio de Janeiro, 1937); *História de Dois Golpes de Estado* (Rio de Janeiro, 1939); *Diogo Antônio Feijó (1763–1843)* (Rio de Janeiro, 1942); *José Bonifácio (1763–1848)* (Rio de Janeiro, 1945); *O pensamento vivo de José Bonifácio* (São Paulo, 1945); *A vida de D. Pedro* I, 3 vols. (Rio de Janeiro, 1952); *História dos fundadores do Império do Brasil* 10 vols. (Rio de Janeiro, 1957).

B. Pedro Moacyr Campos, "Outline of Brazilian Historiography," in E. Bradford Burns, *Perspectives on Brazilian History* (New York, 1967), p. 88; Percy Alvin Martin, *Who's Who in Latin America*, 2d ed. rev. (Stanford, 1940), pp. 499–500; "Octavio Tarquinio de Sousa (1889–1959)," *Hispanic American Historical Review*, 40, No. 3 (August 1960), pp. 431–434; José Honorio Rodrigues, *Historia e historiadores do Brasil* (São Paulo, 1965), pp. 148–157; and Stanley Stein, "Historiography of Brazil, 1808–1889," *Hispanic American Historical Review*, 40, No. 2 (May 1960), pp. 234–278.

TAUNAY, AFONSO D'ESCRAGNOLLE (11 June 1876, Nossa Senhora do Desterro, Brazil—20 March 1958, São Paulo). *Education*: Studied civil engineering at the Escola Politécnica do Rio, 1900; chemical and physical education degree in the course of Engenheiros Industriais da Escola Politecnica de São Paulo, 1901. *Career*: Taught at the Escola Politecnica do São Paulo and at the School of Sciences and Letters, University of São Paulo; Director, Museo Paulista, 1917; President, Consejo de Bibliotecas y Museos.

Taunay was a student and lifelong admirer of the great Brazilian historian *Capistrano de Abreu, and his work parallelled some of the studies of the other leading 19th-century historian, *Francisco Adolfo de Varnhagen. In his early studies Taunay remained within the pale of traditional Brazilian history, but as he developed his work he became more revisionist in its outlook and production. He was a careful methodologist who meticulously combed the work of earlier traditional historians, clarifying, expanding, correcting, and bringing their works up to date. A more significant contribution, however, was Taunay's efforts in the area of territorial expansion as he studied the exploits and activities of the *bandeirantes* as they moved the boundaries of Brazil into the interior, creating the vast Brazilian nation. Along the same lines, and within the framework of the same books, Taunay paved the way for historical studies on collective movements that had been of little interest to previous scholars, who concentrated upon political activities. In this way he helped to direct historiographical attention to the social sphere, and later, in his studies on the importance of coffee to the development of Brazil, he pioneered in economic history.

In his histories, Taunay was not particularly interpretative and remained traditional with his narrative style. He devoted his attention to describing what had happened rather than trying to analyze why the events occurred, but his reliance upon strict analysis of documents and his determination to find the truth of historical events won for him a place of prominence in the historiographic developments of his nation. Additionally, he continued the practice of 19th century Latin American historians of creating lengthy, multivolume histories of their nations. In his work on the general history of the *paulista bandeirantes* he wrote 11 volumes in 26 years. He added a 15-volume history of coffee and a host of monographs that tended to expand the historical knowledge of his nation. Taunay found the documentation to suport the view of his mentor, Capistrano de Abreu, that the conquest of the Brazilian frontier was the most significant event in the colonial history of Brazil, and in so doing he carved for himself a role as a major historian not only of Brazil but of all of Latin America. Yet Taunay was not without critics. Some charged that he wrote overly long, rambling books so stuffed with narrative detail that no analysis of the topic could be possible. Others deplored his failure to use footnotes in some of his books, making it extremely difficult to learn where his documentation originated. Finally, one observer suggested that Taunay should have included more ideological material in his books so that he could have interpreted as well as narrated the story. When all of these criticisms have been accepted, however, it must be concluded that Taunay's work, for the period in which it was produced, was of benefit to Brazilian historiography.

A. *Grandes vultos da independencia brasileira* (São Paulo, 1922); *Um grande bandi-erante: Bartolomeu Paes de Abreu (1674–1738)* (São Paulo, 1923); *Historia geral das bandeiras paulistas* 11 vols (São Paulo, 1924–1950); *Historia seiscentista de vila de São Paulo*, 4 vols. (São Paulo, 1926–1929); *Visitantes do Brasil colonial (seculos XVI–XVIII)* (São Paulo, 1938); *Historia do café no Brasil*, 15 vols. (Rio de Janeiro, 1939–1943).

B. E. Bradford Burns, *Perspectives on Brazilian History* (New York, 1967), pp. 205–206; Instituto Panamericano de Geografía e Historia, *Guía de personas que cultivan la historia de América* (Mexico City, 1951), pp. 412–413; Richard M. Morse, *The Bandeirantes* (New York, 1965), pp. 180–181; and José Honorio Rodrígues "Alfonso d'Escragnolle Taunay, 1876–1958," *Hispanic American Historical Review*, 38, No. 3 (August 1958), pp. 389–393.

TEJA ZABRE, ALFONSO (23 December 1888, San Luís de la Paz, Mexico—28 February 1962, Mexico City). *Education*: Law degree, University of Mexico, 1908. *Career*: Taught in the Faculty of Philosophy and Letters, National Autonomous University of Mexico, 1942–1962; diplomat in the Dominican Republic, Cuba, and Honduras; novelist and journalist for *El universal*, a daily newspaper.

Although he devoted some of his time to literature and to diplomatic efforts, Teja Zabre was primarily a teacher and a historian. He regarded his discipline as a fount of knowledge where all issues were resolved in the quest to find truth. He was particularly committed to researching and writing the history of his own country. He viewed Mexican history as part of universal history, and he was convinced that the history that had been written required revision in the light of the Mexican revolutions and because of the youthfulness of the nation. He believed that beneath the surface of the sometimes tumultuous history of Mexico was a great culture that had not yet been uncovered by national historians but that he and others of his generation were destined to unearth. In one book he wrote, "Mexican history constitutes an immense field that explorers can still reclaim."

Teja Zabre's historical method was called interpretative realism. This meant that historical research began with documents that were authenticated and verified and then the material contained in the documents was weighed and evaluated in light of other documents or known facts. His philosophy of history was based on the notion that man makes history and that the historian contributes to the cultural development of his age and is, in fact, a kind of civilizing force. This is especially true, he believed, for historians in youthful nations like Mexico, where extensive historical research had not been caried out. He regarded the historiographical opportunities available in his nation to be extensive, noting that there was a wealth of facts, figures, political events, and social and economic activity that needed to be studied and published in carefully researched and well-written books and articles. His own historical production was extensive, and his work was highly regarded by contemporaries in Mexico as well as in other countries. Some of his finest books were translated into English and French and published in Europe and the United States.

A. *Biografía de México* (Mexico City, 1931); *Historia de México: Una moderna interpretación* (Mexico City, 1935); *Panorama histórico de la Revolución Mexicana* (Mexico City, 1939); *Guía de la historia de México* (Mexico City, 1944); *Breve historia de México* (Mexico City, 1947); *Dinámica de la historia y frontera interamericana* (Mexico City, 1947); and *Lecciones de California* (Mexico City, 1962).

B. Arturo Arnaiz y Freg. "Alfonso Teja Zabre: El historiador," *Revista de Historia de América,* Numbers 53–54 (June–December, 1962), pp. 229–231; Manuel Carrera Stampa, "Alfonso Teja Zabre: El hombre," *Revista de Historia de America,* Numbers 53–54 (June–December, 1962), pp. 232–234 and *Diccionario Porrúa* (Mexico City, 1976), II, 2064.

TERÁN, JUAN BENJAMÍN (26 December 1880, Tucumán, Argentina—1938, Tucumán). *Education*: Colegio Nacional of Tucumán; School of Law, University of Buenos Aires. *Career*: Professor of Literature and eventually Rector, University of Tucumán, 1913–1929; President, National Council of Education, 1930–1932.

Terán was primarily a regional essayist. Residing in Tucumán, he spent most of his time developing historical studies on this region, but he was not exclusively a regionalist historian. He also wrote about the period of the discovery of America, not in a narrative, factual way but in an interpretative piece in which he tried to analyze the facts that surrounded the discovery. He wanted to understand the role of America in the total global historical picture. *Rómulo Carbia said that his work in this area was important even if the reader did not agree with his conclusions. The mere effort to place America in a larger historical stream was a rare occurrence in Latin America, where most historians concentrated upon developments in their own countries. In Terán's case it was even more surprising since he was basically a regional historian. But Carbia, while acknowledging the value of Terán's work, pointed out that his conclusions were based on incomplete data and were therefore premature. Carbia ranks Terán among the chroniclers of Argentina rather than among the historians. He concludes that his work was valuable but despite his attempts to delve deeply into his subjects he was basically chronicling Argentine history.

A. *Tucumán y el norte argentino, 1820–1840* (Buenos Aires, 1910); *Descubrimiento de América en la historia de Europa* (Tucumán, Argentina, 1916); *Una nueva universidad* (Tucumán, Argentina, 1919); *La universidad y la vida* (Buenos Aires, 1921); *El nacimiento de la América española* (Tucumán, Mexico, 1927); *José María Paz* (Buenos Aires, 1936).

B. Rómulo D. Carbia, *Historia crítica de la historiografía argentina desde sus orígenes en el siglo XVI* (La Plata, 1939), pp. 280–281; Percy Alvin Martin, *Who's Who in Latin America* (Stanford, 1936), p. 397.

THAYER OJEDA, TOMÁS (16 June 1877, Caldera, Chile—1953, Santiago). *Education*: Attended the Spanish-English school in Taltal, 1885–1889; attended the San Agustin School, Santiago, 1891–1894; studied philosophy and humanities and the physical and chemical sciences at the University of Chile. *Career*: Clerk, National Library of Chile, 1902; Assistant Director, Department of Manuscripts, National Library of Chile; Director, Manuscripts Division, National Library of Congress, 1910–1931; Director General of Libraries, Archives, and Museums and Director, National Library, 1931–1932.

In the mold of *José Toribio Medina, Thayer Ojeda was as much a bibliographer as a historian. The grandson of a New England sea captain, he was educated in a Spanish-English school before moving on to higher education. He did not become involved in government or diplomatic endeavors but instead devoted his entire career to collecting and organizing manuscripts at the National Library and writing history from the documents with which he became so familiar.

Thayer Ojeda based his historical studies on archival material, and he concentrated his talents on the production of a series of monographs dealing with 16th century Chilean colonial history. *Archbishop Crescente Errázuriz, an excellent historian himself, used these monographs extensively when writing his colonial histories of Chile. In addition to his monographs, Thayer Ojeda wrote an important three-volume history of the conquerors of Chile. His work in political history and biography was typical of the historians of his era, but he departed from his peers and delved into the social and economic history of the 16th century, an area that was not of great interest to most Chilean historians until the middle of the 20th century. A more traditionally accepted area to which he devoted his time and effort was historiography, a field in which Thayer Ojeda carefully examined the works of earlier Chilean historians and chroniclers and then wrote critical assessments of their efforts. Much of his work was in the form of articles in which he investigated narrow social and economic themes from the colonial era.

A. *Santiago durante el siglo XVI* (Santiago, 1905); *The Thayer Family of Thornbury* (Santiago, 1907); *Los conquistadores de Chile* 3 vols. (Santiago, 1908–1913); *Las antiguas ciudades de Chile* (Santiago, 1911); *Observaciones acerca del viaje de Don García*

Hurtado de Mendozo a las provincias de los Coronados y Ancud (Santiago, 1913); *Valdivia y sus compañeros* (Santiago, 1950).
B. Francisco Antonio Encina, "Breve bosquejo de la literatura histórica chilena," *Atenea*, 95, Nos. 291–292 (September–October 1949), p. 58; Instituto Panamericano de Geografía e Historia, *Guía de personas que cultivan la historia de América* (Mexico City, 1951), pp. 414–415; Percy Alvin Martin, *Who's Who in Latin America*, 2d ed. rev. (Stanford, 1940), pp. 503–504; and William Belmont Parker, *Chileans of To-Day* (Santiago, 1920), pp. 283–284.

TOBAR DONOSO, JULIO (25 January 1894, Quito—10 March 1981, Quito).*Education*: Attended the Jesuit Colegio de San Gabriel; Doctor of Laws, University of Quito, 1917. *Career*: Juridical consultant, Ministry of Foreign Relations of Ecuador; Minister of Foreign Relations; Ecuadorean delegate to the VIII Interamerican Conference, Lima; Member, Consultative Junta, Ministry of Foreign Relations; and Minister of the Supreme Court, 1957–1969.

In 1918 Tobar Donoso entered the Sociedad Ecuatoriana de Estudios Históricos Americanos, which was directed by the great historian *Jacinto Jijón y Caammaño. As a consequence, he learned the historian's craft from Jijón and indirectly from *Federico González Suárez, under whom Jijón had studied. Tobar was fascinated by the work of Ecuador's master historians and he scrutinized carefully all their books. He especially examined the work of *Roberto Andrade to make certain of its veracity. Meanwhile he worked in the Ministry of Foreign Relations, and when he negotiated the Protocol of Rio de Janeiro, 1942, his government was so unhappy that he was imprisoned temporarily. Despite such adversity he was the most prolific Ecuadorean writer of the last half-century. He wrote books and articles on border disputes, religious matters, the development of education, and history. In his historical monographs he took up the history of Ecuador from the end of González Suárez' seventh volume of his *Historia general de Ecuador*.

In writing about Ecuador's history Tobar reflects the thinking of both Jijón y Caamaño and González Suárez. He used González Suárez' providentialist philosophy to argue that Catholicism will eventually triumph over all other religions because Providence wills it. Religious convictions ran through much of his work, but he maintained that he was objective in his history efforts. This may be true to a degree, but his intense Catholicism led him to downgrade the Indian role in Ecuadorean national development, something that neither González Suárez nor Jijón Caamaño ever included in their histories. In writing about the independence hero, Simón Bolívar, Tobar insisted that the Liberator did more harm than good for Ecuador with his Gran Colombia scheme of linking together Venezuela, Colombia, and Ecuador. Tobar was interested in biography and in the lives of the major figures in Ecuadorean history, and some of his best work was in this genre. He wrote a number of articles on the dictator Gabriel García Moreno in which he focused his attention not on the dictator but on the political consequences of his dictatorship.While biography held some fascination for him he realized that history was far more than simply the lives of its leaders.

A. *Historia de la iglesia ecuatoriana en el siglo XIX* (Quito, 1936); *Monografías históricas* (Quito, 1937); *La invasión peruana y el Protocolo de Río* (Quito, 1945); *Apuntes para la historia de la educación laica en el Ecuador* (Quito, 1948); *La iglesia modeladora de la nacionalidad* (Quito, 1953); and *Derecho territorial ecuatoriano* (Quito, 1961).
B. Albert William Bork and Georg Maier, *Historical Dictionary of Ecuador* (Metuchen, N.J., 1973); Instituto Panamericano de Geografía e Historia, *Guía de personas que cultivan la historia de América* (Mexico City, 1951); and Adam Szaszdi, ''The Historiography of the Republic of Ecuador,'' *Hispanic American Historical Review*, 44, No. 4 (November 1964), pp. 517–518.

U

UDAONDO, ENRIQUE (11 June 1880, Buenos Aires—6 June 1962, Buenos Aires). *Education*: Studied at the British Academy, Buenos Aires; graduated from the South American Institute, Buenos Aires, 1898. *Career*: Director, Colonial and Historical Museum of Buenos Aires Province, Lujan, Argentina, 1923–1962; First Vice-President, Argentine Academy of History; First Vice-President and National Commissioner of Museums and Monuments of the Mitre Institution, 1961–1962.

Argentina was fortunate to have men of the caliber of Enrique Udaondo to enrich its past. Unlike most historians who develop their research around specific events or people, Udaondo focused his attention upon buildings and cities and georgraphic areas of Argentina. This does not mean that he evaded the more traditional types of history, because he did publish his share of articles and books on leaders of the past and on early Argentina activities, but he was more comfortable with what he regarded as works of practical value for the citizen. For example, he published biographical dictionaries, a study of the historical reasons for naming streets and plazas in Buenos Aires, and another book on the military uniforms of Argentine soldiers from the 16th to the 20th centuries.

When Udaondo did write a more traditional type of history he did it very well and in a very professional manner. He used documentation from both public and private archives to develop his theme and he subjected these sources to careful scrutiny. He viewed history as a source of knowledge that people needed to know in order to understand themselves.

A. *Juan de Lezica y Torrezuri* (Buenos Aires, 1914); *Reseña histórica del templo de Nuestra Señora del Pilar (Recoleta)* (Buenos Aires, 1918); *La villa de Lujan en tiempos de la Colonia y en la época de la República* (Buenos Aires, 1927); *Fray Justo Santa María de Oro* (Buenos Aires, 1936); *Diccionario biográfico argentino* (Buenos Aires, 1938); *Guía del Museo de Transportes con numerosas ilustraciones y antecedentes sobre la evolución de los mismos* (Buenos Aires, 1950).

B. Julian Garces, "Enrique Udaondo," *Revista de historia de América*, Nos. 53–54 (June–December 1962), pp. 222–224; Ione S. Wright and Lisa M. Nekhom, *Historical Dictionary of Argentina* (Metuchen, N.J., 1978), pp. 961–962.

URTEAGA, HORACIO H. (19 March 1877, Cajamarca, Peru—11 June 1952, Lima). *Education*: Studied at the Arco School and the Colegio de San Ramon de Cajamarca; Doctor of Philosophy and Letters, School of Law, University of

San Marcos, Lima, 1903. *Career*: Alternate Deputy from Cajamarca, National Congress, 1903; Deputy, 1904–1908; Director, Chalaco Institute; Director, National School of San Carlos, Puno, 1910; taught at the government school in Huancayo; Adjunct Professor of the History of Civilization, University of San Marcos; Professor of Peruvian History, Escuela Normal, Lima; Director, Colegio Nacional de Santa Isabel of Huancayo, 1913; Professor of Peruvian History, Pedagogical Institute for Men, Lima, 1914; Director, National Archives, 1917.

Many Latin American historians were excellent administrators in government, business, and education. Urteaga was an outstanding leader of the National School in Puna, where through his efforts a new building was acquired, standards were elevated, equipment was purchased, and the morale of both faculty and students was improved. Additionally, he reorganized the teaching staff and opened courses in agriculture and stock raising, and he eventually created the Departments of Agriculture and Agronomy. Beyond his educational and political activities he wrote poems and drama. At one time he wrote two plays in verse for a fund-raising effort designed to acquire money for national defense.

Urteaga's historical research efforts differed from those of the majority of Latin Americans in that he did not confine his work to the history of his native country. Instead, he studied and wrote about Greece and the Orient in a series of textbooks on the history of the world. However, his major contribution to the historiography of Peru was the publication of the 12-volume *Colección de libros y documentos para la historia del Perú,* which he compiled in collaboration with Carlos Romero from 1916 to 1919.

A. *Colección de libros y documentos para la historia del Perú,* 12 vols. (Lima, 1916–1919); *Informaciones acerca de la religión y gobierno de los incas* (Lima, 1918); *El imperio incaico en el que se incluye la historia del ayllo y familia de los incas* (Lima, 1919); *La organización judicial en el imperio de los incas* (Lima, 1928); and *Los cronistas de la conquista* (Paris, 1938).

B. Percy Alvin Martin, *Who's Who in Latin America* (Stanford, 1936), pp. 410–411; and William Belmont Parker, *Peruvians of To-Day* (Lima, 1919), pp. 396–398.

V

VALDÉS, JULIO CÉSAR (1862, La Paz—1918, La Paz). *Education*: Law degree, Universidad Mayor de San Andrés. *Career*: Wrote for periodicals after 1886; served in Parliament; President, Chamber of Deputies; diplomat in Chile.

A fine writer, Valdés worked mainly in the literary genre of chronicles. He was also interested in recounting the customs of the Bolivian people, and in this way he found many defects in society and attacked them viciously, but with humor. As a *costumbrista* (writer on customs) he was compared with the Spaniard, Mariano José de Larra, but critics argued that he did not have the sick humor and pessimism of Larra and was far more optimistic in analyzing society. He was more the realist but with a bright outlook on the future of his country. Valdés' literary efforts, in addition to his *costumbrista* activity, tended to shed light upon national characteristics, and his novels introduced the *chola* as a viable character in Bolivian literature. This tendency to look at elements of Bolivian society disdained by earlier writers helped pave the way for the Bolivian creole novel that became a popular literary form in subsequent years. Valdés even gained praise from, and won the admiration of, the then literary giant of Latin America, *Ricardo Palma.

While writing about the customs of his people, often in a sarcastic tone, Valdés also worked in history. He retained his humor in looking at the past. He was not the meticulous researcher who wrote in great detail but rather the scholar who assessed history in the light of his contemporary age and found both past and present lacking. In each case he sought to set forth a cure for the maladies by pointing out the basic problems, but in a pleasant literary style to which few could object. He noted the problems of a racially divided nation and the economic backwardness of a predominently rural, preindustrial society. Combining essays, prose, and history, he managed to build a favorable reputation for himself not only in his own country but throughout Latin America.

A. *La Paz de Ayacucho (relación histórica, descriptiva y comercial)* (La Paz, 1889); *D. Juan Bautista de Sagárnaga, protomártir de la independencia sud-americana* (La Paz, 1894); *Don Crispin Andrade y Portugal: Instrucción cívica. El estado de guerra, obra adoptada para la instrucción de ejército boliviano* (La Paz, 1895); *Asuntos internacionales; Bolivia y Chile; antecedentes históricos; discusión diplomática; estado actual de la cuestión* (Santiago, 1900).

B. Enrique Finot, *Historia de la literatura boliviana* (Mexico City, 1943), pp. 250–251; and Unión Panamericana, *Diccionario de la literatura latinoamericana: Bolivia* (Washington, D.C., 1958).

VALLADARES, JOSÉ ANTÔNIO DO PRADO (3 May 1917, Salvador, Bahía, Brazil—23 December 1959, Rio de Janeiro). *Education*: Bachelor of Law, University of Pernambuco, Recife; studied art at the Graduate Institute of New York University and museology at the Brooklyn Museum. *Career*: Journalist for the *Diário de Pernambuco;* Director Museu do Estado da Bahía, 1939; Professor of Aesthetics, University of Bahía; wrote a series of articles on the arts for the *Diário de notícias* of Bahia.

In the first half of the 20th century the field of museology was little developed in Brazil. Consequently,Valladares, who was deeply involved in the development and preservation of museums in his native land, traveled to the United States to study the history of art and the program of museum creation and maintenance. Back in Brazil he taught at the University of Bahia and eventually became Director of the State Museum of Bahía. As a professor of Aesthetics he introduced a course in the history of art that he taught until his death. In his job as Museum Director he catalogued and photographed collections of the decorative arts of the 18th century while acquiring prized collections of art for the museum. Meanwhile, he initiated a series of monographs published by the museum on the local folk art and on the folklore of Brazil. Later he made a study of the colonial ecclesiastical silver of Bahía and wrote it up as a chapter of a book on the arts of Brazil. He also wrote the definitive history of Portuguese scenic tiles to be found in Brazil. This became a classic of research and study as well as a model for illustrated books of this nature. While his tasks as Museum Director and Professor occupied much of his time and effort, he still was able to write weekly articles on the arts for the *Diario de notícias* of Bahía. This work established his reputation as a literary journalist and won him a measure of fame throughout Brazil.

Although not a historian in the traditional sense of that term, Valladares contributed to Brazilian historiography through his articles and books on the history of art and on museum direction in his home state of Bahía and throughout Brazil. He labored long to popularize the national artistic treasures in an effort to bring enjoyment and knowledge to a wide range of the Brazilian population. He not only gave to the people of Bahía a well-organized and progressive museum in Bahía but through his writing he brought the art collections of the nation to the attention of the entire population of Brazil. In the process he gained a wide personal reputation that spread to Portugal, where he assisted in the creation of a museum of religious art in the Church of Saint Teresa in Salvador. He also wrote about Afro-Brazilian folk customs in bringing Brazil's art history to the attention of the nation. By his work in art history he was able to bind together the ties of Portugal and Brazil in the historical development of both countries, and he won the plaudits of scholars on both sides of the Atlantic for his efforts.

A. *Museu do estado; guía do visitante* (Bahía, Brazil, 1946); *Museu para o povo. Un estudo sobre museus americanos* (Salvador, Bahía, Brazil, 1946); *A galeria Abbot. Primeira pinacoteca da Bahía* (Salvador, Bahía, Brazil, 1951); *Dominicais. Seleção de crônicas de arte, 1945–1950* (Salvador, Bahía, Brazil, 1951); *Arte brasileira; publicações de 1943–1953* (Salvador, Bahía, Brazil, 1955); *Artes maiores e menores. Seleção de crônicas de arte, 1951–1956* (Salvador, Bahía, Brazil, 1957).

B. Robert G. Smith, "José Antônio do Prado Valladares (1917–1959)," *Hispanic American Historical Review*, 40, No. 3 (August 1960), pp. 435–438.

VALLE, RAFAEL HELIODORO (3 July 1891, Tegucigalpa, Honduras—29 July 1959, Mexico City). *Education*: Graduated from the Escuela Normal de Maestros, Mexico City, 1911; Doctor of Historical Sciences, School of Philosophy and Letters, Universidad Nacional Autónoma de Mexico. *Career*: Founded the Academia de la Lengua de Honduras and the Ateneo Americano de Washington; served as Consul or Ambassador in various countries; Honduras Ambassador to the United States, 1949–1955; taught at the Universidad Nacional Autónoma; directed publications of the Mexican National Museum; Director, Bibliographic Section, Secretariat of Education.

After graduation from secondary school, Valle turned to journalism, and following a visit to Mexico he became obsessed with Mexican history. In 1907 he wrote an article on Benito Juárez, which the Mexican Consul in Honduras saw and for which he sought out the young boy. The Consul promised Valle a scholarship to study in Mexico City, but when Valle arrived in the Mexican capital no scholarship was available and he had to support himself by working on Mexican newspapers. *Justo Sierra also promised him a scholarship after he heard him present a paper, but it was awarded just eight months before he graduated. Valle next turned to a career in the Honduran foreign service and was assigned to the consulate at Mobile, Alabama, and later to Belize, British Honduras. Consequently, when he was assigned to the boundary commission in Washington, D.C., that studied Honduran boundary disputes he was already conversant with the subject because of the studies he had carried out in Belize. In Washington for the commission's deliberations he familiarized himself with the materials in the Library of Congress so that his diplomatic foray was beneficial for acquainting him with sources in a wide variety of archives and libraries. In 1947 he headed the Honduran delegation to the UNESCO Conference in Mexico City, and in 1950 he moved to Washington as Ambassador to the United States. While in Washington he continued to write poetry, which he had done throughout his life, gaining stature with each passing year. He was a postmodernist poet whose work flowed smoothly, leading one writer to refer to his poems as verses of honey. Additionally, he wrote essays, bibliographies, and anthologies, along with histories.

In his historical work Valle concentrated upon individuals and on American themes. He was generally objective in his assessment of historical events, and he was ever the realist in examining the past and the lives of prominent historical figures. He wrote monographs on Iturbide, Bolívar and Cristóbal de Olid. He was also interested in uniting the culture of all America and in building cooperation among all American intellectuals. To accomplish this end he founded the Ateneo Americano while Ambassador to Washington. This organization was designed to link all intellectuals, writers, and literary figures in a common movement in which they could assist each other in their work on American themes. As part of this effort he helped Latin American historians find documents and other primary sources with which he was familiar. He was not the erudite historian, despite his recognition of the essential nature of primary documentation, and when he wrote he aimed his words at the general public, not only the professional historians. He did not want to become a world renowned historian but he wanted to be of service to the average citizen who also had an interest in the history of his country. For this type of individual Valle believed he could be useful, and he tried to make his ideas and his research understandable for the nonprofessional historian. In this fashion he linked his storytelling capabilities with his research commitment to produce popular histories. At the same time, unlike other chroniclers and storytellers who worked on themes in a local area, Valle used all of America as a basis for his work. Because of his journalistic training and his reportorial style of writing he could accomplish this objective of reaching the widest possible audience, and he left a legacy of popular history for other Latin American historians of the same inclination to follow.

A. *Cómo era Iturbide* (Mexico City, 1922); *La anexión de Centro América a México (documentos y escritos de 1821)* 6 vols. (Mexico City, 1924–1949); *El espejo historial* (Mexico City, 1937); *Iturbide, varón de Dios* (Mexico City, 1944); *Cristóbal de Olid, conquistador de Mexico y Honduras* (Mexico City, 1960), and *Historia de las ideas contemporáneas en Centro-América* (Mexico City, 1960).

B. William J. Griffith, "The Historiography of Central America Since 1830," *Hispanic American Historical Review*, 40, No. 4 (November 1960), p. 558; Instituto Panamericano de Geografía e Historia, *Guía de personas que cultivan la historia de América* (Mexico City 1951), p. 431; Percy Alvin Martin, *Who's Who in Latin America* (Stanford, 1936), pp. 415–416; Emilia Romero de Valle, *Recuerdo a Rafael Heliodoro Valle en los cincuenta años de su vida literaria* (Mexico City 1957); Lota M. Spell, "Rafael Heliodoro Valle (1891–1959)," *Hispanic American Historical Review*, 40, No. 3 (August 1960), pp. 425–430; and Unión Panamericana, *Diccionario de la literatura latinoamericana: América Central; Honduras, Nicaragua y Panamá* (Washington, D.C., 1963), II, pp. 180–183.

VALLE-ARIZPE, ARTEMIO DE (25 January 1888, Saltillo, Mexico—15 November 1961, Mexico City). *Education*: Studied in the Jesuit Colegio de San Juan and the Ateneo Fuente; law degree, Escuela Nacional de Jurisprudencia, 1910. *Career*: Deputy, National Congress, 1911; Secretary of the Mexican legation in Spain, 1919, Belgium, and Holland; Member, Comision de Investigaciones y Estudios Históricos in Madrid, Spain, for five years; Chronicler of Mexico City, 1942; practiced law.

Throughout his career Valle-Arizpe combined his love for history with his political, diplomatic, literary, and legal practices. He worked in archives and libraries in Spain and in other European countries where he was assigned as a diplomat. He wrote poetry, novels, and stories as well as histories of the colonial age in Mexican development. Only rarely did he write about a historical event outside the colonial period.

For many literary figures and historians, work in the colonial period was a passing interest as they moved on to study the 19th and 20th centuries. But for Valle-Arizpe the colonial age was his career. He personally was immersed in and fascinated by the era, and he developed a deep loyalty to historical events and personages from that period that continued throughout his lifetime. Because of this love for colonial Mexico, he created a style of writing that was similar to that used in the colonial era, and he set his novels in that same period. In his novels he mixed reality with fiction in an imaginative fashion that attracted readers to his work. It was this combination of fiction with history that led to one of his contributions to historiography, in that he presented his material in an effective style, frequently imitative of the archaic colonial language, that was interesting to Mexican readers. Valle-Arizpe's work was picturesque, quaint in the eyes of many of his contemporaries, but fascinating for the reading public. In this way he popularized the history of colonial Mexico for his countrymen.

A. *La muy noble y leal ciudad de Mexico, según relatos de antaño y ogaño* (Mexico City, 1924); *Del tiempo pasado* (Madrid, 1932); *Cirreyes y virreinas de la Nueva España* (Madrid, 1933); *Historias de vivos y muertos* (Madrid, 1936); *Historia de la ciudad de México, según relatos de sus cronistas* (Mexico City, 1939); *Personajes de historia y de leyenda* (Mexico City, 1953); *Historia, tradiciones y leyendas de las calles de Mexico* (Mexico City, 1959).

B. Margaret Mason Bolton, "Artemio de Valle-Arizpe (1884–1961), Creator of the Artistic Colonial Novel in Mexico" (Master's thesis, Texas Christian University, 1965); Percy Alvin Martin, *Who's Who in Latin America* (Stanford, 1936), p. 416; Aurora M. Ocampo de Gómez and Ernesto Prado Velázquez, *Diccionario de escritores mexicanos* (Mexico City, 1967), pp. 400–402; Luis Rublúo "Artemio de Valle Arizpe," *Revista de historia de América*, Nos. 55–56 (January–December 1963), pp. 192–193.

VARNHAGEN, FRANCISCO ADOLFO DE (17 February 1816, Sorocaba, Brazil—29 June 1878, Vienna). *Education*: Real Colegio da Luz, Portugal, 1825–1833; studied engineering, physical science, political economy, paleography, German, French, and English at the Academia da Marinha, Brazil, 1832–1833. *Career*: Diplomat; fought in the civil wars on the side of Dom Pedro I; Lieutenant of Artillery; Attaché to the Brazilian legation in Lisbon; Secretary to the Brazilian legation in Madrid, 1846; served in the Foreign Office in Rio de Janeiro, 1850; Minister to Paraguay, 1859; Minister of New Granada, Venezuela, and Ecuador, 1861; Brazilian diplomatic representative in Vienna, 1868.

When Varnhagen went abroad in the foreign service of his country, he took the opportunity afforded him and spent much of his time in archives and libraries researching historical topics that related to Brazil. He used the Portuguese archives to collect all manner of documentation that he later put to good use in his two-volume general history of Brazil. In this manner, too, he uncovered many new facts that altered the prevailing concepts of Brazilian history, particularly in the 16th century. He was not as successful in finding material for the

17th century, and his coverage of the 18th century was even deficient in many respects. However, it must be pointed out that he was the first Brazilian to explore the 18th century in Brazilian history. Some critics have charged that Varnhagen's general history was a chronicle rather than a true history, but the great Brazilian historian *Capistrano de Abreu suggested that, while Varnhagen chronicled some phases of Brazil's past, he interpreted wisely many others. His studies also clarified the work of earlier historians. Capistrano did criticize Varnhagen, however, for trying to include too much material in the two-volume general history. Because in many respects it was a pioneering effort, Capistrano believed that Varnhagen should have been content with a truly general study without including patches of highly detailed material. Capistrano believed that the book took this form because Varnhagen lacked the skill to synthesize his documentation so that the general history became too specific in spots. Varnhagen was also criticized because he showed a reluctance to cite the work of other historians, and he sometimes chose initials instead of the complete name to refer to his fellow Brazilian historians.

Varnhagen's style was sometimes rough and rude, tending at times to irritate the reader, but there was much original material included that rewarded the reader with enormous insight into Brazil's early history despite the style. Capistrano de Abreu referred to Varnhagen as the "teacher and guide" of Brazilian historiography. For many years after his general history, Varnhagen was ignored by his countrymen and he attained little academic stature for his efforts, but Capistrano resurrected his work with a critical analysis that was fair and objective and that made it clear that no other general history written by a Brazilian could compare with Varnhagen's study. Other historians suggested that Varnhagen wrote "uncritically and unstimulatingly," cluttering his books with unimportant facts and neglecting important events. But even his detractors agreed that he was a good researcher, though his histories might be cold and aloof. He used source materials that had not been exploited by other historians, such as newspapers, pamphlets, and correspondence, which gave his books a sound basis in important sources.

A. *Reflexoes críticas* (Lisbon, 1839); *Memorial orgânico* (Madrid, 1850); *Historia geral do Brasil* 2 vols. (São Paulo, 1852–1857); *O Tobaco de Bahia* (Caracas, 1863); *Sementeira da Herva Mate* (Vienna, 1877); *Historia das lutas com os holandeses no Brasil* (São Paulo, 1942).

B. João Capistrano de Abreu, "A Critique of Francisco Adolfo de Varnhagen," in E. Bradford Burns, *Perspectives on Brazilian History* (New York, 1967), pp. 143–155; Stuart B. Schwartz, "Francisco Adolfo de Varnhagen: Diplomat, Patriot, Historian," *Hispanic American Historical Review*, 48, No. 2 (May 1967), pp. 185–202; Stanley Stein, "Historiography of Brazil, 1808–1889," *Hispanic American Historical Review*, 40, No. 2 (May 1960), p. 236.

VASCONCELOS, JOSÉ (27 February 1882, Oaxaca, Mexico—30 June 1959, Mexico City). *Education*: Studied at the Instituto Campechano and the Escuela Nacional Preparatoria in Mexico City; law degree, School of Law, University of Mexico, 1905. *Career*: Taught music in the Free Conservatory, 1914; Rector, University of Mexico; Secretary of Public Education; ran unsuccessfully for President of the Republic, 1929; lived in Europe, the United States, Asia, and South America; Director of the review, *La antorcha*; Director, Biblioteca Mexico; Professor, School of Social Sciences, University of La Plata, Argentina, 1934.

Many intellectuals and scholars in Mexico, Vasconcelos among them, found their careers shaped by the Revolution of 1910. Vasconcelos joined the influential Ateneo de la Juventud (Athenium of Youth) and became directly involved in the revolution as a supporter of Francisco I. Madero and Pancho Villa, both of whom challenged the government of Porfirio Díaz. When the revolution ended, Vasconcelos was given the task of advancing public education by President Alvaro Obregón. He not only sought to expand and extend educational oportunities among the youth of the nation, but he tried to carry education into the rural areas that had been long neglected by the Mexican government, and Vasconcelos tried to help adults in the villages as well as the youth through a form of community development program. Additionally, he created libraries, promoted mural painting, expanded publications for educational purposes, and even imported scholars, artists, and writers to enhance Mexican education. Because he was a political figure, Vasconcelos had to leave the country from time to time when his opponents gained control of the government, but he managed to return when his side assumed office. His forays into exile, however, proved beneficial because these periods of travel permitted him to observe life in other cultures, which provided him with ideas for his own people when he returned.

Vasconcelos' scholarly activities encompassed philosophy, sociology, and history. He produced a number of thoughtful works on the development of the Hispanic American culture, and he sought to defend the Hispanic contribution to the history of the Western world. He denounced the Indianismo movement in Mexico, which elevated the contribution of native Americans to Mexican development, and he was a rarity in scholarly circles because he suported the anti-liberal school of historiography by charging that 19th-century liberals were mere puppets of the United States. Instead, he championed the conservative historian of the 19th century, *Lucas Alamán. More a philosopher than a historian, Vasconcelos did not spend his time in detailed, rigorous research of primary historical documents. Rather, he was a synthesizer and model builder of the past, somewhat in the same vein as *José Lastarria in Chile and *Vicente Fidel López in Argentina. He endorsed completely their view that history must be forged into a kind of philosophical system to be of any significance to mankind. Additionally, he made a major contribution to historiography through his memoirs, which filled four volumes. These books were not only recollections of his life but somber views of an eyewitness to the chaotic and turbulent years of the Mexican Revolution of 1910. In this respect, Vasconcelos became a chronicler of his age as well as its historian and philosopher.

A. *El movimiento intelectual contemporáneo de México* (Mexico City, 1916); *La caida de Carranza: De la dictadura a la libertad México* (Mexico City, 1920); *La raza cósmica* (Barcelona, Spain 1925); *Aspects of Mexican Civilization* (Chicago, 1926); *Ulises criollo* (Mexico City, 1935); *Breve historia de México* (Mexico City, 1937); *Apuntes para la historia de México, desde la conquista hasta la revolución* (Mexico City, 1943).

B. Helen Delpar, *Encyclopedia of Latin America* (New York, 1974), p. 613; Percy Alvin Martin, *Who's Who in Latin America* (Stanford, 1936), p. 417; Aurora M. Ocampo de Gómez and Ernesto Prado Velázquez, *Diccionario de escritores mexicanos* (Mexico City, 1967), pp. 403–404; and Robert A. Potash, "Historiography of Mexico Since 1821," *Hispanic American Historical Review*, 40, No. 3 (August 1960), pp. 396–397.

VÁZQUEZ-MACHICADO, HUMBERTO (27 April 1904, Santa Cruz de la Sierra, Bolivia—16 December 1957, La Paz). *Education*: Primary, secondary, and college education in Santa Cruz; law degree, University of San Andrés, La Paz. *Career*: Held a variety of governmental positions including Asesor de la Concillería and Secretary of the Yacimientos Petroliferos Fiscales Bolivianos; Member, Board of Directors, Central Bank; President, Comisión Boliviana Demarcadora de Límites con el Brasil; assigned to various official missions in other Latin American countries and to Europe; Professor of History, Economics, and Sociology, University of San Andrés; Director, University Library; lectured at the University of Texas and the University of Florida, 1954.

Vázquez-Machicado was born in the same small city as the great Bolivian historians *Gabriel René-Moreno and *Enrique Finot. From early youth he was devoted to the history of René-Moreno and he worked tirelessly to bring to the public the work of the then neglected historian. Vázquez-Machicado was a member of one of the prominent families of the community, and his father, a teacher, saw to it that he received a solid educational base. Because of his birthplace he was conversant with the Oriente of Bolivia. He loved this lowland region but he also was aware that the history of Bolivia was rooted in the highlands. Because of this understanding of his nation and his awareness of the relative roles of the two major regions, he has been called one of the most representative Bolivian scholars. Like so many other Latin American historians, he combined a teaching career with a position in Bolivia's foreign service, and like the others he took full advantage of his tours of duty outside the country to use libraries, archives, and private documentary collections for his histories. Not only did he make good use of other Latin American resources but he also served in Spain, France, Germany, England, and the Vatican, and at every stop he used the documents available when they pertained to Bolivia. Additionally, he purchased books and manuscripts relative to Bolivia during his travels abroad and added manuscripts that he acquired in his own country. His history collection became one of the outstanding sources for historical research in Bolivia.

As a historian Vázquez-Machicado was committed to research in primary documents. He was impatient with many of his fellow historians who used only secondary sources, and he demanded that they study history only through primary research. He was obsessed with historical research despite his many positions.

Much of his work was published in short articles that were included in the Sunday literary supplements in Bolivian newspapers. Additionally, he published short monographs that included lengthy bibliographies and extensive documentation.When he encountered evidence to refute accepted historical beliefs he generally published his findings, revising current opinion with such extensive documentation that no opportunity for argument remained. His basic work on Bolivian history stands as a monument to the rigorous historic method that he advocated and pursued throughout his career, making him one of the outstanding Bolivian historians of all time.

A. *La sociología de Gabriel René-Moreno* (Buenos Aires, 1936); *Tres ensayos históricos* (La Paz, 1937); *El acta de la fundación de Asunción* (La Paz, 1938); *Blasfemias históricas*. *El mariscal Sucre, el doctor clañeta y la fundación de Bolivia* (La Paz, 1939); *La diplomacia boliviana en la corte de Isabel II* (La Paz, 1941); *Orígenes de nuestro derecho procasal* (La Paz, 1951); *El enigma de Juliano el Apostata* (Oruro, Bolivia, 1955); *La leyenda negra boliviana. La calumnia de la corradura del napa* (La Paz, 1955).

B. Charles W. Arnade, "The Historiography of Colonial and Modern Bolivia," *Hispanic American Historical Review*, 37, No. 3 (August 1962), pp. 333–384; Charles W. Arnade, "Humberto Vázquez-Machicado, 1904–1957," *Hispanic American Historical Review*, 38, No. 2 (May 1958), pp. 268–270; and Dwight B. Heath, *Historical Dictionary of Bolivia* (Metuchen, N.J., 1972), p. 244.

VEDIA Y MITRE, MARIANO DE (29 December 1880, Buenos Aires—19 February 1958, Montevideo). *Education*: Law degree, School of Law and Social Sciences, University of Buenos Aires. *Career*: Taught in the secondary schools of Buenos Aires; Rector, Colegio Nacional Bernardino Rivadavia until 1916; Professor of Argentine History, University of Buenos Aires; Judge; worked in municipal government; journalist; sociologist; and historian.

Vedia y Mitre taught, served in government, and wrote sociology, history, literature, and biography. He also translated the works of Chaucer, Shakespeare, Shelley, Wilde, Eliot, Shaw, and Samuel Johnson. Of all the English literature he translated, he was most fond of the sonnets of Shakespeare, all of which he translated into Spanish, along with Hamlet's monologue. In addition to his translations, he wrote extensive and detailed prologues and introductions that included information not only on the work translated but on the author as well. He believed that to translate was to interpret, and he was careful to bring his interpretation into as close an approximation of the author's intent as possible. For him translations of verse were works of art, and few surpassed his talent for this type of translation.

In his histories Vedia y Mitre reflected the historiographic method of *Bartolomé Mitre with its emphasis upon long, careful examination of primary documents. Following the acquisition of these materials the historian then could proceed to a complete and reasoned explanation of the sources. In this manner he examined the political history of Argentina and produced a 13-volume history on the political ideas in the nation. Instead of focusing upon a short time frame he looked at the broad spectrum of Argentine history against the backdrop of world political ideas, bringing forth a logical, meaningful history of the political ideas of Argentina. In other books Vedia y Mitre wrote about Argentine history in the 19th century, examining the essential events of that era including independence, the early governments, the Rosas era, the collapse of the Rosas dictatorship, and the creation of the united Argentine nation. In all of these books Vedia y Mitre was as careful of detail as he was when translating English poetry, and his general, sweeping analysis of Argentine life presented a panoramic view of his nation's history in the 19th century.

A. *El deán Funes en la historia argentina* (Buenos Aires, 1906); *La presidencia de Rivadavia* (Buenos Aires, 1910); *La revolución de diciembre y sus consecuencias* (Buenos Aires, 1923); *La revolución del 90; origen y fundación de la unión cívica, causas, desarrollo y consecuencias de la revolución de julio* (Buenos Aires, 1929); *Historia general de las ideas políticas (con una introducción sobre la teoría del estado)*, 13 vols. (Buenos Aires, 1946), and *Historia de la unidad nacional* (Buenos Aires, 1952).

B. Julian Garces, ''Mariano de Vedia y Mitre,'' *Revista de historia de América*, No. 45 (June 1958), pp. 152–153; Roberto F. Giusti, *Diccionario de la literatura latinoamericana: Argentina* (Washington, D.C., 1961), pp. 215–218; and Percy Alvin Martin, *Who's Who in Latin America* (Stanford, 1936), pp. 418–419.

VELASCO, JUAN DE (6 January 1727, Riobamba, Ecuador—20 June 1792, Faenza, Italy). *Education*: Studied theology, mathematics, and physics at the Colegio de San Luís. *Career*: Joined the Jesuit order in 1743 and took his vows in 1746; taught at the Colegio de Popayan; left Ecuador when the Jesuit order was banned from Latin America in 1767; and took up residence in exile in Italy.

When the Jesuit order was expelled from Latin America in 1767, the priests made the long, difficult journey back to Europe. Along the way many of the older priests died because of the rigors of the trip. Velasco survived the journey and the exile, but for nine years he was too ill to work. Then, however, the Spanish King wanted a history of the Kingdom of Quito in order to demonstrate to the world the virtues of Spain, and he recognized that the Jesuits had been directly involved in the region and were well equipped to provide him with such a study. Therefore he commissioned Velasco to write the history of the Kingdom of Quito, and the result was the first history of Ecuador, a three-volume study. When the manuscript was completed Velasco sent it to the King, but it was not published at that time and instead found its way into the Royal Archives, where it remained until the middle of the 19th century, when it was finally brought before the reading public.

Velasco's history was constructed from his own experience in Eucador and from his knowledge of the indigenous pre-Hispanic society. He covered the organization of the Indian tribes and revealed for the first time the nature of the political and governmental organization of the Indians in the pre-Columbian era in Ecuador. While Velasco sometimes became overly imaginative in putting his work together, he did preserve the oral legends of the region. While the criticism of his work has been extensive, it is worth noting that he wrote under difficult circumstances. The major obstacle was that he wrote the book in Italy, far removed from the sources that he needed for a definitive, accurate history. But his extensive travels through the backlands of Ecuador furnished him with memories that he could incorporate into his history, and because he was vitally interested in antiquities he retained so much from his visits to remote regions that this part of the history was important. But overall the history has been subjected to intense scrutiny and found lacking in accuracy by modern historians. Nonetheless, this was the first major history of Ecuador, and it served as the foundation for the subsequent national histories written by *Pedro Fermín Cevallos and *Federico González Suárez. For that reason alone Velasco deserves the place of distinction he holds today in Ecuadorean historiography.

A. *Historia del Reino de Quito en la América Meridonal, escrita por el presbitero de Juan de Velasco... año de 1789*, 3 vols. (Quito, 1841–1844); *Historia moderna del Reyno de Quito y crónica de la Provincia de la Compañia de Jesús del mismo Reyno* (Quito, 1941).

B. Marvin Alisky, *Historical Dictionary of Peru* (Metuchen, N.J., 1979), pp. 109–110; Isaac J. Barrera, *Historiografía del Ecuador* (Mexico City, 1956), pp. 29–42; Albert Wiliam Bork and Georg Maier, *Historical Dictionary of Ecuador* (Metuchen, N.J., 1973), p. 153; Adam Szaszdi, "The Historiography of the Republic of Ecuador," *Hispanic American Historical Review*, 44, No. 4 (November 1964), pp. 508–511; and A. Curtis Wilgus, *The Historiography of Latin America: A Guide to Historical Writing, 1500–1800* (Metuchen, N.J., 1975), pp. 109–110.

VICUÑA MACKENNA, BENJAMÍN (25 August 1831, Santiago—25 January 1886, Santa Rosa de Colmo, Chile. *Education*: National Institute, 1846–1848; law degree, Universidad de Chile, 1857. *Career*: Lawyer, teacher; politician; journalist; diplomat; Editor of *La asamblea constituyente*, 1856; Editor of *El mercurio*, 1863; elected Deputy from Santiago, 1863; Special Envoy to the United States, 1865; Special Envoy to Europe, 1870; founded the Partido Democrático Liberal, 1858; candidate for the presidency, 1876.

As the writing of history in Chile expanded in the middle of the 19th century, Vicuña and his fellow historians followed the traditional historical method and philosophy taught by *Andrés Bello. They searched for historic truth by pursuing a thorough and rigorous examination and analysis of primary sources. Publishing his first articles at the age of 17, Vicuña had a long and distinguished career, but he was also committed to political action resulting from his dedication to political freedom and to Chilean Liberalism. Not content simply to write about political issues, Vicuña became embroiled in a Liberal rebellion against the Conservative government at mid-century, when he was just 20 years old. From this experience he gained the material for what became the major account of the 1851 rebellion, *Historia de la jornada del 20 de abril de 1851*. Caught up in the romanticism of the age, he participated in organizing a group of disillusioned young intellectuals dedicated to ending the Conservative domination of the government and establishing a Liberal regime based on the ideals of the French Revolution of 1789. Ultimately the assault on the government failed and Vicuña, along with many other Liberal writers, went into exile. Once again he made use of his experience to publish a work of significance. This time, it was a three-volume travel account of a three-year journey through the United States and Europe. Vicuña proved a perceptive visitor to foreign lands, and many of his observations about the United States are as penetrating as those made by Alexis de Tocqueville, who preceded him through North America 20 years earlier. Returning home Vicuña continued his interest in politics and at the same time launched a successful career in journalism. Nevertheless, his greatest impact on Chile resulted from his historical works.

Vicuña's histories were a departure from the politically motivated studies that predominated in the Latin America of that era. He researched his subjects carefully and attempted a fair and just analysis of the data. More than any of his contemporaries he combined this attention to detail and scholarship with an exciting literary style that gained him a reputation as a popular historian. While other historians were writing primarily for intellectuals, Vicuña produced history that could be read and enjoyed by both scholars and the general public. Perhaps for this reason he chose to work in biography, a genre that the public found stimulating. He concentrated upon the lives of independence war leaders, bringing fresh interpretations to traditional assessments of the independence heroes. Vicuña's penchant for literary quality led to criticism of his work by a few contemporaries who charged that he permitted his imagination free rein, making some of his histories appear closer to fiction than to sound, scholarly studies. Most observers, however, praised his imaginative treatment of history as a significant and welcome change from the staid works of other Chilean historians. Today he is regarded as Chile's finest literary historian of the 19th century.

A. *Páginas de mi diario durante tres años de viaje, 1853–1854–1855* (Santiago, 1856); *El ostracismo de los Carreras* (Santiago, 1857); *Los jirondinos chilenos* (Santiago, 1862); *La historia de los diez años de la administración de Montt* 6 vols. (Santiago, 1868); *Ostracismo de general don Bernardo O'Higgins* (Santiago, 1868); Páginas olvidadas de Vicuña Mackenna en "El Mercurio" (Santiago, 1936).

B. Justo Arteaga Alemparte, *Don Benjamín Vicuña Mackenna* (Santiago, 1832); Ricardo Donoso, *Don Benjamín Vicuña Mackenna: Su vida, sus escritos y su tiempo, 1831–1886* (Santiago, 1925); Guillermo Feliú Cruz, "Interpretación de Vicuña Mackenna: Un historiador de siglo XIX," *Atenea*, 95, Nos. 291–292 (September–October 1949), pp. 144–181; Luís Galdames, *La juventud de Vicuña Mackenna* (Santiago, 1931); Eugenio Orrego Vicuña, *Vicuña Mackenna, vida y trabajos* (Santiago, 1932); and Gertrude Matyoka Yeager, "Barros Arana, Vicuña Mackenna, Amunátegui: The Historian as National Educator," *Journal of Inter-American Studies and World Affairs*, 19, No. 2 (May 1977), pp. 173–199.

VIGIL, JOSÉ MARÍA (11 October 1829, Guadalajara, Mexico—18 February 1909, Mexico City). *Education*: Studied philosophy and Latin at the Seminario Conciliar, Guadalajara, and law at the Universidad de Guadalajara. *Career*: Dramatist; taught Latin and philosophy in the Liceo de Varones de Guadalajara; directed the official periodical, *El país*; formed the Biblioteca Publica; edited *Boletín de noticias*; Deputy five times; taught grammar and philosophy in the

Escuela Nacional Preparatoria and history and geography at the Escuela Nacional de Niñas; Judge, Supreme Court of Justice, 1875; Director, Biblioteca Nacional, 1879–1901; reorganized the library and published eight volumes of its catalog; elected Director, Academia Mexicana de la Lengua, 1894.

Vigil's life spanned the chaotic 19th century of Mexican development as he witnessed the Santa Anna age, the Maximilian imperial period, the Juárez reform era, and finally, the Díaz dictatorship. Vigil was a staunch patriot and republican who went into voluntary exile when Maximilian arrived. From the United States he continued to write in support of the liberal cause and against the empire. Serving in Congress with the restoration of the reform government, he contributed to the republican resurgence but he was primarily committed to the literature and worked in a wide variety of literary disciplines. Early in his life he wrote poetry but soon turned to drama, criticism, translation, and, finally, history. As a teacher of Latin he translated into Spanish a number of Latin books, but because he was able to handle English he also translated some Yankee literature, such as the stories of Washington Irving. Additionally, he compiled bibliographies that were significant to historians of his generation and those who succeeded him as well.

His historiographic activities revolved around events through which he lived, such as the reform era and the French intervention. He was not a profound researcher but chose rather to write about historical events he knew firsthand. Occasionally he wrote articles on colonial subjects or produced a piece honoring historians of Mexico. In some biographies he went back into the colonial period, but these efforts were not well researched and were more in the nature of popular studies of prominent Mexicans. This reflected his humanistic bent of mind coupled with his desire to provide literary works for a wide range of readers. His publication of the catalog of the Biblioteca Nacional was also representative of his desire to make the literature of Mexico available to as many people as possible. Thus, his histories were popular rather than scholarly and erudite.

A. *Flores de Anáhuac* (Guadalajara, Mexico, 1857); *Realidades y quimeras* (Guadalajara, Mexico, 1857); *Ensayo histórico del Ejército de Occidente* (Mexico City, 1874); *Fray Bartolomé de las Casas, Historia de las Indias* (Mexico City 1877), and "Historia de la reforma, de la intervención y del imperio," in *Mexico a través de los siglos* (Barcelona, 1889); *Vigil* (Mexico, 1963).

B. Carlos L. Sierra, *José Maria Vigil* (Mexico City, 1963); Aurora M. Ocampo de Gomez and Ernesto Prado Velazquez, *Diccionario de Escritores Mexicanos* (Mexico City, 1967), pp. 407–408.

VILLARROEL, GASPAR DE (1587, Quito—11 October 1665, Charcas, Bolivia.) *Education*: Doctor of Humanities, University of San Marcos. *Career*: Joined the Augustinian order and worked in Peru and Spain; orator and writer; Bishop of Santiago de Chile, 1638; Bishop of Arequipa, 1651; and Archbishop of Chuquisaca, 1660.

In the colonial period throughout Latin America priests manned the pulpits, taught in the schools, and wrote many of the books that were produced. Among this group Gaspar de Villarroel emerged as an inspired orator, a sound defender of Church doctrine, and a chronicler of historic events. After gaining a measure of fame and respect in Eucador and Peru, he traveled to Spain, where he remained for eight years. As Bishop of Santiago he performed the difficult task of resolving differences between clerical and civil authorities. In 1647 a severe earthquake hit Santiago and the Bishop was seriously wounded, but he nonetheless calmed the panic-stricken citizens and helped to maintain order in the tumultuous region. He was fond of writing from a very early age, and his major themes were theological and the struggle between civil and ecclesiastical authorities that plagued almost all of Latin America. Additionally, he wrote histories of the colonial age.

In his books Villarroel sought to document his positions on theological and historical matters, but his research was not profound. Yet he was significant as a historian because he tried to correlate social, political, and religious questions as they applied to Latin America. These writings could also be used as a source of events that transpired in the era of Villarroel. He sought to trace and interpret the sacred and ecclesiastical histories that were used by priests in their tasks as ministers to the Christian flock. In his study of the earthquake of Santiago he tried to use the event to enhance the loyalty and faith of the followers of the Church. In all of this writing there was a hint of the obscure and obtuse, and critics argued that his work was too vague to be of much value. Supporters and admirers, however, challenged that assessment and insisted that his history was sound, religious scholarship that was of great importance to the chronicles of Ecuador and all of Latin America. To be sure, he was more a chronicler than a historian, but his work did provide some insight into life in Eucuador in the period about which he wrote.

A. *Semana santa, tratados de los cementarios, dificultades y discursos literales y místicos sobre los evangelios de la quaresma* (Sevilla, Spain, 1634); *Gobierno eclesiástico pacífico y unión de los dos cuchillos, pontificio y reglo. Primera parte* (Madrid, 1656); *Segunda parte* (Madrid, 1657); *Primera parte de las historias sagradas y eclesiásticas morales: con quince mysterios de nuestra fé; de que se albran quince coronas a la Virgen Santissima Señora N.* (Madrid, 1660).

B. Unión Panamericana, *Diccionario de la literatura latinoamericana: Ecuador* (Washington, D.C., 1958), pp. 67–70.

VILLAVERDE DE LA PAZ, CIRILO (12 October 1812, San Diego de Nuñez, Cuba—20 October 1894, New York). *Career*: Secretary to General Narcisco Lopez, founded a school near New York City; established the review *La Habana* in 1858; wrote novels, short stories, and textbooks.

Like other Latin American patriots, Villaverde's early life was spent in the effort to win independence from Spanish domination. He was arrested in the 1848 Cuban rebellion against Spain and spent several months in prison. He attempted to overthrow the Spanish government in Cuba by accompanying two other invasions of the island, but both failed. After the second failure he went into exile in New York, but he continued to work for independence even from abroad. He made periodic trips back to Cuba but stayed only briefly and always returned to New York. Unfortunately, he did not live long enough to witness the independence of his homeland, and he died during a trip to New York in 1894. In both New York and Cuba he wrote many novels, short stories, essays, and independence propaganda.

Villaverde's early novels and short stories were brutal, bloody, cruel accounts of life that frequently included seduction and incest. Murder and barbarism marked the pages of this early work, but even in the later period of his writing he was unable to divorce himself completely from violence in his stories. He wrote biography and displayed a major interest in history, but his primary contribution to history was the historical novel. Villaverde has been praised for such works as *Cecilia Valdez*, which one critic insists was the best history of an epoch to come out of Cuba. In this work Villaverde described carefully the life of the slave and explored the social differences between the Cuban classes. In this manner his novel became a social history that won a wider audience than scholarly books on the subject of slavery and social inequalities. With books of this nature Villaverde made a major contribution to Cuban historiography without writing historical monographs. He was also a folklorist who laced his studies with social history.

A. *La joven de la flecna de oro; historia habanera* (Havana, 1841); *Comunicad de nombres y apellidos* (Havana, 1845); *Cecilia Valdes o La Loma del Angel* (Madrid, 1882); *Cuentos de me abuelo* (New York, 1889); *El quajiro* (Havana, 1890); *Excursión a la vuelta abajo* (Havana, 1891).

B. Max Henríquez Ureña, *Panorama histórico de la literatura cubana* (New York, 1963), pp. 225–232; Donald E. Herdeck, ed. *Caribbean Writers: A Bio-Bibliographical-Critical Encyclopedia* (Washington, D.C., 1979), pp. 900–901; Emeterio Santiago Santovenia y Echaide, *Cirilo Villaverde* (Havana, 1911).

W

WIESSE, CARLOS (4 September 1859, Tacna, Peru—1933, Lima). *Education*: Studied in private schools in Tacna; Doctor of Letters, University of San Marcos; Doctor of Political Science and Bachelor of Law, Colegio Dos de Mayo, Cochabamba, Bolivia. *Career*: On the editorial staff of *La opinión*; on the staff of the Peruvian legation in Ecuador, 1880; opened a private school in Chiclayo; Clerk of the Superior Court; taught courses in aesthetics and the history of modern philosophy at the University of San Marcos; Criminal Judge; appointed Chief Clerk, Department of Foreign Affairs, 1894; taught sociology and the history of Peru, University of San Marcos.

A scholar who worked in the area of government service and diplomatic activity, Carlos Wiesse was prepared to accept almost any challenge offered. He represented the Peruvian Corporation Ltd. before the Franco-Chilean Court of Arbitration in Europe. He also carried out many other diplomatic tasks, in the process of which he was able to visit several countries in Latin America and Europe. In addition to his governmental duties he taught sociology and history. In his history courses he paid particular attention to linking archaeology with history, and he also devoted some energy to Inca and Hispanic colonial regional history.

The history in which Wiesse worked was both scholarly and practical. He researched the pre-Columbian and colonial eras of Peruvian development, and he wrote a book on the national period in Peru's history. In these works his approach was traditional history in which he collected primary data and explored the secondary works available and then wrote his history. His practical history revolved around boundary disputes between Peru and its neighbors. His research carried him to a study of the boundary between Peru and Chile, which became a controversial subject following the War of the Pacific between the two countries. In addition, he researched the boundaries between Peru and Brazil, providing his government with information to support its position in the negotiations. Like many other Latin Americans of his epoch he also wrote biography, and at one point he published a text on geography, also a favorite discipline of historians.

A. *Historia y civilización del Perú* (Lima, 1891); *La cuestión de límites entre el Perú y el Brasil* (Lima, 1904); *Apuntes de historia crítica del Perú, época colonial* (Lima, 1909); *Las civilizaciones primitivas del Perú* (Lima, 1913); *Historia del Perú independiente* (Lima, 1930).

B. William Belmont Parker, *Peruvians of To-Day* (Lima, 1919), pp. 226–228.

Y

YNSFRAN, PABLO MAX (30 June 1894, Asunción,—2 May 1972, Austin, Tex.) *Education*: Escuela Normal, 1902–1905; Bachelor of Arts, Colegio Nacional de Asunción, 1906–1911; Escuela de Notariado, 1915–1917; School of Foreign Service, Georgetown University, Washington, D.C., 1930–1931. *Career*: Taught classical literature at the Escuela Normal, 1920–1928; taught philosophy and Roman history at the Colegio Nacional, 1923–1928; Secretary of the Paraguayan delegation to the Fifth Pan American Conference of Santiago de Chile, 1923; Deputy, National Congress, 1924–1928; President, State Bank, 1933; Minister of Public Works under Estigarribia; chargé d'affaires in Washington, D.C., 1929–1939.

By the second quarter of the 20th century Paraguay was beginning to recover from the disastrous War of the Triple Alliance, which had decimated its population in the middle of the 19th century. Unfortunately, the Chaco War exploded in 1932, throwing the nation into another prolonged period of dislocation. Following the war political forces vied for power in the government, and many scholars became embroiled in the clash. Pablo Ynsfran was directly implicated in the political maneuvering, and when the political atmosphere deteriorated in 1940 he fled into exile in the United States. Eventually he was able to secure a teaching position at the University of Texas at Austin, where he remained until his death.

Ynsfran was from the modern school of Paraguayan historiography, displaying far more objectivity in his scholarship than did those of the 19th century or even from the Generation of 1900. Unlike these earlier historians he was not preoccupied with the War of the Triple Alliance or the role of the Paraguayan dictator Francisco Solano López, themes that had dominated earlier historiography in the nation. Instead he examined the value of the Chaco region to Paraguay, explored intellectual history in the 19th century, and brought a greater understanding of Latin America to U.S. students and scholars by virtue of his teaching career at the University of Texas. He also was one of the first Paraguayans to write on the Chaco War. By virtue of the fact that he was in the United States and had been teaching in Texas for a decade, his work on the Chaco War was far more objective than the other initial histories of that war that came from Paraguayan authors.

A. *Sobre latinismo* (Asunción, 1926); *The Epic of the Chaco* (Austin, Texas, 1950); *La expedición norteamericana contra el Paraguay, 1858–1859*, 2 vols. (Mexico City, 1954).

B. Charles J. Kolinski *Historical Dictionary of Paraguay* (Metuchen, N.J., 1973), pp. 266–267; Percy Alvin Martin, *Who's Who in Latin America*, 2d ed. rev. (Stanford, 1940); and William Belmont Parker, *Paraguayans of To-Day* (New York, 1969), pp. 89–90.

Z

ZAMACOIS, NICETO DE (1820, Bilbao, Spain—1885, Mexico City). *Education*: Educated in Mexico but details unknown. *Career*: Returned to Spain from Mexico, 1858; wrote for several periodicals such as *El museo universal;* edited several other periodicals.

When his family emigrated to Mexico while he was still at a young age Zamacois found himself in the midst of the confusion of the immediate post-independence age. A sensitive young man, he wrote poetry and romantic novels, but in 1858, when the political situation became dangerous for him, he fled to Spain, where he continued to write while editing periodicals. Returning to Mexico in the period of the Maximilian empire, he served as editor-in-chief of the periodicals *El cronista* and *La sociedad mercantil*. But when the empire fell he once again made his way back to Spain, where he worked on his monumental study, *Historia de México*. When he returned once again to Mexico, the state of Oaxaca offered to elect him Deputy to the National Congress if he would renounce his Spanish citizenship, but he refused, despite his belief that such an offer constituted a great honor. In addition to history he wrote articles about customs, poetry, drama, and novels.

Zamacois' most significant historical study was his *Historia de México* (1876–1882), which was an effort to clarify many controversial points that had developed in other general histories of the nation. He based his history on unedited documents that he uncovered in both Mexico and Spain. But perhaps more importantly, he provided a source of information about 19th century Mexico, particularly those events in which he took part. He knew personally many of the important figures of Mexican history, and consequently he could write as an eyewitness to many of the events and describe the primary actors from firsthand knowledge.

A. *Los ecos de mi lira* (Mexico City, 1849); *Los misterios de México* (Mexico City, 1851); *El capitán Rossi* (Mexico City, 1864); *El mendigo de San Ángel* (Mexico City, 1864–1865); *La destrucción de Pompeya* (Mexico City, 1871); *Historia de México desde sus tiempos más remotos hasta nuestros dias, escrita en vista de todo lo que de irrecusable han dado a luz los mas caracterizados historiadores, y en virtud de documentos auténticos, no publicados todavia, tomados del Archivo Nacional de México, de las bibliotecas públicas, y de los prediosos manuscritos que, hasta hace poco, existian en las de los conventos de aquel país* (Barcelona, 1876–1882); *La herencia de un barbero* (Mexico City, 1879); *Un angel desterrado del cielo, leyenda religiosa* (Mexico City, 1885); El sitio de Monterrey (Mexico City, n.d.).

B. Aurora M. Ocampo de Gómez and Ernesto Prado Velázquez, *Diccionario de escritores mexicanos* (Mexico City, 1967), pp. 417–418.

ZAMORA, ALONSO DE (24 May 1635, Nuevo Reino, Colombia—June 1717, Rosario de Santafé, Colombia). *Education*: Attended primary school at the Colegio Universitario de Santo Tomás; joined the Dominican order, 1642. *Career*: Assigned to work in a diocese in Panama; procurator in the curias of Madrid and Rome, 1669; Visitador de la Costa, 1672; reader in theology; Provincial Secretary, 1673; Prior, Convento de Las Aguas, Santafé; named official chronicler and teacher, 1691; attained the highest rank within his order, that of Provincial, 1698.

Father Zamora's interest in history and in chronicling the events of his own age coincided with his determination to progress within his own religious order. He was successful at moving up within the Dominican order, but he did not deny his obsession to write the history of New Granada. Praise was heaped upon him by his contemporaries in the Church, most of which depicted him as superhuman. While this was far from the truth, it was true that he was an excellent chronicler of his order and of New Granada.

Zamora wrote down the important facts of the age he described and added a very detailed physical description of New Granada. He wrote with clarity and sincerity in a period when many writers sought to be florid in their styles and obtuse in their philosophy. In addition to the history, he compiled lists of the varieties of plants and animals in the region. He also noted the therapeutic value of many of the plants and wrote about remote areas that even in the 20th century have seldom been penetrated. While his descriptions of fruits and foods were extensive, he managed to overlook some of the more important ones of a later period, like the chirimoya and some varieties of grapes. Then, too, when describing physical features of the area he was even more lax and his style became prosaic. He lacked any kind of imaginative flair when writing about nature. Yet overall the book was informative for a people who knew little of the New World, which was strange and incomprehensible to them. The style was not as rich as that of *Lucas Fernández de Piedrahita, but the complete work was important for the information it contained.

A. *Historia de Nuevo Reino de Granada y de la provincia de San Antonio en la religión de Santo Domingo* (Barcelona, Spain, 1701); *Historia de la provincia de San Antonio del Nuevo Reino de Granada* (Caracas, 1930).

B. Robert H. Davis, *Historical Dictionary of Colombia* (Metuchen, N.J., 1977), p. 230; and Antonio Gómez Restrepo, *Historia de la literatura colombiana* (Bogotá, 1940), II, pp. 173–183.

ZAVALA, LORENZO DE (3 October 1788, Tenoch, Mexico—19 November 1836, San Jacinto, Tex.). *Education*: Studied Latin, theology, and classical philosophy, the Franciscan Seminario de San Ildefonso, in Mérida, studied medicine and English while imprisoned for political activity for three years. *Career*: Elected to represent Yucatan in the Spanish Parliament, 1820; represented Yucatan in the National Congress at Mexico City; President, Chamber of Deputies; first to sign the Federal Constitution, 1824; Governor, State of Mexico, 1827;

Minister of Finance in the Guerrero government; Minister to France, 1833; Governor, State of Mexico, 1832; Deputy for Harrisburg, Texas; Delegate to the U.S.Congress when Texas independence was declared; first Vice-President of the Republic of Texas, 1836; signed the Texas Declaration of Independence.

A liberal from his early youth, Zavala throughout his life fought against first the Spanish control of Mexico and later Mexican control over Texas. He paid for his opposition to Spain with three years' imprisonment in the island prison of San Juan de Ulua. Later, following independence, when conservative forces came to power in Mexico, Zavala went into exile in North America and Europe. He worked in the land development business in Texas, and his time abroad was spent in caring for this enterprise. At the same time he wrote about his travels in an excellent book covering the United States, its people and customs. He was an astute observer who noted many of the same things that Alexis de Tocqueville would later write about in his travels in America. Zavala wrote the book to instruct Mexicans in democracy. While in exile he wrote not only travelogues but in Paris wrote his most famous history, *Essay on the Revolutions of Mexico*. Because his liberalism coincided with the Texas movement against the conservative government of Santa Anna, Zavala threw his support to the Texas rebels, and the result was a prominent position in the new movement. When Texas gained its independence from Mexico, Zavala then was elected its Vice-President. Mexicans long regarded him as a traitor because he gave up his citizenship and supported Texas independence.

Zavala was a literary romantic who used words much as a painter uses his brushes. He described carefully what he observed, and he sought to draw political lessons from the way people lived and from the institutions they created. His histories were slanted toward liberalism and could not be regarded as objective. Instead, he sought to show the value of liberalism over the conservative ideology that was so powerful in the early years of Mexican independent life. He was a man of action, impatient with prosaic research, but he recognized the value of history and sought to use it to instruct his people in what he regarded as the proper political system.

A. *Juicio imparcial sobre los acontecimientos de Mexico en 1828 y 1829* (New York, 1830); *Ensayo histórico de las revoluciones de la Nueva España* (Paris, 1831–1832); *Viaje a los Estados-Unidos del Norte de América* (Paris, 1834); *Albores de la República* (Mexico City, 1949); *Imbral de la independencia* (Mexico City, 1949); and *Venganza de la colonia* (Mexico City, 1950).

B. Raymond Estep, "The Life of Lorenzo de Zavala" (Ph.D diss., University of Texas, Austin, 1942); Louis Wiltz Kemp, *The Signers of the Texas Declaration of Independence* (Houston, Tex., 1944), pp. 371–380; and Michael Rheta Martin and Gabriel Lovett, *Encyclopedia of Latin American History* (Indianapolis, 1968), pp. 346–347.

ZAYAS Y ALFONSO, ALFREDO (21 February 1861, Havana—1934, Havana). *Education*: Studied at the Colegio of Madame Boblag in Havana and the Colegio el Salvador; law degree, University of Havana, 1882. *Career*: Practiced law; wrote for the press; edited a literary magazine; represented the Revolutionary party in Havana; Prosecuting Attorney, 1889; Municipal Judge, 1891; Acting Mayor of Havana, 1901; Senator from the Province of Havana and President of the Senate, 1905; President, Revolutionary Committee, 1906; Member, Committee of Consultation to deal with Cuban–U.S. relations, 1907; Vice-President of the Republic, 1908; President of the Republic, 1921–1925.

Zayas y Alfonso was a member of the Autonomist party and also the Revolutionist party in Havana. Because of his anti-Spanish activities he was arrested and imprisoned in 1896 and sent into exile in 1897. When independence came in 1898, Zayas y Alfonso became involved immediately in political life and began to build his political career. However, he did not accept the new Cuban government, and in 1906 he led a rebellion against the Tomás Estrada Palma regime. In 1921 he was elected President of Cuba. Zayas y Alfonso deplored the U.S. role in the island, but because of the financial and economic conditions of his nation he was obliged to accept aid from Washington. This unpopular act, coupled with charges of graft and corruption in his administration, doomed him to one term as president. Once his political career soured he turned more to literature and history.

Zayas y Alfonso wrote for the press, he wrote poetry, and of course he wrote extensively on political subjects. He was also a linguist who published scholarly works in that discipline. His histories were political in nature, and he was mainly concerned with 19th century Cuban history. He was not a great researcher in primary documents but rather synthesized the works of other historians. Throughout his work there was also a strain of patriotism and nationalism, which is logical since he lived through the independence war and the post-independence turmoil as a major actor in Cuban politics.

A. *El presbitero don José Agustín Caballero y su vida y sus obras* (Havana, 1891); *El sufragio y su ejercicio en Cuba* (Havana, 1910); *Lexicografía antillana* (Havana, 1914); *Un capítulo de la historia general de Cuba (1867–1868)* (Havana, 1916); *El sufragio político de la mujer en Cuba* (Havana, 1930); and *La poesía patriótica en Cuba hasta 1868* (Havana, 1931).

B. Helen Delpar, *Encyclopedia of Latin America* (New York, 1974), p. 641; Michael Rheta Martin and Gabriel Lovett, *Encyclopedia of Latin American History* (Indianapolis, 1968), p. 347; and William Belmont Parker, *Cubans of To-Day* (New York, 1967), pp. 377–379.

ZINNY, ANTONIO (1821, Gibralter, Spain—1890, Buenos Aires). *Career*: Teacher, bibliographer.

Zinny was born in Europe and did not arrive in Buenos Aires until he was 21 years old. Once in his adopted country he taught and devoted a good deal of his time to the study of Argentina's past. He was basically a regional historian whose work resembled that of the chroniclers of earlier ages. However, he did work in unedited documents, especially diaries, and his work bore a resemblance to earlier Jesuit historians. His histories also were similar to those of Gregorio

Funes. In both cases the details of events were simply narrated by the writer without any critical evaluation. Zinny grouped facts, almost entirely political facts, by region. Such a narrative approach was used by regional chroniclers in the 17th and 18th centuries, but as noted, Zinny did rely heavily upon unedited documentation and he frequented the archives to collect data for his work. Moreover, like others of his generation who used extensive primary source material, he frequently flaunted his erudition by including in the books some of the unedited documents, acompanied by his commentary. Sometimes these documents were not closely associated with the narration and appeared simply tossed into the text without reason. Then, too, in this manner Zinny included a large amount of minutiae in his work. He believed everything important had to be included in a history book and he added to his books everything he could find on a given topic, providing the reader with an enormous amount of data that often bore little relation to the main theme.

While Zinny's work was a narrative recounting of political developments without analysis, his history did not lack significance. His studies, and those of others like Dean Funes, paved the way for later, more analytical, sophisticated, and philosophical histories. In particular his extensive research and the inclusion of documents in his texts provided the inspiration for subsequent historians, and his books became the foundation for later histories. He did go to the archives for his data, and while his procedures were simplistic, amounting often to a mere detailed chronicle of events, they aided regional studies in subsequent generations. Like Jesuit chroniclers before him he went to the documents, and this alone, given the stage of Argentine historiography during his lifetime, was important for later, 19th century histories of a higher quality.

A. *Efemeridografía argiroparquiotica o sea de las provincias argentinas* (Buenos Aires, 1868); *Efemeridografía argirometropolitana hasta la caida de Rosas* (Buenos Aires, 1869); *Gaceta de Buenos Aires desde 1810 a 1821* (Buenos Aires, 1875); *Bibliografía histórica de las provincias unidas de Río de la Plata desde 1780 hasta 1821* (Buenos Aires, 1875); *La gaceta mercantil* (Buenos Aires, 1875–1912); *Juan María Gutiérrez: su vida y sus escritos* (Buenos Aires, 1878).

B. Rómulo D. Carbia, *Historia crítica de la historiografía argentina desde (sus origenes en el siglo XVI* (La Plata, 1939), pp. 111–114.

ZORRILLA DE SAN MARTÍN, JUAN (28 December 1855, Montevideo—4 November 1931, Montevideo). *Education*: Primary education at the Colegio de la Immaculado Concepción de Santa Fé, Argentina; attended the Universidad de Montevideo for three years; graduated from the Colegio de la Immaculado Concepción de Santa Fé, 1873; law degree, Universidad de Chile, 1877. *Career*: Judge, Department of Montevideo; Judge of the First Instance; private practice of law; Deputy, 1887–1890; Minister Plenipotentiary to Madrid; President, commission to represent Uruguay at the American Historical Exposition; Minister Plenipotentiary to the Holy See, 1898; represented Uruguay in Argentina and Chile in commemoration of the centenary of independence; University Professor;

represented Uruguay at the inauguration of President Gondra of Paraguay; founded the periodical, *El bien público*; Minister to France; Minister to the Hague Tribunal; founder and President, Instituto Histórico y Geográfico del Uruguay; Professor, University of Montevideo.

Zorrilla de San Martín served his country well in a number of academic and diplomatic posts. Having been educated partially in Chile he brought a broader view of history to Uruguay than did many of his contemporaries, as he encompassed the entire hemisphere in his thinking rather than simply one country. His diplomatic career was extensive, but his fame resulted more from his literary efforts than public service. He participated in political action in Montevideo for which he was forced into exile in Buenos Aires. Here again, as in time spent in Spain and Paris, Zorrilla was able to fashion a world view of history that was not always present among Latin American historians.

Zorrilla began his literary career as a journalist writing for the press in both Chile and Uruguay. He then founded his own newspaper, *El bien público,* which supported the Catholic church in its political maneuvering. As a poet he wrote a patriotic verse in 1879, entitled *La leyenda patria*. In 1888 he wrote another well-received poetic legend, *Tabaré*, which won the attention of his countrymen and gained him a wide reputation as a fine epic poet. *Tabaré* was an effort to acquaint Uruguayans with the Indians who had inhabited the land before the Europeans arrived. It was not only a great piece of poetry but an informative historical document as well. Other poems followed, and many of them had a patriotic and historical bent. Zorrilla was also involved in writing history and biography although his major interest remained poetry. His history was not based on extensive research in primary documents but instead synthesized the work of others. His importance lay in his linking poetry with history, making it an artistic as well as informative endeavor. His work on José Artigas glorified that national hero of independence. While the style was romantic and novelesque, the study did present a fairly accurate picture of Artigas' life, and it became a classic in Uruguayan literature.

A. *Notas de un himno* (Santiago, 1876); *La leyenda patria* (Montevideo, 1879); *Tabaré* (Montevideo, 1898); *La epopeya de Artigas,* 2 vols. (Montevideo, 1910); *La profecía de Ezequiel* (Montevideo, 1921); *Tabaré: An Epic Poem of the Early Days of Uruguay,* trans. Ralph Walter Huntington (Buenos Aires, 1934).

B. Helen Delpar, *Encyclopedia of Latin America* (New York, 1974, p. 652); Michael Rheta Martin and Gabriel Lovett, *Encyclopedia of Latin American History* (Indianapolis, 1968), p. 347; "Notes and Comment," *Hispanic American Historical Review,* 12, No. 3 (August 1932), pp. 355–356; William Belmont Parker, *Uruguayans of To-Day* (New York, 1967), pp. 567–570; Jean L. Willis, *Historical Dictionary of Uruguay* (Metuchen, N.J., 1974), p. 652.

ZUM FELDE, ALBERTO (30 May 1888, Montevideo,—18 September 1951, Montevideo). *Career*: Chief Clerk, Ministry of Foreign Affairs; Secretary, National Library; head of the editorial staff of the newspaper, *El diario*; Editor-in-

Chief, *El día*; orator; Member, Chamber of Deputies; First Official, Ministry of Foreign Affairs.

One of Uruguay's most famous literary critics and social historians, Zum Felde was instrumental in journalistic activity and public service along with his historical and literary work. He served in elective posts, and he emerged as one of the outstanding orators of his age. Writing extensively in journals and reviews in the La Plata region, he became deservedly famous. But his greatest acclaim resulted from his novels and histories.

In his research Zum Felde liked to study the broad sweep of Uruguayan history and to analyze historical events and ages. His first major historical study, *Evolución histórica del Uruguay,* was published in 1920, and it was continued in subsequent editions until the fifth, which appeared in 1967, making it a classic in Uruguayan literature. Another study, *Proceso intelectual del Uruguay y crítica de su literatura,* written in 1930, became one of the most widely distributed books in South America. For these and other works Zum Felde has become known as Uruguay's foremost intellectual of the 20th century. Concentrating on the history of ideas, he studied the political philosophy and the thinking of politicians who led Uruguay in the 19th and 20th centuries. At the same time, unlike some of his famous countrymen, he did not view the United States as a major threat to Latin America. José Enrique Rodo had led the way in anti-U.S. sentiment, but Zum Felde argued that Latin America could build its own culture only after it had ceased its reliance on Europe and had curbed the extreme nationalism that pervaded the region.

A. *El Uruguay ante el concepto sociológico* (Montevideo, 1911); *Proceso histórico del Uruguay* (Montevideo, 1919); *Evolucíon historica del Uruguay* ((Montevideo, 1920); *Critica de la literatura uruguaya* (Montevideo, 1921); *Proceso intelectual del Uruguay y crítica de su literatura* (3 vols.) (Montevideo, 1930); *El problema de la cultura americana* (Buenos Aires, 1943).

B. Joseph R. Barager, "The Historiography of the Río de La Plata Area, Since 1830," *Hispanic American Historical Review*, 39, No. 4 (November 1959), p. 629; Percy Alvin Martin, *Who's Who in Latin America* (Stanford, 1936), p. 557; William Belmont Parker, *Uruguayans of To-Day* (New York, 1967), p. 575; Jean L. Willis, *Historical Dictionary of Uruguay* (Metuchen, N.J., 1974), pp. 259–260.

Appendices

Listing by Birthplace

NAME	BIRTHDATE	BIRTHPLACE
	ARGENTINA	
Caillet-Bois, Ricardo R.	7 September 1903	Buenos Aires
Carbia, Rómulo D.	15 September 1885	Buenos Aires
Funes, Gregorio	26 May 1749	Córdoba
Fúrlong Cárdiff, Guillermo	21 June 1889	Villa Constitución Santa Fé
García, Juan Agustín	12 April 1862	Buenos Aires
Garzón Maceda, Ceferino	25 August 1895	Córdoba
Gutiérrez, Juan María	6 May 1809	Buenos Aires
Ibarguren, Carlos	18 April 1877	Salta
Lafuente Machain, Ricardo de	4 January 1882	Buenos Aires
Leguizamón, Martiniano	28 April 1858	Buenos Aires
Levene, Ricardo	7 February 1885	Buenos Aires
López, Vicente Fidel	25 April 1815	Buenos Aires
Mitre, Bartolomé	26 July 1821	Buenos Aires
Pueyrredón, Carlos Alberto	18 July 1887	Buenos Aires
Quesada, Ernesto	1 June 1858	Buenos Aires
Quesada, Vicente Gregorio	7 April 1830	Buenos Aires
Ramos Mejía, José María	24 December 1849	Buenos Aires
Ravignani, Emilio	15 January 1886	Buenos Aires
Rojas, Ricardo	16 September 1882	Tucumán
Sarmiento, Domingo Faustino	15 February 1811	San Juan
Terán, Juan Benjamín	26 December 1880	Tucumán
Udaondo, Enrique	11 June 1880	Buenos Aires
Vedia y Mitre, Mariano de	29 December 1880	Buenos Aires
	BOLIVIA	
Arguedas, Alcides	15 July 1879	La Paz
Cortés, Manuel José	10 April 1815	Coragaita del Distrito de Potosí
Díez de Medina, Eduardo	8 February 1881	La Paz
Finot, Enrique	16 September 1891	Santa Cruz de la Sierra
Gutiérrez, Alberto	18 September 1863	Sucre
Mendoza, Jaime	25 July 1874	Sucre
Omiste, Modesto	6 June 1840	Potosí

NAME	BIRTHDATE	BIRTHPLACE
Otero Vértiz, Gustavo Adolfo	8 September 1896	La Paz
Pazos Kanki, Vicente	30 December 1779	Ilabaya
Pinto, Manuel María	1872	Yungas de la Paz
René-Moreno, Gabriel	7 November 1836	Santa Cruz de la Sierra
Taborga, Miguel de los Santos	5 July 1833	Sucre
Valdés, Julio César	1862	La Paz
Vázquez-Machicado, Humberto	27 April 1904	Santa Cruz de la Sierra

BRAZIL

Abreu y Lima, José Inácio	6 April 1794	Recife
Alcântara Machado D'Oliveira, José de	19 October 1875	Piracicaba
Capistrano de Abreu, João	23 October 1853	Maranguape
Cunha, Euclides da	20 January 1866	Province of Rio de Janeiro
García, Rodolfo	25 May 1873	Ceará Mirim
Gonzaga Jaeger, Luís	10 July 1889	Bom Jargim
Lôbo, Hélio	17 October 1883	Juiz de Fora
Melo Morais, Alexandre José de	23 July 1816	Alogoas
Oliveira Lima, Manuel de	1867	São Paulo
Oliveira Vianna, Francisco José de	20 June 1883	Rio de Janeiro
Rangel, Alberto	29 May 1871	Recife
Simonsen, Roberto Cochrane	18 February 1889	Santos
Tarquinio de Sousa, Octávio	7 September 1889	Rio de Janeiro
Taunay, Afonso D'Escragnolle	11 June 1876	Nossa Senhora do Desterro
Valladares, José Antonio do Prado	3 May 1917	Salvador
Varnhagen, Francisco Adolfo de	17 February 1816	Sorocaba

CHILE

Amunátegui, Miguel Luís	11 January 1828	Santiago
Amunátegui Solar, Domingo	21 October 1860	Santiago
Barros Arana, Diego	16 August 1830	Santiago
Barros Borgoño, Luís	1858	Santiago
Bilbao, Francisco	9 January 1823	Santiago
Bilbao, Manuel	1827	Santiago
Bulnes, Gonzalo	19 November 1851	Santiago
Edwards, Alberto	1873	Valparaiso
Encina y Armanet, Francisco Antonio	10 September 1874	Talca
Errázuriz Valdivieso, Crescente	28 November 1839	Santiago

NAME	BIRTHDATE	BIRTHPLACE
Eyzaguirre Gutiérrez, Jaime	1908	Santiago
Fuenzalida Grandón, Alejandro	21 December 1865	Copiapó
Galdames, Luís	1881	Santiago
Irarrázaval Larrain, José Miguel	28 January 1881	Santiago
Jobet Búrquez, Julio César	1912	Santiago
Lastarria Santander, José Victorino	22 March 1817	Santiago
Letelier, Valentín	1852	Santiago
Medina, José Toribio	21 October 1852	Santiago
Oña, Pedro de	1570	Valdivia
Ovalle, Alonso de	1601	Santiago
Riquelme, Daniel	1875	Santiago
Sotomayor Valdés, Ramón	30 April 1830	Santiago
Thayer Ojeda, Tomás	16 June 1877	Caldera
Vicuña Mackenna, Benjamín	25 August 1831	Santiago

COLOMBIA

Cuervo, Luís Augusto	14 February 1893	San José de Cúcuta
Díaz Díaz, Oswaldo	1910	Gachetá
Fernández de Piedrahita, Lucas	6 March 1624	Bogotá
García del Río, Juan	1794	Cartagena
García Ortiz, Laureano	19 July 1867	Río Negro
Groot, José Manuel	25 December 1800	Bogotá
Ospina Vásquez, Luís	1906	Medellín
Picón Salas, Mariano	26 January 1901	Mérida
Posada Gutiérrez, Joaquín	1797	Cartagena
Restrepo, José Manuel	31 December 1781	Emvigada
Restrepo Posada, José	1908	Bogotá
Samper Ortega, Daniel	1895	Bogotá
Zamora, Alonso de	24 May 1635	Nuevo Reino

COSTA RICA

Arguello Mora, Manuel	5 July 1845	San José
Dobles Segreda, Luís	17 January 1890	Heredia
Fernández Guardia, Ricardo	4 January 1867	Alajuela
González Víquez, Cleto	1858	San José
Jiménez, Manuel de Jesús	20 June 1854	Cartago

CUBA

Figarola-Caneda, Domingo	17 January 1852	Havana
Guerra y Sánchez, Ramiro	1880	Havana
Justiz y del Valle, Tomás Juan de	12 July 1871	Santiago
Llaverías Martínez, Joaquín	27 July 1875	Havana
Peraza Sarausa, Fermín	7 July 1907	Guara

NAME	BIRTHDATE	BIRTHPLACE
Ramos, José Antonio	4 April 1885	Havana
Santovenia y Echaide, Emeterio	23 May 1889	Mantua, Pinar del Río
Villaverde de La Paz, Cirilo	12 October 1812	San Diego de Río Núñez
Zayas y Alfonso, Alfredo	21 February 1861	Havana

DOMINICAN REPUBLIC

Henríquez Ureña, Max	16 November 1885	Santo Domingo
Henríquez Ureña, Pedro	29 June 1884	Santo Domingo
Henríquez y Carvajal, Federico	16 September 1848	Santo Domingo

ECUADOR

Andrade, Roberto	26 October 1852	Parroquía
Barrera, Isaac J.	4 February 1884	Otavalo
Cevallos, Pedro Fermín	7 July 1812	Ambato
González Suárez, Federico	12 April 1844	Quito
Jaramillo Alvarado, Pío	1889	Loja
Jijón y Caamaño, Jacinto	11 December 1890	Quito
Mera, Juan León	28 July 1832	Ambato
Moncayo, Pedro	1807	Ibarra
Reyes, Oscar Efrén	18 June 1896	Baños de Tungurahua
Tobar Donoso, Julio	25 January 1894	Quito
Velasco, Juan de	6 January 1727	Riobamba
Villarroel, Gaspar de	1587	Quito

EL SALVADOR

Batres Montúfar, José	18 March 1809	San Salvador
Gavidia, Francisco	27 December 1863	San Miguel

ENGLAND

Cararera Stampa, Manuel	20 October 1917	Portsmouth

FRANCE

Gay, Claudio	18 March 1800	Draguignan
Gay, João Pedro	20 November 1815	Altos Pirineus
Groussac, Pablo	15 February 1848	Toulouse
Levillier, Roberto	1886	Paris

GUATEMALA

Fuentes y Guzmán, Francisco Antonio de	1643	Santiago de los Caballeros
Gómez Carrillo, Enrique	27 February 1873	Guatemala City
Marure, Alejandro	28 February 1806	Guatemala City

NAME	BIRTHDATE	BIRTHPLACE
Milla y Vidaurre, José	4 August 1822	Guatemala City
Montúfar, Lorenzo	11 March 1823	Guatemala City
Montúfar y Coronado, Manuel	1791	Guatemala City
Pardo Gallardo, José Joaqín	29 December 1905	Guatemala City

HAITI

Pressoir, Jacques Catts	2 April 1892	Port-au-Prince

HONDURAS

Coello, Augusto C.	1 September 1884	Tegucigalpa
Durón, Rómulo E.	6 July 1865	Comayagua
Valle, Rafael Heliodoro	3 July 1891	Tegucigalpa

ITALY

Ingenieros, José	24 April 1877	Palermo

MEXICO

Alamán, Lucas	17 October 1792	Guanajuato
Alegre, Francisco Javier	12 November 1729	Veracruz
Alessio Robles, Vito	14 August 1879	Saltillo
Alva Ixtlilxochitl, Fernando de	1557	Teotihuacán
Ancona, Eligio	1 December 1836	Mérida, Yucatán
Bustamante, Carlos María de	4 November 1774	Oaxaca
Cavo, Andrés	13 February 1739	Guadalajara
Chávez Orozco, Luís	15 April 1901	Irapuato
Clavijero, Francisco Javier	6 September 1731	Veracruz
Cosío Villegas, Daniel	23 July 1898	Mexico City
Cue Cánovas, Agustín	28 August 1913	Villahermosa
Eguiarna Eguren, Juan José de	February 1696	Mexico City
Elguero, Francisco	24 March 1856	Morelia
García, Genaro	17 August 1867	Fresnillo
García Granados, Rafael	20 February 1893	Mexico City
García Icazbalceta, Joaquín	21 August 1825	Mexico City
Garibay K., Ángel María	18 June 1892	Toluca
Gómez Haro, Enrique	14 July 1877	Puebla
González Obregón, Luís	25 August 1865	Guanajuato
Icaza, Francisco A. de	2 February 1863	Mexico
Iguíniz, Juan B.	29 August 1881	Guadalajara
López Portillo y Rojas, José	26 May 1850	Guadalajara
Meade Sáinz-Trápaga, Joaquín Felipe	5 February 1896	San Luis Potosí
Mora, José María Luís	1794	San Francisco de Chamacuero
Orozco y Berra, Manuel	8 June 1816	Mexico City

NAME	BIRTHDATE	BIRTHPLACE
Paso y Troncoso, Francisco del	8 October 1842	Veracruz
Pereyra, Carlos	3 November 1871	Saltillo
Pimentel, Francisco	2 December 1832	Aguscalientes
Prieto, Guillermo	10 February 1818	Mexico City
Quintano Roo, Andrés	30 November 1787	San Bernabé de Mérida
Ramírez de Aguilar, Fernando	4 August 1887	Oaxaca
Riva Palacio, Vicente	16 October 1832	Mexico City
Salado Álvarez, Victoriano	30 September 1867	Teocaltiche
Sierra, Justo	26 January 1848	Campeche
Sierra O'Reilly, Justo	24 September 1814	Tixcacaltuyú
Sigüenza y Góngora, Carlos de	1645	Mexico City
Sosa, Francisco	2 April 1848	San Francisco de Campeche
Teja Zabre, Alfonso	23 December 1888	San Luís de la Paz
Valle-Arizpe, Artemio de	25 January 1888	Saltillo
Vasconcelos, José	27 February 1882	Oaxaca
Vigil, José María	11 October 1829	Guadalajara
Zavala, Lorenzo de	3 October 1788	Tenoch

NICARAGUA

Chamorro, Pedro Joaquín	1891	Managua
Gámez, José Dolores	12 July 1851	Granada

PANAMA

Alfaro, Ricardo Joaquín	20 August 1882	Panama City
Méndez Pereira, Octavio	30 August 1887	Aguadulce

PARAGUAY

Baez, Cecilio	1 February 1862	Asunción
Cardoza, Ramón Indalecio	16 May 1876	Villarrica
Cardozo, Efraím	16 October 1906	Villarrica
Decoud, Hector Francisco	9 July 1855	Asunción
Domínguez, Manuel	1869	Asunción
Godoi, Juansilvano	12 November 1850	Asunción
Moreno, Fulgencio R.	9 November 1872	Asunción
O'Leary, Juan Emiliano	13 June 1880	Asunción
Ynsfran, Pablo Max	30 June 1894	Asunción

PERU

Basadre, Jorge	12 February 1903	Tacna
Cosío, José Gabriel	18 March 1886	Accha
Garcilaso de la Vega	12 November 1539	Cuzco
Huamán Poma de Ayala, Felipe	1530	Unknown
Jaimes Freyre, Ricardo	12 May 1868	Tacna

NAME	BIRTHDATE	BIRTHPLACE
Palma, Ricardo	7 February 1833	Lima
Paz-Soldán, Juan Pedro	20 June 1869	Lima
Porras Barrenechea, Raúl	23 March 1897	Pisco
Prado y Ugarteche, Javier	3 December 1871	Lima
Riva Aguero y Osma, José de la	26 February 1885	Lima
Urteaga, Horacio H.	19 March 1877	Cajamarca
Wiesse, Carlos	4 September 1859	Tacna

PUERTO RICO

Abril y Ostalo, Mariano	25 May 1862	San Juan

SPAIN

Aguirre, Juan Francisco	18 August 1758	Doña Maria
Alvear y Ponce de León, Diego de	13 November 1749	Montilla
Azara, Feliz de	18 May 1752	Barbunales
Balbuena, Bernardo de	1562	Valdepeñas
Benavente, Fray Toribio	1520	Villa de Benavente
Cervantes de Salazar, Francisco	1514	Toledo
Cieza de León, Pedro de	1519	Sevilla
Comas Camps, Juan	1900	Alajar, Menorca, Baleares
Díaz del Castillo, Bernal	1492	Medina del Campo
Ercilla y Zúñiga, Alonso de	7 August 1533	Madrid
Gómara, Francisco López de	2 February 1511	Gomara
Iglesia y Parga, Ramón	3 July 1905	Santiago de Compostela
Jiménez de Quesada, Gonzalo	1506	Córdoba
Las Casas, Bartolomé de	11 November 1484	Sevilla
Leturia, Pedro de	26 November 1891	Zumárraga
Oviedo y Valdés, Gonzalo Fernández	1478	Madrid
Pizarro, Pedro	1515	Toledo
Sahagún, Bernardino de	1500	Sahagún
Sarmiento de Gambóa, Pedro	1530	Alcala de Henares
Zamacois, Niceto de	1820	Bilbao
Zinny, Antonio	1821	Gibralter

URUGUAY

Acevedo Díaz, Eduardo	20 April 1851	Unión
Favaro, Edmundo J.	25 June 1907	Montevideo
Ferreira, Mariano	24 January 1834	Montevideo
Lamas, Andrés	10 November 1817	Montevideo
Martínez, José Luciano	1870	Montevideo
Nin Frías, Alberto Augusto Antonio	9 November 1882	Montevideo

NAME	BIRTHDATE	BIRTHPLACE
Pereda Setembrino, Ezequiel	10 April 1859	Paysandu
Real de Azúa, Carlos	1916	Montevideo
Salgado, José	29 March 1875	Montevideo
Zorrilla de San Martín, Juan	28 December 1855	Montevideo
Zum Felde, Alberto	30 May 1888	Montevideo

VENEZUELA

Acosta, Cecilio	1 February 1818	San Diego de los Altos
Baralt, Rafael María	3 July 1810	Maracaibo
Bello, Andrés	30 November 1781	Caracas
Blanco, Eduardo	1839	Caracas
Blanco-Fombona, Rufino	17 June 1874	Caracas
Briceño-Iragorry, Mario	15 September 1897	Trujillo
Gil Fortoul, José	17 November 1861	Barquisimeto
González, Juan Vicente	28 May 1811	Caracas
Larrazábal, Felipe	1818	Caracas
Mendoza, Cristóbal L.	9 October 1866	Caracas
Rojas, Arístides	November 1826	Caracas

APPENDIX II
Listing by Year of Birth

1478
Oviedo y Valdés, Gonzalo Fernández
(Spain)

1484
Las Casas, Bartolomé de (Spain)

1492
Díaz del Castillo, Bernal (Spain)

1500
Sahagún, Bernardino de (Spain)

1511
Gómara, Francisco López (Spain)

1514
Cervantes de Salazar, Francisco (Spain)

1515
Pizarro, Pedro (Spain)

1519
Cieza de León, Pedro de (Spain)

1520
Benavente, Fray Toribio (Spain)

1530
Huamán Poma de Ayala, Felipe (Peru)
Sarmiento de Gambóa, Pedro (Spain)

1533
Ercilla y Zúñiga, Alonso de (Spain)

1539
Garcilaso de la Vega (Peru)

1562
Balbuena, Bernardo de (Spain)

1570
Oña, Pedro de (Chile)

1577
Alva Ixtlilxochitl, Fernando de (Mexico)

1579
Jiménez de Quesada, Gonzalo (Spain)

1587
Villarroel, Gaspar de (Ecuador)

1601
Ovalle, Alonso de (Chile)

1624
Fernández de Piedrahita, Lucas
(Colombia)

1635
Zamora, Alonso de (Colombia)

1643
Fuentes y Guzmán, Francisco Antonio de
(Guatemala)

1645
Sigüenza y Góngora, Carlos de (Mexico)

1696
Eguiara Eguren, Juan José de (Mexico)

1727
Velasco, Juan de (Ecuador)

1729

Alegre, Francisco Javier (Mexico)

1731

Clavijero, Francisco Javier (Mexico)

1749

Alvear y Ponce de León, Deigo de (Spain)
Funes, Gregorio (Argentina)

1752

Azara, Feliz de (Spain)

1758

Aguirre, Juan Francisco (Spain)

1765

Mier Noriega y Guerra, Fray José Servando Teresa de (Mexico)

1774

Bustamante, Carlos María de (Mexico)

1779

Pazos Kanki, Vicente (Bolivia)

1781

Bello, Andrés (Venezuela)
Restrepo, José Manuel (Colombia)

1787

Quintano Roo, Andrés (Mexico)

1788

Zavala, Lorenzo de (Mexico)

1791

Montúfar y Coronado, Manuel (Guatemala)

1792

Alamán, Lucas (Mexico)

1794

Abreu y Lima, José Inácio (Brazil)
García del Río, Juan (Colombia)
Mora, José María Luís (Mexico)

1797

Posada Gutiérrez, Joaquín (Colombia)

1800

Gay, Claudio (France)
Groot, José Manuel (Colombia)

1803

Cavo, Andrés (Mexico)

1804

Ramírez, José Fernando (Mexico)

1806

Marure, Alejandro (Guatemala)

1809

Batres Montúfar, José (El Salvador)
Gutiérrez, Juan María (Argentina)

1810

Baralt, Rafael María (Venezuela)

1811

González, Juan Vicente (Venezuela)
Sarmiento, Domingo Faustino (Argentina)

1812

Cevallos, Pedro Fermín (Ecuador)
Villaverde y de La Paz, Cirilo (Cuba)

1814

Sierra O'Reilly, Justo (Mexico)

1815

Cortés, Manuel José (Bolivia)
Gay, João Pedro (France)
López, Vicente Fidel (Argentina)

1816

Melo Morais, Alexandre José de (Brazil)
Orozco y Berra, Manuel (Mexico)
Varnhagen, Francisco Adolfo de (Brazil)

1817

Lamas, Andrés (Uruguay)

1818

Acosta, Cecilio (Venezuela)
Larrazábal, Felipe (Venezuela)
Lastarria Santander, José Victorino
(Chile)
Prieto, Guillermo (Mexico)

1820

Zamacois, Niceto de (Spain)

1821

Mitre, Bartolomé (Argentina)
Zinny, Antonio (Spain)

1822

Milla y Vidaurre, José (Guatemala)

1823

Bilbao, Francisco (Chile)
Montúfar, Lorenzo (Guatemala)

1825

García Icazbalceta, Joaquín (Mexico)

1826

Rojas, Arístides (Venezuela)

1827

Bilbao, Manuel (Chile)

1828

Amunátegui, Miguel Luís (Chile)

1829

Vigil, José María (Mexico)

1830

Barros Arana, Diego (Chile)
Quesada, Vicente Gregorio (Argentina)
Sotomayor Valdés, Ramón (Chile)

1831

Vicuña Mackenna, Benjamín (Chile)

1832

Mera, Juan León (Ecuador)
Pimentel, Francisco (Mexico)
Riva Palacio, Vicente (Mexico)

1833

Palma, Ricardo (Peru)
Taborga, Miguel de los Santos (Bolivia)

1834

Ferreira, Mariano (Uruguay)

1836

Ancona, Eligio (Mexico)
René-Moreno, Gabriel (Bolivia)

1838

Sierra, Justo (Mexico)

1839

Blanco, Eduardo (Venezuela)
Errázuriz Valdivieso, Crescente (Chile)

1840

Omiste, Modesto (Bolivia)

1842

Paso y Troncoso, Francisco del (Mexico)

1844

González Suárez, Federico (Ecuador)

1845

Arguello Mora, Manuel (Costa Rica)

1848

Groussac, Pablo (France)
Henríquez y Carvajal, Federico (Dominican Republic)
Sosa, Francisco (Mexico)

1849

Ramos Mejía, José María (Argentina)

1850

Godoi, Juansilvano (Paraguay)
López Portillo y Rojas, José (Mexico)

1851

Acevedo Díaz, Eduardo (Uruguay)
Bulnes, Gonzalo (Chile)
Gámez, José Dolores (Nicaragua)

1852

Andrade, Roberto (Ecuador)
Figarola-Caneda, Domingo (Cuba)
Letelier, Valentín (Chile)
Medina, José Toribio (Chile)

1853

Capistrano de Abreu, João (Brazil)

1854

Jiménez, Manuel de Jesús (Costa Rica)

1855

Decoud, Hector Francisco (Paraguay)
Zorrilla de San Martín, Juan (Uruguay)

1856

Elguero, Francisco (Mexico)

1857

Riquelme, Daniel (Chile)

1858

Barros Borgoño, Luís (Chile)
González Víquez, Cleto (Costa Rica)
Leguizamón, Martiniano (Argentina)
Quesada, Ernesto (Argentina)

1859

Pereda Setembrino, Ezequiel (Uruguay)
Wiesse, Carlos (Peru)

1860

Amunátegui Solar, Domingo (Chile)

1861

Gil Fortoul, José (Venezuela)
Zayas y Alfonso, Alfredo (Cuba)

1862

Abril y Ostalo, Mariano (Puerto Rico)
Baez, Cecilio (Paraguay)
García, Juan Agustín (Argentina)
Valdés, Julio César (Bolivia)

1863

Gavidia, Francisco (El Salvador)
Gutiérrez, Alberto (Bolivia)
Icaza, Francisco A. de (Mexico)

1865

Durón, Rómulo E. (Honduras)
Fuenzalida Grandón, Alejandro (Chile)
González Obregón, Luís (Mexico)

1866

Cunha, Euclides da (Brazil)
Mendoza, Cristóbal L. (Venezuela)

1867

Fernández Guardia, Ricardo (Costa Rica)
García, Genaro (Mexico)
García Ortiz, Laureano (Colombia)
Oliveira Lima, Manuel de (Brazil)
Salado Álvarez, Victoriano (Mexico)

1868

Jaimes Freyre, Ricardo (Peru)

1869

Domínguez, Manuel (Paraguay)
Paz-Soldán, Juan Pedro (Peru)

1870

Martínez, José Luciano (Uruguay)

1871

Justiz y del Valle, Tomás Juan de (Cuba)
Pereyra, Carlos (Mexico)
Prado y Ugarteche, Javier (Peru)
Rangel, Alberto (Brazil)

1872

Moreno, Fulgencio R. (Paraguay)
Pinto, Manuel María (Bolivia)

1873

Edwards, Alberto (Chile)
García, Rodolfo (Brazil)
Gómez Carrillo, Enrique (Guatemala)

1874

Blanco-Fombona, Rufino (Venezuela)
Encina y Armanet, Francisco Antonio
(Chile)
Mendoza, Jaime (Bolivia)

1875

Alcântara Machado D'Oliveira, José de (Brazil)
Llaverías Martínez, Joaquín (Cuba)
Salgado, José (Uruguay)

1876

Cardoza, Ramón Indalecio (Paraguay)
Taunay, Alfonso D'Escragnolle (Brazil)

1877

Gómez Haro, Enrique (Mexico)
Ibarguren, Carlos (Argentina)
Ingenieros, José (Argentina)
Thayer Ojeda, Tomás (Chile)
Urteaga, Horacio H. (Peru)

1879

Alessio Robles, Vito (Mexico)
Arguedas, Alcides (Bolivia)

1880

Guerra y Sánchez, Ramiro (Cuba)
O'Leary, Juan Emiliano (Paraguay)
Terán, Juan Benjamín (Argentina)
Udaondo, Enrique (Argentina)
Vedia y Mitre, Mariano de (Argentina)

1881

Díez de Medina, Eduardo (Bolivia)
Galdames, Luís (Chile)
Iguíniz, Juan B. (Mexico)
Irarrázaval Larrain, José Miguel (Chile)

1882

Alfaro, Ricardo Joaquín (Panama)
Lafuente Machain, Ricardo de (Argentina)
Nin Frías, Alberto Augusto Antonio (Uruguay)
Rojas, Ricardo (Argentina)
Vasconcelos, José (Mexico)

1883

Lôbo, Hélio (Brazil)
Oliveira Vianna, Francisco José de (Brazil)

1884

Barrera, Isaac J. (Ecuador)
Coello, Augusto C. (Honduras)
Henríquez Ureña, Pablo (Dominican Republic)

1885

Carbia, Rómulo D. (Argentina)
Henríquez Ureña, Max (Dominican Republic)
Levene, Ricardo (Argentina)
Ramos, José Antonio (Cuba)
Riva Aguero y Osma, José de la (Peru)

1886

Cosío, José Gabriel (Peru)
Levillier, Roberto (France)
Ravignani, Emilio (Argentina)

1887

Méndez Pereira, Octavio (Panama)
Pueyrredón, Carlos Alberto (Argentina)
Ramírez de Aguilar, Fernando (Mexico)

1888

Moncayo, Pedro (Ecuador)
Teja Zabre, Alfonso (Mexico)
Valle-Arizpe, Artemio de (Mexico)
Zum Felde, Alberto (Uruguay)

1889

Fúrlong Cárdiff, Guillermo (Argentina)
Gonzaga Jaeger, Luís (Brazil)
Jaramillo Alvarado, Pío (Ecuador)
Santovenia y Echaide, Emeterio (Cuba)
Simonsen, Roberto Cochrane (Brazil)
Tarquinio de Sousa, Octávio (Brazil)

1890

Dobles Segreda, Luís (Costa Rica)
Jijón y Caamaño, Jacinto (Ecuador)

1891

Chamorro, Pedro Joaquín (Nicaragua)
Finot, Enrique (Bolivia)
Leturia, Pedro de (Spain)
Valle, Rafael Heliodoro (Honduras)

1892

Garibay K., Ángel María (Mexico)
Pressoir, Jacques Catts (Haiti)

1893

Cuervo, Luís Augusto (Colombia)
García Granados, Rafael (Mexico)

1894

Tobar Donoso, Julio (Ecuador)
Ynsfran, Pablo Max (Paraguay)

1895

Garzón Maceda, Ceferino (Argentina)
Samper Ortega, Daniel (Colombia)

1896

Meade Sáinz-Trápaga, Joaquín Felipe
(Mexico)
Otero Vértiz, Gustavo Adolfo (Bolivia)
Reyes, Oscar Efrén (Ecuador)

1897

Briceño-Iragorry, Mario (Venezuela)

1898

Cosío Villegas, Daniel (Mexico)

1900

Comas Camps, Juan (Spain)

1901

Chávez Orozco, Luís (Mexico)
Picón Salas, Mariano (Colombia)

1903

Basadre, Jorge (Peru)
Caillet-Bois, Ricardo R. (Argentina)

1904

Vázquez-Machicado, Humberto (Bolivia)

1905

Iglesia y Parga, Ramón (Spain)
Pardo Gallardo, José Joaquín (Guatemala)

1906

Cardozo, Efraím (Paraguay)
Ospina Vásquez, Luís (Colombia)

1907

Favaro, Edmundo J. (Uruguay)
Paraza Sarausa, Fermín (Cuba)

1908

Eyzaguirre Gutiérrez, Jaime (Chile)
Restrepo Posada, José (Colombia)

1910

Díaz Díaz, Oswaldo (Colombia)

1912

Jobet Búrquez, Julio César (Chile)

1913

Cue Canovas, Agustín (Mexico)

1916

Real de Azúa, Carlos (Uruguay)

1917

Carrera Stampa, Manuel (Mexico)
Valladares, José Antonio do Prado
(Brazil)

APPENDIX III
Careers of the Historians

Throughout Latin America those who wrote history supported themselves in a variety of ways other than by teaching history in universities, which is the primary means of support in the United States. In the following appendix most historians are listed under several different categories because they frequently changed careers during their lifetimes. Their home countries are listed in the parentheses following the names.

Archivist

Alamán, Lucas (Mexico)
Carrera Stampa, Manuel (Mexico)
Domínguez, Manuel (Paraguay)
Godoi, Juansilvano (Paraguay)
Gómez Haro, Enrique (Mexico)
González Obregón, Luís (Mexico)
Iguíniz, Juan B. (Mexico)
Llaverías Martínez, Joaquín (Cuba)
Rangel, Alberto (Brazil)
Santovenia y Echaide, Emeterio (Cuba)

Artist

Mera, Juan León (Ecuador)

Attorney General

Cortés, Manuel José (Bolivia)

Businessman

Alamán, Lucas (Mexico)
García Ortiz, Laureano (Colombia)
Jijón y Caamaño, Jacinto (Ecuador)
Jiménez, Manuel de Jesús (Costa Rica)
López, Vicente Fidel (Argentina)
Rojas, Arístides (Venezuela)
Santovenia y Echaide, Emeterio (Cuba)
Simonsen, Roberto Cochrane (Brazil)
Vázquez-Machicado, Humberto (Bolivia)
Ynsfran, Pablo Max (Paraguay)

Cabinet Officer

Alfaro, Ricardo Joaquín (Panama)
Amunátegui Solar, Domingo (Chile)
Barros Borgoño, Luís (Chile)
Cevallos, Pedro Fermín (Ecuador)
Díez de Medina, Eduardo (Bolivia)
Dobles Segreda, Luís (Costa Rica)
Domínguez, Manuel (Paraguay)
Durón, Romulo E. (Honduras)
Edwards, Alberto (Chile)
Fernández Guardia, Ricardo (Costa Rica)
García del Rio, Juan (Colombia)
Gutiérrez, Juan María (Argentina)
Ibarguren, Carlos (Argentina)
Lamas, Andrés (Uruguay)
Méndez Pereira, Octavio (Panama)
Orozco y Berra, Manuel (Mexico)
Prado y Ugarteche, Javier (Peru)
Prieto, Guillermo (Mexico)
Quesada, Vicente Gregorio (Argentina)
Quintano Roo, Andrés (Mexico)
Restrepo, José Manuel (Colombia)
Ynsfran, Pablo Max (Paraguay)
Zavala, Lorenzo de (Mexico)

Chronicler

Cieza de León, Pedro de (Spain)

Clergy

Alegre, Francisco Javier (Mexico)
Balbuena, Bernardo de (Puerto Rico)

Benavente, Fray Toribio (Mexico)
Cavo, Andrés (Mexico)
Cervantes de Salazar, Francisco (Mexico)
Clavijero, Francisco Javier (Mexico)
Errázuriz Valdivieso, Crescente (Chile)
Fernández de Piedrahita, Lucas (Colombia)
Funes, Gregorio (Argentina)
Fúrlong Cárdiff, Guillermo (Argentina)
Garibay K., Ángel María (Mexico)
Gay, João Pedro (Uruguay)
Gómara, Francisco López de (Spain)
González Suárez, Federico (Ecuador)
Las Casas, Bartolomé de (Spain)
Leturia, Pedro de (Spain)
Mier Noriega y Guerra,
    Fray José Servando Teresa de (Mexico)
Ovalle, Alonso de (Chile)
Pazos Kanki, Vicente (Bolivia)
Restrepo Posada, José (Colombia)
Sahagún, Bernardino de (Spain)
Sigüenza y Góngora, Carlos de (Mexico)
Taborga, Miguel de los Santos (Bolivia)
Velasco, Juan de (Ecuador)
Villarroel, Gaspar de (Ecuador)
Zamora, Alonso de (Colombia)

Cosmographer

Sarmiento de Gambóa, Pedro (Spain)

Costumbrista (Writer of Customs)

Groot, José Manuel (Colombia)

Diplomat

Acevedo Díaz, Eduardo (Uruguay)
Alamán, Lucas (Mexico)
Alfaro, Ricardo Joaquín (Panama)
Alessio Robles, Vito (Mexico)
Arguedas, Alcides (Bolivia)
Baez, Cecilio (Paraguay)
Baralt, Rafael María (Venezuela)
Barros Arana, Diego (Chile)
Barros Borgoño, Luís (Chile)
Blanco-Fombona, Rufino (Venezuela)
Briceño-Iragorry, Mario (Venezuela)
Caillet-Bois, Ricardo R. (Argentina)
Cardozo, Efraím (Paraguay)
Chamorro, Pedro Joaquín (Nicaragua)
Coello, Augusto C. (Honduras)

Cortés, Manuel José (Bolivia)
Cosío Villegas, Daniel (Mexico)
Cuervo, Luís Augusto (Colombia)
Díez de Medina, Eduardo (Bolivia)
Dobles Segreda, Luís (Costa Rica)
Domínguez, Manuel (Paraguay)
Encina y Armanet, Francisco Antonio (Chile)
Ercilla y Zúñiga, Alonso de (Spain)
Favaro, Edmundo J. (Uruguay)
Fernández Guardia, Ricardo (Costa Rica)
Ferreira, Mariano (Uruguay)
Finot, Enrique (Bolivia)
García Ortiz, Laureano (Colombia)
Gil Fortoul, José (Venezuela)
Godoi, Juansilvano (Paraguay)
Gómez Carrillo, Enrique (Guatemala)
Gómez Haro, Enrique (Mexico)
Gonzlez Víquez, Cleto (Costa Rica)
Guerra y Sánchez, Ramiro (Cuba)
Gutiérrez, Alberto (Bolivia)
Henríquez Ureña, Max (Dominican Republic)
Icaza, Francisco A. de (Mexico)
Jaimes Freyre, Ricardo (Peru)
Jaramillo Alvarado, Pío (Ecuador)
Jiménez, Manuel de Jesús (Costa Rica)
Lamas, Andrés (Uruguay)
Lastarria Santander, José Victorino (Chile)
Levillier, Roberto (Argentina)
Lôbo, Hélio (Brazil)
Meade Sáinz-Trápaga, Joaquín Felipe (Mexico)
Medina, José Toribio (Chile)
Méndez Pereira, Octavio (Panama)
Milla y Vidaurre, José (Guatemala)
Montúfar, Lorenzo (Guatemala)
Mora, José María Luís (Mexico)
Moreno, Fulgencio R. (Paraguay)
Nin Frías, Alberto Augusto Antonio (Uruguay)
O'Leary, Juan Emiliano (Paraguay)
Oliveira Lima, Manuel de (Brazil)
Omiste, Modesto (Bolivia)
Otero Vértiz, Gustavo Adolfo (Bolivia)
Pazos Kanki, Vicente (Bolivia)
Paz-Soldán, Juan Pedro (Peru)
Pereyra, Carlos (Mexico)

Picón Salas, Mariano (Colombia)
Porras Barrenechea, Raúl (Peru)
Prado y Ugarteche, Javier (Peru)
Quesada, Ernesto (Argentina)
Quesada, Vicente Gregorio (Argentina)
Ramos, José Antonio (Cuba)
Rangel, Alberto (Brazil)
Reyes, Oscar Efrén (Ecuador)
Riva Palacio, Vicente (Mexico)
Salado Álvarez, Victoriano (Mexico)
Sarmiento, Domingo Faustino (Argentina)
Sierra, Justo (Mexico)
Sierra O'Reilly, Justo (Mexico)
Sotomayor Valdés, Ramón (Chile)
Teja Zabre, Alfonso (Mexico)
Tobar Donoso, Julio (Ecuador)
Valdés, Julio César (Bolivia)
Valle, Rafael Heliodoro (Honduras)
Valle-Arizpe, Artemio de (Mexico)
Varnhagen, Francisco Adolfo de (Brazil)
Vázquez-Machicado, Humberto (Bolivia)
Vicuña Mackenna, Benjamín (Chile)
Wiesse, Carlos (Peru)
Ynsfran, Pablo Max (Paraguay)
Zorrilla de San Martín, Juan (Uruguay)

Director, National Archives

González Obregón, Luís (Mexico)
O'Leary, Juan Emiliano (Paraguay)
Orozco y Berra, Manuel (Mexico)
Pardo Gallardo, José Joaquín (Guatemala)
Urteaga, Horacio H. (Peru)

Director, National Library

Basadre, Jorge (Peru)
Chávez Orozco, Luís (Mexico)
Figarola-Caneda, Domingo (Cuba)
García, Rodolfo (Brazil)
Godoi, Juansilvano (Paraguay)
Iguíniz, Juan B. (Mexico)
Sosa, Francisco (Mexico)
Thayer Ojeda, Tomás (Chile)
Vasconcelos, José (Mexico)
Vigil, José María (Mexico)

Director, National Museum

Edwards, Alberto (Chile)
García, Genaro (Mexico)

García, Rodolfo (Brazil)
Godoi, Juansilvano (Paraguay)
Paso y Troncoso, Francisco del (Mexico)
Pueyrredón, Carlos Alberto (Argentina)
Udaondo, Enrique (Argentina)
Valladares, José Antonio do Prado (Brazil)

Editor

Barrera, Isaac J. (Ecuador)
Bilbao, Manuel (Chile)
Bustamante, Carlos María de (Mexico)
Caillet-Bois, Ricardo R. (Argentina)
Cardozo, Efraím (Paraguay)
Cosío, José Gabriel (Peru)
Cuervo, Luis Augusto (Colombia)
Decoud, Hector Francisco (Paraguay)
Durón, Rómulo E. (Honduras)
Errázuriz Valdivieso, Crescente (Chile)
Favaro, Edmundo J. (Uruguay)
Fúrlong Cárdiff, Guillermo (Argentina)
García del Río, Juan (Colombia)
García Ortiz, Laureano (Colombia)
Gómez Haro, Enrique (Mexico)
Gonzaga Jaeger, Luís (Brazil)
Groussac, Pablo (Argentina)
Guerra y Sánchez, Ramiro (Cuba)
Henríquez Ureña, Pedro (Dominican Republic)
Henríquez y Carvajal, Federico (Dominican Republic)
Ingenieros, José (Argentina)
Jaimes Freyre, Ricardo (Peru)
Justiz y del Valle, Tomás Juan de (Cuba)
Lamas, Andés (Uruguay)
Larrazábal, Felipe (Venezuela)
Levillier, Roberto (Argentina)
Llaverías Martínez, Joaquín (Cuba)
Méndez Pereira, Octavio (Panama)
Mendoza, Cristóbal L. (Venezuela)
Mera, Juan León (Ecuador)
Milla y Vidaurre, José (Guatemala)
Moreno, Fulgencio (Paraguay)
Omiste, Modesto (Bolivia)
Palma, Ricardo (Peru)
Pazos Kanki, Vicente (Bolivia)
Paz-Soldán, Juan Pedro (Peru)
Pereda Setembrino, Ezequiel (Uruguay)
Riquelme, Daniel (Chile)

Samper Ortega, Daniel (Colombia)
Santovenia y Echaide, Emeterio (Cuba)
Sotomayor Valdés, Ramón (Chile)
Vasconcelos, José (Mexico)
Vicuña Mackenna, Benjamín (Chile)
Vigil, José Mariá (Mexico)
Wiesse, Carlos (Peru)
Zamacois, Niceto de (Mexico)
Zayas y Alfonso, Alfredo (Cuba)
Zum Felde, Alberto (Uruguay)

Educational Administrator

Alcântara Machado D'Oliveira, José de (Brazil)
Amunátegui Solar, Domingo (Chile)
Andrade, Roberto (Ecuador)
Arguello Mora, Manuel (Costa Rica)
Baez, Cecilio (Paraguay)
Barros Arana, Diego (Chile)
Caillet-Bois, Ricardo R. (Argentina)
Cardoza, Ramón Indalecio (Paraguay)
Cervantes de Salazar, Francisco (Mexico)
Chávez Orozco, Luís (Mexico)
Clavijero, Francisco Javier (Mexico)
Comas Camps, Juan (Mexico)
Cosío, José Gabriel (Peru)
Cosío Villegas, Daniel (Mexico)
Dobles Segreda, Luís (Costa Rica)
Domínguez, Manuel (Paraguay)
Durón, Rómulo E. (Honduras)
Eguiara Eguren, Juan José de (Mexico)
Fernández Guardia, Ricardo (Costa Rica)
Finot, Enrique (Bolivia)
Funes, Gregorio (Argentina)
Galdames, Luís (Chile)
García, Genaro (Mexico)
García Granados, Rafael (Mexico)
Garibay K., Ángel María (Mexico)
Garzón Maceda, Ceferino (Argentina)
Groot, José Manuel (Colombia)
Groussac, Pablo (Argentina)
Gutiérrez, Juan María (Argentina)
Henríquez Ureña, Max (Dominican Republic)
Henríquez Ureña, Pedro (Dominican Republic)
Henríquez y Carvajal, Federico (Dominican Republic)

Ibarguren, Carlos (Argentina)
Letelier, Valentín (Chile)
Levene, Ricardo (Argentina)
López, Vicente Fidel (Argentina)
Méndez Pereira, Octavaio (Panama)
Mendoza, Jaime (Bolivia)
Montúfar, Lorenzo (Guatemala)
O'Leary, Juan Emiliano (Paraguay)
Oliveira Vianna, Francisco José de (Brazil)
Otero Vértiz, Gustavo Adolfo (Bolivia)
Ovalle, Alonso de (Chile)
Picón Salas, Mariano (Colombia)
Pimentel, Francisco (Mexico)
Posada Gutiérrez, Joaquín (Colombia)
Prado y Ugarteche, Javier (Peru)
Ramírez, José Fernando (Mexico)
Ramos Mejía, José María (Argentina)
Ravignani, Emilio (Argentina)
Reyes, Oscar Efrén (Ecuador)
Rojas, Ricardo (Argentina)
Samper Ortega, Daniel (Colombia)
Terán, Juan Benjamín (Argentina)
Urteaga, Horacio H. (Peru)
Vedia y Mitre, Mariano de (Argentina)
Villaverde y de La Paz, Cirilo (Cuba)
Wiesse, Carlos (Peru)

Elected Municipal Official

Cosío, José Gabriel (Peru)
Cuervo, Luís Augusto (Colombia)
Decoud, Hector Francisco (Paraguay)
Eguiara Eguren, Juan José de (Mexico)
Fuentes y Guzmán, Francisco (Guatemala)
Jijón y Caamaño, Jacinto (Ecuador)
Omiste, Modesto (Bolivia)
Oña, Pedro de (Chile)
Oroczo y Berra, Manuel (Mexico)
Oviedo y Valdés, Gonzalo Fernández (Spain)
Pimentel, Francisco (Mexico)
Pueyrredón, Carlos Alberto (Argentina)
Ramírez de Aguilar, Fernando (Mexico)
Ravignani, Emilio (Argentina)
Riva Agauero y Osma, José de la (Peru)
Riva Palacio, Vicente (Mexico)
Vedia y Mitre, Mariano de (Argentina)
Zayas y Alfonso, Alfredo (Cuba)

Engineer

Azara, Feliz de (Spain)
Batres Montúfar, José (El Salvador)
Cunha, Euclides de (Brazil)
Rangel, Alberto (Brazil)

Functionary in the National Government

Amunátegui, Miguel Luís (Chile)
Andrade, Roberto (Ecuador)
Baralt, Rafael María (Venezuela)
Bilbao, Francisco (Chile)
Briceño-Iragorry, Mario (Venezuela)
Bulnes, Gonzalo (Chile)
Cervantes de Salazar, Francisco (Mexico)
Edwards, Alberto (Chile)
Favaro, Edmundo J. (Uruguay)
Fernández Guardia, Ricardo (Costa Rica)
Fuenzalida Grandón, Alejandro (Chile)
Godoi, Juansilvano (Paraguay)
Ibarguren, Carlos (Argentina)
Leguizamón, Martiniano (Argentina)
Marure, Alejandro (Guatemala)
Milla y Vidaurre, José (Guatemala)
Otero Vértiz, Gustavo Adolfo (Bolivia)
Palma, Ricardo (Peru)
Pereyra, Carlos (Mexico)
Ramos Mejía, José María (Argentina)
Reyes, Oscar Efrén (Ecuador)
Riquelme, Daniel (Chile)
Salado Álvarez, Victoriano (Mexico)
Sotomayor Valdés, Ramón (Chile)
Tarquinio de Sousa, Octávio (Brazil)
Vázquez-Machicado, Humberto (Bolivia)
Zum Felde, Alberto (Uruguay)

Journalist

Abril y Ostalo, Mariano (Puerto Rico)
Acevedo Díaz, Eduardo (Uruguay)
Amunátegui, Miguel Luís (Chile)
Amunátegui Solar, Domingo (Chile)
Ancona, Eligio (Mexico)
Arguedas, Alcides (Bolivia)
Arguello Mora, Manuel (Costa Rica)
Baralt, Rafael María (Venezuela)
Bello, Andrés (Chile)
Bilbao, Francisco (Chile)
Bilbao, Manuel (Chile)
Blanco-Fombona, Rufino (Venezuela)

Bulnes, Gonzalo (Chile)
Capistrano de Abreu, João (Brazil)
Carbia, Rómulo D. (Argentina)
Cardozo, Efraím (Paraguay)
Coello, Augusto C. (Honduras)
Cosío, José Gabriel (Peru)
Cunha, Euclides da (Brazil)
Decoud, Hector Francisco (Paraguay)
Edwards, Alberto (Chile)
Elguero, Francisco (Mexico)
Fuenzalida Grandón, Alejandro (Chile)
Gámez, José Dolores (Nicaragua)
García, Rodolfo (Brazil)
García del Río, Juan (Colombia)
Gómez Carrillo, Enrique (Guatemala)
González, Juan Vicente (Venezuela)
González Obregón, Luís (Mexico)
Groot, José Manuel (Colombia)
Groussac, Pablo (Argentina)
Gutiérrez, Alberto (Bolivia)
Henríquez Ureña, Max (Dominican Republic)
Ingenieros, José (Argentina)
Jaramillo Alvarado, Pío (Ecuador)
Lamas, Andrés (Uruguay)
Larrazábal, Felipe (Venezuela)
Leguizamón, Martiniano (Argentina)
Levillier, Roberto (Argentina)
Llaverías, Martínez, Joaquín
Lôbo, Hélio (Brazil)
López Portillo y Rojas, José (Mexico)
Mendoza, Cristóbal L. (Venezuela)
Mier Noriega y Guerra, Fray José Servando Teresa de (Mexico)
Mitre, Bartolomé (Argentina)
Moncayo, Pedro (Ecuador)
Montúfar y Coronado, Manuel (Guatemala)
Mora, José María Luís (Mexico)
Moreno, Fulgencio (Paraguay)
Otero Vértiz, Gustavo Adolfo (Bolivia)
Pazos Kanki, Vicente (Bolivia)
Paz-Soldán, Juan Pedro (Peru)
Pereyra, Carlos (Mexico)
Prieto, Guillermo (Mexico)
Quintano Roo, Andrés (Mexico)
Rangel, Alberto (Brazil)
René-Moreno, Gabriel (Bolivia)
Restrepo, José Manuel (Colombia)

Riquelme, Daniel (Chile)
Rojas, Ricardo (Argentina)
Salado Álvarez, Victoriano (Mexico)
Sarmiento, Domingo Faustino (Argentina)
Sierra, Justo (Mexico)
Sierra O'Reilily, Justo (Mexico)
Sosa, Francisco (Mexico)
Sotomayor Valdés, Ramón (Chile)
Tarquinio de Sousa, Octávio (Brazil)
Teje Zabre, Alfonso (Mexico)
Valdés, Julio César (Bolivia)
Valladares, José Antonio do Prado (Brazil)
Vedia y Mitre, Mariano de (Argentina)
Vicuña Mackenna, Benjamín (Chile)
Zayas Alfonso, Alfredo (Cuba)
Zamacois, Niceto de (Mexico)
Zum Felde, Alberto (Uruguay)

Judge

Ancona, Eligio (Mexico)
Arguello Mora, Manuel (Costa Rica)
Báez, Cecilio (Paraguay)
Cortés, Manuel José (Bolivia)
Durón, Rómulo E. (Honduras)
Elguero, Francisco (Mexico)
Gómez Haro, Enrique (Mexico)
Larrazábal, Felipe (Venezuela)
Mera, Juan León (Ecuador)
Montúfar, Lorenzo (Guatemala)
Porras Barrenechea, Raúl (Peru)
Prado y Ugarteche, Javier (Peru)
Quesada, Ernesto (Argentina)
Quintano Roo, Andrés (Mexico)
Ramírez, José Fernando (Mexico)
Restrepo, José Manuel (Colombia)
Riva Palacio, Vicente (Mexico)
Sierra, Justo (Mexico)
Sierra O'Reilly, Justo (Mexico)
Vedia y Mitre, Mariano de (Argentina)
Vigil, José María (Mexico)
Wiesse, Carlos (Peru)
Zayas y Alfonso, Alfredo (Cuba)
Zorrilla de San Martín, Juan (Uruguay)

Landed Estate Owner

Alva Ixtlilxochitl, Fernando de (Mexico)
Bulnes, Gonzalo (Chile)

Las Casas, Bartolomé de (Spain)
Pizarro, Pedro (Ecuador)

Lawyer (Private Practice)

Baralt, Rafael María (Venezuela)
Bello, Andrés (Chile)
Bustamante, Carlos María de (Mexico)
Elguero, Francisco (Mexico)
Galdames, Luís (Chile)
González Haro, Enrique (Mexico)
González Víquez, Cleto (Costa Rica)
Henríquez Ureña, Max (Dominican Republic)
Irarrázaval Larrain, José Miguel (Chile)
Jaramillo Alvarado, Pío (Ecuador)
Lafuente Machain, Ricardo de (Argentina)
Leguizamón, Martiniano (Argentina)
Medina, José Toribio (Chile)
Orozco y Berra, Manuel (Mexico)
Pereda Setembrino, Ezequiel (Uruguay)
Pinto, Manuel María (Bolivia)
Porras Barrenechea, Raúl (Peru)
Ramírez, José Fernando (Mexico)
Santovenia y Echaide, Emeterio (Cuba)
Valle-Arizpe, Artemio de (Mexico)
Vicuña Mackenna, Benjamín (Chile)
Zayas y Alfonso, Alfredo (Cuba)
Zorrilla de San Martín, Juan (Uruguay)

Legislator

Abril y Ostalo, Mariano (Puerto Rico)
Acevedo Díaz, Eduardo (Uruguay)
Acosta, Cecilio (Venezuela)
Alamán, Lucas (Mexico)
Alcântara Machado D'Oliveira, José de (Brazil)
Amunátegui Solar, Domingo (Chile)
Andrade, Roberto (Ecuador)
Arguedas, Alcides (Bolivia)
Barrera, Isaac J. (Ecuador)
Batres Montúfar, José (El Salvador)
Bello, Andrés (Chile)
Bulnes, Gonzalo (Chile)
Bustamante, Carlos María de (Mexico)
Cevallos, Pedro Fermín (Ecuador)
Coello, Augusto C. (Honduras)
Cortés, Manuel José (Bolivia)
Cuervo, Luís Augusto (Colombia)

Decoud, Hector Francisco (Paraguay)
Dobles Segreda, Luís (Costa Rica)
Durón, Rómulo E. (Honduras)
Edwards, Alberto (Chile)
Elguero, Francisco (Mexico)
Encina y Armanet, Francisco Antonio (Chile)
Gámez, José Dolores (Nicaragua)
García del Río, Juan (Colombia)
García Ortiz, Laureano (Colombia)
González, Juan Vicente (Venezuela)
González Suárez, Federico (Ecuador)
Groot, José Manuel (Colombia)
Gutiérrez, Alberto (Bolivia)
Henríquez y Carvajal, Federico (Dominican Republic)
Jijón y Caamaño, Jacinto (Ecuador)
Jiménez, Manuel de Jesús (Costa Rica)
Larrazábal, Felipe (Venezuela)
Lastarria Santander, José Victorino (Chile)
López, Vicente Fidel (Argentina)
López Portillo y Rojas, José (Mexico)
Marure, Alejandro (Guatemala)
Mendoza, Jaime (Bolivia)
Mera, Juan León (Ecuador)
Mier Noriega y Guerra, Fray José Servando Teresa de (Mexico)
Milla y Vidaurre, José (Guatemala)
Montúfar, Lorenzo (Guatemala)
Montúfar y Coronado, Manuel (Guatemala)
Moreno, Fulgencio (Paraguay)
O'Leary, Juan Emiliano (Paraguay)
Omiste, Modesto (Bolivia)
Ospina Vásquez, Luís (Colombia)
Pereda Setembrino, Ezequiel (Uruguay)
Prado y Ugarteche, Javier (Peru)
Prieto, Guillermo (Mexico)
Pueyrredón, Carlos Alberto (Buenos Aires)
Quesada, Vicente Gregorio (Argentina)
Quintano Roo, Andrés (Mexico)
Ramírez, José Fernando (Mexico)
Ravignani, Emilio (Argentina)
Restrepo, José Manuel (Colombia)
Riva Palacio, Vicente (Mexico)
Salado Álvarez, Victoriano (Mexico)
Salgado, José (Uruguay)
Santovenia y Echaide, Emeterio (Cuba)
Sierra, Justo (Mexico)

Simonsen, Roberto Cochrane (Brazil)
Sosa, Francisco (Mexico)
Sotomayor Valdés, Ramón (Chile)
Urteaga, Horacio (Peru)
Valdés, Julio César (Bolivia)
Valle-Arizpe, Artemio de (Mexico)
Vicuña Mackenna, Benjamín (Chile)
Vigil, José María (Mexico)
Ynsfran, Pablo Max (Paraguay)
Zavala, Lorenzo de (Mexico)
Zayas y Alfonso, Alfredo (Cuba)
Zorrilla de San Martín, Juan (Uruguay)

Librarian

Basadre, Jorge (Peru)
Carbia, Rómulo D. (Argentina)
Chávez Orozco, Luís (Mexico)
Errázuriz Valdivieso, Crescente (Chile)
García, Rodolfo (Brazil)
García del Río, Juan (Colombia)
Gómez Haro, Enrique (Mexico)
Groussac, Pablo (Argentina)
Iguíniz, Juan B. (Mexico)
Nin Frías, Alberto Augusto Antonio (Uruguay)
Palma, Ricardo (Peru)
Paso y Troncoso, Francisco del (Mexico)
Peraza Sarausa, Fermín (Cuba)
Picón Salas, Mariano (Colombia)
Quesada, Ernesto (Argentina)
Quesada, Vicente Gregorio (Argentina)
Ramos, José Antonio (Cuba)
René-Moreno, Gabriel (Bolivia)
Samper Ortega, Daniel (Colombia)
Taunay, Afonso D'Escragnolle (Brazil)
Thayer Ojeda, Tomás (Chile)
Zum Felde, Alberto (Uruguay)

Literary Critic

Real de Azúa, Carlos (Uruguay)
Tarquinio de Sousa, Octávio (Brazil)

Minister of Foreign Relations

Fernández Guardia, Ricardo (Costa Rica)
Ferreira, Mariano (Uruguay)
Finot, Enrique (Bolivia)
Gámez, José Dolores (Nicaragua)
García Ortiz, Laureano (Colombia)

González Víquez, Cleto (Costa Rica)
Jiménez, Manuel de Jesús (Costa Rica)
Lamas, Andrés (Uruguay)
López Portillo y Rojas, José (Mexico)
Mitre, Bartolomé (Argentina)
Montúfar, Lorenzo (Guatemala)
Moreno, Fulgencio (Paraguay)
Ramírez, José Fernando (Mexico)
Tobar Donoso, Julio (Ecuador)

Minister of Public Education

Blanco, Eduardo (Venezuela)
Cosío Villegas, Daniel (Mexico)
Durón, Rómulo E. (Honduras)
Fernández Guardia, Ricardo (Costa Rica)
Gavidia, Francisco (El Salvador)
Gil Fortoul, José (Venezuela)
Ibarguren, Carlos (Argentina)
López, Vicente Fidel (Argentina)
López Portillo y Rojas, José (Mexico)
Samper Ortega, Daniel (Colombia)
Sierra, Justo (Mexico)
Vasconcelos, José (Mexico)

Musician

Larrazábal, Felipe (Venezuela)

National President

Alfaro, Ricardo Joaquín (Panama)
Baez, Cecilio (Provisional) (Paraguay)
Barros Borgoño, Luís (Interim) (Chile)
Gil Fortoul, José (Venezuela)
González Víquez, Cleto (Costa Rica)
Mitre, Bartolomé (Argentina)
Sarmiento, Domingo Faustino (Argentina)
Zayas y Alfonso, Alfredo (Cuba)

Novelist

Gómez Carrillo, Enrique (Guatemala)
Henríquez Ureña, Max (Dominican Republic)
Leguizamón, Martiniano (Argentina)
Sierra, Justo (Mexico)
Teja Zabre, Alfonso (Mexico)
Villaverde y de La Paz, Cirilo (Cuba)

Naval Officer

Aguirre, Juan Francisco (Spain)
Alvear y Ponce de León, Diego de (Spain)
Palma, Ricardo (Peru)

Physician

Melo Morais, Alexandre José de (Brazil)
Mendoza, Jaime (Bolivia)
Ramos Mejía, José María (Argentina)
Rojas, Arístides (Venezuela)

Playwright

Díaz Díaz, Oswaldo (Colombia)
Henríquez Ureña, Max (Dominican Republic)
Ramos, José Antonio (Cuba)
Vigil, José María (Mexico)

Poet

Acosta, Cecilio (Venezuela)
Baralt, Rafael María (Venezuela)
Batres Montúfar, José (El Salvador)
Bello, Andrés (Chile)
Blanco-Fombona, Rufino (Venezuela)
Durón, Rómulo E. (Honduras)
Ercilla y Zúñiga, Alonso de (Spain)
Groot, José Manuel (Colombia)
Henríquez Ureña, Max (Dominican Republic)
Oña, Pedro de (Chile)
Pinto, Manuel María (Bolivia)
Sierra, Justo (Mexico)

Police Official

Alessio Robles, Vito (Mexico)

Publisher

Blanco-Fombona, Rufino (Venezuela)
Cardozo, Efraím (Paraguay)
Chamorro, Pedro Joaquín (Nicaragua)
Gámez, José Dolores (Nicaragua)
García Icazbalceta, Joaquín (Mexico)
García Ortiz, Laureano (Colombia)
Godoi, Juansilvano (Paraguay)
González, Juan Vicente (Venezuela)
Henríquez y Carvajal, Federico (Dominican Republic)
Jaimes Freyre, Ricardo (Peru)

Lamas, Andrés (Uruguay)
Larrazábal, Felipe (Venezuela)
Lastarria Santander, José Victorino (Chile)
López, Vicente Fidel (Argentina)
López Portillo y Rojas, José (Mexico)
Medina, José Toribio (Chile)
Milla y Vidaurre, José (Guatemala)
Mitre, Bartolomé (Argentina)
Otero Vértiz, Gustavo Adolfo (Bolivia)
Paz-Soldán, Juan Pedro (Peru)
Pereyra, Carlos (Mexico)
Pinto, Manuel María (Bolivia)
Quesada, Vicente Gregorio (Argentina)
Riquelme, Daniel (Chile)
Sierra O'Reilly, Justo (Mexico)
Villaverde y de La Paz, Cirilo (Cuba)
Zorrilla de San Martín, Juan (Uruguay)

Secondary School Teacher

Alegre, Francisco Javier (Mexico)
Alfaro, Ricardo Joaquín (Panama)
Alessio Robles, Vito (Mexico)
Amunátegui, Miguel Luís (Chile)
Amunátegui Solar, Domingo (Chile)
Barrera, Isaac J. (Ecuador)
Barros Arana, Diego (Chile)
Barros Borgoño, Luís (Chile)
Bello, Andrés (Chile)
Briceño-Iragorry, Mario (Venezuela)
Caillet-Bois, Ricardo R. (Argentina)
Capistrano de Abreu, João (Brazil)
Cardoza, Ramón Indalecio (Paraguay)
Cavo, Andrés (Mexico)
Clavijero, Francisco Javier (Mexico)
Cosío, José Gabriel (Peru)
Cosío Villegas, Daniel (Mexico)
Cue Cánovas, Agustin (Mexico)
Cunha, Euclides da (Brazil)
Díaz Díaz, Oswaldo (Colombia)
Dobles Segreda, Luís (Costa Rica)
Domínguez, Manuel (Paraguay)
Durón, Rómulo E. (Honduras)
Eguiara Eguren, Juan José de (Mexico)
Elguero, Francisco (Mexico)
Finot, Enrique (Bolivia)
Fuenzalida Grandón, Alejandro (Chile)
Fúrlong Cárdiff, Guillermo (Argentina)
García Ortiz, Laureano (Colombia)

Garibay K., Ángel María (Mexico)
Garzón Maceda, Ceferino (Argentina)
Gavidia, Francisco (El Salvador)
Gay, Claudio (France)
Gay, João Pedro (Uruguay)
Gonzaga Jaeger, Luís (Brazil)
González, Juan Vicente (Venezuela)
Groot, José Manuel (Colombia)
Groussac, Pablo (Argentina)
Gutiérrez, Juan María (Argentina)
Huamán Poma de Ayala, Felipe (Peru)
Iglesia y Parga, Ramón (Spain)
Iguíniz, Juan B. (Mexico)
Jaimes Freyre, Ricardo (Peru)
Jaramillo Alvarado, Pío (Ecuador)
Jiménez, Manuel de Jesús (Costa Rica)
Jobet Búrquez, Julio César (Chile)
Leguizamón, Martiniano (Argentina)
Leturia, Pedro de (Spain)
Levene, Ricardo (Argentina)
Lôbo, Hélio (Brazil)
Marure, Alejandro (Guatemala)
Mera, Juan León (Ecuador)
O'Leary, Juan Emiliano (Paraguay)
Orozco y Berra, Manuel (Mexico)
Paso y Troncoso, Francisco del (Mexico)
Pereyra, Carlos (Mexico)
Porras Barrenechea, Raúl (Peru)
Quesada, Ernesto (Argentina)
Ramos, José Antonio (Cuba)
René-Moreno, Gabriel (Bolivia)
Rojas, Ricardo (Argentina)
Sahagún, Bernardino de (Spain)
Salado Álvarez, Victoriano (Mexico)
Santovenia y Echaide, Emeterio (Cuba)
Sarmiento, Domingo Faustino (Argentina)
Sierra, Justo (Mexico)
Taunay, Afonso D'Escragnolle (Argentina)
Vasconcelos, José (Mexico)
Vedia y Mitre, Mariano de (Argentina)
Velasco, Juan de (Ecuador)
Vicuña Mackenna, Benjamín (Chile)
Vigil, José María (Mexico)
Ynsfran, Pablo Max (Paraguay)
Zinny, Antonio (Argentina)

Secretary to the President of the Republic

Blanco, Eduardo (Venezuela)
Cardozo, Efraím (Paraguay)

Coello, Augusto C. (Honduras)
Henríquez Ureña, Max (Dominican Republic)
Jaimes Freyre, Ricardo (Peru)

Soldier

Abreu y Lima, José Inácio (Brazil)
Alessio Robles, Vito (Mexico)
Azara, Feliz de (Spain)
Baralt, Rafael María (Venezuela)
Barros Borgoño, Luís (Chile)
Batres Montúfar, José (El Salvador)
Blanco, Eduardo (Venezuela)
Bustamante, Carlos María de (Mexico)
Cieza de León, Pedro (Spain)
Cunha, Euclides da (Brazil)
Díaz del Castillo, Bernal (Spain)
Fuentes y Guzmán, Francisco (Guatemala)
Garcilaso de la Vega (Peru)
Iglesia y Parga, Ramón (Spain)
Jiménez de Quesada, Gonzalo (Spain)
Llaverías Martínez, Joaquín (Cuba)
Martínez, José Luciano (Uruguay)
Meade Sáinz-Trápaga, Joaquín Felipe (Mexico)
Medina, José Toribio (Chile)
Mendoza, Jaime (Bolivia)
Mitre, Bartolomé (Argentina)
Posada Gutiérrez, Joaquín (Colombia)
Rangel, Alberto (Brazil)
Riva Palacio, Vicente (Mexico)
Varnhagen, Francisco Adolfo de (Brazil)

State or Provincial Governor

Alva Ixtlilxochitl, Fernando de (Mexico)
Ancona, Eligio (Mexico)
Blanco-Fombona, Rufino (Venezuela)
Bulnes, Gonzalo (Chile)
Cuervo, Luís Augusto (Colombia)
Fernández de Piedrahita, Lucas (Colombia)
Jaramillo Alvarado, Pío (Ecuador)
Larrazábal, Felipe (Venezuela)
Mera, Juan León (Ecuador)
Mitre, Bartolomé (Argentina)
Oviedo y Valdés, Gonzalo Fernández (Spain)
Restrepo, José Manuel (Colombia)
Riva Palacio, Vicente (Mexico)

Sarmiento, Domingo Faustino (Argentina)
Zavala, Lorenzo de (Mexico)

University Professor

Acosta, Cecilio (Venezuela)
Alcântara Machado D'Oliveira, José de (Brazil)
Amunátegui, Miguel Luís (Chile)
Amunátegui Solar, Domingo (Chile)
Andrade, Roberto (Ecuador)
Baez, Cecilio (Paraguay)
Basadre, Jorge (Peru)
Batres Montúfar, José (El Salvador)
Caillet-Bois, Ricardo R. (Argentina)
Capistrano de Abreu, João (Brazil)
Carbia, Rómulo D. (Argentina)
Cardoza, Ramón Indalecio (Paraguay
Cardozo, Efraím (Paraguay)
Carrera Stampa, Manuel (Mexico)
Cervantes de Salazar, Francisco (Mexico)
Cevallos, Pedro Fermín (Ecuador)
Comas Camps, Juan (Mexico)
Díez de Medina, Eduardo (Bolivia)
Dobles Segreda, Luís (Costa Rica)
Domínguez, Manuel (Paraguay)
Eyzaguirre Gutiérrez, Jaime (Chile)
Fuenzalida Grandón, Alejandro (Chile)
Galdames, Luís (Chile)
García, Genaro (Mexico)
García Granados, Rafael (Mexico)
García, Juan Agustín (Argentina)
García, Rodolfo (Brazil)
García Ortiz, Laureano (Colombia)
Guerra y Sánchez, Ramiro (Cuba)
Henríquez Ureña, Pedro (Argentina)
Henríquez y Carvajal, Federico (Dominican Republic)
Ibarguren, Carlos (Argentina)
Ingenieros, José (Argentina)
Jaimes Freyre, Ricardo (Peru)
Jaramillo Alvarado, Pío (Ecuador)
Jijón y Caamaño, Jacinto (Ecuador)
Jobet Búrquez, Julio César (Chile)
Justiz y del Valle, Tomás Juan de (Cuba)
Levene, Ricardo (Argentina)
López, Vicente Fidel (Argentina)
López Portillo y Rojas, José (Mexico)
Méndez Pereira, Octavio (Panama)

Mendoza, Cristóbal L. (Venezuela)
Mendoza, Jaime (Bolivia)
Montúfar, Lorenzo (Guatemala)
Mora, José María Luís (Mexico)
Oliveira Vianna, Francisco José de (Brazil)
Ospina Vásquez, Luís (Colombia)
Pardo Gallardo, José Joaquín (Guatemala)
Peraza Sarausa, Fermín (Cuba)
Picón Salas, Mariano (Colombia)
Pressoir, Jacques Catts (Haiti)
Quesada, Ernesto (Argentina)
Ramírez de Aguilar, Fernando (Mexico)
Ramos, José Antonio (Cuba)
Ravignani, Emilio (Argentina)
Reyes, Oscar Efrén (Ecuador)
Riva Aguero y Osma, José de la (Peru)

Rojas, Ricado (Argentina)
Salgado, José (Uruguay)
Sigüenza y Góngora, Carlos de (Mexico)
Simonsen, Roberto Cochrane (Brazil)
Taunay, Afonso D'Escragnolle (Brazil)
Teja Zabre, Alfonso (Mexico)
Terán, Juan Benjamín (Argentina)
Urteaga, Horacio H. (Peru)
Vallardares, José Antonio do Prado (Brazil)
Valle, Rafael Heliodoro (Honduras)
Vasconcelos, José (Mexico)
Vázquez-Machicado, Humberto (Bolivia)
Vedia y Mitre, Mariano de (Argentina)
Wiesse, Carlos (Peru)
Ynsfran, Pablo Max (Paraguay)
Zorrilla de San Martín, Juan (Uruguay)

APPENDIX IV
Subjects Researched by the Major Historians

In addition to the general national histories that were written in every Latin American nation, historians produced a variety of monographic and biographical themes. The following appendix of subject matter contains the names of the historians who wrote on the theme, along with their native countries.

Agriculture

Zinny, Antonio	Spain

José Manuel Balmaceda

Irarrázaval Larrain, José Miguel	Chile

José Ballivián y Segurola

René-Moreno, Gabriel	Bolivia

Bandeirantes of Brazil

Alcântara Machado D'Oliveira, José de	Brazil
Gonzaga Jaeger, Luís	Brazil

Manuel Belgrano

Mitre, Bartolomé	Argentina

Andrés Bello

Amunátegui, Miguel Luís	Chile
Mendoza, Cristóbal L.	Venezuela

Bibliography

Figarola-Caneda, Domingo	Cuba
García, Genaro	Mexico
García, Rodolfo	Brazil
Peraza Sarausa, Fermín	Cuba

Simón Bolívar

Blanco-Fombona, Rufino	Venezuela
García del Río, Juan	Colombia
Jaramillo Alvarado, Pío	Ecuador
Larrazábal, Felipe	Venezuela
Leturia, Pedro de	Spain
Méndez Pereira, Octavio	Panama
Mendoza, Cristóbal L.	Venezuela

Mera, Juan León	Ecuador
Otero Vértiz, Gustavo Adolfo	Bolivia
Pereyra, Carlos	Mexico
Rojas, Arístides	Venezuela

Boundary Issues

Alvear y Ponce de León, Diego de	Spain
Alegre, Francisco Javier	Mexico
Cardozo, Efraím	Paraguay
Chamorro, Pedro Joaquín	Nicaragua
Díez de Medina, Eduardo	Bolivia
Moncayo, Pedro	Ecuador
Porras Barrenechea, Raúl	Peru
Wiesse, Carlos	Peru

Central American Federation

Chamorro, Pedro Joaquín	Nicaragua
Montúfar, Lorenzo	Guatemala

Colonial Era

Azara, Feliz de	Spain
Batres Montúfar, José	El Salvador
Capistrano de Abreu, João	Brazil
Cervantes de Salazar, Francisco	Spain
Jaramillo Alvarado, Pío	Ecuador
Medina, José Toribio	Chile
Salgado, José	Uruguay
Taborga, Miguel de los Santos	Bolivia
Wiesse, Carlos	Peru
Zavala, Lorenzo	Mexico

Conquest of America

Amunátegui, Miguel Luís	Chile
Cieza de León, Pedro de	Spain
Clavijero, Francisco Javier	Mexico
Díaz del Castillo, Bernal	Spain
Ercilla y Zúñiga, Alonso de	Spain
Errázuriz Valdivieso, Crescente	Chile
Eyzaguirre Gutiérrez, Jaime	Chile
Fernández Guardia, Ricardo	Costa Rica
Fernández de Piedrahita, Lucas	Colombia
Ferreira, Mariano	Uruguay
García, Genaro	Mexico
García Icazbalceta, Joaquín	Mexico
Gómara, Francisco López de	Spain
Icaza, Francisco A. de	Mexico
Iglesia y Parga, Ramón	Peru
Jaimes Freyre, Ricardo	Peru

Jijón y Caamaño, Jacinto	Ecuador
Jiménez de Quesada, Gonzalo	Spain
Lafuente Machaín, Ricardo de	Argentina
Lamas, Andrés	Uruguay
Las Casas, Bartolomé de	Spain
Levillier, Roberto	France
Leturia, Pedro de	Spain
Oliveira Lima, Manuel de	Brazil
Oviedo y Valdés, Gonzalo Fernández	Spain
Pizarro, Pedro	Spain
Porras Barrenechea, Raúl	Peru
Reyes, Oscar Efrén	Ecuador
Sahagún, Bernardino de	Spain
Sosa, Francisco	Mexico
Thayer Ojeda, Tomás	Chile

Constitutional History

Cosío Villegas, Daniel	Mexico
Galdames, Luís	Chile
Gil Fortoul, José	Venezuela
Lastarria Santander, José Victorino	Chile
Sierra O'Reilly, Justo	Mexico

Hernán Cortés

Orozco y Berra, Manuel	Mexico
Sigüenza y Góngora, Carlos de	Mexico

Cuadros de Costumbres (Articles about Customs)

Jiménez, Manuel de Jesús	Costa Rica

Culture

Henríquez Ureña, Pedro	Dominican Republic
Icaza, Francisco A. de	Mexico
Méndez Pereira, Octaviio	Panama
Picón Salas, Mariano	Colombia
Prado y Ugarteche, Javier	Peru
Ramírez de Aguilar, Fernando	Mexico
Riva Aguero y Osma, José de la	Peru
Rojas, Ricardo	Argentina
Samper Ortega, Daniel	Colombia
Valladares, José Antonio do Prado	Brazil
Zum Felde, Alberto	Uruguay

Porfirio Díaz

Cosío Villegas, Daniel	Mexico
García Granados, Rafael	Mexico

Diplomacy

Alfaro, Ricardo Joaquín	Panama
Caillet-Bois, Ricardo R.	Argentina
Chamorro, Pedro Joaquín	Nicaragua
Coello, Augusto C.	Honduras
Comas Camps, Juan	Spain
Cue Cánovas, Agustín	Mexico
Gámez, José Dolores	Nicaragua
Godoi, Juansilvano	Paraguay
Gutiérrez, Alberto	Bolivia
Henríquez Ureña, Max	Dominican Republic
Lôbo, Hélio	Brazil
Méndez Pereira, Octavio	Panama
Moreno, Fulgencio R.	Paraguay
Pereyra, Carlos	Mexico
Quesada, Ernesto	Argentina
Quesada, Vicente Gregorio	Argentina
Salgado, José	Uruguay
Valdés, Julio	Bolivia

Discovery of America

Capistrano de Abreu, João	Brazil
Carbia, Rómulo D.	Argentina
Sarmiento de Gambóa, Pedro	Spain

Economic History

Encina y Armanet, Francisco Antonio	Chile
Garzón Maceda, Ceferino	Argentina
Guerra y Sánchez, Ramiro	Cuba
Jobet Búrquez, Julio César	Chile
Levene, Ricardo	Argentina
Lôbo, Hélio	Brazil
Moreno, Fulgencio R.	Paraguay
Ospina Vásquez, Luís	Colombia
Pimentel, Francisco	Mexico
Simonsen, Roberto Cochrane	Brazil
Taunay, Afonso D'Escragnolle	Brazil
Varnhagen, Francisco Adolfo de	Brazil

Education

Amunátegui Solar, Domingo	Chile
Cardoza, Ramón Indalecio	Paraguay
García, Juan Agustín	Argentina
Guerra y Sánchez, Ramiro	Cuba
Gutiérrez, Juan María	Argentina
Prado y Ugarteche, Javier	Peru
Tobar Donoso, Julio	Ecuador

Epic Poetry

Balbuena, Bernardo de	Puerto Rico
Baralt, Rafael María	Venezuela
Ercilla y Zúñiga, Alonso de	Spain
Prieto, Guillermo	Mexico
Quintano Roo, Andrés	Mexico
Rojas, Arístides	Venezuela
Zorrilla de San Martín, Juan	Uruguay

Ethnography

Aguirre, Juan Francisco	Spain
Cosío, José Gabriel	Peru

Gabriel García Moreno

Andrade, Roberto	Ecuador
Mera, Juan León	Ecuador

Gauchos

Acevedo Díaz, Eduardo	Uruguay
Leguizamón, Martiniano	Argentina

Historical Novels

Acevedo Díaz, Eduardo	Uruguay
Ancona, Eligio	Mexico
Arguello Mora, Manuel	Costa Rica
Gómez Carrillo, Enrique	Guatemala
Milla y Vidaurre, José	Guatemala
Ramos, José Antonio	Cuba
Riva Palacio, Vicente	Mexico

Historiography

Barrera, Isaac J.	Ecuador
Basadre, Jorge	Peru
Carbia, Rómulo D.	Argentina
Cardozo, Efraím	Paraguay
Fuentes y Guzmán, Francisco Antonio	Guatemala
Galdames, Luís	Chile
Iglesia y Parga, Ramón	Spain .
Pardo Gallardo, José Joaquín	Guatemala
Pressoir, Jacques Catts	Haiti
Vedia y Mitre, Mariano de	Argentina

Agustín de Iturbide

Valle, Rafael Heliodoro	Honduras

Independence

Abril y Ostalo, Mariano	Puerto Rico
Acevedo Díaz, Eduardo	Uruguay

Alamán, Lucas	Mexico
Alfaro, Ricardo Joaquín	Panama
Barros Arana, Diego	Chile
Blanco, Eduardo	Venezuela
Bustamante, Carlos María de	Mexico
Cevallos, Pedro Fermín	Ecuador
Díaz Díaz, Oswaldo	Colombia
Fernández Guardia, Ricardo	Costa Rica
Gay, Claudio	France
Henríquez y Carvajal, Federico	Dominican Republic
Lastarria Santander, José Victorino	Chile
Levene, Ricardo	Argentina
López, Vicente Fidel	Argentina
Marure, Alejandro	Guatemala
Melo Morais, Alexandre José de	Brazil
Mier Noriega y Guerra, Fray José Servando Teresa de	Mexico
Mitre, Bartolomé	Argentina
Montúfar y Coronado, Manuel	Guatemala
Mora, José María Luís	Mexico
Moreno, Fulgencio R.	Paraguay
Pereda Setembrino, Ezequiel	Uruguay
Quintano Roo, Andrés	Mexico
Restrepo, José Manuel	Colombia
Riva Aguero y Osma, José de la	Peru
Tarquinio de Sousa, Octávio	Brazil
Taunay, Afonso D'Escragnolle	Brazil
Valdés, Julio César	Bolivia
Zavala, Lorenzo de	Mexico

Indian History

Alva Ixtlilxochitl, Fernando de	Mexico
Garcilaso de la Vega	Peru
Garibay K., Ángel María	Mexico
González Suárez, Federico	Ecuador
Huamán Poma de Ayala, Felipe	Unknown
Jaramillo Alvarado, Pío	Ecuador
Las Casas, Bartolomé de	Spain
López Portillo y Rojas, José	Mexico
Mera, Juan León	Ecuador
Oña, Pedro de	Chile
Paso y Troncoso, Francisco del	Mexico
Pimentel, Francisco	Mexico
Quesada, Vicente Gregorio	Argentina
Reyes, Oscar Efrén	Ecuador
Sahagún, Bernardino de	Spain
Sarmiento de Gambóa, Pedro	Spain
Sierra O'Reilly, Justo	Mexico
Urteaga, Horacio H.	Peru

Vigil, José María	Mexico
Wiesse, Carlos	Peru

Inquisition

Palma, Ricardo	Peru

Intellectual History

Vasconcelos, José	Mexico
Vedia y Mitre, Mariano	Argentina
Zum Felde, Alberto	Uruguay

International Law

Bello, Andrés	Venezuela

Jesuit Order

Alegre, Francisco Javier	Mexico
Fúrlong Cárdiff, Guillermo	Argentina
Gay, João Pedro	France
Gonzaga Jaeger, Luís	Brazil
Ovalle, Alonso de	Chile
Velasco, Juan de	Ecuador

Benito Juárez

Cue Cánovas, Agustín	Mexico
Salado Álvarez, Victoriano	Mexico

Legal History

Basadre, Jorge	Peru
Leteliler, Valentín	Chile
Levene, Ricardo	Argentina
Ravignani, Emilio	Argentina
Riva Aguero y Osma, José de la	Peru

Lyric Poetry

Batres Montúfar, José	El Salvador
Coello, Augusto C.	Honduras
Mera, Juan León	Ecuador
Pimentel, Francisco	Mexico
Pinto, Manuel María	Bolivia
Zayas y Alfonso, Alfredo	Cuba

Hernando de Magallanes

Barros Arana, Diego	Chile

Malvinas Islands

Caillet-Bois, Ricardo R.	Argentina

José Martí

Henríquez y Carvajal, Federico   Dominican Republic
Llaverias Martínez, Joaquín   Cuba

Mexican Revolution of 1910

Elguero, Francisco   Mexico

Military History

Cunha, Euclides da   Brazil
Martínez, José Luciano   Uruguay
Posada Gutiérrez, Joaquín   Colombia
Ramírez, José Fernando   Mexico
Riquelme, Daniel   Chile
Sotomayor Valdés, Ramón   Chile
Vigil, José María   Mexico

Francisco de Miranda

Picón Salas, Mariano   Colombia
Pueyrredón, Carlos Alberto   Argentina

Missionary History

Alvear y Ponce de Leon, Diego de   Spain

Manuel Montt

Barros Arana, Diego   Chile

Monroe Doctrine

López Portillo y Rojas, José   Mexico

Municipal History

Briceño-Iragorry, Mario   Venezuela
Carrera Stampa, Manuel   England
Cosío, José Gabriel   Peru
Dobles Segreda, Luís   Costa Rica
Funes, Gregorio   Argentina
González Obregón, Luís   Mexico
González Víquez, Cleto   Costa Rica
Lafuente Machain, Ricardo de   Argentina
Lamas, Andrés   Uruguay
Meade Sáinz-Trápaga, Joaquín Felipe   Mexico
Orozco y Berra, Manuel   Mexico
Pardo Gallardo, José Joaquín   Guatemala
Paz-Soldán, Juan Pedro   Peru
Quesada, Ernesto   Argentina
Ramírez de Aguilar, Fernando   Mexico
Rojas, Arístides   Venezuela
Santovenia y Echaide, Emeterio   Cuba

Taunay, Afonso D'Escragnolle	Brazil
Thayer Ojeda, Tomás	Chile
Valle-Arizpe, Aratemio de	Mexico
Vázquez-Machicado, Humberto	Bolivia
Villaverde de La Paz, Cirilo	Cuba

National Archives

Llaverías Martínez, Joaquín	Cuba

Bernardo O'Higgins

Amunátegui, Miguel Luís	Chile
Eyzaguirre Gutiérrez, Jaime	Chile
Vicuña Mackenna, Benjamín	Chile

Dom Pedro I

Tarquinio de Sousa, Octávio	Brazil

Dom Pedro II

Rangel, Alberto	Brazil

Philosophy of History

Cuervo, Luís Augusto	Colombia
Gavidia, Francisco	El Salvador
Groussac, Pablo	Argentina

Diego Portales

Encino y Armanet, Francisco Antonio	Chile

Protestantism in Latin America

Pressoir, Jacques Catts	Haiti

Provincial, State, and Local History

Alessio Robles, Vito	Mexico
Barrera, Isaac J.	Ecuador
Cardoza, Ramón Indalecio	Paraguay
Durón, Rómulo E.	Honduras
Gómez Haro, Enrique	Mexico
González Suárez, Federico	Ecuador
Iguíniz, Juan B.	Mexico
Jaimes Freyre, Ricardo	Peru
Ravignani, Emilio	Argentina
Sarmiento, Domingo Faustino	Argentina
Terán, Juan Benjamín	Argentina
Zamora, Alonso de	Colombia

Psychohistory

Ingenieros, José	Italy
Oliveira Vianna, Francisco José de	Brazil
Ramos Mejía, José María	Argentina

Roman Catholic Church

Ancona, Elligio	Mexico
Benavente, Fray Toribio	Spain
Bilbao, Francisco	Chile
Carbia, Rómulo D.	Argentina
Eguiara Eguren, Juan José de	Mexico
Elguero, Francisco	Mexico
Errázuriz Valdivieso, Crescente	Chile
García, Juan Agustín	Argentina
García Icazbalceta, Joaquín	Mexico
González Suárez, Federico	Ecuador
Groot, José Manuel	Colombia
Iguíniz, Juan B.	Mexico
Larrazábal, Felipe	Venezuela
Mora, José María Luís	Mexico
Nin Frías, Alberto Augusto Antonio	Uruguay
Oña, Pedro de	Chile
Pazos Kanki, Vicente	Bolivia
Restrepo Posada, José	Colombia
Tobar Donoso, Julio	Ecuador
Udaondo, Enrique	Argentina
Villarroel, Gaspar de	Ecuador
Zamacois, Niceto de	Spain
Zamora, Alonso de	Colombia
Zorrilla de San Martín, Juan	Uruguay

Juan Manuel de Rosas

Bilbao, Manuel	Chile
Ibarguren, Carlos	Argentina
Quesada, Ernesto	Argentina
Ramos Mejía, José María	Argentina

Salvador Sanfuentes

Amunátegui, Miguel Luís	Chile

José de San Martín

García del Rio, Juan	Colombia
Gutiérrez, Juan María	Argentina
Irarrázaval Larrain, José Miguel	Chile
Jaramillo Alvarado, Pío	Ecuador
Mitre, Bartolomé	Argentina
Pueyrredón, Carlos Alberto	Argentina
Rojas, Ricardo	Argentina

Antonio López de Santa Anna

Bustamante, Carlos María de	Mexico

Francisco de Paula Santander

Cuervo, Luís Augusto	Colombia
García Ortiz, Laureano	Colombia

Domingo Faustino Sarmiento

Rojas, Ricardo	Argentina

Social History

Ramos, José Antonio	Cuba
Sarmiento, Domingo Faustino	Argentina
Sierra, Justo	Mexico

Socialism

Abreu y Lima, José Inácio	Brazil
Abril y Ostalo, Mariano	Puerto Rico
Acosta, Cecilio	Venezuela
Chávez Orozco, Luis	Mexico
Jobet Búrquez, Julio César	Chile

Sociology of Latin America

Arguedas, Alcides	Bolivia
Edwards, Alberto	Chile
Finot, Enrique	Bolivia
Fuenzalida Grandón, Alejandro	Chile
González Obregón, Luís	Mexico
Ingenieros, José	Italy
Jobet Búrquez, Julio César	Chile
Nin Frías, Alberto Augusto Antonio	Uruguay
Vázquez-Machicado, Humberto	Bolivia
Zum Felde, Alberto	Uruguay

Francisco Solano López

Báez, Cecilio	Paraguay
Decoud, Hector Francisco	Paraguay
Domínguez, Manuel	Paraguay
Godoi, Juansilvano	Paraguay
O'Leary, Juan Emiliano	Paraguay

Antonio José de Sucre

Andrade, Roberto	Ecuador
Otero Vértiz, Gustavo Adolfo	Bolivia
Vázquez-Machicado, Humberto	Bolivia

War of the Pacific

Barros Borgoño, Luís	Chile
Bulnes, Gonzalo	Chile
Gutiérrez, Alberto	Bolivia

Pinto, Manuel María   Bolivia
Riquelme, Daniel   Chile

War of the Triple Alliance

Báez, Cecilio   Paraguay

Women in History

García, Genaro   Mexico
Omiste, Modesto   Bolivia
Zayas y Alfonso, Alfredo   Cuba

Bibliography

Acuña, Angel. *Mitre historiador*. 2 vols. Buenos Aires: Coni, 1936.

Aiken, Henry David. *The Age of Ideology*. New York: Mentor Books, 1956.

Alisky, Marvin. *Historical Dictionary of Peru*. Metuchen, N.J.: Scarecrow Press, 1979.

Almela Melía, Juan. *Guía de personas que cultivan la historia de América*. Mexico City: Pan American Institute of History and Geography, 1951.

Altamirano, Ignacio M. "Dos Palabras." *Calvario y Tabor: Memorias de la lucha de la intervención*, by Vicente Riva Palacio. Vol. 1. Mexico City: Editorial Nacional, 1953.

Amador, Elias. "Prólogo." In *Diario histórico de México*, by Carlos María de Bustamante. Zacatecas, Mexico. Tip. de la Escuela de Artes y Oficios de la Penitenciaría, 1896.

Amunátegui Solar, Domingo. *Don Andrés Bello enseña a los chilenos a narrar la historia nacional*. Santiago: Prensas de la Universidad de Chile, 1938.

———. *El Instituto Nacional bajo los rectorados de don Manuel Montt, don Francisco Puente y don Antonio Varas, 1835–1845*. Santiago: Cervantes, 1891.

———. *Los primeros años de Instituto Nacional, 1813–1835*. Santiago: Cervantes, 1889.

Antuña, José G. "Prólogo: Juan Zorrilla de San Martín, El Tribuno." In *Conferencias y discursos, by Juan Zorrilla de San Martín*. Vol. 1. Montevideo: Ministerio de Instrucción Pública y Previsión Social, 1965.

Apuntes para la biografía del d. Lucas Alamán. Mexico City: Imprenta del Sagrado Corazón de Jesús, 1897.

Arcila Farias, Eduardo. "Prólogo." In *Tres autores en la historia de Baralt*, by Antonio Mieres. Caracas: Instituto Estudios Hispanoamericanos, Facultad de Humanidades y Educación, Universidad Central de Venezuela, 1966.

Arciniegas, Germán. *El pensamiento vivo de Andrés Bello*. Buenos Aires: Losada, 1946.

Arias Robalino, Augusto. *Biografía de Pedro Fermín Cevallos*. Quito: Editorial Colegio Central Técnico, 1948.

———. *Vida de Pedro Fermín Cevallos*. Quito: Editorial Escuela Central Tecnica, 1946.

Arnade, Charles. "The Historiography of Colonial and Modern Bolivia." *Hispanic American Historical Review*, 42, No. 3 (August 1962), pp. 333–384.

Arnáiz y Freg, Arturo. "Prólogo." In *Semblanzas e ideario*, by Lucas Alamán. Mexico City: Ediciones de la Universidad Nacional Autónoma, 1939.

———. "Prólogo y selección." *Ensayos, ideas y retratos*, by José María Luís Mora. Mexico City: Ediciones de la Universidad Nacional Autónoma, 1941.

Arzú, José. "Manuel Montúfar y Coronado." *Memorias para la historia de la revolución de Centro-América*, by Manuel Montúfar. 4th ed. Guatemala City: Tipografía Sánchez y de Guise, 1934.

Barager, Joseph R. "The Historiography of the Río de la Plata Area, Since 1830." *Hispanic American Historical Review*, 39, No. 4 (November 1959), pp. 588–642.

Barba, Francisco Esteve. *Historiografía indiana*. Madrid: Gredos, 1964.

Barbieri, Antonio. "Prólogo." In *Discursos apologéticos*, by Francisco Bauzá. Montevideo: Mosca Hnos., 1952.

Barrera, Isaac J. *Historiografía del Ecuador*. Mexico City: Instituto Pan Americano de Geografía e Historia, 1956.

———. *Pedro Fermín Cevallos: Estudio y selecciones*. Puebla, Mexico: J. M. Cajica Jr., 1960.

Blakemore, Harold. "The Chilean Revolution of 1891 and Its Historiography." *Hispanic American Historical Review*, 45, No. 3 (August 1965), pp. 393–421.

Blanco Acevedo, Pablo. "Prólogo." In *Escritos selectos del dr. Andrés Lamas*, by Andrés Lamas. Montevideo: Tipografía Moderna de Arduino Hnos., 1922.

Blanco-Fombona, Rufino. *The Man of Gold*. Translated by Isaac Goldberg. New York: Brentano's, 1920.

Bork, Albert William and Georg Maier. *Historical Dictionary of Ecuador*. Metuchen, N.J.: Scarecrow Press, 1973.

Briggs, Donald C. and Marvin Alisky. *Historical Dictionary of Mexico*. Metuchen, N.J.: Scarecrow Press, 1981.

Bronner, Fred. "José de la Riva Aguero (1885–1944) Peruvian Historian," *Hispanic American Historical Review*, 36, No. 4 (November 1956), pp. 490–502.

Bulnes, Alfonso. "Bello y la historiografía chilena." *Atenea*, 160, No. 410 (October–December 1965), pp. 33–40.

Burns, E. Bradford. "Ideology in Nineteenth-Century Latin American Historiography." *Hispanic American Historical Review*, 58, No. 3 (August 1978), pp. 409–431.

———. *Perspectives on Brazilian History*. New York: Columbia University Press, 1967.

Caicedo Rojas, José. "Don José Manuel Groot." In *Historia eclesiástica y civil de Nueva Granada*, by José Manuel Groot. Vol. 1 Bogotá: Biblioteca de Autores Colombianos, 1953.

Carbia, Rómulo D. *Historia crítica de la historiografía argentina desde sus origenes en el siglo XVI*. Buenos Aires: Coni, 1925.

———. *Historia de la historiografía argentina*. La Plata: Imprenta López, 1939.

Carbonell, Diego. *Escuelas de historia en América*. Buenos Aires: López, 1943.

Cardozo, Efraím. *Historiografía paraguaya*. Mexico City: Instituto Panamericano de Geografía e Historia, 1959.

Caro, Miguel Antonio. *D. José Manuel Groot*. Bogotá: Prensas del Ministerio de Educación Nacional, 1950.

Carranza, Angel, J. "Introducción." In *Escritos políticos y literarios*, by Andrés Lamas. Buenos Aires: Casa Editora, 1877.

Carreras, Carlos N. "Al lector." In *Tradiciones y leyendas puertorriqueñas*, by Cayetano Coll y Toste. Barcelona, Spain: Maucci, 1928.

Caso, Antonio. "Prólogo." In *Prosas,* by Justo Sierra. Mexico City: Universidad Autónoma de Mexico, 1963.

Castro Leal, Antonio. "Prólogo."In *Don Fray Juan de Zumárraga: Primer obispo y arzobispo de Mexico,* by Joaquín García Icazbalceta. Vol. 1. Mexico City: Porrúa, 1947.

———. "Prólogo." In *Fray Toribio de Motolinía y otros estudios*, by José Fernando Ramírez. 2d ed. rev. Mexico City: Porrúa, 1957.

———. "Prólogo." In *Monja y Casada, virgen y martir,* by Vicente Riva Palacio. Vol. 1, Mexico City: Porrúa, 1958.

Chinchilla Aguilar, Ernesto. *El historiador guatemalteco don Alejandro Marure*. Mexico City: Instituto Panamericano de Geografía e Historia, 1966.

Cieza de León, Pedro de. *Civil Wars in Peru: The War of Las Salinas*. Translated by Sir Clements Markham. London: Hakluyt Society, 1923.

————. *The Travels of Pedro de Cieza de Leon*. Translated by Clements R. Markham. London: Hakluyt Society, 1864.

Cosío, José Gabriel. *Cuzco: The Historical and Monumental City of Peru*. Lima: n.p., 1924.

Coto Conde, José Luís. *Don Ricardo Fernández Guardia: Ensayo biográfico*. San José; Imprenta Nacional, 1957.

Cox, Isaac Joslin. *Some of Chile's Historians as Viewed by Their Fellow Craftsmen*. New York: H.W.Wilson, 1939.

Cruz, Fernando. "Prólogo de la segunda edición."In *Elementos de la historia de Centro-América*, by Agustín Gómez Carrillo. 5th ed. Guatemala City: Encuadernación y Tip. Musical, 1895.

———— and Antonio Machado. *José Batres Montúfar y Alejandro Marure*. 2d ed. Guatemala City: Editorial del Ministerio de Educación Pública, 1957.

Cunha, Euclides da. *Rebellion in the Backlands*. Translated by Samuel Putnam. Chicago: University of Chicago Press, 1944.

Davis, Robert H. *Historical Dictionary of Colombia*. Metuchen, N.J.: Scarecrow Press, 1977.

Díaz, Victor Miguel. "Prólogo." In *Memorias para la historia del Antigua Reino de Guatemala*, by Francisco de Paula García Pelaez. Vol. 1. 2d ed. Guatemala City: Tipografía Nacional, 1943.

Díaz Arrieta, Hernán. *Historia personal de la literatura chilean desde don alonso de Ercilla hasta Pablo Neruda*. 2d ed. Santiago: Zig-Zag, 1962.

Díaz del Castillo, Bernal. *Cortez and the Conquest of Mexico*. Translated by B.G. Herzog. New York: W. R. Scott, 1942.

————. *The Discovery and Conquest of Mexico, 1517–1521*. Translated by A. P. Maudslay. Mexico City: Tolteca, 1953.

Donoso, Ricardo. *Don Benjamín Vicuña Mackenna: Su vida, sus escritos y su tiempo, 1831–1886*. Santiago: Imprenta Universitaria, 1925.

Encina, Francisco. "Breve bosquejo de la literatura histórica chilena." *Atenea*, 75, Nos. 291–292 (September–October 1949), pp. 27–75.

————. *La literatura histórica chilena y el concepto actual de la historia*. Santiago: Nascimento, 1935.

Ercilla y Zúñiga, Alonso de. *The Araucaniad*. Translated by Charles Maxwell Lancaster and Paul Thomas Lancaster. Nashville, Tenn.: Vanderbilt University Press, 1945.

Farr, Kenneth R. *Historical Dictionary of Puerto Rico and the U.S. Virgin Islands*. Metuchen, N.J.: Scarecrow Press, 1973.

Feliú Cruz, Guillermo. *Barros Arana, historiador*. 5 vols. Santiago: Ediciones de los Anales de la Universidad de Chile, 1959.

————. *Benjamín Vicuña Mackenna: El Historiador*. Santiago: Ediciones de los Anales de la Universidad de Chile, 1958.

————. "Interpretación de Vicuña Mackenna: Un historiador del siglo XIX."*Atenea*, 95, Nos. 291–292 (September–October 1949), pp. 144–181.

————. "La literatura histórica chilena: Notas sobre su desenvolvimiento." *Atenea*, 68, No. 203 (May 1942), pp. 254–268.

Fernández y Medina, Benjamín. "Apuntes biográficos del dr. d. Andrés Lamas." In *La obra económica de Bernardino Rivadavia*, by Andrés Lamas. Buenos Aires: Comité Sudamericano para el Impuesto Único, 1917.

————"Prólogo de la primera edición." In *Conferencias y Discursos,* by Juan Zorrilla de San Martín. Vol. 1. Montevideo: Ministerio de Instrucción Pública y Previsión Social, 1965.

Ferrer del Rio, Antonio. "D Lucas Alamán: Su vida y sus escritos." In *Disertaciones sobre la historia de la República Mexicana,* by Lucas Alamán. Mexico City: Jus, 1942.

Flemion, Philip F. *Historical Dictionary of El Salvador.* Metuchen, N.J.: Scarecrow Press, 1972.

Fombona-Pachano, J. "Alvarado visto por J. Fombona-Pachano." In *Los delitos políticos en la historia de Venezuela,* by Lisandro Alvarado. Caracas: Biblioteca de Cultura Venezolana, 1954.

Fuenzalida Grandón, Alejandro. *Lastarria y su tiempo (1817–1888): Su vida, obras e influencia en el desarrollo políticio e intelectual de Chile.* Santiago: Barcelona, 1911.

Galdames, Luis. "Concepto de la historia."*Atenea*, 95, Nos. 291–292 (September–October 1949), pp. 297–308.

————. *A History of Chile.* Translated by Isaac Joslin Cox. Chapel Hill: University of North Carolina Press, 1941.

Gall, Francis. *José Milla y Vidaurre.* Mexico City: Instituto Panamericano de Geografía e Historia, 1966.

Gaos, José. *De antropología e historiografía.* Veracruz, Mexico: Universidad Veracruzana, 1967.

Garcilaso de la Vega. *First Part of the Royal Commentaries of the Yncas.* Translated by Clements R. Markham. London: Hakluyt Society, 1869–1871.

————. *Works: A Critical Text.* Translated by Hady Ward Keniston. New York: Hispanic Society of America, 1925.

Gibson, Charles, "Writings on Colonial Mexico." *Hispanic American Historical Review*, 55, No. 2 (May 1975), pp. 287–323.

Giusti, Roberto F. *Diccionario de la literatura latinoamericana: Argentina.* Washington, D.C.: Unión Panamericana, 1961.

Glauert, Earl. "Ricardo Rojas and the Emergence of Argentine Cultural Nationalism." *Hispanic American Historical Review,* 43, No. 1 (February 1963), pp. 1–13.

Gómara, Francisco López. *Annals of the Emperor Charles V.* Translated by Roger Bigelow Merriman. Oxford: Clarendon Press, 1912.

Gómez Millas, Juan. "Las tendencias del pensamiento histórico." *Atenea*, 95, Nos. 291–292 (September–October 1949), pp. 11–26.

Gómez Restrepo, Antonio. *Historia de la literatura colombiana.* 4 vols. Bogotá: Publicaciones de la Biblioteca Nacional Colombia, 1938–1946.

————. *La literatura colombiana.* Bogotá: Talleres de ediciones, Colombia, 1926.

González, Ariosto D. "Estudio preliminar." In *Escritos*, by Andrés Lamas. Vol. 3. Montevideo: Imprenta Nacional, 1952.

————. "Prólogo." In *Escritos*, by Andrés Lamas. Vol. 2. Montevideo: Imprenta L.I.G.U., 1943.

González Obregón, Luís. "Datos bio-bibliográficos." In *Obras del lic. Don Fernando Ramírez*, by José Fernando Ramírez. Vol. 1. Mexico City: V. Agueros, 1898.

Grases, Pedro. *Rafael María Baralt (1810–1860)*. Caracas: Ediciones de la Fundación Eugenio Mendoza, 1959.

Griffin, Charles C. "Francisco Encina and Revisionism in Chilean History." *Hispanic American Historical Review*, 37, No. 1 (February 1957), pp. 1–26.

Griffith, William J. "The Historiography of Central America Since 1830," *Hispanic American Historical Review*, 40, No. 4 (November 1960), pp. 548–569.

Hale, Charles A. *Mexican Liberalism in the Age of Mora, 1821–1853*. New Haven: Yale University Press, 1968.

Heath, Dwight B. *Historical Dictionary of Bolivia*. Metuchen, N.J.: Scarecrow Press, 1972.

Hedrick, Anne K. and Basil C. *Historical Dictionary of Panama*. Metuchen, N.J.: Scarecrow Press, 1970.

Henestrosa, Andrés. "Prólogo." In *Conversaciones, cartas y ensayos*, by Justo Sierra. Mexico City: Secretaria de Educación Pública, 1947.

Henríquez, Ureña, Pedro. *Literary Currents in Hispanic America*. Cambridge: Harvard University Press, 1949.

Herdeck, Donald E., ed. *Caribbean Writers: A Bio-Bibliographical-Critical Encyclopedia*. Washington, D.C.: Three Continents Press, 1979.

Herrera y Reissig, Manuel. "Prólogo." In *La obra económica de Bernardino Rivadavia*, by Andrés Lamas. Buenos Aires: Comité Sudamericano para el Impuesto Único, 1917.

Higham, John. *History: Professional Scholarship in America*. New York: Harper Row, 1965.

Huneeus y Gana, Jorge. *Cuadro histórico de la producción intelectual de Chile*. Santiago: Biblioteca de Escritores de Chile, 1910.

Iglesias, Agusto. *Benjamín Vicuña Mackenna aprendiz de revolucionario*. Santiago: Universidad de Chile, 1946.

Instituto Panamericano de Geografía e Historia. *Guía de personas que cultivan la historia de América*. Mexico City: Instituto Panamericano de Geografía e Historia, 1951.

Jeffrey, William H. *Mitre and Argentina*. New York: Library Publishers, 1952.

Jijón y Caamaño, Jacinto. "Prólogo." In *Obras escogidas*, by Federico González Suárez. Quito: Imprenta de Ministerio de Gobierno, 1944.

Jiménez, Nicolás. *Biografía de ilustrisimo Federico González Suárez*. Quito: Talleres Tipográficos Municipales, 1936.

Jobet, Julio César. "Notas sobre la historiografía chilena." *Atenea*, 95, Nos. 291–292 (September–October 1949), pp. 345–377.

Juarros, Domingo. *A Statistical and Commercial History of the Kingdom of Guatemala in Spanish America*. Translated by J. Baily. London: John Mearne, 1823.

Kaempffer Villagran, Guillermo. *Asi sucedió: Sangrientos episodios de la lucha obrera en Chile, 1850–1925*. Santiago: Arancibia Hermanos, 1962.

Key-Ayala, Santiago. "La X-esima dimensión." In *Los delitos políticos en la historia de Venezuela*, by Lisandro Alvarado. Caracas: Biblioteca de Cultura Venezolana, 1954.

Kolinski, Charles J. *Historical Dictionary of Paraguay*. Metuchen, N.J.: Scarecrow Press, 1973.

Laferrere, Alfonso. "Noticia Preliminar." In *Páginas de Groussac*, by Pablo Groussac. Buenos Aires: Talleres Gráficos Argentinos L. J. Rosso, 1928.

Larrabure Unanue, Eugenio. "Juan de Arona." In *Cuadros y episodios peruanos y otras poesías, nacionales y diversas*, by Juan de Arona. Lima: Calle de Melchormalo, 1867.

Las Casas, Bartolomé de. *A Brief Narration of the Destruction of the Indies by the Spaniards*. London: n.p., 1625.

Lemus, George. *Francisco Bulnes: Su vida y sus obras*. Mexico City: Ediciones de Andres, 1965.

Leon, N. "Noticia biográfica del autor." In *Obras,* by Alfredo Chavero. Mexico City: Tipografía de Victoriano Agueros, 1904.

Levene, Ricardo. *Las ideas históricas de Mitre*. Buenos Aires: Coni, 1948.

―――. *Mitre y los estudios históricos en la Argentina*. Buenos Aires: Academia Nacional de la Historia, 1944.

Lillo, Samuel A. *Literatura chilena*. 2d ed. Santiago, Minerva, 1920.

Lugones, Leopoldo. "Introducción."In *Calchaqui*, by Adán Quiroga. Buenos Aires: La Cultura Argentina, 1923.

Machado, José E. "Preambulo." In *Historia moderna*, by Juan Vicente González. Caracas: Bolívar, 1925.

Martin, Michael Rheta and Gabriel Lovett. *Encyclopedia of Latin American History*. Indianapolis: Bobbs-Merrill, Inc., 1968.

Martin, Percy Alvin, *Who's Who in Latin America*. Stanford: Stanford University Press, 1936.

―――. *Who's Who in Latin America*. 2d. ed. rev. Stanford: Stanford University Press, 1940.

Martínez Delgado, Luís. "Carlos Martínez Silva." In *Prosa política*, by Carlos Martínez Silva. Bogotá: Minerva, 1936.

―――. "Prólogo."In *Escritos varios,* by Carlos Martínez Silva. Bogotá: Kelly, 1954.

Martínez Santamaria, Hernando. "Advertencia preliminar."In *Por que caen los partidos políticos,* by Carlos Martínez Silva. Bogotá: Camacho Roldan, 1934.

Meyer, Harvey K. *Historical Dictionary of Honduras*. Metuchen, N.J.: Scarecrow Press, 1976.

―――. *Historical Dictionary of Nicaragua*. Metuchen, N.J.: Scarecrow Press, 1972.

Mieres, Antonio. *Tres autores en la historia de Baralt*. Caracas: Instituto de Estudios Hispanoamericanos, Facultad de Humanidades y Educación, Universidad Central de Venezuela, 1966.

Mijares, Augusto. "Baralt historiador."In *Obras completas*, by Rafael María Baralt. Vol. 1. Maracaibo, Venezuela: Universidad de Zulia, 1960.

Moore, Richard. *Historical Dictionary of Guatemala*. rev. ed. Metuchen, N.J.: Scarecrow Press, 1973.

Montúfar, Rafael. "Prólogo." In *Discursos del doctor Lorenzo Montúfar*, by Lorenzo Montúfar. Guatemala City: Impreso en los Talleres Sánchez & De Guise, 1923.

―――. "Prólogo." In *El general Francisco Morazán*, by Lorenzo Montúfar. Guatemala City: Tipografía Americana, 1896.

Morales, Ernesto. "Noticia biográfica."In *La cruz en América*, by Adán Quiroga. Buenos Aires: Editorial Americana, 1901.

Muñoz Gonzáles, Luís. "Andrés Bello y los origenes de la epopeya Romanesca." *Atenea*, 160, No. 40 (October–December 1965), pp. 125–133.

Newton, Jorge. *Mitre: Una vida al servicio de la libertad*. Buenos Aires: Claridad, 1965.

Ocampo de Gómez, Aurora M. and Ernesto Prado Velázquez. *Diccionario de escritores mexicanos*. Mexico City: Universidad Nacional Autónoma de Mexico, 1967.

Orgaz, Raúl A. *Alberdi y el historicismo*. Córdoba, Argentina: Argentina, 1937.

―――. *Sarmiento y el naturalismo histórico*. Córdoba, Argentina: Rossi, 1940.

————. *Vicente F. López y la filosofía de la historia*. Córdoba, Argentina: Rossi, 1938.

Orrego Barros, Carlos. *Diego Barros Arana*. Santiago: Universidad de Chile, 1952.

Ortega Pena, Rodolfo and Eduardo Luís Duhalde. *Las guerras civiles argentinas y la historiografía*. Buenos Aires: Sudestada, 1967.

Ortega y Medina, Juan A. *Polémicas y ensayos mexicanos en torna a la historia*. Mexico City: Autónoma de Mexico Instituto de Investigaciones Históricas, 1970.

Oyarzún, Luís. *El pensamiento de Lastarria*. Santiago: Editorial Jurídica de Chile, 1952.

Palma, Ricardo. *The Knights of the Cape*. Translated by Harriet de Onis. New York: Knopf, 1945.

Parker, William Belmont. *Argentines of To-Day*. 2 vols. Buenos Aires: Hispanic Society of America, 1920.

————. *Bolivians of To-Day*. 2d ed. rev. New York: Kraus Reprint, 1967.

————. *Chileans of To-Day*. Santiago: Hispanic Society of America, 1920.

————. *Cubans of To-Day*. New York: Putnam, 1919.

————. *Paraguayans of To-Day*. New York: Kraus Reprint, 1967.

————. *Peruvians of To-Day*. New York: Kraus Reprint, 1967.

————. *Uruguayans of To-Day*. New York: Kraus Reprint, 1967.

Pazos Kanki, Vicente. *Letters on the United Provinces of South America*. Translated by Platt Crosby. New York: Seymour, 1819.

Perusse, Roland I. *Historical Dictionary of Haiti*. Metuchen, N.J.: Scarecrow Press, 1977.

Phelan, John. "The Apologetic History of Fray Bartolomé de Las Casas." *Hispanic American Historical Review*, 49, No. 1 (February 1969), pp. 94–99.

Picón Salas, Mariano. "Nota sintética sobre el escritor." In *Páginas escogidas*, by Juan Vicente González. Caracas: Antologías "Victoria," 1921.

————. *On Being Good Neighbors*. Translated by Muna Lee. Washington, D.C.: Pan American Union, 1944.

Potash, Robert A. "Historiography of Mexico Since 1821," *Hispanic American Historical Review*, 40, No. 3 (August 1960), pp. 383–424.

Prieto, Guillermo. *San Francisco in the Seventies: The City as Viewed by a Mexican Political Exile*. San Francisco: n.p., 1938.

Puerta Flores, Ismael. "Bello y la escondida senda de historiador." *Revista de historia*, 2, No. 7 (1961), pp. 27–37.

Quirozz, Alberto. *Lucas Alamán*. Mexico City: Cuadernos de Lectura Popular, 1967.

Ratcliff, Dillwyn. *Venezuelan Prose Fiction*. New York: Institutos de las Españas en los Estados Unidos, 1933.

Read, J. Lloyd. *The Mexican Historical Novel, 1826–1910*. New York: Instituto de las Españas en los Estados Unidos, 1939.

Riva Aguero y Osma, José de. "El general don Manuel de Mendiburu: Su vida y caracter." In *Diccionario histórico-biográfico del Perú*, by Manuel Mendiburu. 2d ed. Vol. 1. Lima: Enrique Palacios, 1931.

Rodrígues, José Honorio. *Historia e historiadores do Brasil*. São Paulo: Fulgor, 1965.

Rodríguez Monegal, Emir. *Eduardo Acevedo Díaz*. Montevideo: Ediciones del Río de la Plata, 1963.

Rojas, Ricardo. "Prólogo." In *Comprobaciones históricas*, by Bartolomé Mitre. Vol. 1. Buenos Aires: La Facultad de Juan Roldán, 1916.

Romero, José Luís. "Estudio preliminar." In *Memoria sobre...las diversas escuelas de historia social*, by Vicente Fidel López. Buenos Aires: Nova, 1943.

Ross, Stanley R. "Cosío Villegas' Historia Moderna de Mexico." *Hispanic American Historical Review*, 46, No. 3 (August 1966), pp. 274–282.

Rudolf, Donna Keyse and G.A. Rudolf. *Historical Dictionary of Venezuela*. Metuchen, N.J.: Scarecrow Press, 1971.

Sahagún, Bernardino de. *A History of Ancient Mexico*. Nashville, Tenn.: Fiske University Press, 1932.

Samayoa Guevara, Hector Humberto. *La enseñanza de la historia en Guatemala*. Guatemala City: Imprenta Universitaria, 1959.

Sánchez Roca, Mariano. "Nota introductoria." In *El juego y la vangancia en Cuba y estudio sobre la esclavitud*, by José Antonio Saco. Havana: Lex, 1960.

Sanin Cano, B. "Joaquín Acosta." In *Descubrimiento y colonización de la Nueva Granada*, by Joaquín Acosta. Bogotá: Biblioteca Popular de Cultura Colombiana, 1942.

Sarmiento, Domingo Faustino. *Life in the Argentine Republic in the Days of the Tyrants*. New York: Hurd and Houghton, 1869.

———. *A Sarmiento Anthology*. Translated by Stuart Edgar Grummon. Princeton: Princeton University Press, 1948.

Schwartz, Stuart B. "Francisco Adolfo de Varnhagen: Diplomat, Patriot, Historian." *Hispanic American Historical Review*, 47, No. 2 (May 1967), pp. 185–202.

Sierra, Carlos J. "Prólogo." In *José María Vigil*, by José María Vigil. Mexico City: Club de Periodistas de México, 1963.

Sierra, Justo. *Mexico: Its Social Evolution*. Translated by G. Sentinon. 2 vols. Mexico City: J.Ballesca, 1900–1904.

Sigüenza y Góngora, Carlos de. *The Mercurio Volante of Don Carlos de Sigüenza y Góngora*. Translated by Irving A. Leonard. Los Angeles: Quivira Society, 1932.

Silva Castro, Raúl. "Ensayo sobre Lastarria." *Cuadernos americanos*, 16, No. 1 (1957), pp. 235–255.

Skidmore, Thomas E., "The Historiography of Brazil, 1889–1964, Part I." *Hispanic American Historical Review*, 55, No. 4 (November 1975), pp. 716–748.

Soto, César Humberto. *Personajes célebres de Venezuela*. Caracas: Impresores Unidos, 1946.

Stein, Stanley. "Historiography of Brazil, 1808–1889." *Hispanic American Historical Review*, 40, No. 2 (May 1962), pp. 234–278.

———. "The Tasks Ahead for Latin American Historians." *Hispanic American Historical Review*, 41, No. 3 (August 1961), pp. 424–433.

Szaszdi, Adam. "The Historiography of the Republic of Ecuador." *Hispanic American Historical Review*, 44, No. 4 (November 1964), pp. 503–550.

Thomas, Jack Ray. "The Impact of the Generation of 1842 on Chilean Historiography." *The Historian*, 41, No. 4 (August 1979), pp. 705–720.

———. "The Role of Private Libraries and Public Archives in Nineteenth-Century Spanish American Historiography." *The Journal of Library History*, 9, No. 4 (October 1974), p. 334–351.

Toro, Alfonso. "Don Lorenzo de Zavala y su obra." In *Ensayo histórico de las revoluciones de México desde 1808 hasta 1830*, by Lorenzo de Zavala. 3d ed. Mexico City: Oficina Impresora de Hacienda Dept. Editorial, 1918.

Torres Caicedo, J.M. "Don José Manuel Groot." In *Historia eclesiástica y civil de Nueva Granada*, by José Manuel Groot. Bogotá: Biblioteca de Autores Colombianos, 1953.

Unión Panamericana, *Diccionario de la literatura latinoamericana: América Central; Costa Rica, El Salvador y Guatemala*. Washington, D.C.: Unión Panamericana, 1963.

———. *Diccionario de la literatura latinoamericana: América Central; Honduras, Nicaragua y Panamá*.Washington, D.C.: Unión Panamericana, 1963.

———. *Diccionario de la literatura latinoamericana: Bolivia*. Washington D.C.: Unión Panamericana, 1958.

———. *Diccionario de la literatura latinoamericana: Chile*. Washington, D.C.: Unión Panamericana, 1958.

———. *Diccionario de la literatura latinoamericana: Colombia*. Washington D.C.: Unión Panamericana, 1959.

Uslar Pietri, Arturo. *Letras y hombres de Venezuela*. Mexico City: Fondo de Cultura Económica, 1948.

Valades, José C. *Alamán, estadista y historiador*. Mexico City: José Porrúa y Hijos, 1918.

Vasconcelos, José. *Aspects of Mexican Civilization*. Chicago: University of Chicago Press, 1926.

Vildosola, C. Silva. "Introducción." In *Páginas olvidades de Vicuña Mackenna en "El Mercurio,"* by Benjamín Vicuña Mackenna. Santiago: Nascimento, 1931.

Villalobos Rivera, Sergio. "La historiografía económica en Chile, sus comienzos." *Historia*, 10 (1971), pp. 7–32.

Visca, Arturo Sergio, "Prólogo." In *Estudios literarios,* by Francisco Bauzá. Montevideo: Ministerio de Instrucción Pública y Prevision Social, 1953.

Wilgus, A. Curtis. *The Historiography of Latin America: A Guide to Historical Writing, 1500–1800*. Metuchen, N.J.: Scarecrow Press, 1975.

Willis, Jean L. *Historical Dictionary of Uruguay*. Metuchen, N.J.: Scarecrow Press, 1974.

Woll, Allen. "For God and Country: History Textbooks and the Secularization of Chilean Society." *Journal of Latin American Studies,* 7 (May 1975), pp. 23–43.

———. "The Philosophy of History in Nineteenth Century Chile: The Lastarria–Bello Controversy." *History and Theory*, 13 (October 1974), pp. 273–290.

———. "Positivism and History in Nineteenth Century Chile: José Victorino Lastarria and Valentín Letelier." *Journal of the History of ideas*, 37 (July–September 1976), pp. 493–506.

Wright, Ione S. and Lisa M. Nekom. *Historical Dictionary of Argentina*. Metuchen, N.J.: Scarecrow Press, 1978.

Yañez, Agustín. "Introducción." In *Juárez: Su obra y su tiempo,* by Justo Sierra. Mexico City: Universidad Nacional Autónoma de Mexico, 1956.

———. "Prólogo." In *Mexico y sus revoluciones*, by José María Luís Mora. Mexico City: Porrúa, 1950.

Yeager, Gertrude Matyoka. "Barros Arana, Vicuña Mackenna, Amunátegui: The Historian as National Educator." *Journal of Inter-American Studies and World Affairs*, 19, No. 2 (May 1977), pp. 173–199.

Zorrilla de San Martín, Juan. *Tabare: An Epic Poem of the Early Days of Uruguay*. Translated by Ralph Walter Huntington. Buenos Aires: n.p., 1934.

Index

Note: The location of main entries in the dictionary is indicated in the index by italic page numbers.

About the Author

JACK RAY THOMAS is Professor of History at Bowling Green State University. He is the author of *Varieties and Problems of Twentieth Century Socialism* (with Louis Patsouias) and *Latin America*. Thomas has written articles for many publications including the *Hispanic American Historical Review*, the *Journal of Inter-American Studies*, *The Historian*, and *Revista/Review Interamericana*.